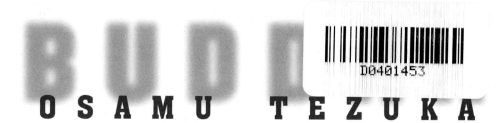

BUDD

OSAMU TEZUKA

VERTICAL.

4: The Forest of Uruvela

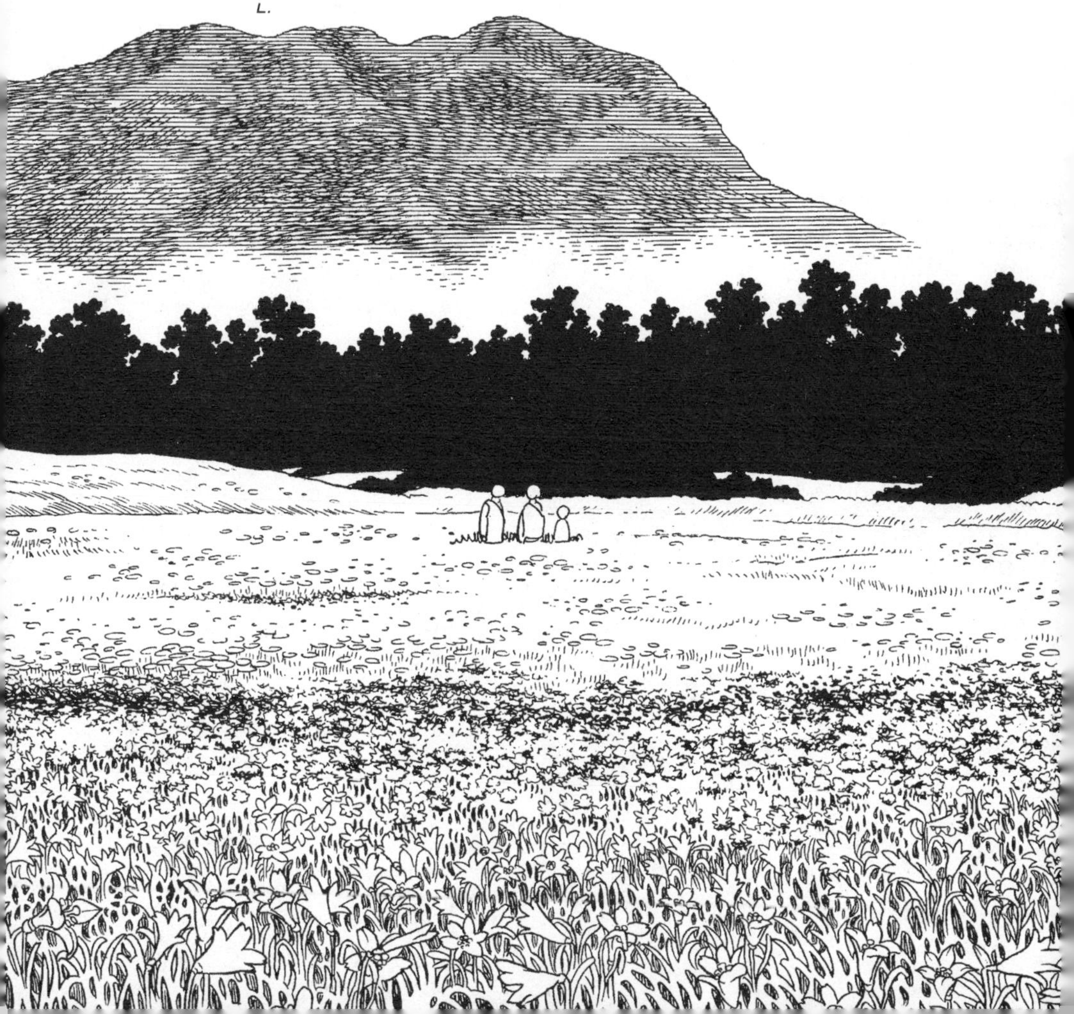

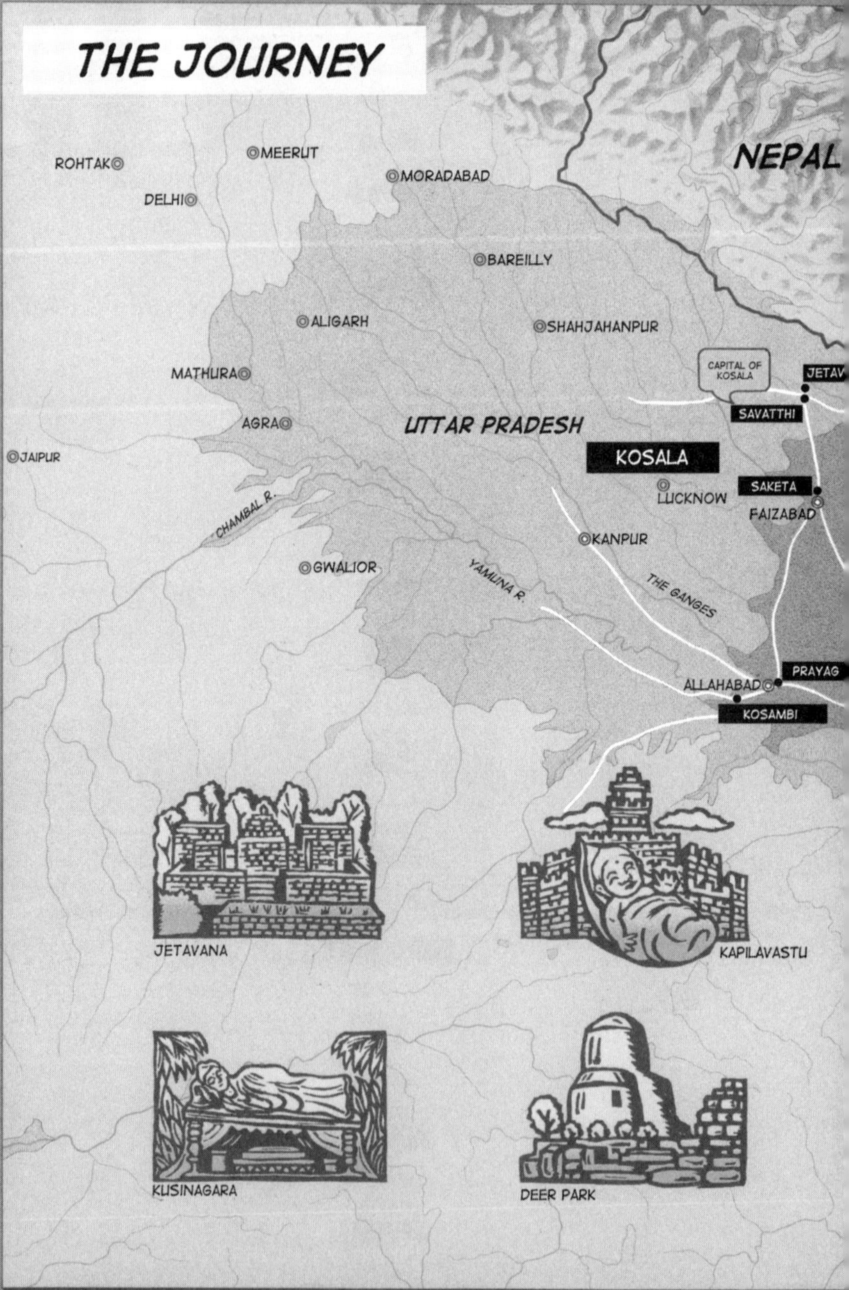
THE JOURNEY
NEPAL
ROHTAK
MEERUT
MORADABAD
DELHI
BAREILLY
ALIGARH
SHAHJAHANPUR
CAPITAL OF KOSALA
JETAV
MATHURA
SAVATTHI
AGRA
UTTAR PRADESH
JAIPUR
KOSALA
SAKETA
LUCKNOW
FAIZABAD
CHAMBAL R.
KANPUR
GWALIOR
YAMUNA R.
THE GANGES
PRAYAG
ALLAHABAD
KOSAMBI
JETAVANA
KAPILAVASTU
KUSINAGARA
DEER PARK

LUMBINI ANCIENT PLACE NAMES — MAJOR ROUTES ● PLACES VISITED BY THE BUDDHA

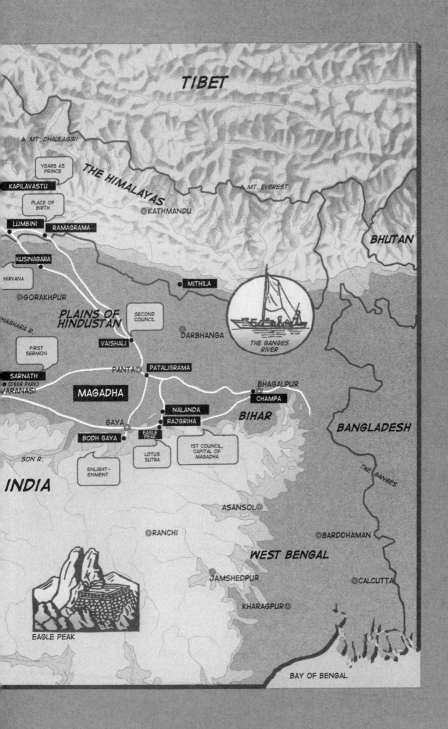

TIBET

THE HIMALAYAS

▲ MT. DHAULAGIRI

MT. EVEREST

BHUTAN

◎ KATHMANDU

YEARS AS PRINCE

KAPILAVASTU

PLACE OF BIRTH

LUMBINI   RAMAGRAMA

KUSINAGARA

NIRVANA

◎ GORAKHPUR

AGHARA R.

PLAINS OF HINDUSTAN

MITHILA

SECOND COUNCIL

◎ DARBHANGA

THE GANGES RIVER

VAISHALI

FIRST SERMON

PANTA ◎   PATALIGRAMA

SARNATH
(DEER PARK)
VARANASI

MAGADHA

BHAGALPUR

CHAMPA

BANGLADESH

NALANDA

GAYA ◎   RAJGRIHA

BIHAR

BODH GAYA

EAGLE PEAK

LOTUS SUTRA

1ST COUNCIL, CAPITAL OF MAGADHA

THE GANGES

SON R.

ENLIGHT-ENMENT

INDIA

ASANSOL ◎

◎ RANCHI

◎ BARDDHAMAN

WEST BENGAL

◎ JAMSHEDPUR

◎ CALCUTTA

EAGLE PEAK

KHARAGPUR ◎

BAY OF BENGAL

PUBLISHED BY VERTICAL, INC., NEW YORK.

ORIGINALLY PUBLISHED IN JAPANESE AS *BUDDA DAI YONKAN URUBERA NO MORI* BY USHIO SHUPPANSHA, TOKYO, 1987.

ISBN 978-1-932234-59-6

MANUFACTURED IN THE UNITED STATES OF AMERICA

FIRST PAPERBACK EDITION. THE ARTWORK OF THE ORIGINAL HAS BEEN PRODUCED AS A MIRROR-IMAGE IN ORDER TO CONFORM WITH THE ENGLISH LANGUAGE. THIS WORK OF FICTION CONTAINS CHARACTERS AND EPISODES THAT ARE NOT PART OF THE HISTORICAL RECORD.

SIXTH PRINTING

VERTICAL, INC.
451 PARK AVENUE SOUTH 7TH FLOOR
NEW YORK, NY 10016
WWW.VERTICAL-INC.COM

 CONTENTS

PART THREE (CONTINUED)

PART THREE (CONTINUED)

CHAPTER SIX

IN THE FOREST OF TRIALS

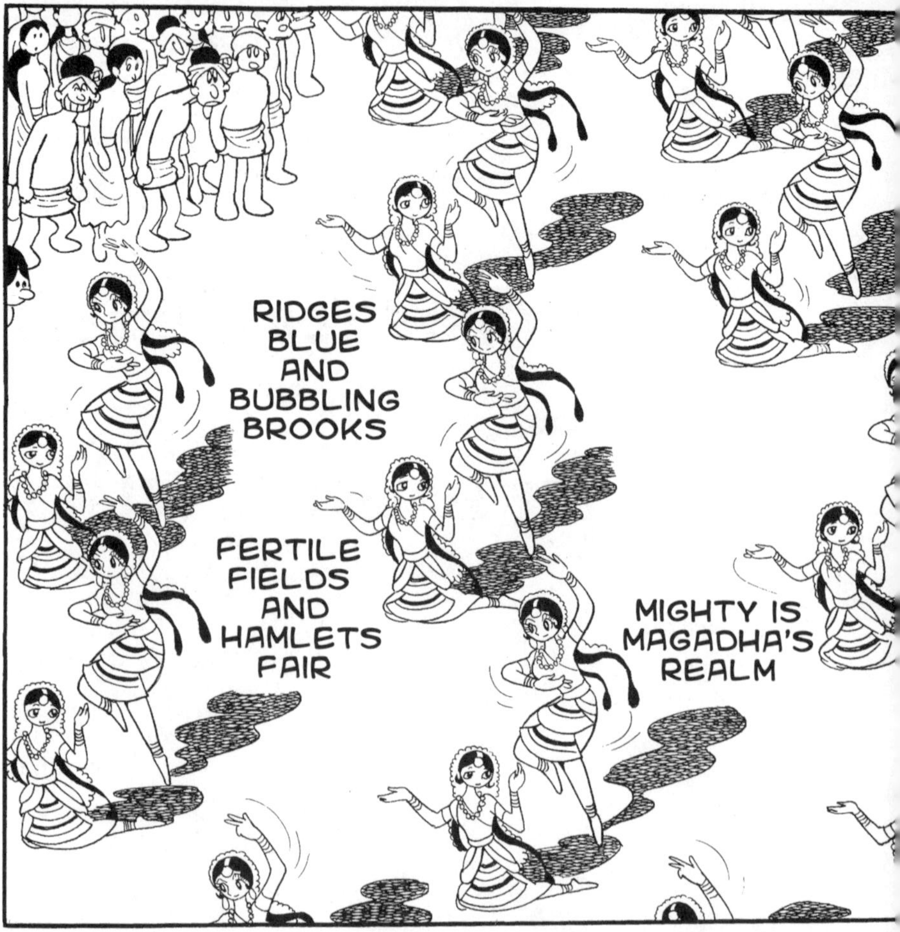
RIDGES BLUE AND BUBBLING BROOKS
FERTILE FIELDS AND HAMLETS FAIR
MIGHTY IS MAGADHA'S REALM

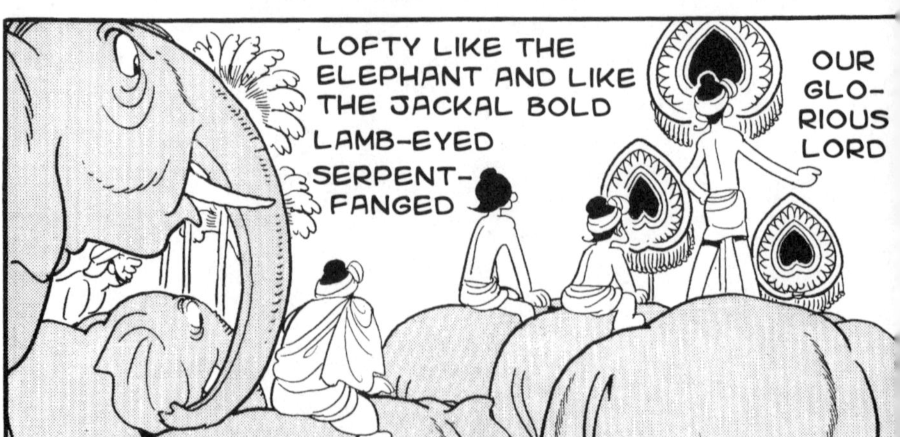
LOFTY LIKE THE ELEPHANT AND LIKE THE JACKAL BOLD
LAMB-EYED
SERPENT-FANGED
OUR GLO-RIOUS LORD

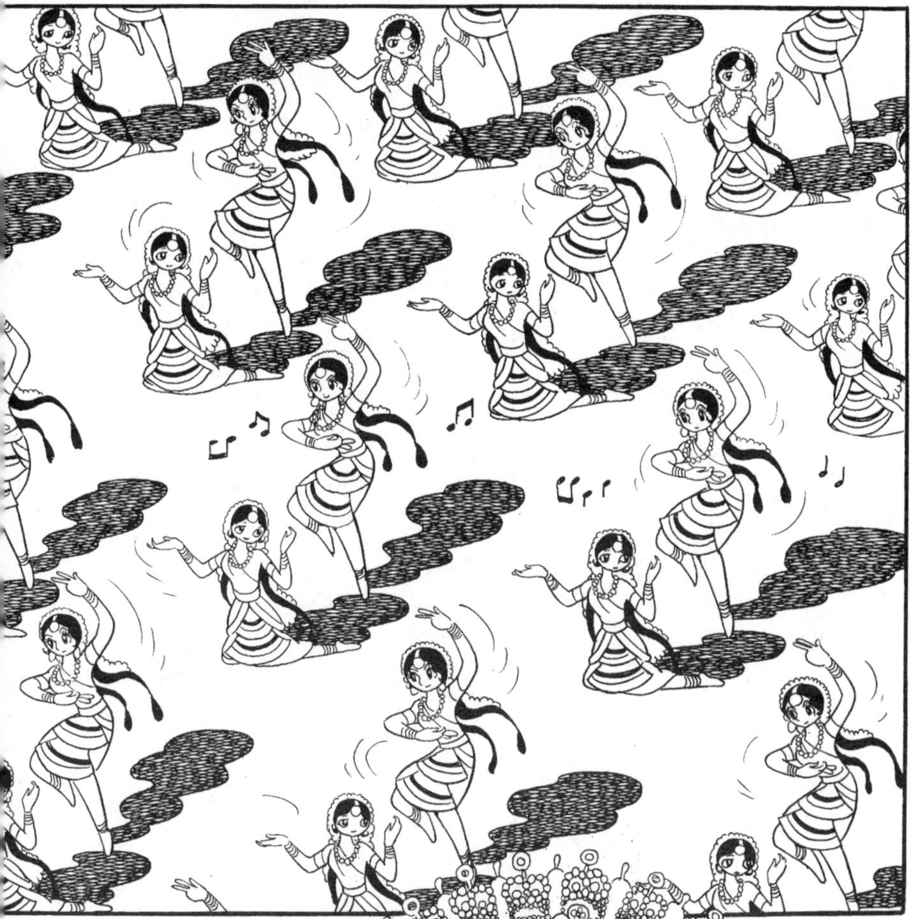

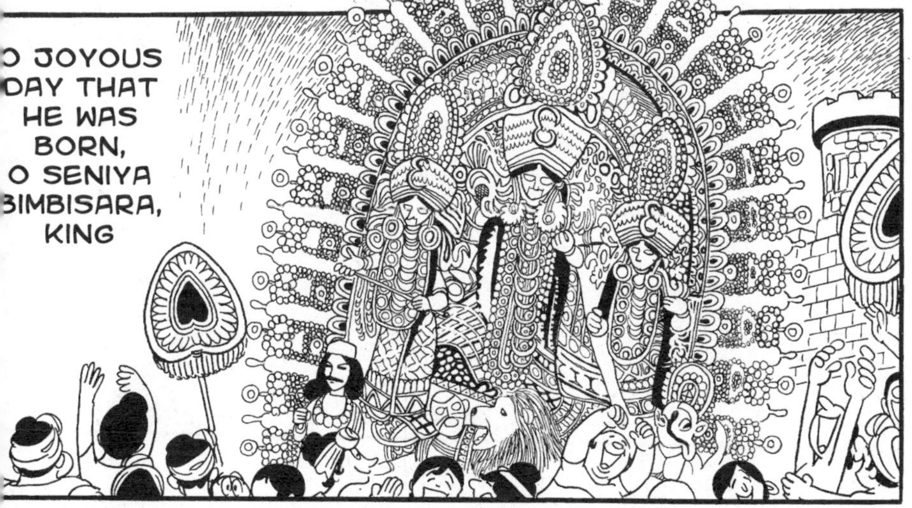
O JOYOUS DAY THAT HE WAS BORN, O SENIYA BIMBISARA, KING

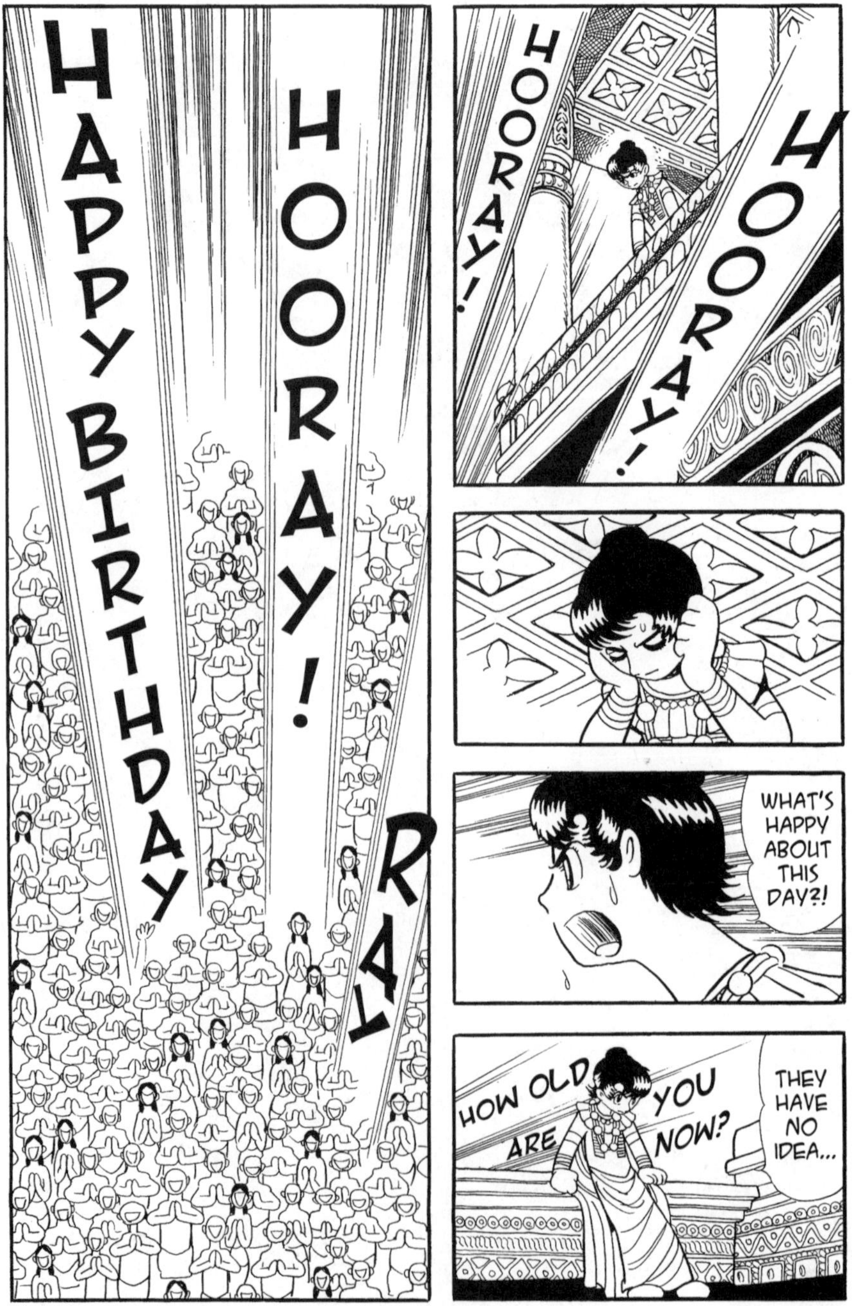
HAPPY BIRTHDAY
HOORAY!
RA
HOORAY!
HOORAY!
HOO
WHAT'S HAPPY ABOUT THIS DAY?!
HOW OLD ARE YOU NOW?
THEY HAVE NO IDEA...

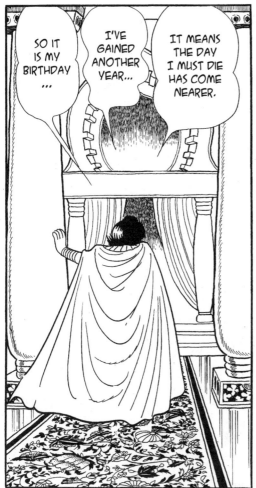

SO IT IS MY BIRTHDAY...

I'VE GAINED ANOTHER YEAR...

IT MEANS THE DAY I MUST DIE HAS COME NEARER.

THOSE CHEERS SOUND TO ME LIKE THE REAPER'S JEERS...

NO MAN KNOWS EXACTLY WHEN HE WILL DIE.

HE GOES ABOUT HIS LIFE, STUDYING, PLAYING, FALLING IN LOVE, WORKING...

AND ONE DAY, LIKE A BLAST OF WIND,

COMES DEATH!

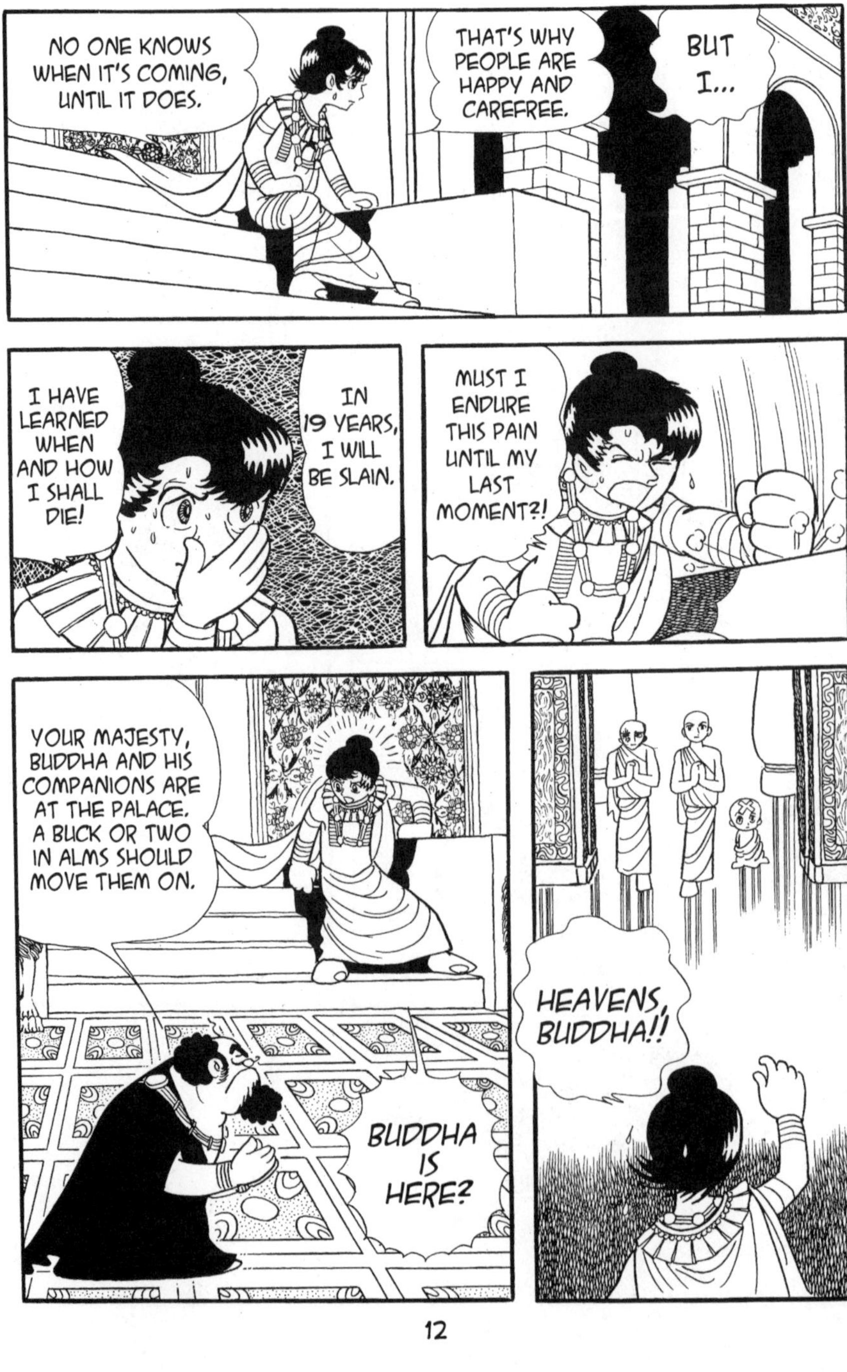
NO ONE KNOWS WHEN IT'S COMING, UNTIL IT DOES.
THAT'S WHY PEOPLE ARE HAPPY AND CAREFREE.
BUT I...
I HAVE LEARNED WHEN AND HOW I SHALL DIE!
IN 19 YEARS, I WILL BE SLAIN.
MUST I ENDURE THIS PAIN UNTIL MY LAST MOMENT?!
YOUR MAJESTY, BUDDHA AND HIS COMPANIONS ARE AT THE PALACE. A BUCK OR TWO IN ALMS SHOULD MOVE THEM ON.
BUDDHA IS HERE?
HEAVENS, BUDDHA!!

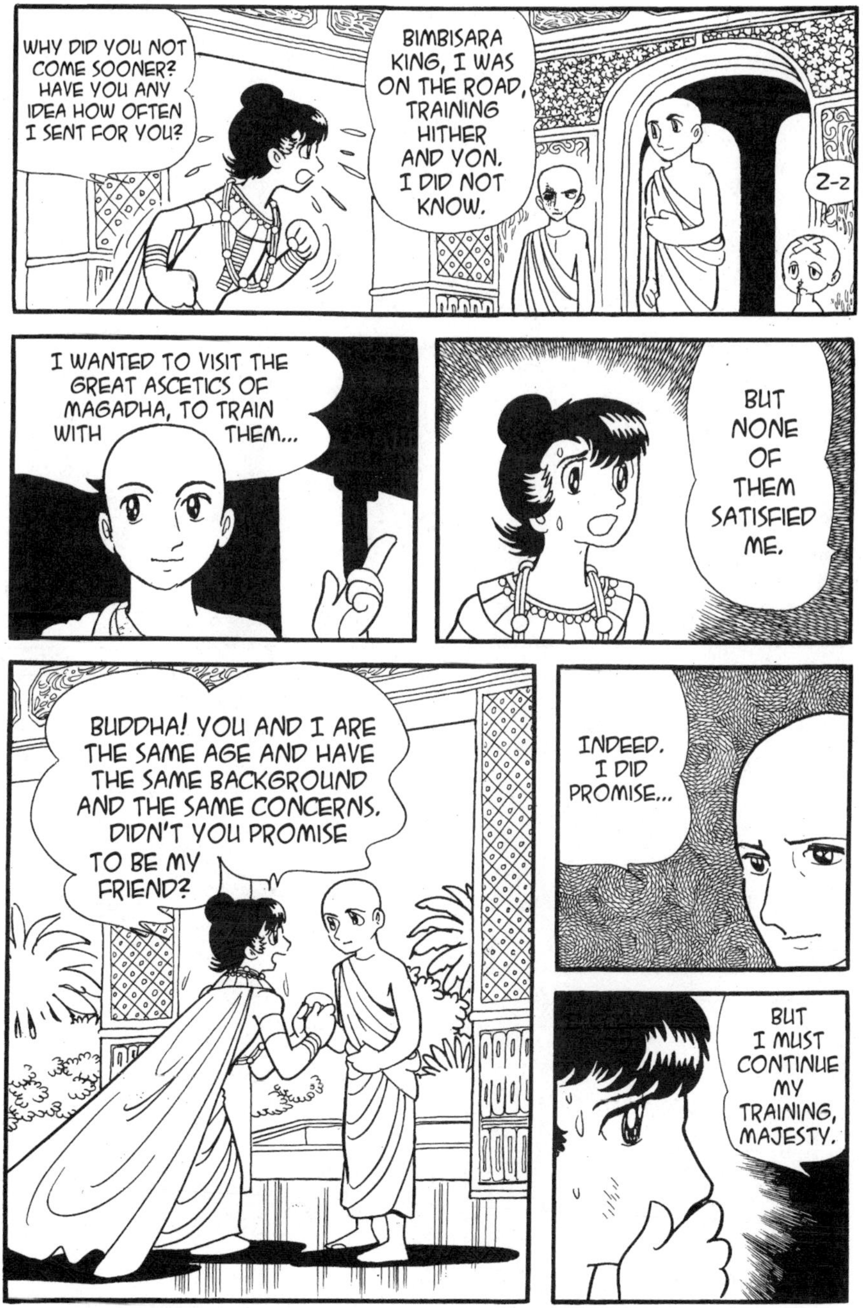
WHY DID YOU NOT COME SOONER? HAVE YOU ANY IDEA HOW OFTEN I SENT FOR YOU?
BIMBISARA KING, I WAS ON THE ROAD, TRAINING HITHER AND YON. I DID NOT KNOW.
Z-z
I WANTED TO VISIT THE GREAT ASCETICS OF MAGADHA, TO TRAIN WITH THEM...
BUT NONE OF THEM SATISFIED ME.
BUDDHA! YOU AND I ARE THE SAME AGE AND HAVE THE SAME BACKGROUND AND THE SAME CONCERNS. DIDN'T YOU PROMISE TO BE MY FRIEND?
INDEED. I DID PROMISE...
BUT I MUST CONTINUE MY TRAINING, MAJESTY.

DON'T "MAJESTY" ME. PLEASE, JUST CALL ME BY NAME.

IT'S SENIYA.

OH, RIGHT.

MAYBE I OUGHT TO DROP MY ROYAL AIRS, TOO, HUH?

'TIS ONLY FAIR.

SINCE WE FIRST MET, MY TORMENT HAS GROWN ONLY MORE INTOLERABLE WITH EACH PASSING DAY.

AS FOR ME, I HAVE MET VARIOUS ASCETICS SINCE THEN.

IS THAT SO? CARRY ON!

FIRST, I WENT TO THE TOWN OF VAISHALI TO SEEK OUT THE SAGE ALARA.

MASTER ALARA IS A RENOWNED ASCETIC WITH THREE HUNDRED DISCIPLES IN VAISHALI.

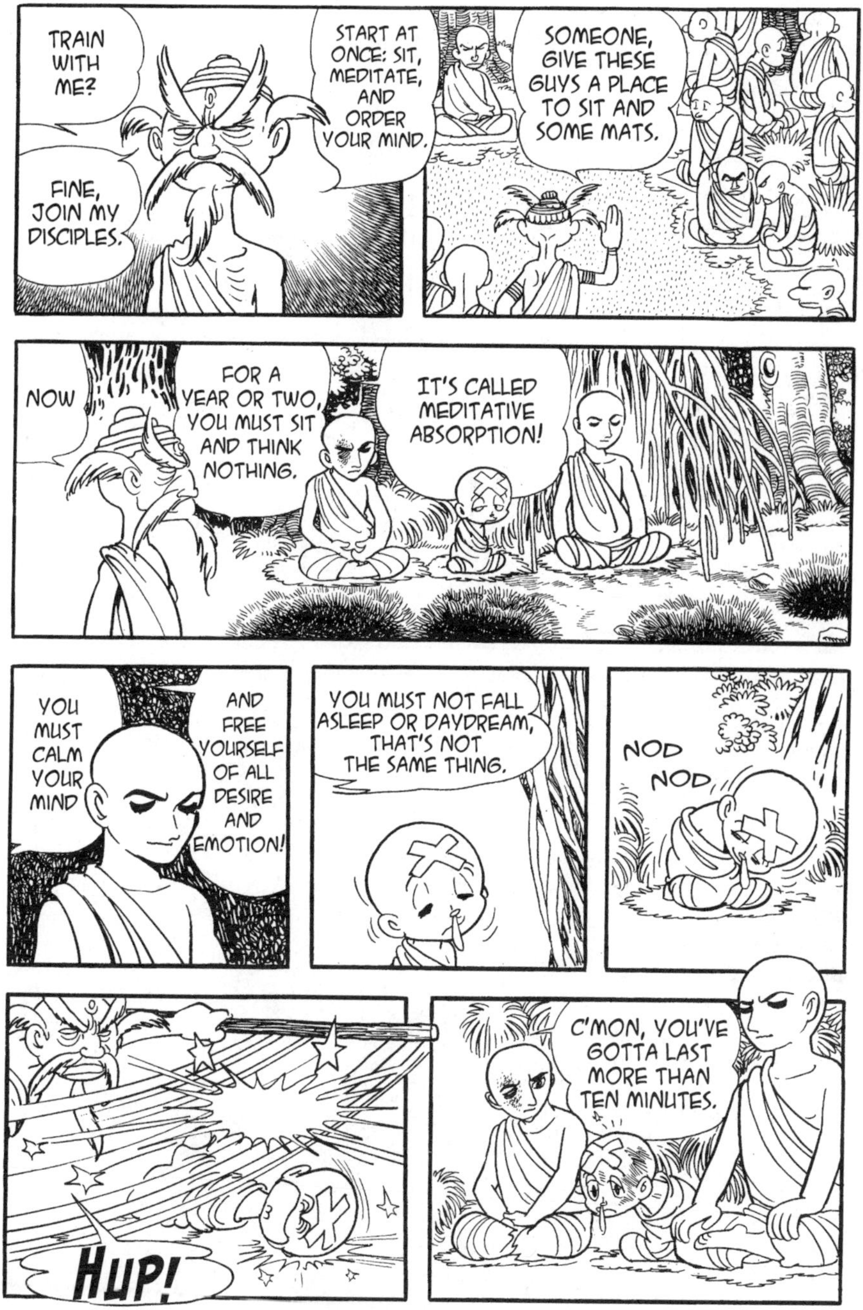
TRAIN WITH ME?
FINE, JOIN MY DISCIPLES.
START AT ONCE: SIT, MEDITATE, AND ORDER YOUR MIND.
SOMEONE, GIVE THESE GUYS A PLACE TO SIT AND SOME MATS.
NOW
FOR A YEAR OR TWO, YOU MUST SIT AND THINK NOTHING.
IT'S CALLED MEDITATIVE ABSORPTION!
YOU MUST CALM YOUR MIND
AND FREE YOURSELF OF ALL DESIRE AND EMOTION!
YOU MUST NOT FALL ASLEEP OR DAYDREAM, THAT'S NOT THE SAME THING.
NOD
NOD
HUP!
C'MON, YOU'VE GOTTA LAST MORE THAN TEN MINUTES.

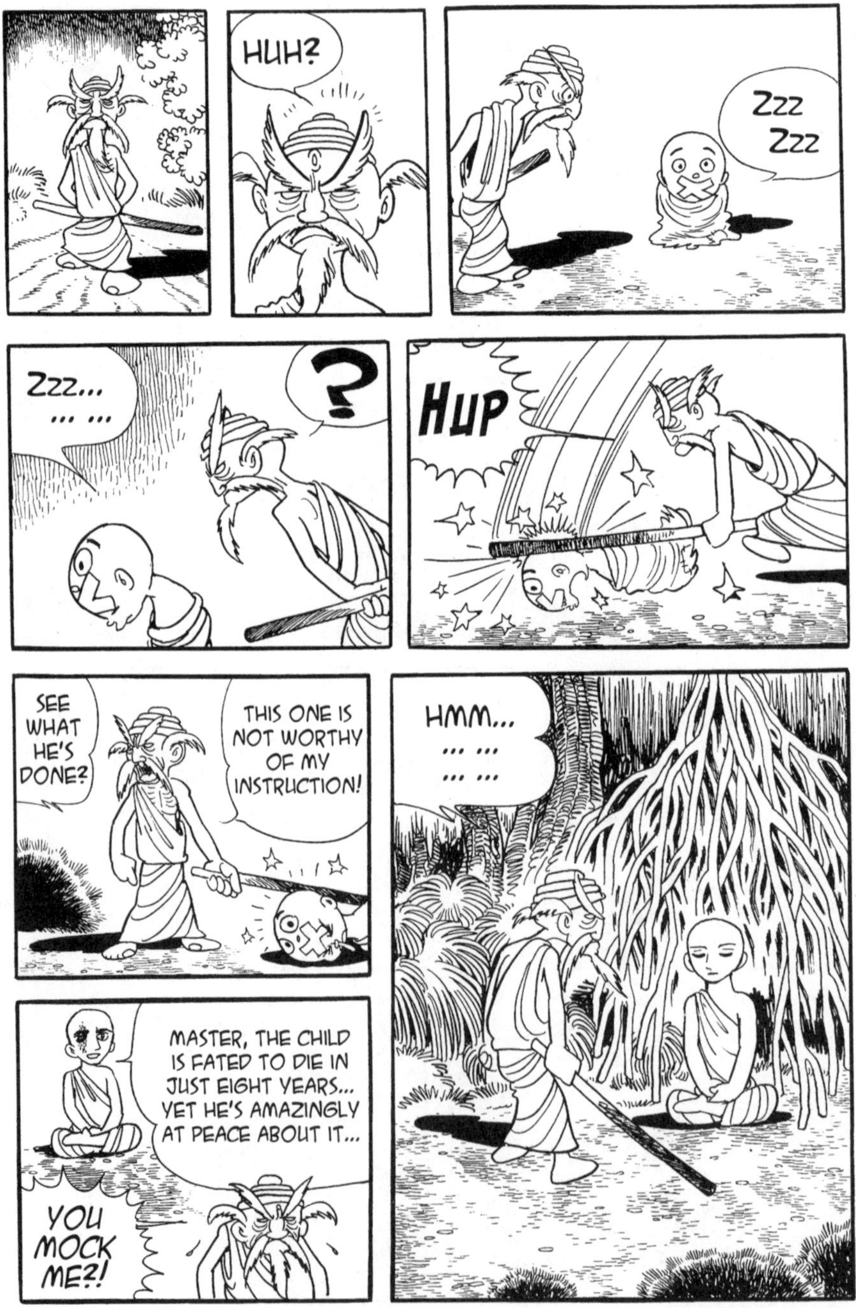
HUH?
Zzz
Zzz
Zzz...
... ...
?
HUP
SEE WHAT HE'S DONE?
THIS ONE IS NOT WORTHY OF MY INSTRUCTION!
MASTER, THE CHILD IS FATED TO DIE IN JUST EIGHT YEARS... YET HE'S AMAZINGLY AT PEACE ABOUT IT...
YOU MOCK ME?!
HMM...
... ...
... ...

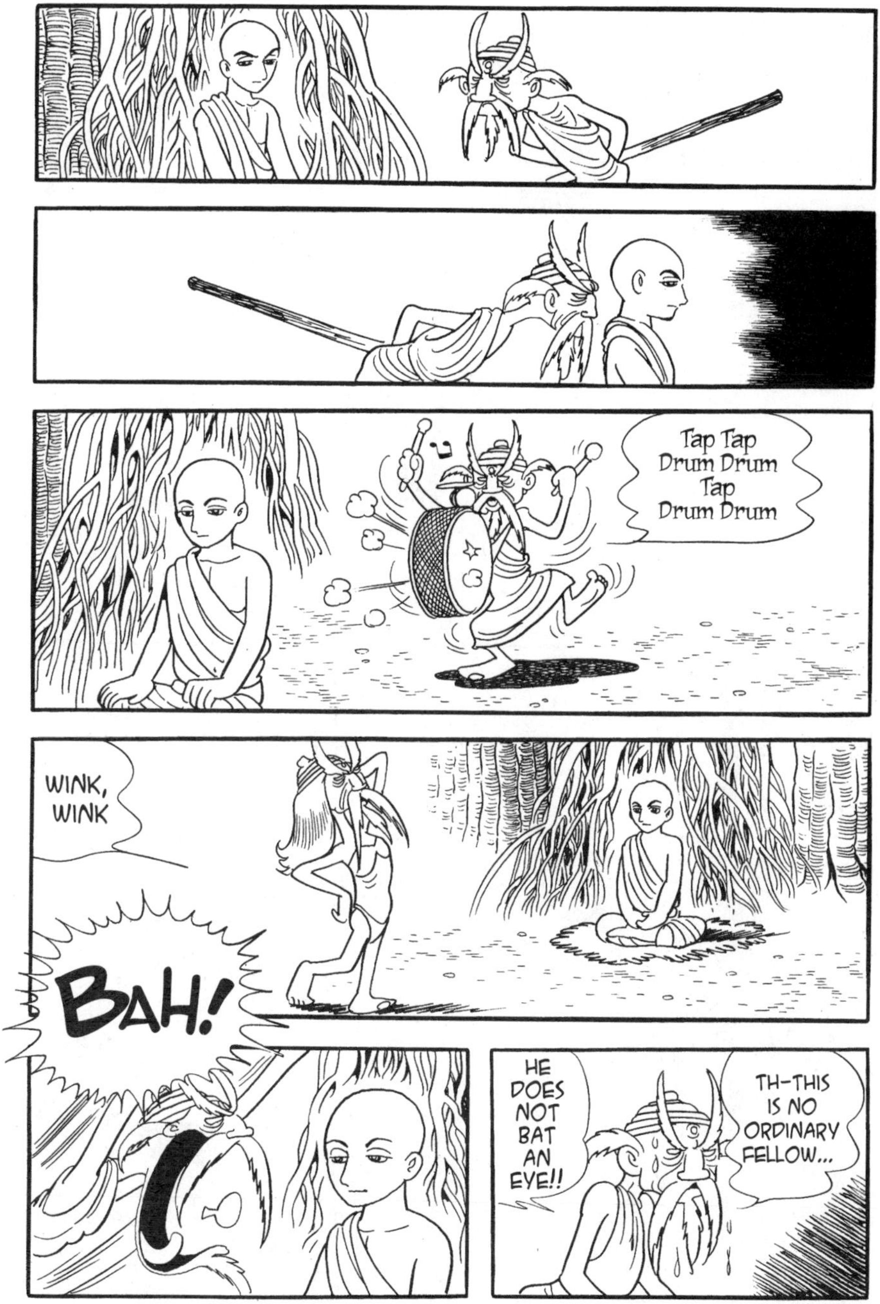

Tap Tap Drum Drum Tap Drum Drum
WINK, WINK
BAH!
HE DOES NOT BAT AN EYE!!
TH-THIS IS NO ORDINARY FELLOW...

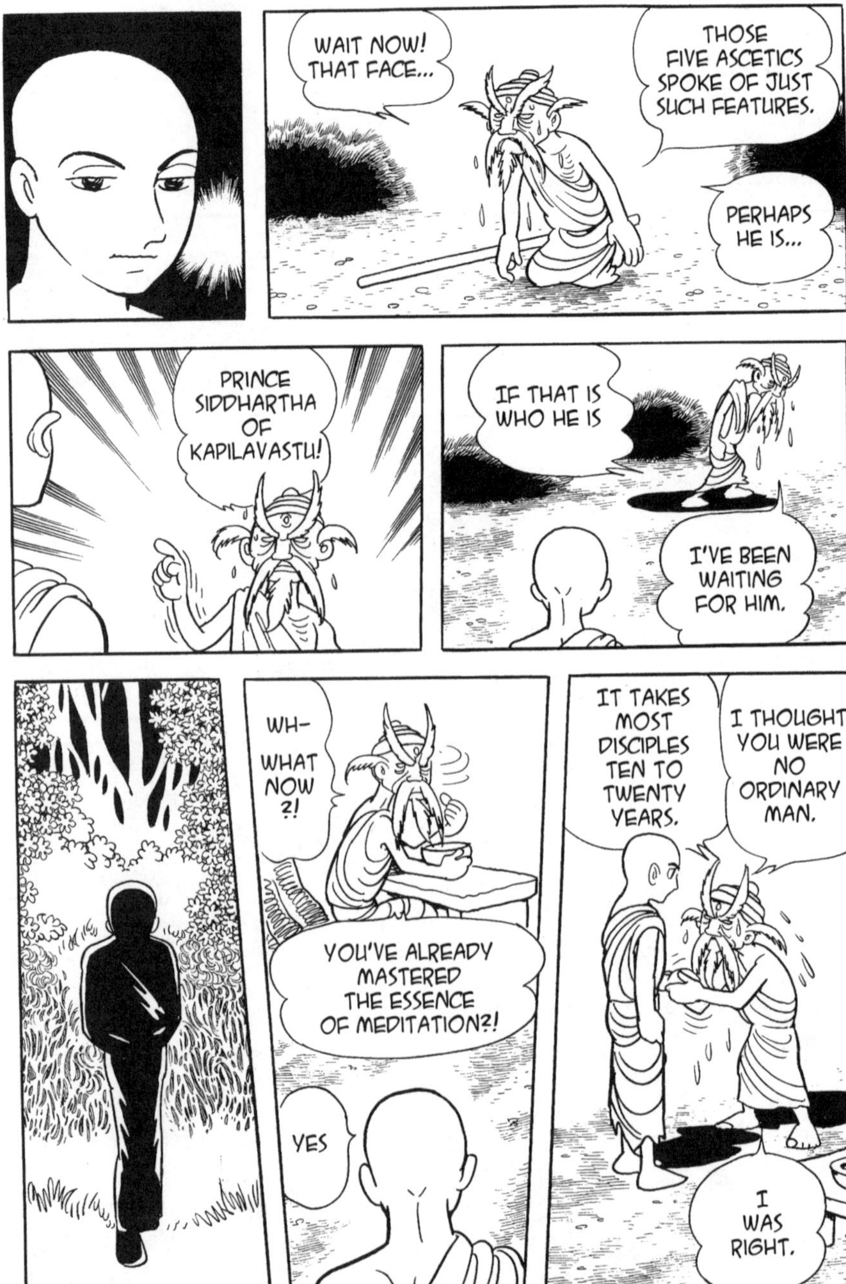
WAIT NOW! THAT FACE...
THOSE FIVE ASCETICS SPOKE OF JUST SUCH FEATURES.
PERHAPS HE IS...
PRINCE SIDDHARTHA OF KAPILAVASTU!
IF THAT IS WHO HE IS
I'VE BEEN WAITING FOR HIM.
WH- WHAT NOW ?!
YOU'VE ALREADY MASTERED THE ESSENCE OF MEDITATION?!
YES
IT TAKES MOST DISCIPLES TEN TO TWENTY YEARS.
I THOUGHT YOU WERE NO ORDINARY MAN.
I WAS RIGHT.

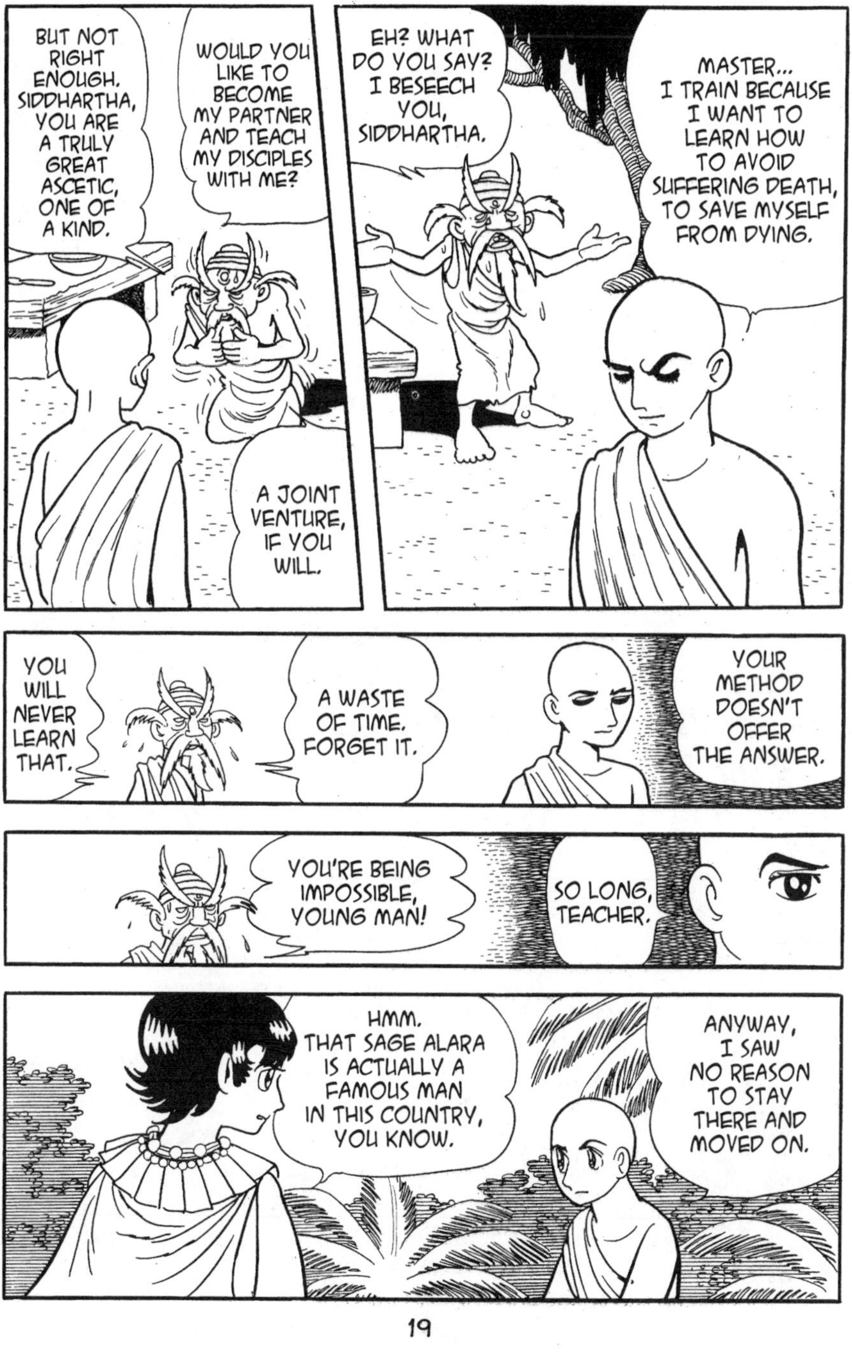
BUT NOT RIGHT ENOUGH. SIDDHARTHA, YOU ARE A TRULY GREAT ASCETIC, ONE OF A KIND.
WOULD YOU LIKE TO BECOME MY PARTNER AND TEACH MY DISCIPLES WITH ME?
A JOINT VENTURE, IF YOU WILL.
EH? WHAT DO YOU SAY? I BESEECH YOU, SIDDHARTHA.
MASTER... I TRAIN BECAUSE I WANT TO LEARN HOW TO AVOID SUFFERING DEATH, TO SAVE MYSELF FROM DYING.
YOU WILL NEVER LEARN THAT.
A WASTE OF TIME. FORGET IT.
YOUR METHOD DOESN'T OFFER THE ANSWER.
YOU'RE BEING IMPOSSIBLE, YOUNG MAN!
SO LONG, TEACHER.
HMM. THAT SAGE ALARA IS ACTUALLY A FAMOUS MAN IN THIS COUNTRY, YOU KNOW.
ANYWAY, I SAW NO REASON TO STAY THERE AND MOVED ON.

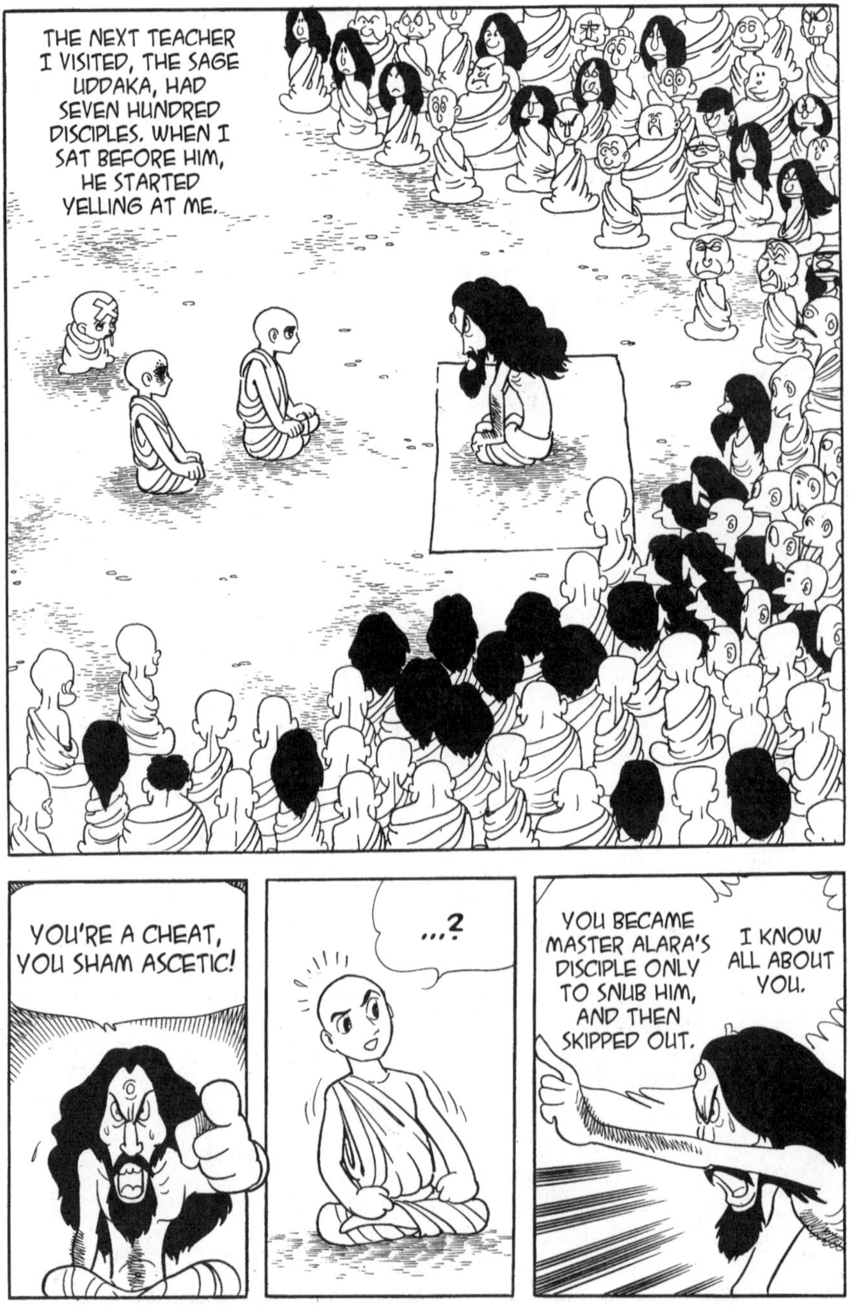
THE NEXT TEACHER I VISITED, THE SAGE UDDAKA, HAD SEVEN HUNDRED DISCIPLES. WHEN I SAT BEFORE HIM, HE STARTED YELLING AT ME.
YOU'RE A CHEAT, YOU SHAM ASCETIC!
...?
YOU BECAME MASTER ALARA'S DISCIPLE ONLY TO SNUB HIM, AND THEN SKIPPED OUT.
I KNOW ALL ABOUT YOU.

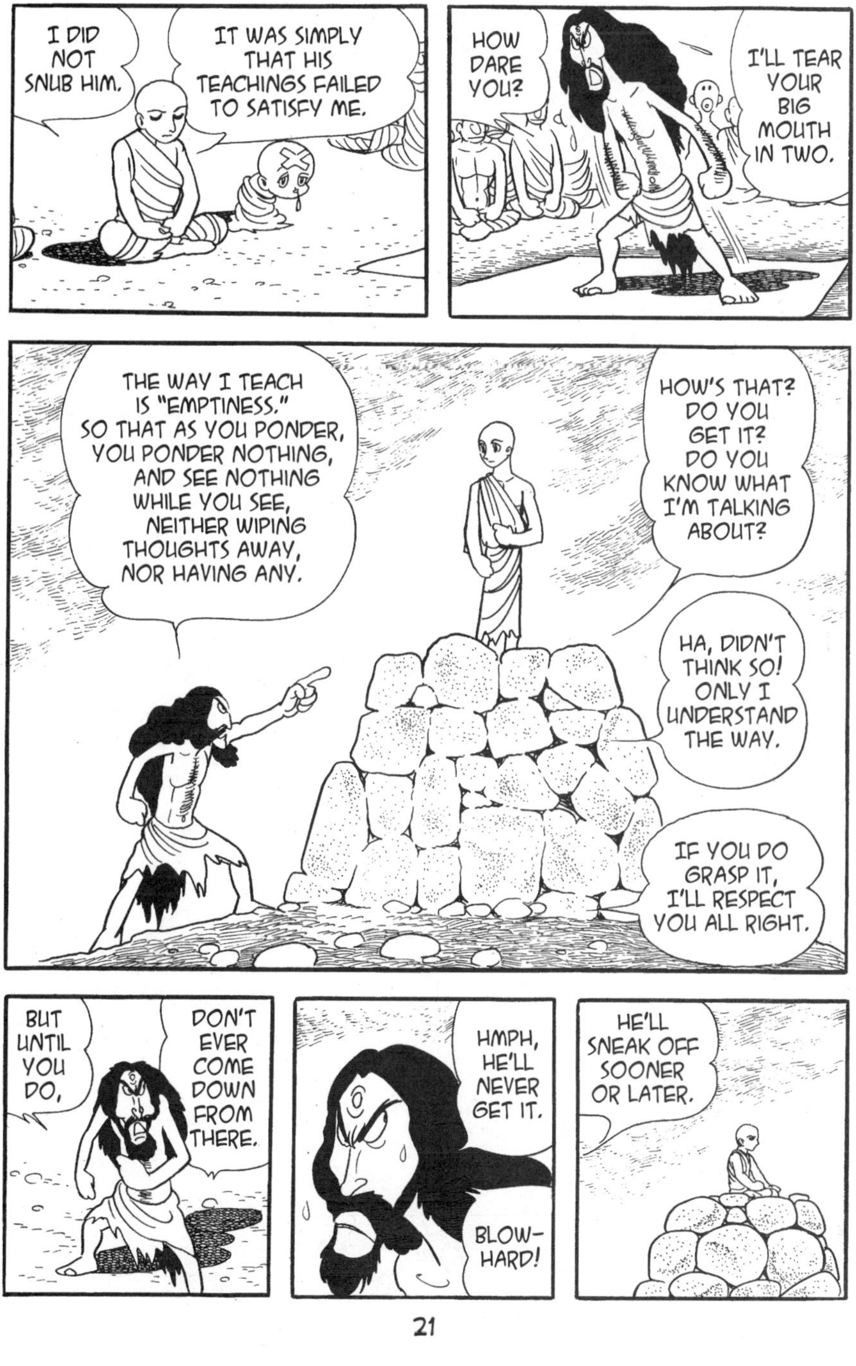
I DID NOT SNUB HIM.
IT WAS SIMPLY THAT HIS TEACHINGS FAILED TO SATISFY ME.
HOW DARE YOU?
I'LL TEAR YOUR BIG MOUTH IN TWO.
THE WAY I TEACH IS "EMPTINESS." SO THAT AS YOU PONDER, YOU PONDER NOTHING, AND SEE NOTHING WHILE YOU SEE, NEITHER WIPING THOUGHTS AWAY, NOR HAVING ANY.
HOW'S THAT? DO YOU GET IT? DO YOU KNOW WHAT I'M TALKING ABOUT?
HA, DIDN'T THINK SO! ONLY I UNDERSTAND THE WAY.
IF YOU DO GRASP IT, I'LL RESPECT YOU ALL RIGHT.
BUT UNTIL YOU DO,
DON'T EVER COME DOWN FROM THERE.
HMPH, HE'LL NEVER GET IT.
BLOW-HARD!
HE'LL SNEAK OFF SOONER OR LATER.

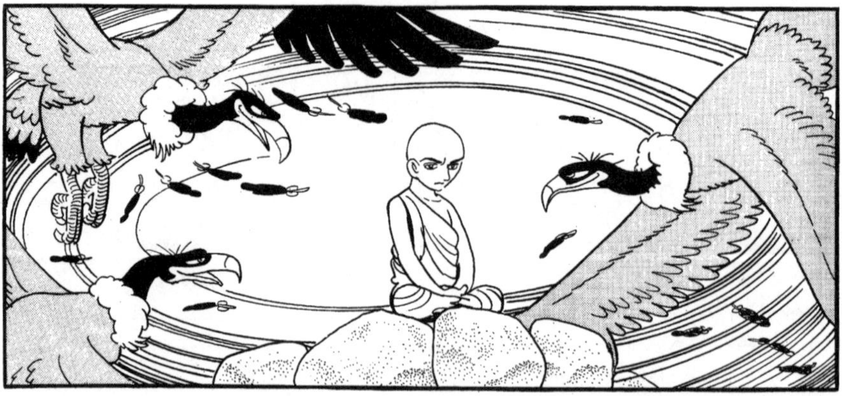

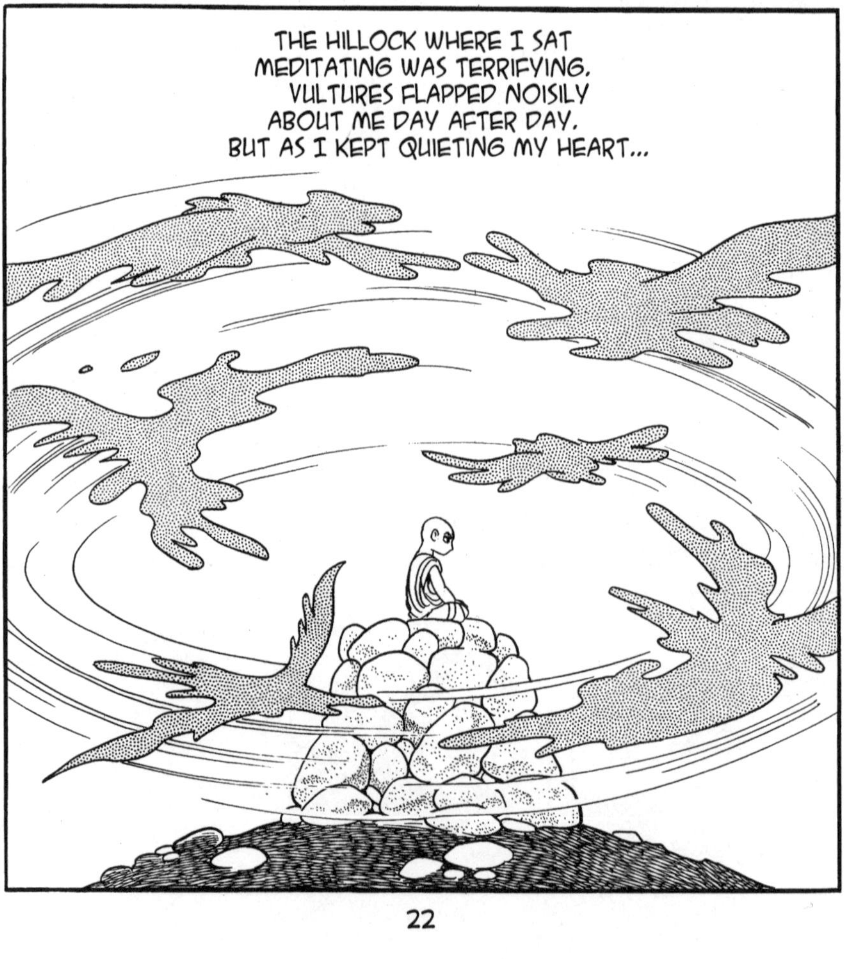
THE HILLOCK WHERE I SAT MEDITATING WAS TERRIFYING. VULTURES FLAPPED NOISILY ABOUT ME DAY AFTER DAY. BUT AS I KEPT QUIETING MY HEART...

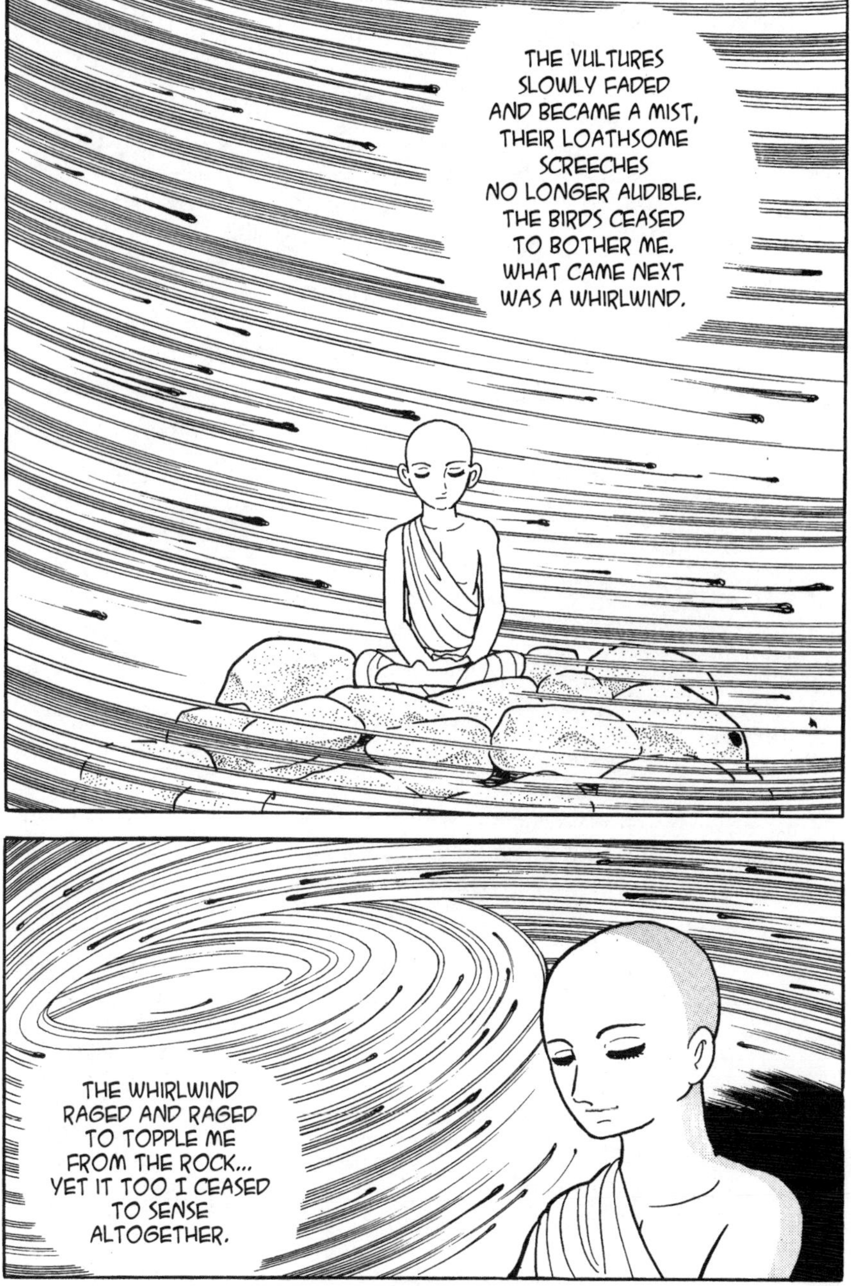
THE VULTURES SLOWLY FADED AND BECAME A MIST, THEIR LOATHSOME SCREECHES NO LONGER AUDIBLE. THE BIRDS CEASED TO BOTHER ME. WHAT CAME NEXT WAS A WHIRLWIND.
THE WHIRLWIND RAGED AND RAGED TO TOPPLE ME FROM THE ROCK... YET IT TOO I CEASED TO SENSE ALTOGETHER.

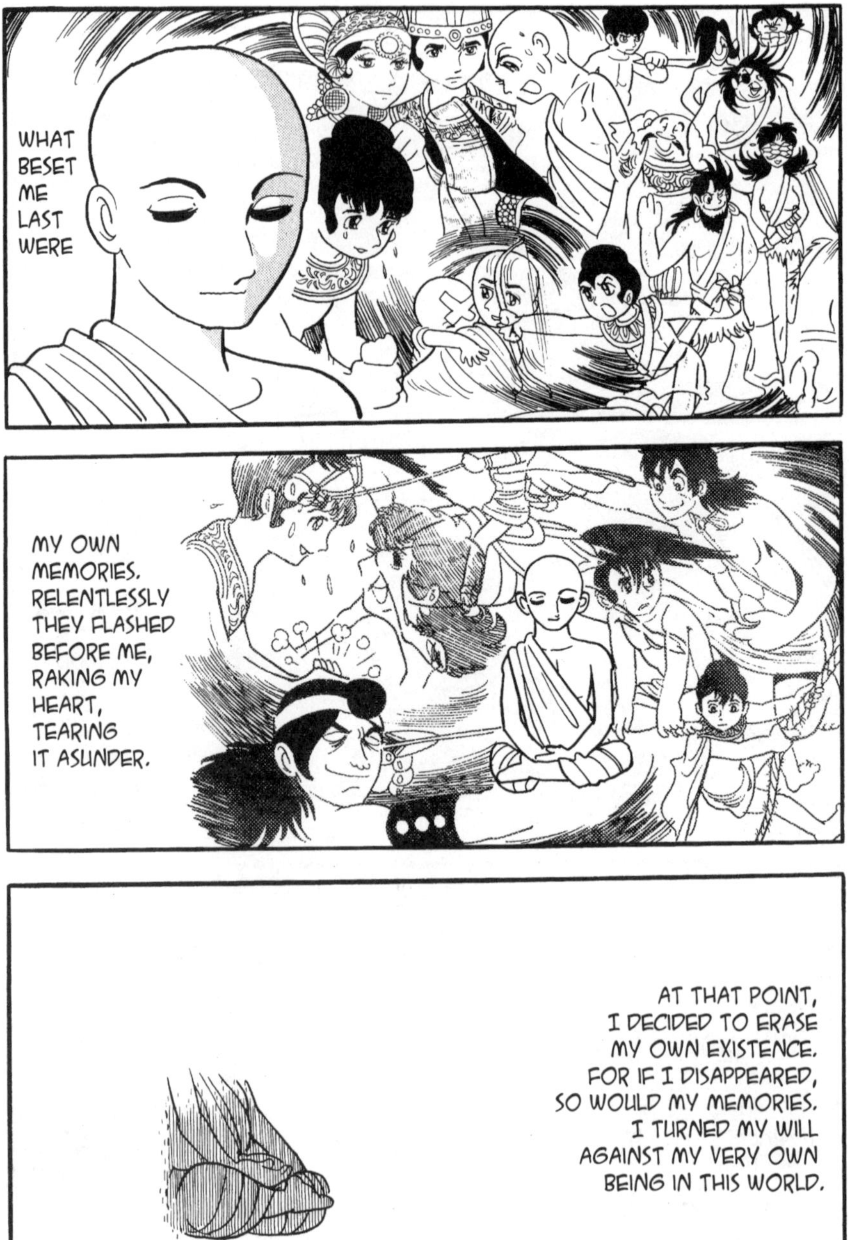
WHAT BESET ME LAST WERE
MY OWN MEMORIES. RELENTLESSLY THEY FLASHED BEFORE ME, RAKING MY HEART, TEARING IT ASUNDER.
AT THAT POINT, I DECIDED TO ERASE MY OWN EXISTENCE. FOR IF I DISAPPEARED, SO WOULD MY MEMORIES. I TURNED MY WILL AGAINST MY VERY OWN BEING IN THIS WORLD.

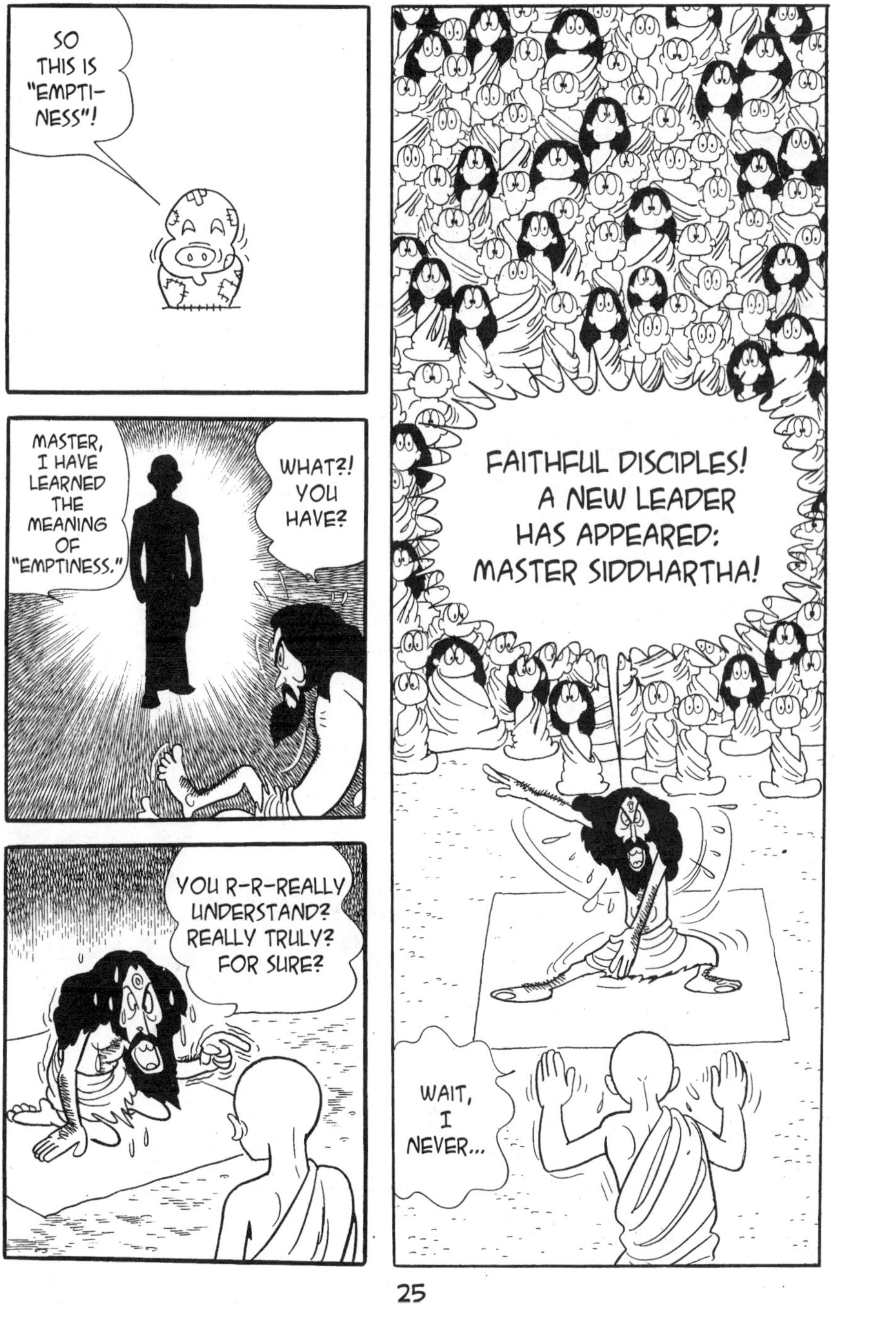
SO THIS IS "EMPTI-NESS"!
MASTER, I HAVE LEARNED THE MEANING OF "EMPTINESS."
WHAT?! YOU HAVE?
YOU R-R-REALLY UNDERSTAND? REALLY TRULY? FOR SURE?
FAITHFUL DISCIPLES! A NEW LEADER HAS APPEARED: MASTER SIDDHARTHA!
WAIT, I NEVER...

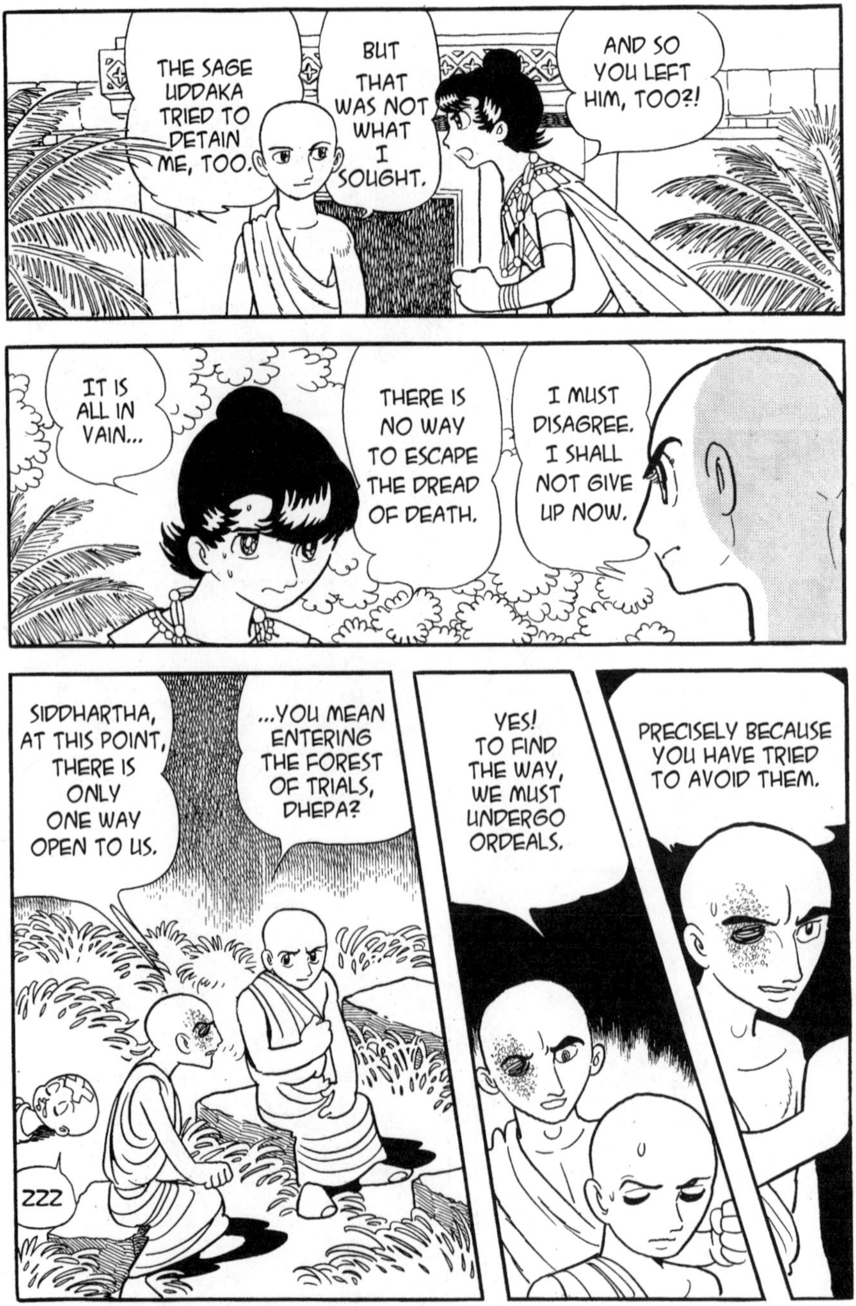
THE SAGE UDDAKA TRIED TO DETAIN ME, TOO.
BUT THAT WAS NOT WHAT I SOUGHT.
AND SO YOU LEFT HIM, TOO?!
IT IS ALL IN VAIN...
THERE IS NO WAY TO ESCAPE THE DREAD OF DEATH.
I MUST DISAGREE. I SHALL NOT GIVE UP NOW.
SIDDHARTHA, AT THIS POINT, THERE IS ONLY ONE WAY OPEN TO US.
...YOU MEAN ENTERING THE FOREST OF TRIALS, DHEPA?
ZZZ
YES! TO FIND THE WAY, WE MUST UNDERGO ORDEALS.
PRECISELY BECAUSE YOU HAVE TRIED TO AVOID THEM.

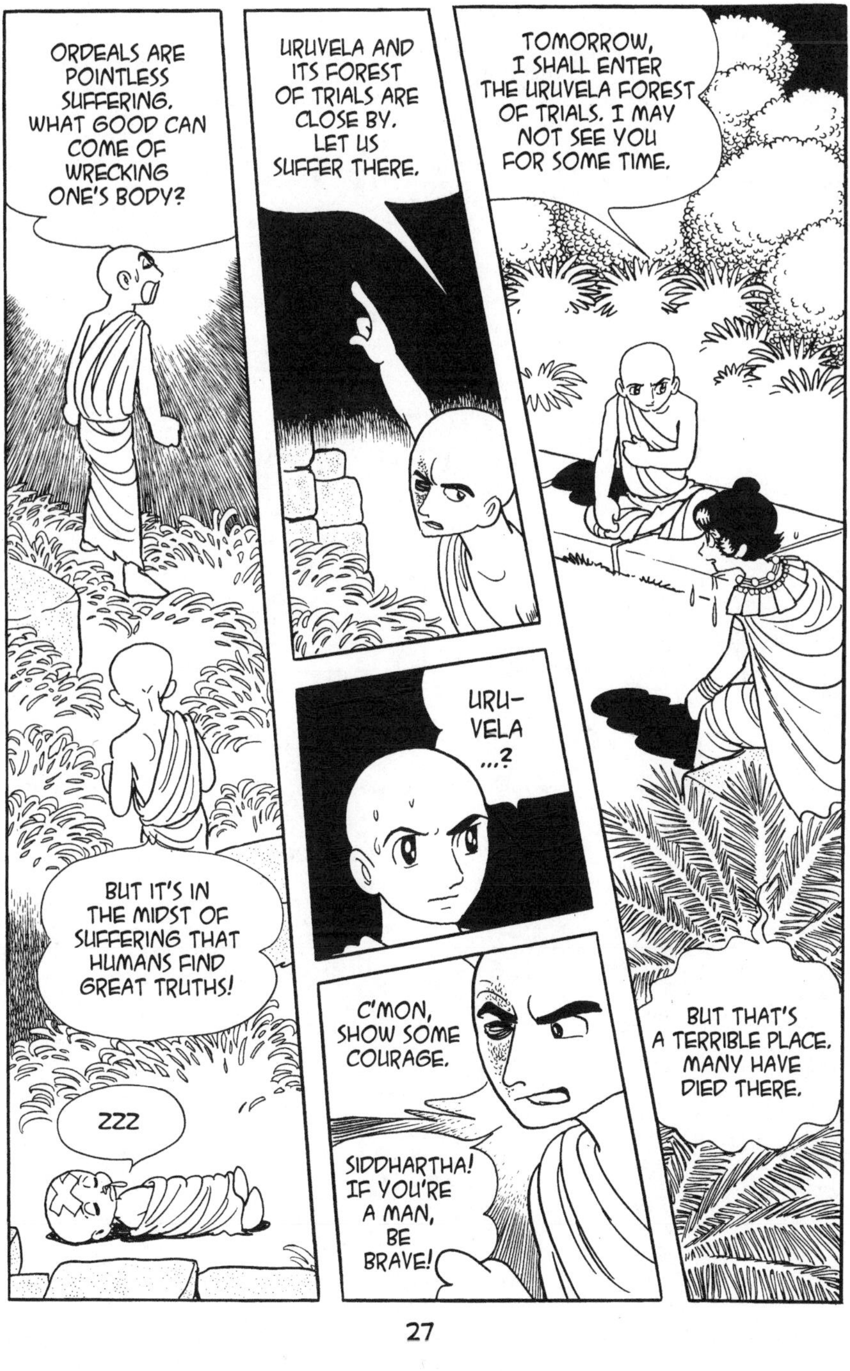
ORDEALS ARE POINTLESS SUFFERING. WHAT GOOD CAN COME OF WRECKING ONE'S BODY?
BUT IT'S IN THE MIDST OF SUFFERING THAT HUMANS FIND GREAT TRUTHS!
ZZZ
URUVELA AND ITS FOREST OF TRIALS ARE CLOSE BY. LET US SUFFER THERE.
URU-VELA ...?
C'MON, SHOW SOME COURAGE.
SIDDHARTHA! IF YOU'RE A MAN, BE BRAVE!
TOMORROW, I SHALL ENTER THE URUVELA FOREST OF TRIALS. I MAY NOT SEE YOU FOR SOME TIME.
BUT THAT'S A TERRIBLE PLACE. MANY HAVE DIED THERE.

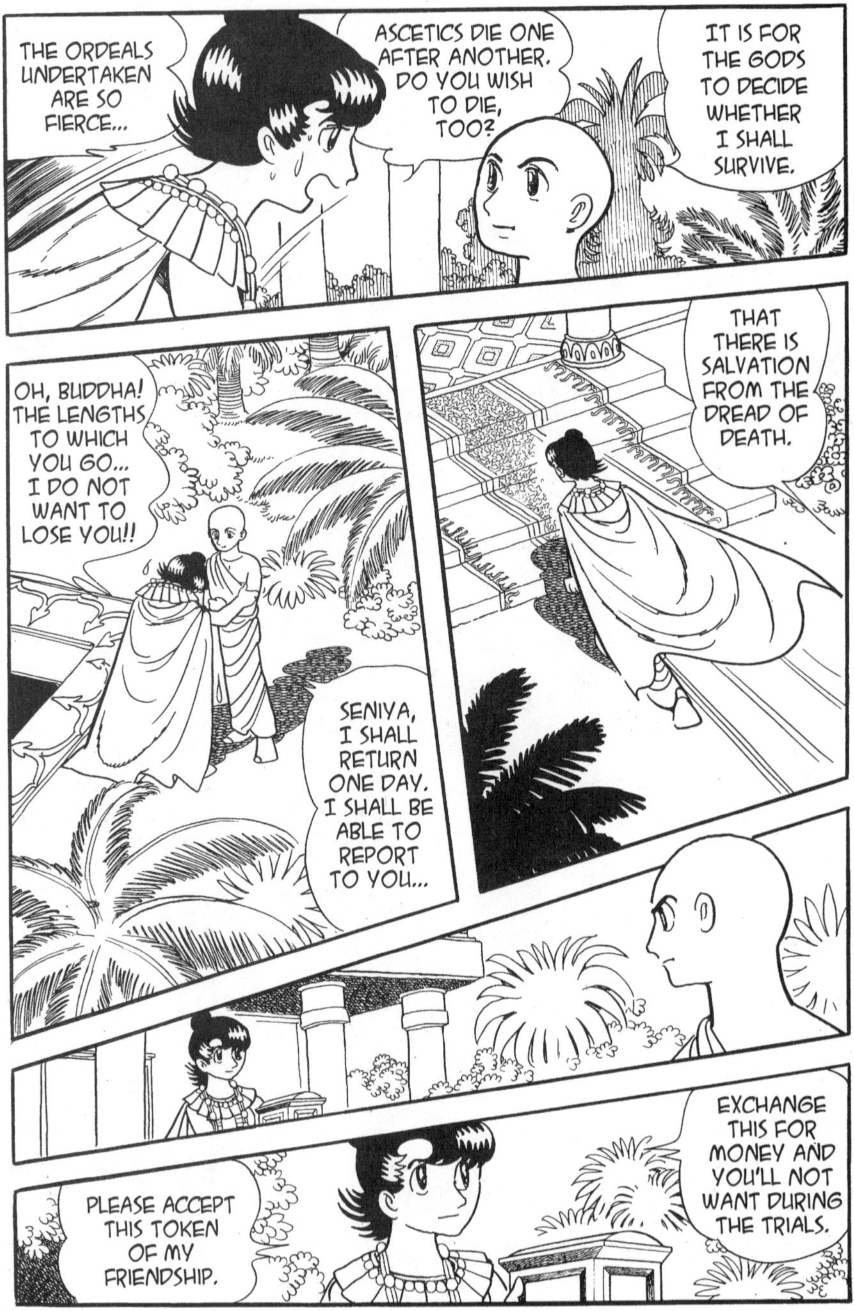
THE ORDEALS UNDERTAKEN ARE SO FIERCE...
ASCETICS DIE ONE AFTER ANOTHER. DO YOU WISH TO DIE, TOO?
IT IS FOR THE GODS TO DECIDE WHETHER I SHALL SURVIVE.
OH, BUDDHA! THE LENGTHS TO WHICH YOU GO... I DO NOT WANT TO LOSE YOU!!
SENIYA, I SHALL RETURN ONE DAY. I SHALL BE ABLE TO REPORT TO YOU...
THAT THERE IS SALVATION FROM THE DREAD OF DEATH.
PLEASE ACCEPT THIS TOKEN OF MY FRIENDSHIP.
EXCHANGE THIS FOR MONEY AND YOU'LL NOT WANT DURING THE TRIALS.

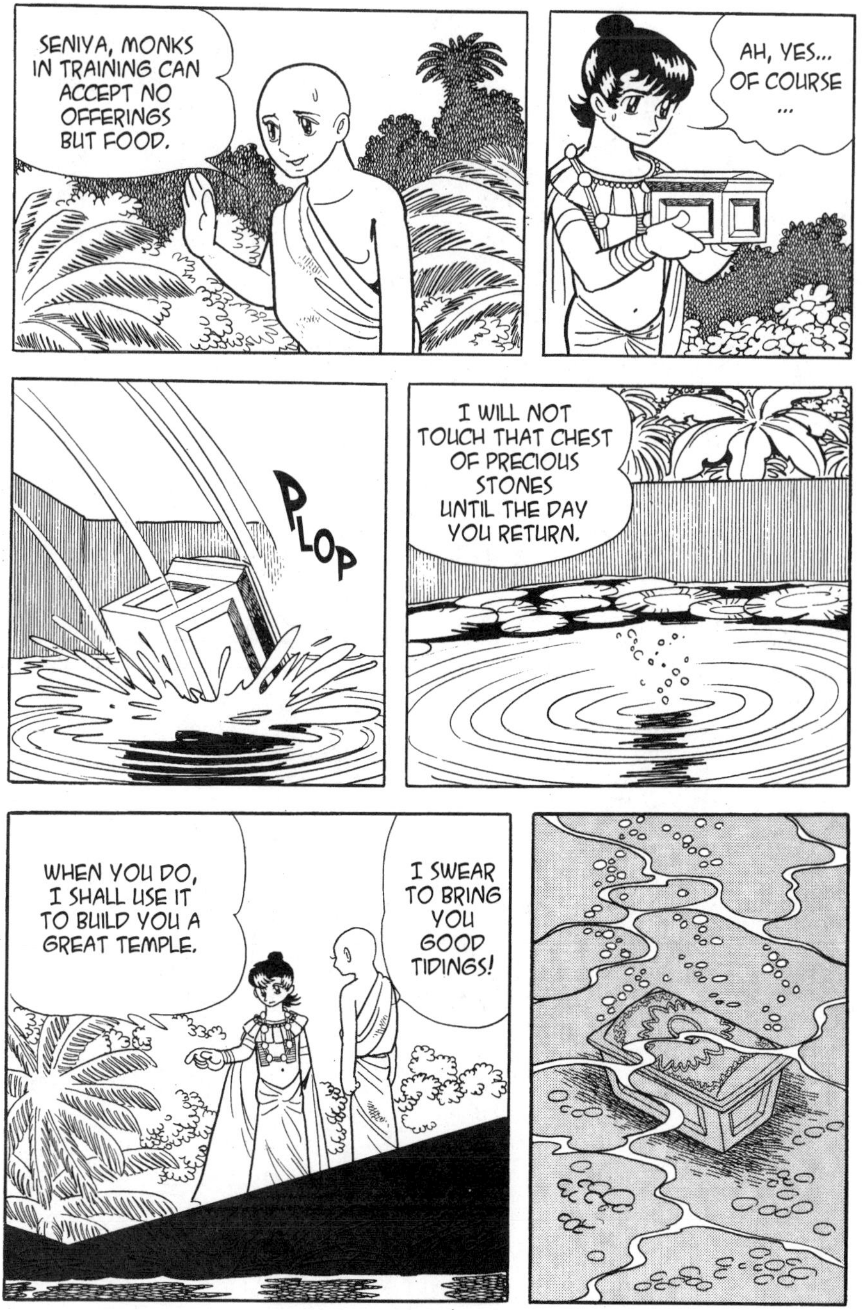
SENIYA, MONKS IN TRAINING CAN ACCEPT NO OFFERINGS BUT FOOD.
AH, YES... OF COURSE ...
PLOP
I WILL NOT TOUCH THAT CHEST OF PRECIOUS STONES UNTIL THE DAY YOU RETURN.
WHEN YOU DO, I SHALL USE IT TO BUILD YOU A GREAT TEMPLE.
I SWEAR TO BRING YOU GOOD TIDINGS!

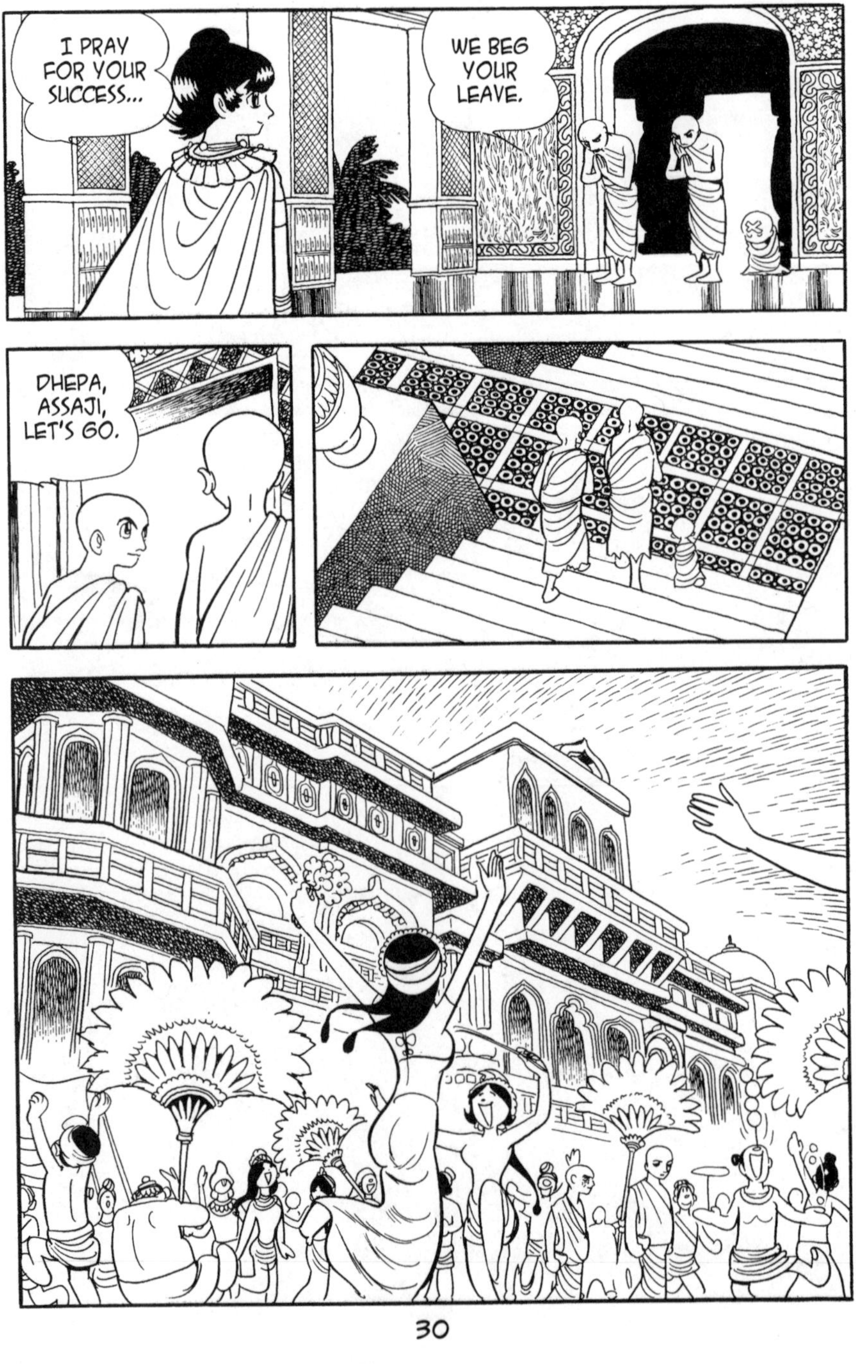
I PRAY FOR YOUR SUCCESS...
WE BEG YOUR LEAVE.
DHEPA, ASSAJI, LET'S GO.

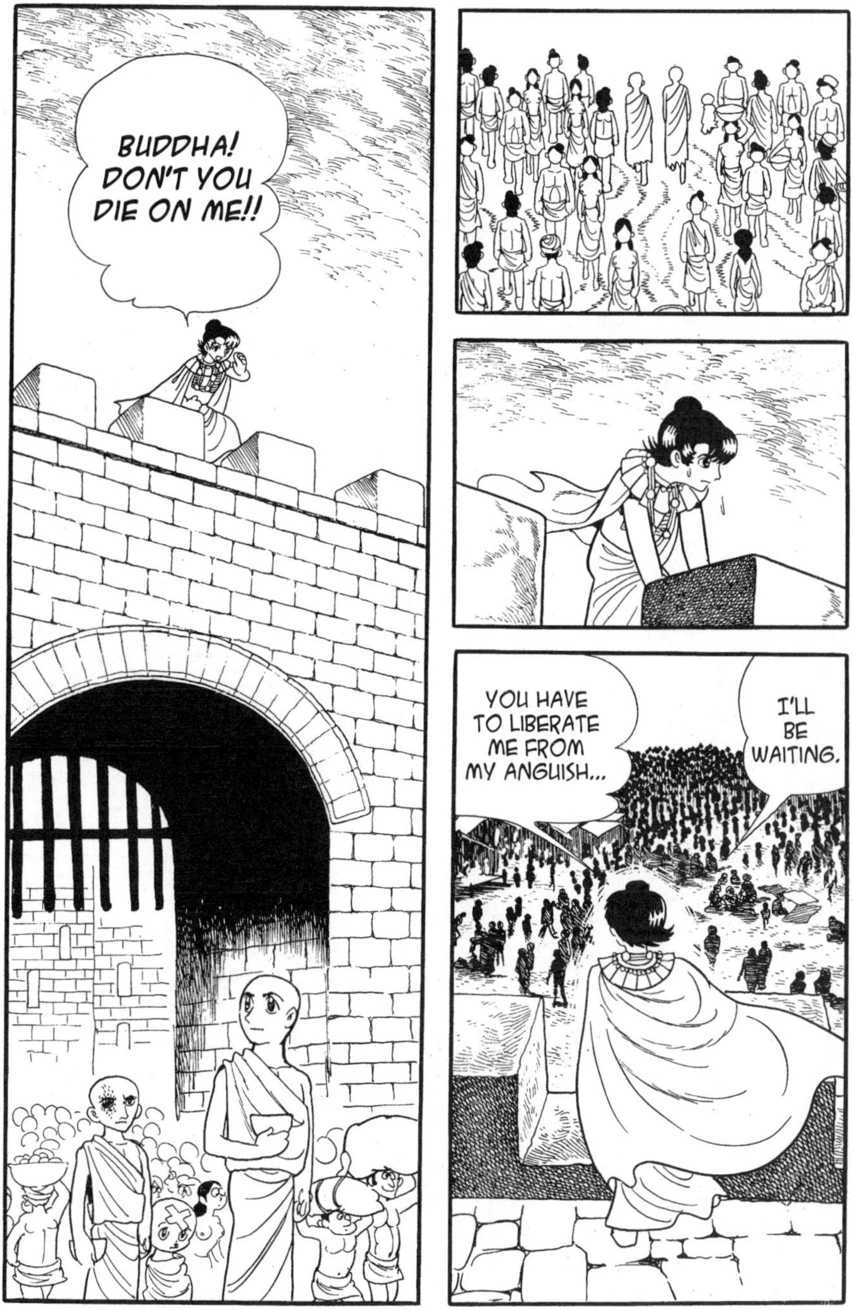
BUDDHA! DON'T YOU DIE ON ME!!
YOU HAVE TO LIBERATE ME FROM MY ANGUISH...
I'LL BE WAITING.

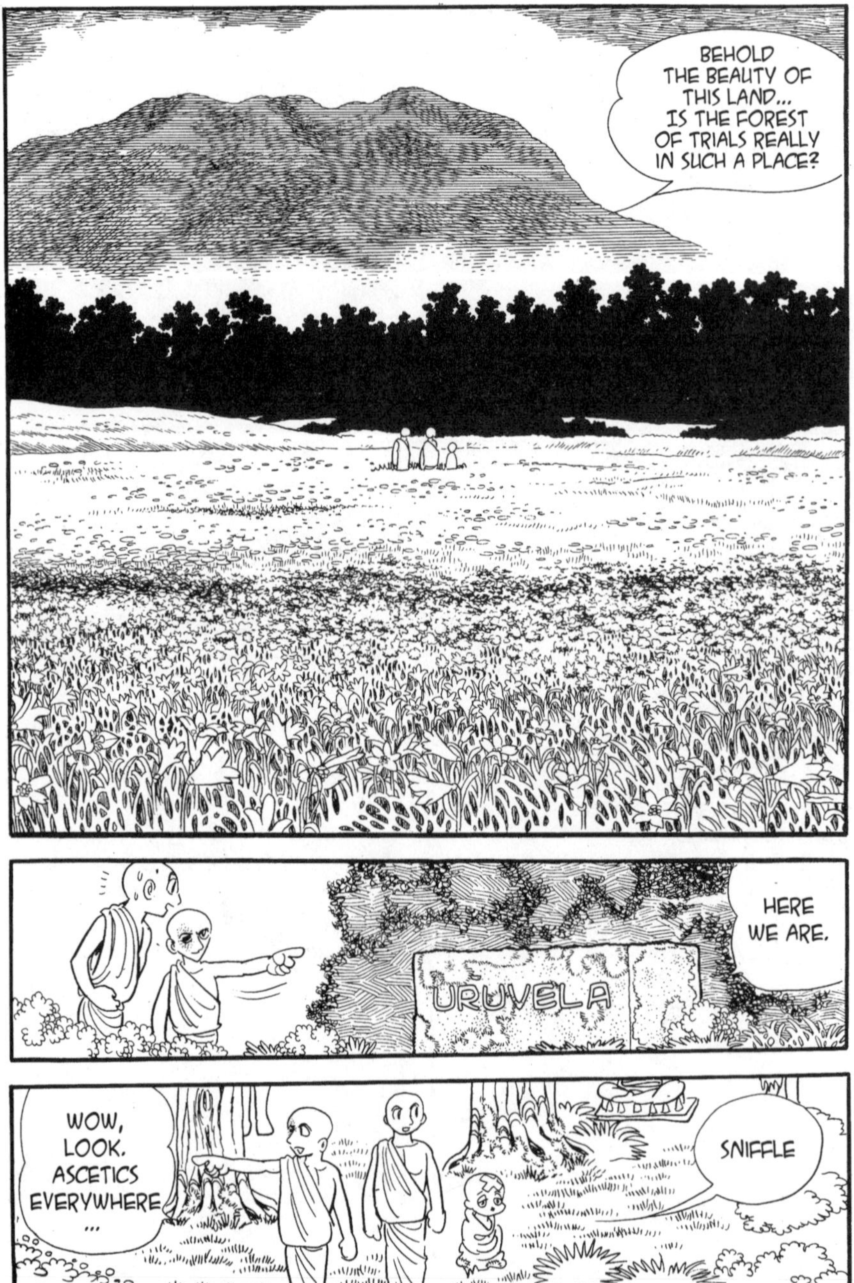
BEHOLD THE BEAUTY OF THIS LAND... IS THE FOREST OF TRIALS REALLY IN SUCH A PLACE?
URUVELA
HERE WE ARE.
WOW, LOOK. ASCETICS EVERYWHERE ...
SNIFFLE

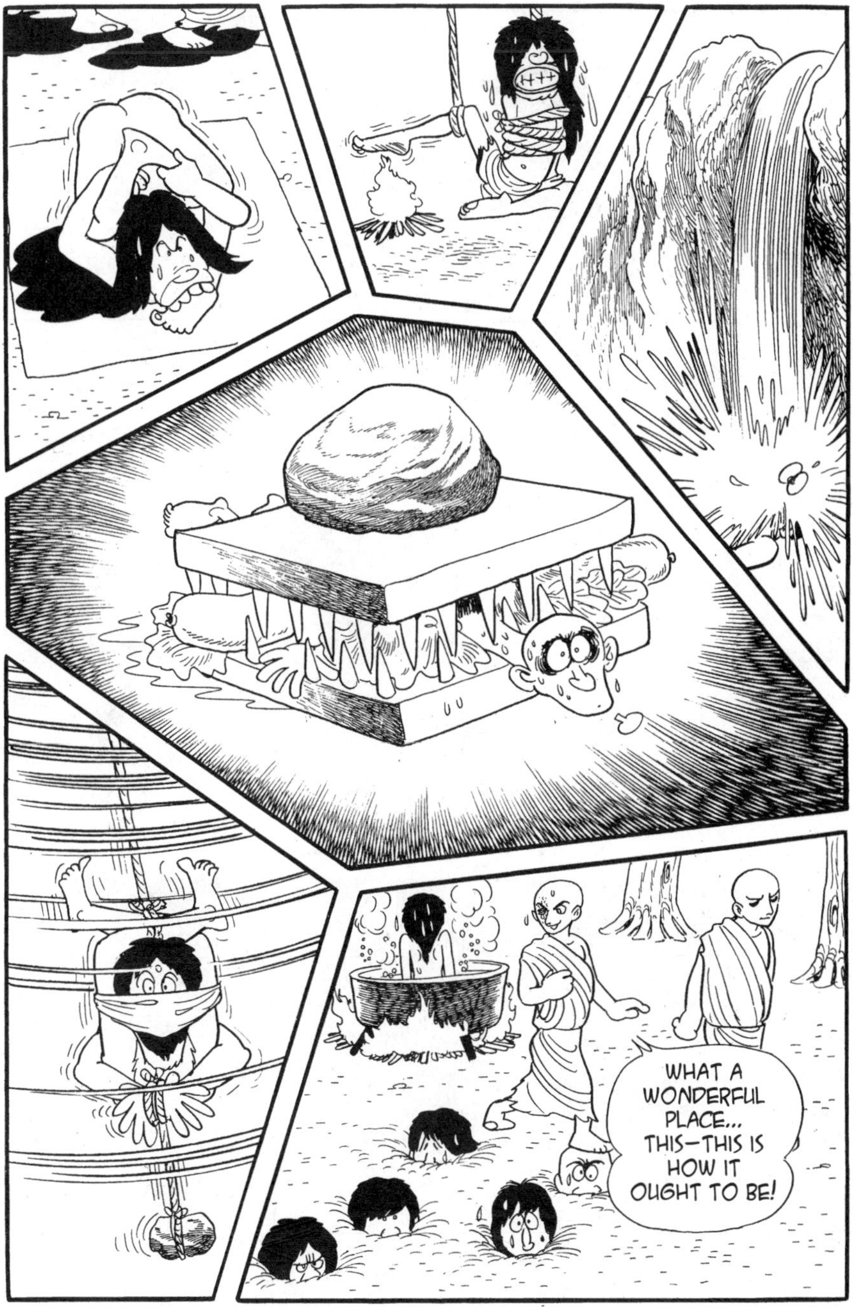
WHAT A WONDERFUL PLACE... THIS—THIS IS HOW IT OUGHT TO BE!

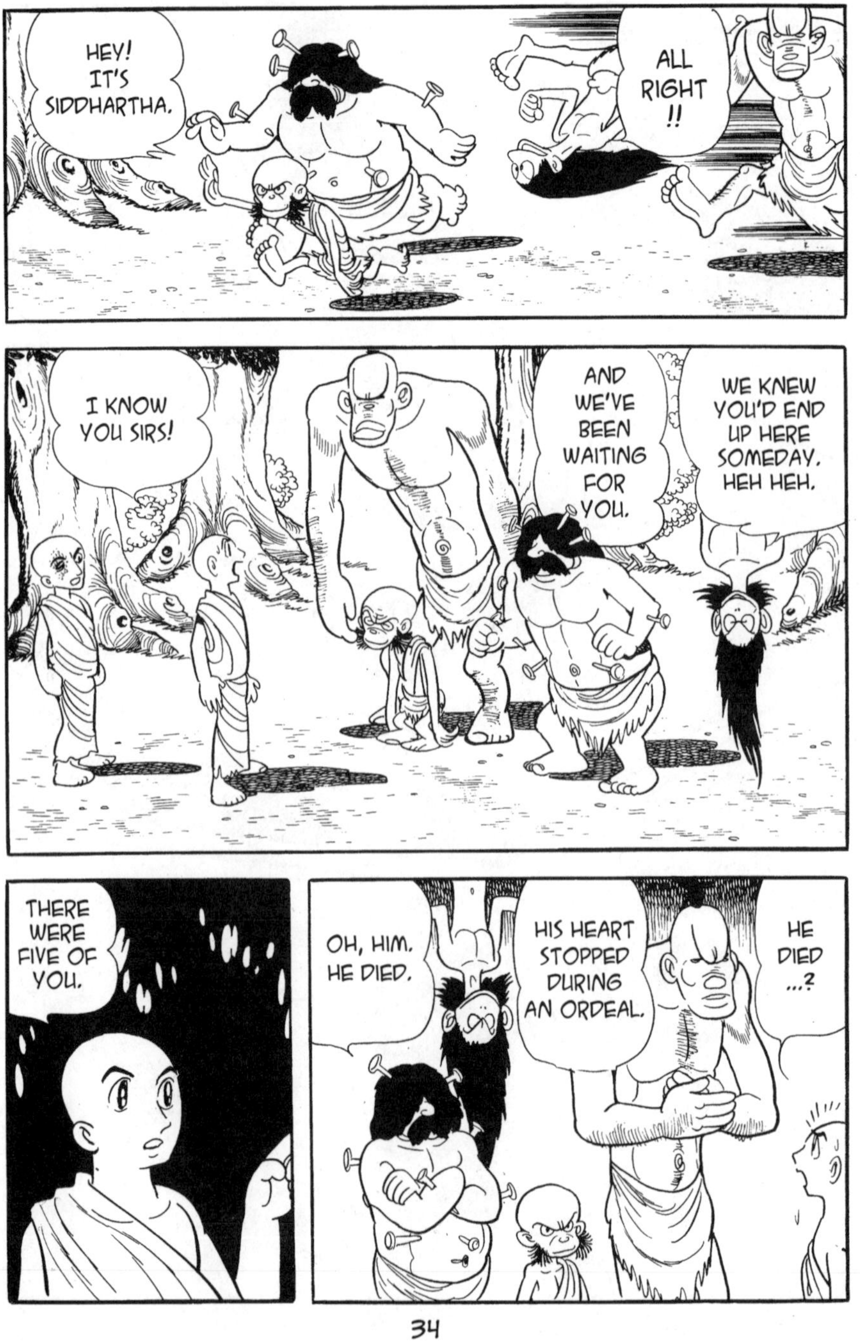
HEY! IT'S SIDDHARTHA.
ALL RIGHT !!
I KNOW YOU SIRS!
AND WE'VE BEEN WAITING FOR YOU.
WE KNEW YOU'D END UP HERE SOMEDAY. HEH HEH.
THERE WERE FIVE OF YOU.
OH, HIM. HE DIED.
HIS HEART STOPPED DURING AN ORDEAL.
HE DIED ...?

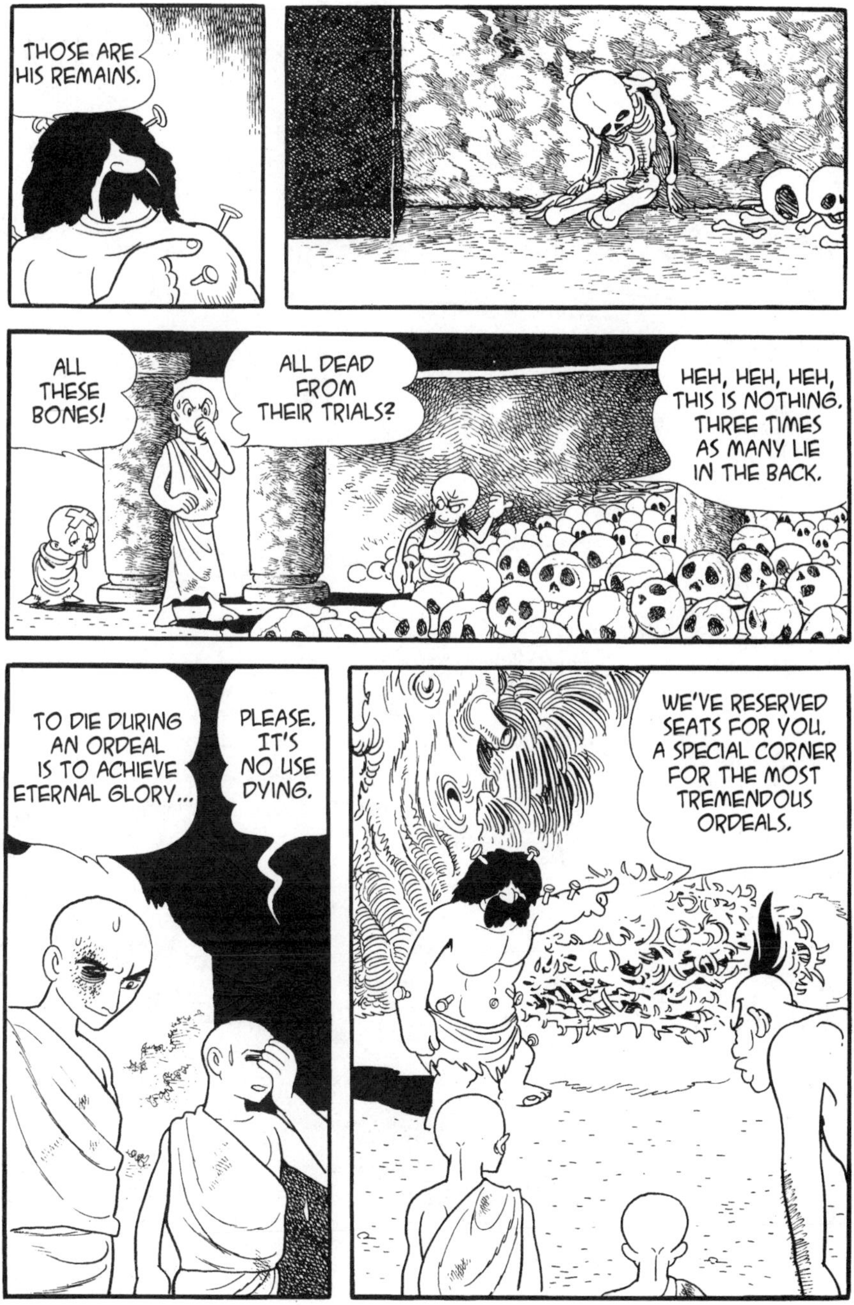
THOSE ARE HIS REMAINS.
ALL THESE BONES!
ALL DEAD FROM THEIR TRIALS?
HEH, HEH, HEH, THIS IS NOTHING. THREE TIMES AS MANY LIE IN THE BACK.
TO DIE DURING AN ORDEAL IS TO ACHIEVE ETERNAL GLORY...
PLEASE. IT'S NO USE DYING.
WE'VE RESERVED SEATS FOR YOU. A SPECIAL CORNER FOR THE MOST TREMENDOUS ORDEALS.

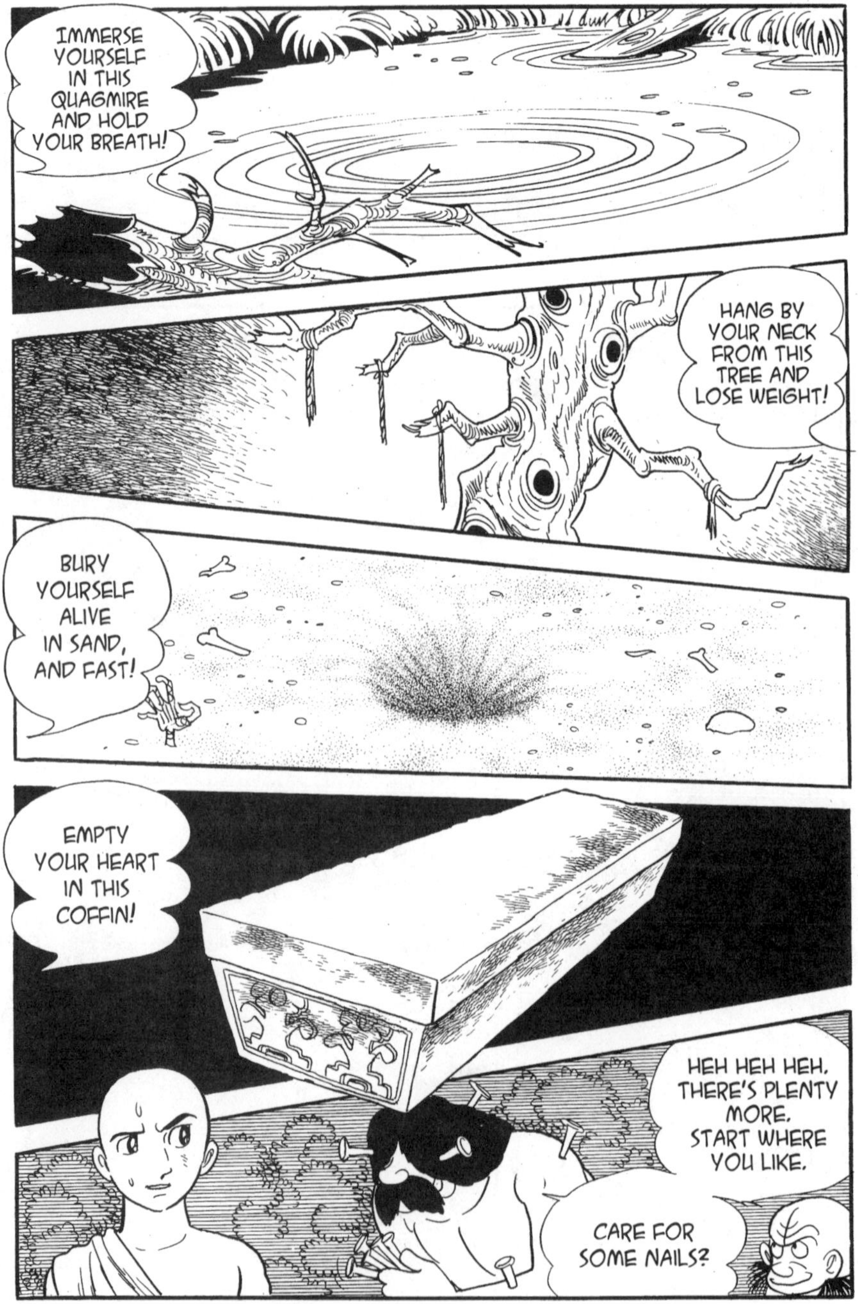
IMMERSE YOURSELF IN THIS QUAGMIRE AND HOLD YOUR BREATH!
HANG BY YOUR NECK FROM THIS TREE AND LOSE WEIGHT!
BURY YOURSELF ALIVE IN SAND, AND FAST!
EMPTY YOUR HEART IN THIS COFFIN!
HEH HEH HEH. THERE'S PLENTY MORE. START WHERE YOU LIKE.
CARE FOR SOME NAILS?

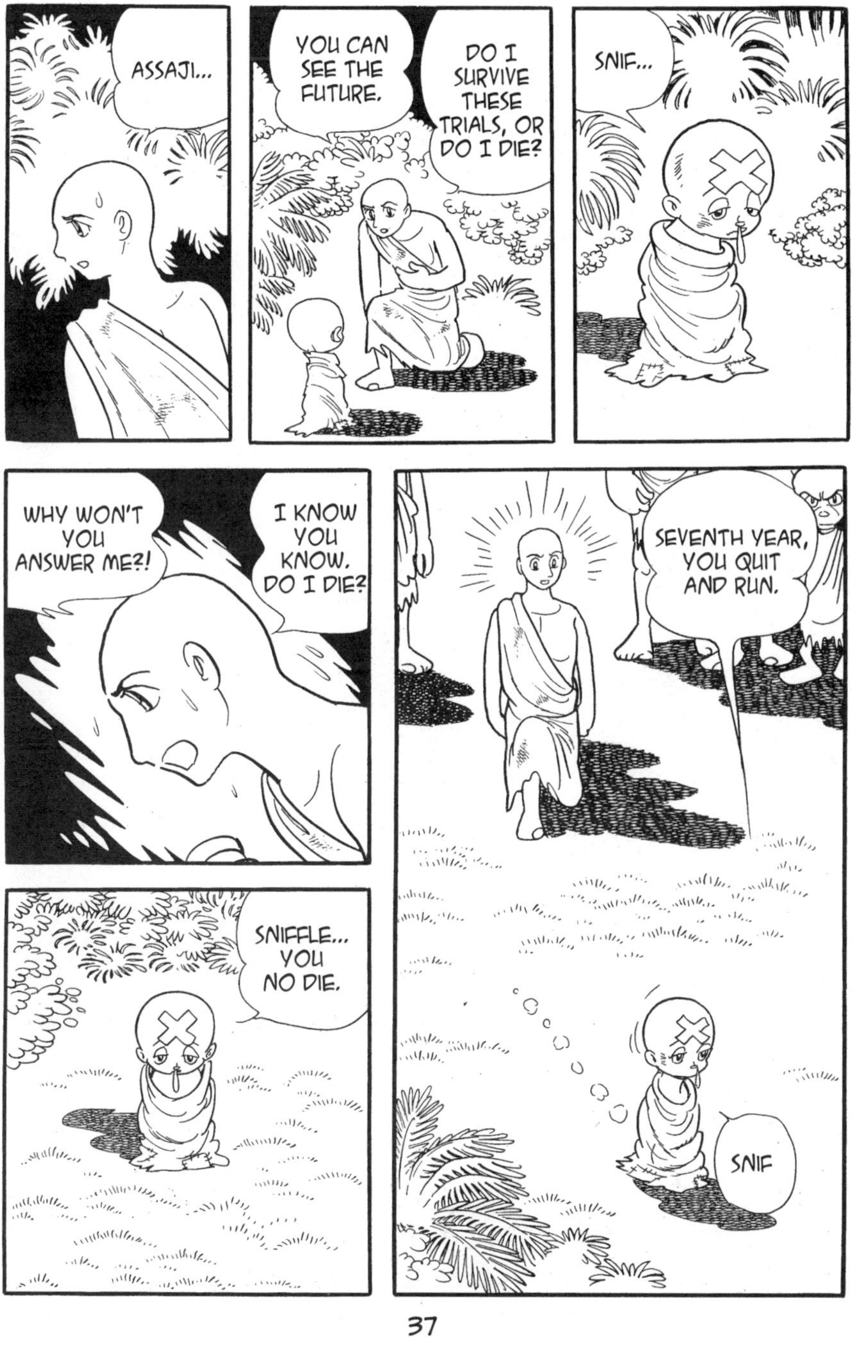
ASSAJI...
YOU CAN SEE THE FUTURE.
DO I SURVIVE THESE TRIALS, OR DO I DIE?
SNIF...
WHY WON'T YOU ANSWER ME?!
I KNOW YOU KNOW. DO I DIE?
SNIFFLE... YOU NO DIE.
SEVENTH YEAR, YOU QUIT AND RUN.
SNIF

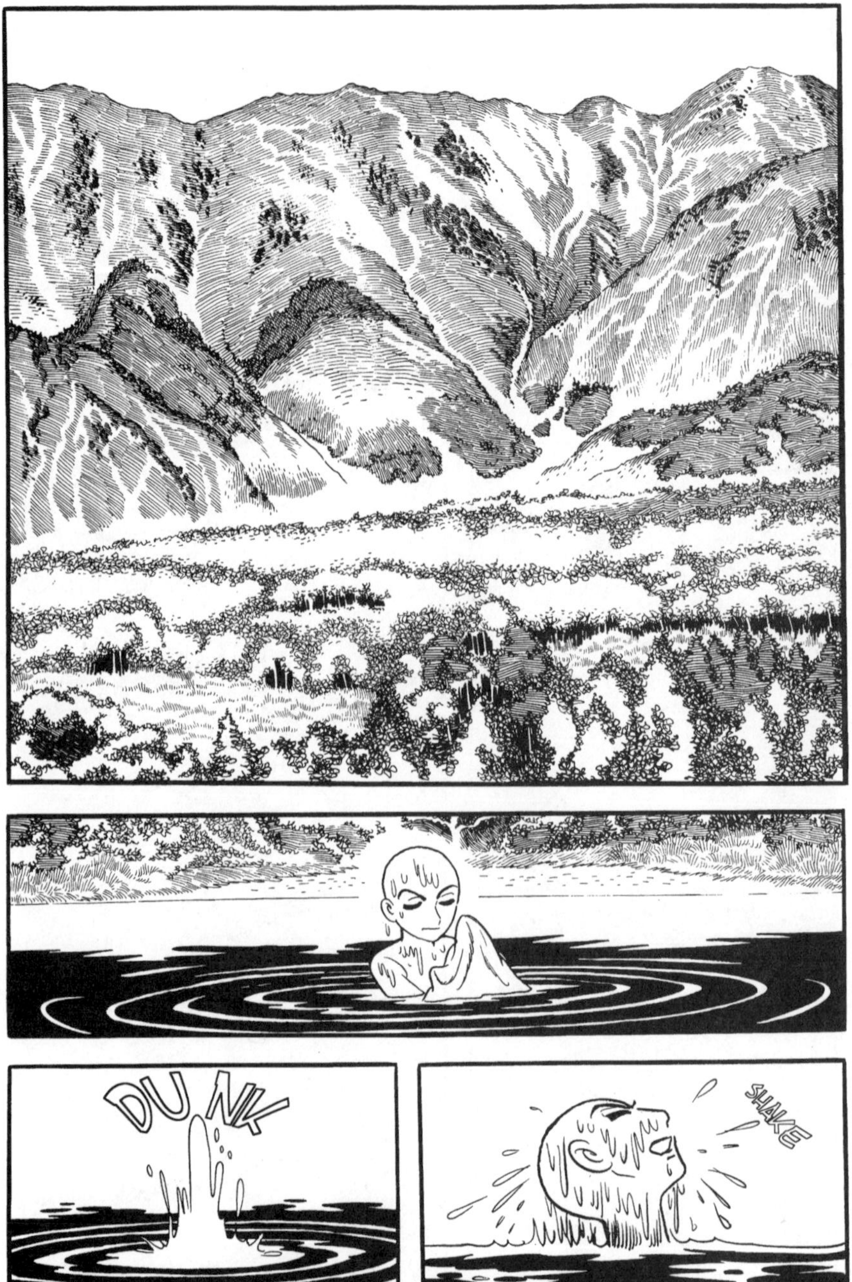
DUNK
SHAKE

HELLO...

HI

I'M SUJATA.

MY NAME'S SIDDHARTHA.

IT'S YOUR FIRST TIME IN THESE WOODS...

I JUST ARRIVED YESTERDAY. HOW COULD YOU TELL?

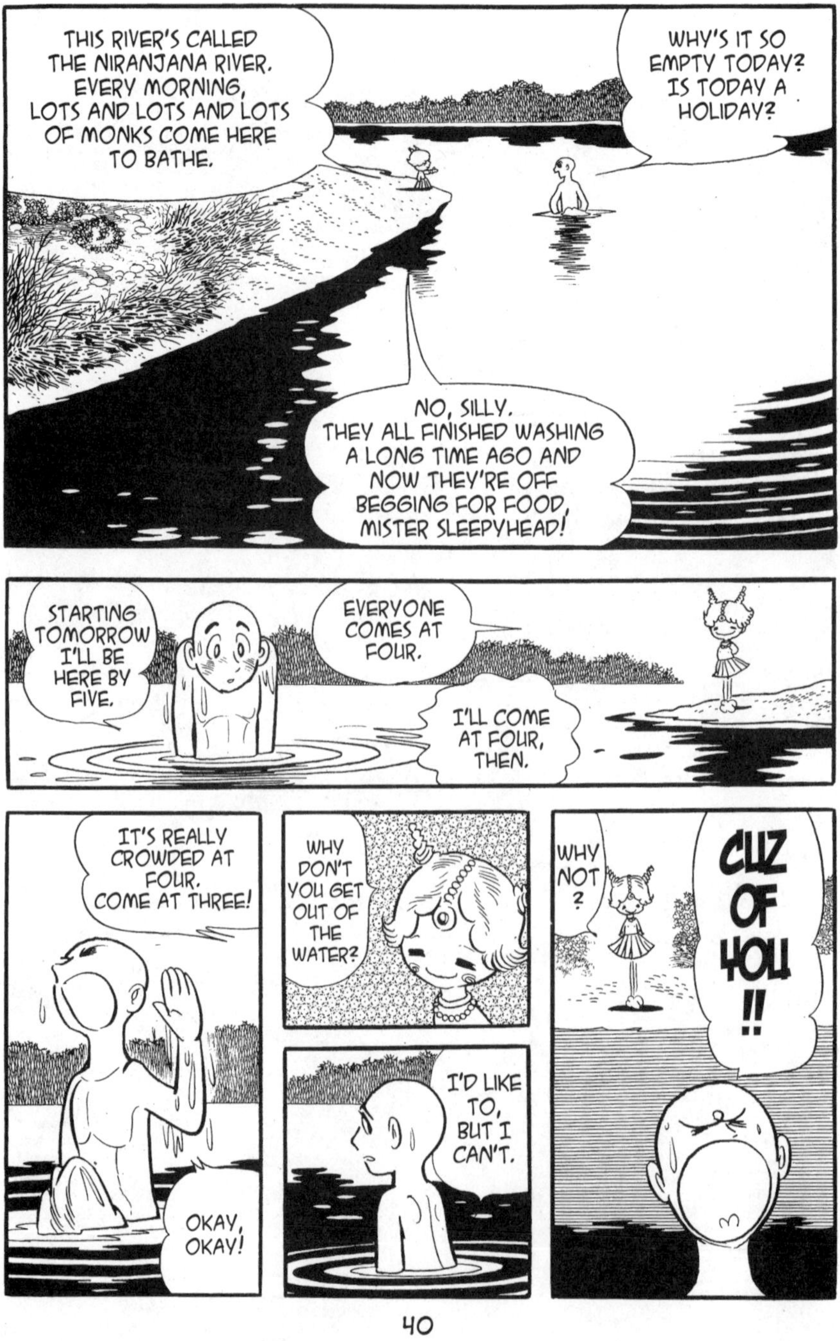
THIS RIVER'S CALLED THE NIRANJANA RIVER. EVERY MORNING, LOTS AND LOTS AND LOTS OF MONKS COME HERE TO BATHE.
WHY'S IT SO EMPTY TODAY? IS TODAY A HOLIDAY?
NO, SILLY. THEY ALL FINISHED WASHING A LONG TIME AGO AND NOW THEY'RE OFF BEGGING FOR FOOD, MISTER SLEEPYHEAD!
STARTING TOMORROW I'LL BE HERE BY FIVE.
EVERYONE COMES AT FOUR.
I'LL COME AT FOUR, THEN.
IT'S REALLY CROWDED AT FOUR. COME AT THREE!
OKAY, OKAY!
WHY DON'T YOU GET OUT OF THE WATER?
I'D LIKE TO, BUT I CAN'T.
WHY NOT?
CUZ OF YOU!!

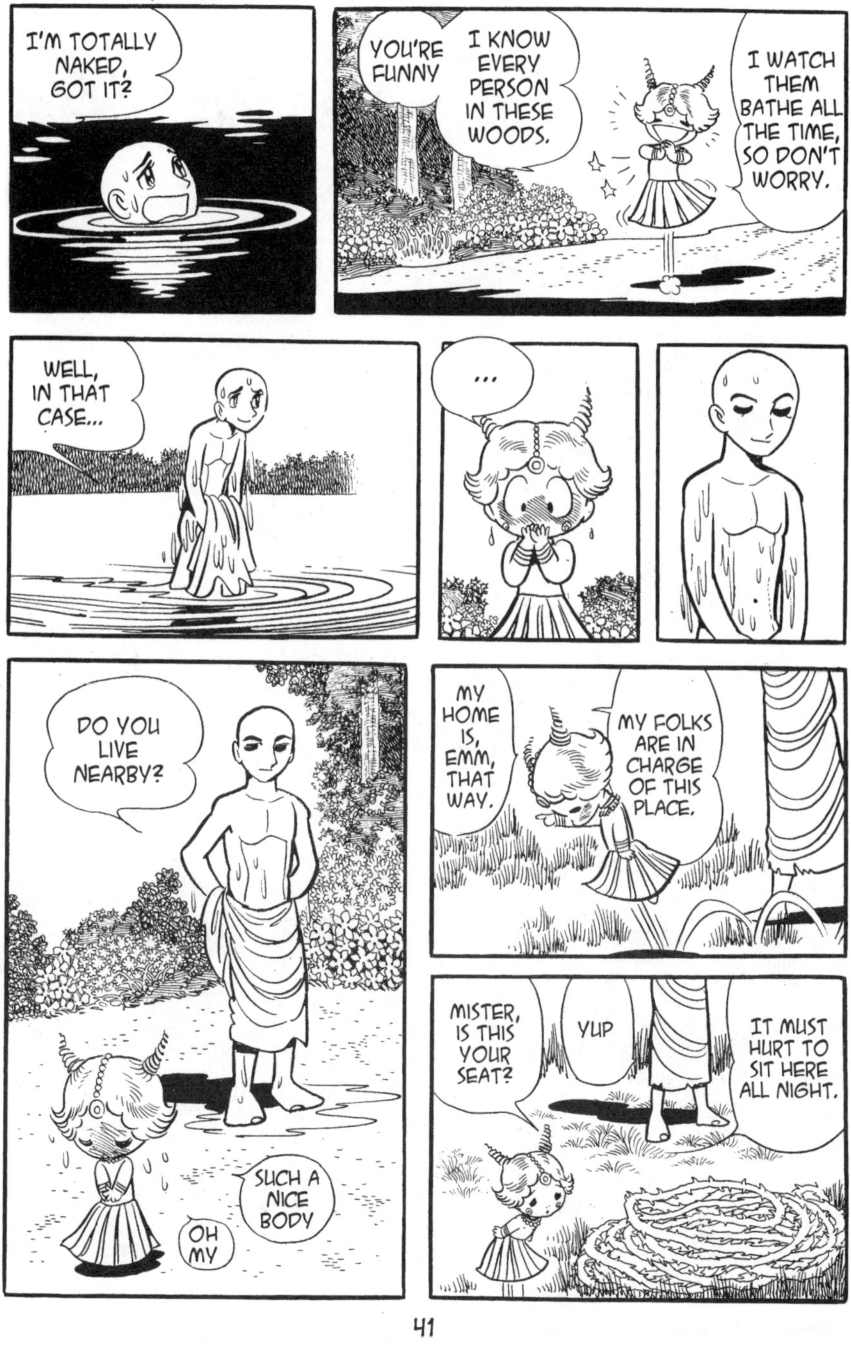
I'M TOTALLY NAKED, GOT IT?
YOU'RE FUNNY
I KNOW EVERY PERSON IN THESE WOODS.
I WATCH THEM BATHE ALL THE TIME, SO DON'T WORRY.
WELL, IN THAT CASE...
...
DO YOU LIVE NEARBY?
SUCH A NICE BODY
OH MY
MY HOME IS, EMM, THAT WAY.
MY FOLKS ARE IN CHARGE OF THIS PLACE.
MISTER, IS THIS YOUR SEAT?
YUP
IT MUST HURT TO SIT HERE ALL NIGHT.

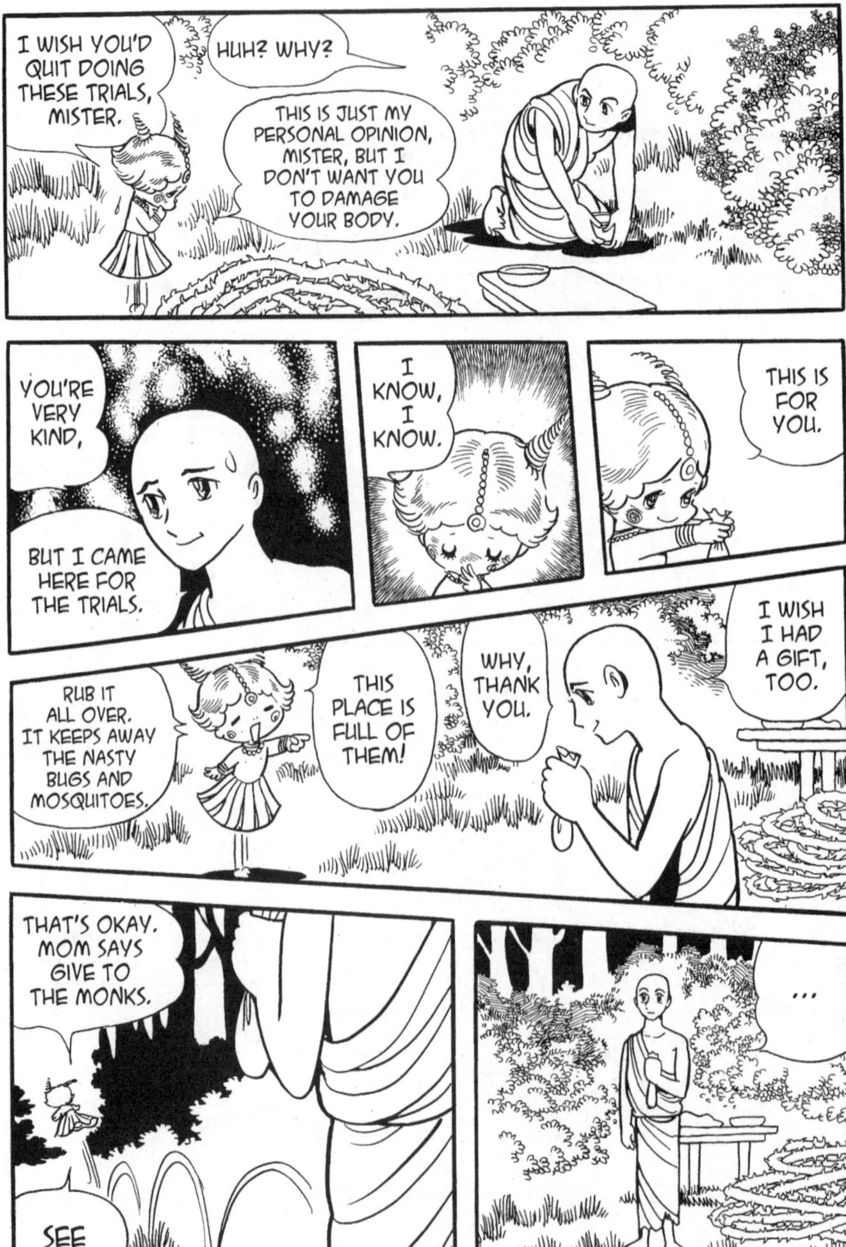
I WISH YOU'D QUIT DOING THESE TRIALS, MISTER.
HUH? WHY?
THIS IS JUST MY PERSONAL OPINION, MISTER, BUT I DON'T WANT YOU TO DAMAGE YOUR BODY.
YOU'RE VERY KIND,
BUT I CAME HERE FOR THE TRIALS.
I KNOW, I KNOW.
THIS IS FOR YOU.
RUB IT ALL OVER. IT KEEPS AWAY THE NASTY BUGS AND MOSQUITOES.
THIS PLACE IS FULL OF THEM!
WHY, THANK YOU.
I WISH I HAD A GIFT, TOO.
THAT'S OKAY. MOM SAYS GIVE TO THE MONKS.
SEE YA
...

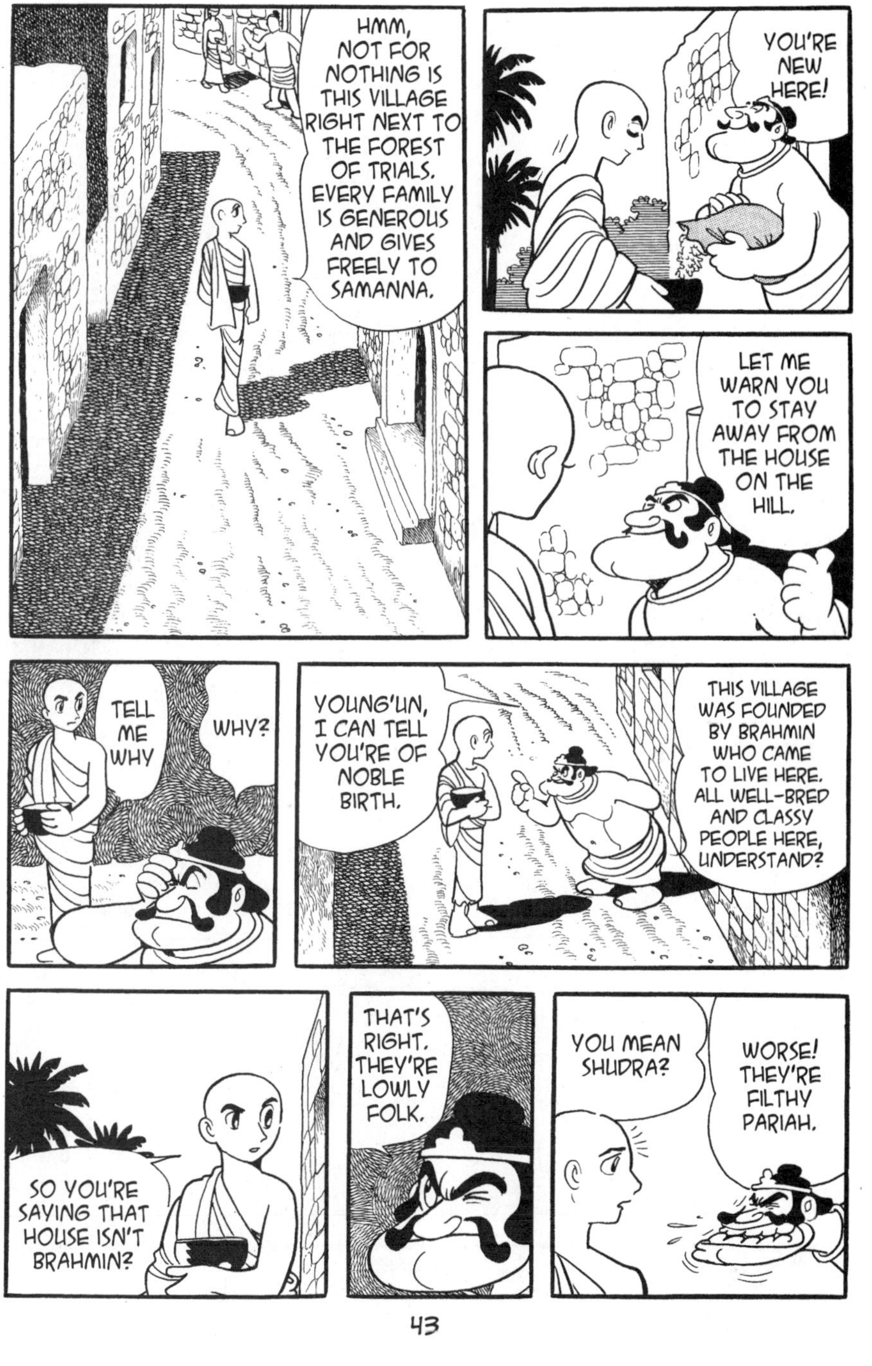
HMM, NOT FOR NOTHING IS THIS VILLAGE RIGHT NEXT TO THE FOREST OF TRIALS. EVERY FAMILY IS GENEROUS AND GIVES FREELY TO SAMANNA.
YOU'RE NEW HERE!
LET ME WARN YOU TO STAY AWAY FROM THE HOUSE ON THE HILL.
TELL ME WHY
WHY?
YOUNG'UN, I CAN TELL YOU'RE OF NOBLE BIRTH.
THIS VILLAGE WAS FOUNDED BY BRAHMIN WHO CAME TO LIVE HERE. ALL WELL-BRED AND CLASSY PEOPLE HERE, UNDERSTAND?
SO YOU'RE SAYING THAT HOUSE ISN'T BRAHMIN?
THAT'S RIGHT. THEY'RE LOWLY FOLK.
YOU MEAN SHUDRA?
WORSE! THEY'RE FILTHY PARIAH.

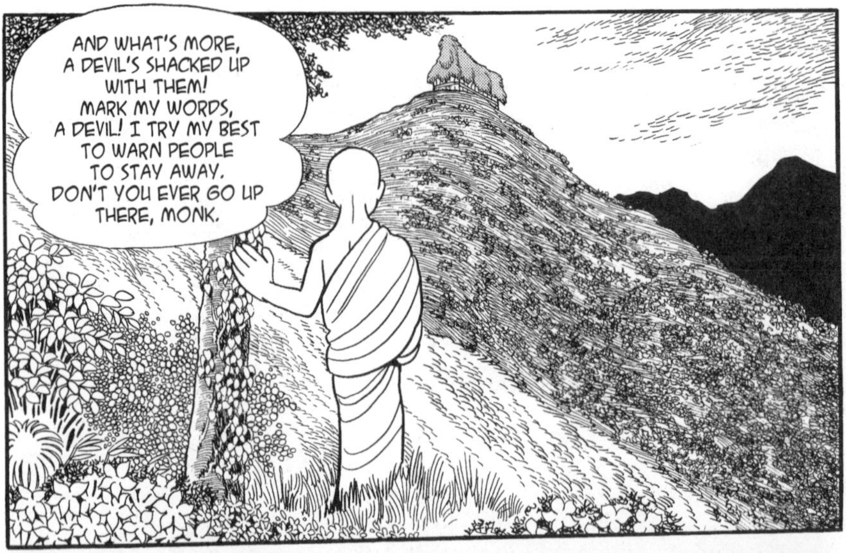
AND WHAT'S MORE, A DEVIL'S SHACKED UP WITH THEM! MARK MY WORDS, A DEVIL! I TRY MY BEST TO WARN PEOPLE TO STAY AWAY. DON'T YOU EVER GO UP THERE, MONK.

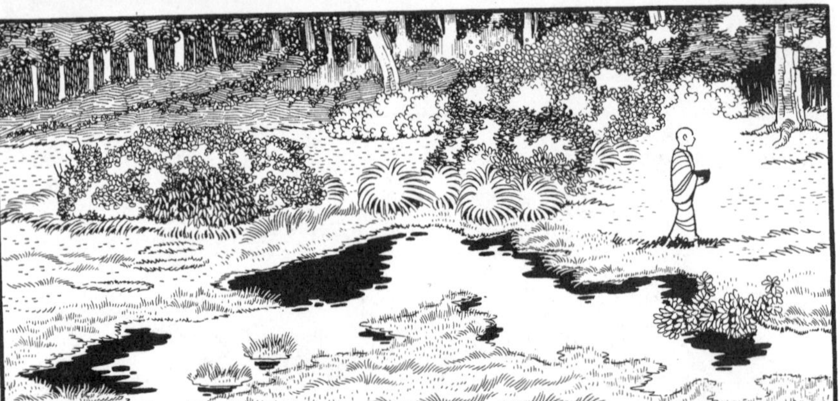

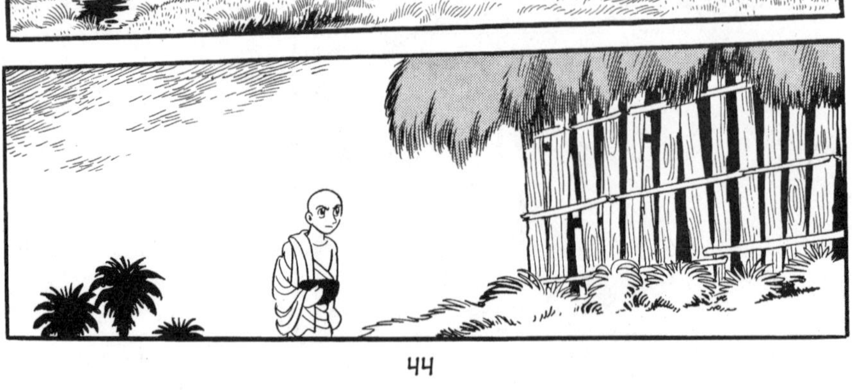

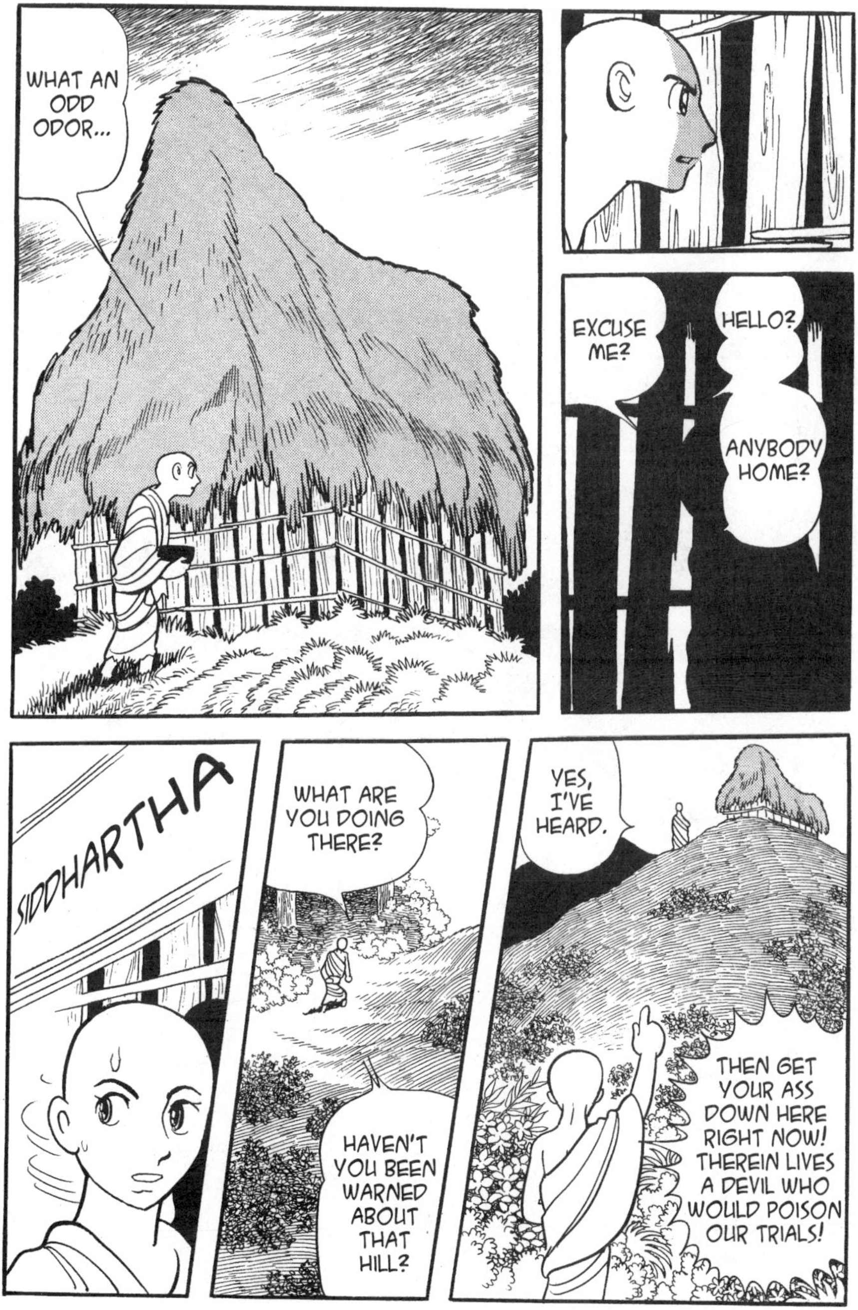
WHAT AN ODD ODOR...
EXCUSE ME?
HELLO?
ANYBODY HOME?
SIDDHARTHA
WHAT ARE YOU DOING THERE?
HAVEN'T YOU BEEN WARNED ABOUT THAT HILL?
YES, I'VE HEARD.
THEN GET YOUR ASS DOWN HERE RIGHT NOW! THEREIN LIVES A DEVIL WHO WOULD POISON OUR TRIALS!

CURIOSITY KILLED THE CAT, SIDDHARTHA!
I'M NOT A CAT.
AND I BET IT'S JUST PEOPLE IN THERE...
HERE I AM. MY FIRST NIGHT OF TRIALS...
THAT GIRL SAID THIS'LL REPEL THE BUGS.

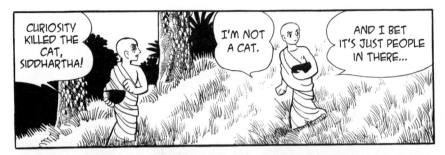

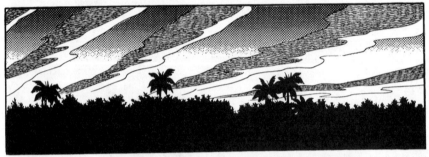

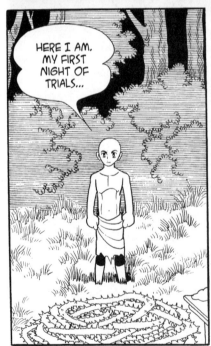

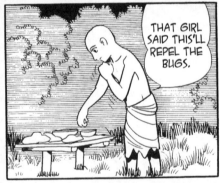

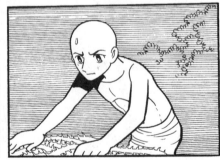

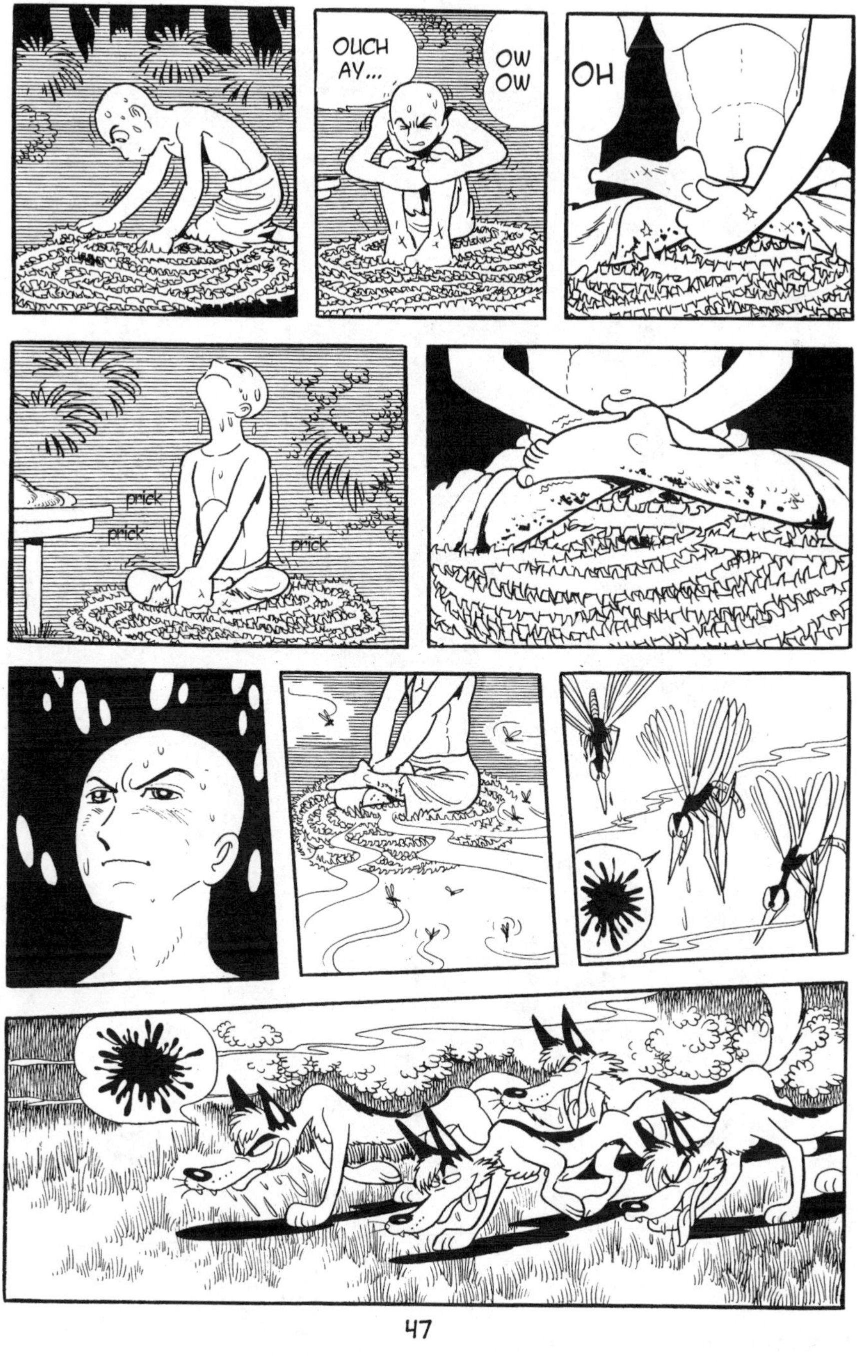
OUCH
AY...
OW
OW
OH
prick
prick
prick

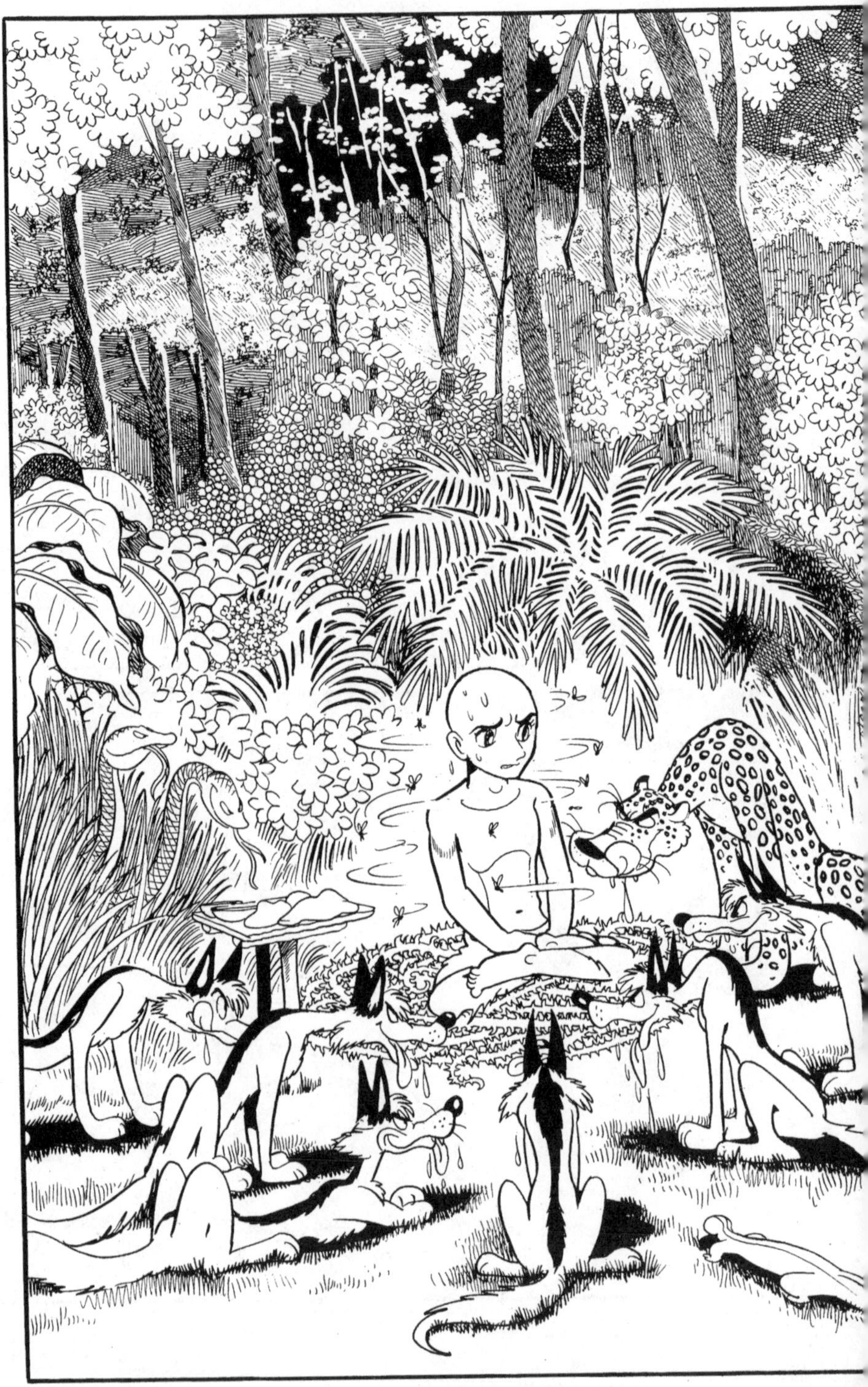

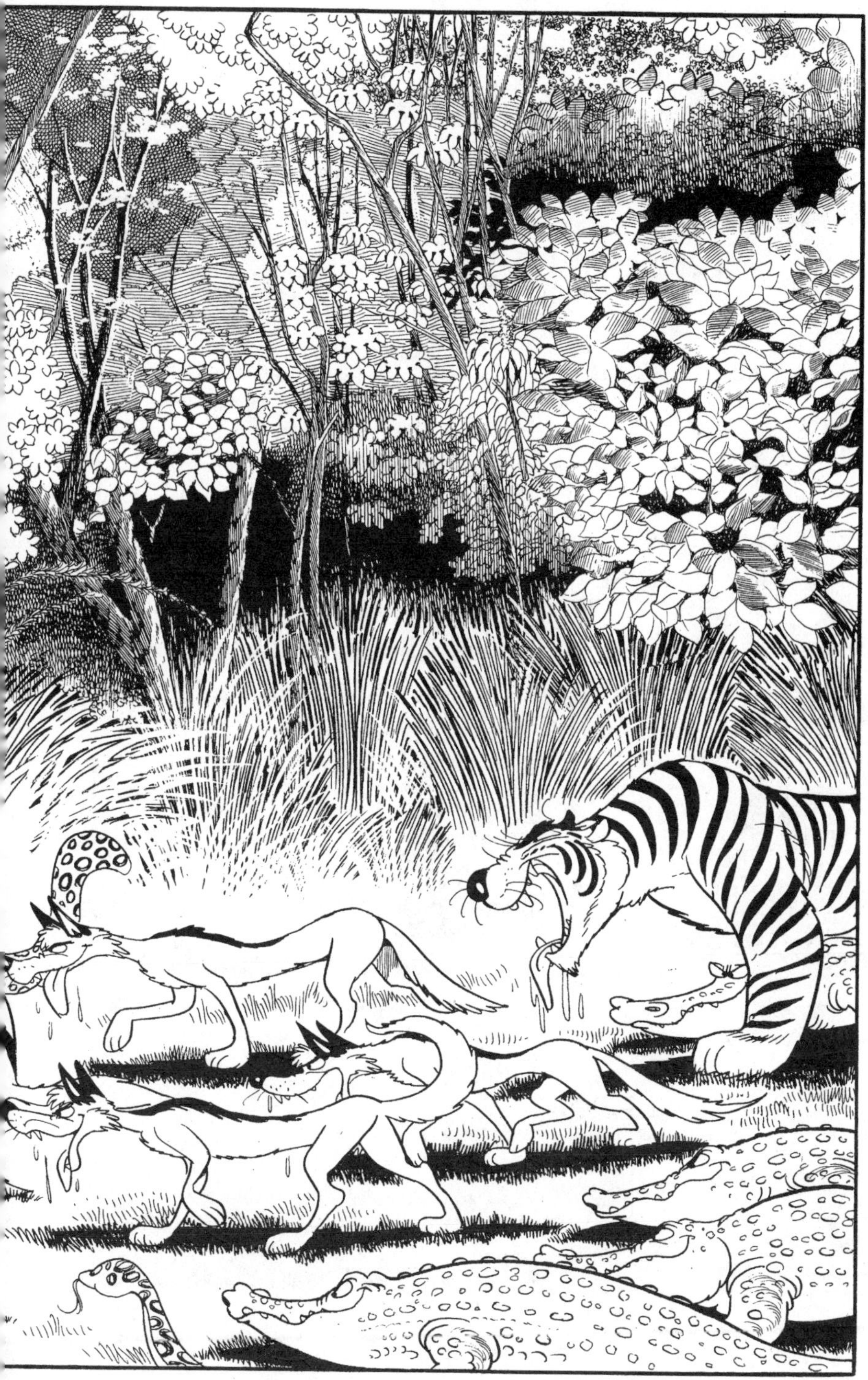

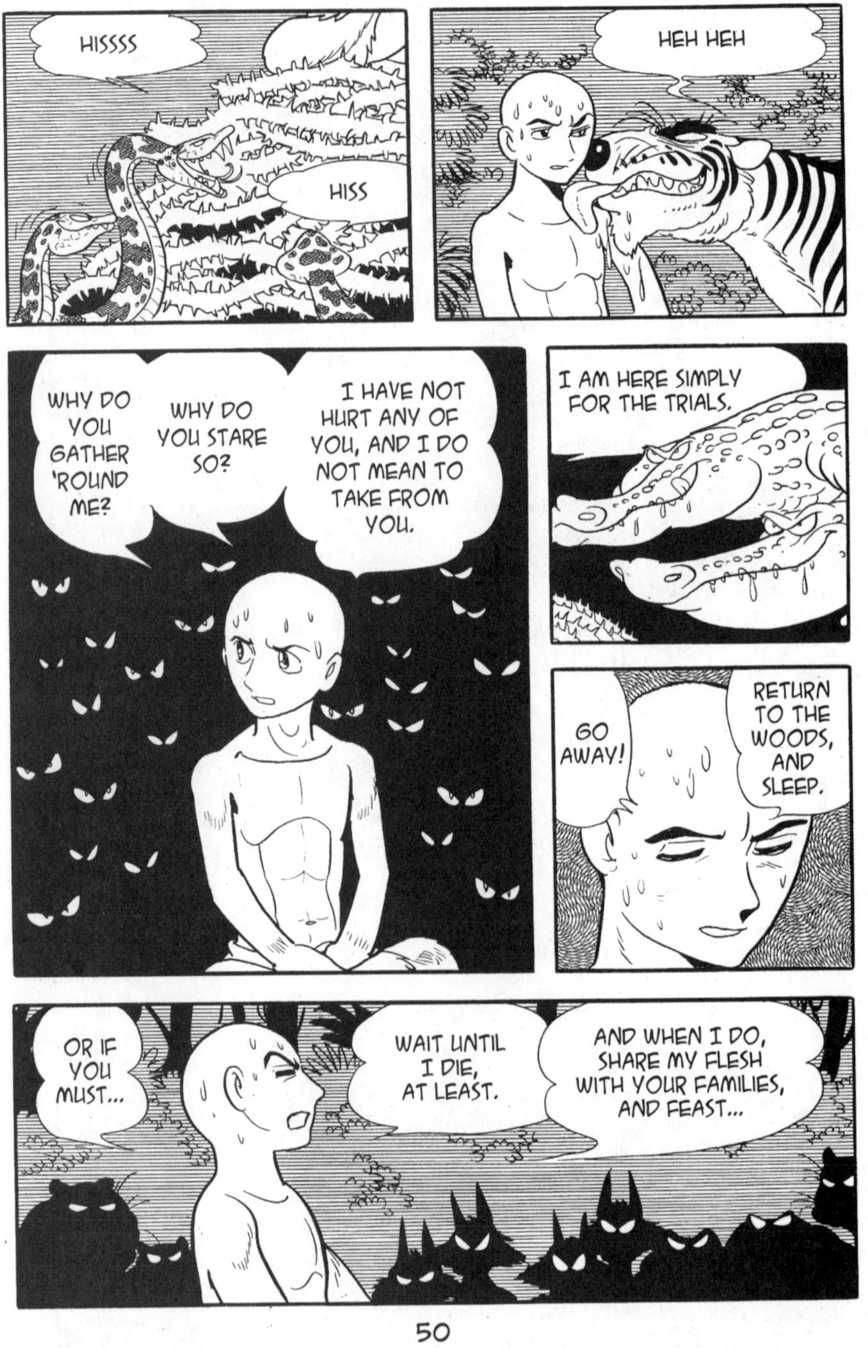
HISSSS
HISS
HEH HEH
WHY DO YOU GATHER 'ROUND ME?
WHY DO YOU STARE SO?
I HAVE NOT HURT ANY OF YOU, AND I DO NOT MEAN TO TAKE FROM YOU.
I AM HERE SIMPLY FOR THE TRIALS.
GO AWAY!
RETURN TO THE WOODS, AND SLEEP.
OR IF YOU MUST...
WAIT UNTIL I DIE, AT LEAST.
AND WHEN I DO, SHARE MY FLESH WITH YOUR FAMILIES, AND FEAST...

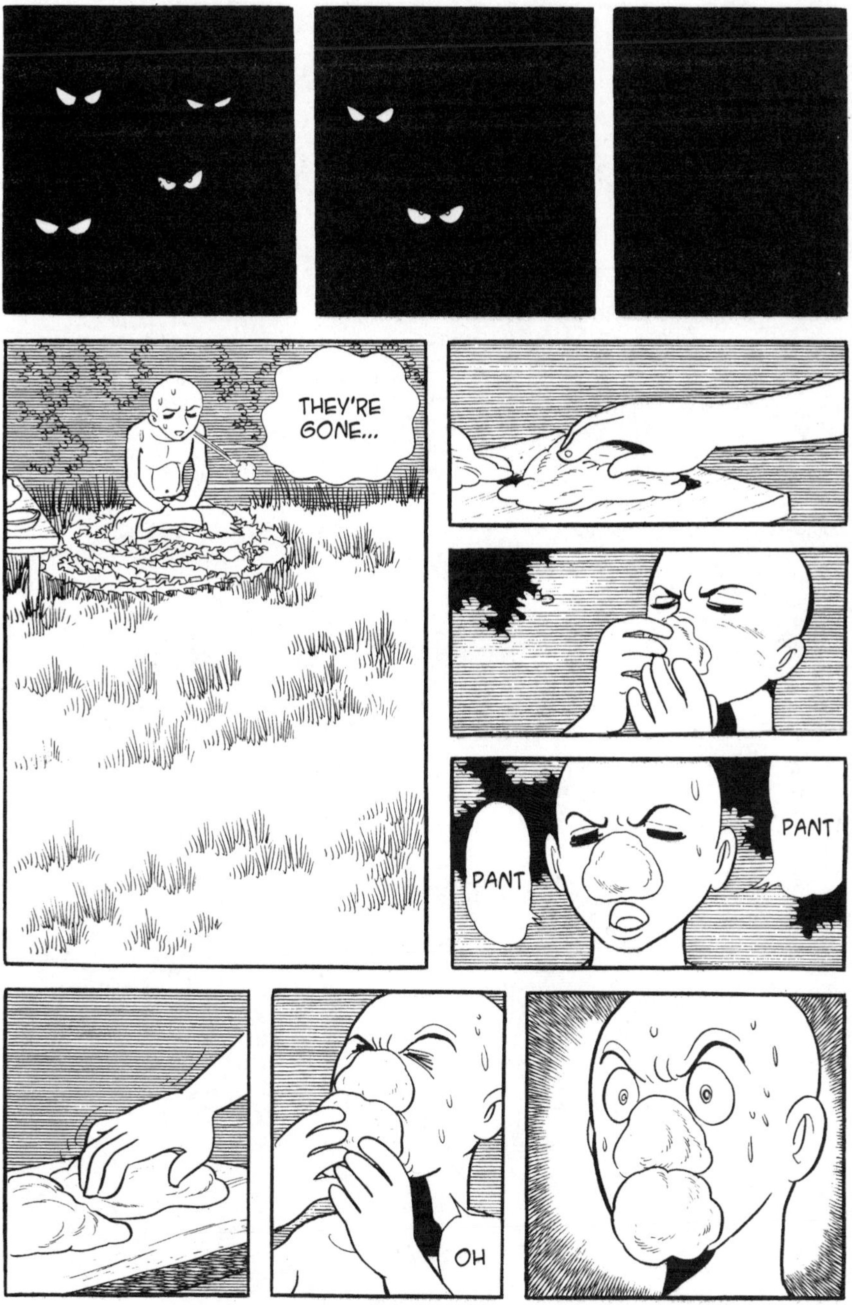
THEY'RE GONE...
PANT
PANT
OH

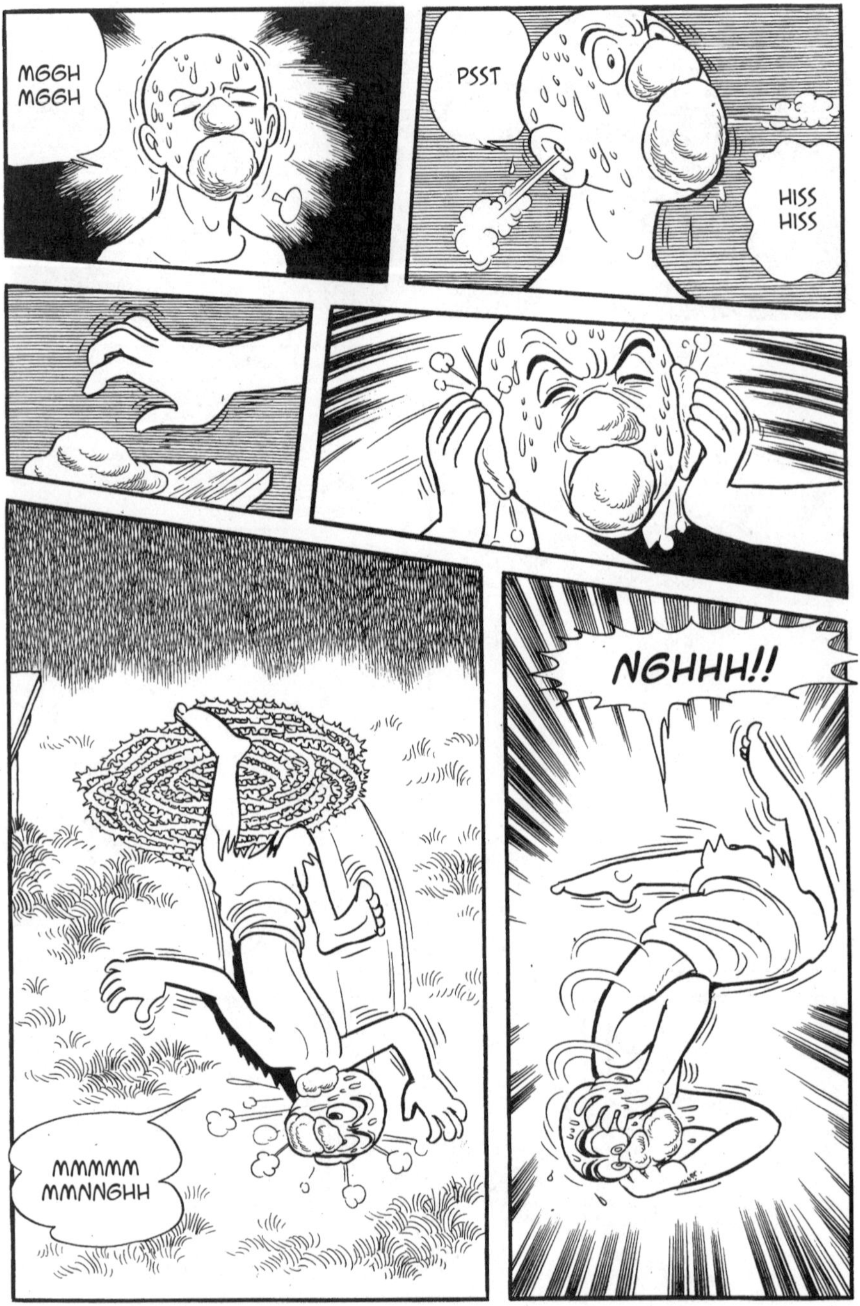
MGGH
MGGH
PSST
HISS
HISS
NGHHH!!
MMMMM
MMNNGHH

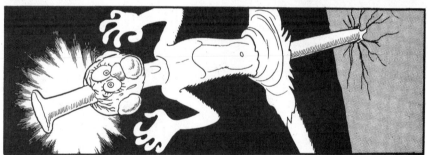

SIDDHARTHA?!
SIDDHARTHA!!

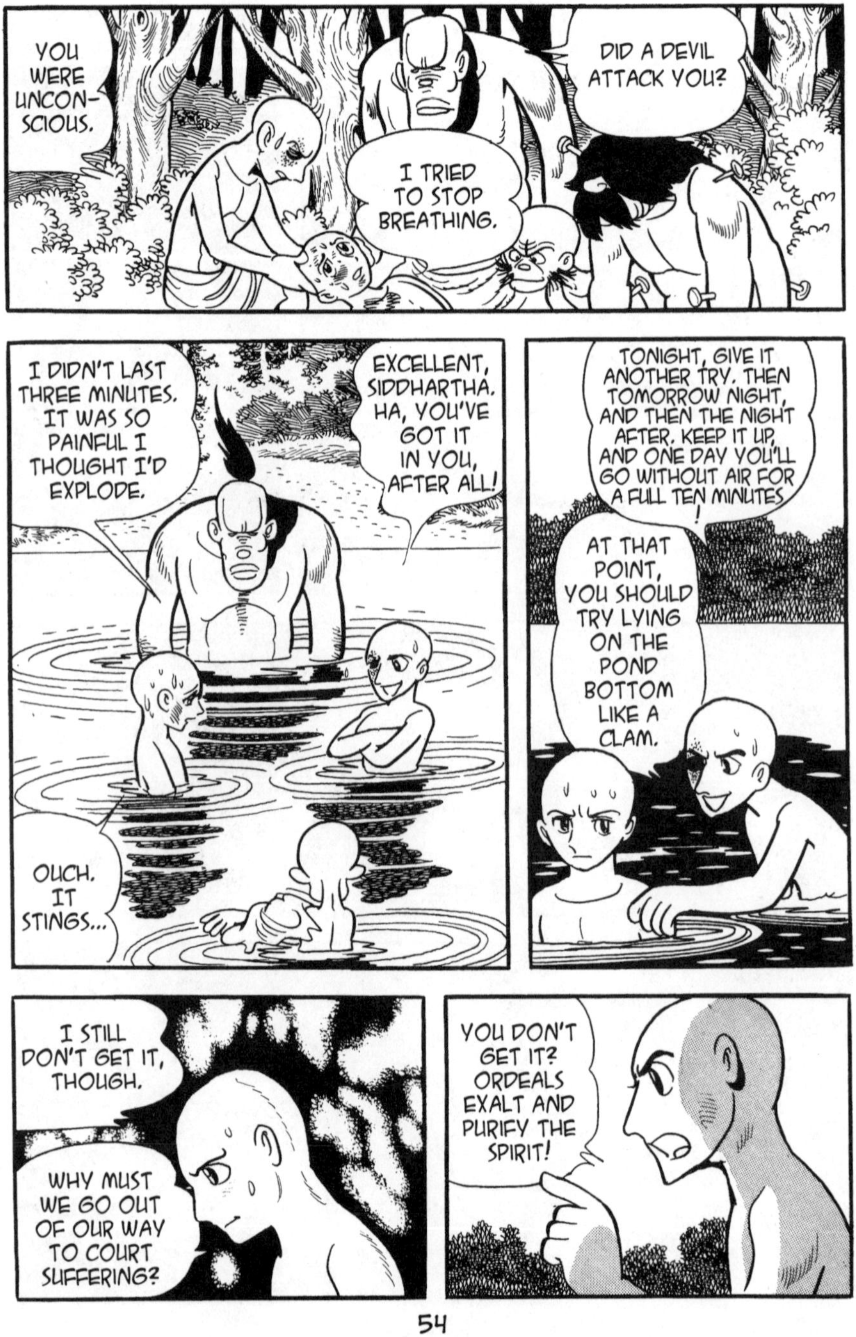
YOU WERE UNCON-SCIOUS.
DID A DEVIL ATTACK YOU?
I TRIED TO STOP BREATHING.
I DIDN'T LAST THREE MINUTES. IT WAS SO PAINFUL I THOUGHT I'D EXPLODE.
EXCELLENT, SIDDHARTHA. HA, YOU'VE GOT IT IN YOU, AFTER ALL!
OUCH. IT STINGS...
TONIGHT, GIVE IT ANOTHER TRY. THEN TOMORROW NIGHT, AND THEN THE NIGHT AFTER. KEEP IT UP, AND ONE DAY YOU'LL GO WITHOUT AIR FOR A FULL TEN MINUTES!
AT THAT POINT, YOU SHOULD TRY LYING ON THE POND BOTTOM LIKE A CLAM.
I STILL DON'T GET IT, THOUGH.
WHY MUST WE GO OUT OF OUR WAY TO COURT SUFFERING?
YOU DON'T GET IT? ORDEALS EXALT AND PURIFY THE SPIRIT!

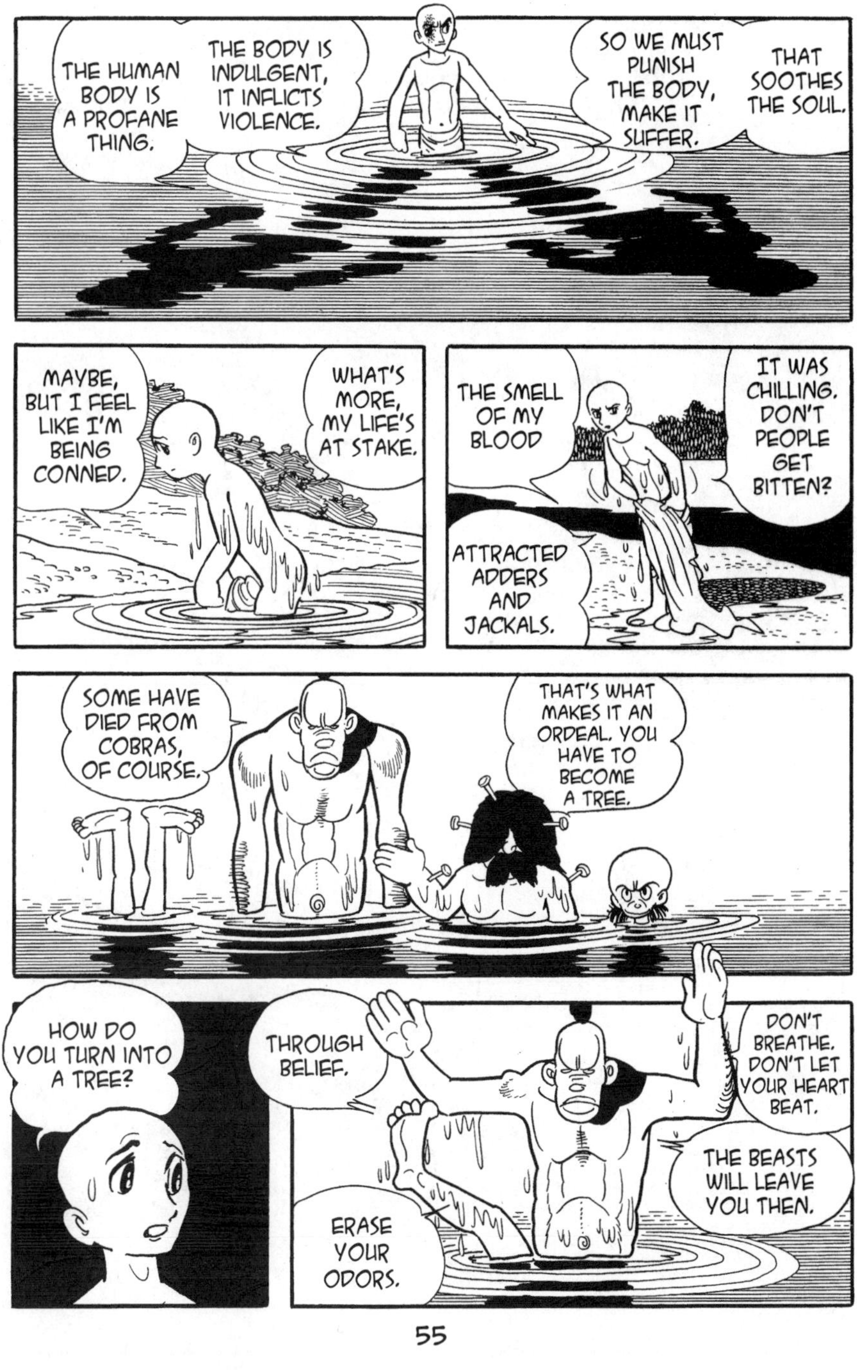
THE HUMAN BODY IS A PROFANE THING.
THE BODY IS INDULGENT, IT INFLICTS VIOLENCE.
SO WE MUST PUNISH THE BODY, MAKE IT SUFFER.
THAT SOOTHES THE SOUL.
MAYBE, BUT I FEEL LIKE I'M BEING CONNED.
WHAT'S MORE, MY LIFE'S AT STAKE.
THE SMELL OF MY BLOOD
ATTRACTED ADDERS AND JACKALS.
IT WAS CHILLING. DON'T PEOPLE GET BITTEN?
SOME HAVE DIED FROM COBRAS, OF COURSE.
THAT'S WHAT MAKES IT AN ORDEAL. YOU HAVE TO BECOME A TREE.
HOW DO YOU TURN INTO A TREE?
THROUGH BELIEF.
DON'T BREATHE. DON'T LET YOUR HEART BEAT.
THE BEASTS WILL LEAVE YOU THEN.
ERASE YOUR ODORS.

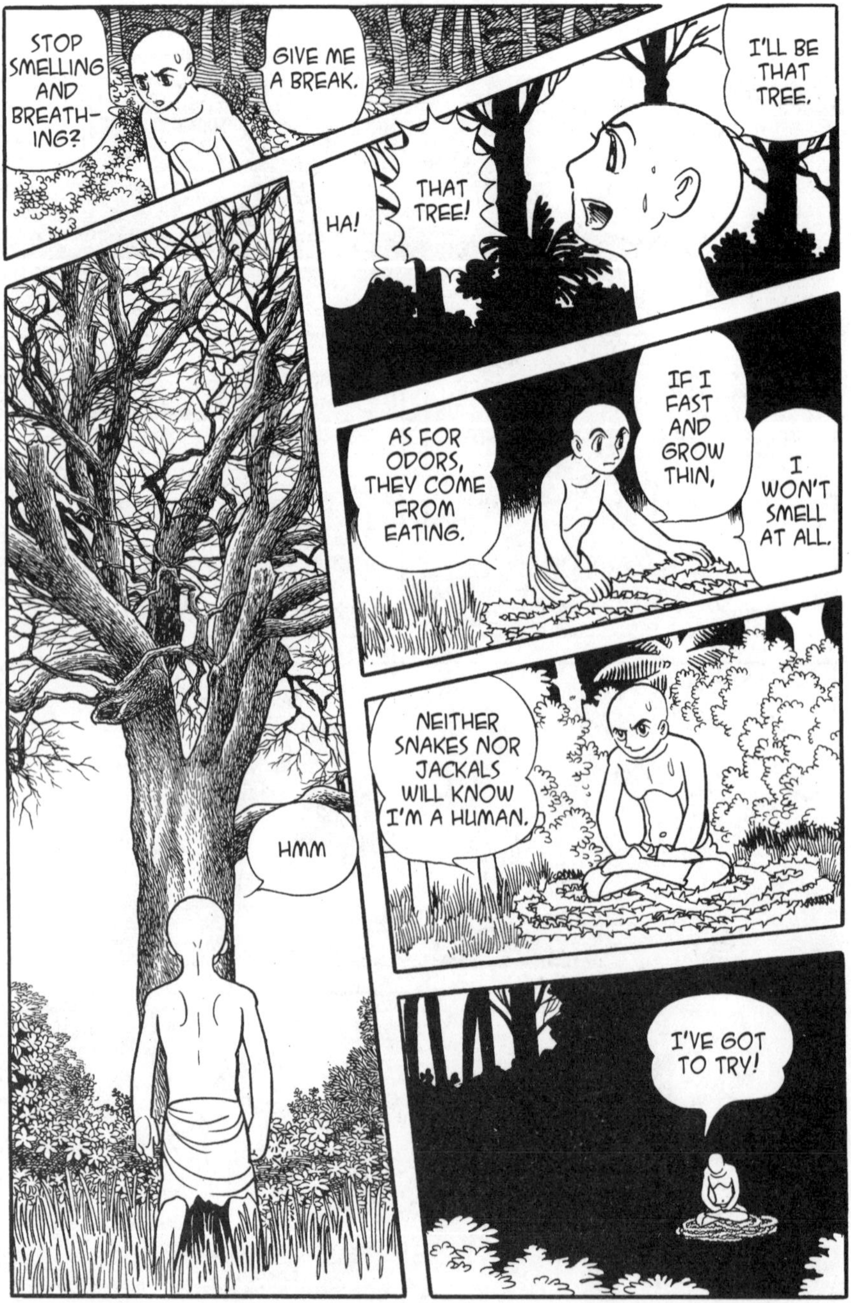
STOP SMELLING AND BREATHING?
GIVE ME A BREAK.
HA!
THAT TREE!
I'LL BE THAT TREE.
HMM
AS FOR ODORS, THEY COME FROM EATING.
IF I FAST AND GROW THIN,
I WON'T SMELL AT ALL.
NEITHER SNAKES NOR JACKALS WILL KNOW I'M A HUMAN.
I'VE GOT TO TRY!

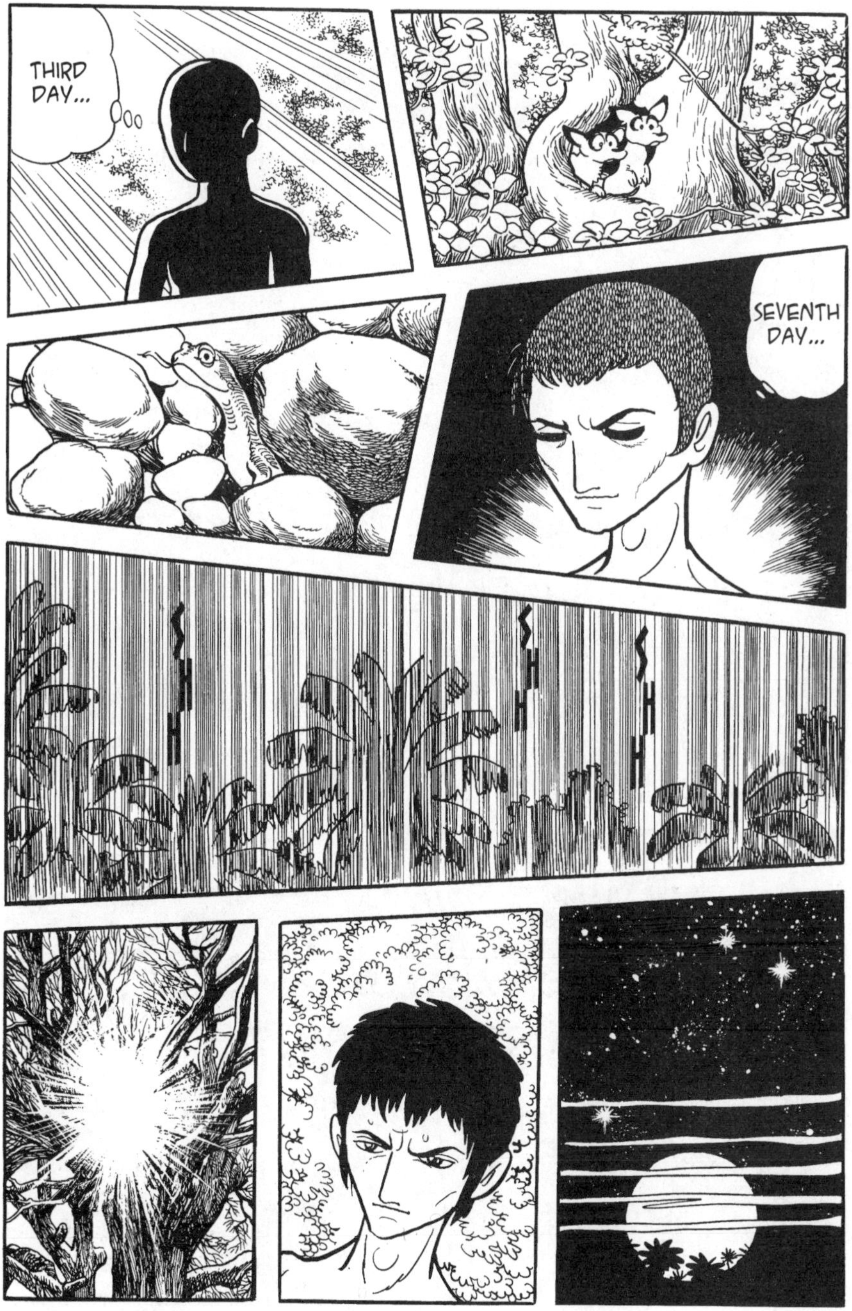
THIRD DAY...
SEVENTH DAY...
SHH
SHH
SHH

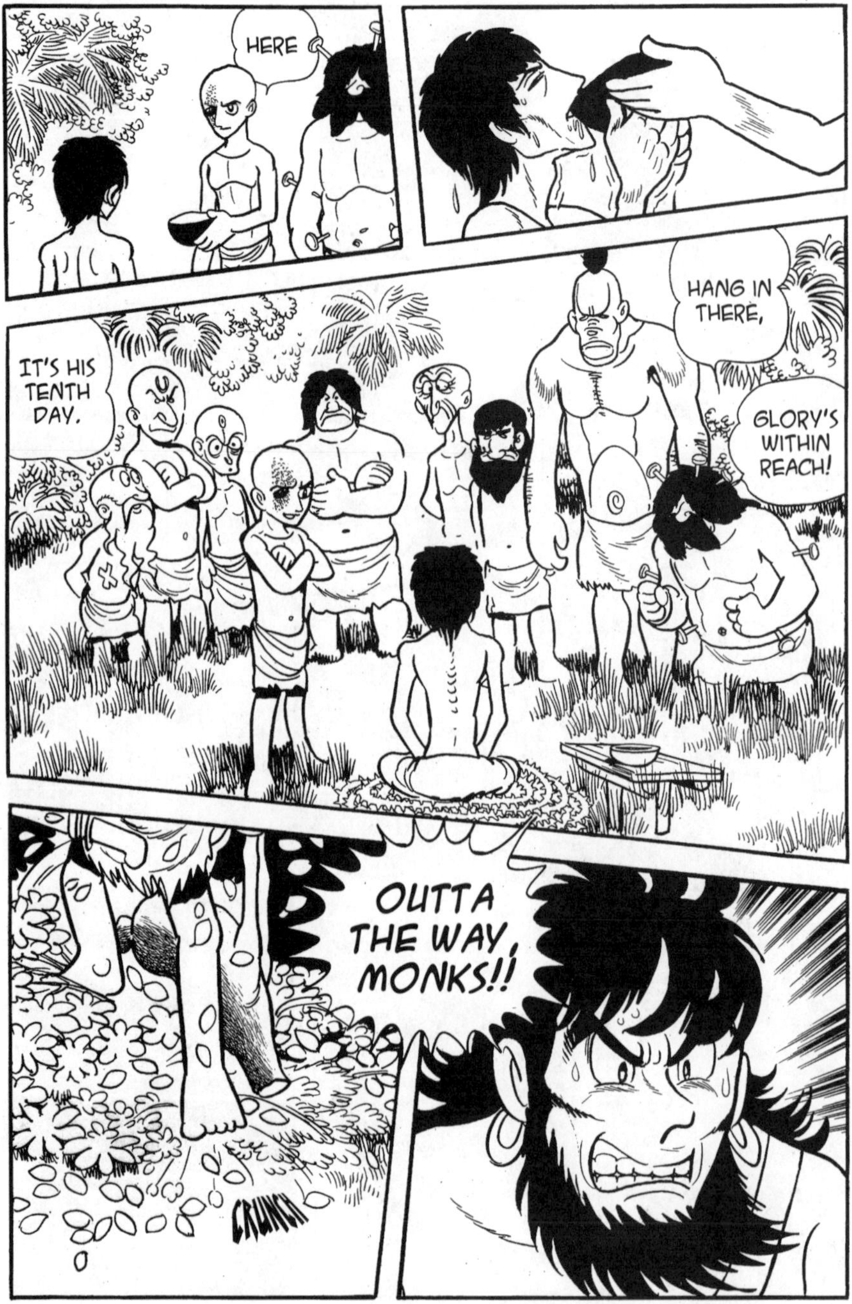
HERE
IT'S HIS TENTH DAY.
HANG IN THERE,
GLORY'S WITHIN REACH!
CRUNCH
OUTTA THE WAY, MONKS!!

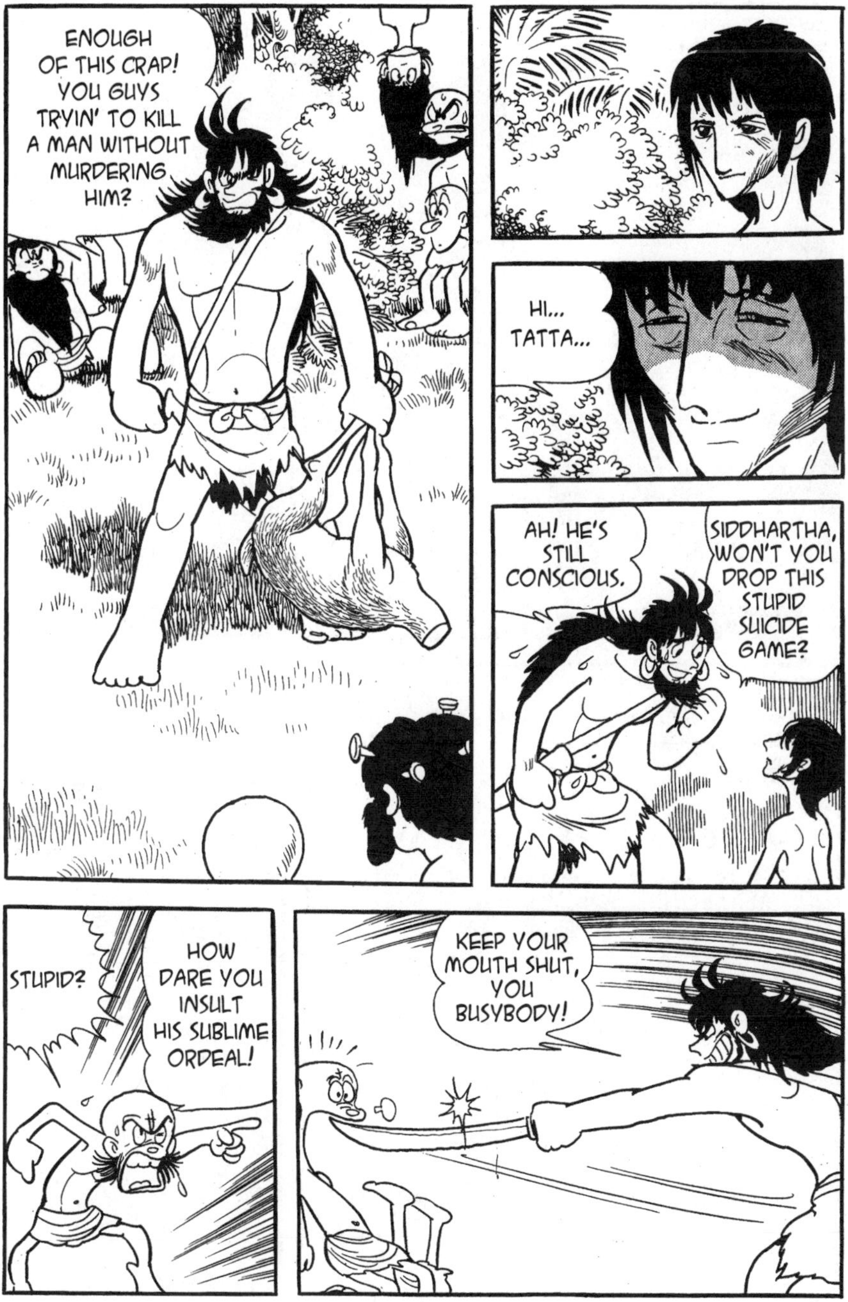
ENOUGH OF THIS CRAP! YOU GUYS TRYIN' TO KILL A MAN WITHOUT MURDERING HIM?
HI... TATTA...
AH! HE'S STILL CONSCIOUS.
SIDDHARTHA, WON'T YOU DROP THIS STUPID SUICIDE GAME?
STUPID?
HOW DARE YOU INSULT HIS SUBLIME ORDEAL!
KEEP YOUR MOUTH SHUT, YOU BUSYBODY!

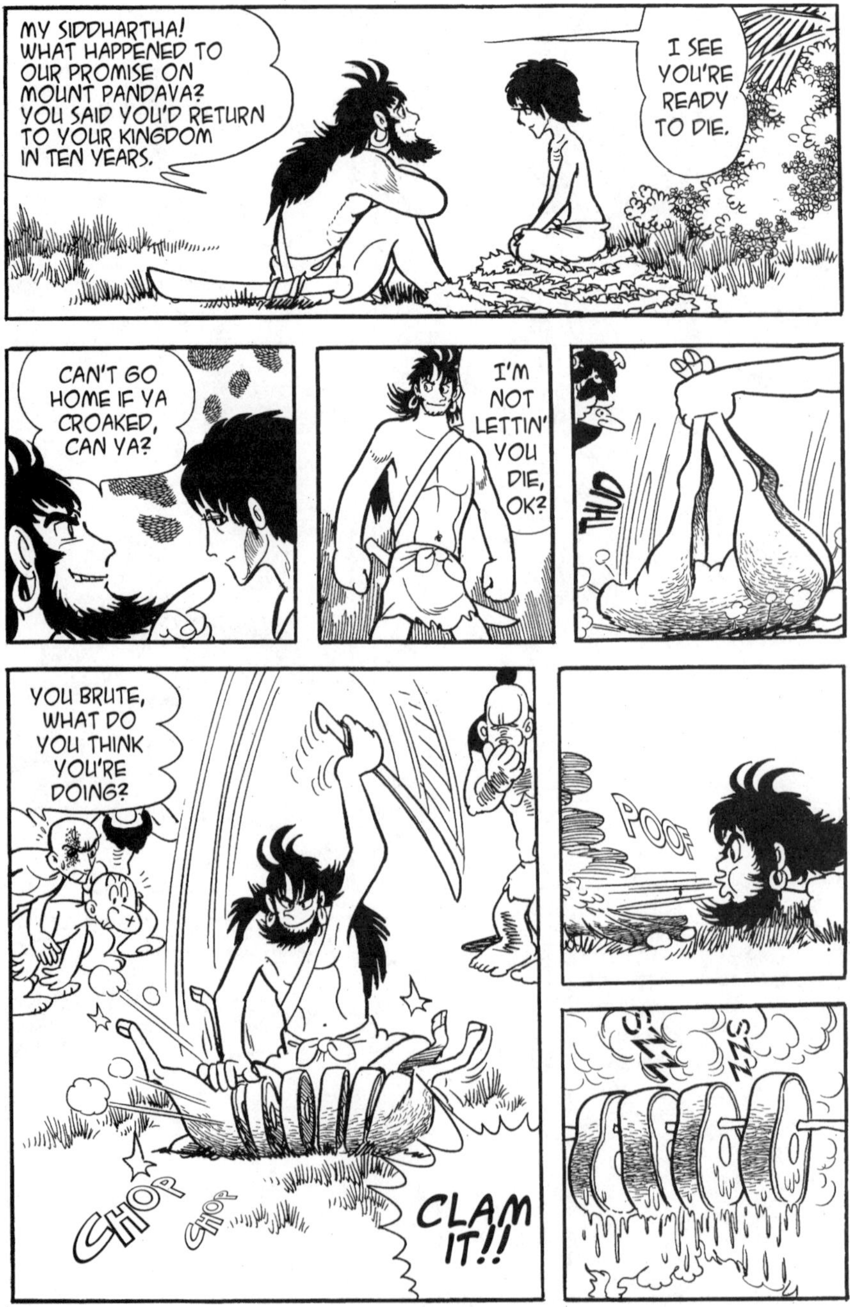
MY SIDDHARTHA! WHAT HAPPENED TO OUR PROMISE ON MOUNT PANDAVA? YOU SAID YOU'D RETURN TO YOUR KINGDOM IN TEN YEARS.
I SEE YOU'RE READY TO DIE.
CAN'T GO HOME IF YA CROAKED, CAN YA?
I'M NOT LETTIN' YOU DIE, OK?
THUD
YOU BRUTE, WHAT DO YOU THINK YOU'RE DOING?
CHOP
CHOP
CLAM IT!!
POOF
SZZ
SZZ

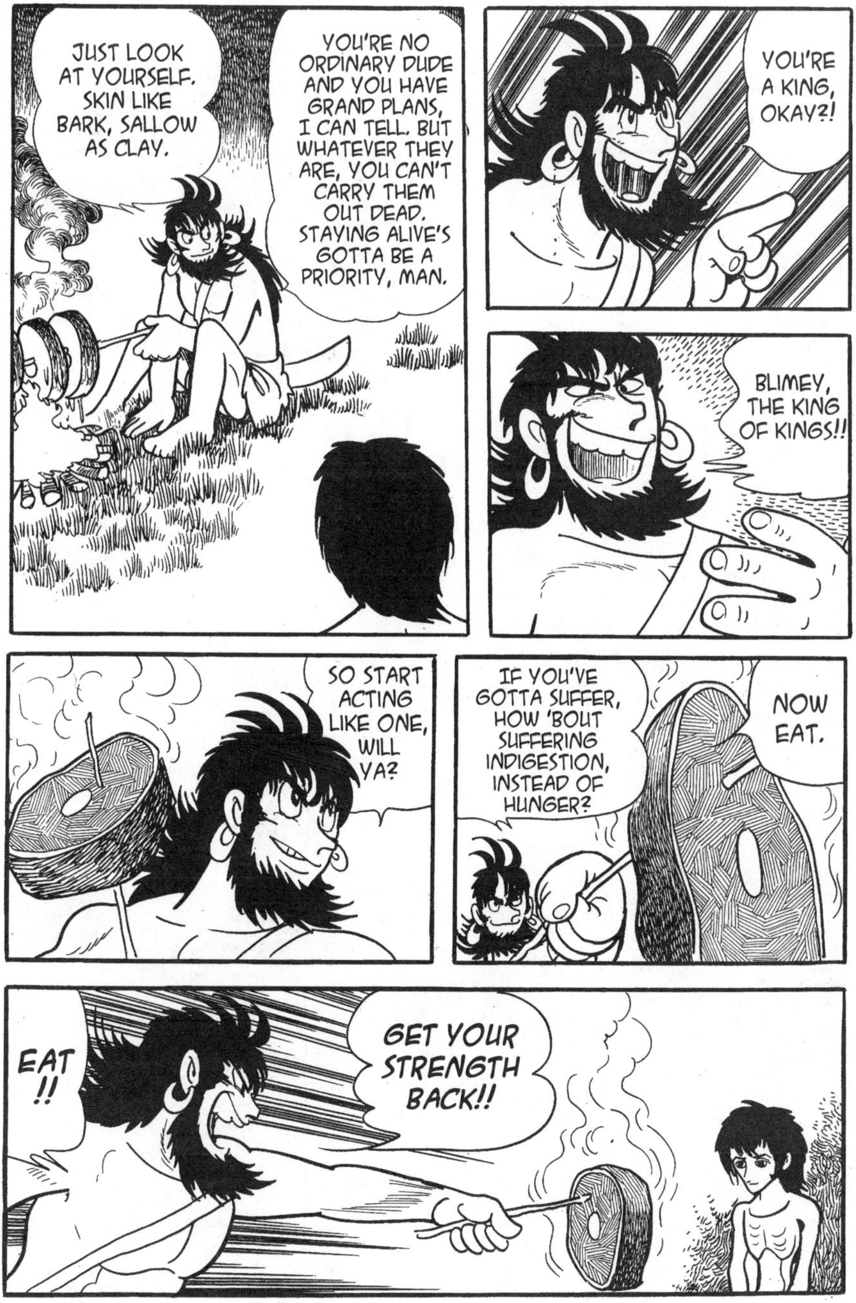
JUST LOOK AT YOURSELF. SKIN LIKE BARK, SALLOW AS CLAY.
YOU'RE NO ORDINARY DUDE AND YOU HAVE GRAND PLANS, I CAN TELL. BUT WHATEVER THEY ARE, YOU CAN'T CARRY THEM OUT DEAD. STAYING ALIVE'S GOTTA BE A PRIORITY, MAN.
YOU'RE A KING, OKAY?!
BLIMEY, THE KING OF KINGS!!
SO START ACTING LIKE ONE, WILL YA?
IF YOU'VE GOTTA SUFFER, HOW 'BOUT SUFFERING INDIGESTION, INSTEAD OF HUNGER?
NOW EAT.
EAT!!
GET YOUR STRENGTH BACK!!

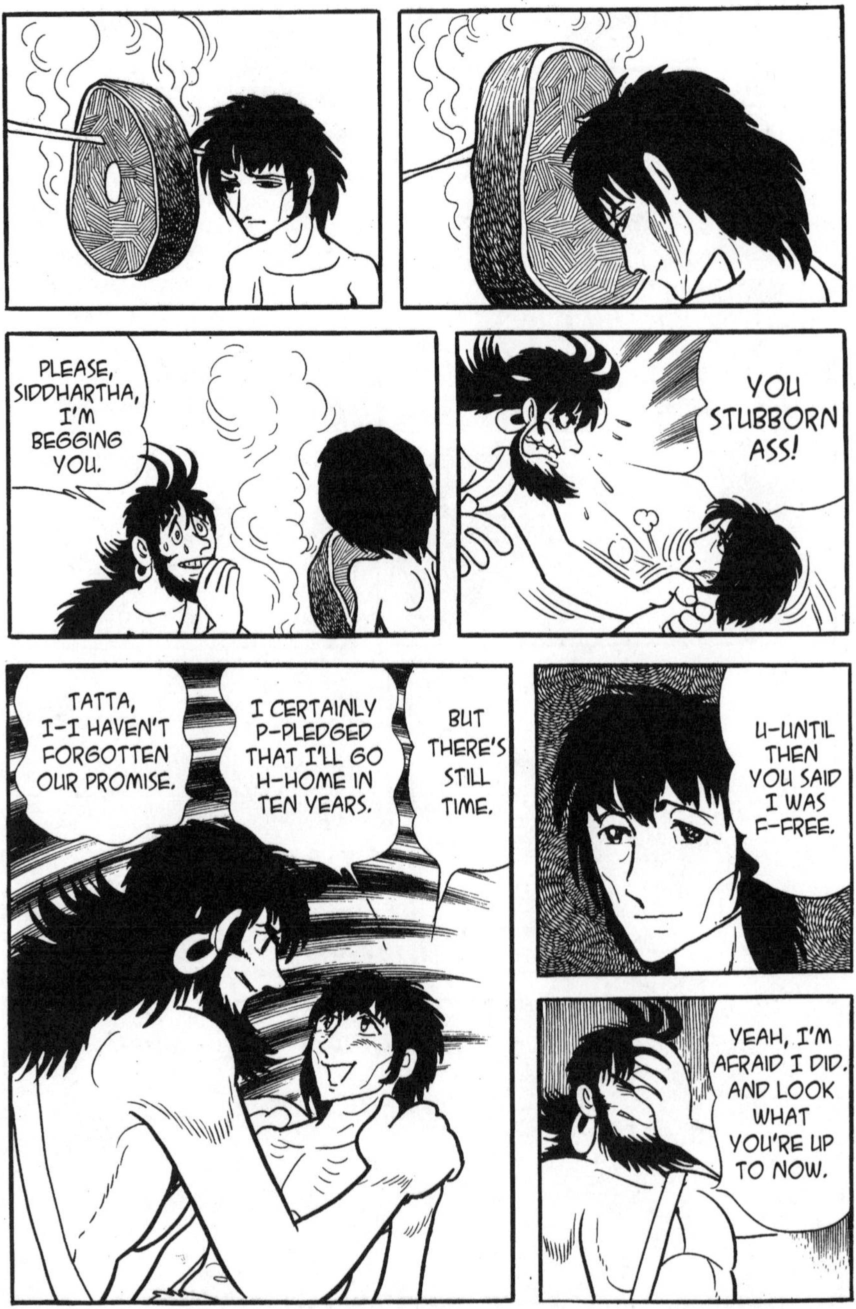
PLEASE, SIDDHARTHA, I'M BEGGING YOU.
YOU STUBBORN ASS!
TATTA, I-I HAVEN'T FORGOTTEN OUR PROMISE.
I CERTAINLY P-PLEDGED THAT I'LL GO H-HOME IN TEN YEARS.
BUT THERE'S STILL TIME.
U-UNTIL THEN YOU SAID I WAS F-FREE.
YEAH, I'M AFRAID I DID. AND LOOK WHAT YOU'RE UP TO NOW.

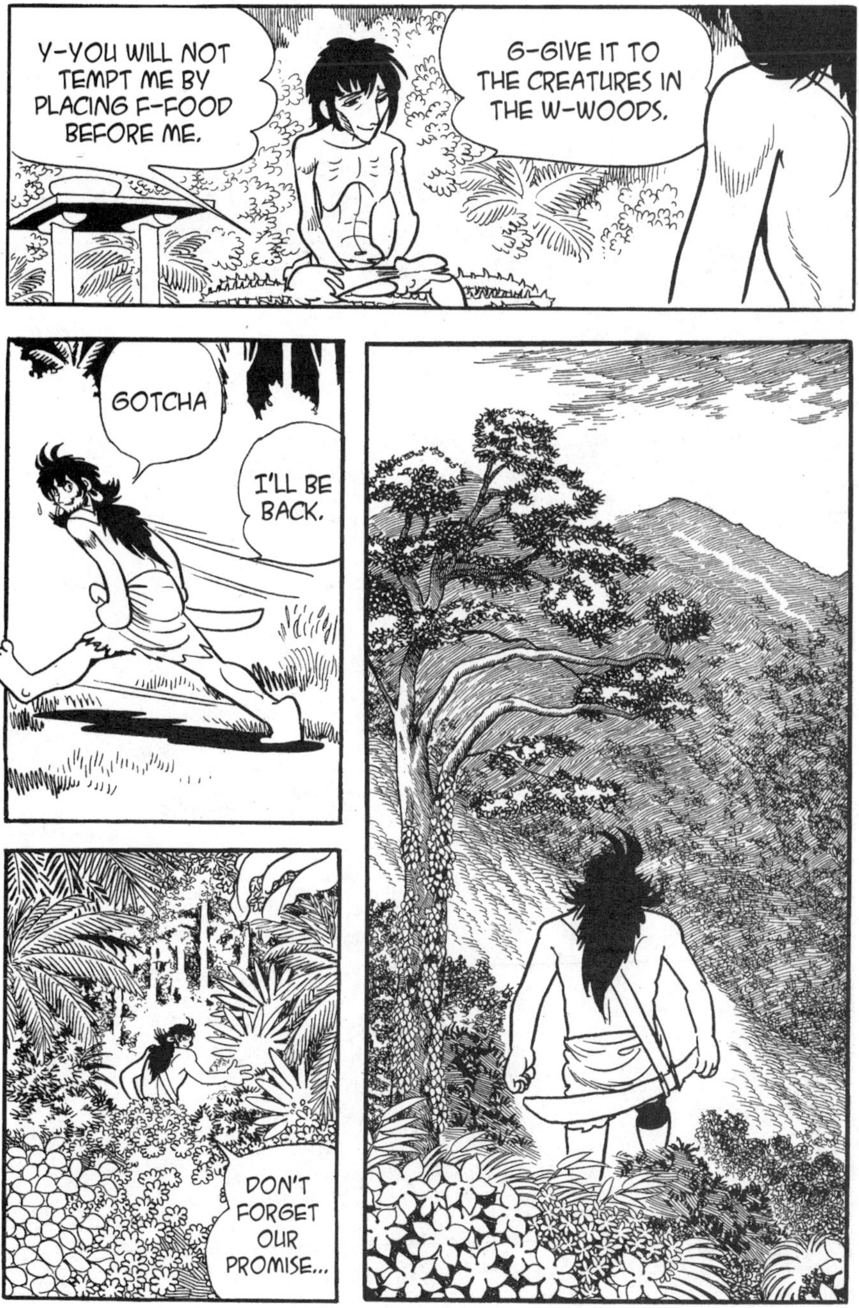
Y-YOU WILL NOT TEMPT ME BY PLACING F-FOOD BEFORE ME.
G-GIVE IT TO THE CREATURES IN THE W-WOODS.
GOTCHA
I'LL BE BACK.
DON'T FORGET OUR PROMISE...

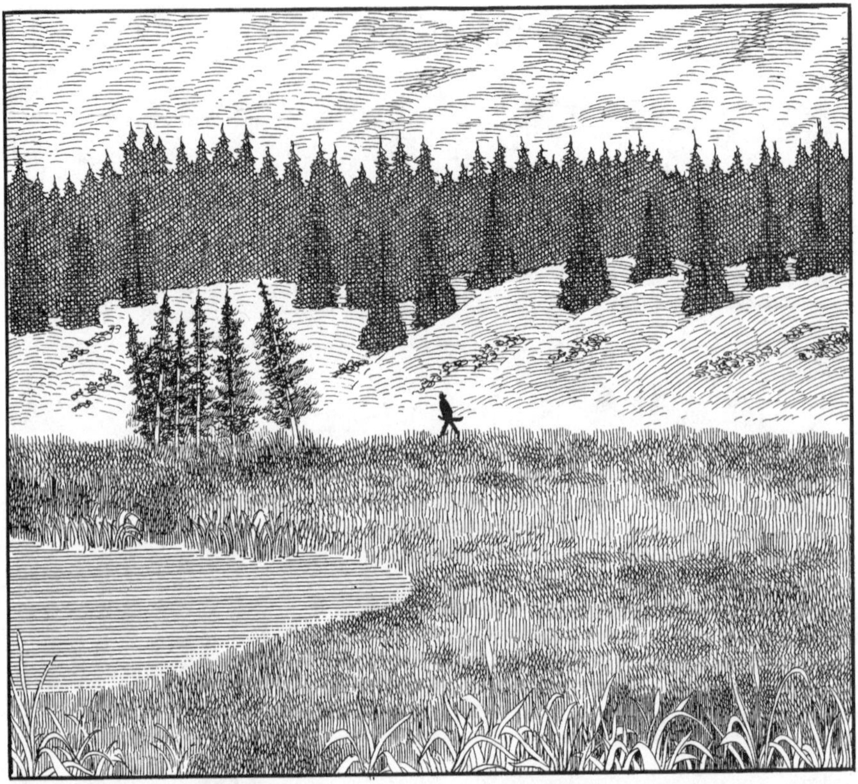

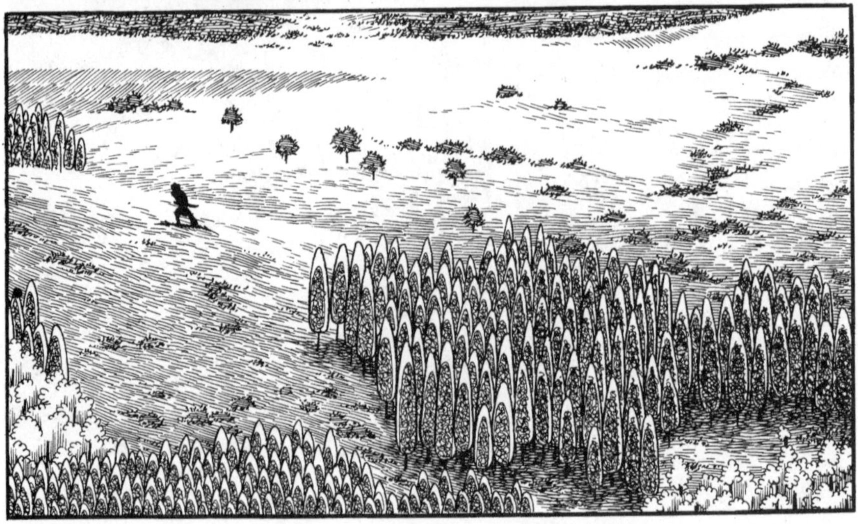

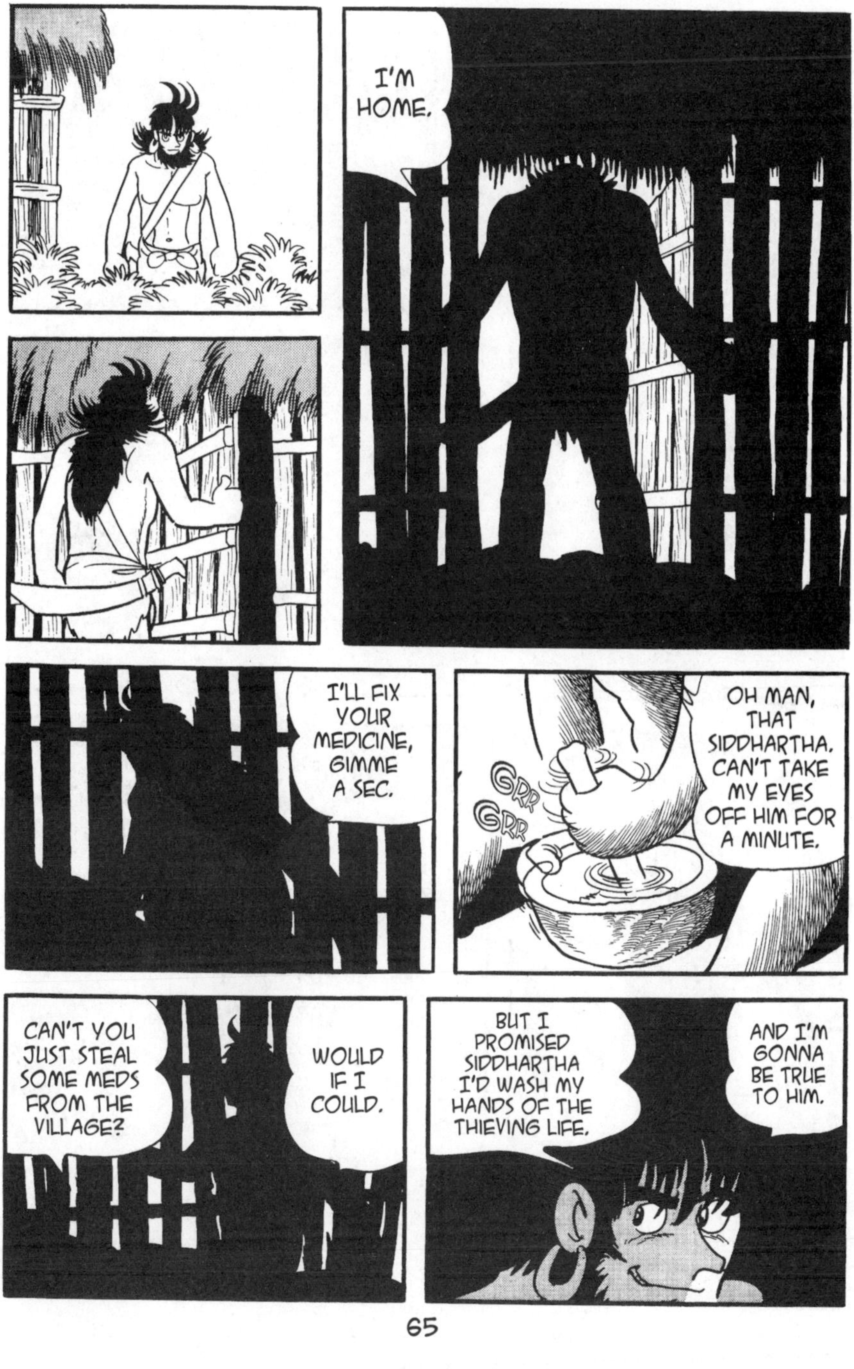
I'M HOME.
I'LL FIX YOUR MEDICINE, GIMME A SEC.
GRR GRR
OH MAN, THAT SIDDHARTHA. CAN'T TAKE MY EYES OFF HIM FOR A MINUTE.
CAN'T YOU JUST STEAL SOME MEDS FROM THE VILLAGE?
WOULD IF I COULD.
BUT I PROMISED SIDDHARTHA I'D WASH MY HANDS OF THE THIEVING LIFE.
AND I'M GONNA BE TRUE TO HIM.

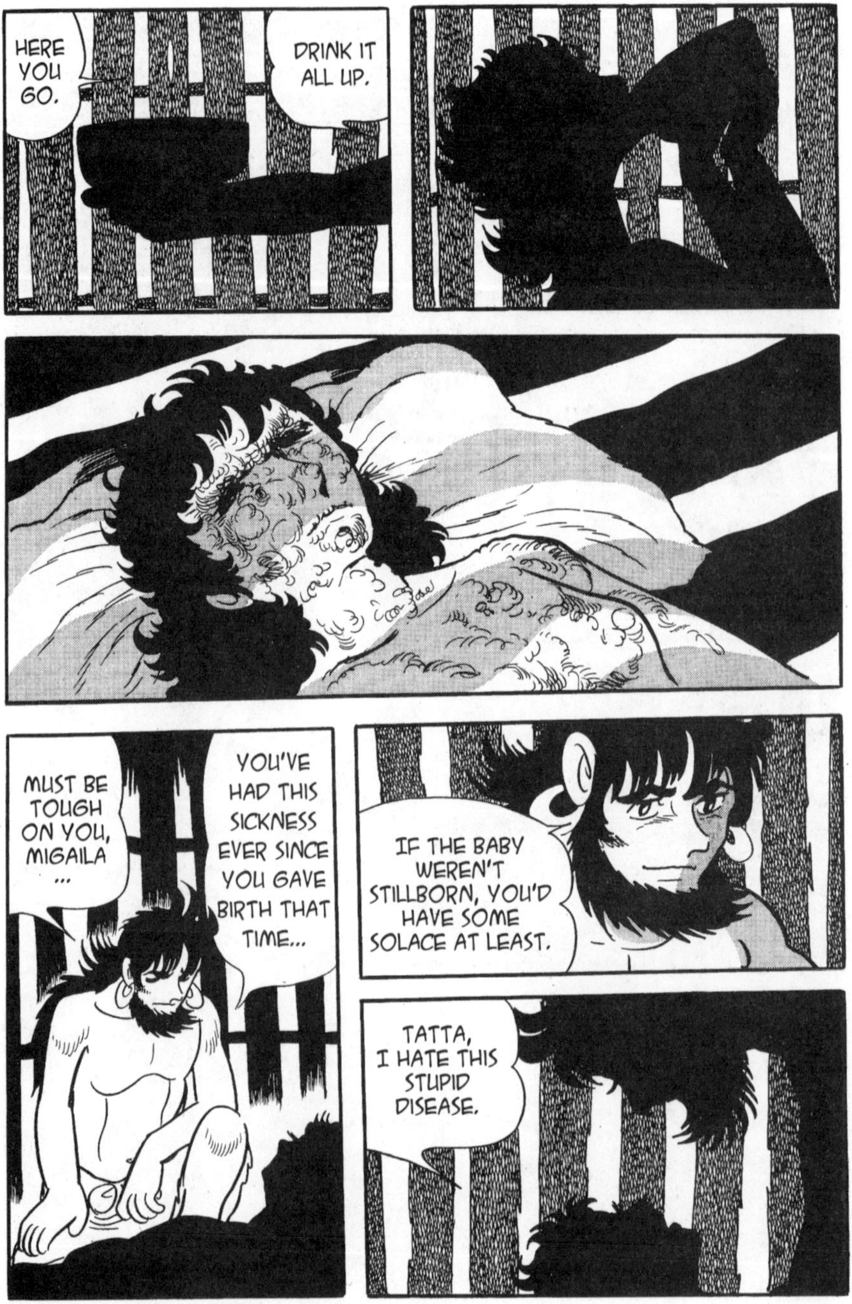
HERE YOU GO.
DRINK IT ALL UP.
MUST BE TOUGH ON YOU, MIGAILA ...
YOU'VE HAD THIS SICKNESS EVER SINCE YOU GAVE BIRTH THAT TIME...
IF THE BABY WEREN'T STILLBORN, YOU'D HAVE SOME SOLACE AT LEAST.
TATTA, I HATE THIS STUPID DISEASE.

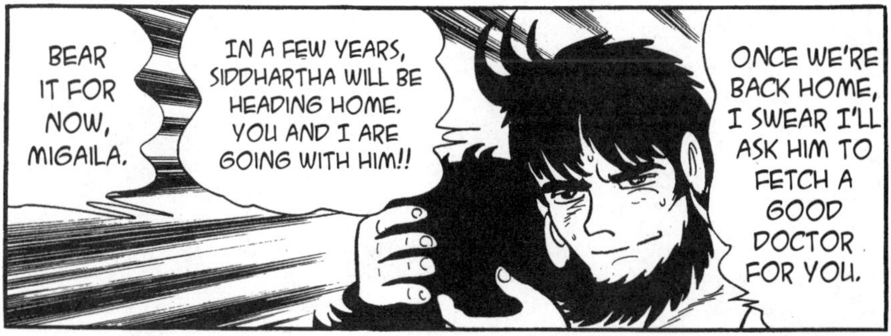
BEAR IT FOR NOW, MIGAILA.
IN A FEW YEARS, SIDDHARTHA WILL BE HEADING HOME. YOU AND I ARE GOING WITH HIM!!
ONCE WE'RE BACK HOME, I SWEAR I'LL ASK HIM TO FETCH A GOOD DOCTOR FOR YOU.

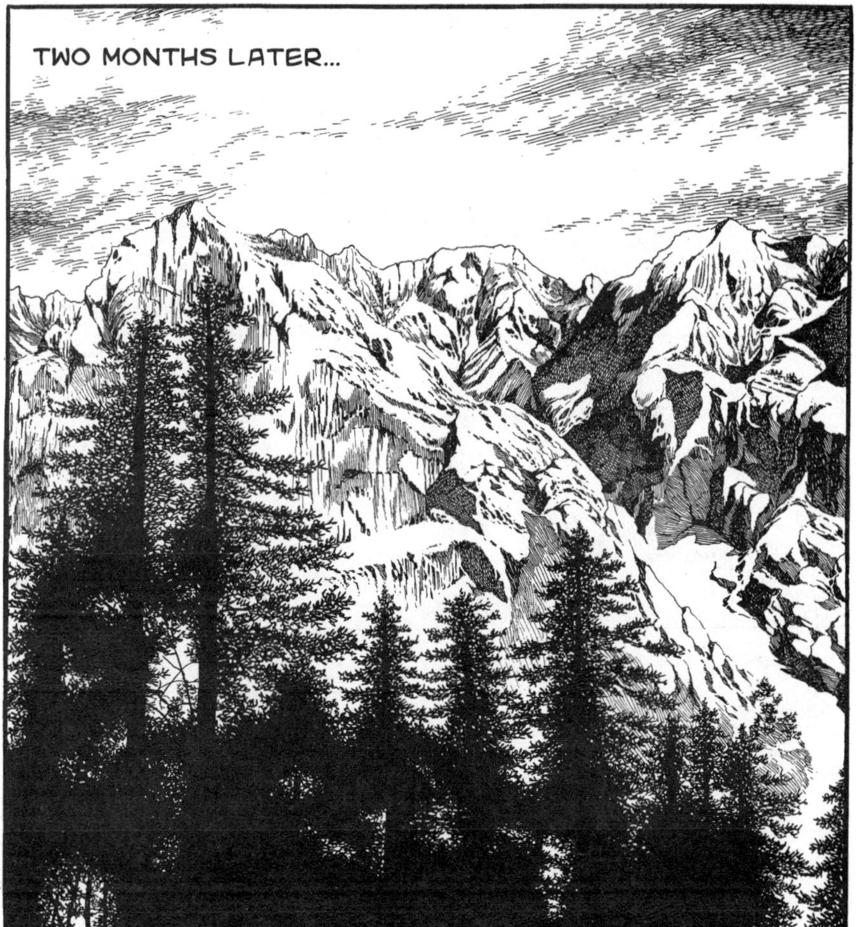
TWO MONTHS LATER...

WHERE'S SIDDHAR-THA?
HE'S GOING THROUGH A TRIAL.
DON'T GO TO HIM. HE NEEDS TO FOCUS!
HE'S BEEN FASTING. NOTHING BUT WATER FOR THE LAST COUPLE OF MONTHS.
HUH ?!
NOTHING? FOR TWO MONTHS?
POOR, POOR MAN...
EEEEK! OH NO!!

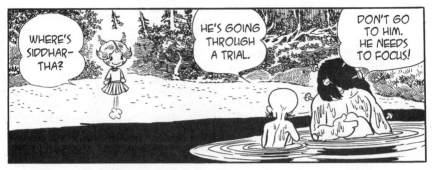

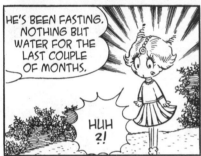

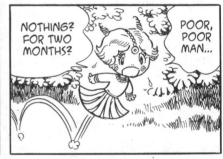

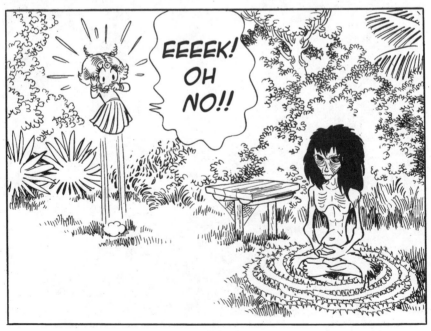

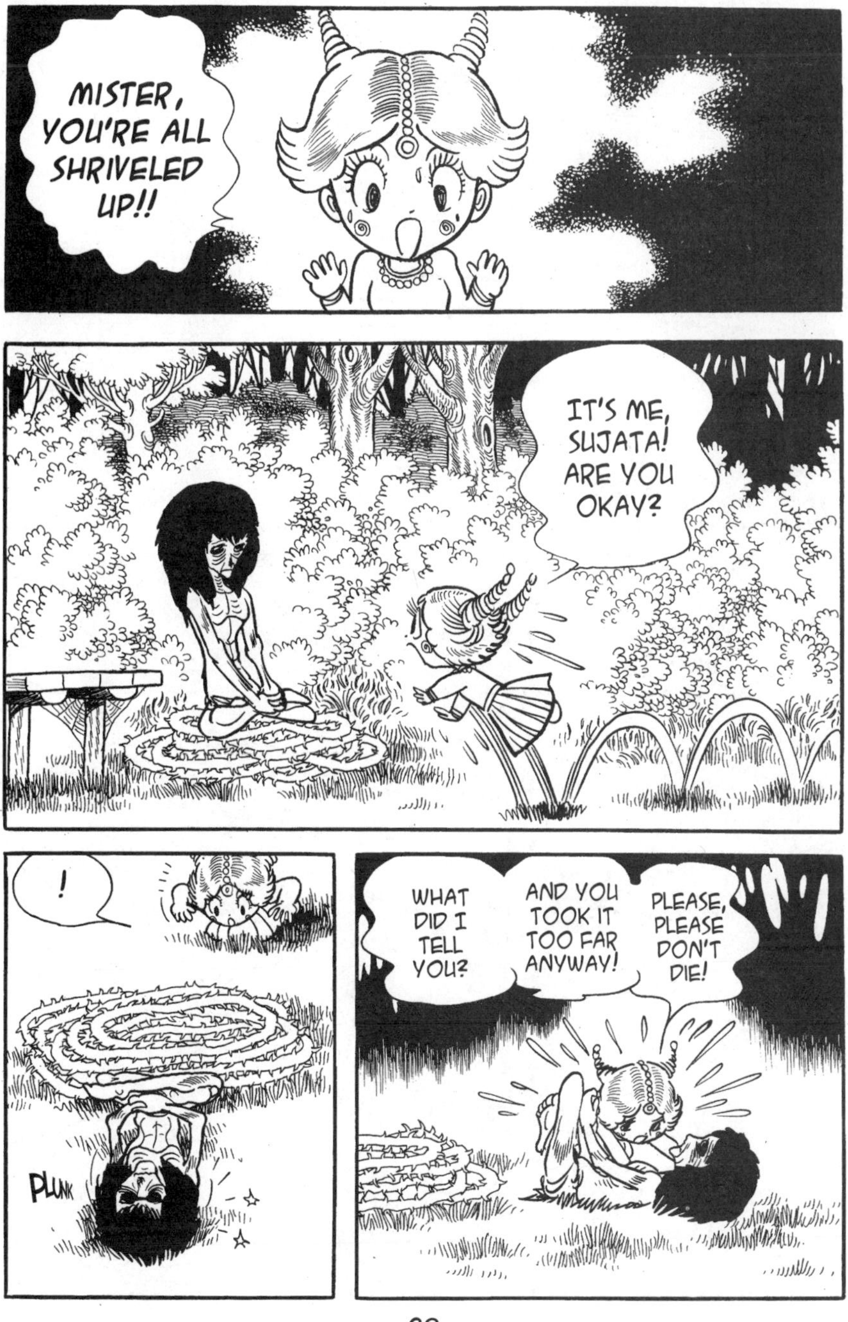
MISTER, YOU'RE ALL SHRIVELED UP!!
IT'S ME, SUJATA! ARE YOU OKAY?
!
PLUNK
WHAT DID I TELL YOU?
AND YOU TOOK IT TOO FAR ANYWAY!
PLEASE, PLEASE DON'T DIE!

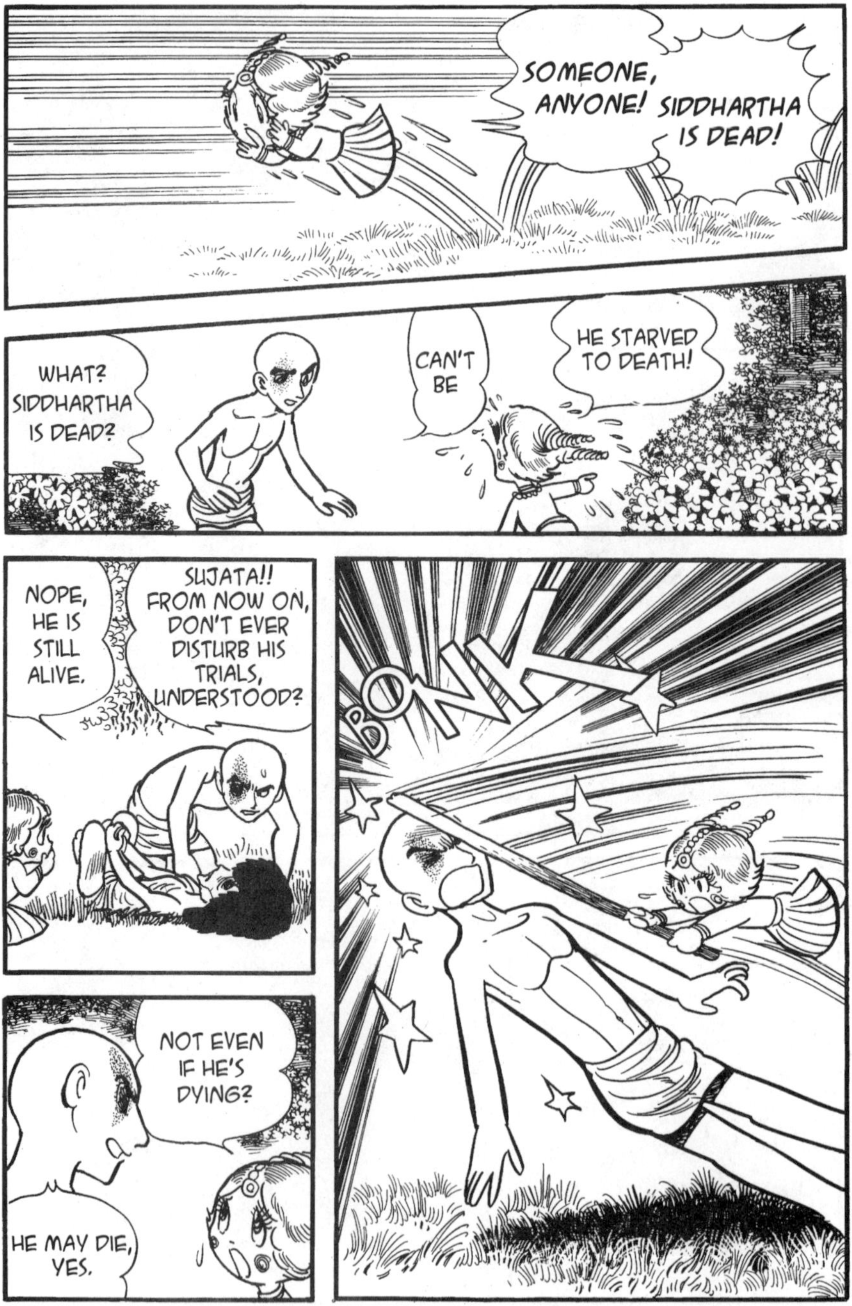
SOMEONE, ANYONE! SIDDHARTHA IS DEAD!
WHAT? SIDDHARTHA IS DEAD?
CAN'T BE
HE STARVED TO DEATH!
NOPE, HE IS STILL ALIVE.
SUJATA!! FROM NOW ON, DON'T EVER DISTURB HIS TRIALS, UNDERSTOOD?
NOT EVEN IF HE'S DYING?
HE MAY DIE, YES.
BONK

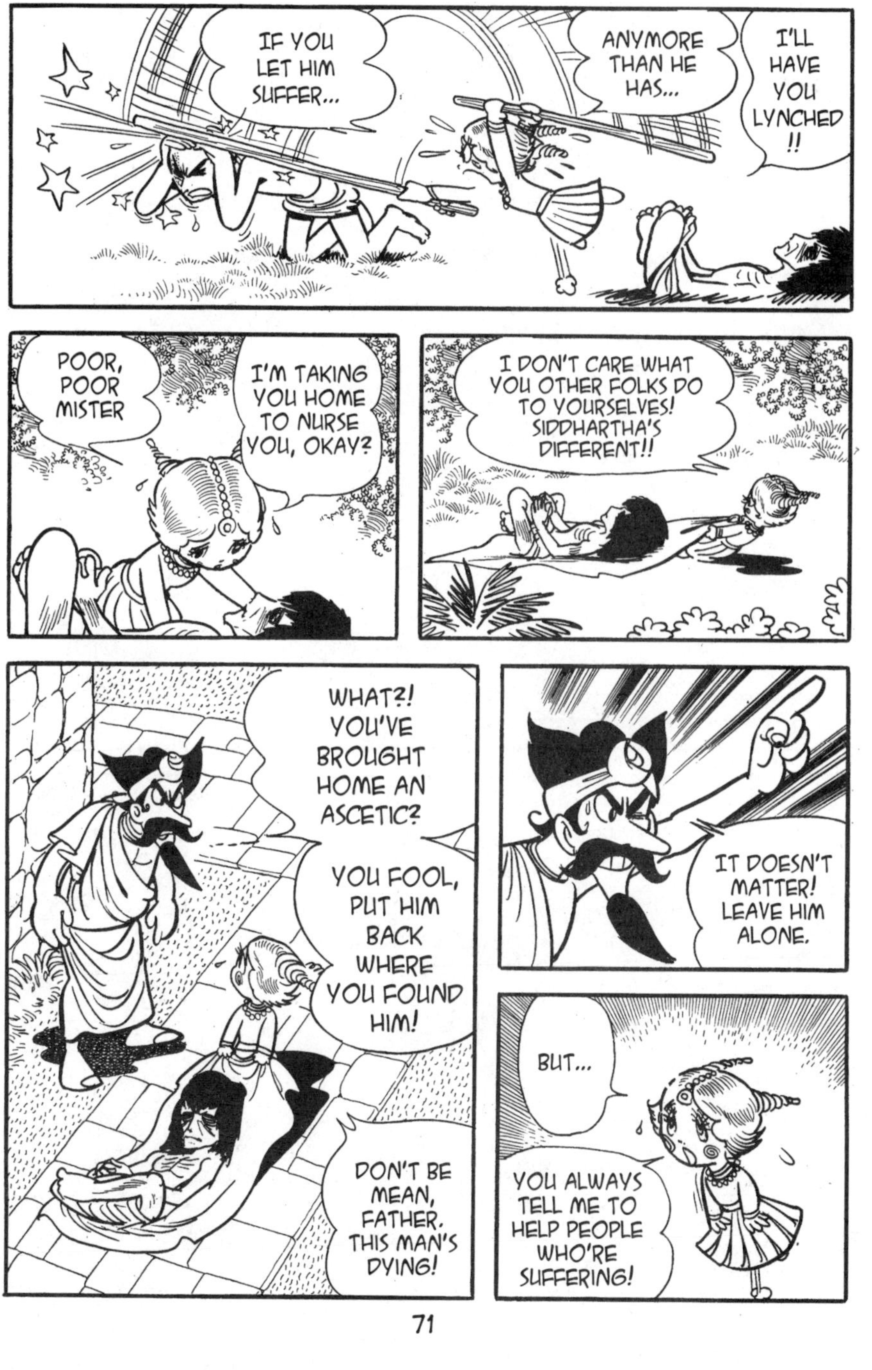
IF YOU LET HIM SUFFER...
ANYMORE THAN HE HAS...
I'LL HAVE YOU LYNCHED !!
POOR, POOR MISTER
I'M TAKING YOU HOME TO NURSE YOU, OKAY?
I DON'T CARE WHAT YOU OTHER FOLKS DO TO YOURSELVES! SIDDHARTHA'S DIFFERENT!!
WHAT?! YOU'VE BROUGHT HOME AN ASCETIC?
YOU FOOL, PUT HIM BACK WHERE YOU FOUND HIM!
DON'T BE MEAN, FATHER. THIS MAN'S DYING!
IT DOESN'T MATTER! LEAVE HIM ALONE.
BUT...
YOU ALWAYS TELL ME TO HELP PEOPLE WHO'RE SUFFERING!

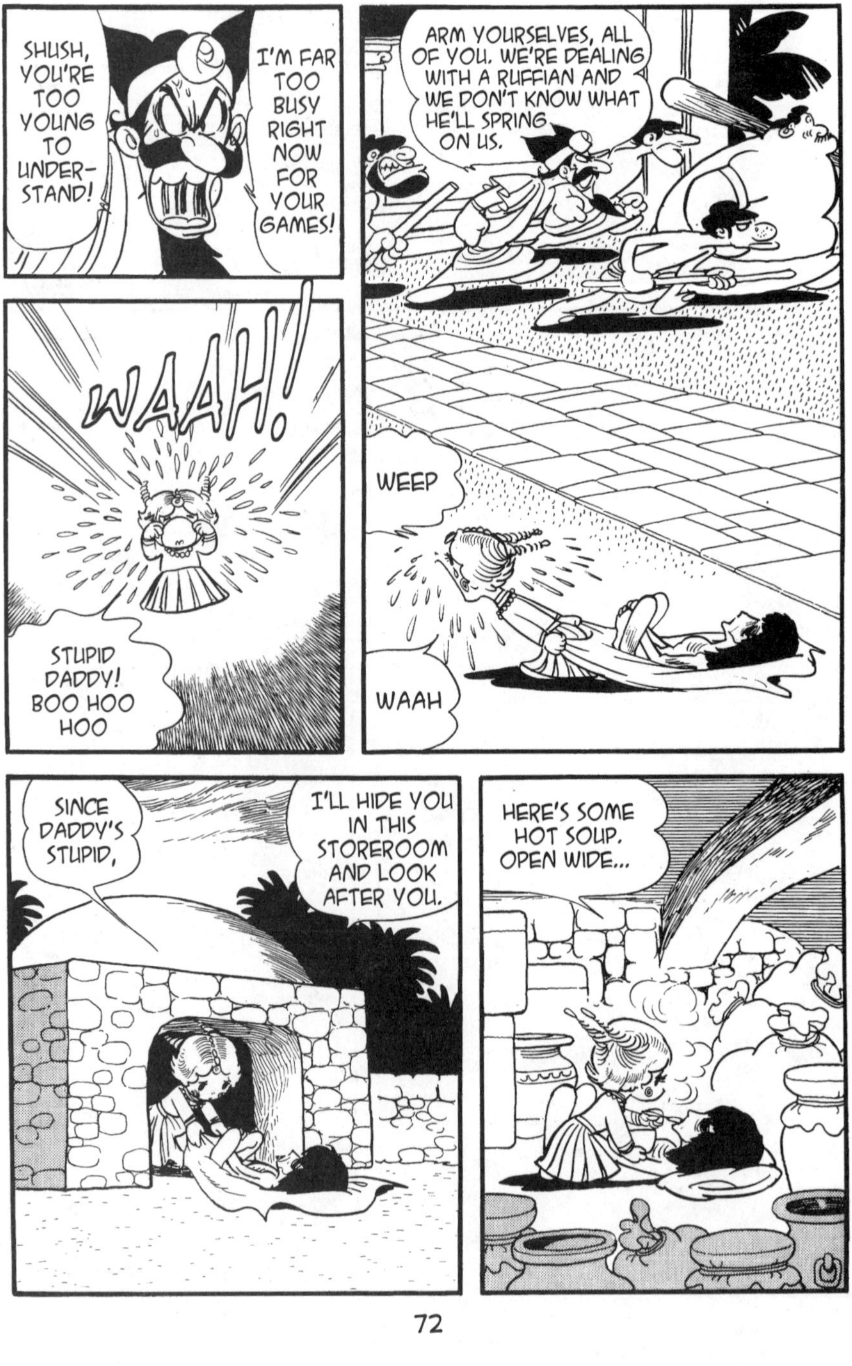
SHUSH, YOU'RE TOO YOUNG TO UNDER-STAND!
I'M FAR TOO BUSY RIGHT NOW FOR YOUR GAMES!
ARM YOURSELVES, ALL OF YOU. WE'RE DEALING WITH A RUFFIAN AND WE DON'T KNOW WHAT HE'LL SPRING ON US.
WAAH!
STUPID DADDY! BOO HOO HOO
WEEP
WAAH
SINCE DADDY'S STUPID,
I'LL HIDE YOU IN THIS STOREROOM AND LOOK AFTER YOU.
HERE'S SOME HOT SOUP. OPEN WIDE...

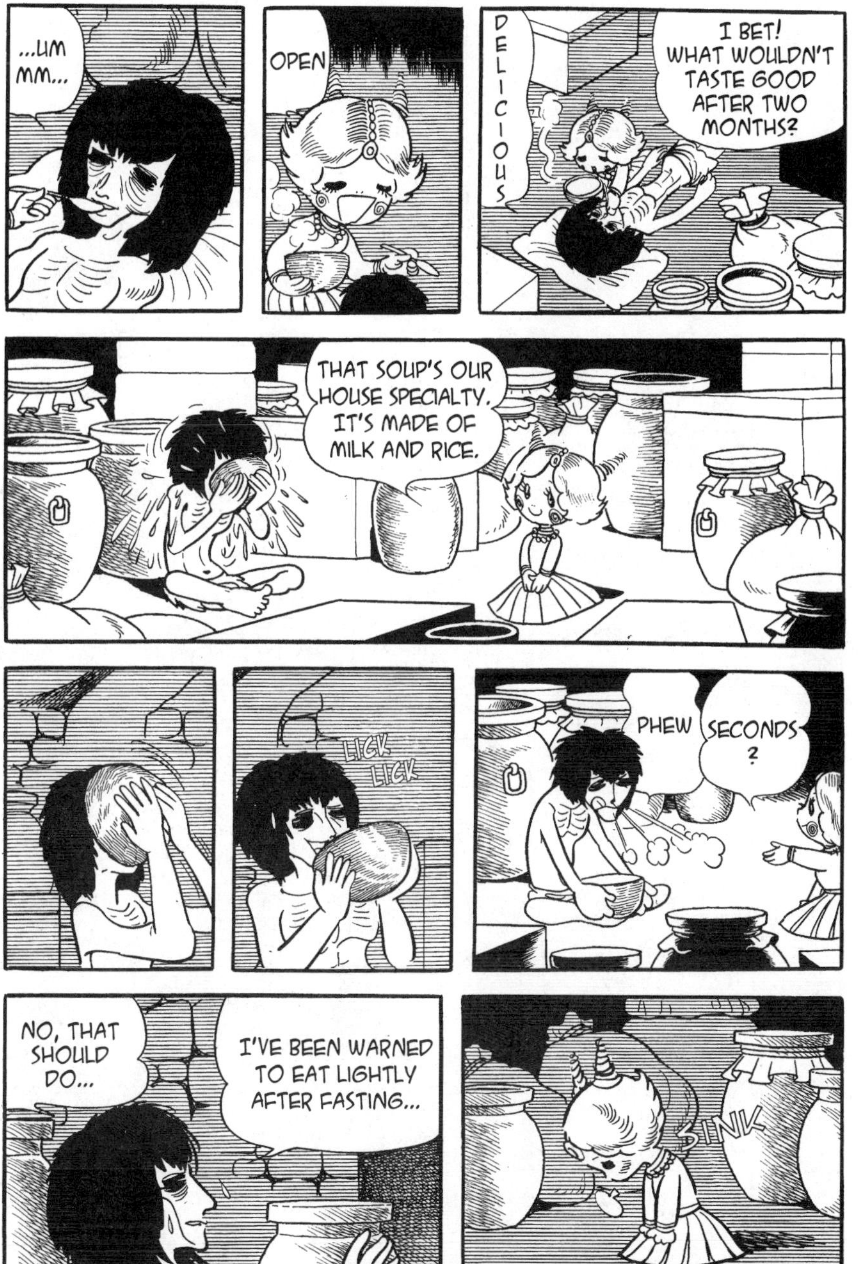

...UM MM...
OPEN
DELICIOUS
I BET! WHAT WOULDN'T TASTE GOOD AFTER TWO MONTHS?
THAT SOUP'S OUR HOUSE SPECIALTY. IT'S MADE OF MILK AND RICE.
LICK LICK
PHEW
SECONDS?
NO, THAT SHOULD DO...
I'VE BEEN WARNED TO EAT LIGHTLY AFTER FASTING...
SINK

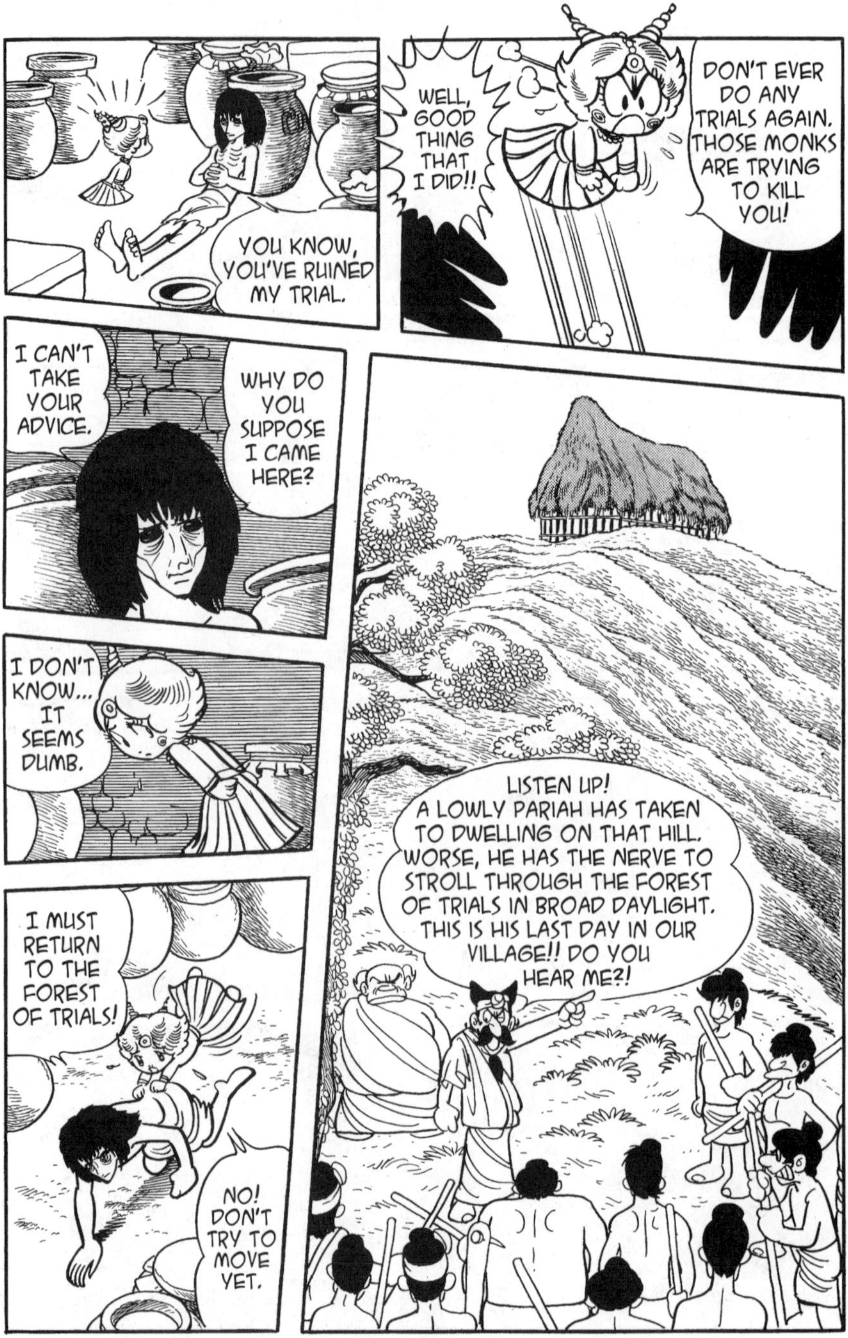
YOU KNOW, YOU'VE RUINED MY TRIAL.
WELL, GOOD THING THAT I DID!!
DON'T EVER DO ANY TRIALS AGAIN. THOSE MONKS ARE TRYING TO KILL YOU!
I CAN'T TAKE YOUR ADVICE.
WHY DO YOU SUPPOSE I CAME HERE?
I DON'T KNOW... IT SEEMS DUMB.
I MUST RETURN TO THE FOREST OF TRIALS!
NO! DON'T TRY TO MOVE YET.
LISTEN UP! A LOWLY PARIAH HAS TAKEN TO DWELLING ON THAT HILL. WORSE, HE HAS THE NERVE TO STROLL THROUGH THE FOREST OF TRIALS IN BROAD DAYLIGHT. THIS IS HIS LAST DAY IN OUR VILLAGE!! DO YOU HEAR ME?!

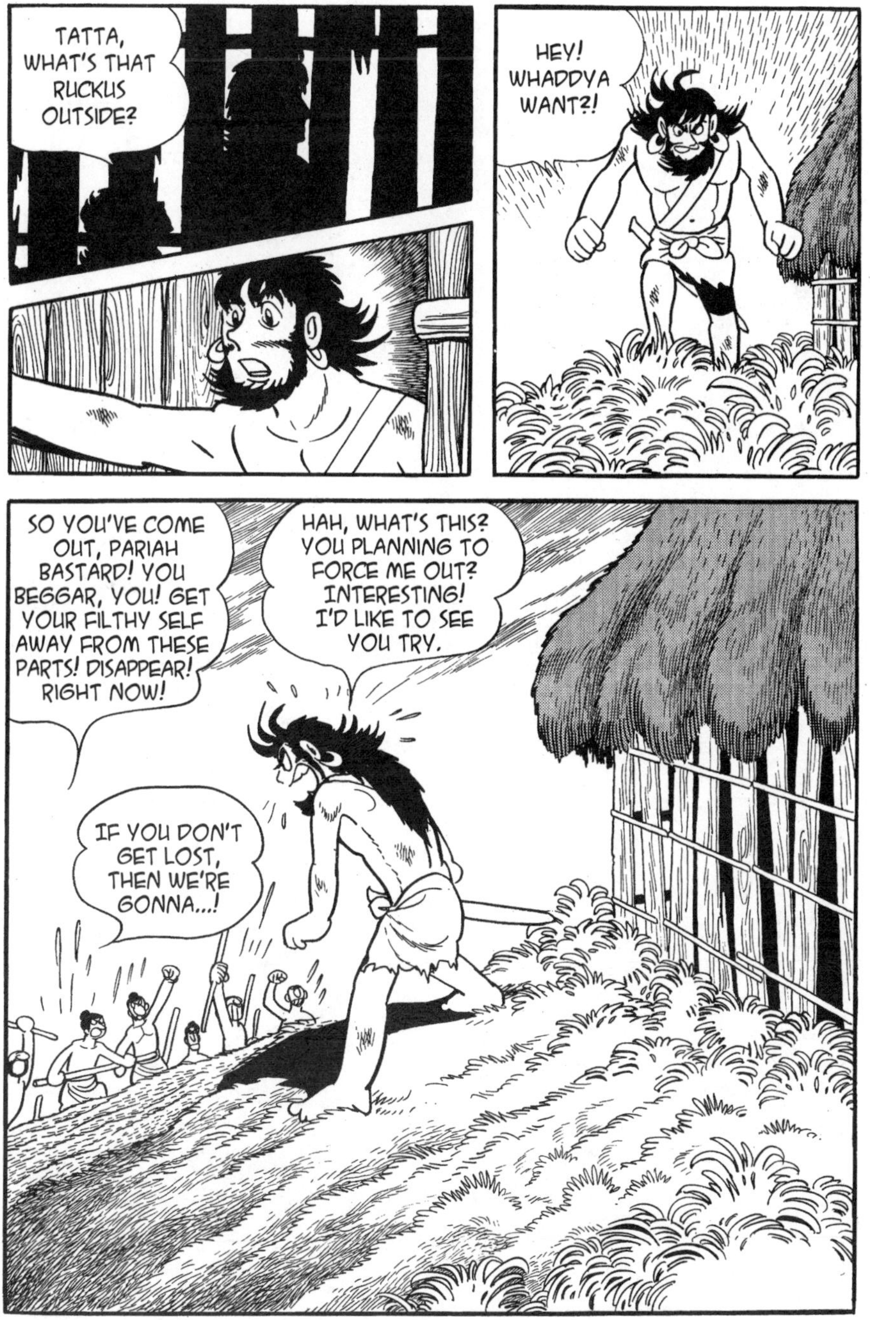
TATTA, WHAT'S THAT RUCKUS OUTSIDE?
HEY! WHADDYA WANT?!
SO YOU'VE COME OUT, PARIAH BASTARD! YOU BEGGAR, YOU! GET YOUR FILTHY SELF AWAY FROM THESE PARTS! DISAPPEAR! RIGHT NOW!
HAH, WHAT'S THIS? YOU PLANNING TO FORCE ME OUT? INTERESTING! I'D LIKE TO SEE YOU TRY.
IF YOU DON'T GET LOST, THEN WE'RE GONNA...!

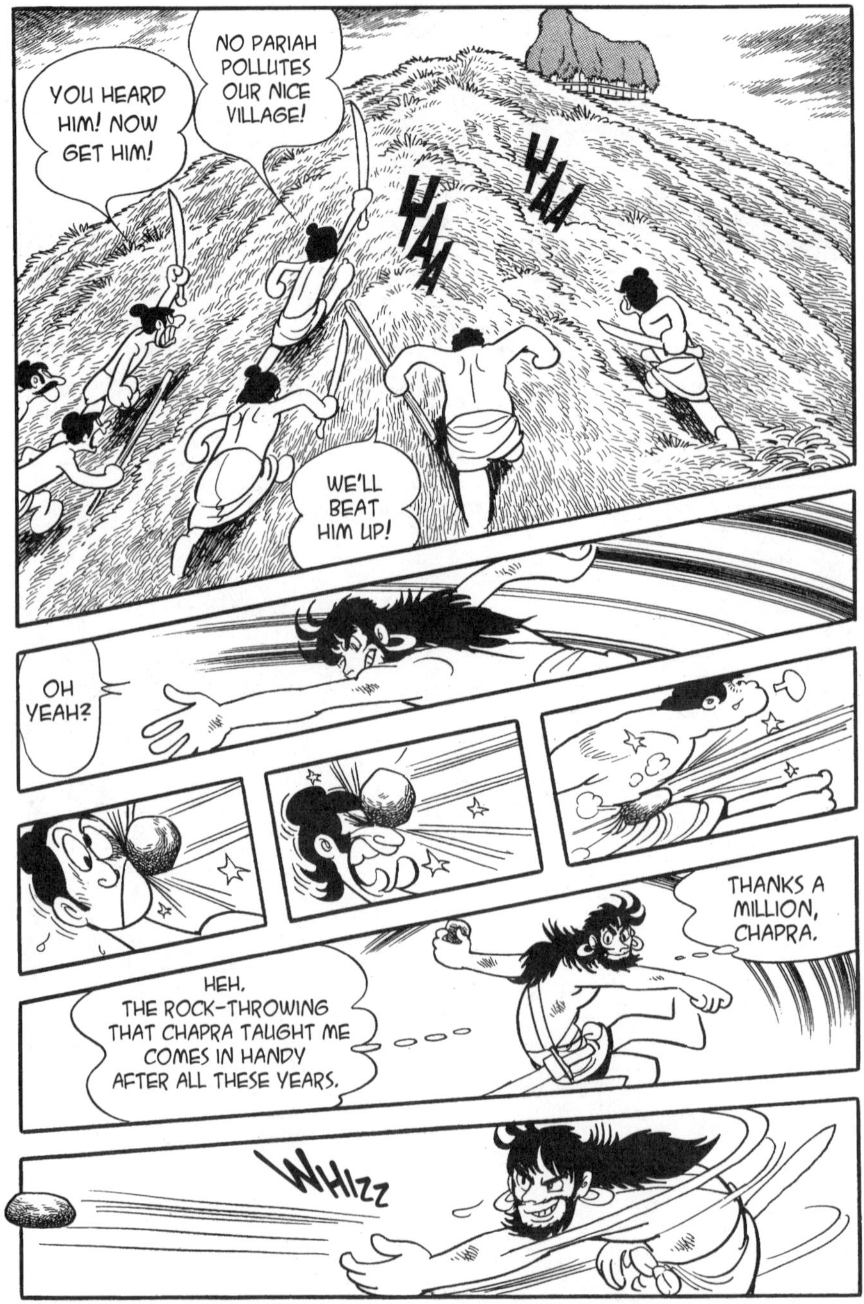

YOU HEARD HIM! NOW GET HIM!
NO PARIAH POLLUTES OUR NICE VILLAGE!
YAAA
YAAA
WE'LL BEAT HIM UP!
OH YEAH?
THANKS A MILLION, CHAPRA.
HEH. THE ROCK-THROWING THAT CHAPRA TAUGHT ME COMES IN HANDY AFTER ALL THESE YEARS.
WHIZZ

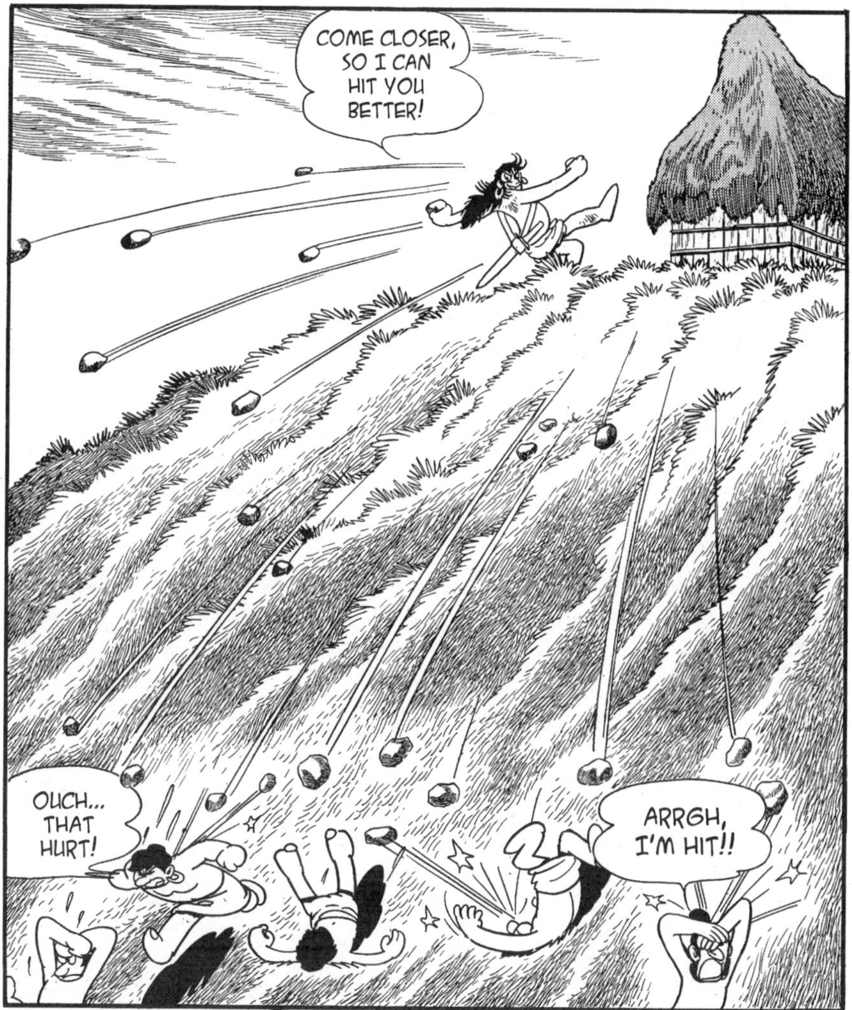
COME CLOSER, SO I CAN HIT YOU BETTER!
OUCH... THAT HURT!
ARRGH, I'M HIT!!
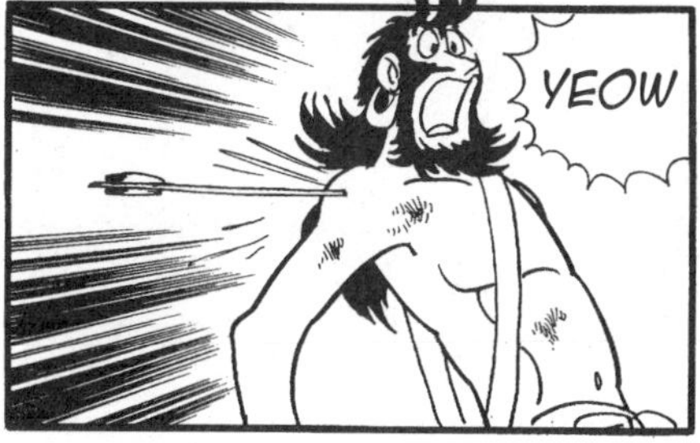
YEOW
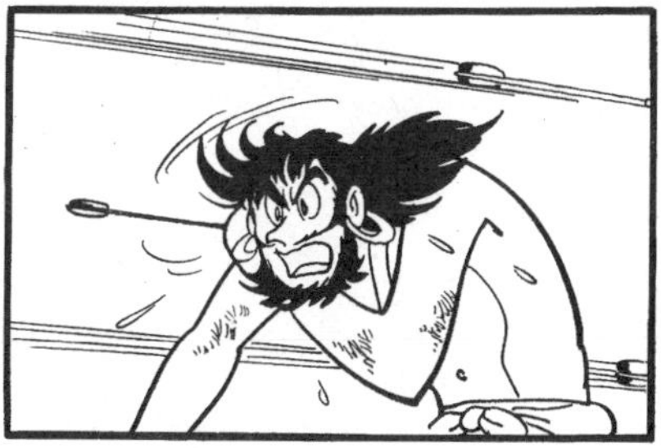

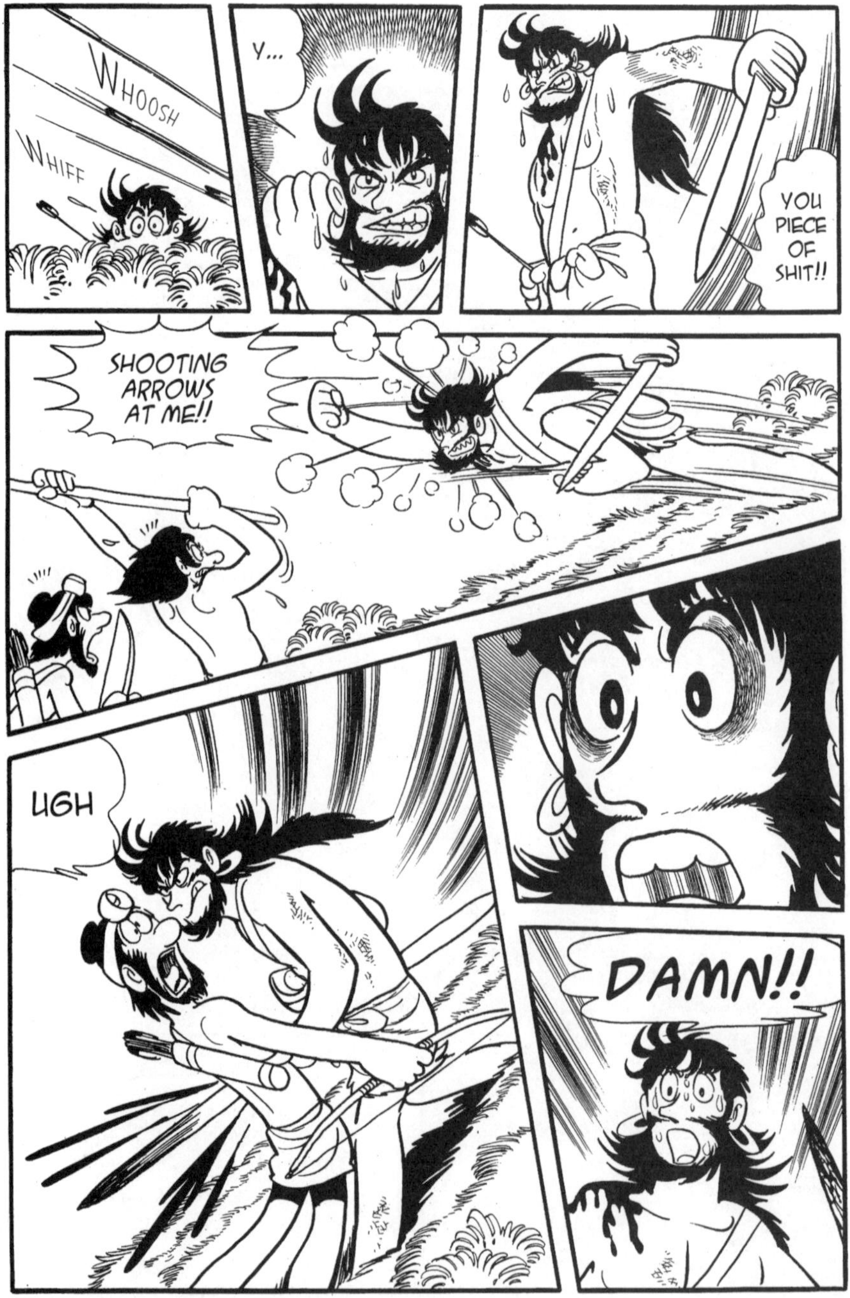
WHOOSH
WHIFF
Y...
YOU PIECE OF SHIT!!
SHOOTING ARROWS AT ME!!
UGH
DAMN!!

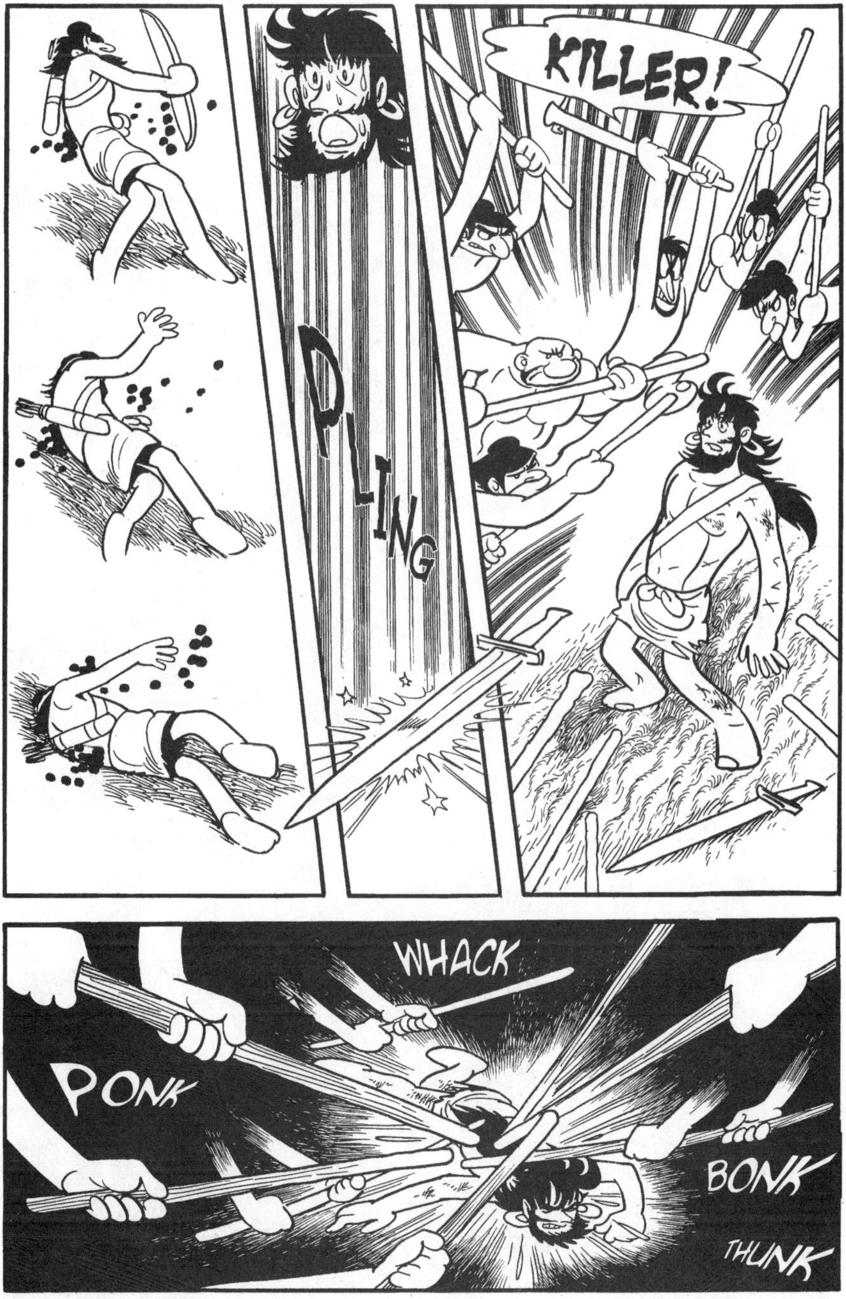

PLING
KILLER!
WHACK
PONK
BONK
THUNK

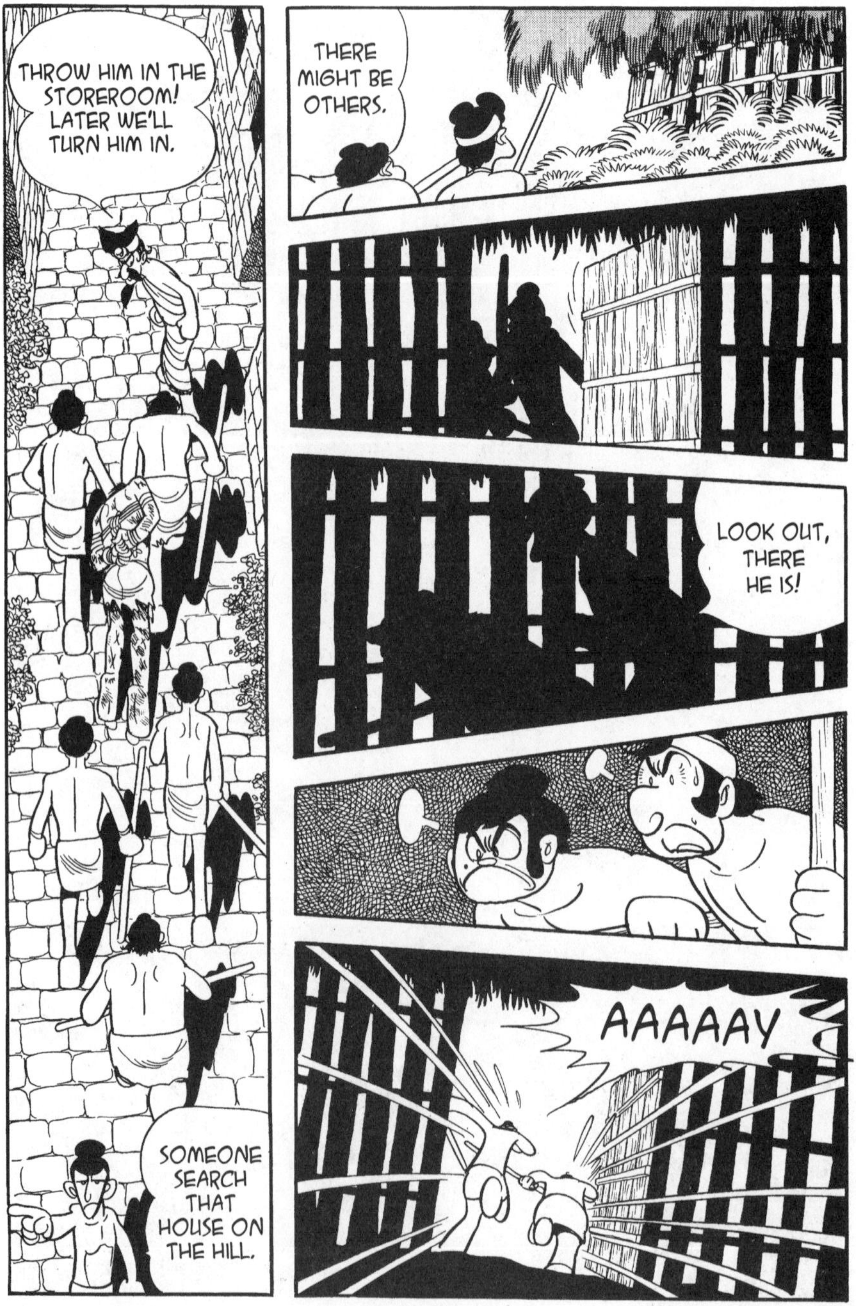
THROW HIM IN THE STOREROOM! LATER WE'LL TURN HIM IN.
SOMEONE SEARCH THAT HOUSE ON THE HILL.
THERE MIGHT BE OTHERS.
LOOK OUT, THERE HE IS!
AAAAAY

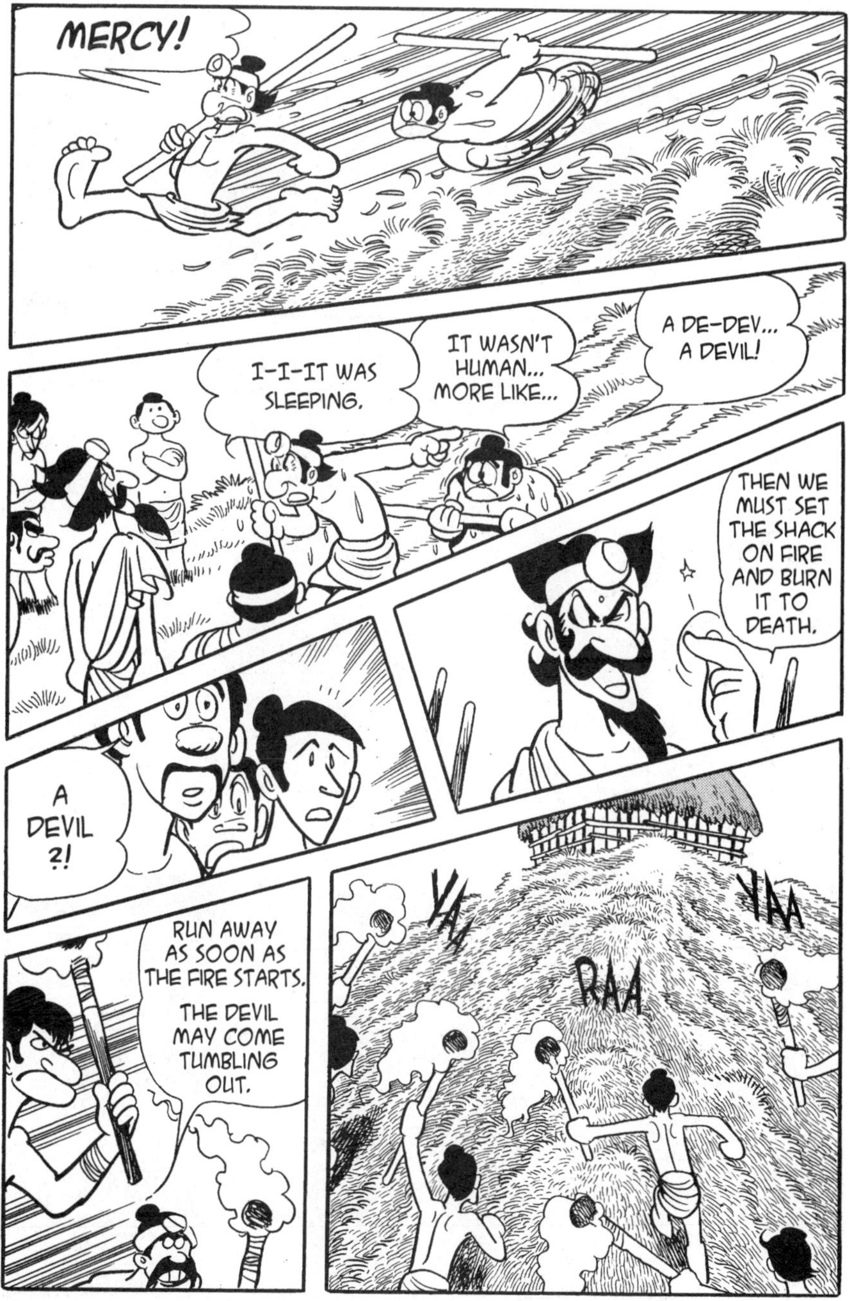
MERCY!
I-I-IT WAS SLEEPING.
IT WASN'T HUMAN... MORE LIKE...
A DE-DEV... A DEVIL!
THEN WE MUST SET THE SHACK ON FIRE AND BURN IT TO DEATH.
A DEVIL ?!
RUN AWAY AS SOON AS THE FIRE STARTS.
THE DEVIL MAY COME TUMBLING OUT.
YAA
RAA
YAA

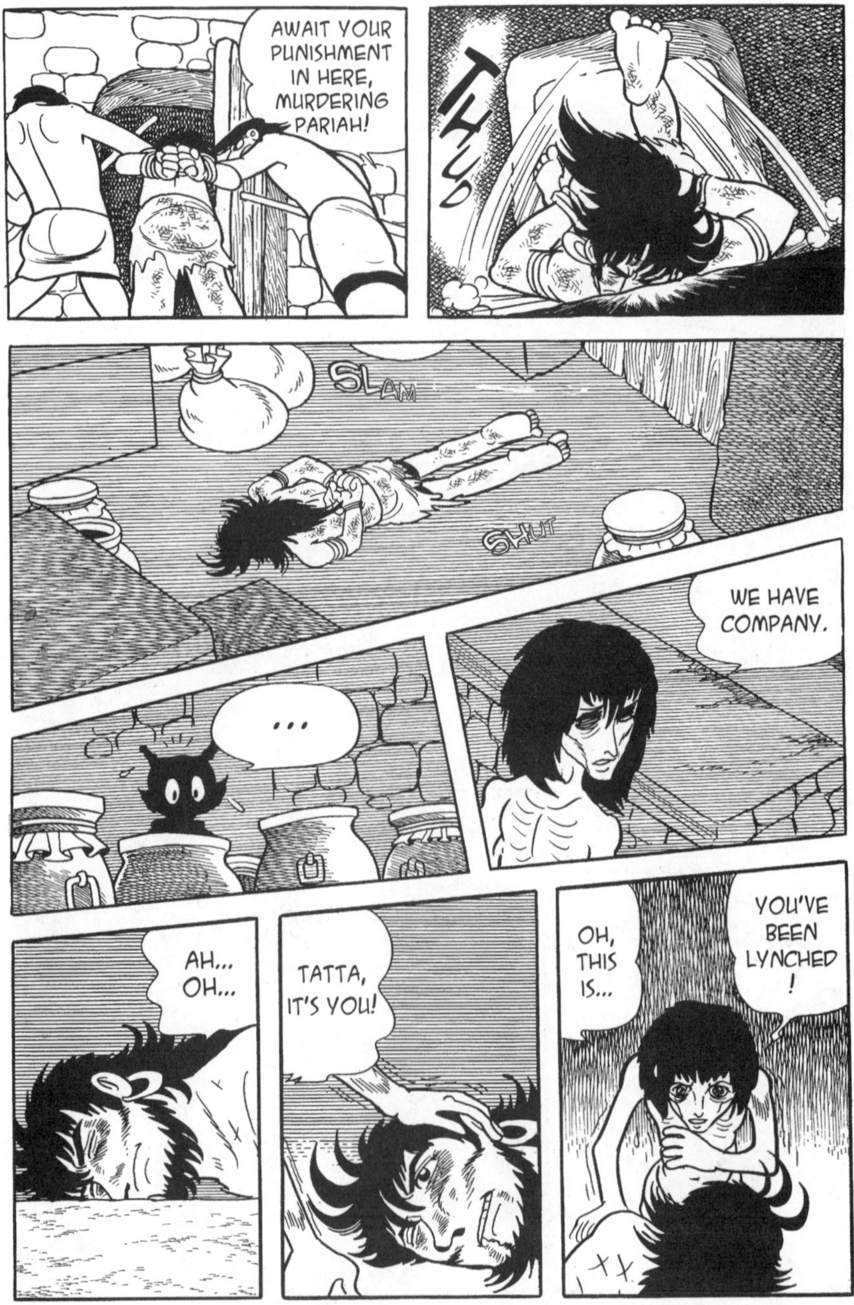
AWAIT YOUR PUNISHMENT IN HERE, MURDERING PARIAH!
THUD
SLAM
SHUT
...
WE HAVE COMPANY.
AH... OH...
TATTA, IT'S YOU!
OH, THIS IS...
YOU'VE BEEN LYNCHED!

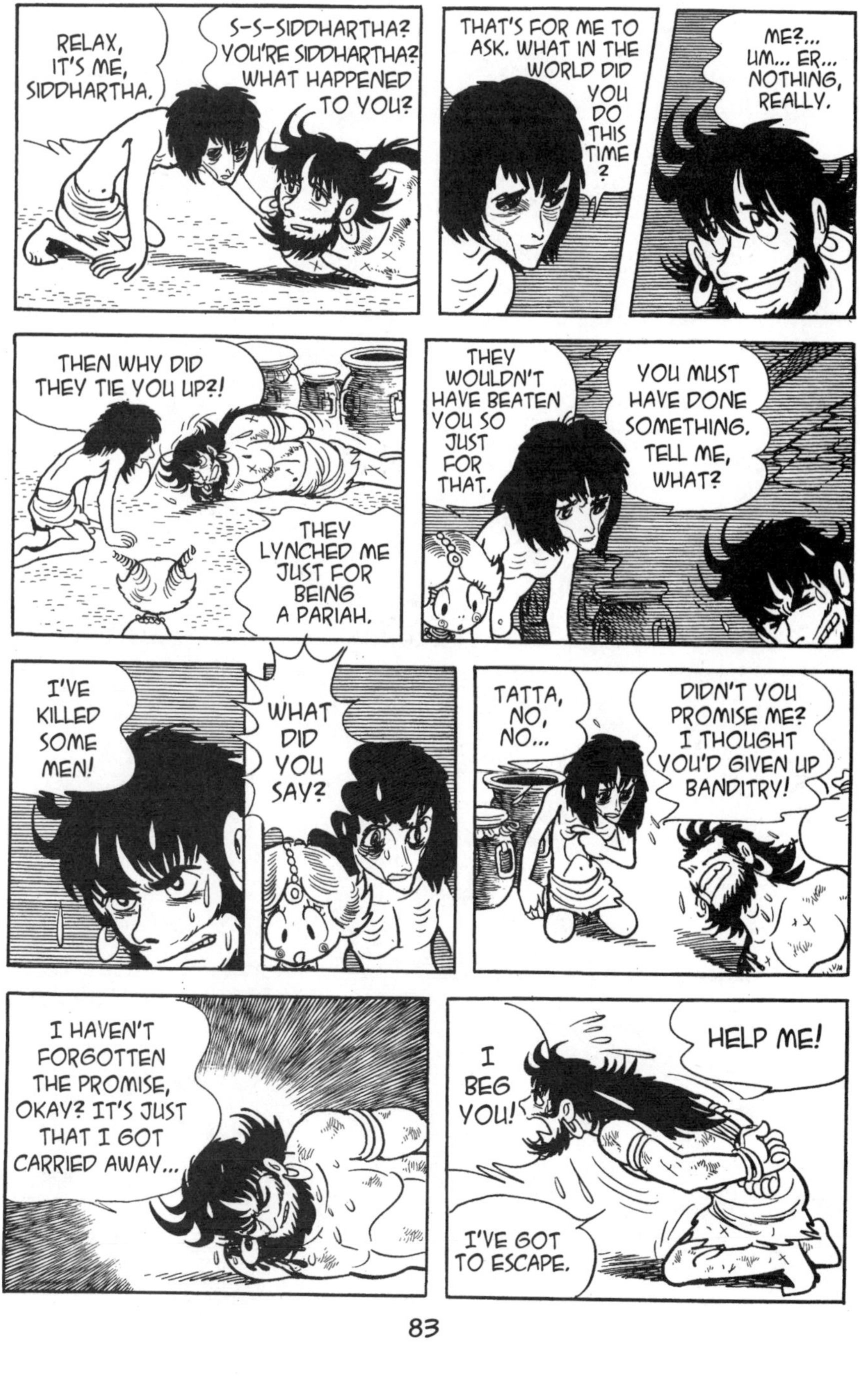
RELAX, IT'S ME, SIDDHARTHA.
S-S-SIDDHARTHA? YOU'RE SIDDHARTHA? WHAT HAPPENED TO YOU?
THAT'S FOR ME TO ASK. WHAT IN THE WORLD DID YOU DO THIS TIME?
ME?... UM... ER... NOTHING, REALLY.
THEN WHY DID THEY TIE YOU UP?!
THEY LYNCHED ME JUST FOR BEING A PARIAH.
THEY WOULDN'T HAVE BEATEN YOU SO JUST FOR THAT.
YOU MUST HAVE DONE SOMETHING. TELL ME, WHAT?
I'VE KILLED SOME MEN!
WHAT DID YOU SAY?
TATTA, NO, NO...
DIDN'T YOU PROMISE ME? I THOUGHT YOU'D GIVEN UP BANDITRY!
I HAVEN'T FORGOTTEN THE PROMISE, OKAY? IT'S JUST THAT I GOT CARRIED AWAY...
I BEG YOU!
HELP ME!
I'VE GOT TO ESCAPE.

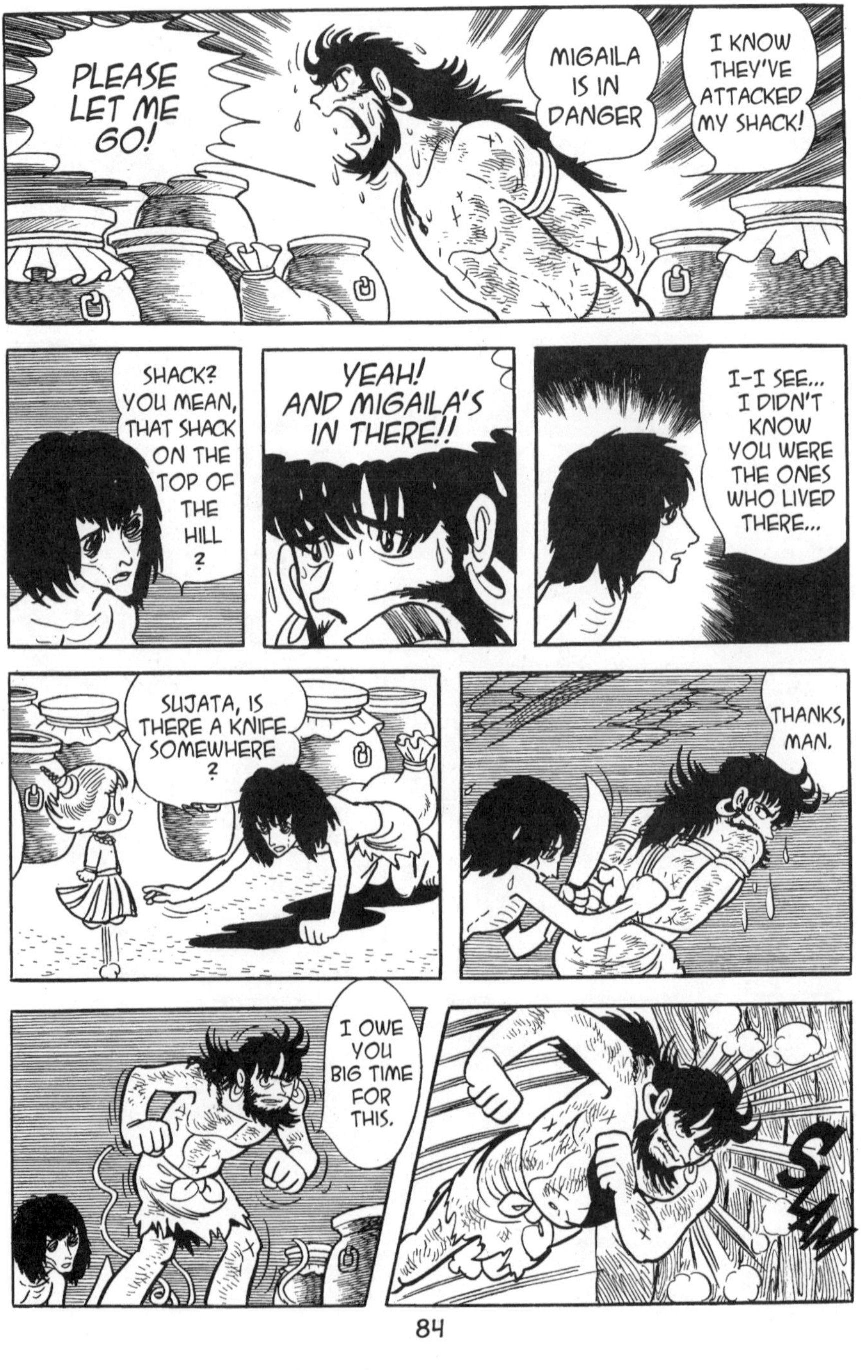
PLEASE LET ME GO!
MIGAILA IS IN DANGER
I KNOW THEY'VE ATTACKED MY SHACK!
SHACK? YOU MEAN, THAT SHACK ON THE TOP OF THE HILL?
YEAH! AND MIGAILA'S IN THERE!!
I-I SEE... I DIDN'T KNOW YOU WERE THE ONES WHO LIVED THERE...
SUJATA, IS THERE A KNIFE SOMEWHERE?
THANKS, MAN.
I OWE YOU BIG TIME FOR THIS.
SLAM

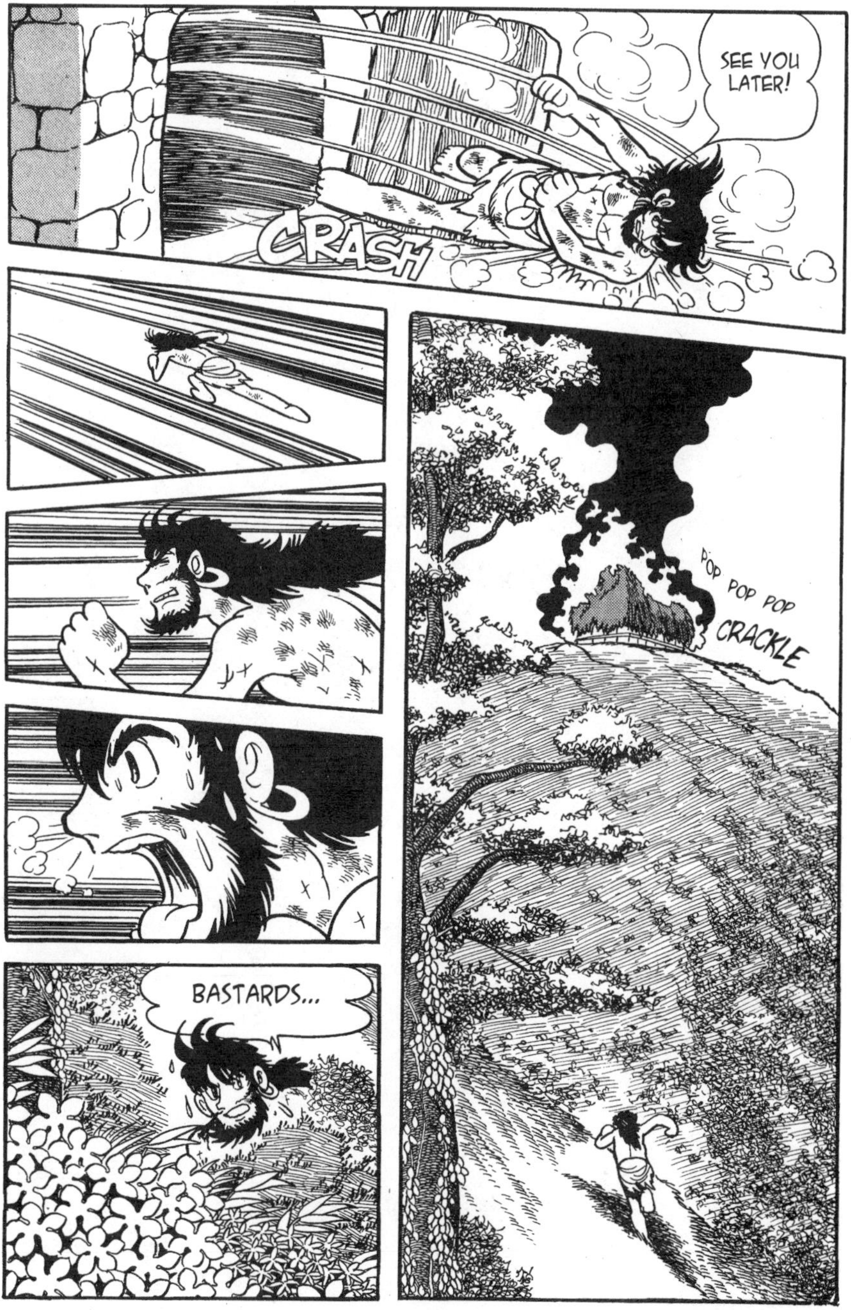
SEE YOU LATER!
CRASH
POP POP POP
CRACKLE
BASTARDS...

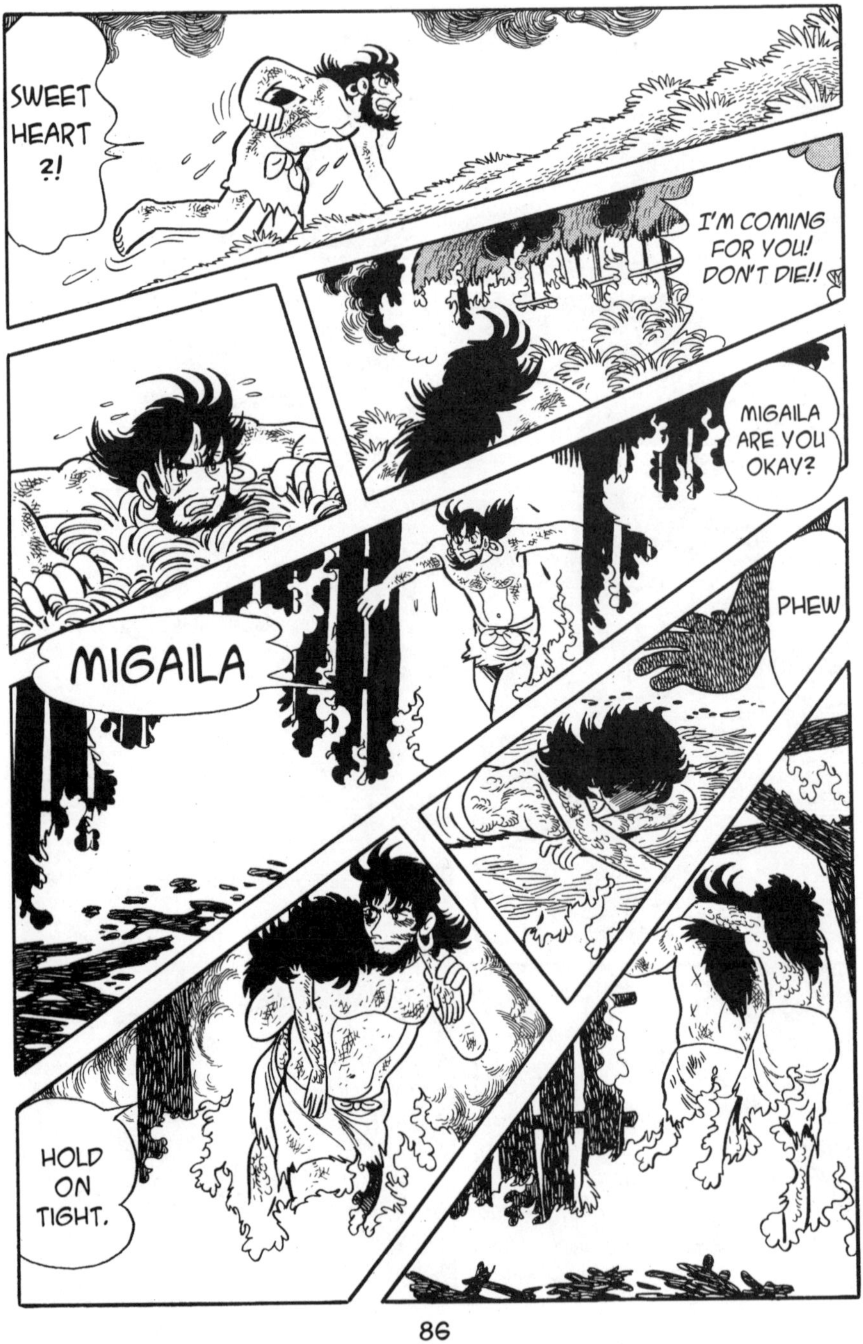
SWEET HEART ?!
I'M COMING FOR YOU! DON'T DIE!!
MIGAILA
MIGAILA ARE YOU OKAY?
PHEW
HOLD ON TIGHT.

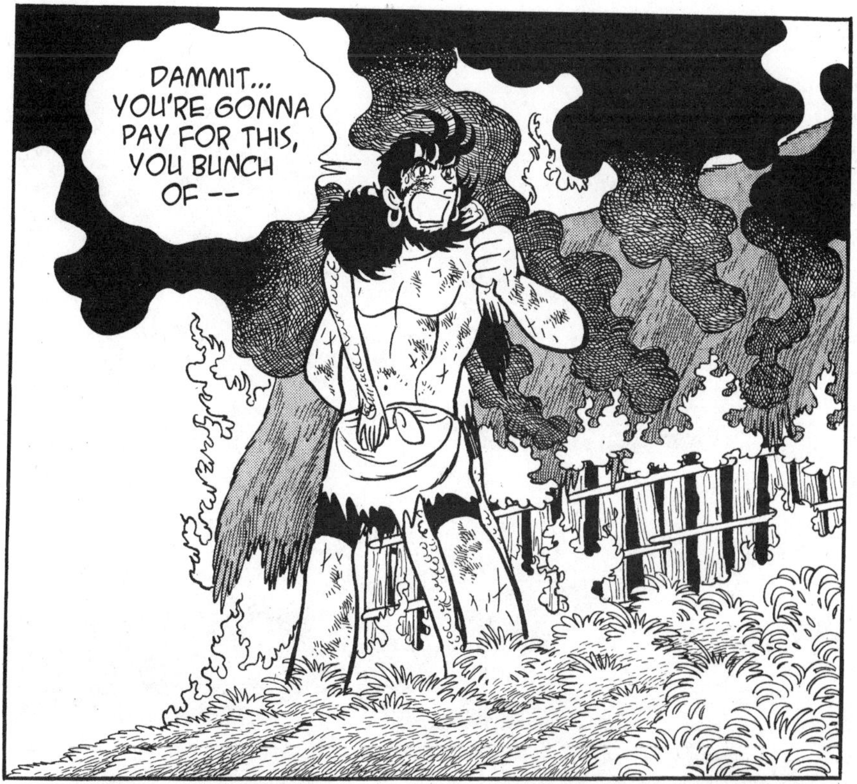
DAMMIT... YOU'RE GONNA PAY FOR THIS, YOU BUNCH OF --

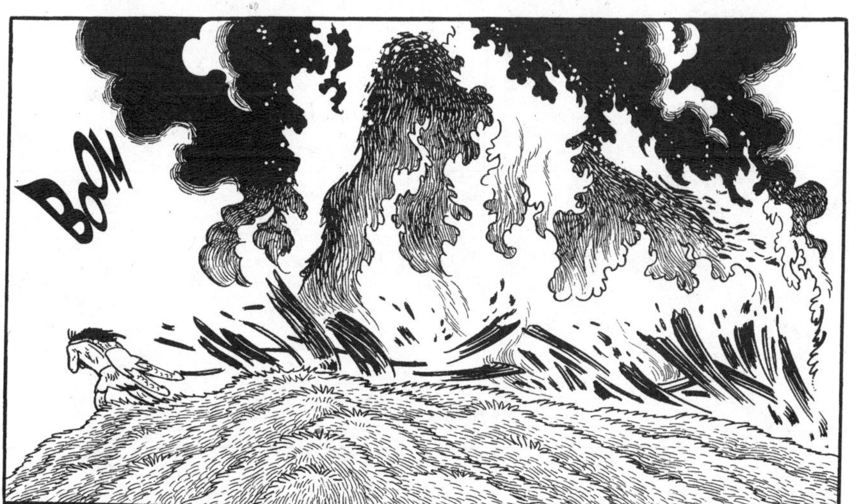
BOOM

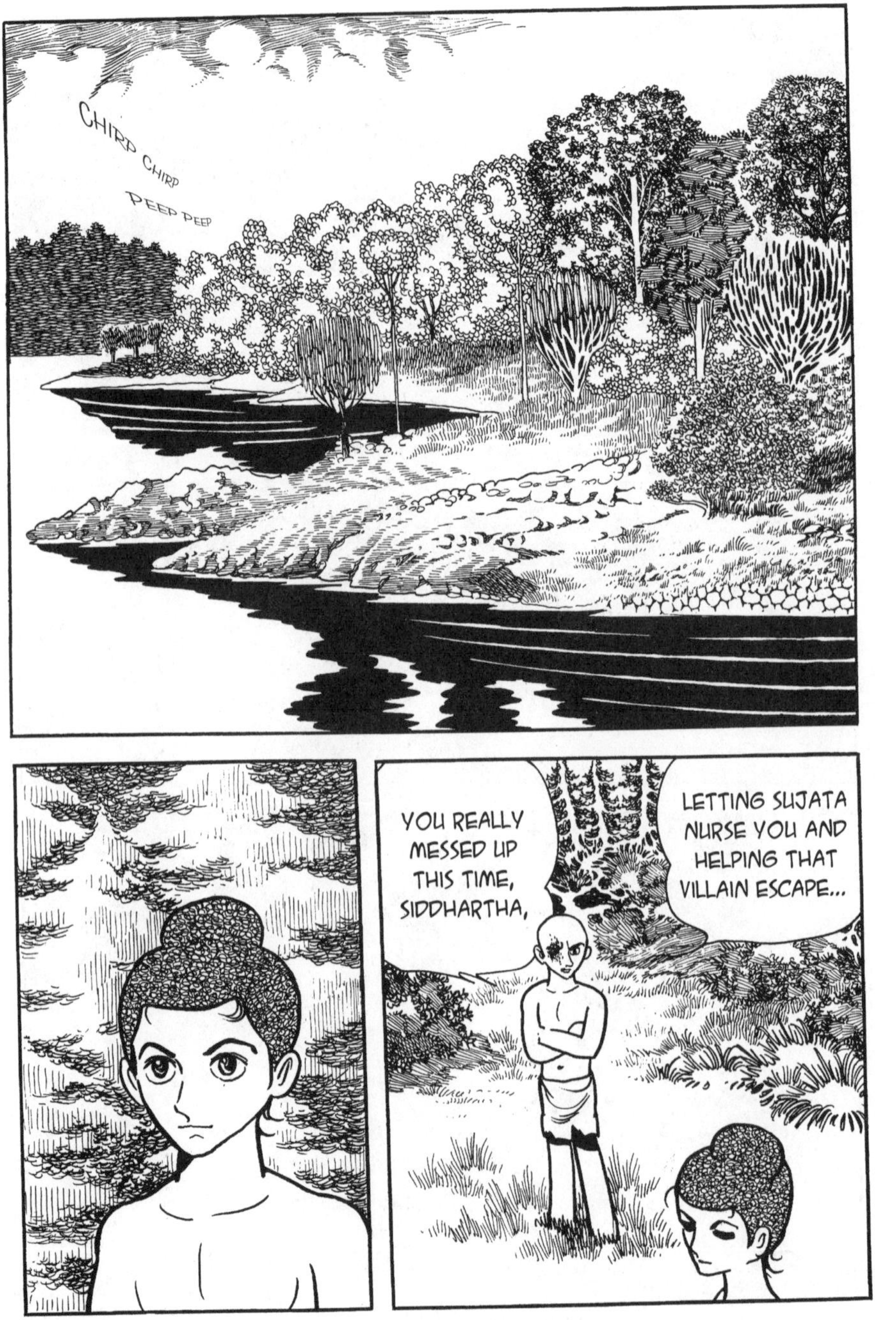
CHIRP CHIRP
PEEP PEEP
YOU REALLY MESSED UP THIS TIME, SIDDHARTHA,
LETTING SUJATA NURSE YOU AND HELPING THAT VILLAIN ESCAPE...

WHAT PAINS ME MOST IS THAT YOU QUIT YOUR FAST...
AND HAD MILK PAP. PATHETIC.
NO ASCETIC TOUCHES MEAT OR FISH, NOR MILK, EGGS AND SUCH.
A LITTLE GRAIN, NUTS AND WATER ARE ALL WE PERMIT OURSELVES.
YET YOU GOBBLED DOWN MILK PAP!
DO YOU STILL CONSIDER YOURSELF AN ASCETIC?!
I SLOWLY BEGAN TO HAVE MY DOUBTS.
FINE AND WELL TO PUNISH THE BODY...
IF THAT REDUCES HUMAN MISERY. BE THAT AS IT MAY...
WHY ARE HUMANS MORTAL? WHY ARE THERE CASTES?

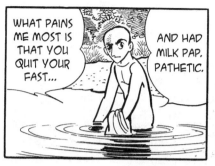

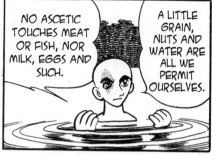

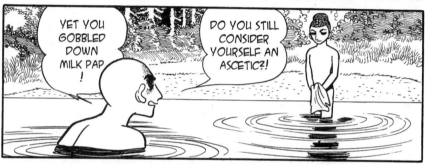

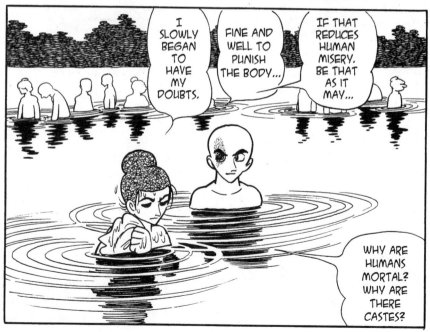

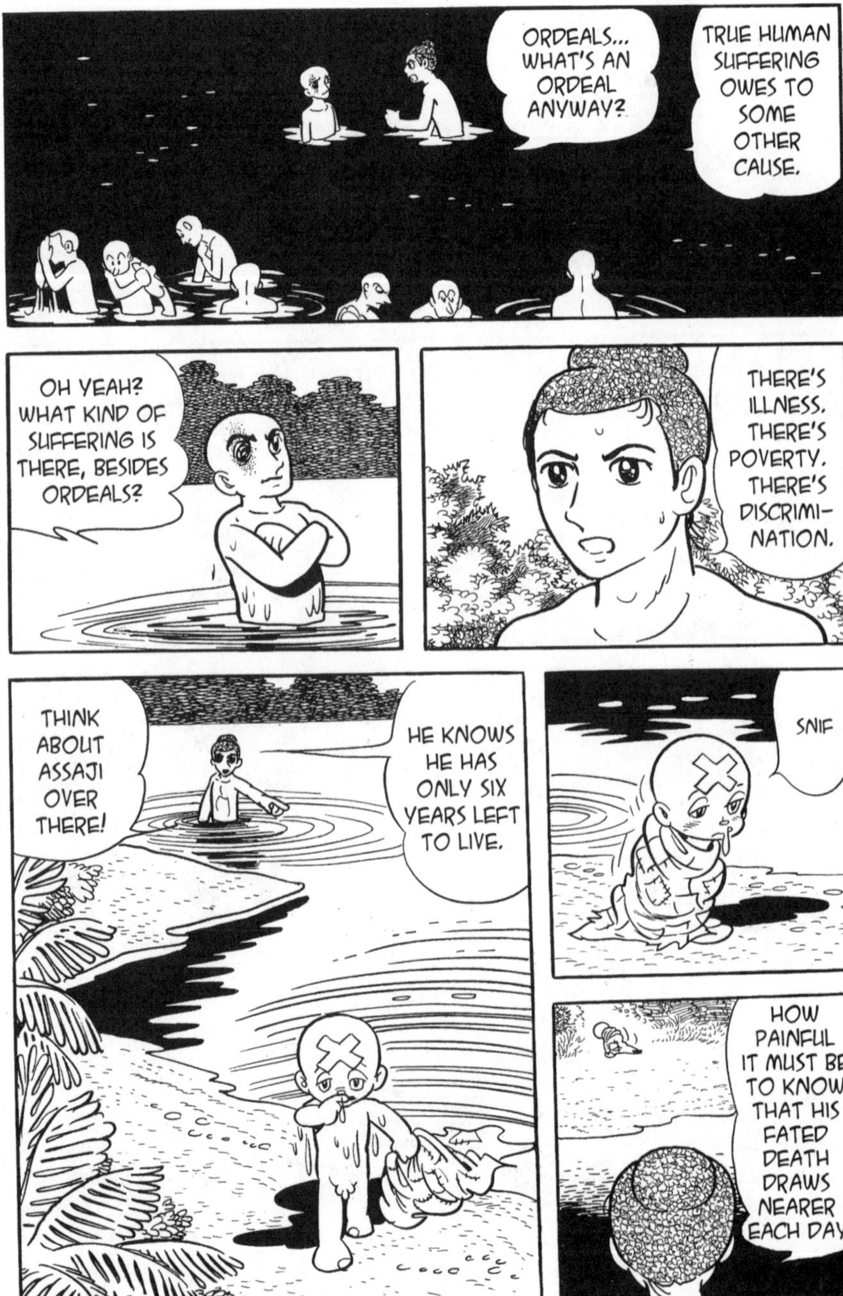
ORDEALS... WHAT'S AN ORDEAL ANYWAY?
TRUE HUMAN SUFFERING OWES TO SOME OTHER CAUSE.
OH YEAH? WHAT KIND OF SUFFERING IS THERE, BESIDES ORDEALS?
THERE'S ILLNESS. THERE'S POVERTY. THERE'S DISCRIMI-NATION.
THINK ABOUT ASSAJI OVER THERE!
HE KNOWS HE HAS ONLY SIX YEARS LEFT TO LIVE.
SNIF
HOW PAINFUL IT MUST BE TO KNOW THAT HIS FATED DEATH DRAWS NEARER EACH DAY.

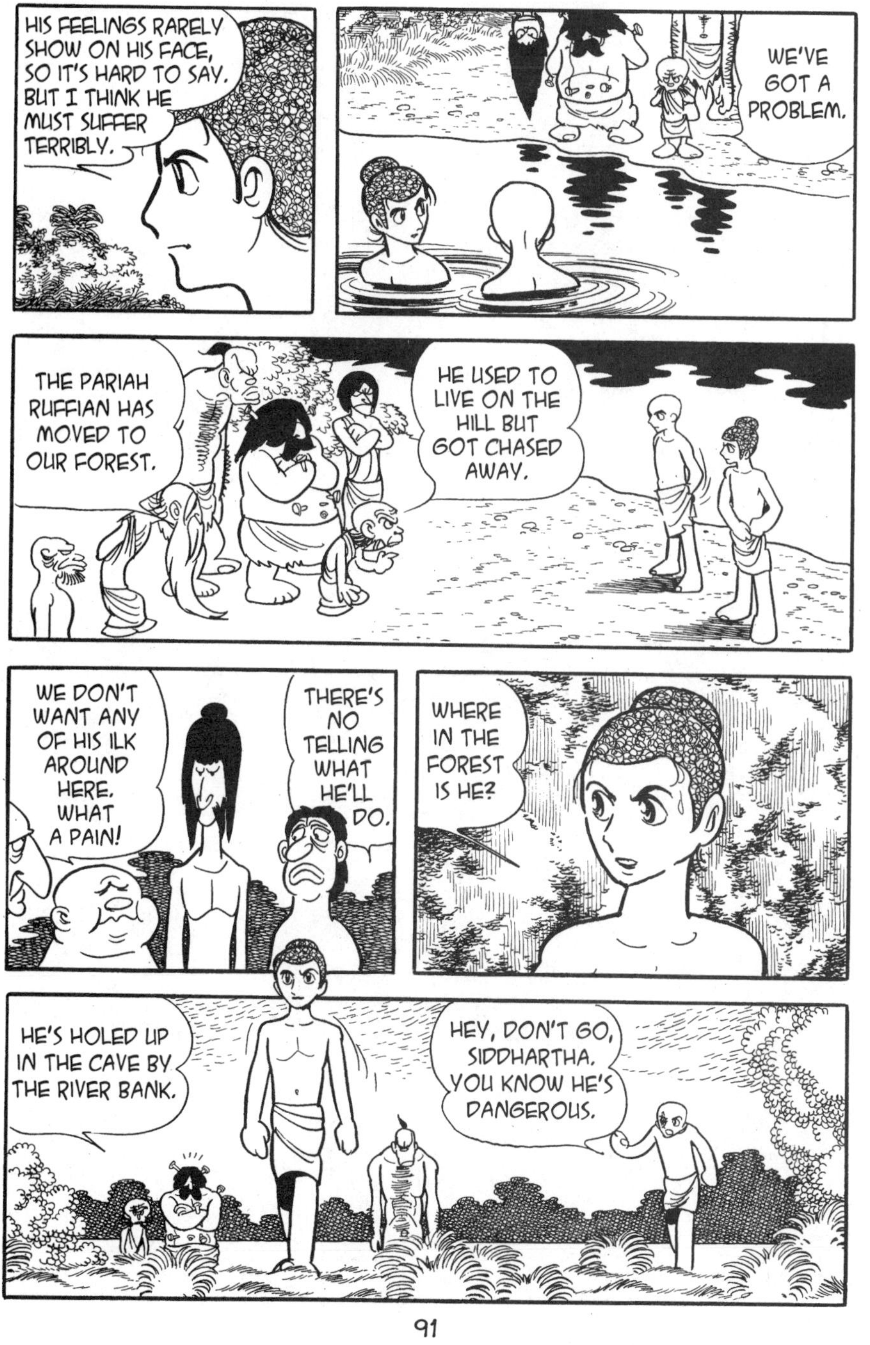
HIS FEELINGS RARELY SHOW ON HIS FACE, SO IT'S HARD TO SAY. BUT I THINK HE MUST SUFFER TERRIBLY.
WE'VE GOT A PROBLEM.
THE PARIAH RUFFIAN HAS MOVED TO OUR FOREST.
HE USED TO LIVE ON THE HILL BUT GOT CHASED AWAY.
WE DON'T WANT ANY OF HIS ILK AROUND HERE. WHAT A PAIN!
THERE'S NO TELLING WHAT HE'LL DO.
WHERE IN THE FOREST IS HE?
HE'S HOLED UP IN THE CAVE BY THE RIVER BANK.
HEY, DON'T GO, SIDDHARTHA. YOU KNOW HE'S DANGEROUS.

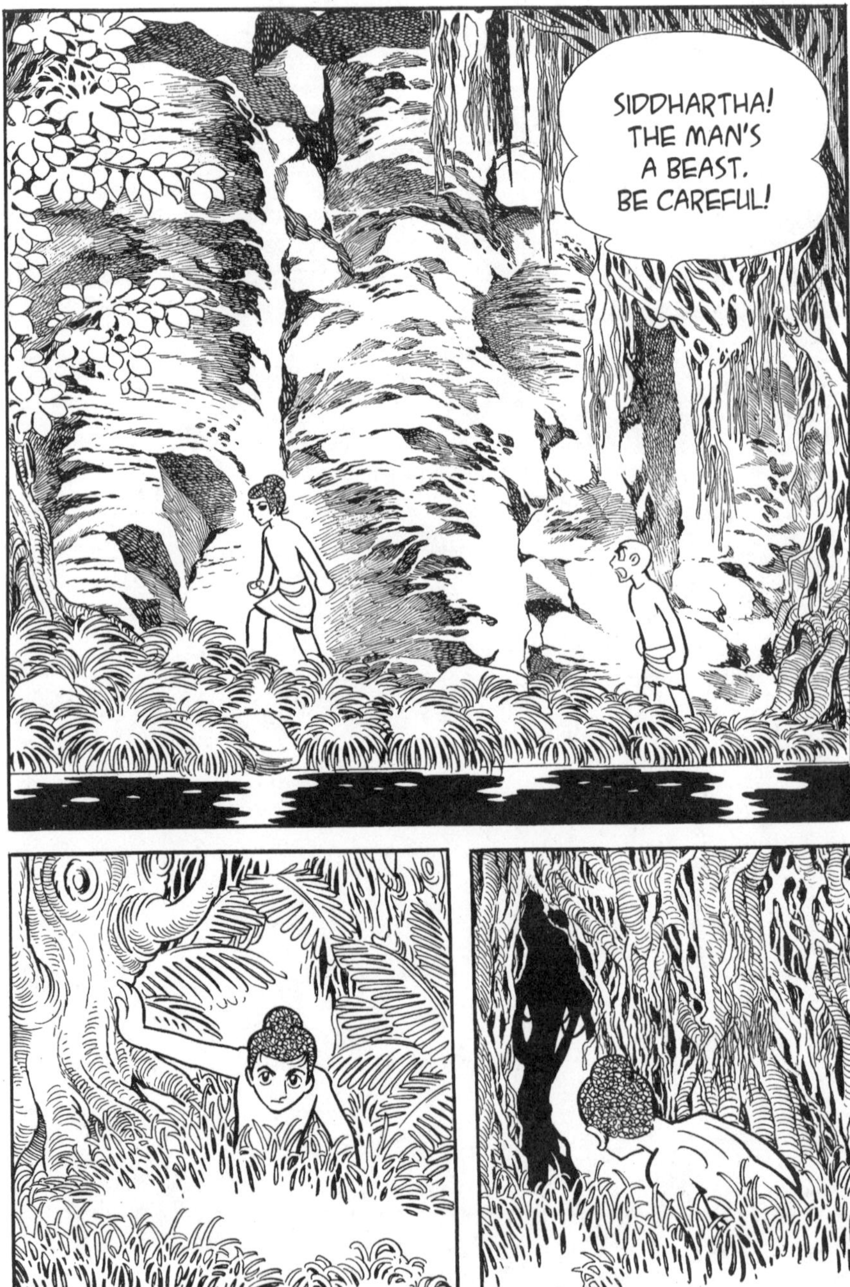
SIDDHARTHA! THE MAN'S A BEAST. BE CAREFUL!

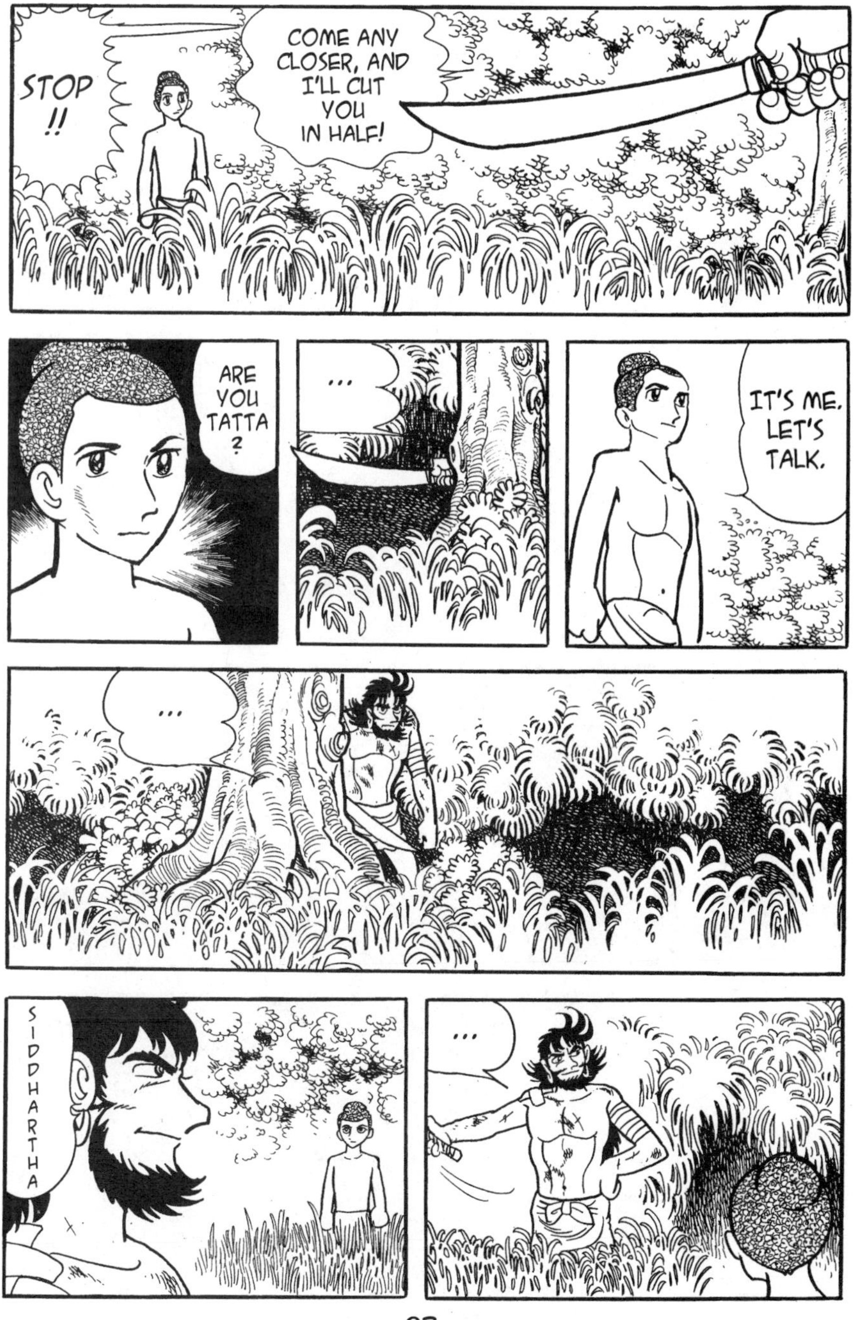
STOP !!
COME ANY CLOSER, AND I'LL CUT YOU IN HALF!
ARE YOU TATTA ?
...
IT'S ME. LET'S TALK.
...
SIDDHARTHA
...

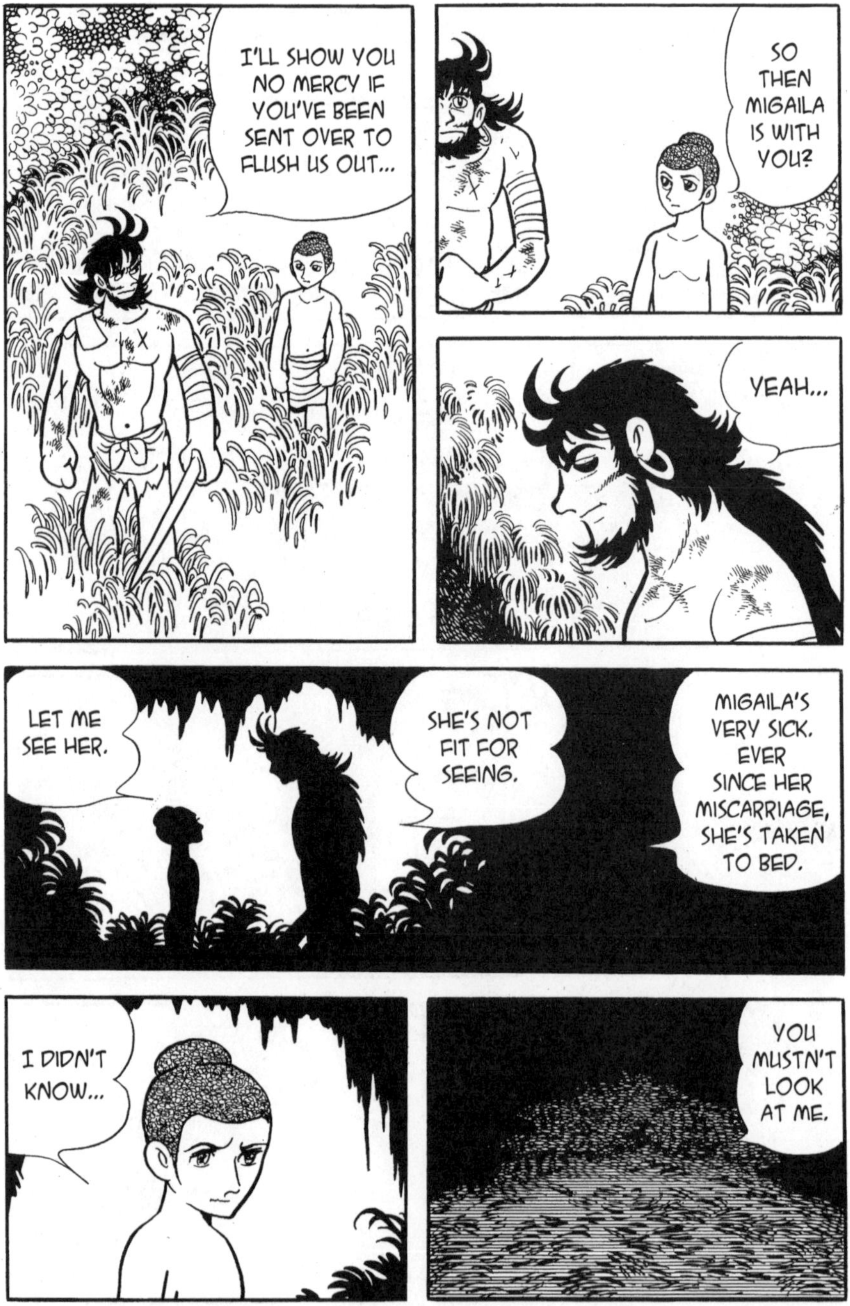
I'LL SHOW YOU NO MERCY IF YOU'VE BEEN SENT OVER TO FLUSH US OUT...
SO THEN MIGAILA IS WITH YOU?
YEAH...
LET ME SEE HER.
SHE'S NOT FIT FOR SEEING.
MIGAILA'S VERY SICK. EVER SINCE HER MISCARRIAGE, SHE'S TAKEN TO BED.
I DIDN'T KNOW...
YOU MUSTN'T LOOK AT ME.

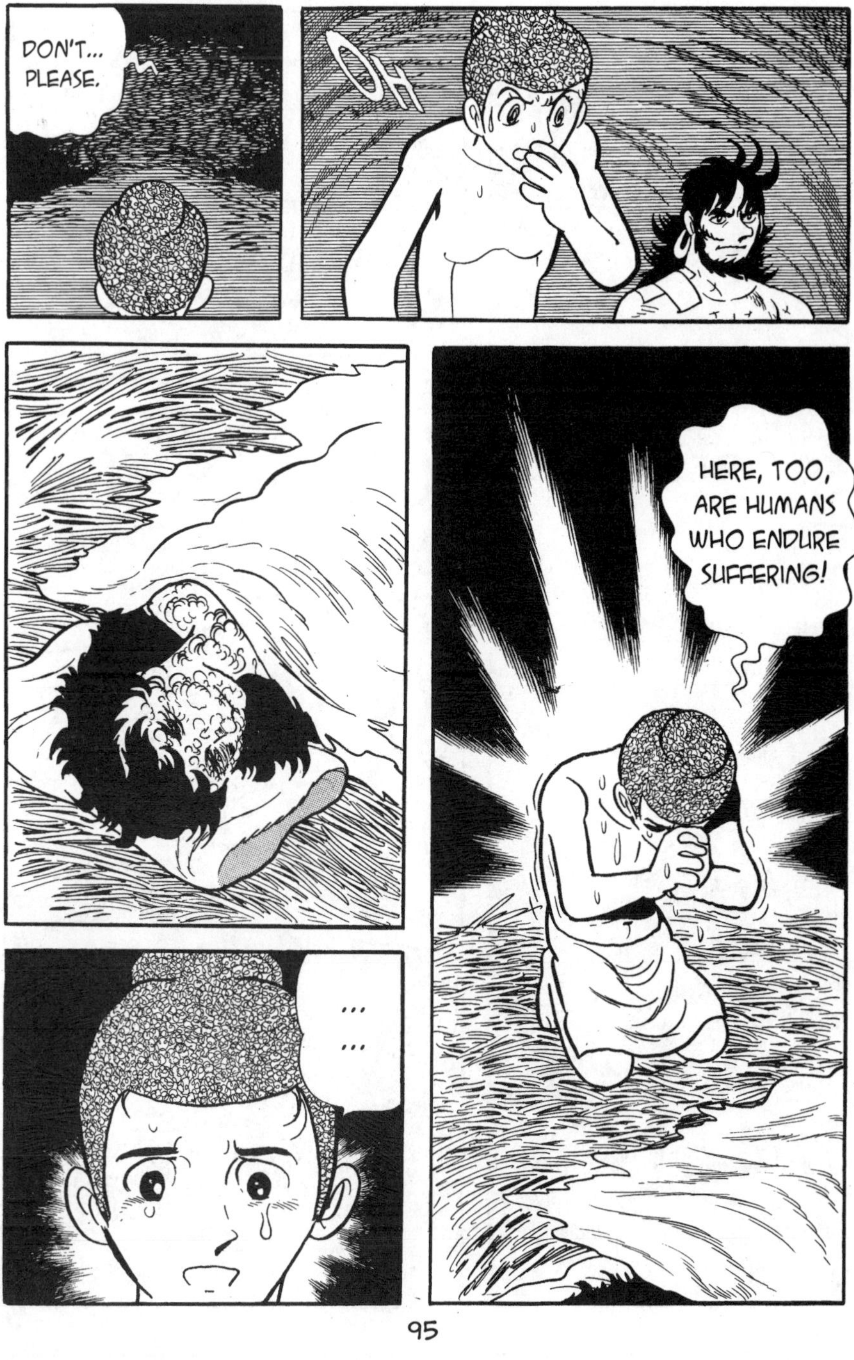
DON'T... PLEASE.
OH
HERE, TOO, ARE HUMANS WHO ENDURE SUFFERING!
...
...

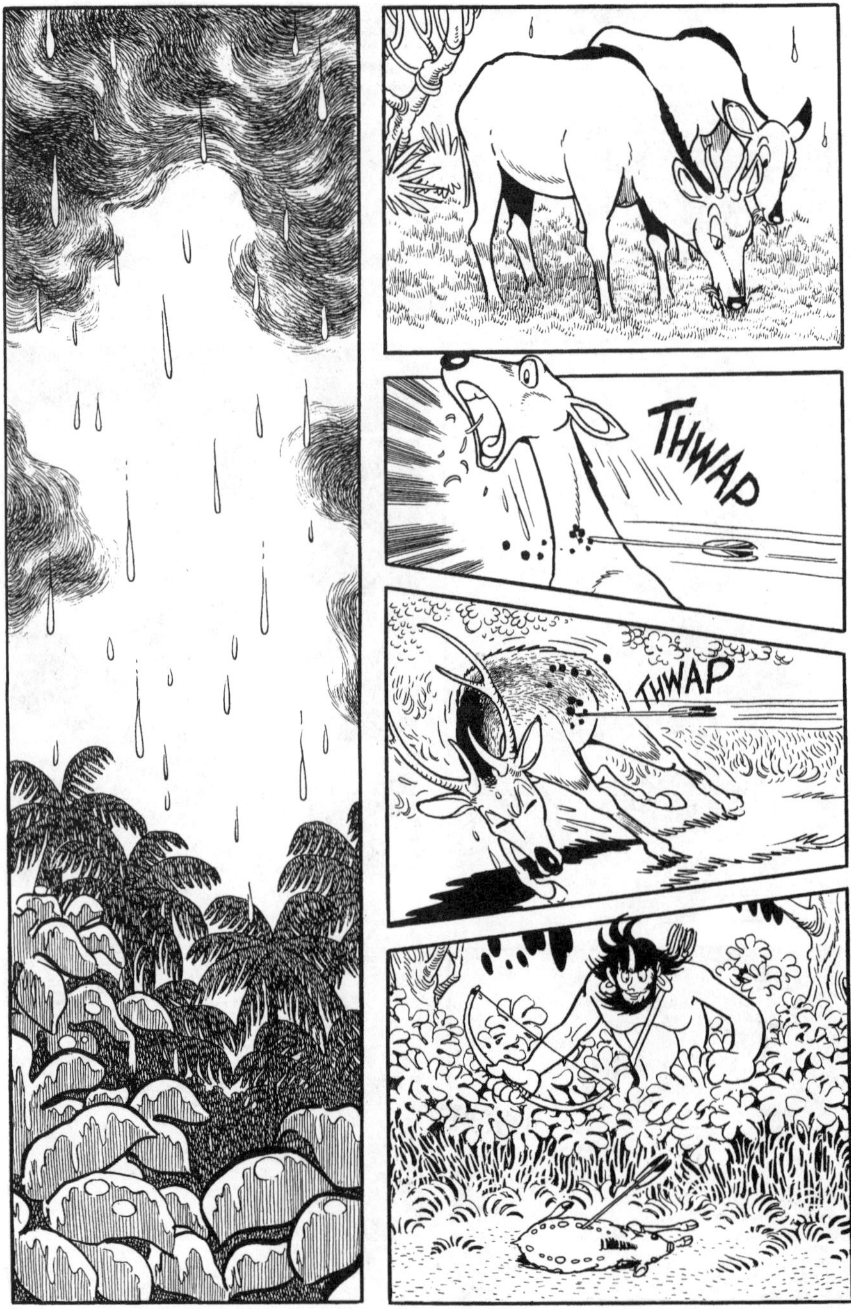
THWAP
THWAP

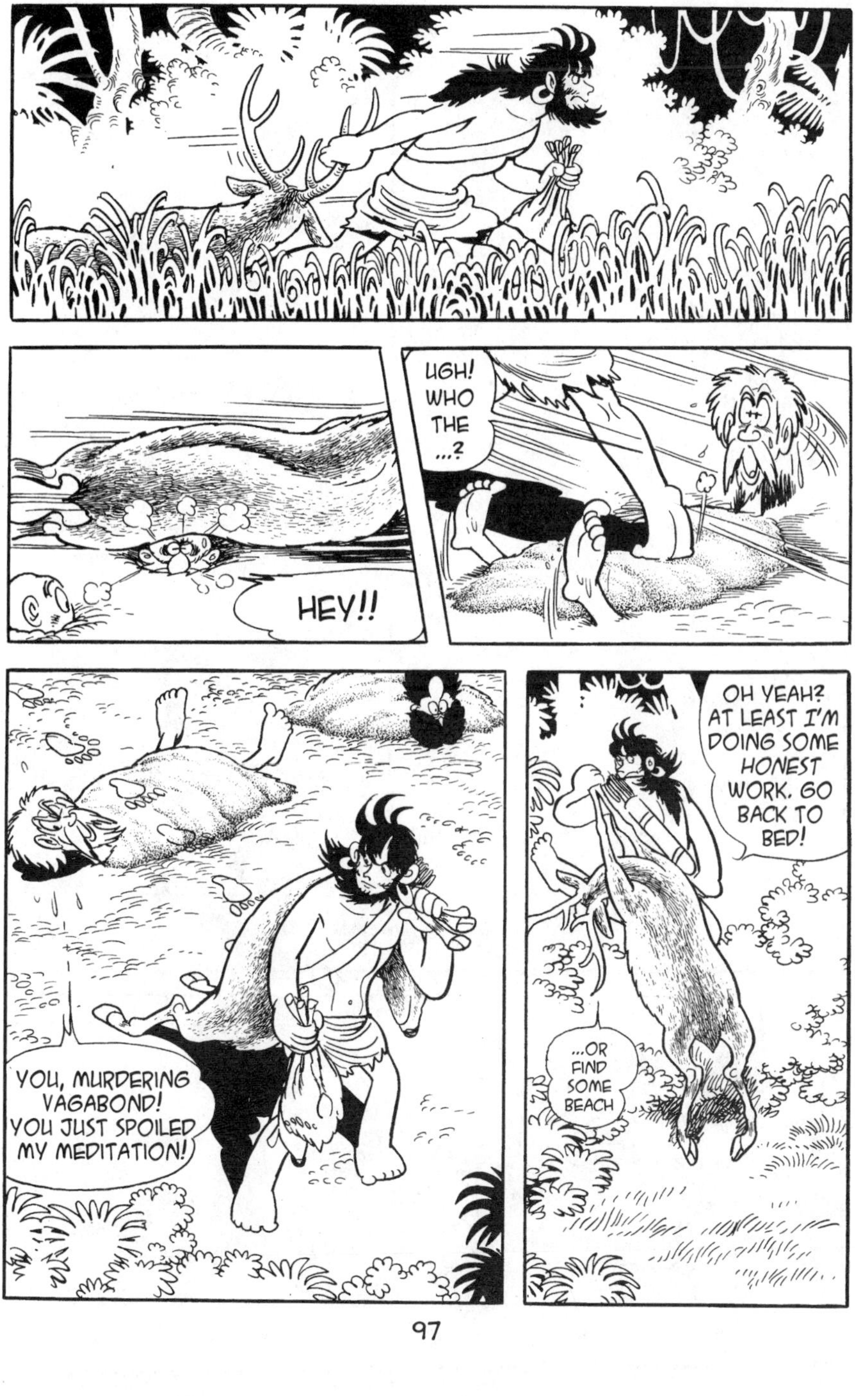
HEY!!
UGH! WHO THE ...?
YOU, MURDERING VAGABOND! YOU JUST SPOILED MY MEDITATION!
OH YEAH? AT LEAST I'M DOING SOME HONEST WORK. GO BACK TO BED!
...OR FIND SOME BEACH

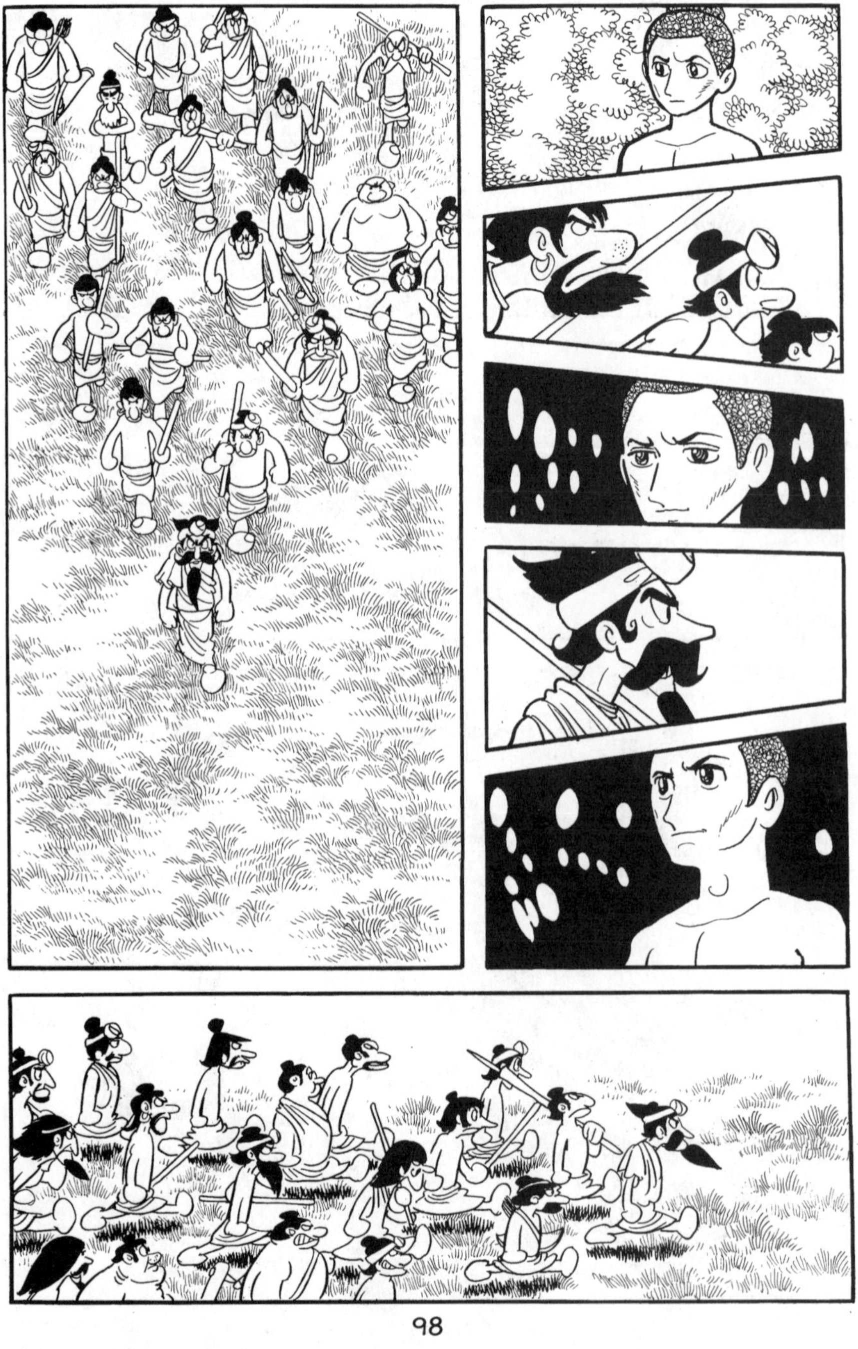

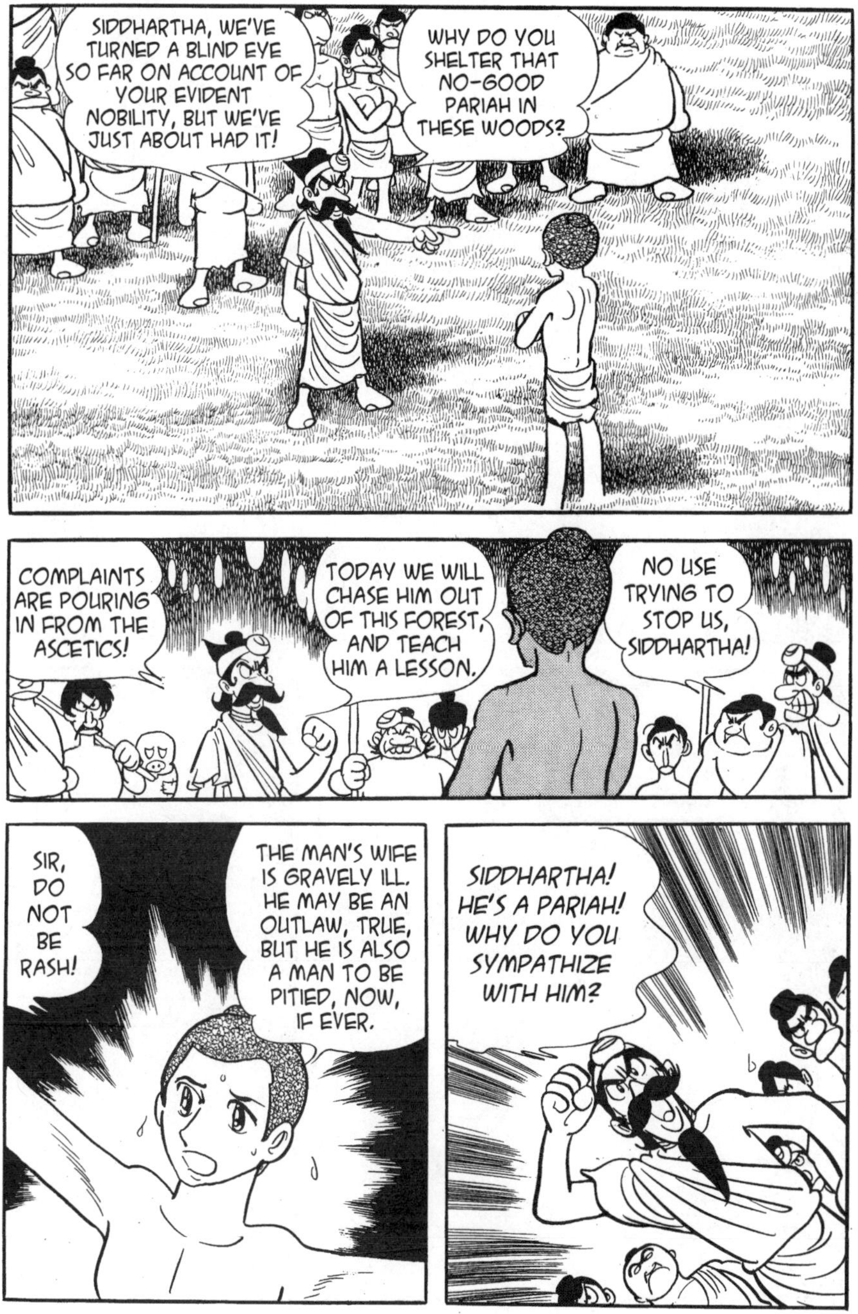
SIDDHARTHA, WE'VE TURNED A BLIND EYE SO FAR ON ACCOUNT OF YOUR EVIDENT NOBILITY, BUT WE'VE JUST ABOUT HAD IT!
WHY DO YOU SHELTER THAT NO-GOOD PARIAH IN THESE WOODS?
COMPLAINTS ARE POURING IN FROM THE ASCETICS!
TODAY WE WILL CHASE HIM OUT OF THIS FOREST, AND TEACH HIM A LESSON.
NO USE TRYING TO STOP US, SIDDHARTHA!
SIR, DO NOT BE RASH!
THE MAN'S WIFE IS GRAVELY ILL. HE MAY BE AN OUTLAW, TRUE, BUT HE IS ALSO A MAN TO BE PITIED, NOW, IF EVER.
SIDDHARTHA! HE'S A PARIAH! WHY DO YOU SYMPATHIZE WITH HIM?

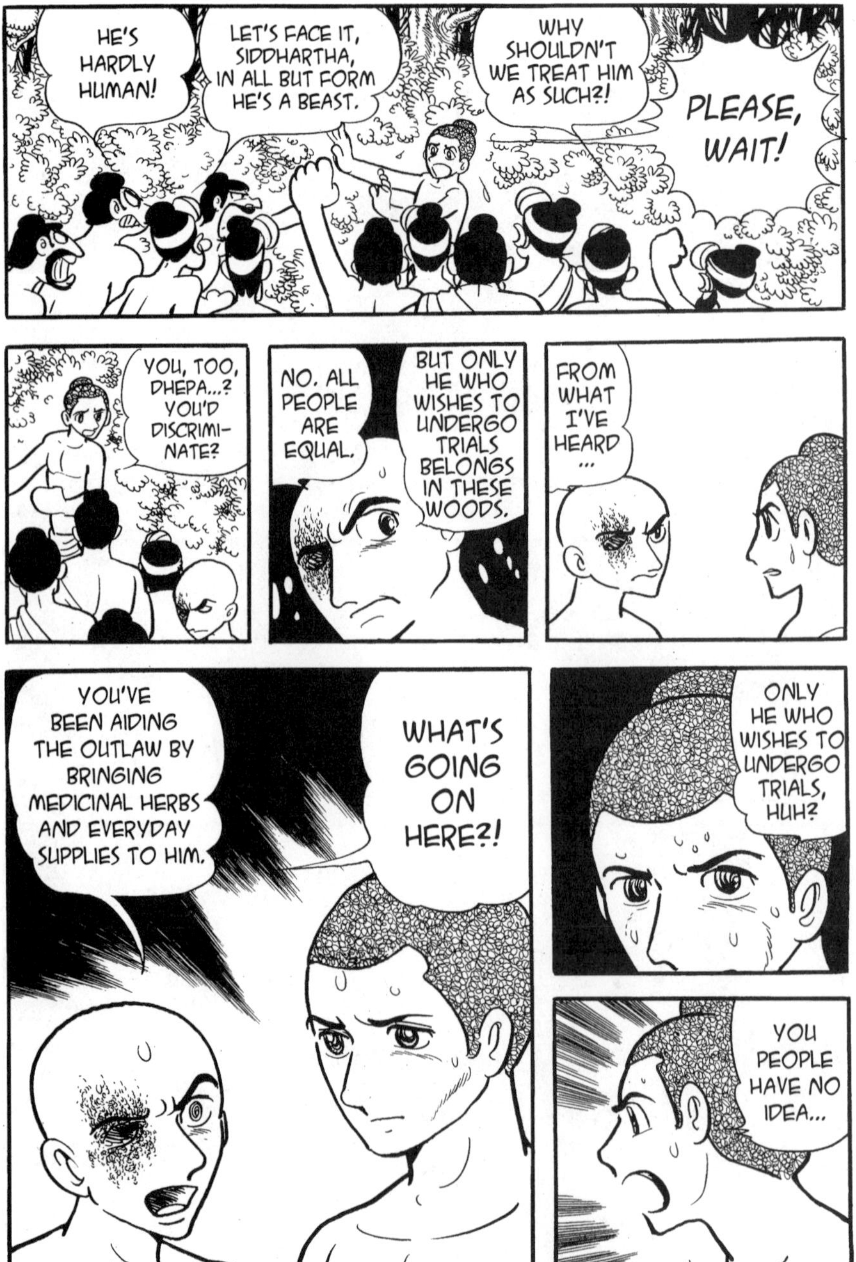
HE'S HARDLY HUMAN!
LET'S FACE IT, SIDDHARTHA, IN ALL BUT FORM HE'S A BEAST.
WHY SHOULDN'T WE TREAT HIM AS SUCH?!
PLEASE, WAIT!
YOU, TOO, DHEPA...? YOU'D DISCRIMINATE?
NO. ALL PEOPLE ARE EQUAL.
BUT ONLY HE WHO WISHES TO UNDERGO TRIALS BELONGS IN THESE WOODS.
FROM WHAT I'VE HEARD ...
YOU'VE BEEN AIDING THE OUTLAW BY BRINGING MEDICINAL HERBS AND EVERYDAY SUPPLIES TO HIM.
WHAT'S GOING ON HERE?!
ONLY HE WHO WISHES TO UNDERGO TRIALS, HUH?
YOU PEOPLE HAVE NO IDEA...

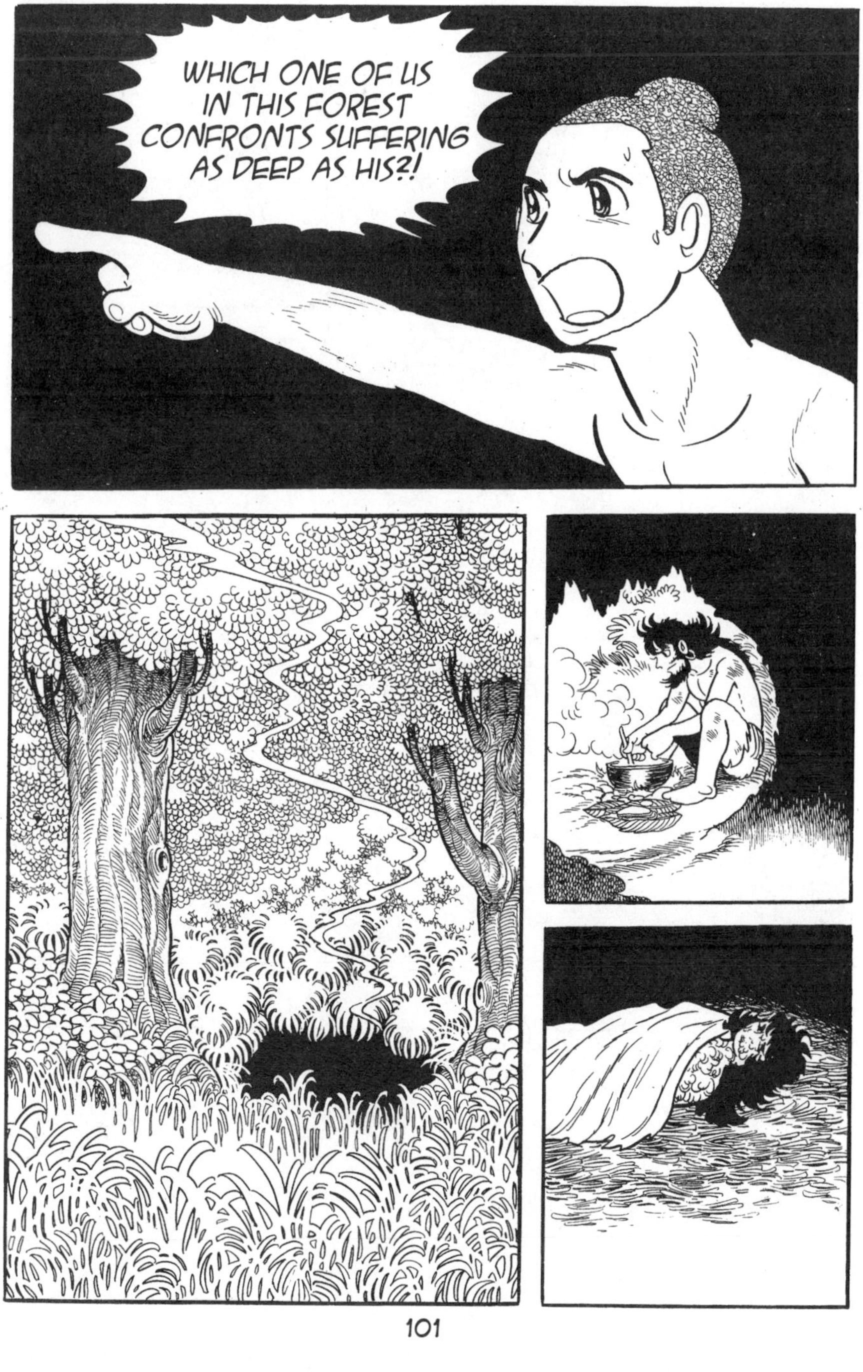
WHICH ONE OF US IN THIS FOREST CONFRONTS SUFFERING AS DEEP AS HIS?!

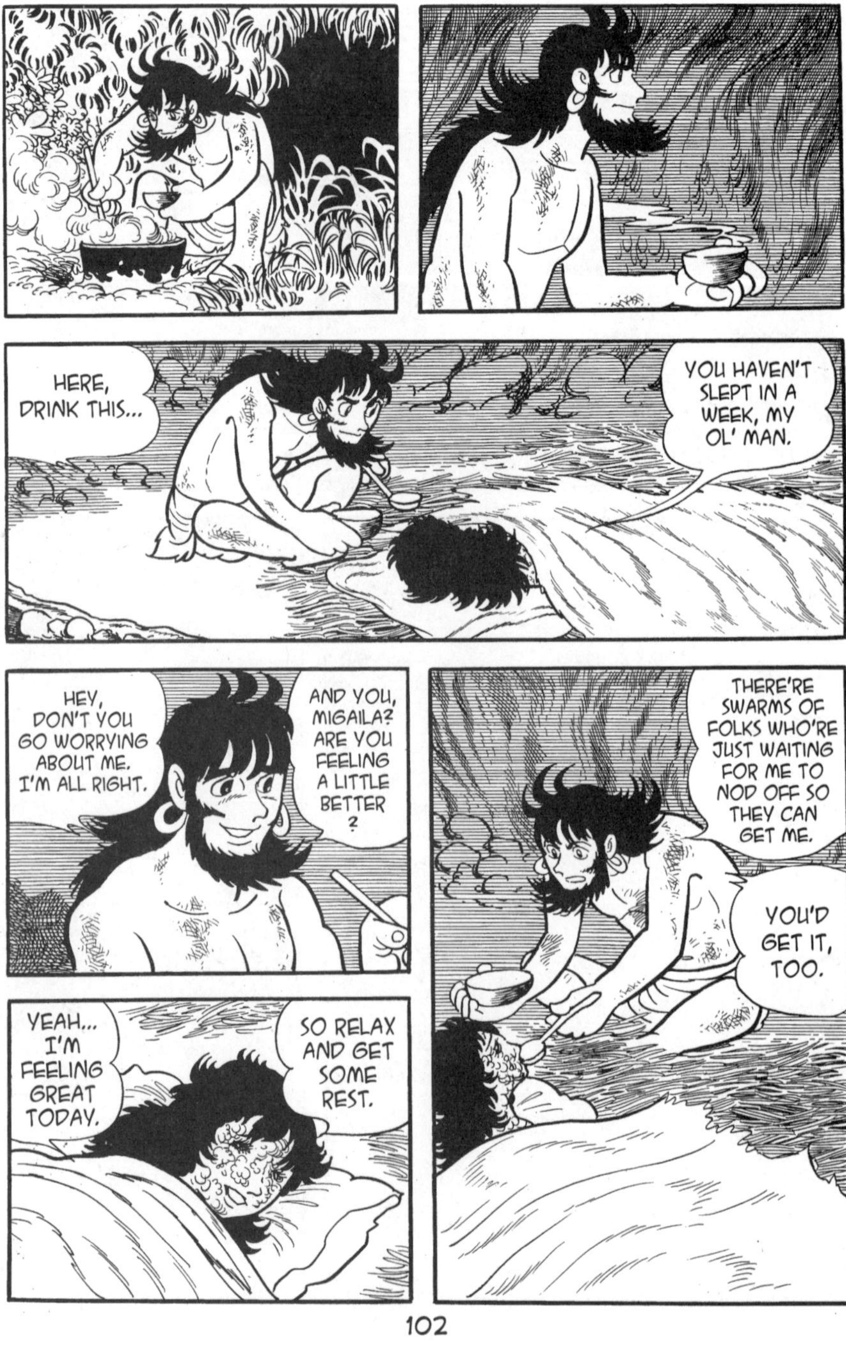
HERE, DRINK THIS...
YOU HAVEN'T SLEPT IN A WEEK, MY OL' MAN.
HEY, DON'T YOU GO WORRYING ABOUT ME. I'M ALL RIGHT.
AND YOU, MIGAILA? ARE YOU FEELING A LITTLE BETTER?
YEAH... I'M FEELING GREAT TODAY.
SO RELAX AND GET SOME REST.
THERE'RE SWARMS OF FOLKS WHO'RE JUST WAITING FOR ME TO NOD OFF SO THEY CAN GET ME.
YOU'D GET IT, TOO.

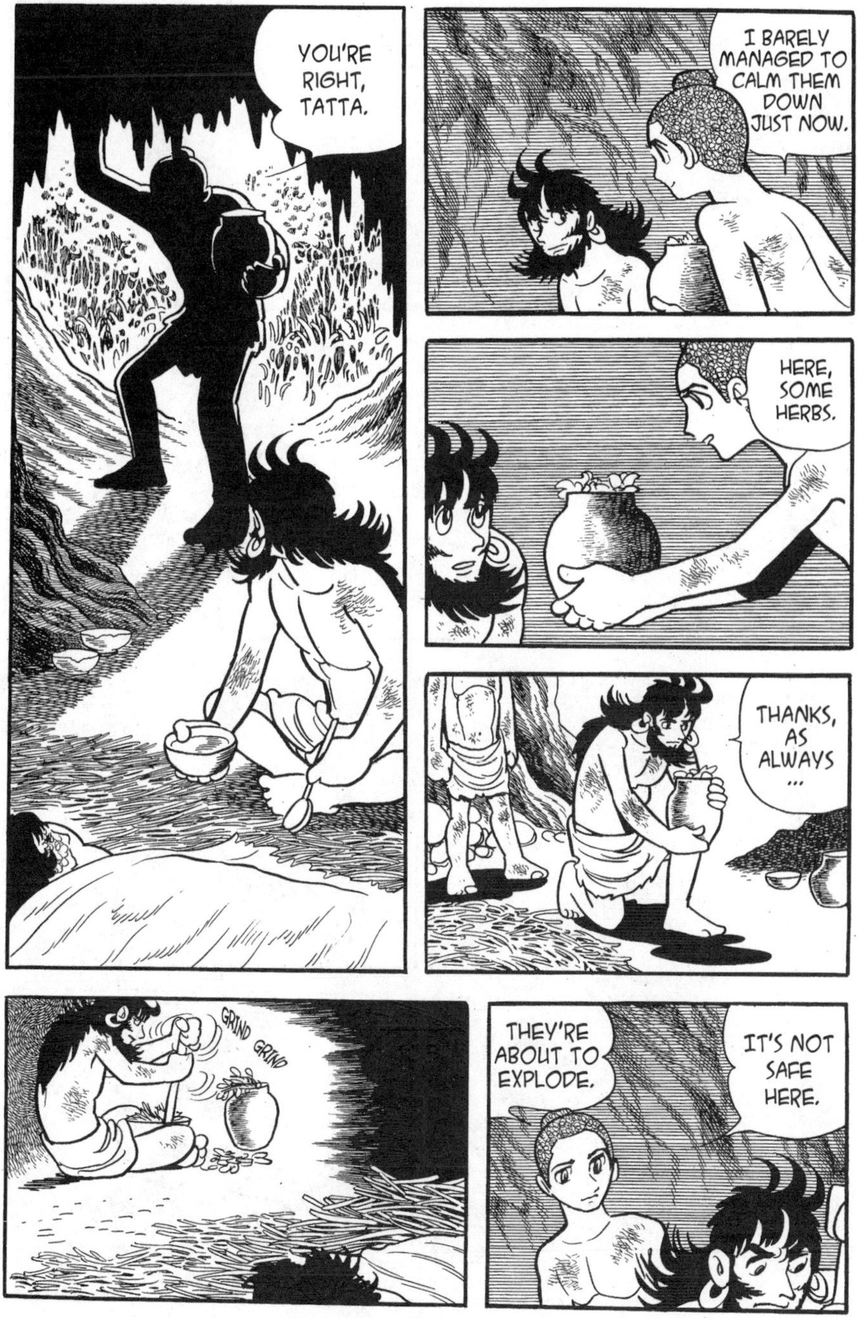
YOU'RE RIGHT, TATTA.
I BARELY MANAGED TO CALM THEM DOWN JUST NOW.
HERE, SOME HERBS.
THANKS, AS ALWAYS ...
GRIND GRIND
THEY'RE ABOUT TO EXPLODE.
IT'S NOT SAFE HERE.

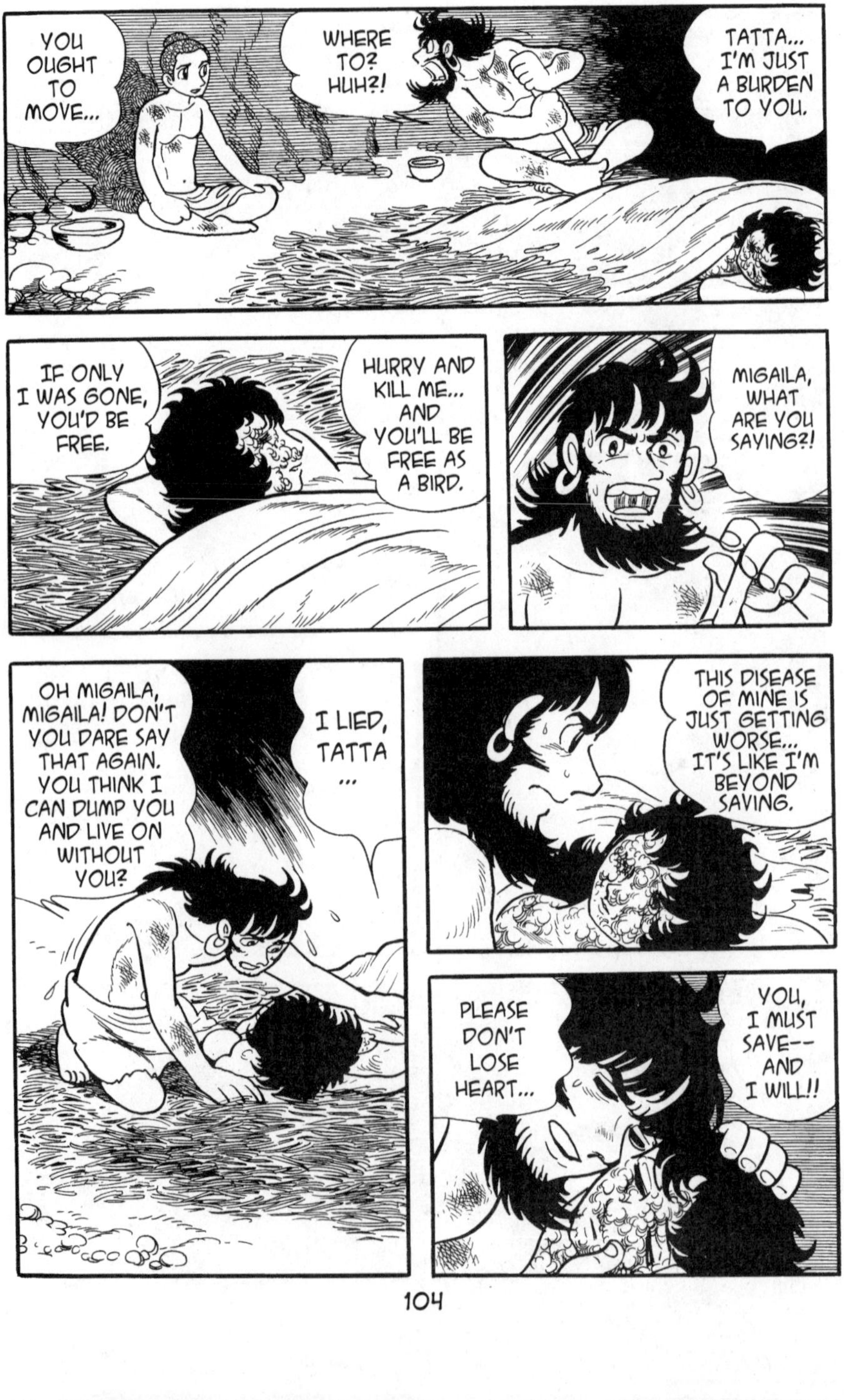
YOU OUGHT TO MOVE...
WHERE TO? HUH?!
TATTA... I'M JUST A BURDEN TO YOU.
IF ONLY I WAS GONE, YOU'D BE FREE.
HURRY AND KILL ME... AND YOU'LL BE FREE AS A BIRD.
MIGAILA, WHAT ARE YOU SAYING?!
OH MIGAILA, MIGAILA! DON'T YOU DARE SAY THAT AGAIN. YOU THINK I CAN DUMP YOU AND LIVE ON WITHOUT YOU?
I LIED, TATTA ...
THIS DISEASE OF MINE IS JUST GETTING WORSE... IT'S LIKE I'M BEYOND SAVING.
PLEASE DON'T LOSE HEART...
YOU, I MUST SAVE-- AND I WILL!!

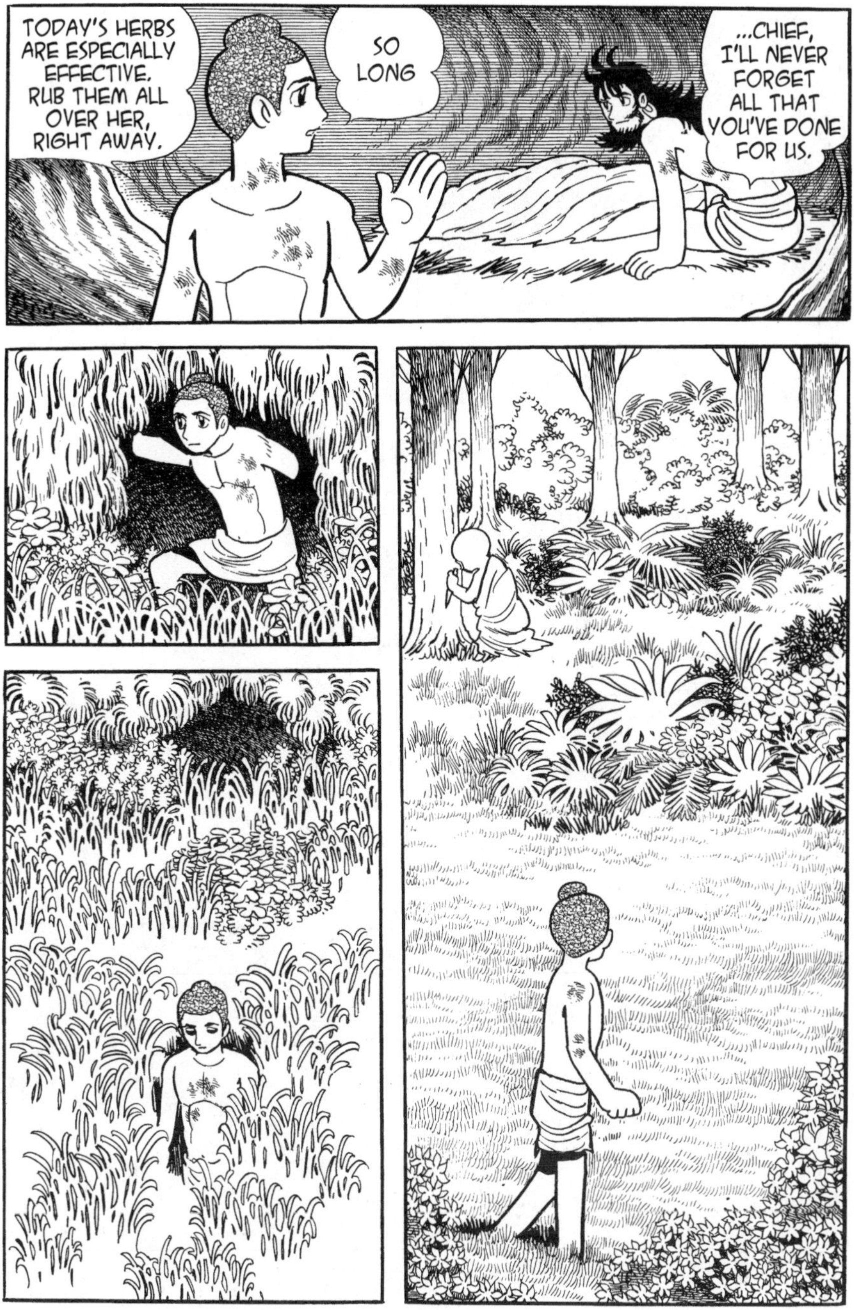
TODAY'S HERBS ARE ESPECIALLY EFFECTIVE. RUB THEM ALL OVER HER, RIGHT AWAY.
SO LONG
...CHIEF, I'LL NEVER FORGET ALL THAT YOU'VE DONE FOR US.

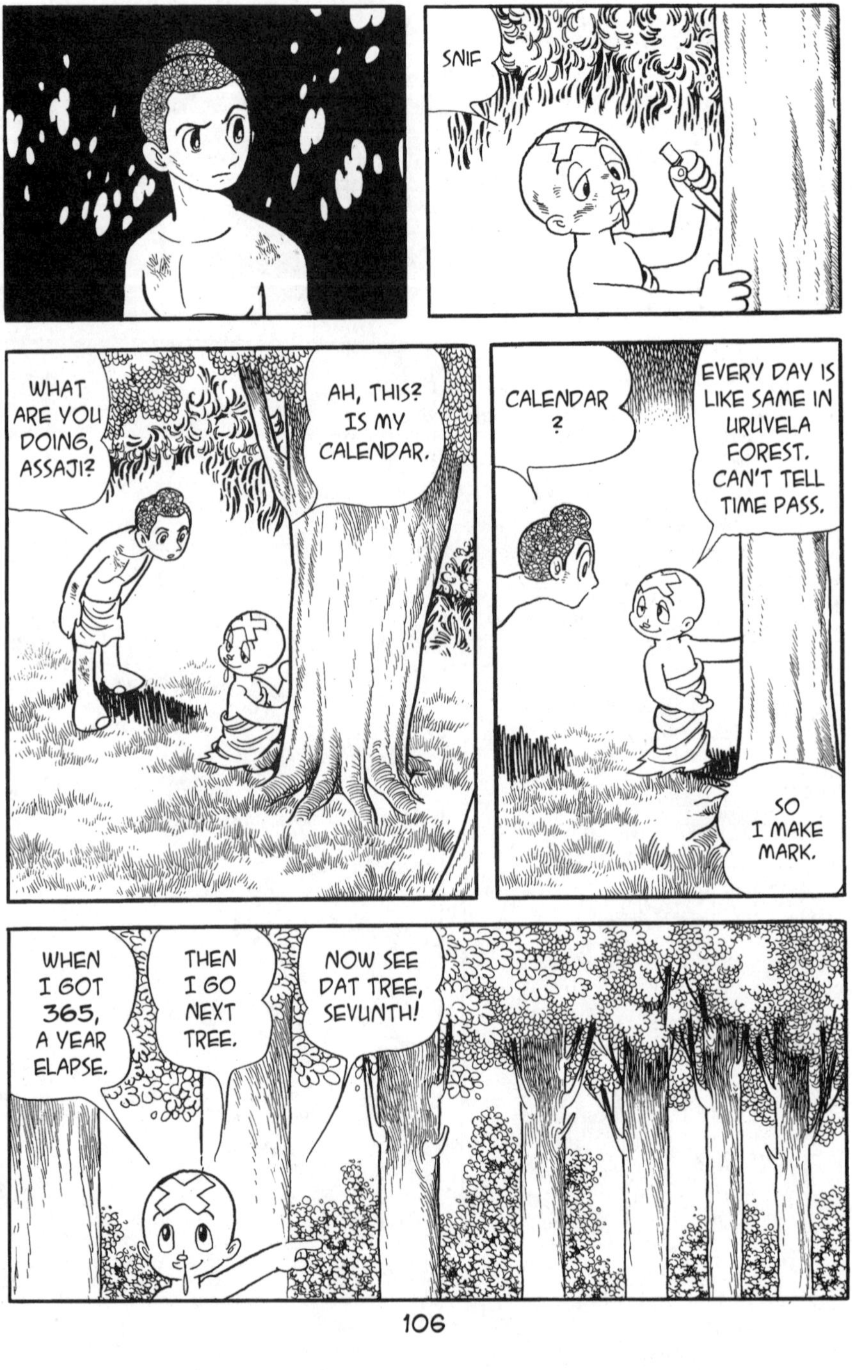
SNIF
WHAT ARE YOU DOING, ASSAJI?
AH, THIS? IS MY CALENDAR.
CALENDAR?
EVERY DAY IS LIKE SAME IN URUVELA FOREST. CAN'T TELL TIME PASS.
SO I MAKE MARK.
WHEN I GOT 365, A YEAR ELAPSE.
THEN I GO NEXT TREE.
NOW SEE DAT TREE, SEVUNTH!

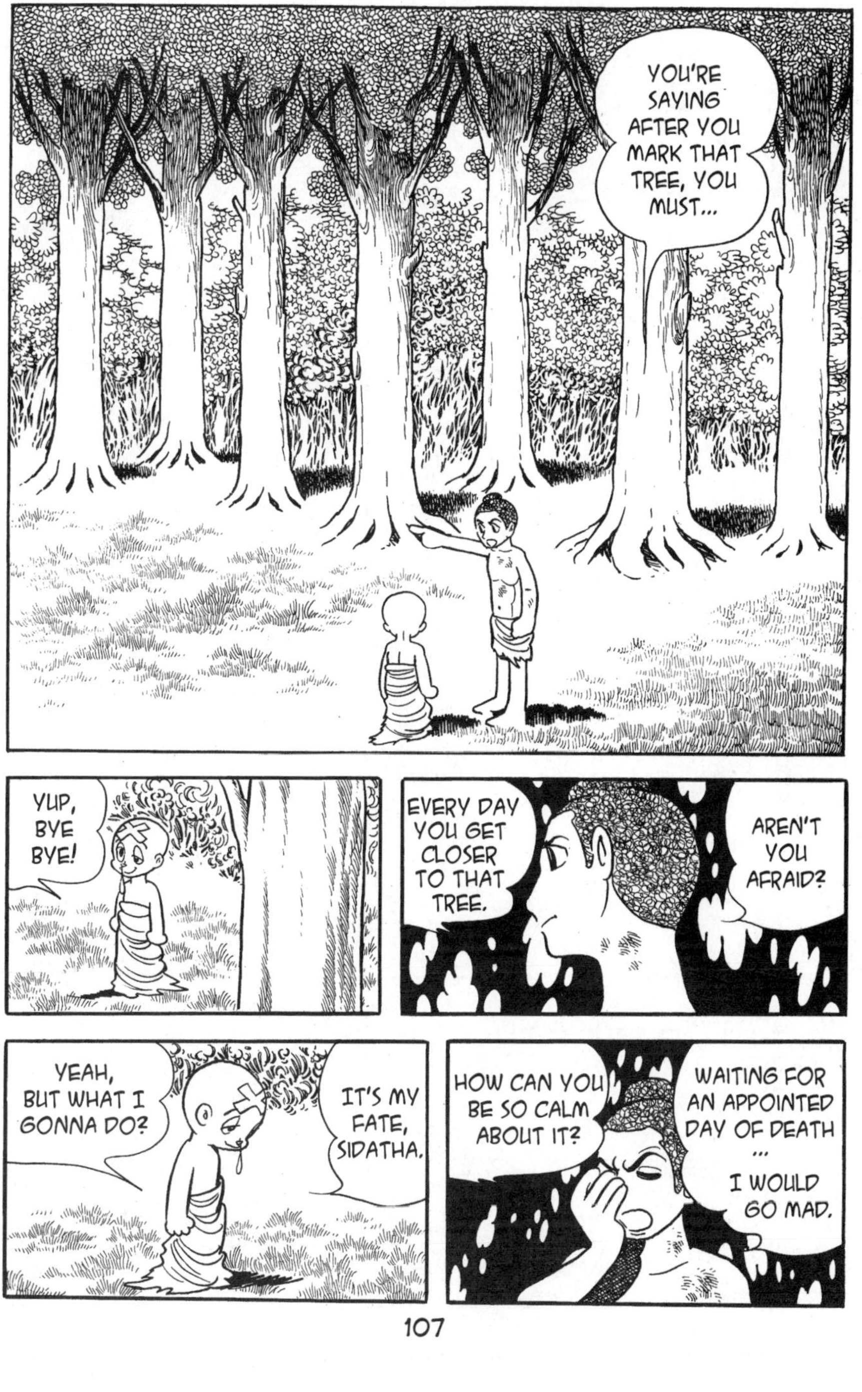

YOU'RE SAYING AFTER YOU MARK THAT TREE, YOU MUST...
YUP, BYE BYE!
EVERY DAY YOU GET CLOSER TO THAT TREE.
AREN'T YOU AFRAID?
YEAH, BUT WHAT I GONNA DO?
IT'S MY FATE, SIDATHA.
HOW CAN YOU BE SO CALM ABOUT IT?
WAITING FOR AN APPOINTED DAY OF DEATH ...
I WOULD GO MAD.

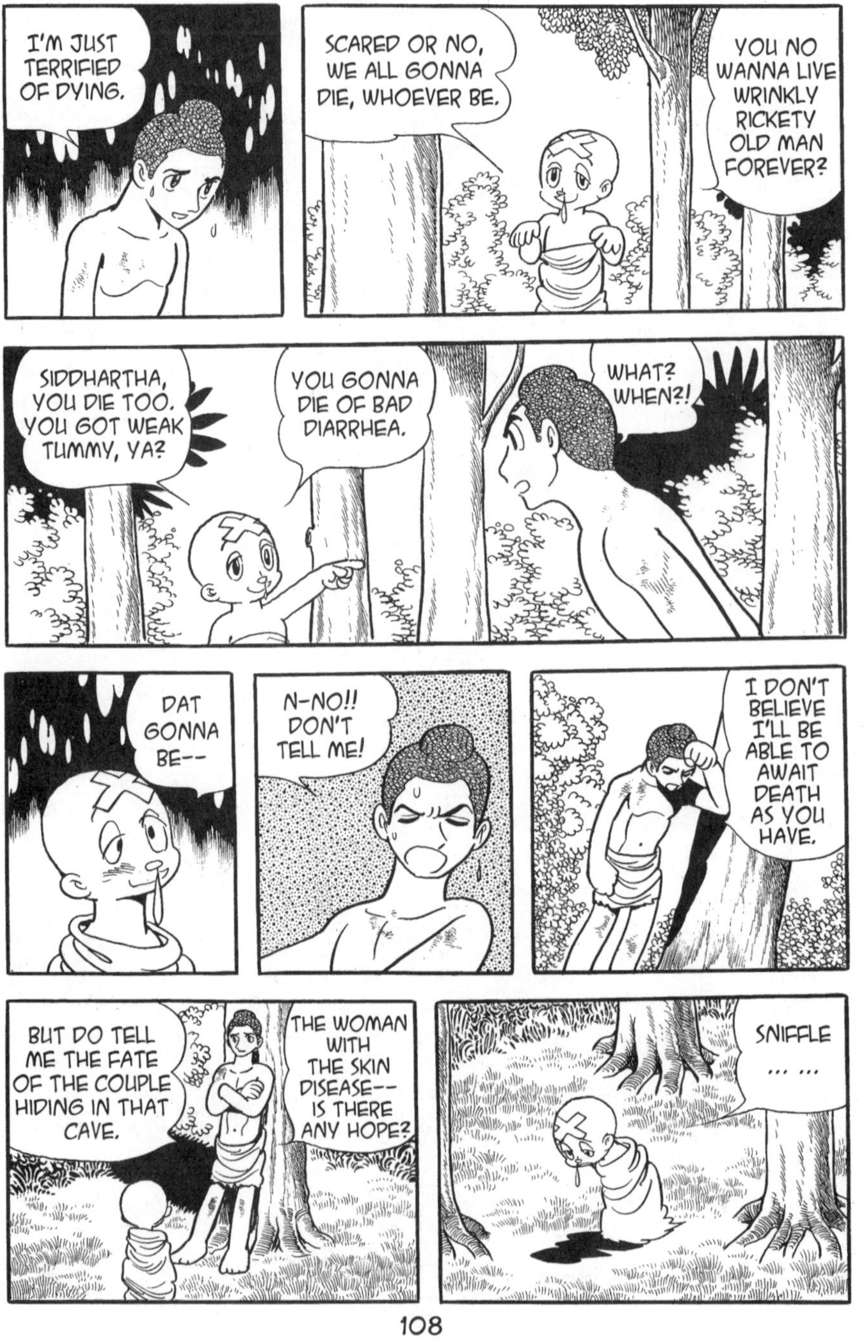
I'M JUST TERRIFIED OF DYING.
SCARED OR NO, WE ALL GONNA DIE, WHOEVER BE.
YOU NO WANNA LIVE WRINKLY RICKETY OLD MAN FOREVER?
SIDDHARTHA, YOU DIE TOO. YOU GOT WEAK TUMMY, YA?
YOU GONNA DIE OF BAD DIARRHEA.
WHAT? WHEN?!
DAT GONNA BE--
N-NO!! DON'T TELL ME!
I DON'T BELIEVE I'LL BE ABLE TO AWAIT DEATH AS YOU HAVE.
BUT DO TELL ME THE FATE OF THE COUPLE HIDING IN THAT CAVE.
THE WOMAN WITH THE SKIN DISEASE-- IS THERE ANY HOPE?
SNIFFLE
... ...

SHE'LL DIE?

YUP, IF YOU NO HELP HER.

ME?! YOU MEAN WITH HERBS?

UH-UH

LIKE YOU DO TO ME ONCE.

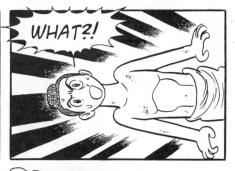

WHAT?!

LIKE YOU DO TO ME WHEN I DIE, DO TO HER AND SHE LIVE. BUT GONNA TAKE A YEAR.

YOU MEAN WHEN I SUCKED THE POISON FROM YOUR WOUND...

THAT IS WHAT I MUST DO?!

109

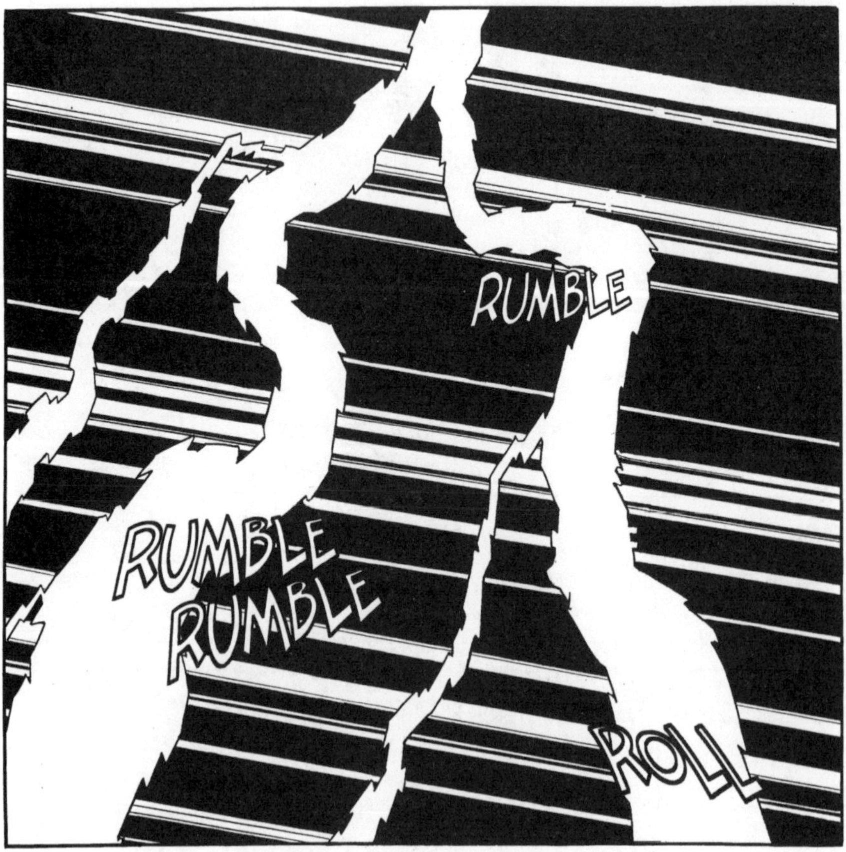
RUMBLE
RUMBLE
RUMBLE
ROLL

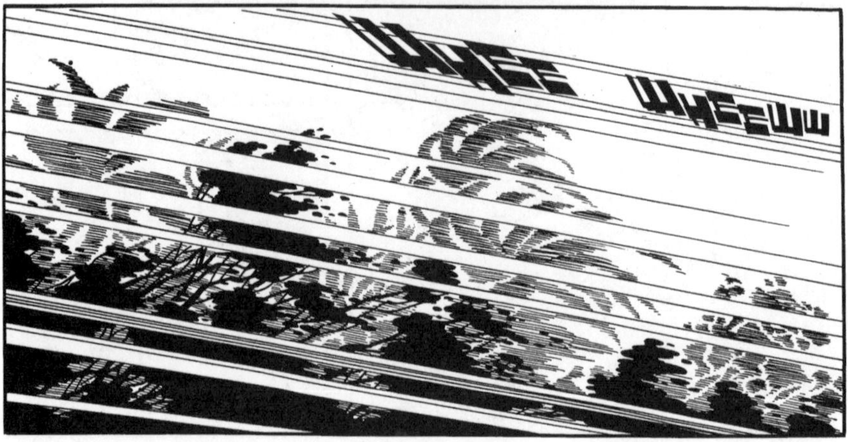
WHEE
WHEEWW

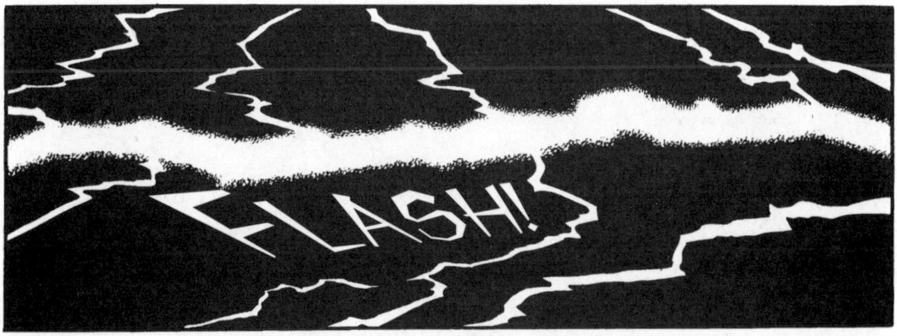
FLASH!
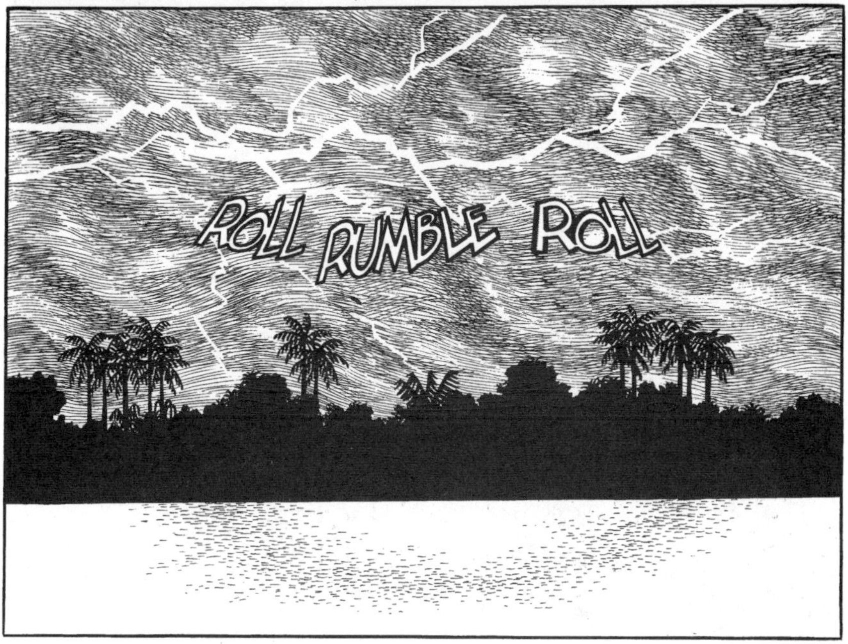
ROLL RUMBLE ROLL
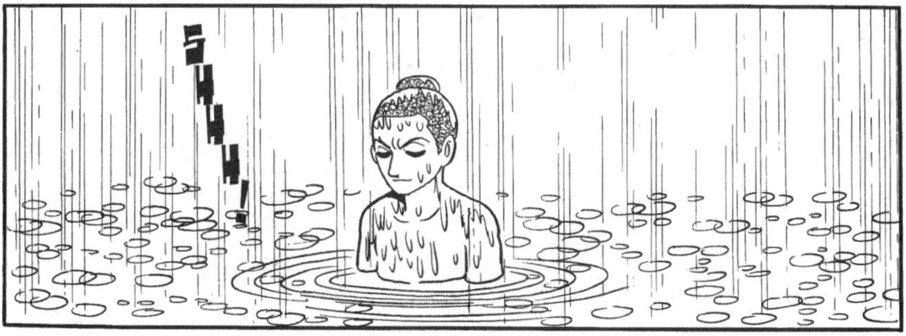
SHHH!

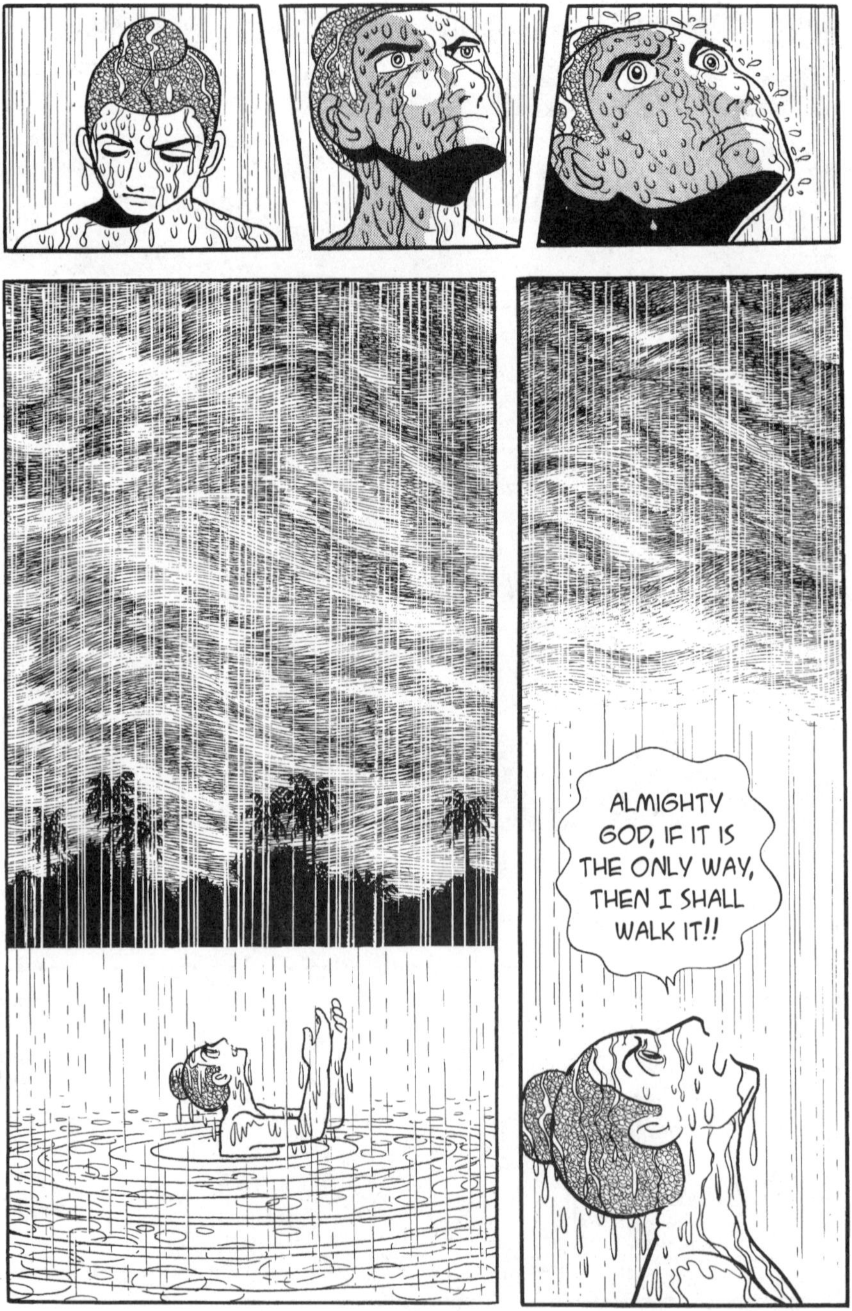
ALMIGHTY GOD, IF IT IS THE ONLY WAY, THEN I SHALL WALK IT!!

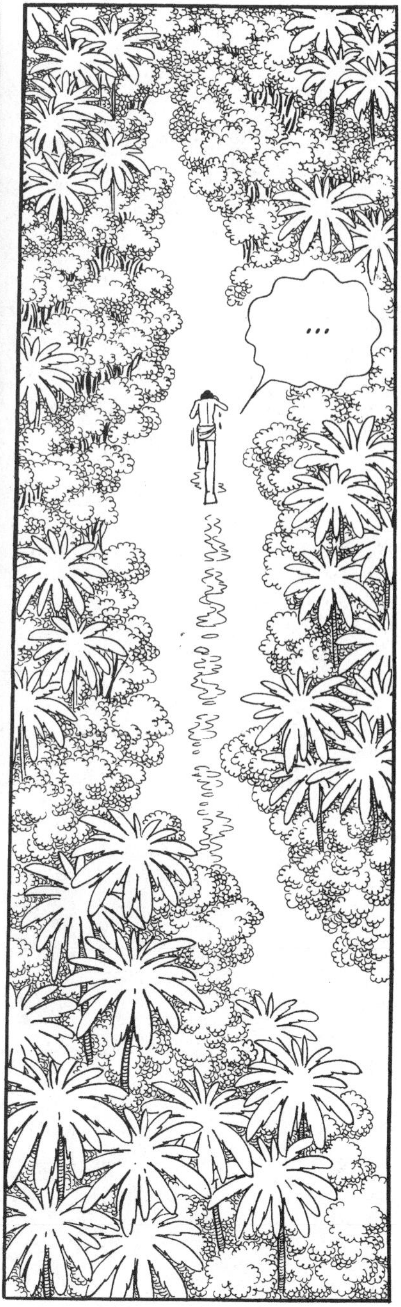
...
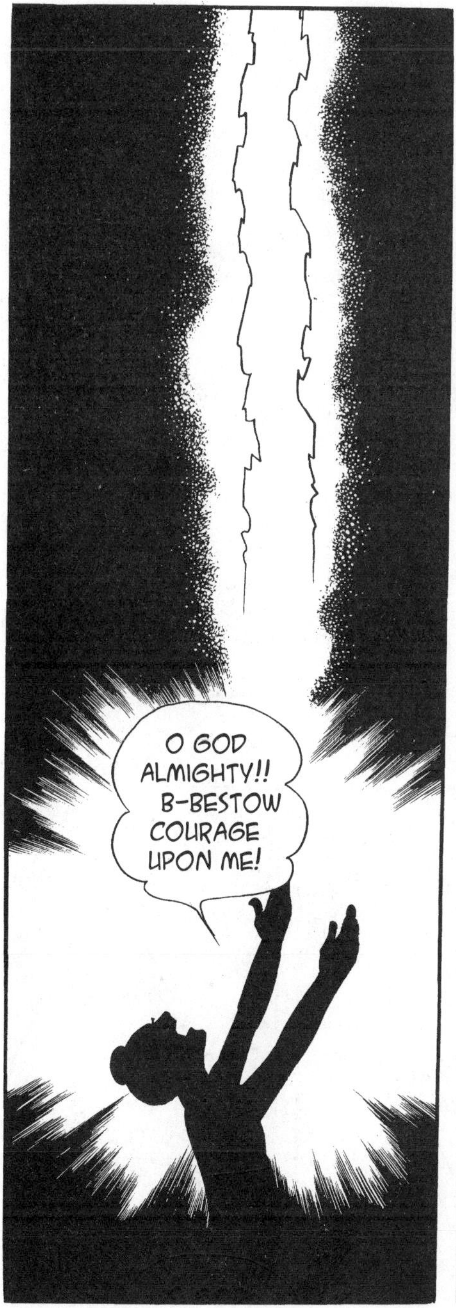
O GOD ALMIGHTY!! B-BESTOW COURAGE UPON ME!

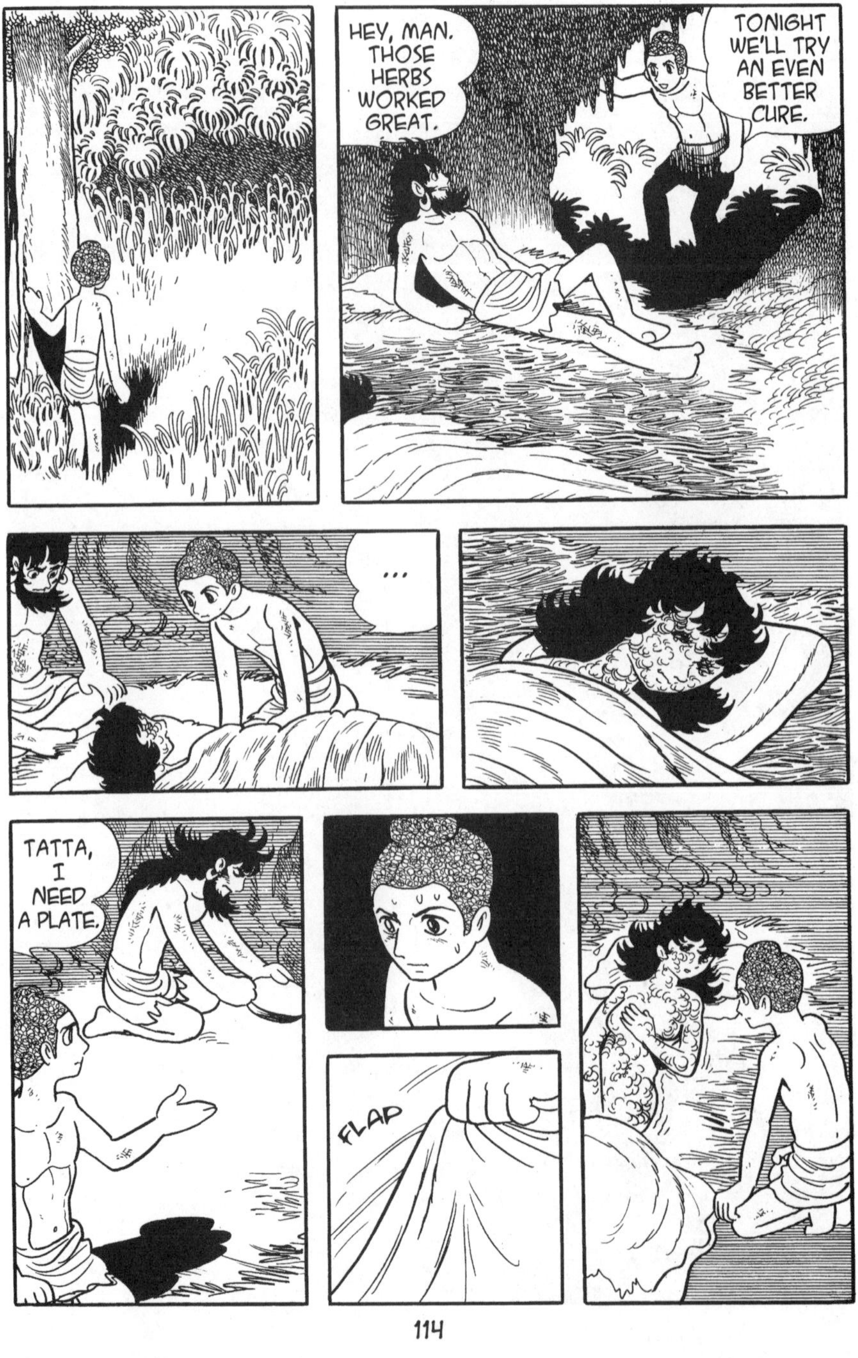
HEY, MAN. THOSE HERBS WORKED GREAT.
TONIGHT WE'LL TRY AN EVEN BETTER CURE.
...
TATTA, I NEED A PLATE.
FLAP

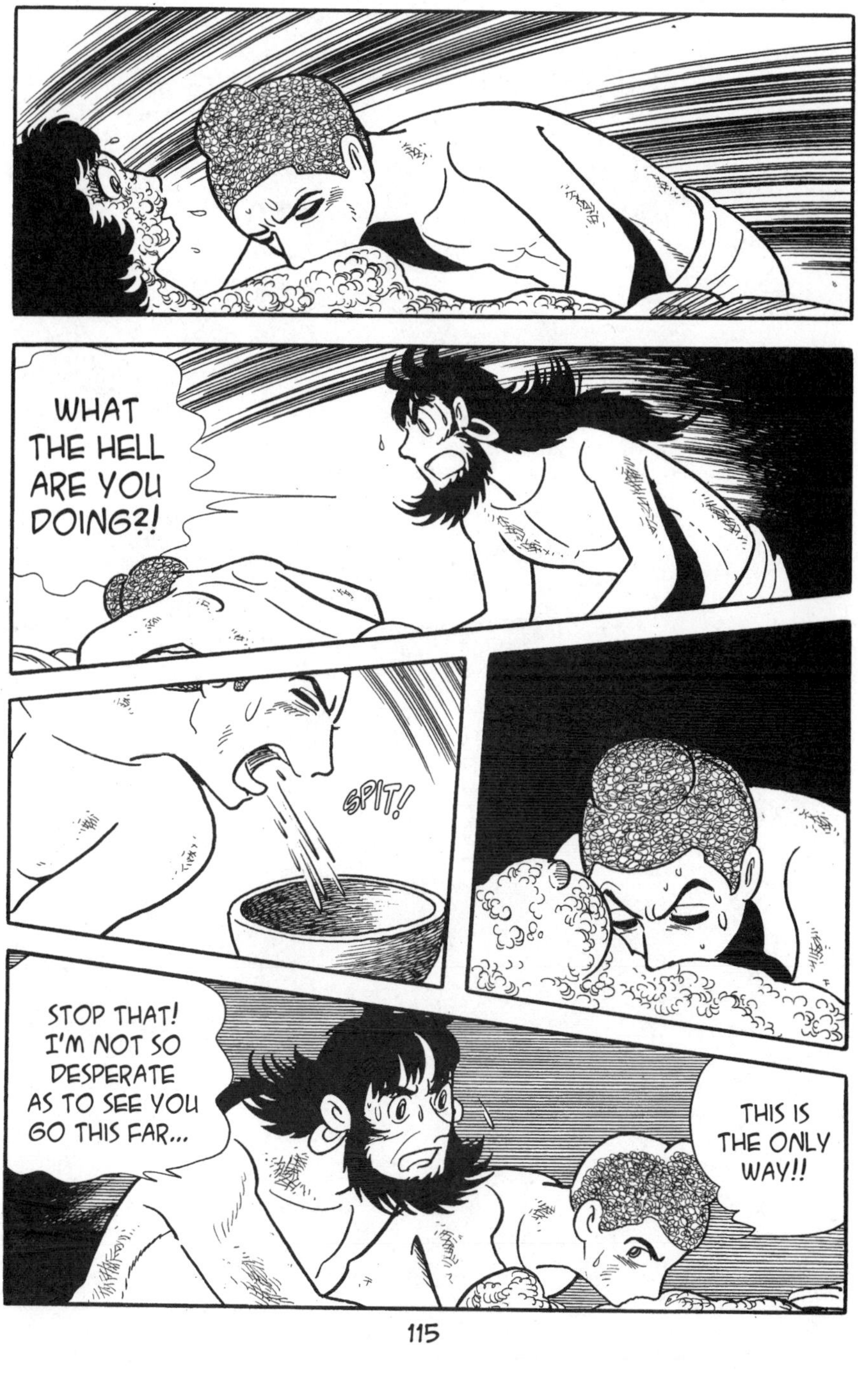

WHAT THE HELL ARE YOU DOING?!
SPIT!
STOP THAT! I'M NOT SO DESPERATE AS TO SEE YOU GO THIS FAR...
THIS IS THE ONLY WAY!!

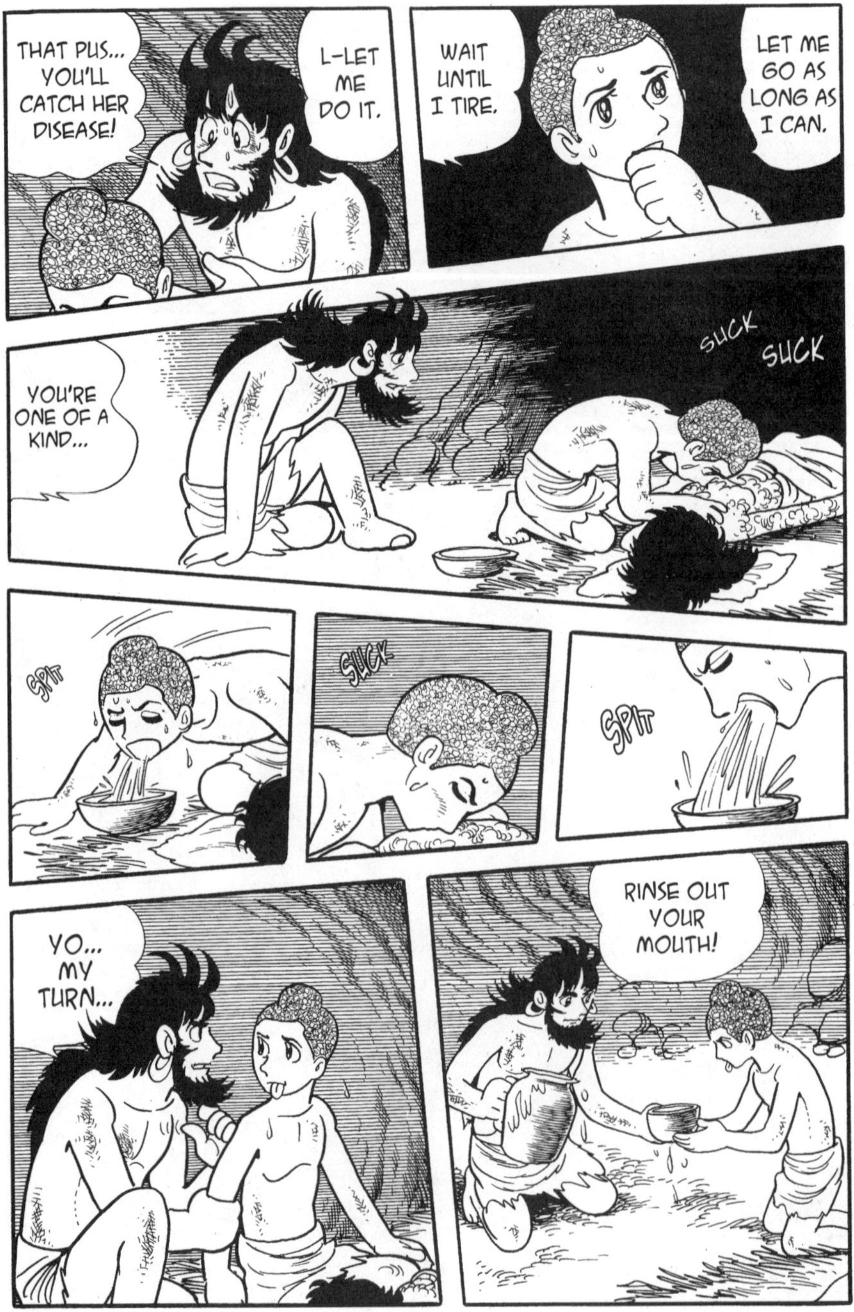
THAT PUS... YOU'LL CATCH HER DISEASE!
L-LET ME DO IT.
WAIT UNTIL I TIRE.
LET ME GO AS LONG AS I CAN.
YOU'RE ONE OF A KIND...
SUCK
SUCK
SPIT
SUCK
SPIT
YO... MY TURN...
RINSE OUT YOUR MOUTH!

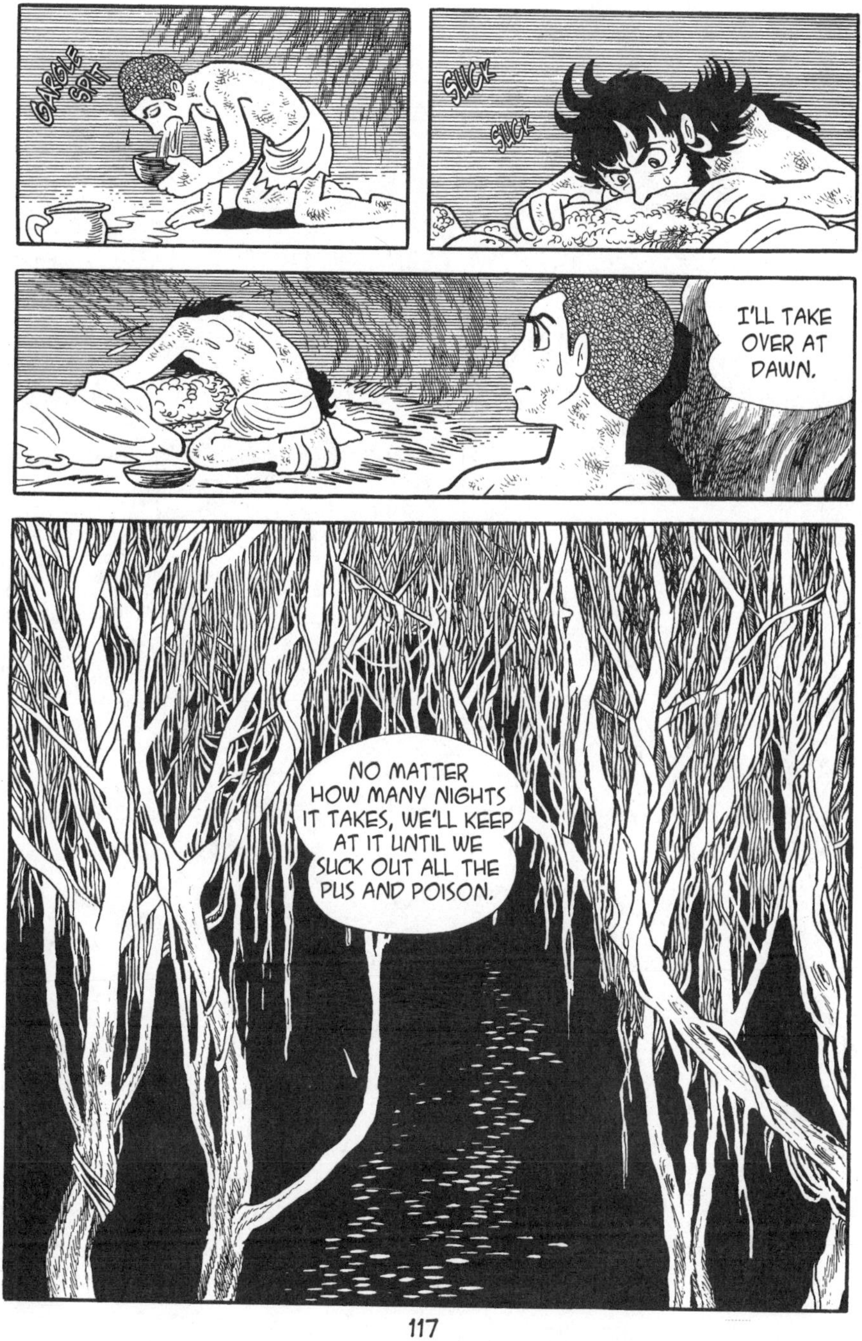
GARGLE SPIT
SUCK SUCK
I'LL TAKE OVER AT DAWN.
NO MATTER HOW MANY NIGHTS IT TAKES, WE'LL KEEP AT IT UNTIL WE SUCK OUT ALL THE PUS AND POISON.

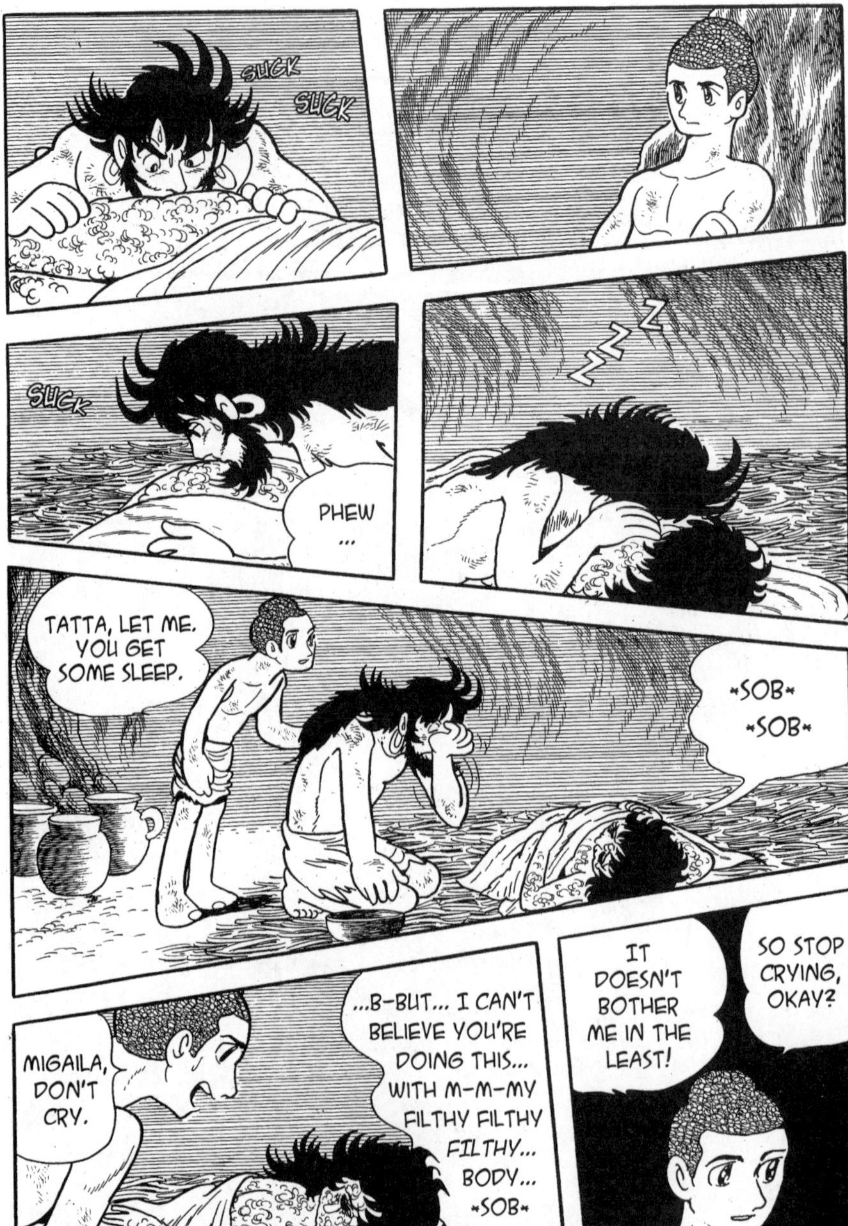
SLICK
SLICK
SLICK
PHEW ...
TATTA, LET ME. YOU GET SOME SLEEP.
SOB *SOB*
MIGAILA, DON'T CRY.
...B-BUT... I CAN'T BELIEVE YOU'RE DOING THIS... WITH M-M-MY FILTHY FILTHY FILTHY... BODY... *SOB*
IT DOESN'T BOTHER ME IN THE LEAST!
SO STOP CRYING, OKAY?

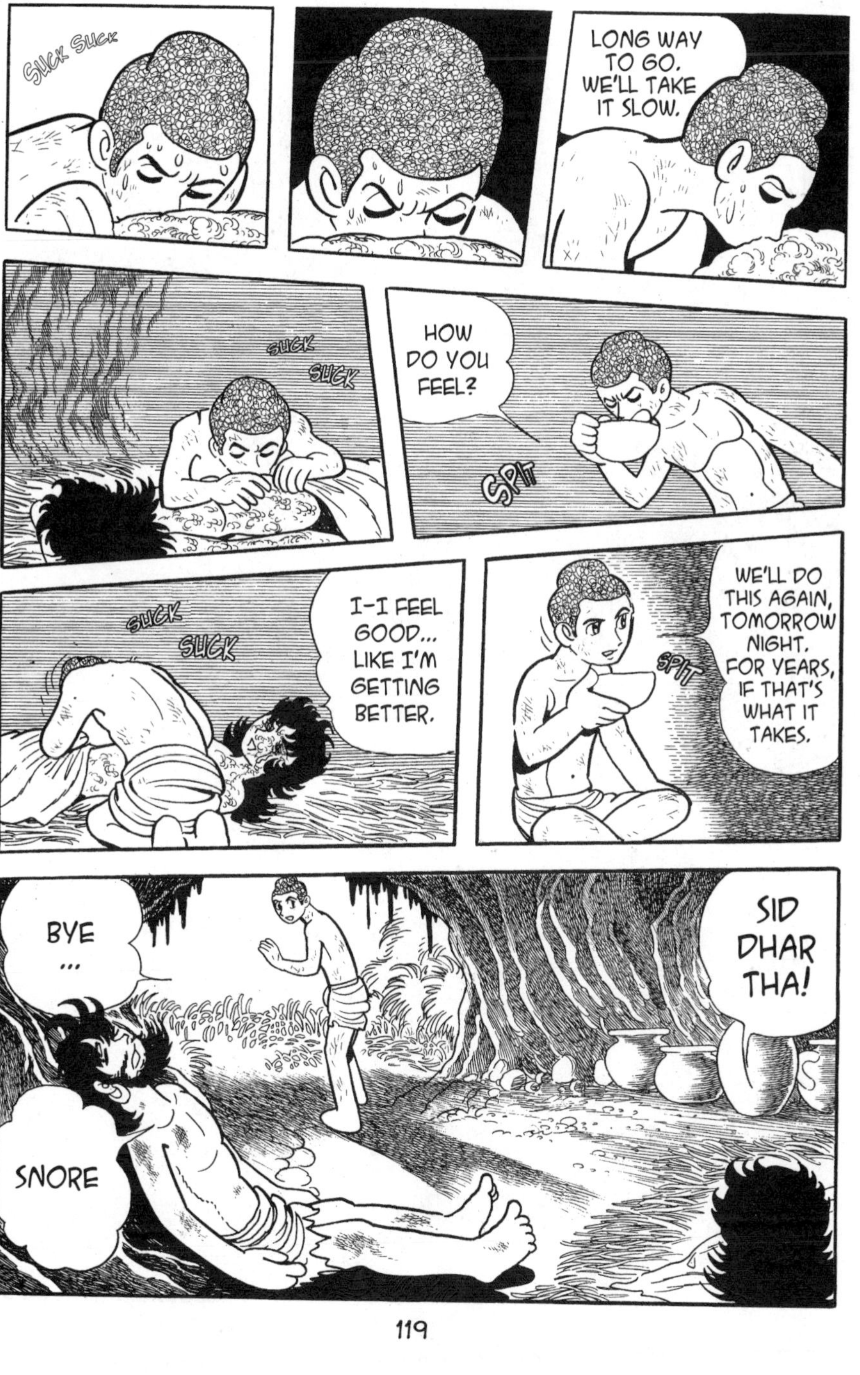
SUCK SUCK
LONG WAY TO GO. WE'LL TAKE IT SLOW.
SUCK
SUCK
HOW DO YOU FEEL?
SPIT
SUCK
SUCK
I-I FEEL GOOD... LIKE I'M GETTING BETTER.
SPIT
WE'LL DO THIS AGAIN, TOMORROW NIGHT. FOR YEARS, IF THAT'S WHAT IT TAKES.
BYE ...
SNORE
SID DHAR THA!

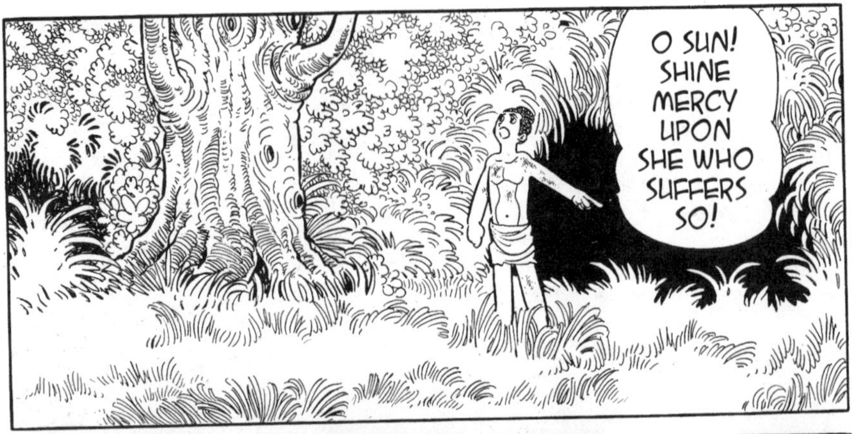
O SUN! SHINE MERCY UPON SHE WHO SUFFERS SO!

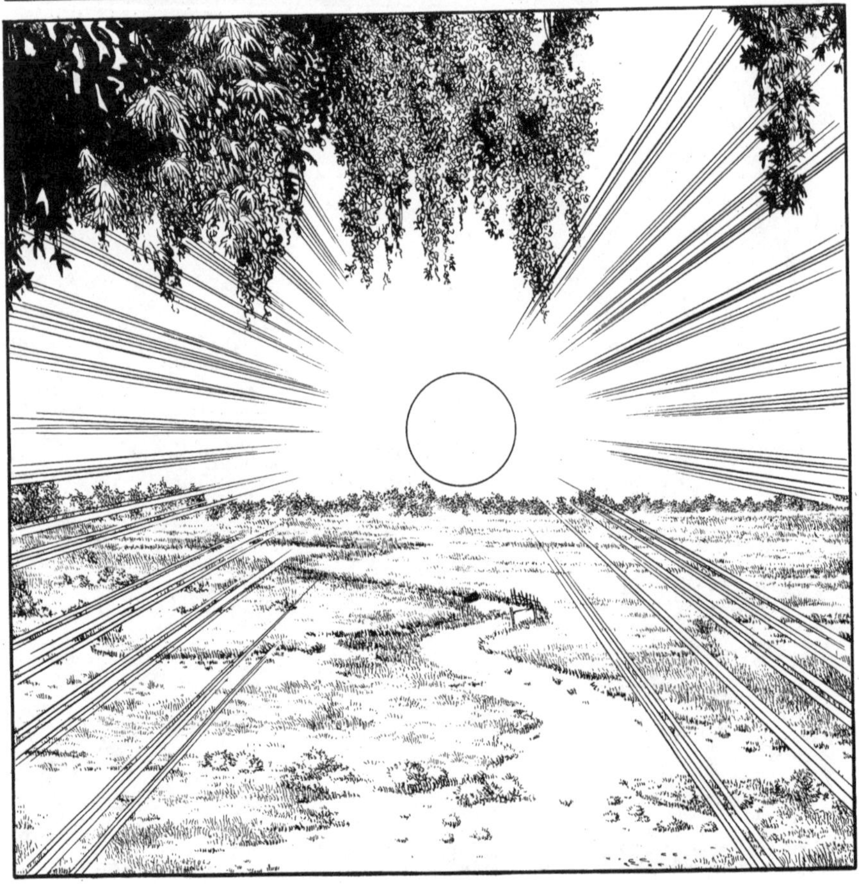

CHAPTER SEVEN

CHASTISED

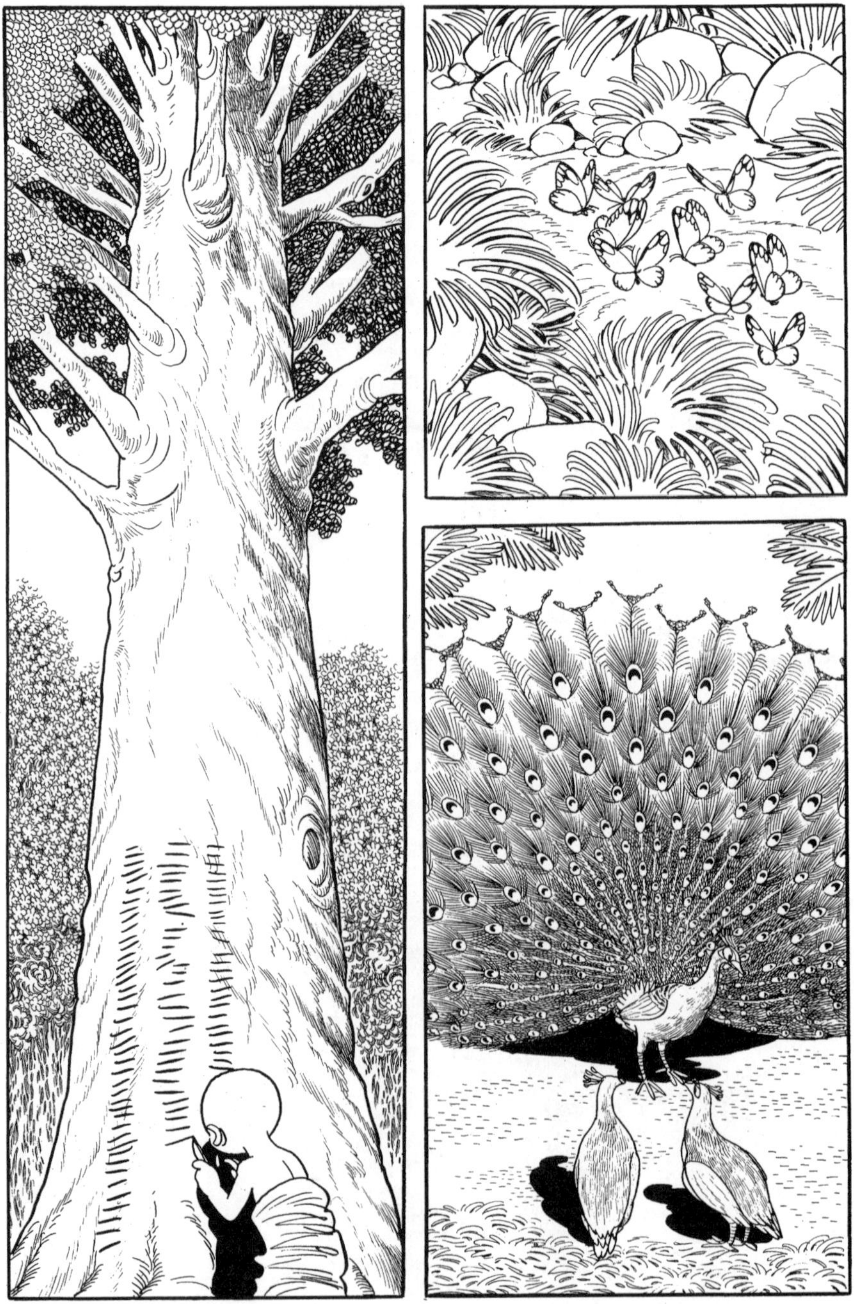

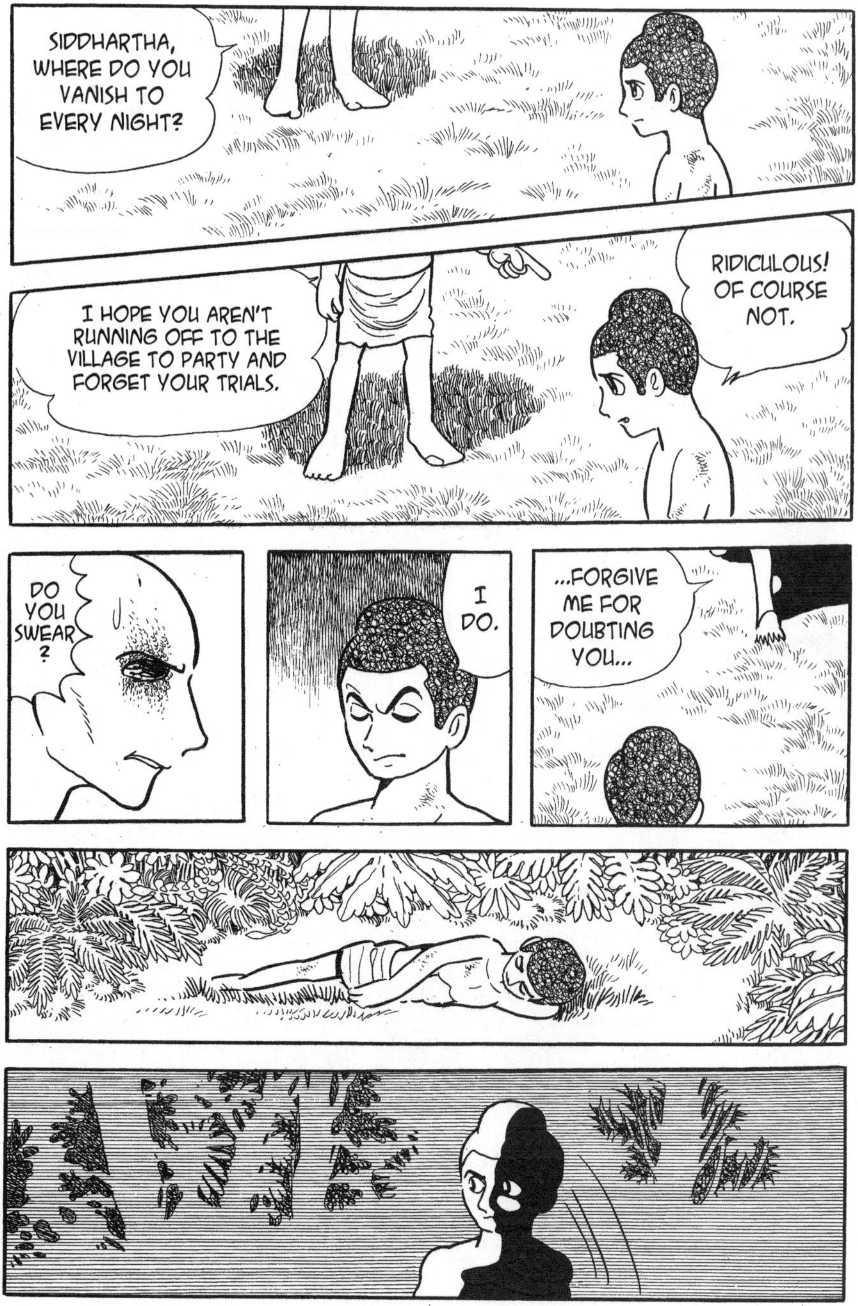
SIDDHARTHA, WHERE DO YOU VANISH TO EVERY NIGHT?
I HOPE YOU AREN'T RUNNING OFF TO THE VILLAGE TO PARTY AND FORGET YOUR TRIALS.
RIDICULOUS! OF COURSE NOT.
DO YOU SWEAR?
I DO.
...FORGIVE ME FOR DOUBTING YOU...

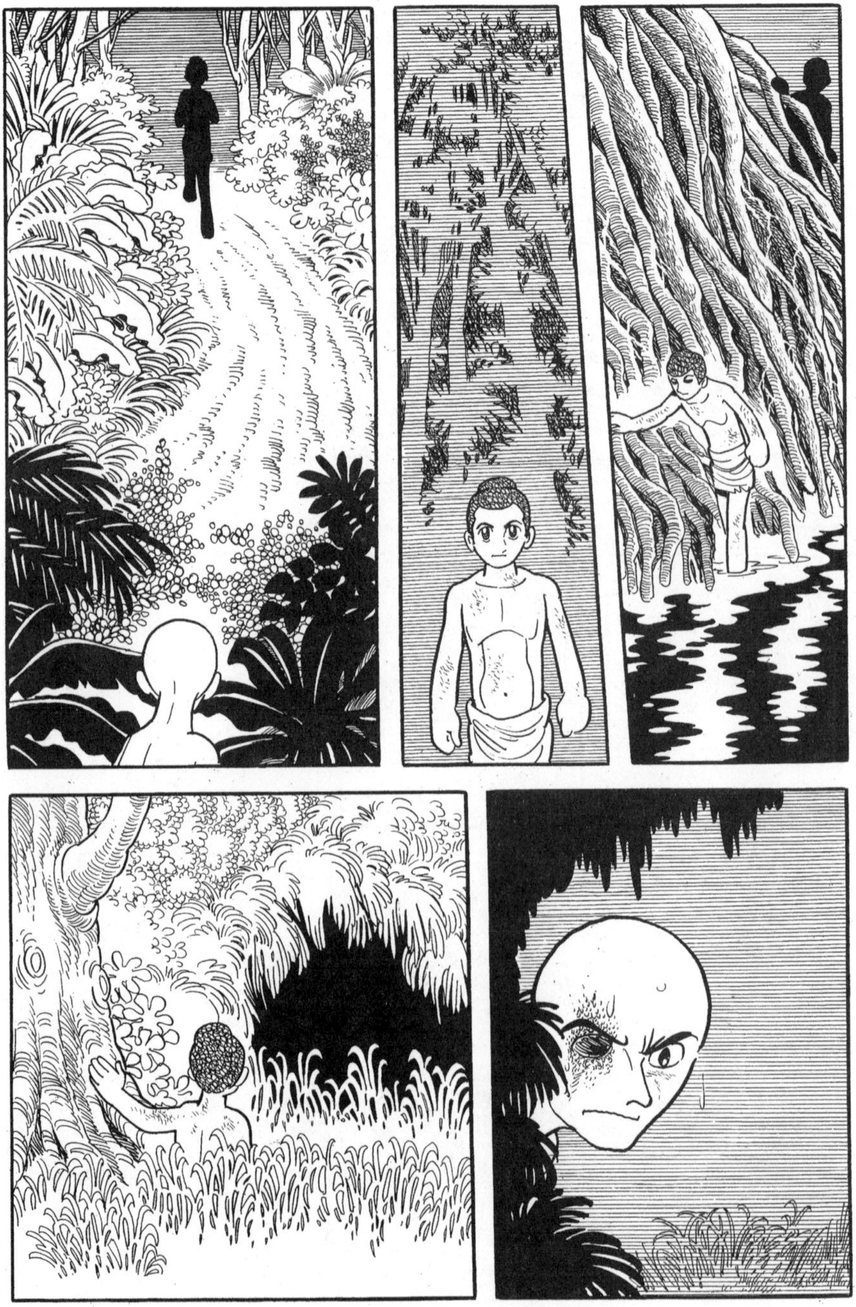

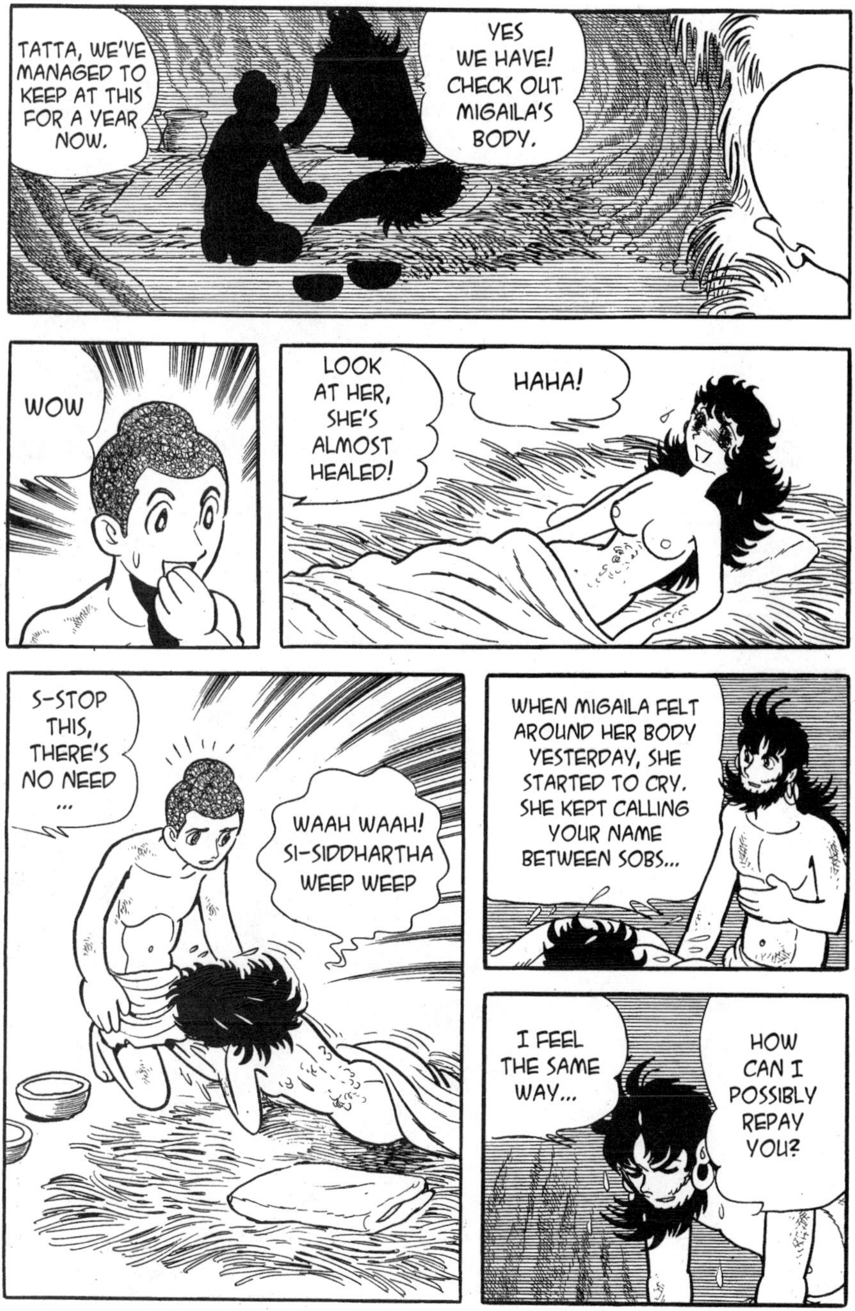
TATTA, WE'VE MANAGED TO KEEP AT THIS FOR A YEAR NOW.
YES WE HAVE! CHECK OUT MIGAILA'S BODY.
WOW
LOOK AT HER, SHE'S ALMOST HEALED!
HAHA!
S-STOP THIS, THERE'S NO NEED ...
WAAH WAAH! SI-SIDDHARTHA WEEP WEEP
WHEN MIGAILA FELT AROUND HER BODY YESTERDAY, SHE STARTED TO CRY. SHE KEPT CALLING YOUR NAME BETWEEN SOBS...
I FEEL THE SAME WAY...
HOW CAN I POSSIBLY REPAY YOU?

OH PLEASE, TATTA. I COULDN'T HAVE DONE IT IF YOU DIDN'T TRUST ME.

PERVERT!! YOU'VE BEEN AT THIS FOR A YEAR?!

DHEPA ...!!

EVEN IF IT'S TO CURE HER, I'VE BEEN KISSING ANOTHER MAN'S WIFE ALL OVER HER BODY.

SKIP THE DIALOGUE, AND THIS PANEL WOULD LOOK LIKE--

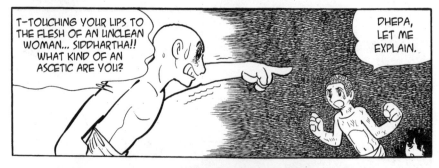

T-TOUCHING YOUR LIPS TO THE FLESH OF AN UNCLEAN WOMAN... SIDDHARTHA!! WHAT KIND OF AN ASCETIC ARE YOU?

DHEPA, LET ME EXPLAIN.

EXPLAIN WHAT?!

THIS ALONE WARRANTS THAT YOU APPEAR BEFORE THE DISCIPLINARY COUNCIL.

YOU'VE LET ME DOWN.

HEY...!! YOU THICKSKULLED FOOL! YOU CALL THIS MAN A PERVERT?

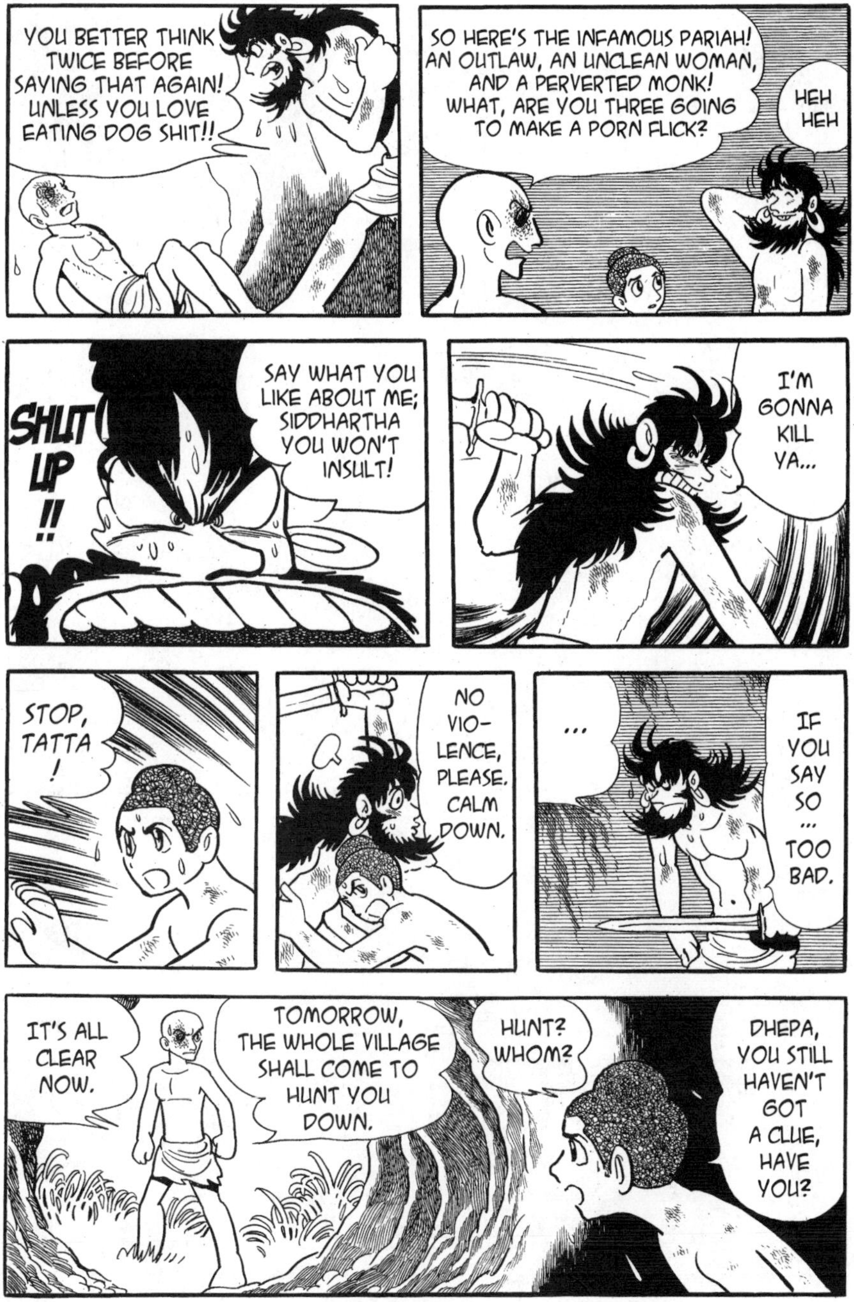
YOU BETTER THINK TWICE BEFORE SAYING THAT AGAIN! UNLESS YOU LOVE EATING DOG SHIT!!
SO HERE'S THE INFAMOUS PARIAH! AN OUTLAW, AN UNCLEAN WOMAN, AND A PERVERTED MONK! WHAT, ARE YOU THREE GOING TO MAKE A PORN FLICK?
HEH HEH
SHUT UP !!
SAY WHAT YOU LIKE ABOUT ME; SIDDHARTHA YOU WON'T INSULT!
I'M GONNA KILL YA...
STOP, TATTA !
NO VIO-LENCE, PLEASE. CALM DOWN.
...
IF YOU SAY SO ... TOO BAD.
IT'S ALL CLEAR NOW.
TOMORROW, THE WHOLE VILLAGE SHALL COME TO HUNT YOU DOWN.
HUNT? WHOM?
DHEPA, YOU STILL HAVEN'T GOT A CLUE, HAVE YOU?

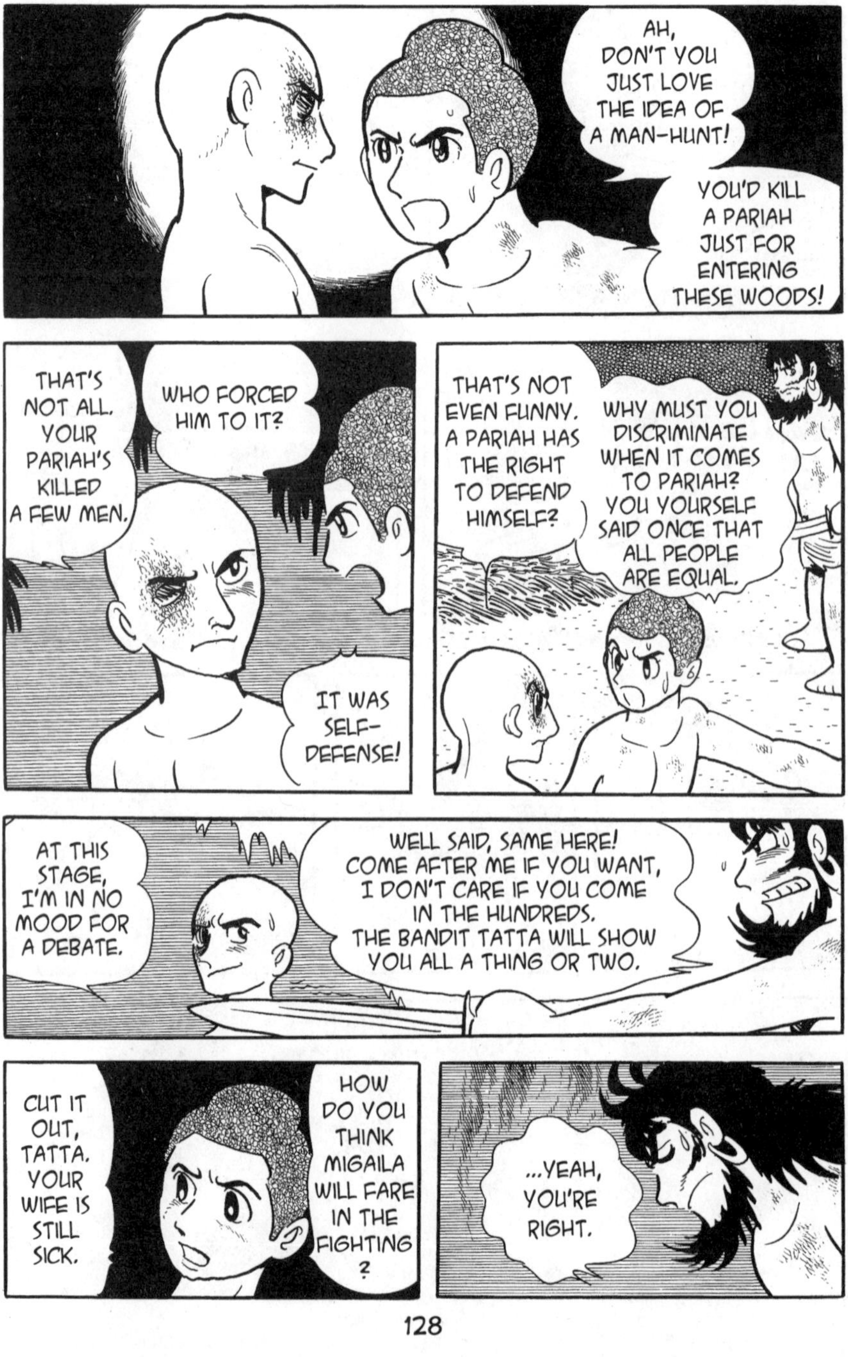
AH, DON'T YOU JUST LOVE THE IDEA OF A MAN-HUNT!
YOU'D KILL A PARIAH JUST FOR ENTERING THESE WOODS!
THAT'S NOT ALL. YOUR PARIAH'S KILLED A FEW MEN.
WHO FORCED HIM TO IT?
IT WAS SELF-DEFENSE!
THAT'S NOT EVEN FUNNY. A PARIAH HAS THE RIGHT TO DEFEND HIMSELF?
WHY MUST YOU DISCRIMINATE WHEN IT COMES TO PARIAH? YOU YOURSELF SAID ONCE THAT ALL PEOPLE ARE EQUAL.
AT THIS STAGE, I'M IN NO MOOD FOR A DEBATE.
WELL SAID, SAME HERE! COME AFTER ME IF YOU WANT, I DON'T CARE IF YOU COME IN THE HUNDREDS. THE BANDIT TATTA WILL SHOW YOU ALL A THING OR TWO.
CUT IT OUT, TATTA. YOUR WIFE IS STILL SICK.
HOW DO YOU THINK MIGAILA WILL FARE IN THE FIGHTING?
...YEAH, YOU'RE RIGHT.

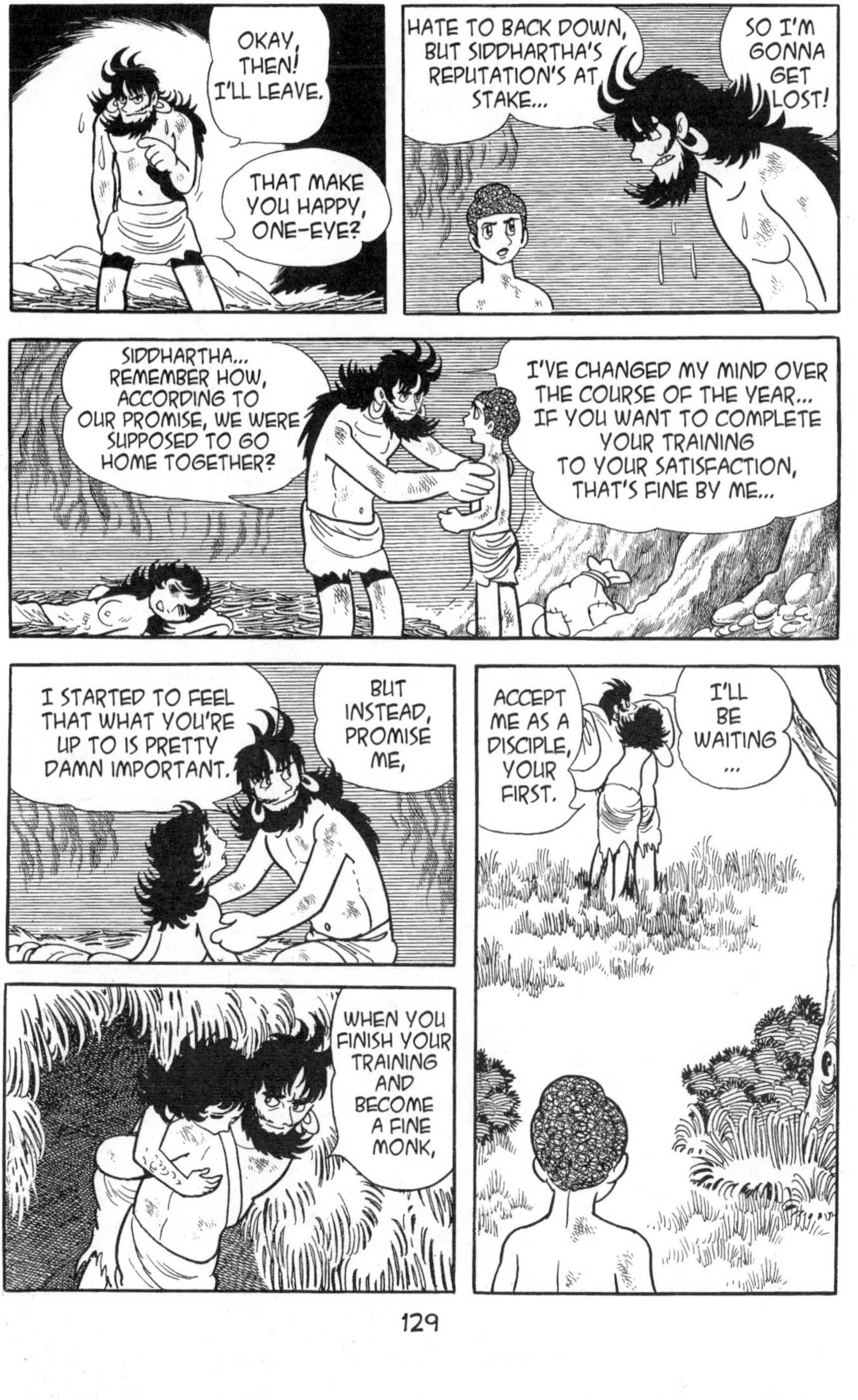
OKAY, THEN! I'LL LEAVE.
THAT MAKE YOU HAPPY, ONE-EYE?
HATE TO BACK DOWN, BUT SIDDHARTHA'S REPUTATION'S AT STAKE...
SO I'M GONNA GET LOST!
SIDDHARTHA... REMEMBER HOW, ACCORDING TO OUR PROMISE, WE WERE SUPPOSED TO GO HOME TOGETHER?
I'VE CHANGED MY MIND OVER THE COURSE OF THE YEAR... IF YOU WANT TO COMPLETE YOUR TRAINING TO YOUR SATISFACTION, THAT'S FINE BY ME...
I STARTED TO FEEL THAT WHAT YOU'RE UP TO IS PRETTY DAMN IMPORTANT.
BUT INSTEAD, PROMISE ME,
WHEN YOU FINISH YOUR TRAINING AND BECOME A FINE MONK,
ACCEPT ME AS A DISCIPLE, YOUR FIRST.
I'LL BE WAITING ...

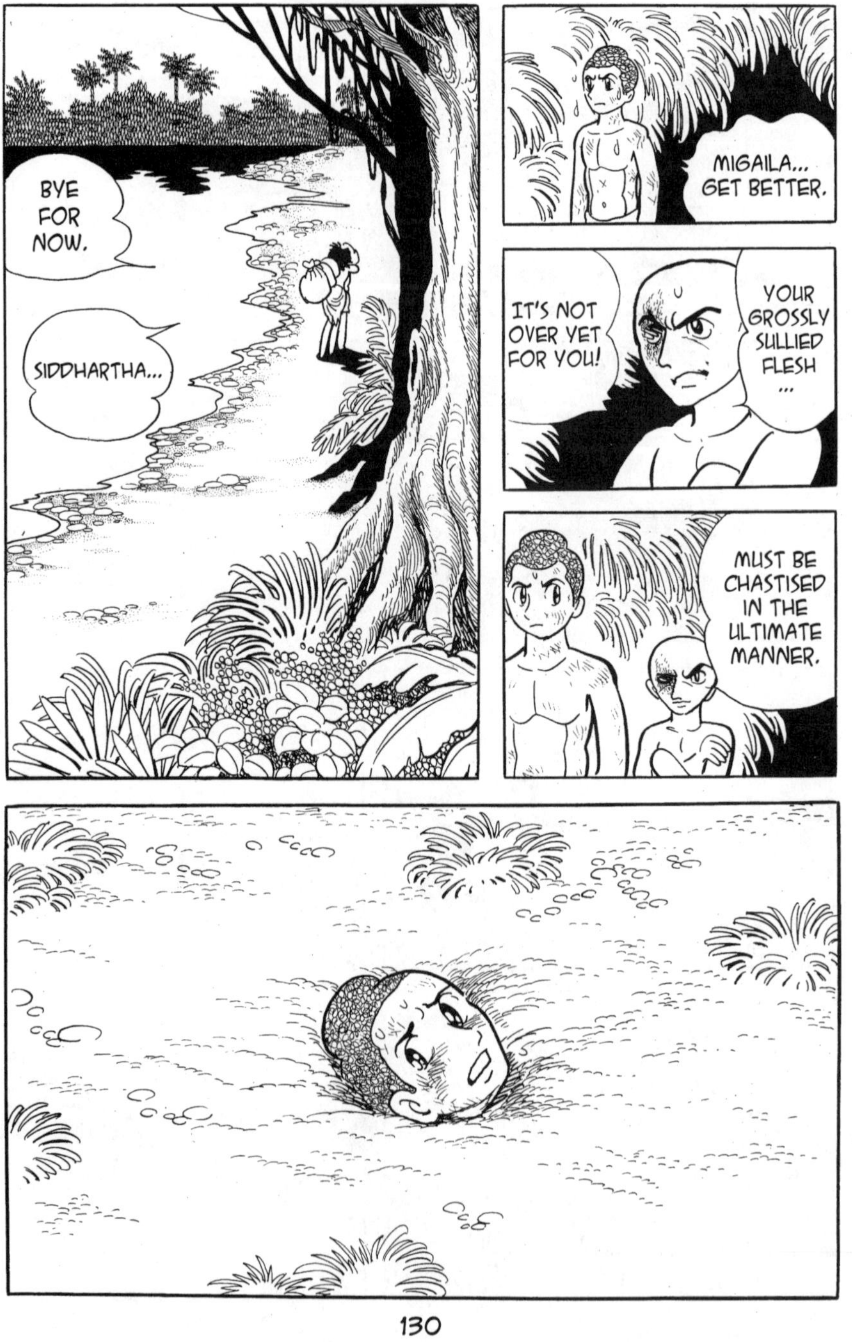
BYE FOR NOW.
SIDDHARTHA...
MIGAILA... GET BETTER.
IT'S NOT OVER YET FOR YOU!
YOUR GROSSLY SULLIED FLESH ...
MUST BE CHASTISED IN THE ULTIMATE MANNER.

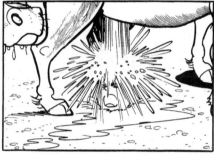

HELP!!

GLUG GLUG GLUG...

131

AHH! AGH!
GAG COUGH
HUMMM
HUMM
HOW DO YOU LIKE THE PAIN? SUFFER, SUFFER AND SUFFER SOME MORE. RELEASE YOUR SOUL FROM YOUR PUTRID FLESH. AT THIS POINT, YOU CAN'T BE SAVED ANY OTHER WAY.

YOU'RE TELLING ME TO DIE...

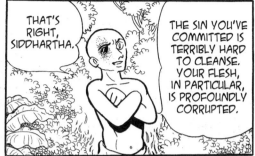

THAT'S RIGHT, SIDDHARTHA.

THE SIN YOU'VE COMMITTED IS TERRIBLY HARD TO CLEANSE. YOUR FLESH, IN PARTICULAR, IS PROFOUNDLY CORRUPTED.

NO!

WHY SHOULD I!

I REMEMBER HOW THE HERMIT BHAGAVA DIED FROM HIS TRIAL. I DON'T WANT TO END UP LIKE HIM!

DIE!!

YOU MUST DIE!

I WON'T.

AH, YOU ARE A HOPELESS FOOL.

WHO'S THE FOOL ?!

IT'S THE BUNCH OF YOU!

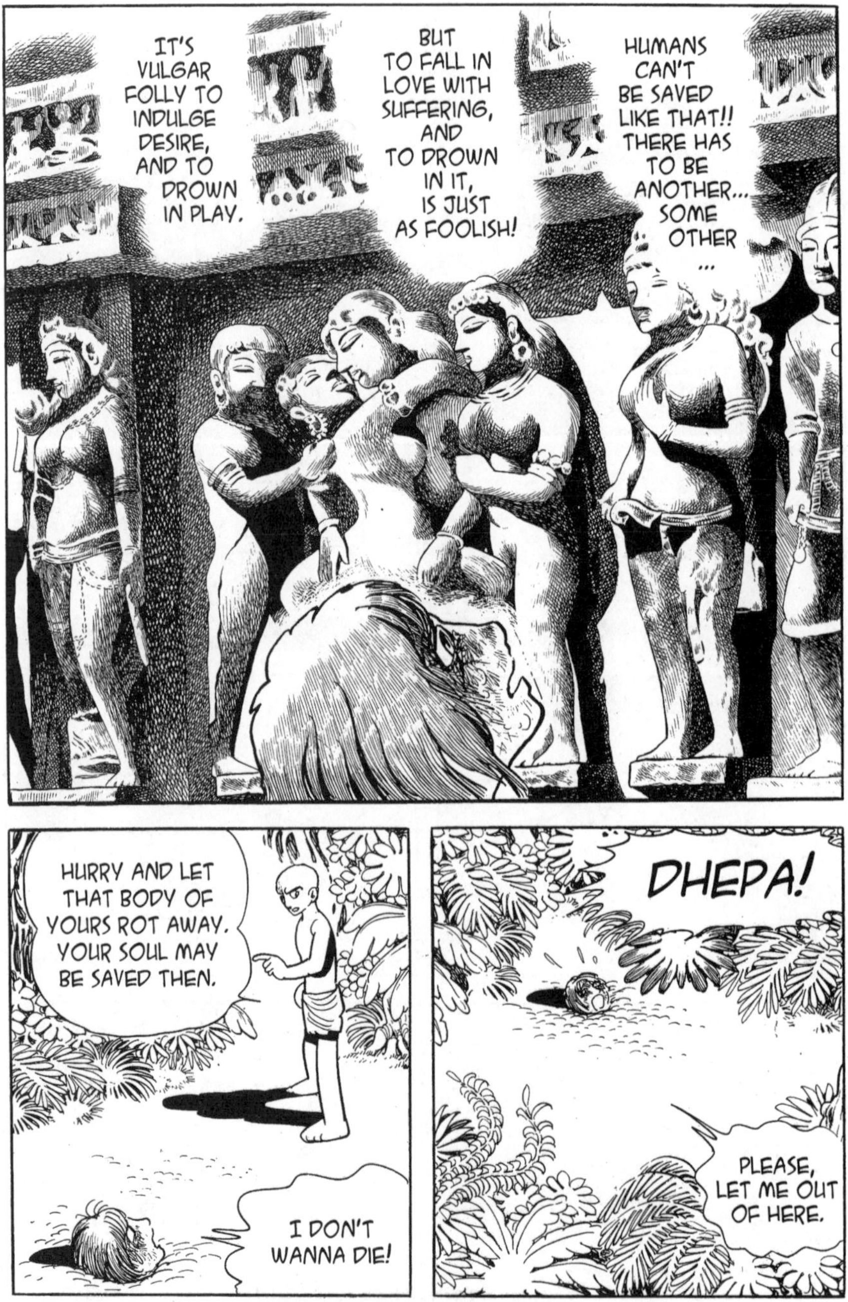
IT'S VULGAR FOLLY TO INDULGE DESIRE, AND TO DROWN IN PLAY.
BUT TO FALL IN LOVE WITH SUFFERING, AND TO DROWN IN IT, IS JUST AS FOOLISH!
HUMANS CAN'T BE SAVED LIKE THAT!! THERE HAS TO BE ANOTHER... SOME OTHER ...
HURRY AND LET THAT BODY OF YOURS ROT AWAY. YOUR SOUL MAY BE SAVED THEN.
I DON'T WANNA DIE!
DHEPA!
PLEASE, LET ME OUT OF HERE.

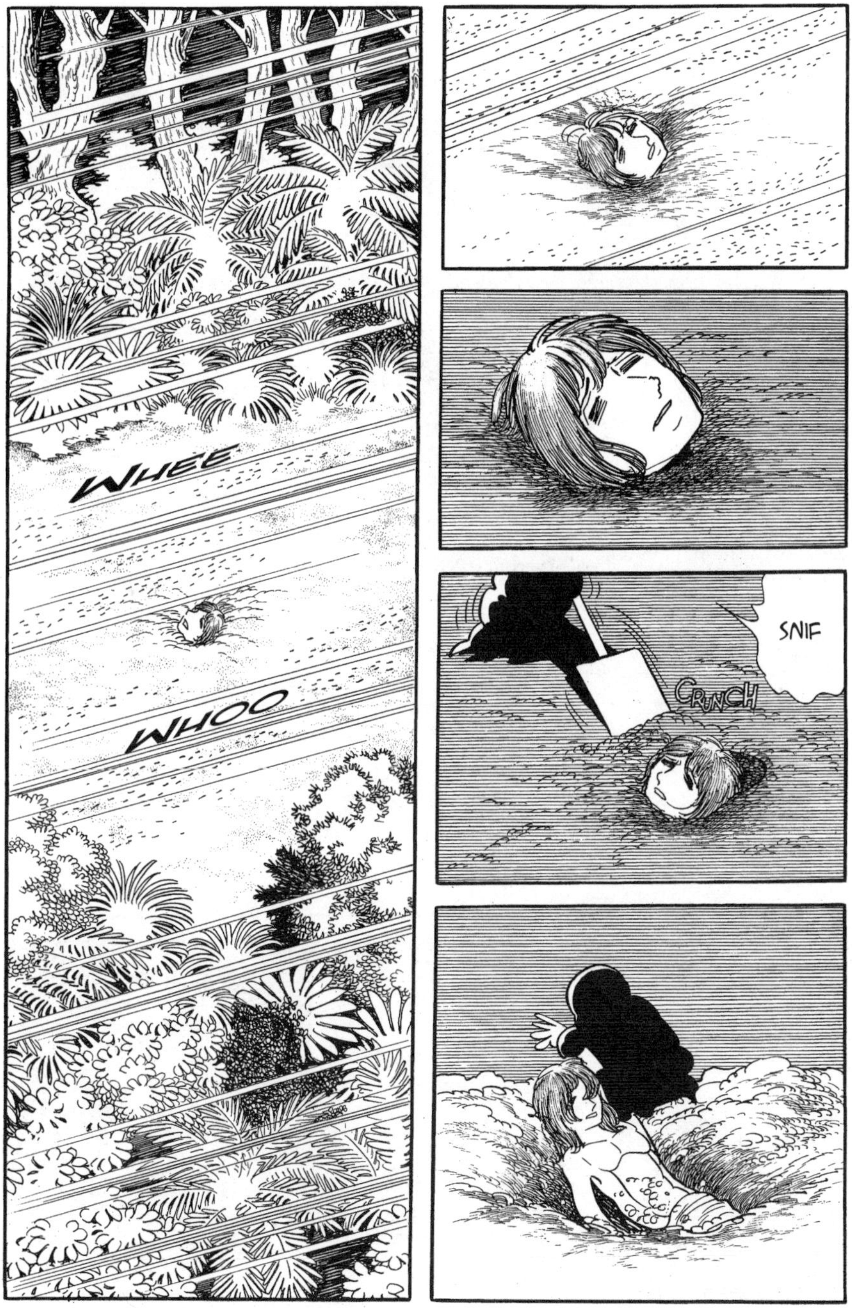
WHEE
WHOO
SNIF
CRUNCH

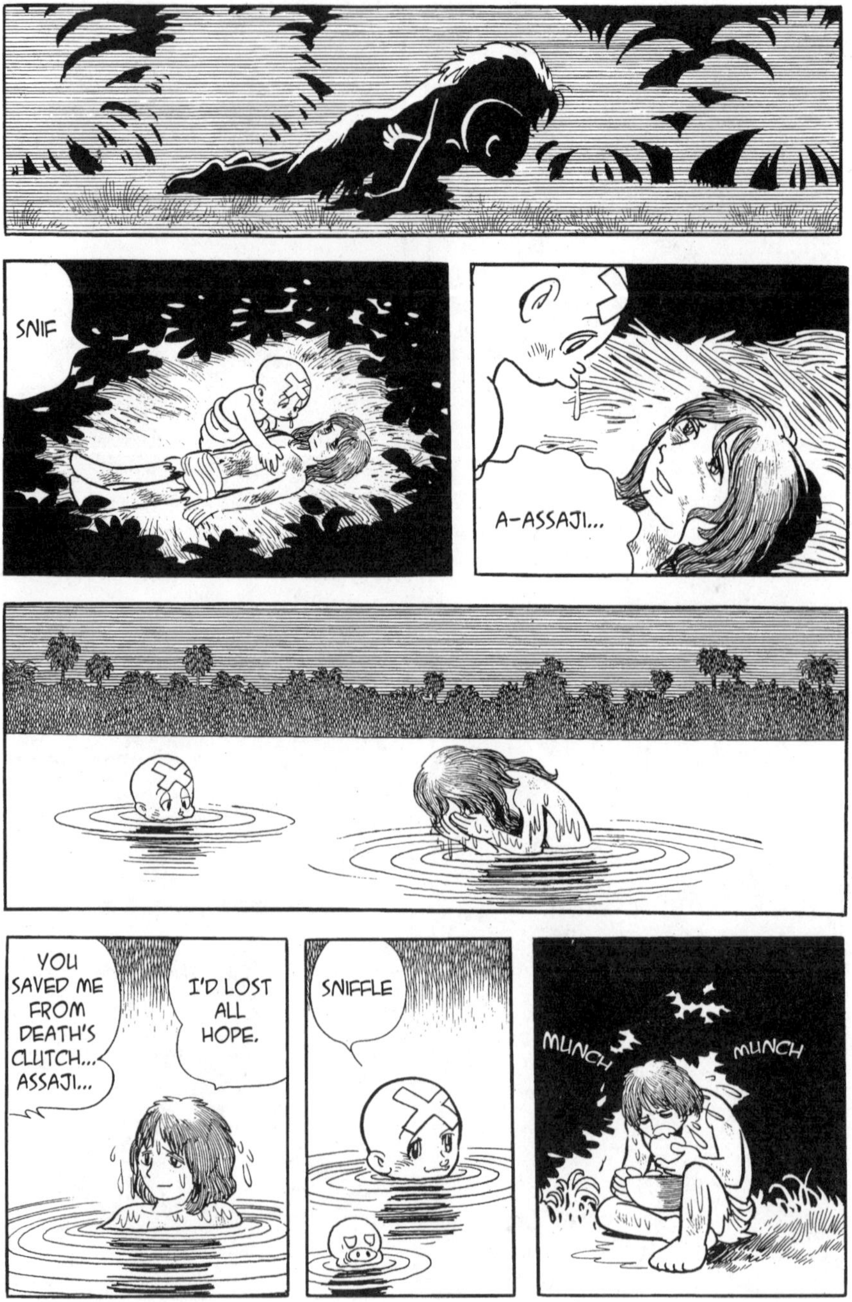
SNIF
A-ASSAJI...
YOU SAVED ME FROM DEATH'S CLUTCH... ASSAJI...
I'D LOST ALL HOPE.
SNIFFLE
MUNCH
MUNCH

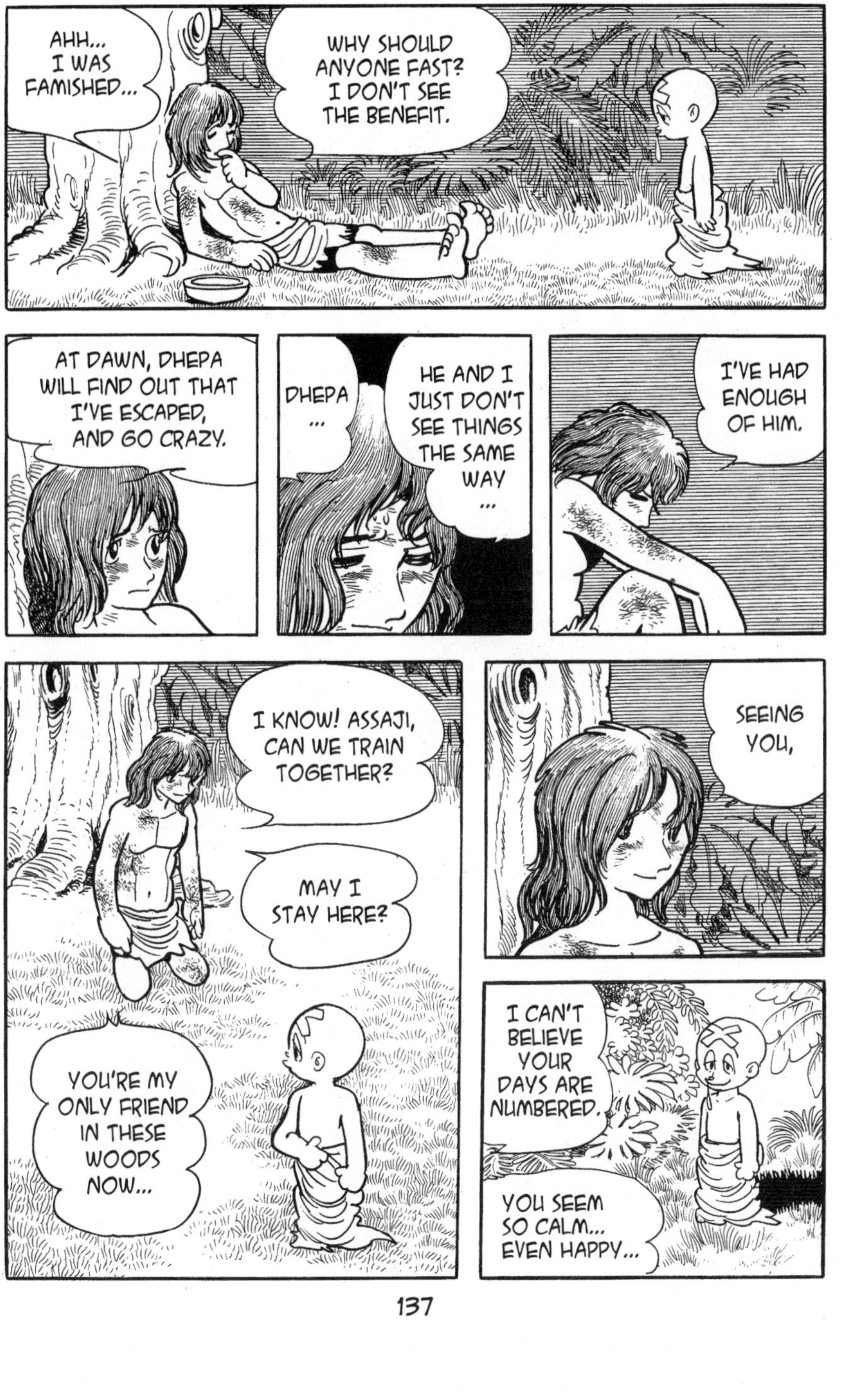
AHH... I WAS FAMISHED...
WHY SHOULD ANYONE FAST? I DON'T SEE THE BENEFIT.
AT DAWN, DHEPA WILL FIND OUT THAT I'VE ESCAPED, AND GO CRAZY.
DHEPA ...
HE AND I JUST DON'T SEE THINGS THE SAME WAY ...
I'VE HAD ENOUGH OF HIM.
I KNOW! ASSAJI, CAN WE TRAIN TOGETHER?
MAY I STAY HERE?
YOU'RE MY ONLY FRIEND IN THESE WOODS NOW...
SEEING YOU,
I CAN'T BELIEVE YOUR DAYS ARE NUMBERED.
YOU SEEM SO CALM... EVEN HAPPY...

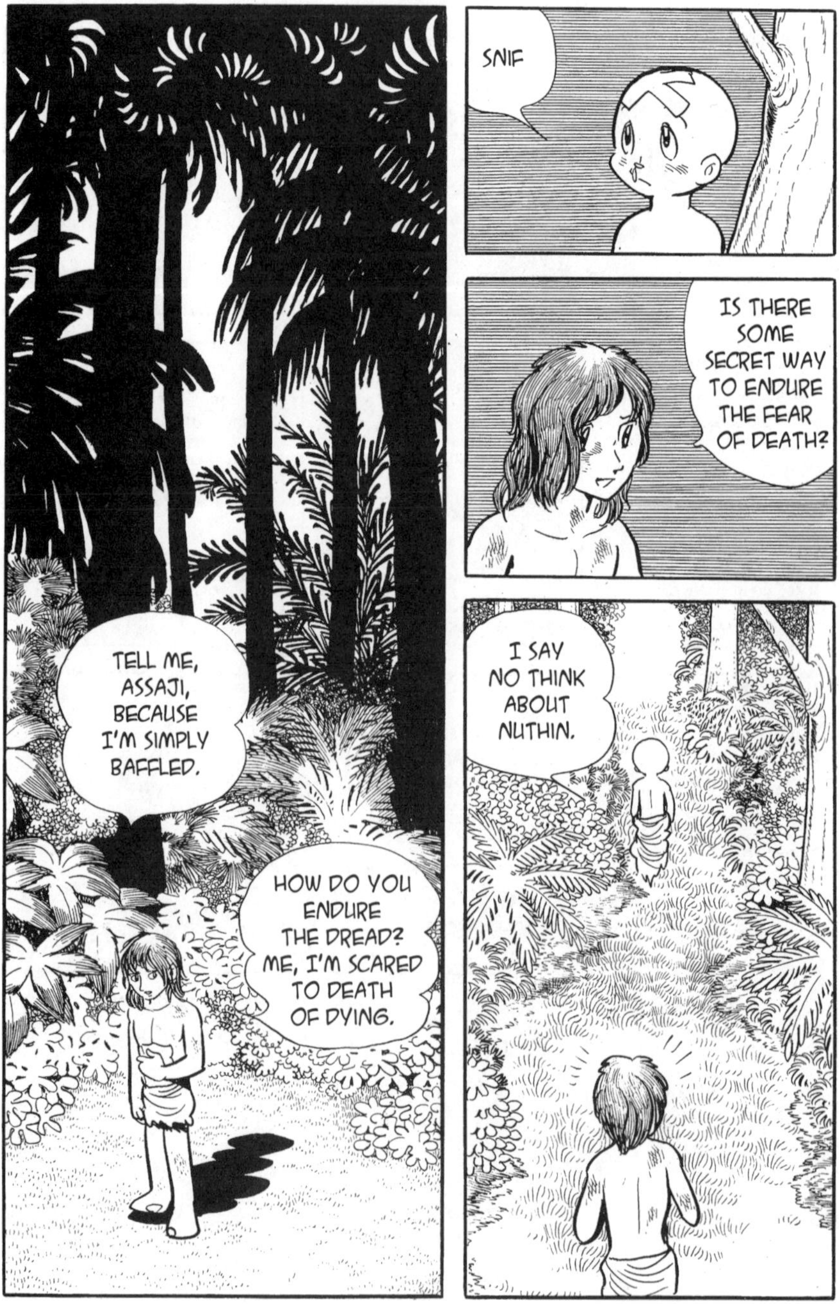
TELL ME, ASSAJI, BECAUSE I'M SIMPLY BAFFLED.
HOW DO YOU ENDURE THE DREAD? ME, I'M SCARED TO DEATH OF DYING.
SNIF
IS THERE SOME SECRET WAY TO ENDURE THE FEAR OF DEATH?
I SAY NO THINK ABOUT NUTHIN.

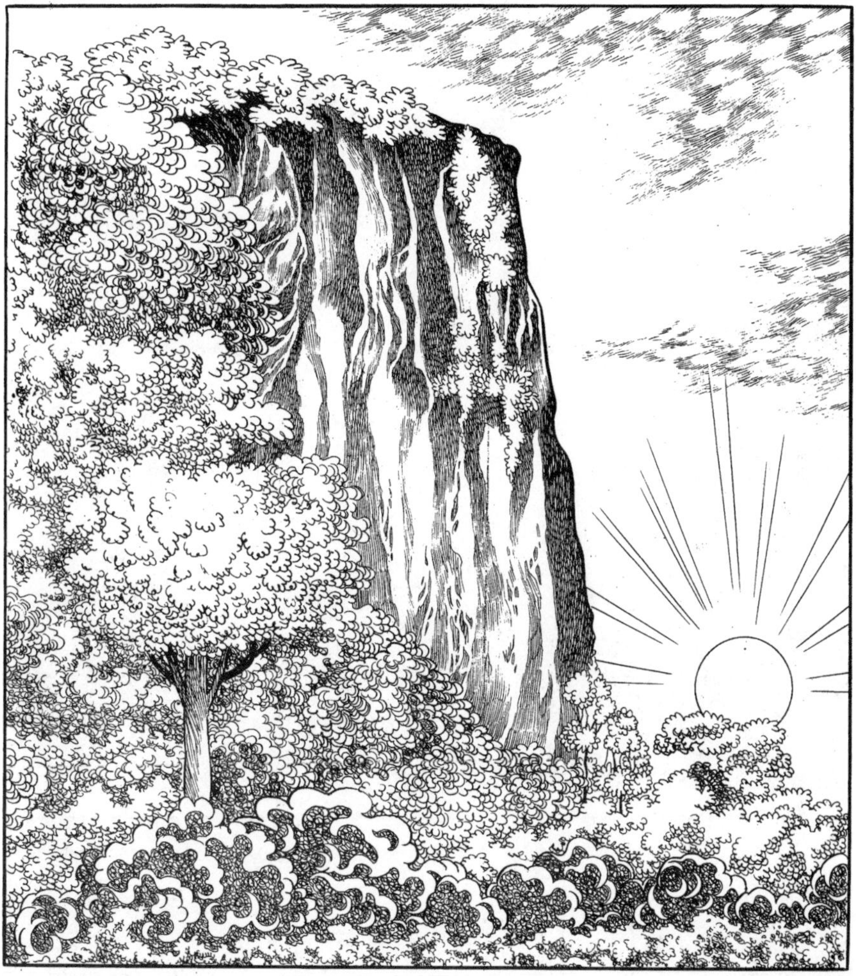

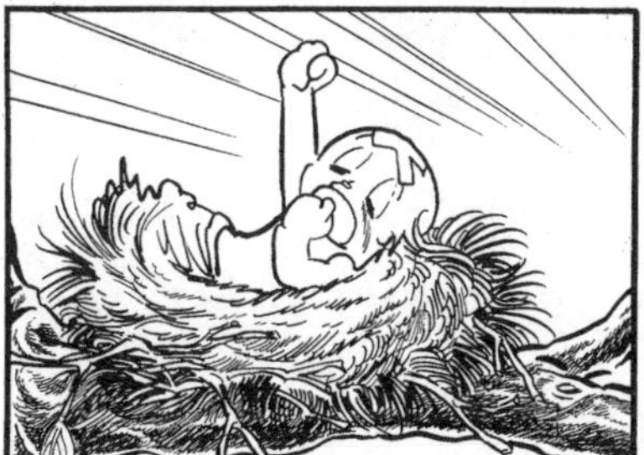

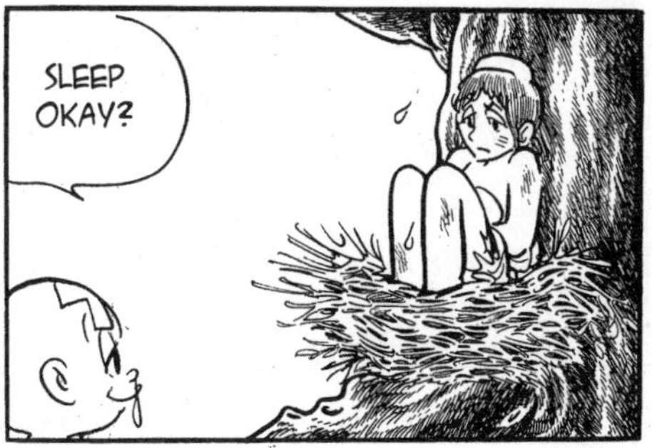
SLEEP OKAY?

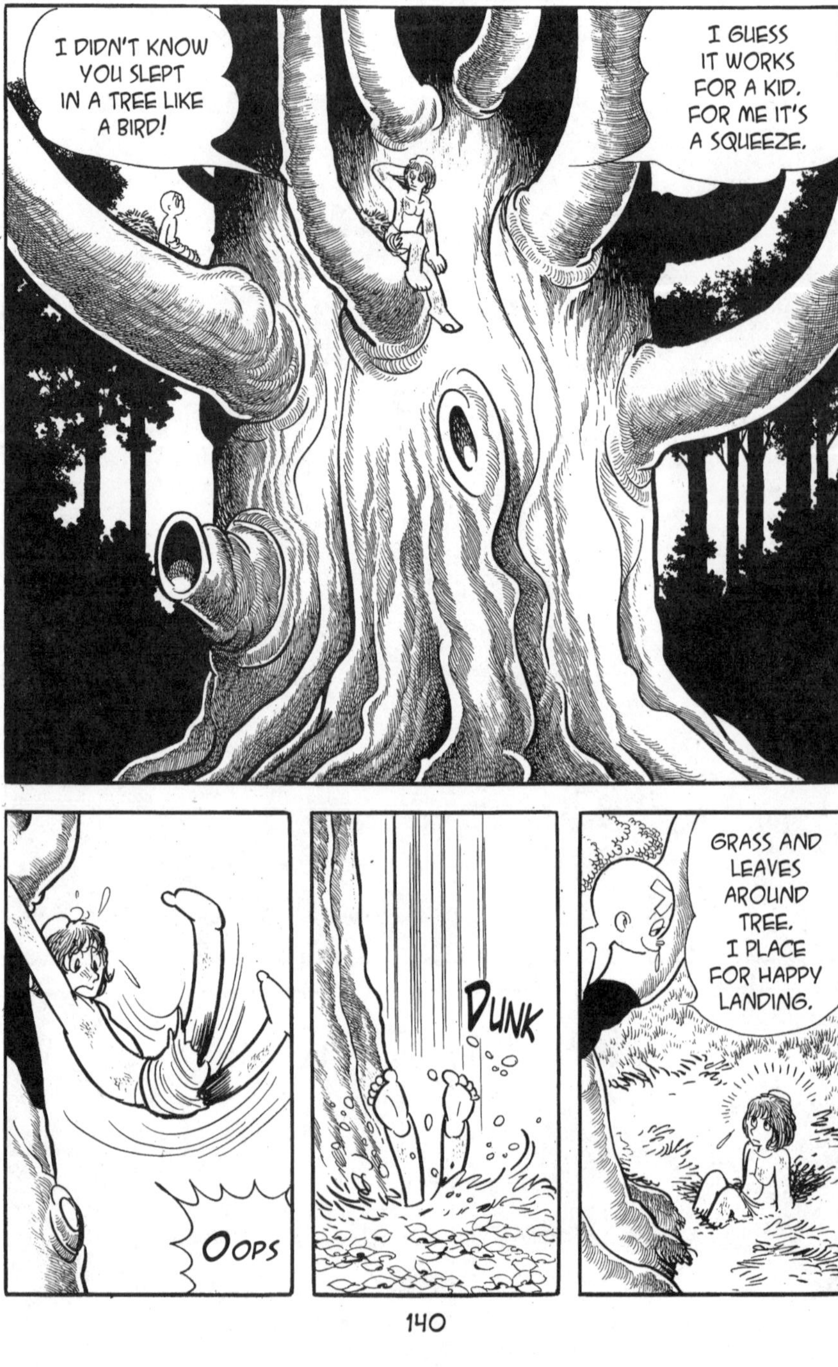
I DIDN'T KNOW YOU SLEPT IN A TREE LIKE A BIRD!
I GUESS IT WORKS FOR A KID. FOR ME IT'S A SQUEEZE.
OOPS
DUNK
GRASS AND LEAVES AROUND TREE. I PLACE FOR HAPPY LANDING.

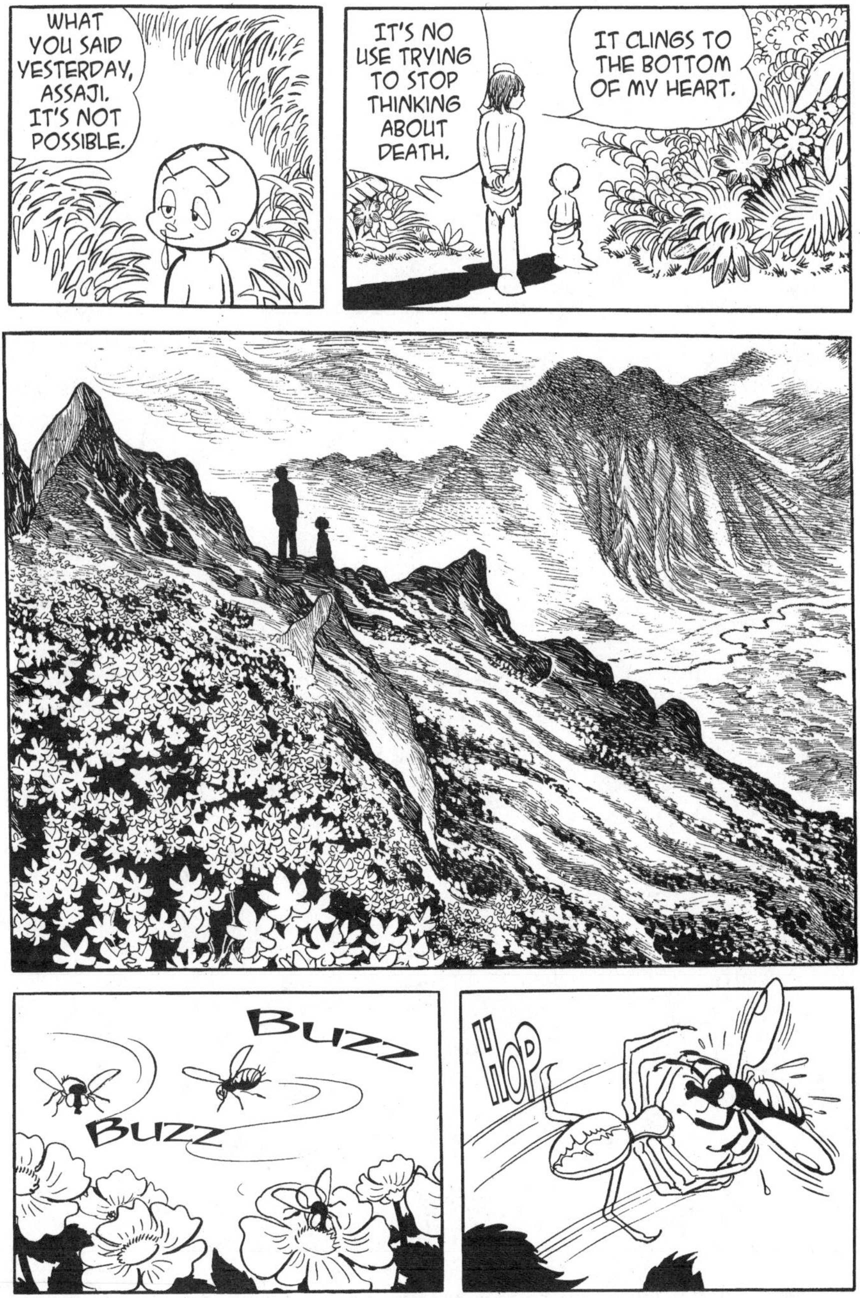
WHAT YOU SAID YESTERDAY, ASSAJI. IT'S NOT POSSIBLE.
IT'S NO USE TRYING TO STOP THINKING ABOUT DEATH.
IT CLINGS TO THE BOTTOM OF MY HEART.
BUZZ
BUZZ
HOP

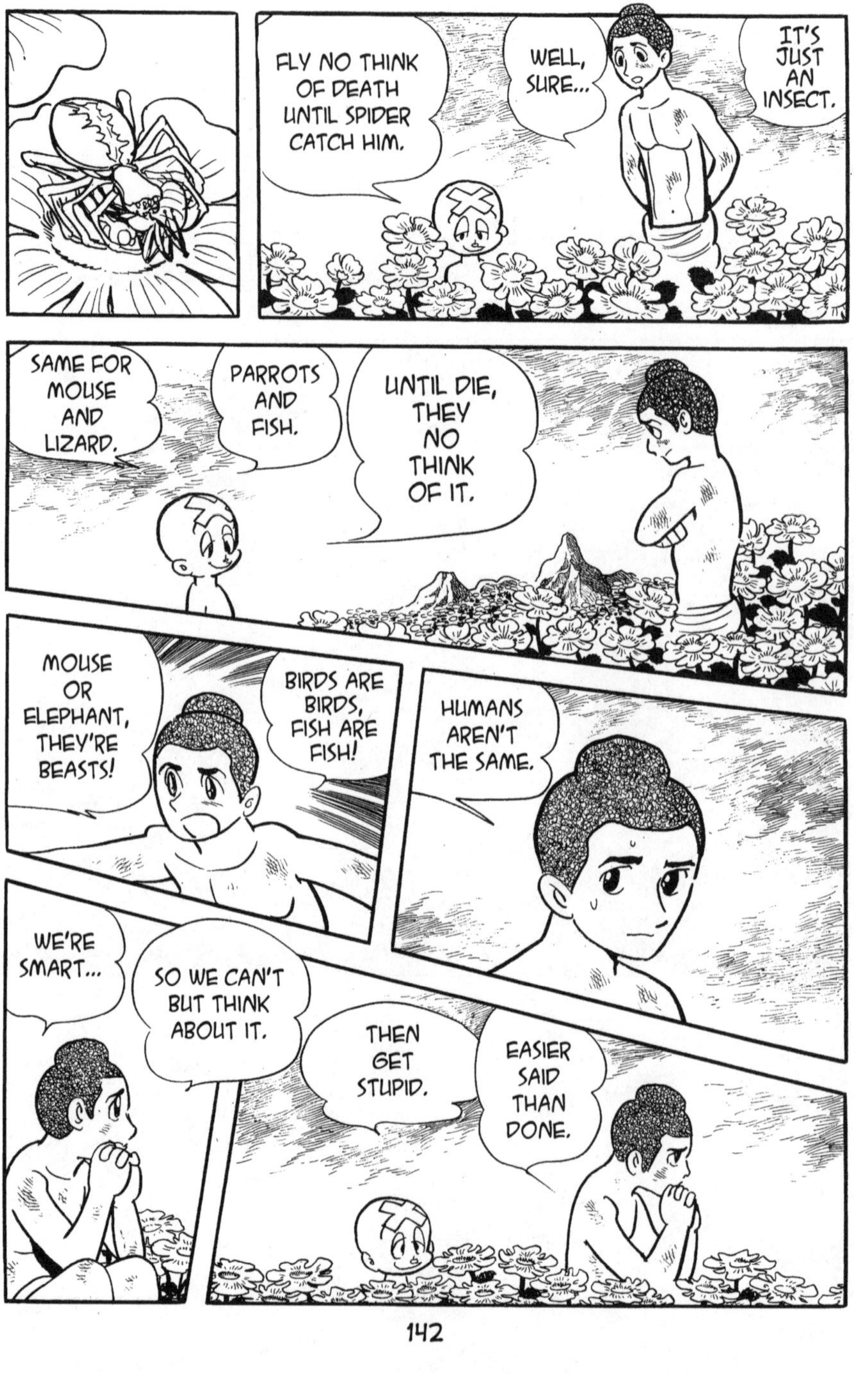
FLY NO THINK OF DEATH UNTIL SPIDER CATCH HIM.
WELL, SURE...
IT'S JUST AN INSECT.
SAME FOR MOUSE AND LIZARD.
PARROTS AND FISH.
UNTIL DIE, THEY NO THINK OF IT.
MOUSE OR ELEPHANT, THEY'RE BEASTS!
BIRDS ARE BIRDS, FISH ARE FISH!
HUMANS AREN'T THE SAME.
WE'RE SMART...
SO WE CAN'T BUT THINK ABOUT IT.
THEN GET STUPID.
EASIER SAID THAN DONE.

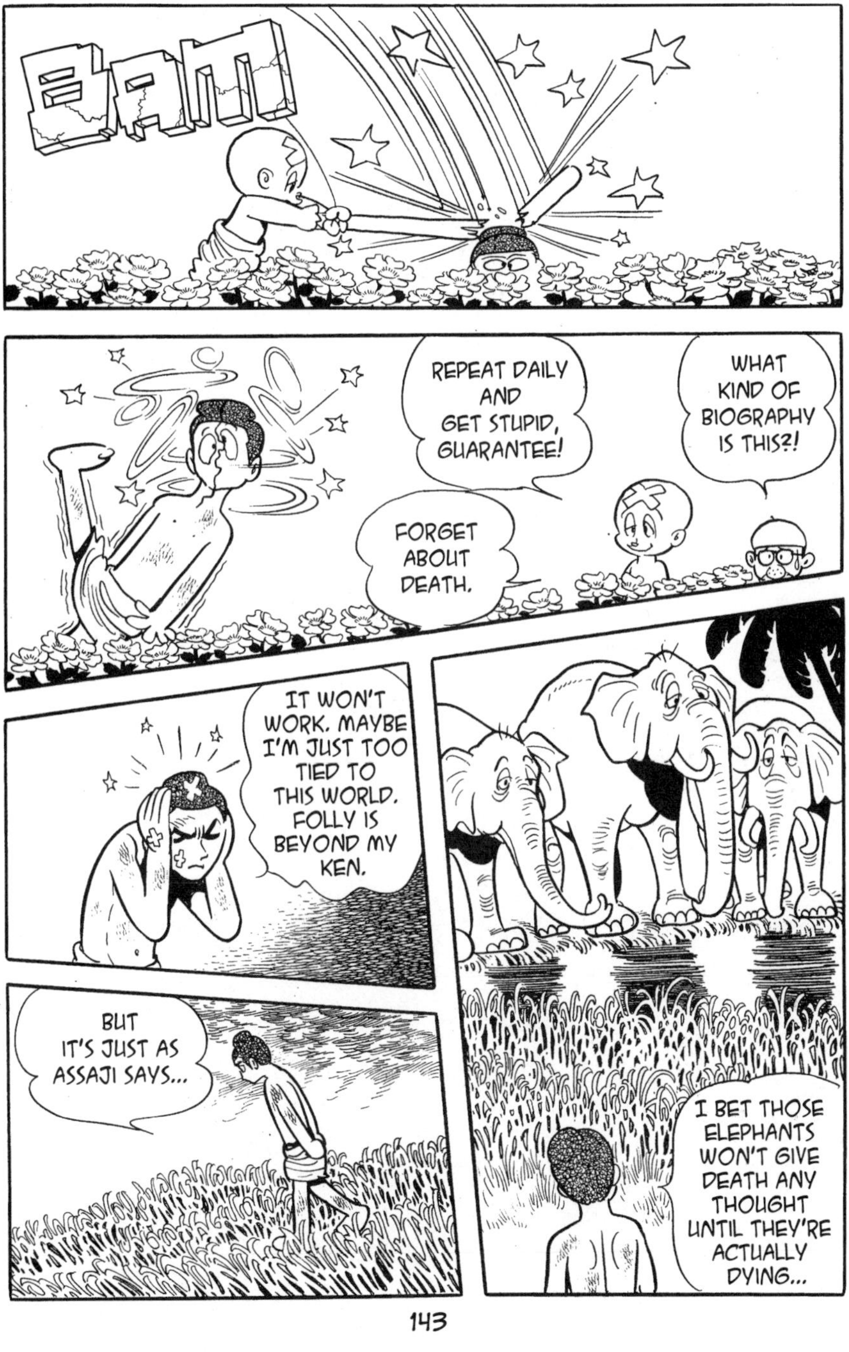
BAM
REPEAT DAILY AND GET STUPID, GUARANTEE!
WHAT KIND OF BIOGRAPHY IS THIS?!
FORGET ABOUT DEATH.
IT WON'T WORK. MAYBE I'M JUST TOO TIED TO THIS WORLD. FOLLY IS BEYOND MY KEN.
BUT IT'S JUST AS ASSAJI SAYS...
I BET THOSE ELEPHANTS WON'T GIVE DEATH ANY THOUGHT UNTIL THEY'RE ACTUALLY DYING...

CHAPTER EIGHT

ASSAJI'S END

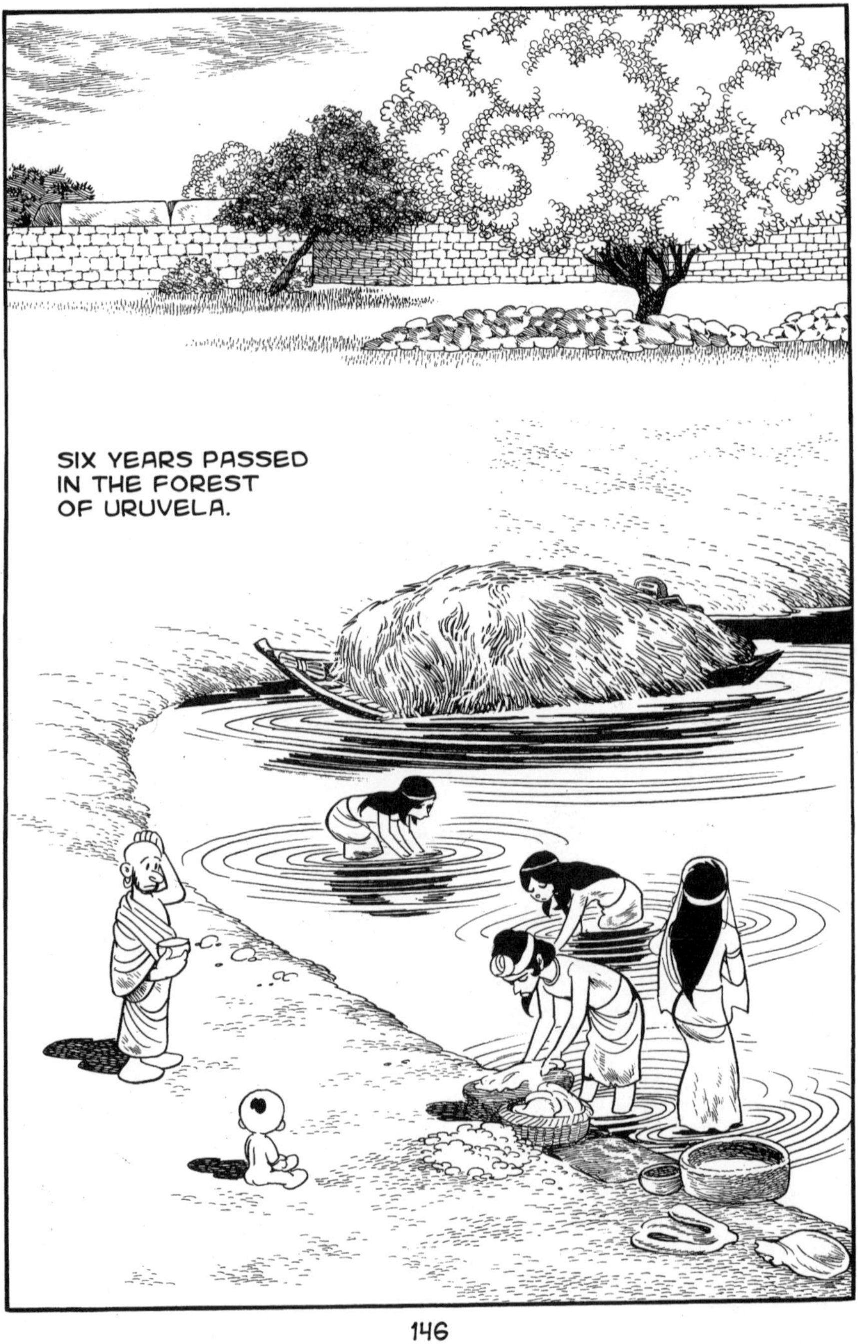
SIX YEARS PASSED IN THE FOREST OF URUVELA.

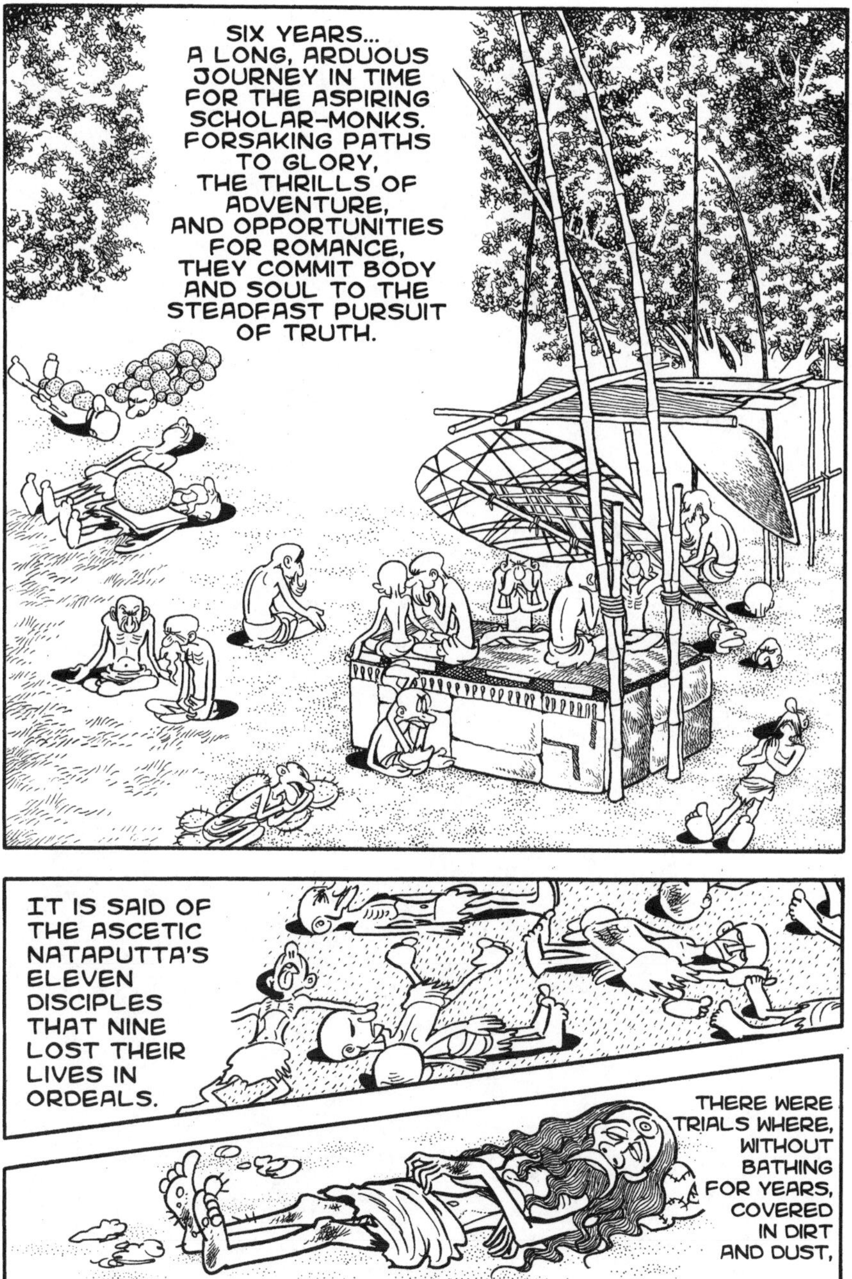
SIX YEARS... A LONG, ARDUOUS JOURNEY IN TIME FOR THE ASPIRING SCHOLAR-MONKS. FORSAKING PATHS TO GLORY, THE THRILLS OF ADVENTURE, AND OPPORTUNITIES FOR ROMANCE, THEY COMMIT BODY AND SOUL TO THE STEADFAST PURSUIT OF TRUTH.
IT IS SAID OF THE ASCETIC NATAPUTTA'S ELEVEN DISCIPLES THAT NINE LOST THEIR LIVES IN ORDEALS.
THERE WERE TRIALS WHERE, WITHOUT BATHING FOR YEARS, COVERED IN DIRT AND DUST,

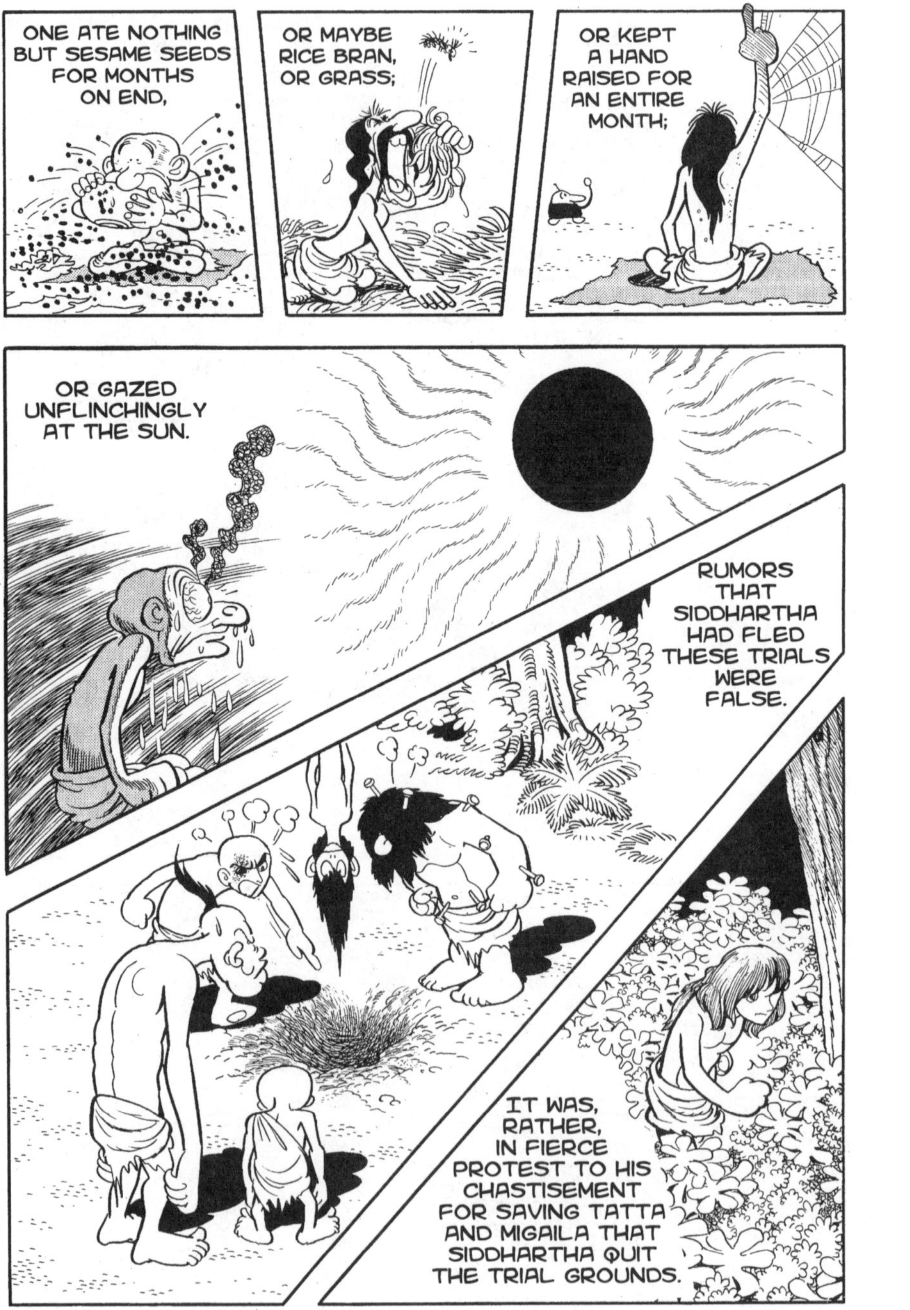
ONE ATE NOTHING BUT SESAME SEEDS FOR MONTHS ON END,
OR MAYBE RICE BRAN, OR GRASS;
OR KEPT A HAND RAISED FOR AN ENTIRE MONTH;
OR GAZED UNFLINCHINGLY AT THE SUN.
RUMORS THAT SIDDHARTHA HAD FLED THESE TRIALS WERE FALSE.
IT WAS, RATHER, IN FIERCE PROTEST TO HIS CHASTISEMENT FOR SAVING TATTA AND MIGAILA THAT SIDDHARTHA QUIT THE TRIAL GROUNDS.

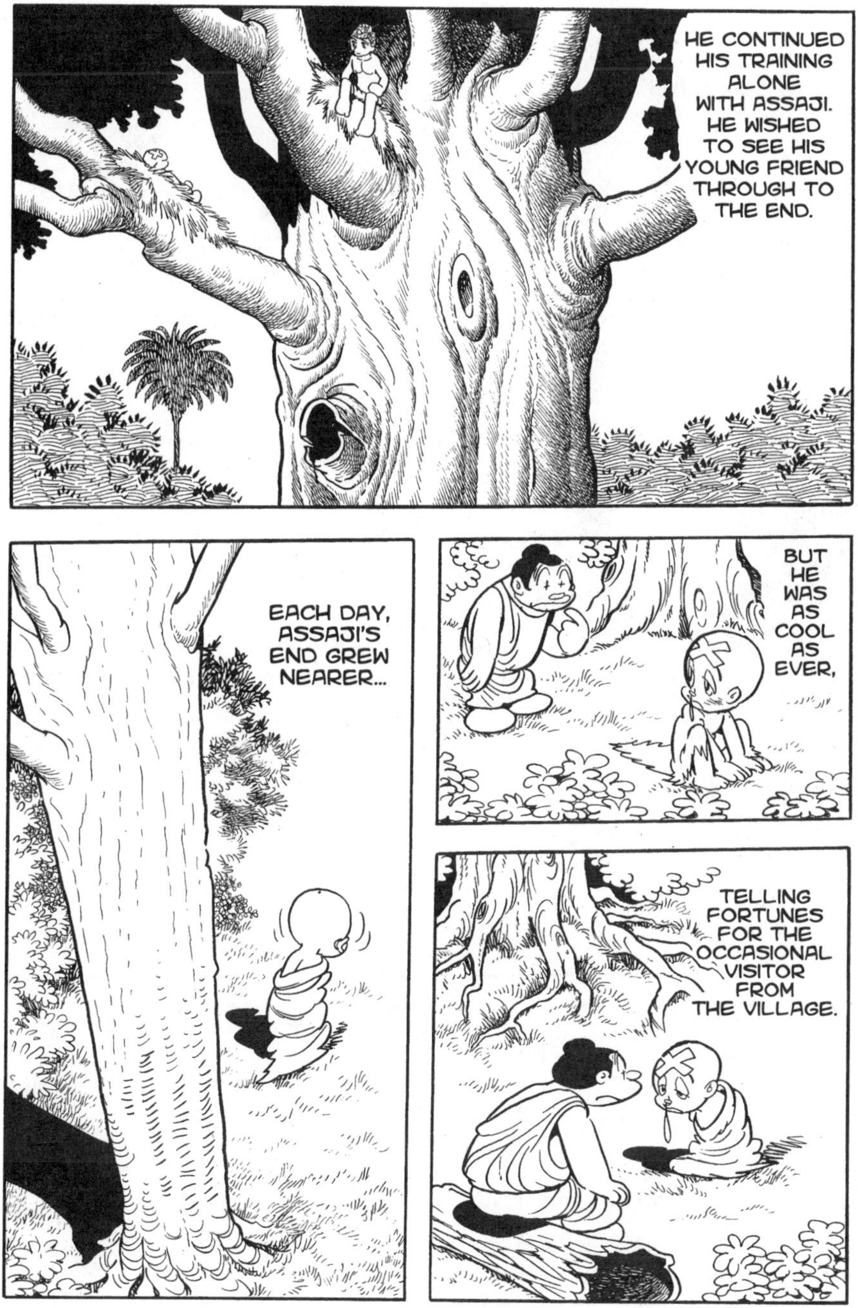
HE CONTINUED HIS TRAINING ALONE WITH ASSAJI. HE WISHED TO SEE HIS YOUNG FRIEND THROUGH TO THE END.
EACH DAY, ASSAJI'S END GREW NEARER...
BUT HE WAS AS COOL AS EVER,
TELLING FORTUNES FOR THE OCCASIONAL VISITOR FROM THE VILLAGE.

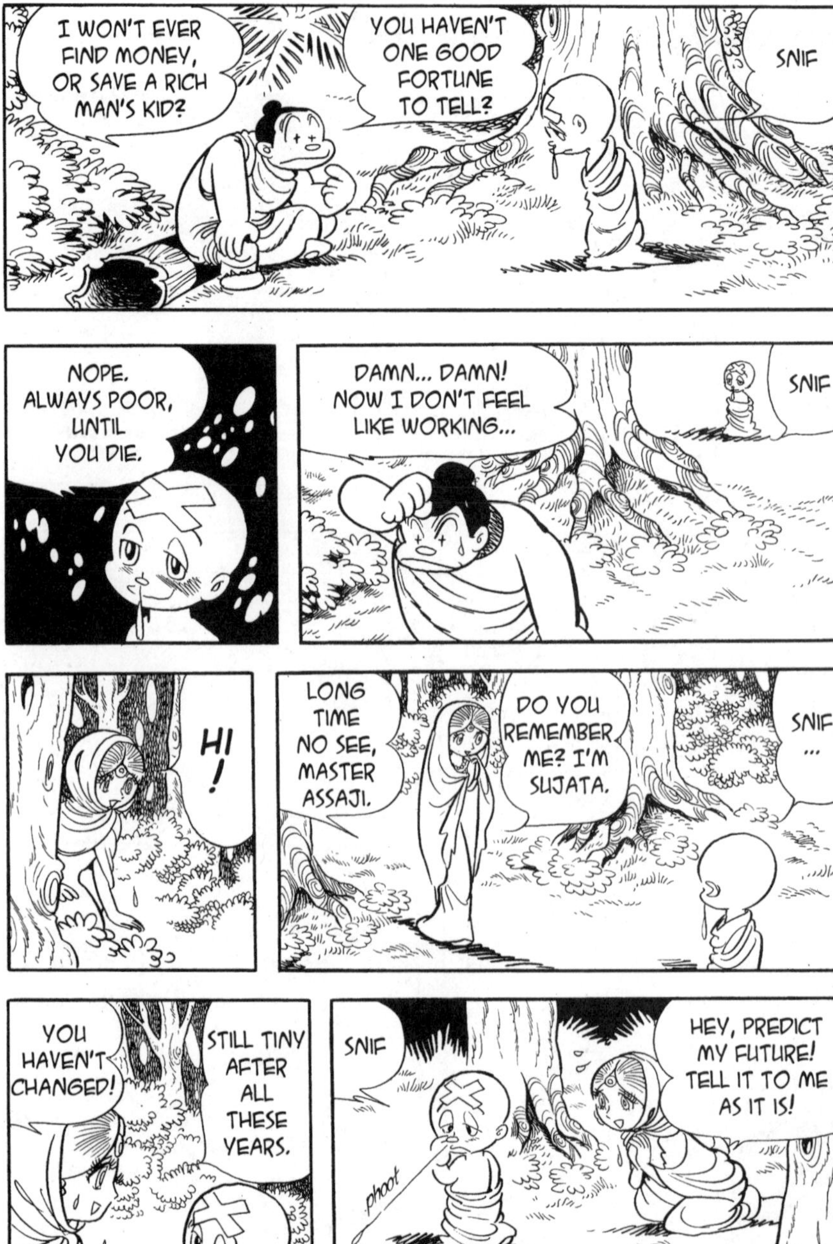
I WON'T EVER FIND MONEY, OR SAVE A RICH MAN'S KID?
YOU HAVEN'T ONE GOOD FORTUNE TO TELL?
SNIF
NOPE. ALWAYS POOR, UNTIL YOU DIE.
DAMN... DAMN! NOW I DON'T FEEL LIKE WORKING...
SNIF
HI!
LONG TIME NO SEE, MASTER ASSAJI.
DO YOU REMEMBER ME? I'M SUJATA.
SNIF ...
YOU HAVEN'T CHANGED!
STILL TINY AFTER ALL THESE YEARS.
SNIF
phoot
HEY, PREDICT MY FUTURE! TELL IT TO ME AS IT IS!

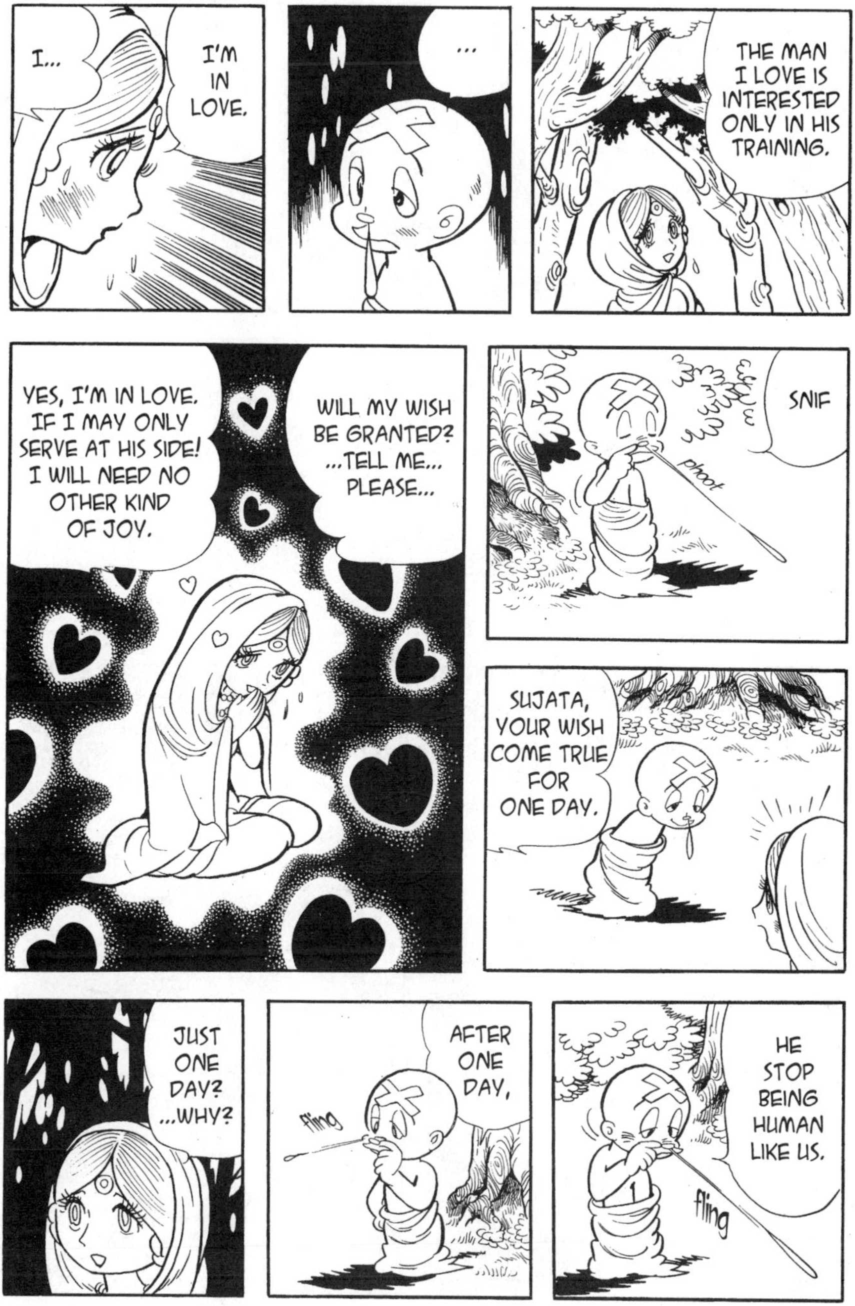
I...
I'M IN LOVE.
...
THE MAN I LOVE IS INTERESTED ONLY IN HIS TRAINING.
YES, I'M IN LOVE. IF I MAY ONLY SERVE AT HIS SIDE! I WILL NEED NO OTHER KIND OF JOY.
WILL MY WISH BE GRANTED? ...TELL ME... PLEASE...
SNIF
phoot
SUJATA, YOUR WISH COME TRUE FOR ONE DAY.
JUST ONE DAY? ...WHY?
AFTER ONE DAY,
fling
HE STOP BEING HUMAN LIKE US.
fling

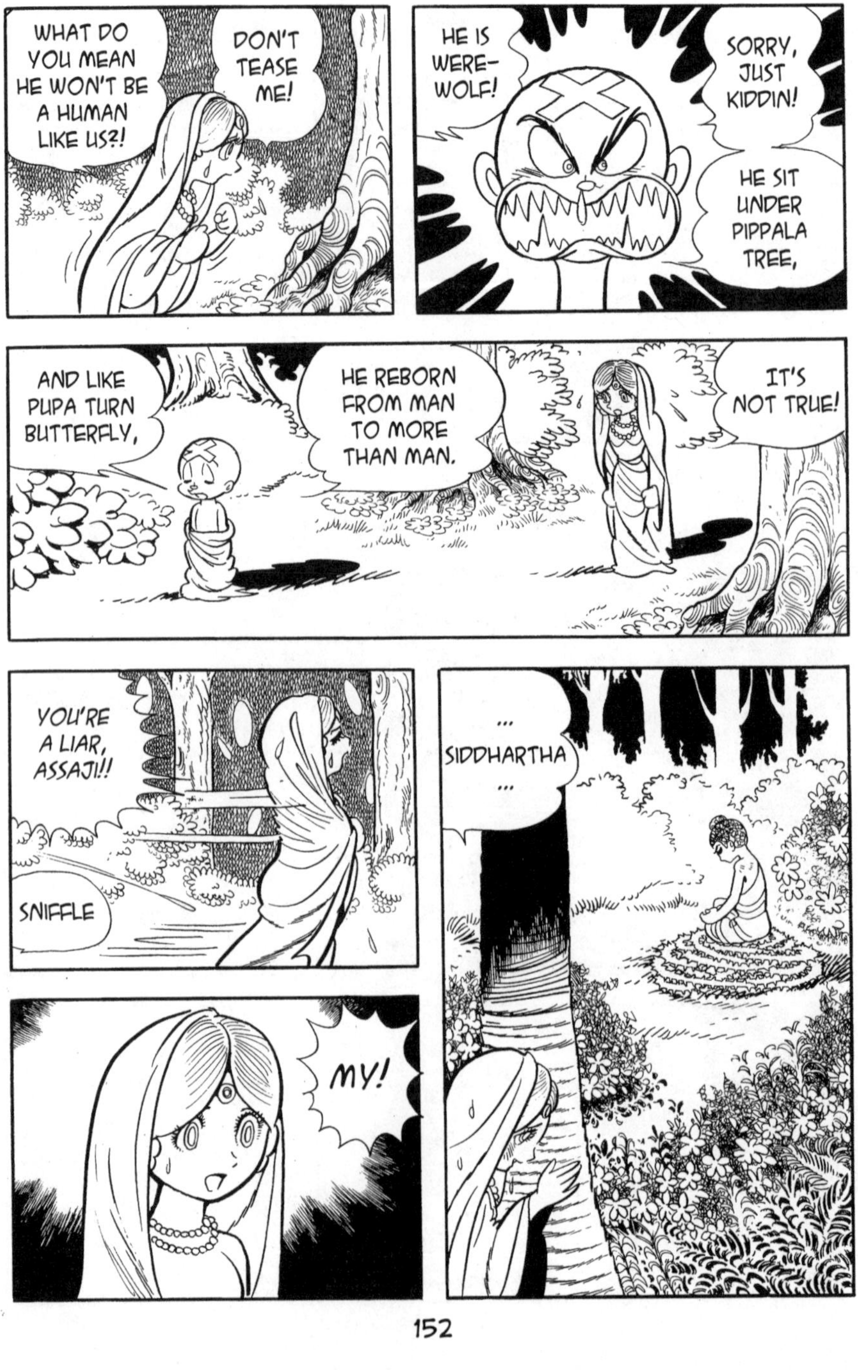
WHAT DO YOU MEAN HE WON'T BE A HUMAN LIKE US?!
DON'T TEASE ME!
HE IS WERE-WOLF!
SORRY, JUST KIDDIN!
HE SIT UNDER PIPPALA TREE,
AND LIKE PUPA TURN BUTTERFLY,
HE REBORN FROM MAN TO MORE THAN MAN.
IT'S NOT TRUE!
YOU'RE A LIAR, ASSAJI!!
SNIFFLE
MY!
... SIDDHARTHA ...

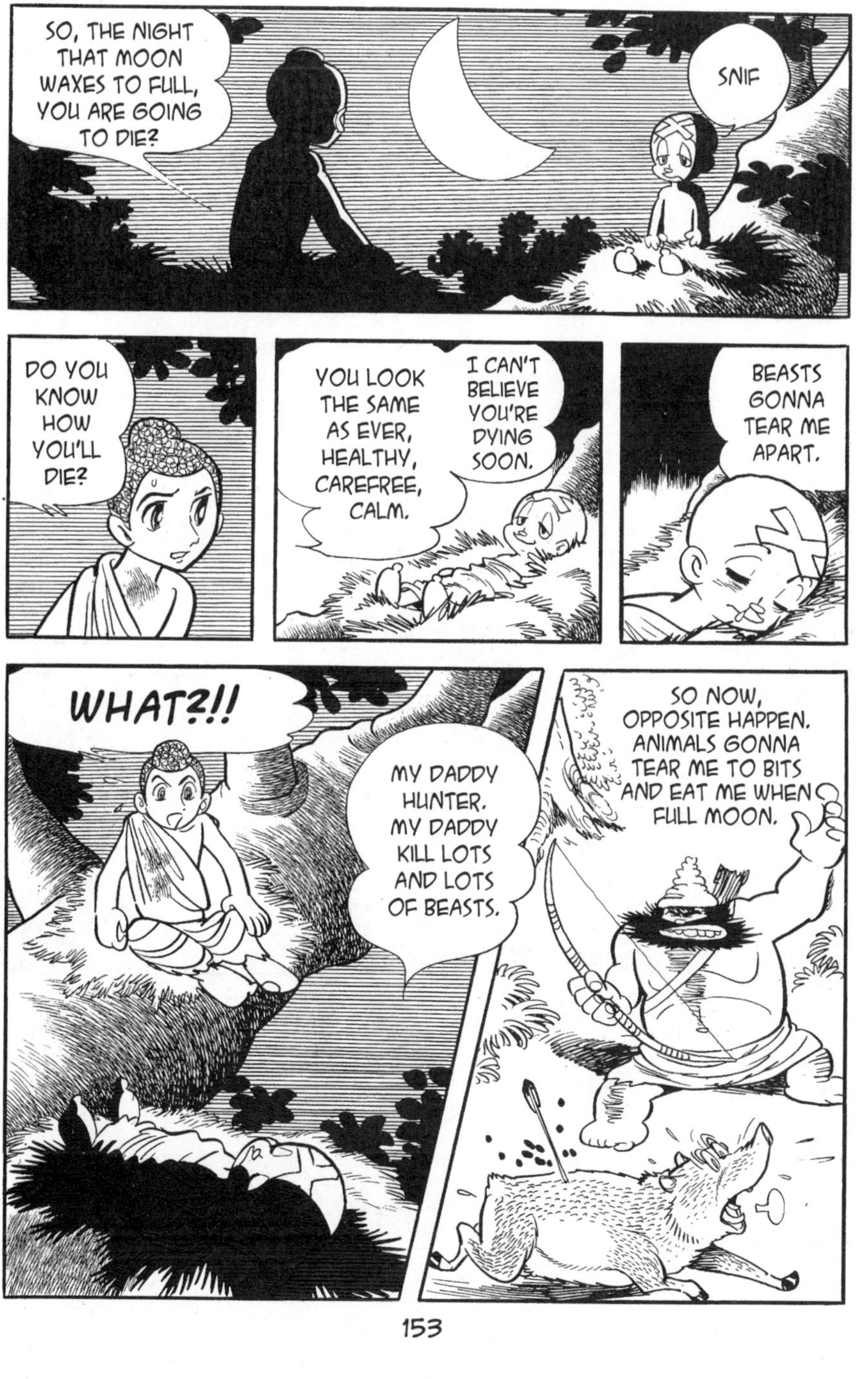
SO, THE NIGHT THAT MOON WAXES TO FULL, YOU ARE GOING TO DIE?
SNIF
DO YOU KNOW HOW YOU'LL DIE?
YOU LOOK THE SAME AS EVER, HEALTHY, CAREFREE, CALM.
I CAN'T BELIEVE YOU'RE DYING SOON.
BEASTS GONNA TEAR ME APART.
WHAT?!!
MY DADDY HUNTER. MY DADDY KILL LOTS AND LOTS OF BEASTS.
SO NOW, OPPOSITE HAPPEN. ANIMALS GONNA TEAR ME TO BITS AND EAT ME WHEN FULL MOON.

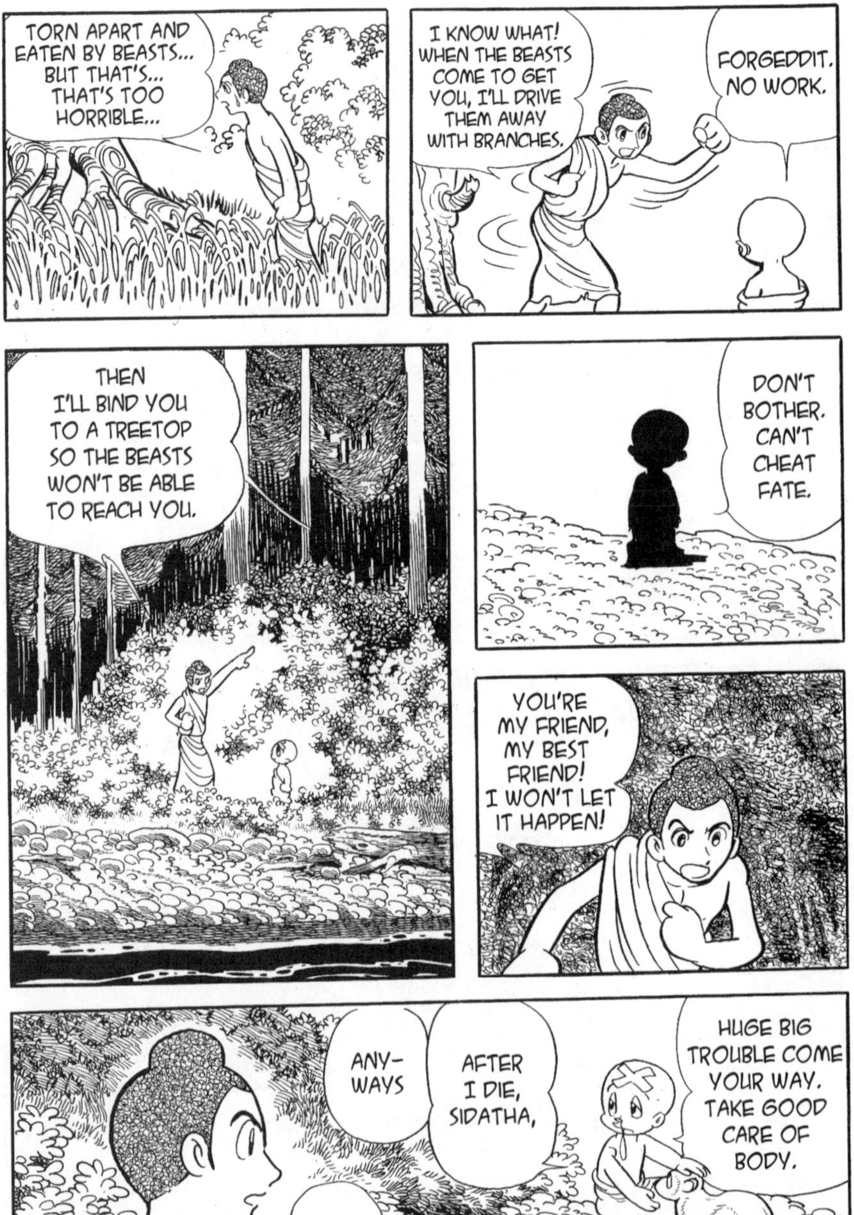
TORN APART AND EATEN BY BEASTS... BUT THAT'S... THAT'S TOO HORRIBLE...
I KNOW WHAT! WHEN THE BEASTS COME TO GET YOU, I'LL DRIVE THEM AWAY WITH BRANCHES.
FORGEDDIT. NO WORK.
THEN I'LL BIND YOU TO A TREETOP SO THE BEASTS WON'T BE ABLE TO REACH YOU.
DON'T BOTHER. CAN'T CHEAT FATE.
YOU'RE MY FRIEND, MY BEST FRIEND! I WON'T LET IT HAPPEN!
ANY-WAYS
AFTER I DIE, SIDATHA,
HUGE BIG TROUBLE COME YOUR WAY. TAKE GOOD CARE OF BODY.
?

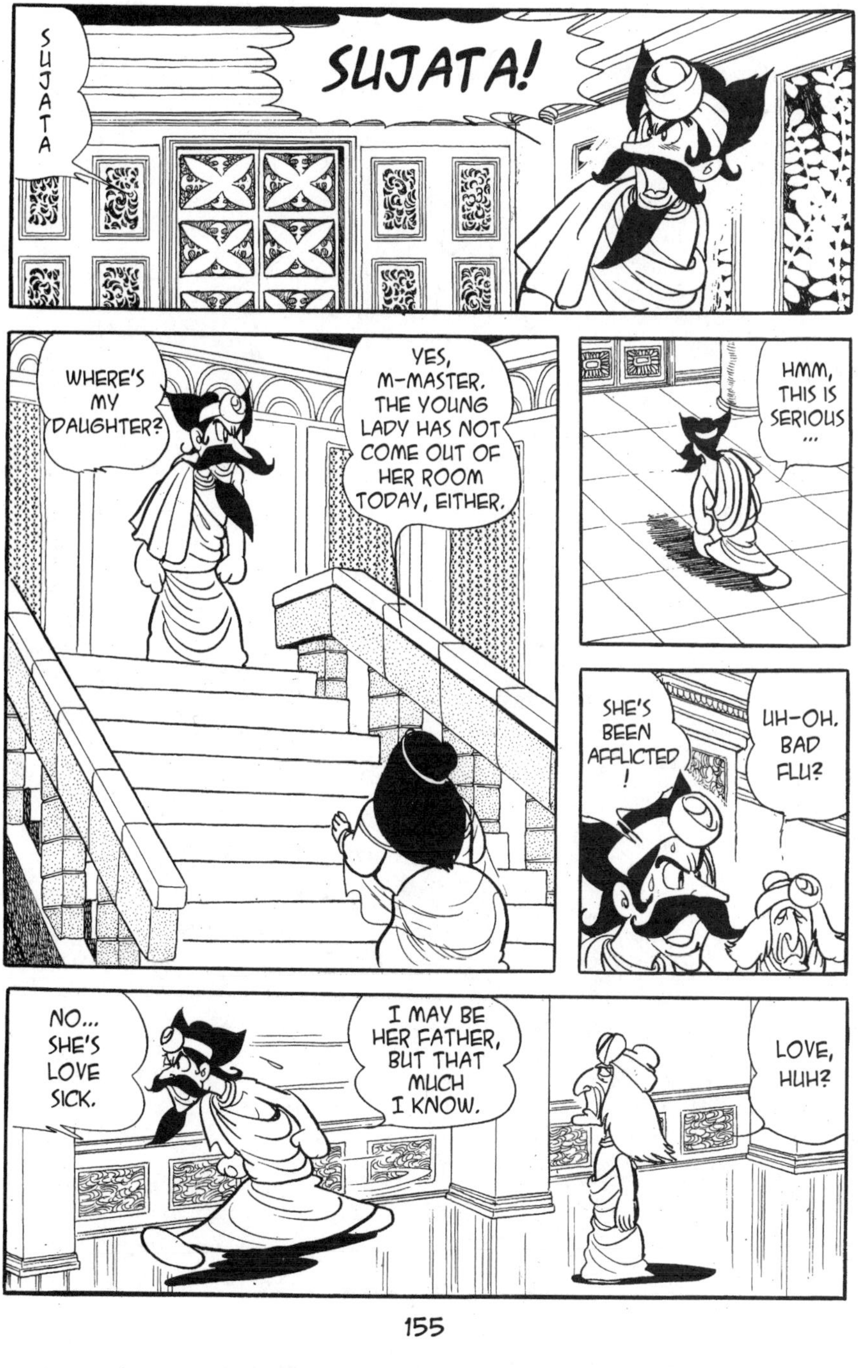
SUJATA
SUJATA!
WHERE'S MY DAUGHTER?
YES, M-MASTER. THE YOUNG LADY HAS NOT COME OUT OF HER ROOM TODAY, EITHER.
HMM, THIS IS SERIOUS ...
SHE'S BEEN AFFLICTED!
UH-OH. BAD FLU?
NO... SHE'S LOVE SICK.
I MAY BE HER FATHER, BUT THAT MUCH I KNOW.
LOVE, HUH?

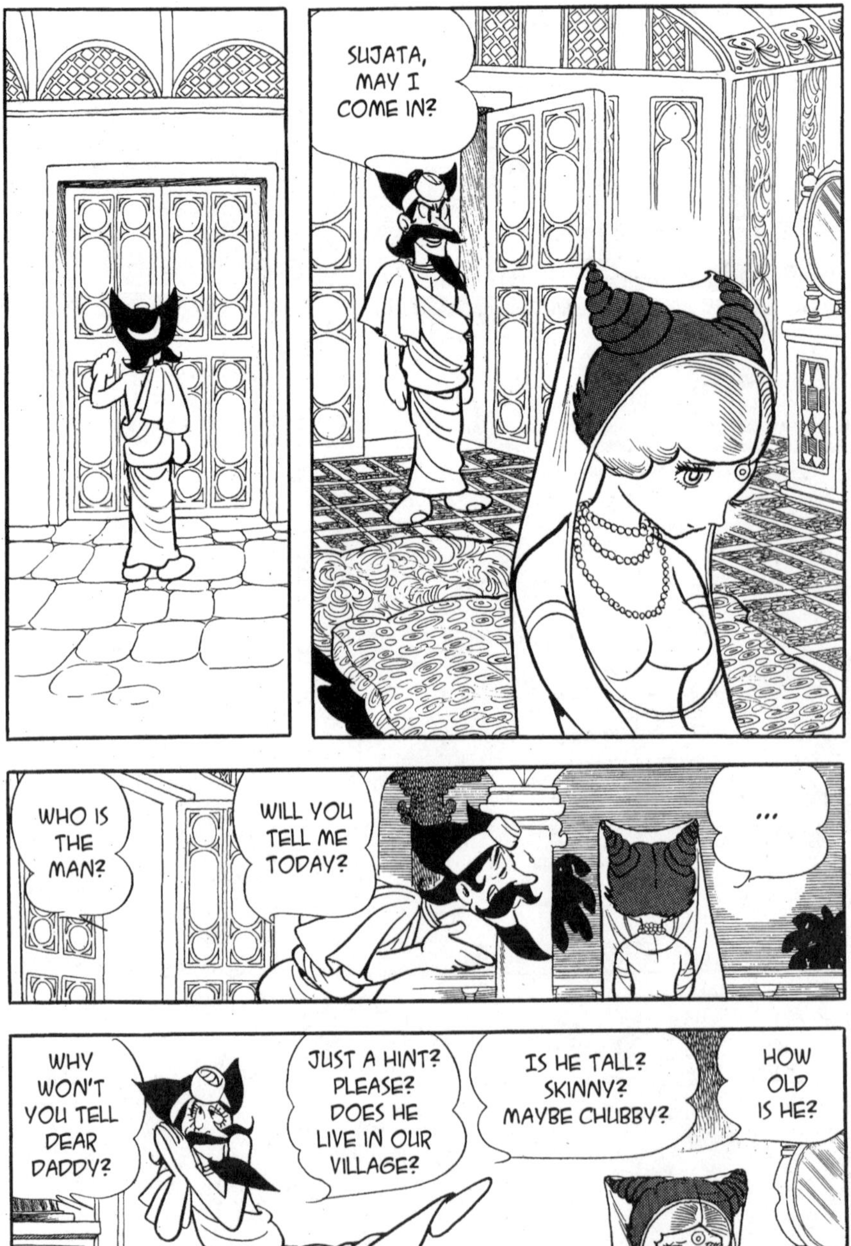
SUJATA, MAY I COME IN?
WHO IS THE MAN?
WILL YOU TELL ME TODAY?
...
WHY WON'T YOU TELL DEAR DADDY?
JUST A HINT? PLEASE? DOES HE LIVE IN OUR VILLAGE?
IS HE TALL? SKINNY? MAYBE CHUBBY?
HOW OLD IS HE?

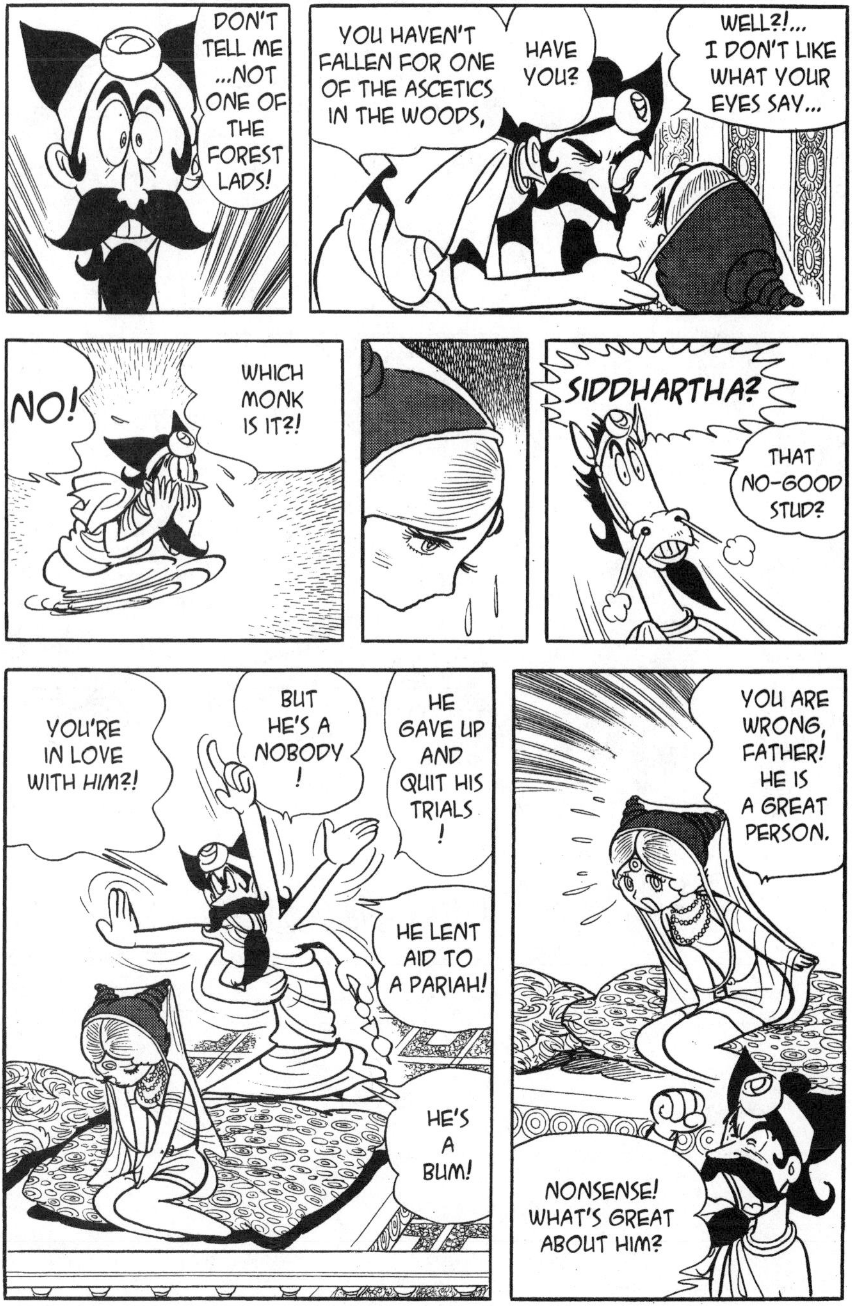
DON'T TELL ME ...NOT ONE OF THE FOREST LADS!
YOU HAVEN'T FALLEN FOR ONE OF THE ASCETICS IN THE WOODS,
HAVE YOU?
WELL?!... I DON'T LIKE WHAT YOUR EYES SAY...
NO!
WHICH MONK IS IT?!
SIDDHARTHA?
THAT NO-GOOD STUD?
YOU'RE IN LOVE WITH HIM?!
BUT HE'S A NOBODY!
HE GAVE UP AND QUIT HIS TRIALS!
HE LENT AID TO A PARIAH!
HE'S A BUM!
YOU ARE WRONG, FATHER! HE IS A GREAT PERSON.
NONSENSE! WHAT'S GREAT ABOUT HIM?

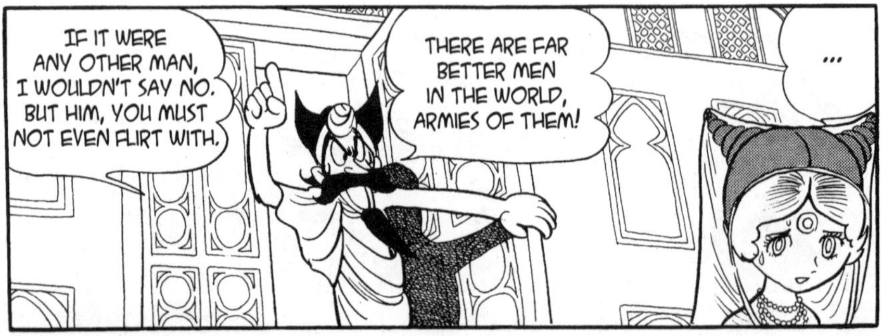
IF IT WERE ANY OTHER MAN, I WOULDN'T SAY NO. BUT HIM, YOU MUST NOT EVEN FLIRT WITH.
THERE ARE FAR BETTER MEN IN THE WORLD, ARMIES OF THEM!
...

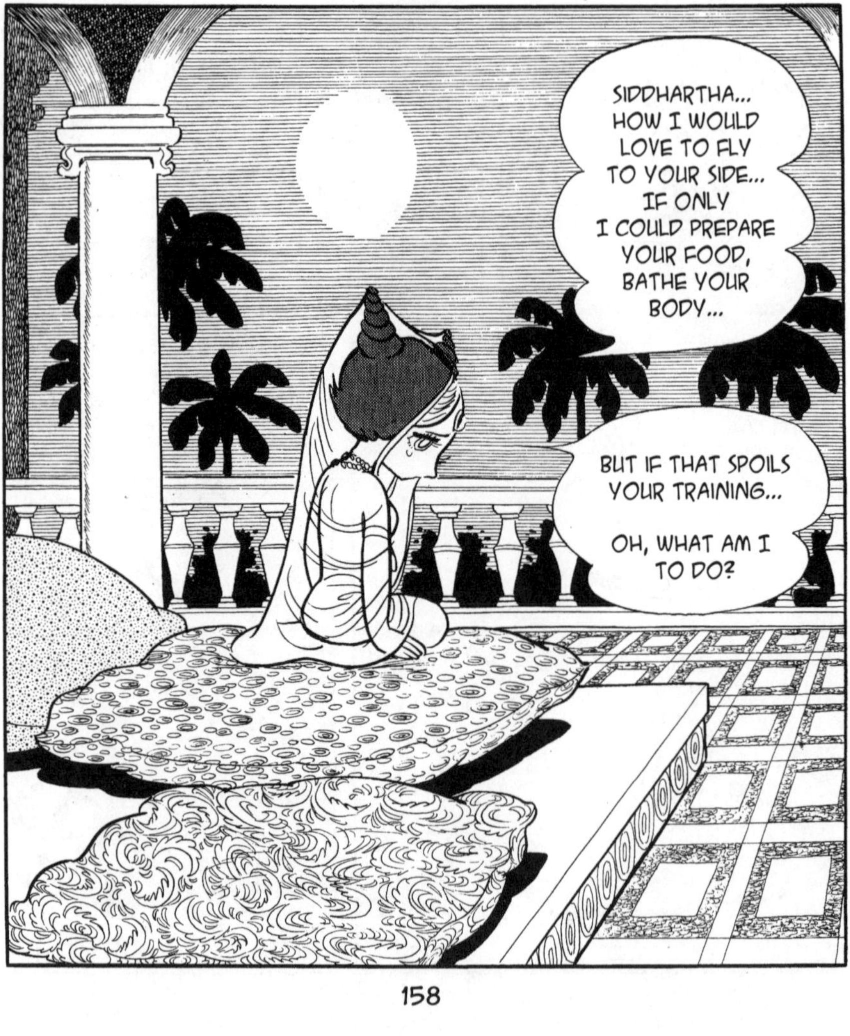
SIDDHARTHA... HOW I WOULD LOVE TO FLY TO YOUR SIDE... IF ONLY I COULD PREPARE YOUR FOOD, BATHE YOUR BODY...
BUT IF THAT SPOILS YOUR TRAINING...
OH, WHAT AM I TO DO?

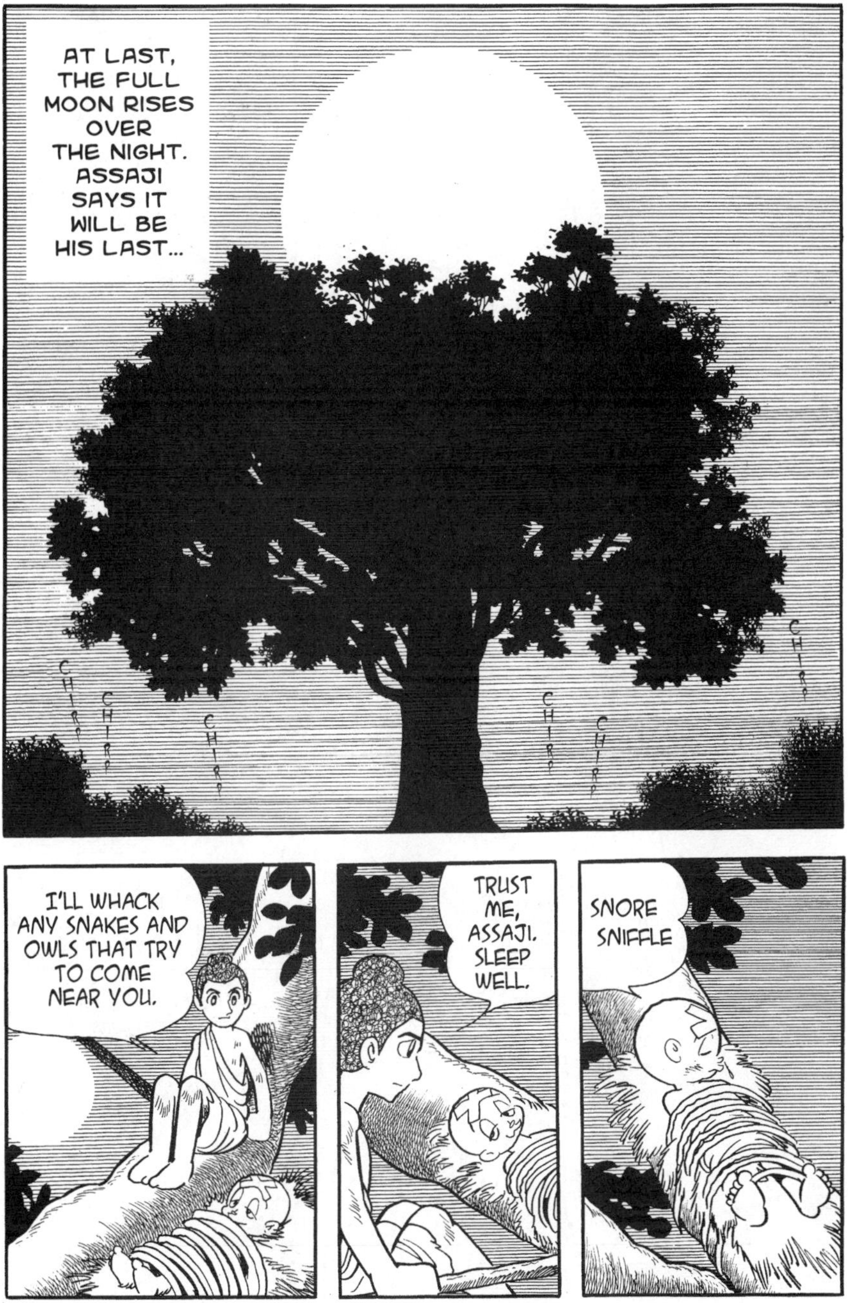
AT LAST, THE FULL MOON RISES OVER THE NIGHT. ASSAJI SAYS IT WILL BE HIS LAST...
CHIRP
CHIRP
CHIRP
CHIRP
CHIRP
CHIRP
I'LL WHACK ANY SNAKES AND OWLS THAT TRY TO COME NEAR YOU.
TRUST ME, ASSAJI. SLEEP WELL.
SNORE SNIFFLE

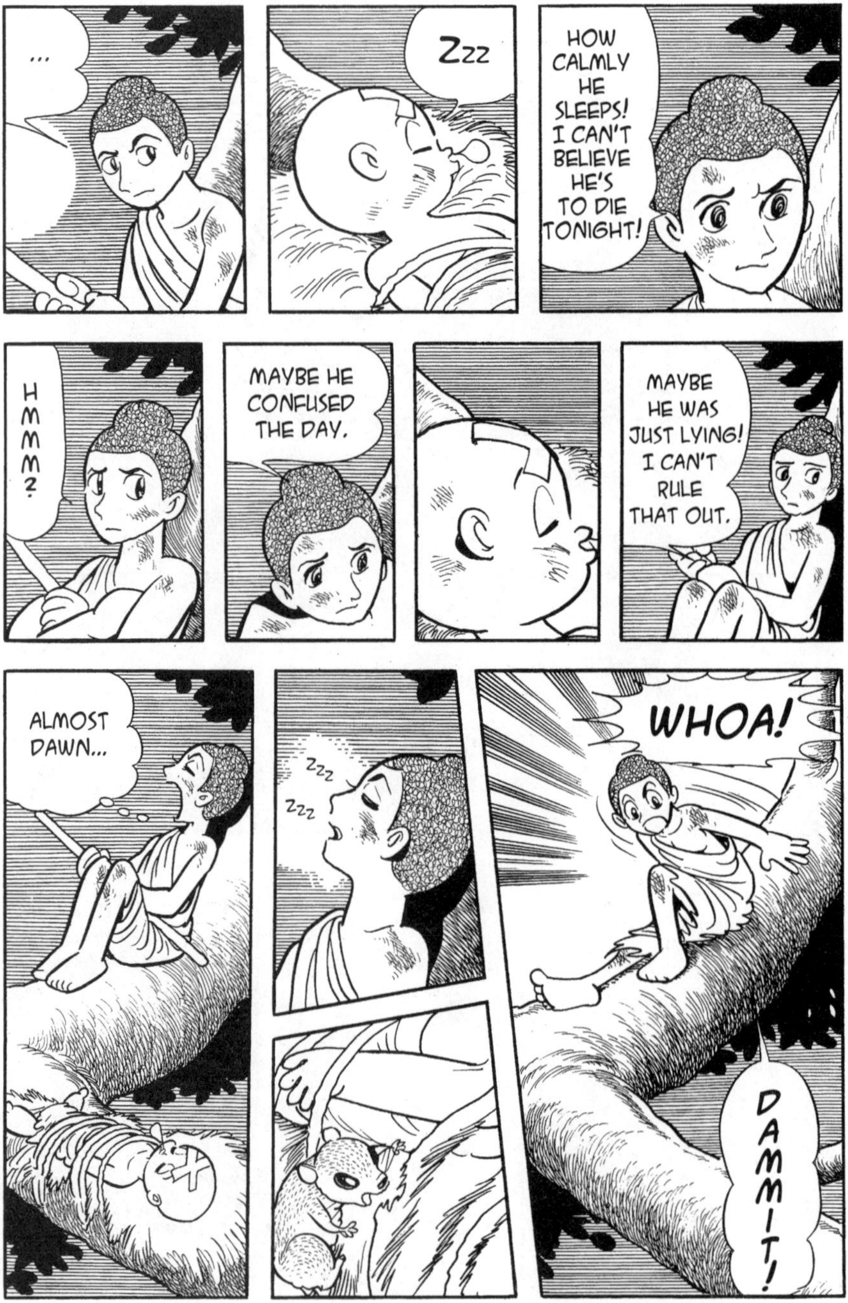
...
Zzz
HOW CALMLY HE SLEEPS! I CAN'T BELIEVE HE'S TO DIE TONIGHT!
HMMM?
MAYBE HE CONFUSED THE DAY.
MAYBE HE WAS JUST LYING! I CAN'T RULE THAT OUT.
ALMOST DAWN...
Zzz
Zzz
WHOA!
DAMMIT!

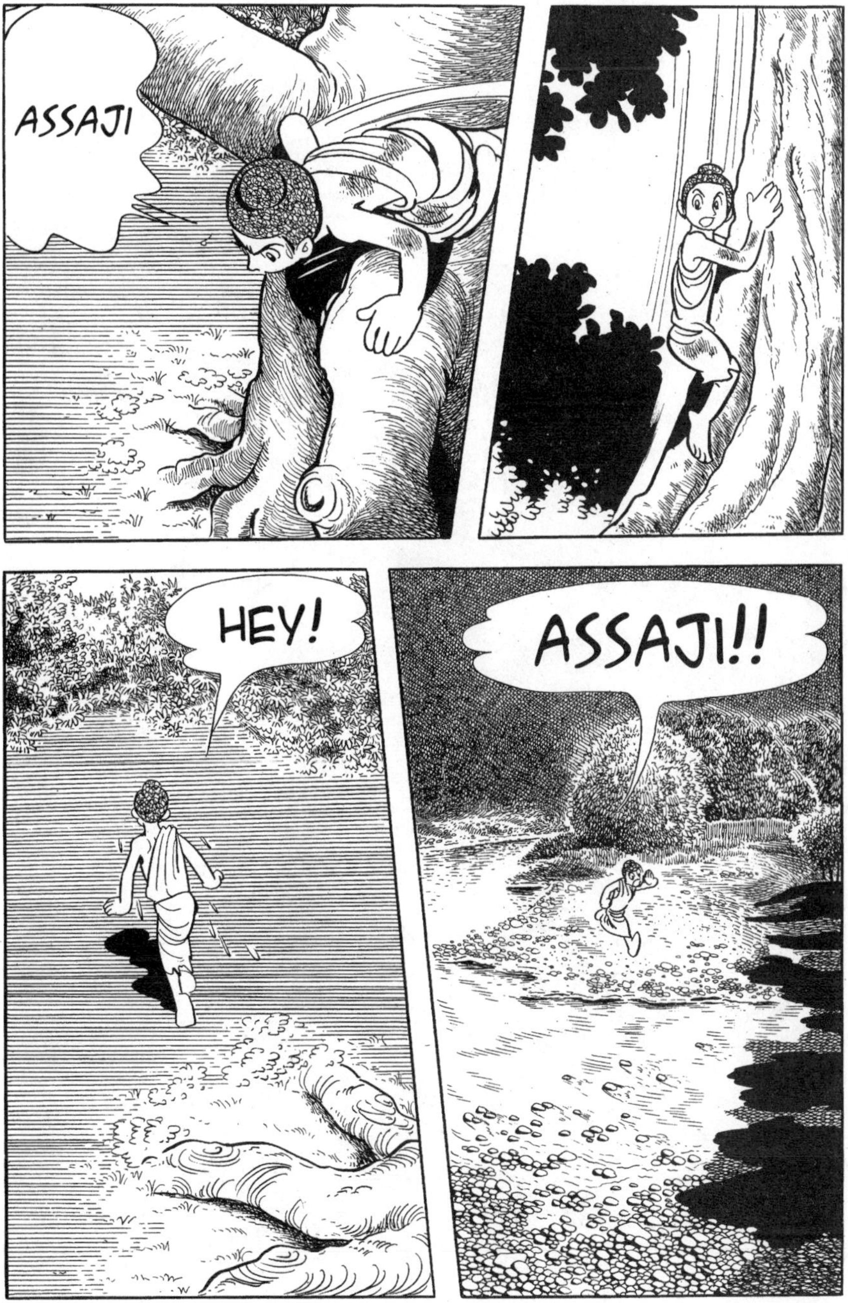
ASSAJI
HEY!
ASSAJI!!

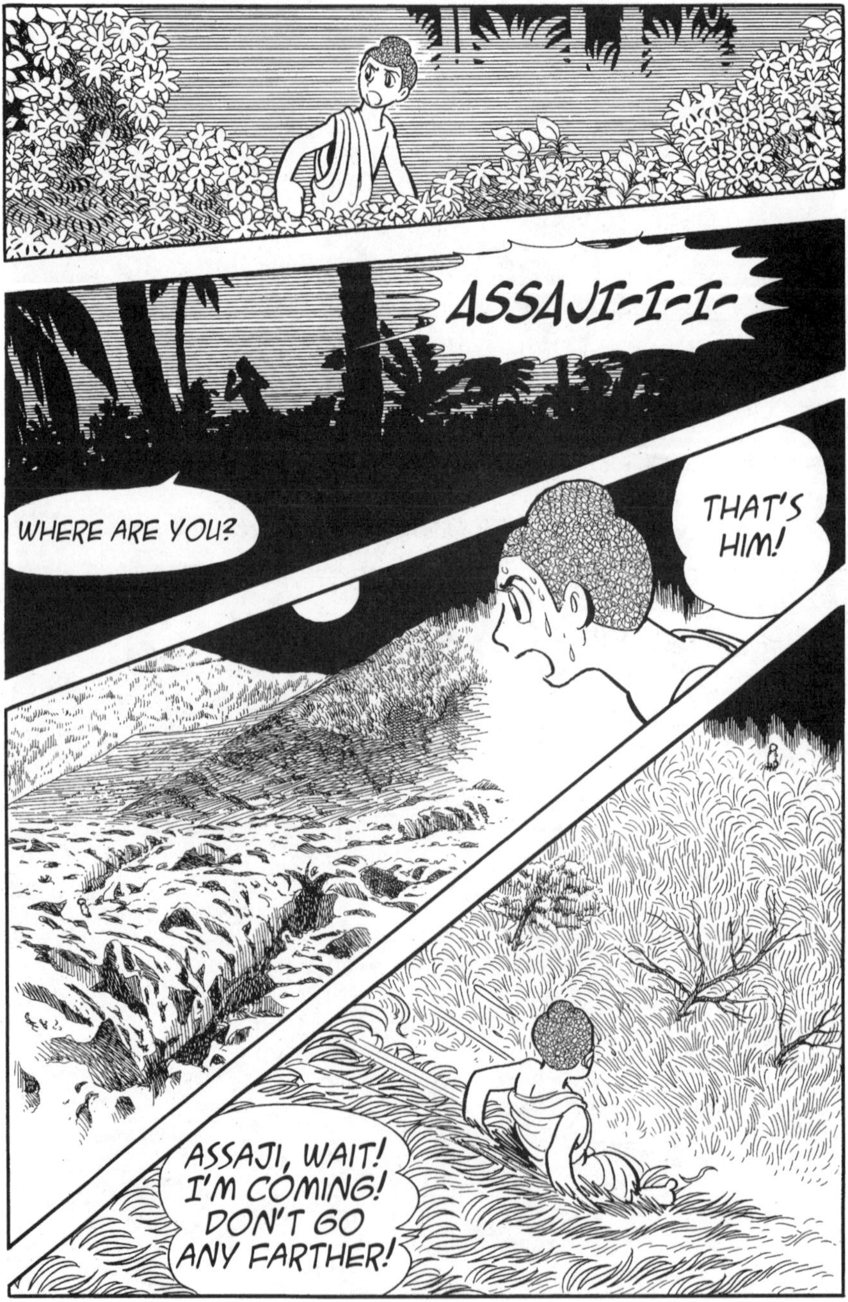
ASSAJI-I-I-
WHERE ARE YOU?
THAT'S HIM!
ASSAJI, WAIT! I'M COMING! DON'T GO ANY FARTHER!

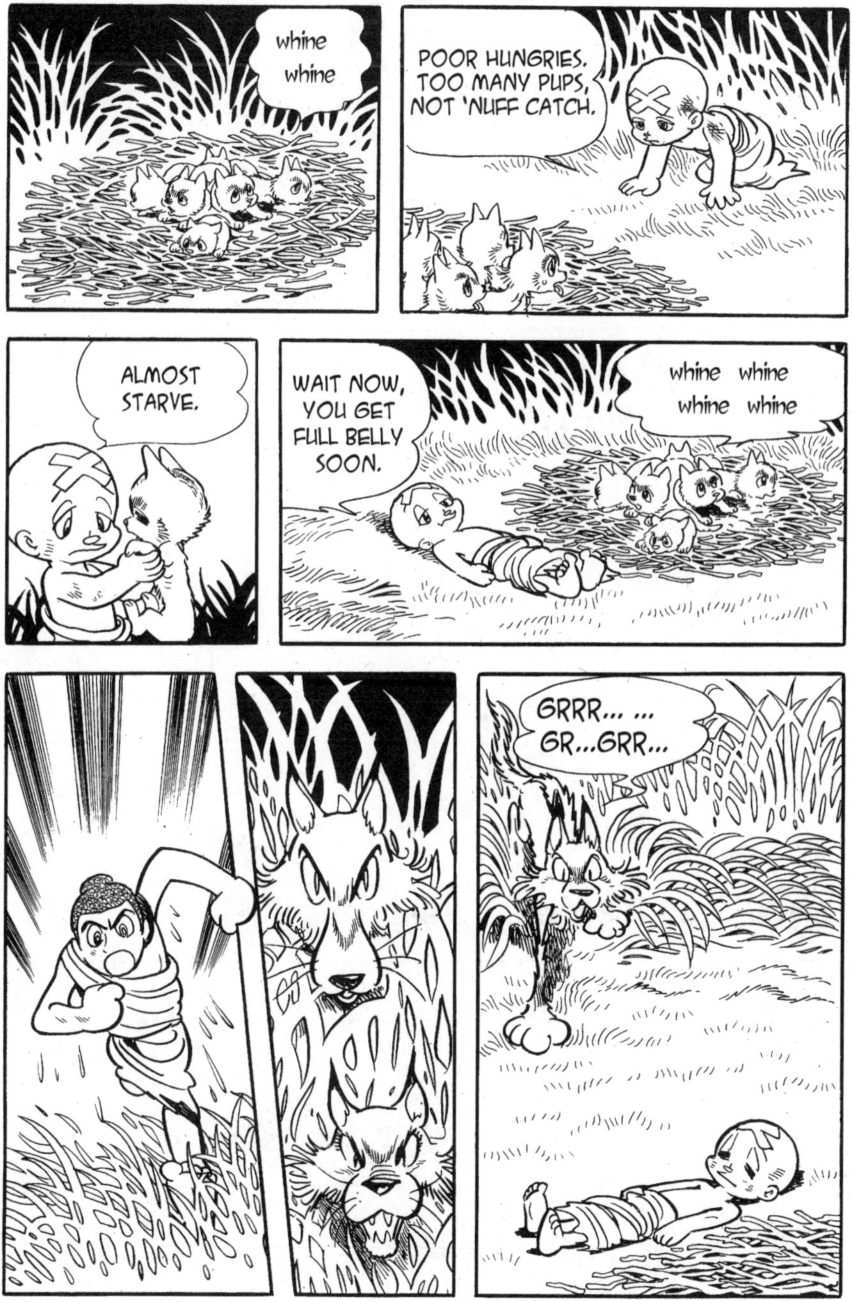
whine
whine
POOR HUNGRIES. TOO MANY PUPS, NOT 'NUFF CATCH.
ALMOST STARVE.
WAIT NOW, YOU GET FULL BELLY SOON.
whine whine whine whine
GRRR... ... GR...GRR...

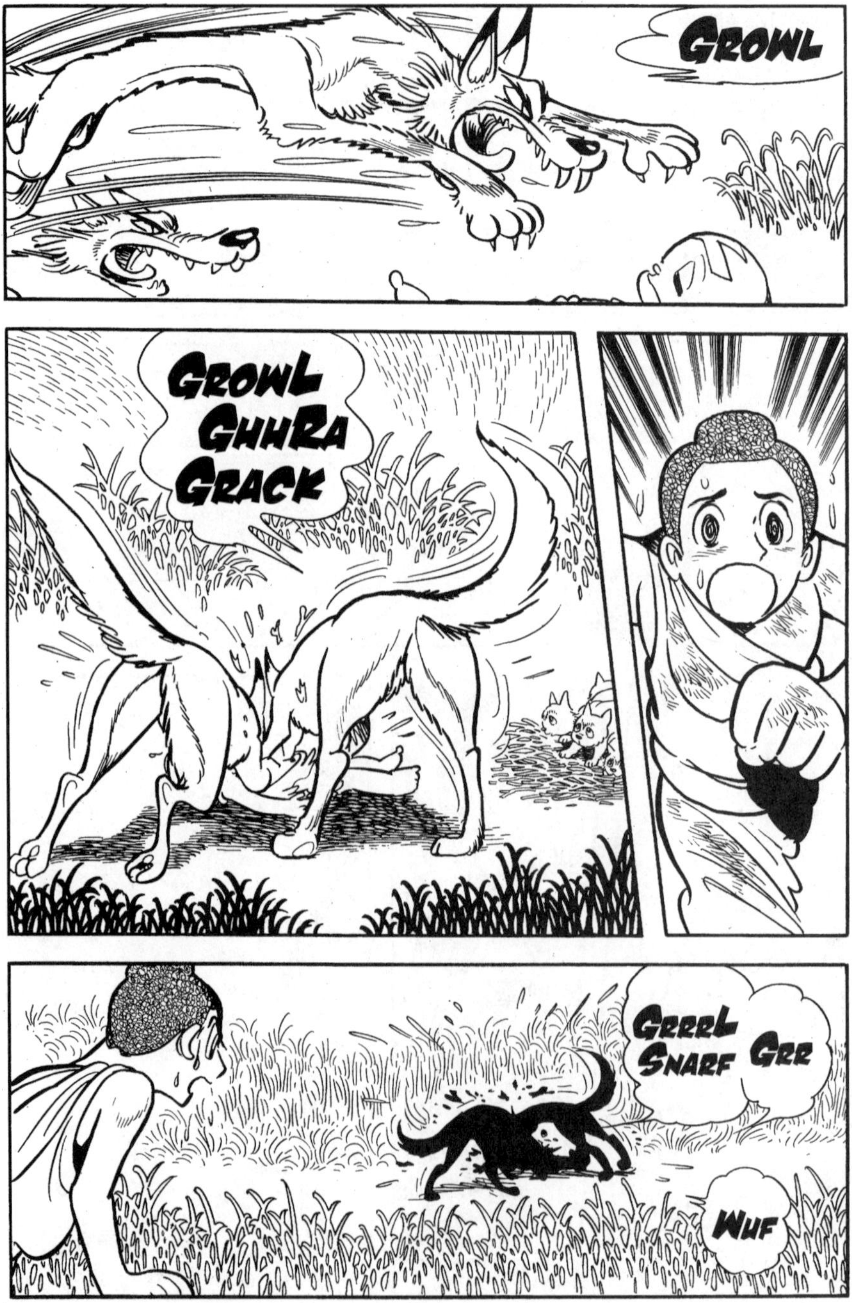
GROWL
GROWL GHHRA GRACK
GRRRL SNARF GRR
WUF

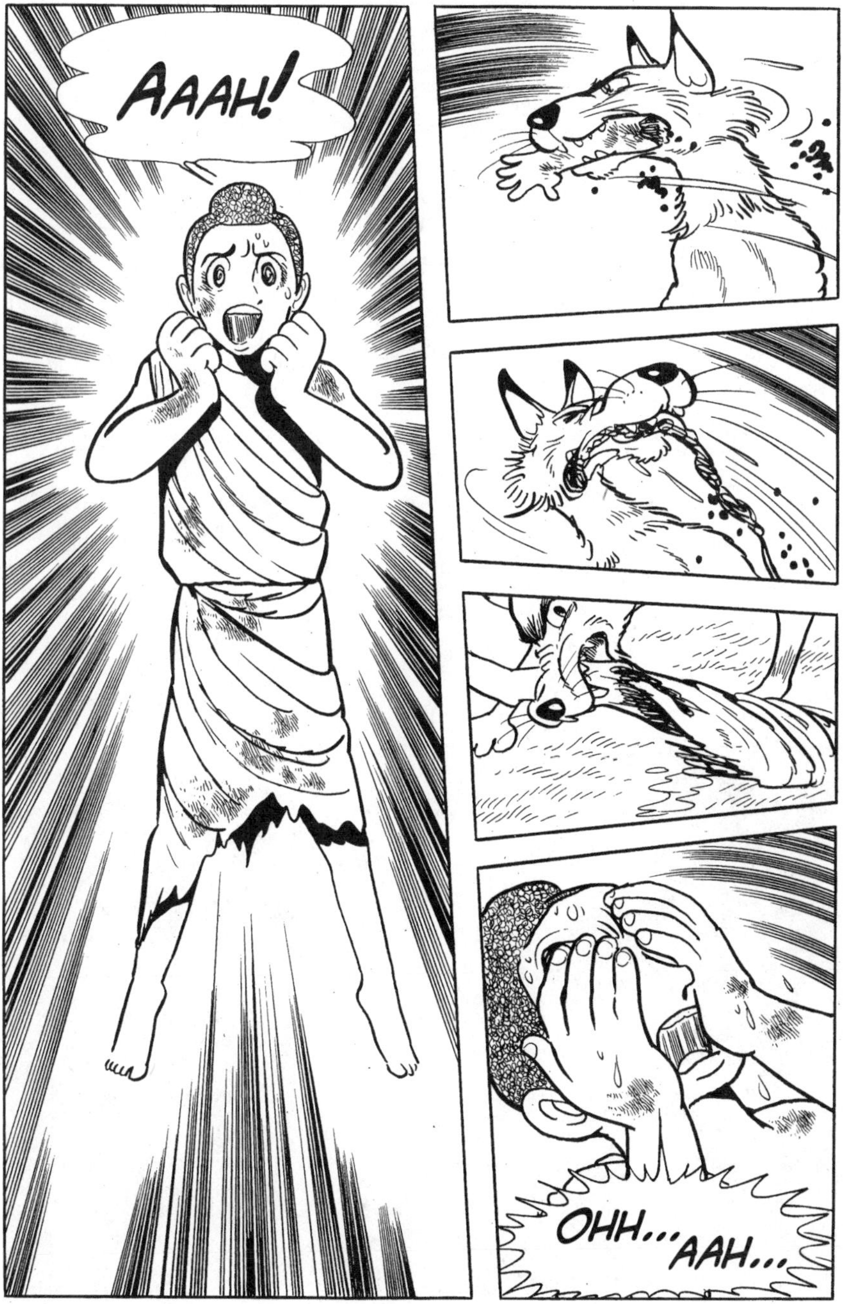
AAAH!
OHH... AAH...

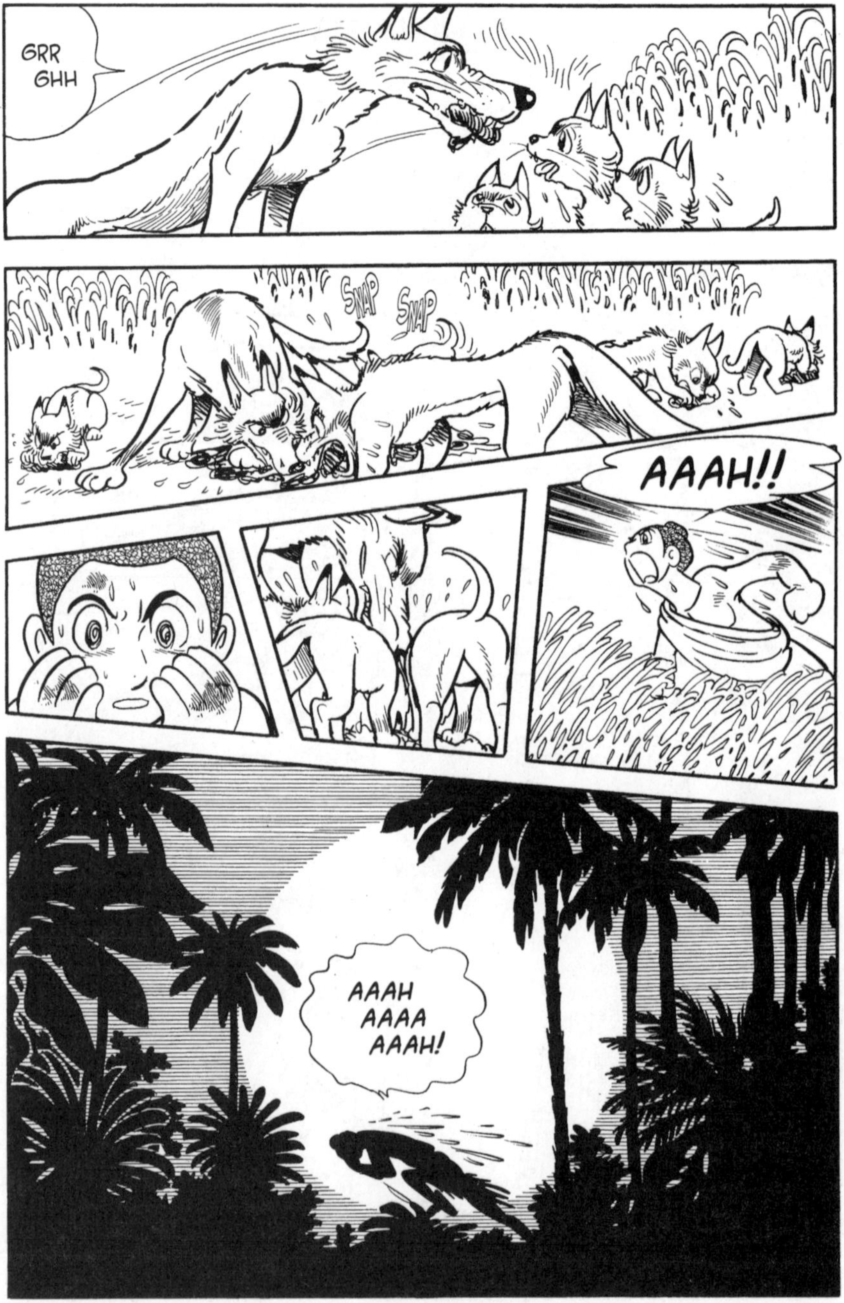
GRR GHH
SNAP
SNAP
AAAH!!
AAAH AAAA AAAH!

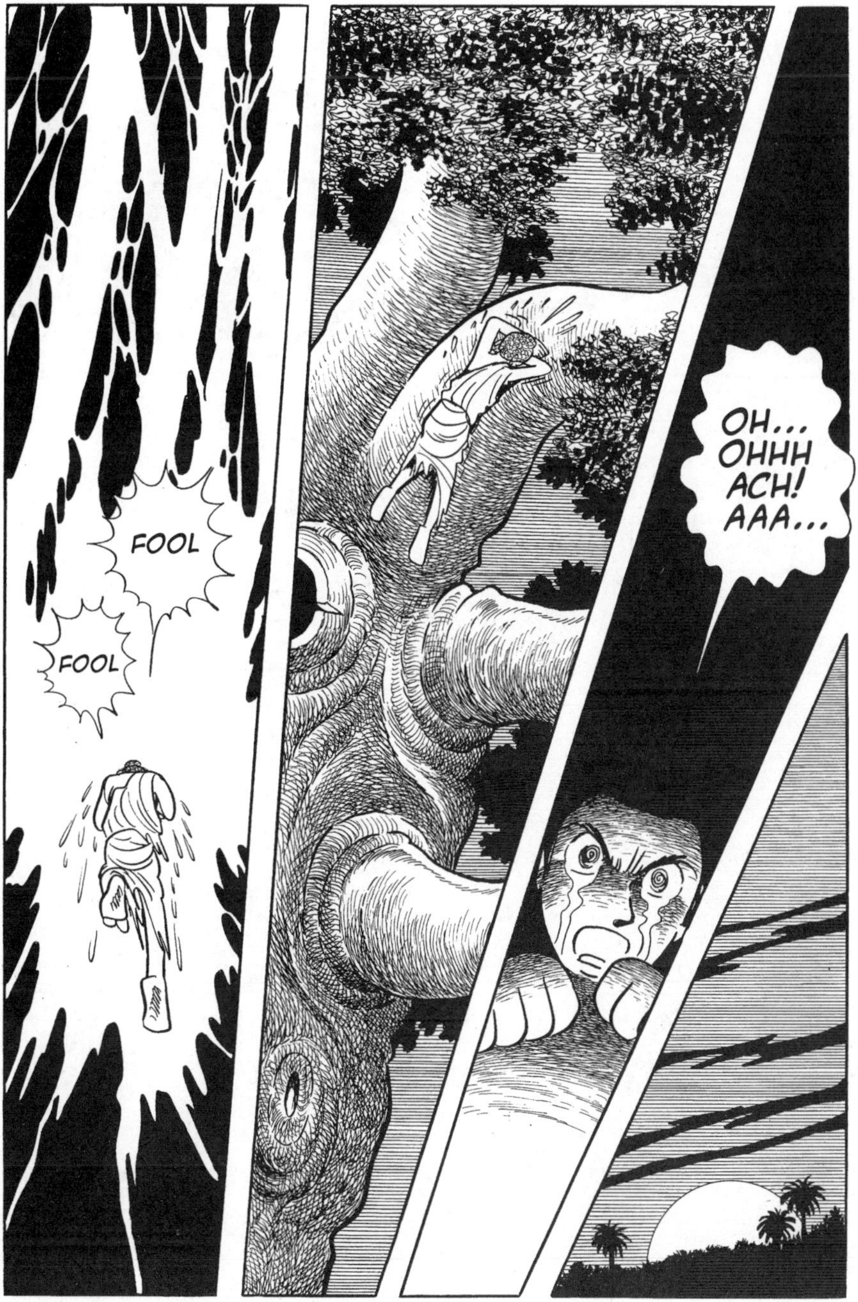
FOOL
FOOL
OH... OHHH ACH! AAA...

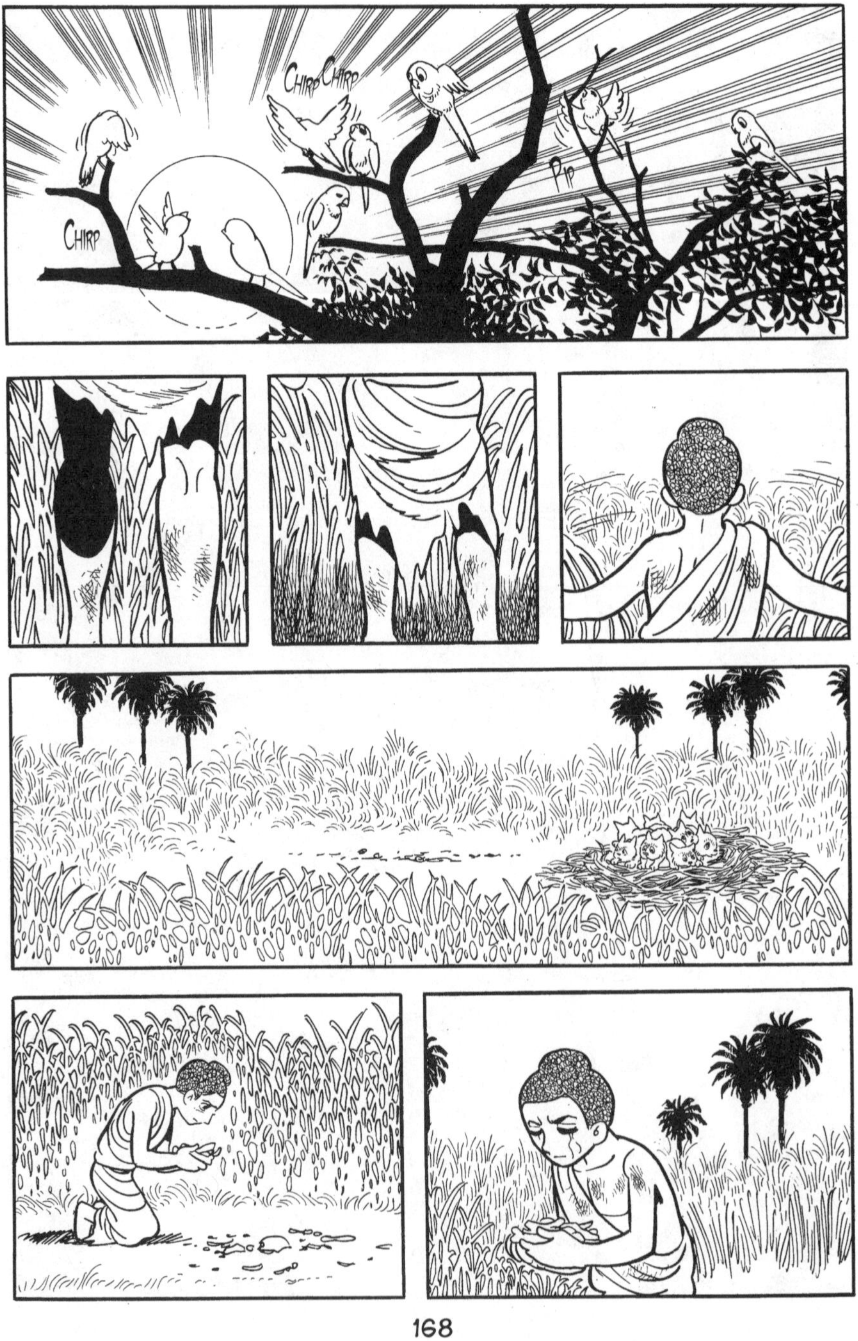
CHIRP CHIRP
CHIRP
PIP

CHAPTER NINE

SUJATA

FLOP
AGH
SIZZLE SIZZLE
OW! OH... SHIT!
PANT PANT

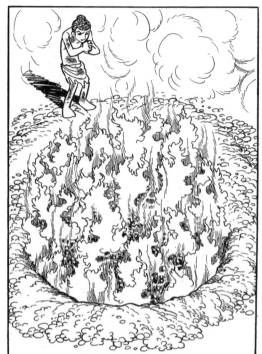

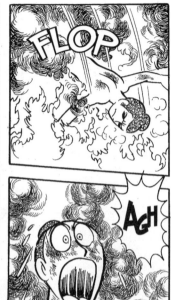

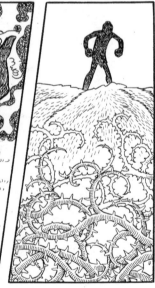

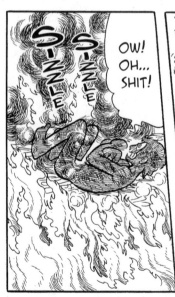

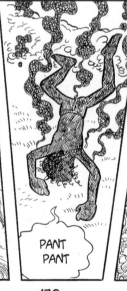

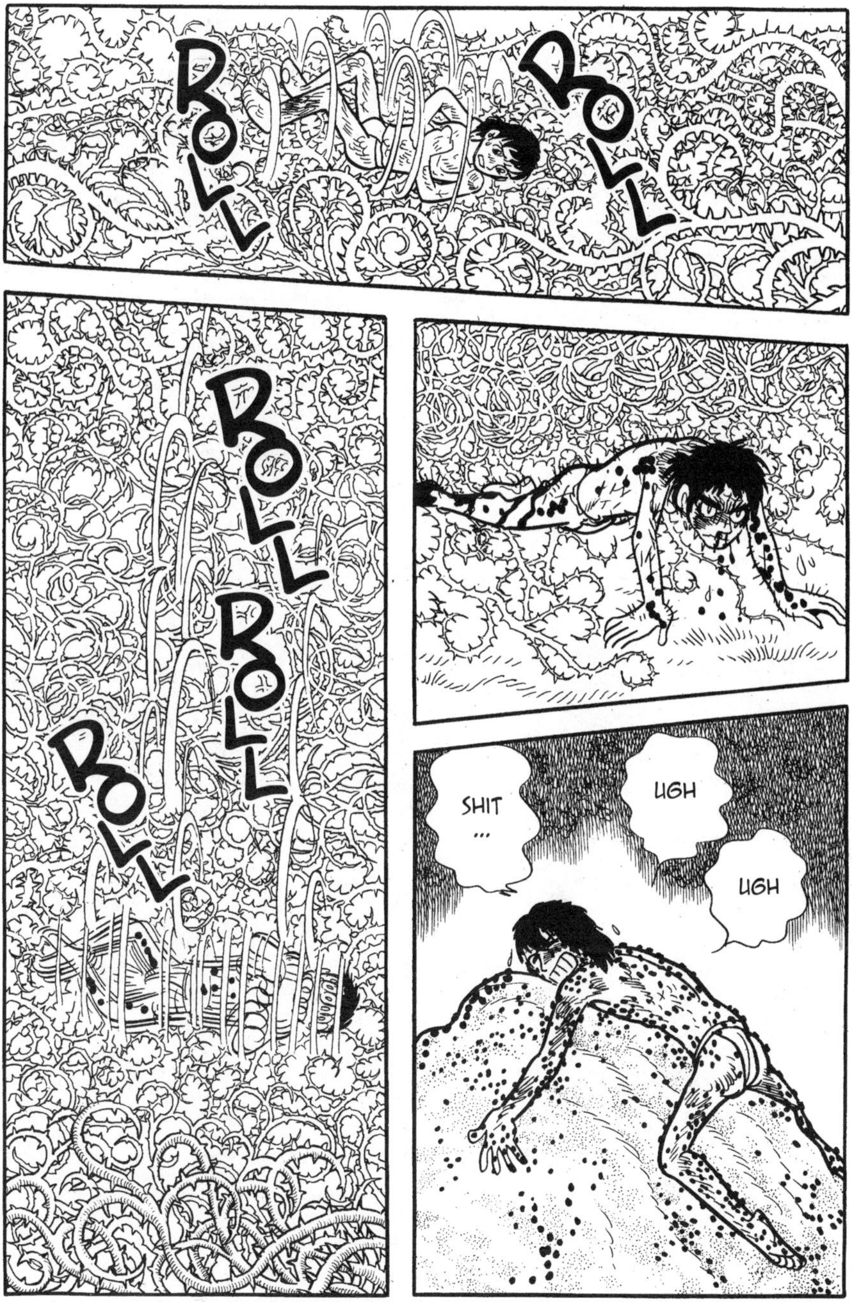
ROLL
ROLL
ROLL
ROLL
ROLL
SHIT ...
UGH
UGH

LOOK AT THAT FELLOW, HE'S EATING COW DUNG.

CRAZY BASTARD!

LET'S PELT HIM!

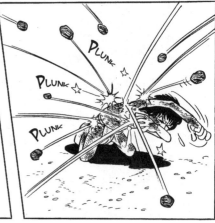

PLUNK

PLUNK

PLUNK

PLUNK

PLUNK

PLUNK

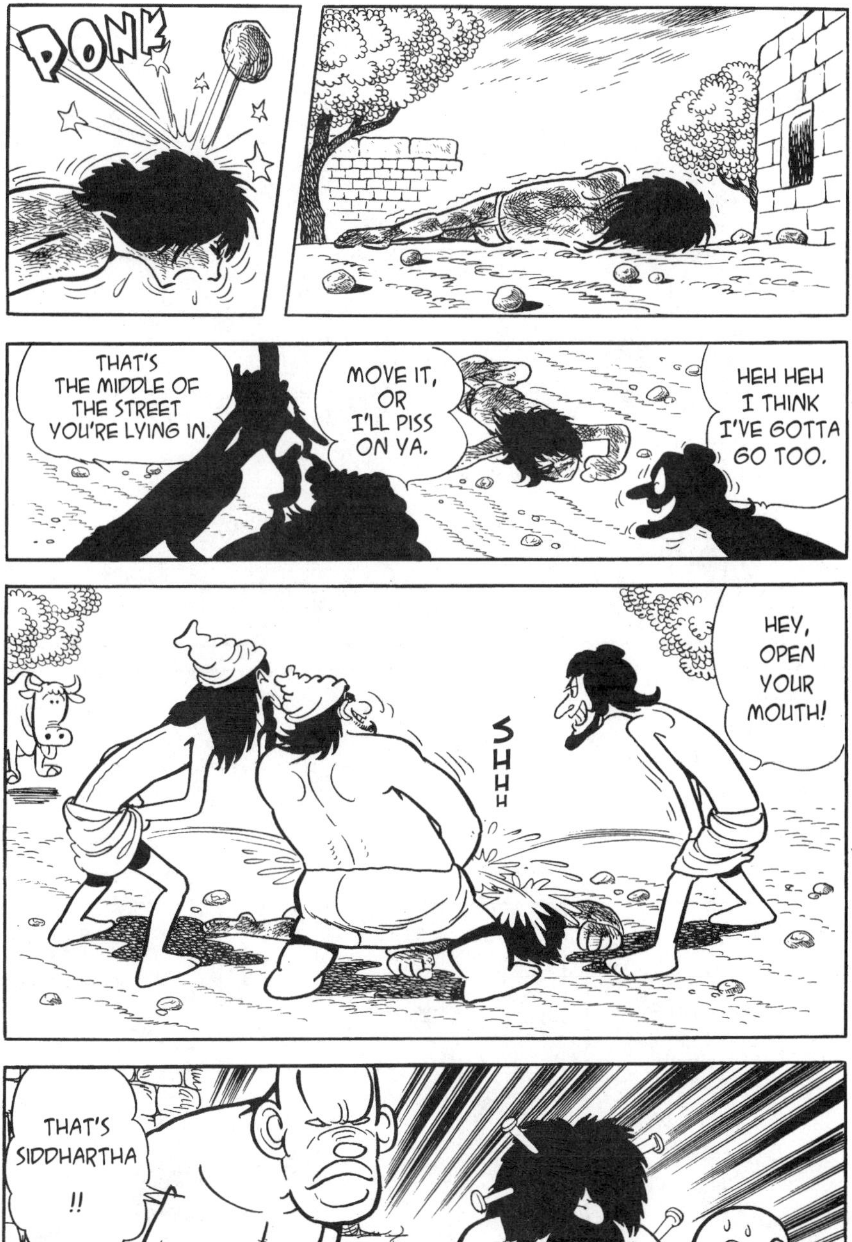
PONK
THAT'S THE MIDDLE OF THE STREET YOU'RE LYING IN.
MOVE IT, OR I'LL PISS ON YA.
HEH HEH I THINK I'VE GOTTA GO TOO.
HEY, OPEN YOUR MOUTH!
SHHH
THAT'S SIDDHARTHA !!

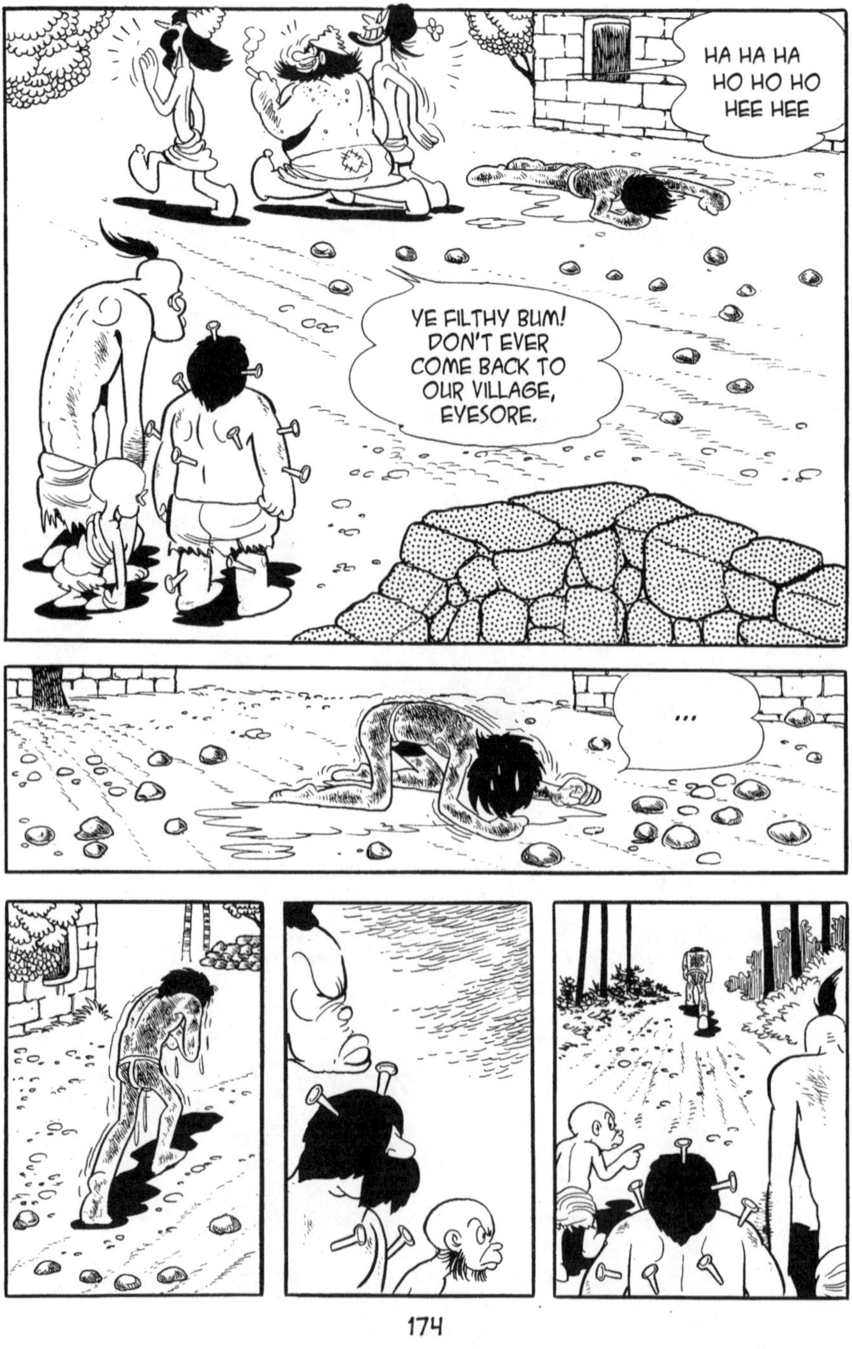
HA HA HA
HO HO HO
HEE HEE
YE FILTHY BUM! DON'T EVER COME BACK TO OUR VILLAGE, EYESORE.
...

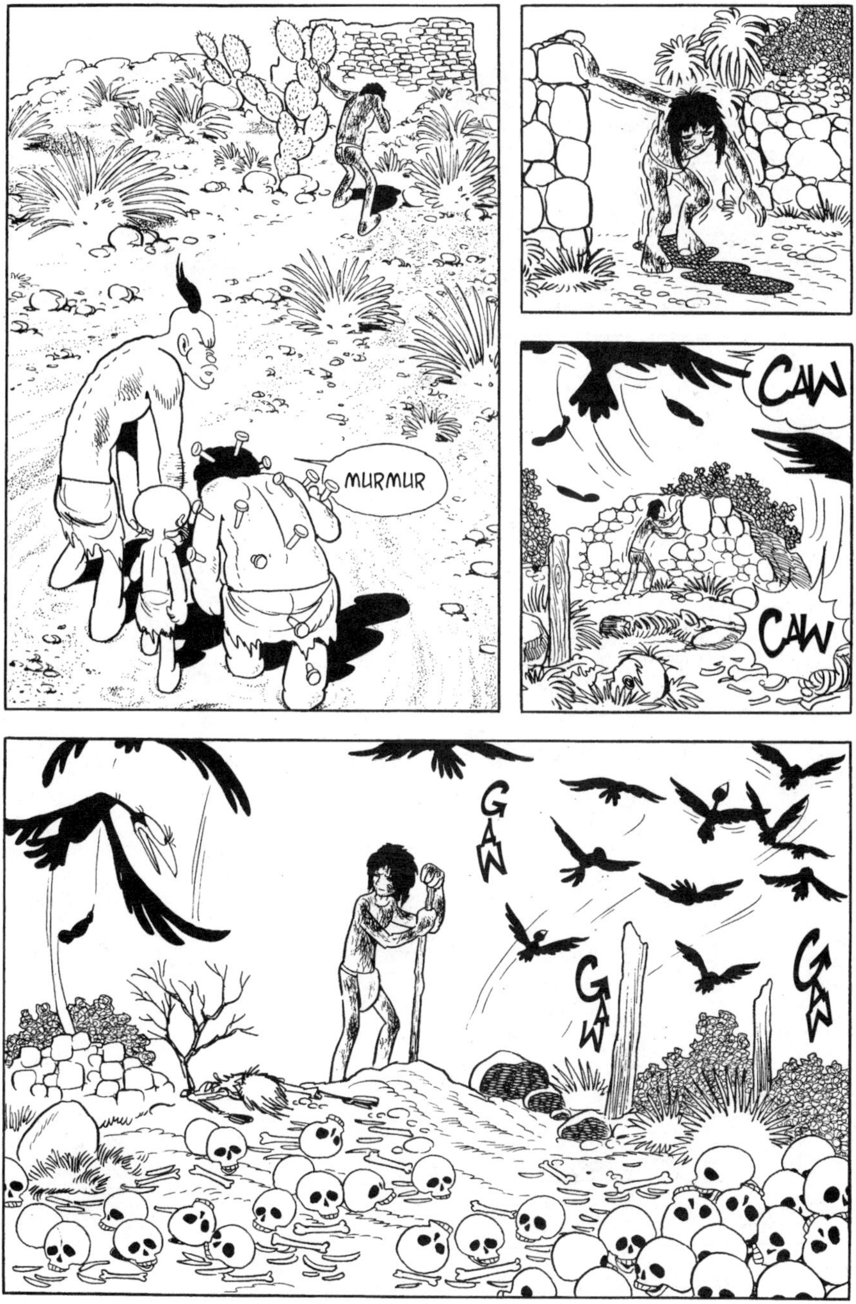
MURMUR
CAW
CAW
GAW
GAW
GAW

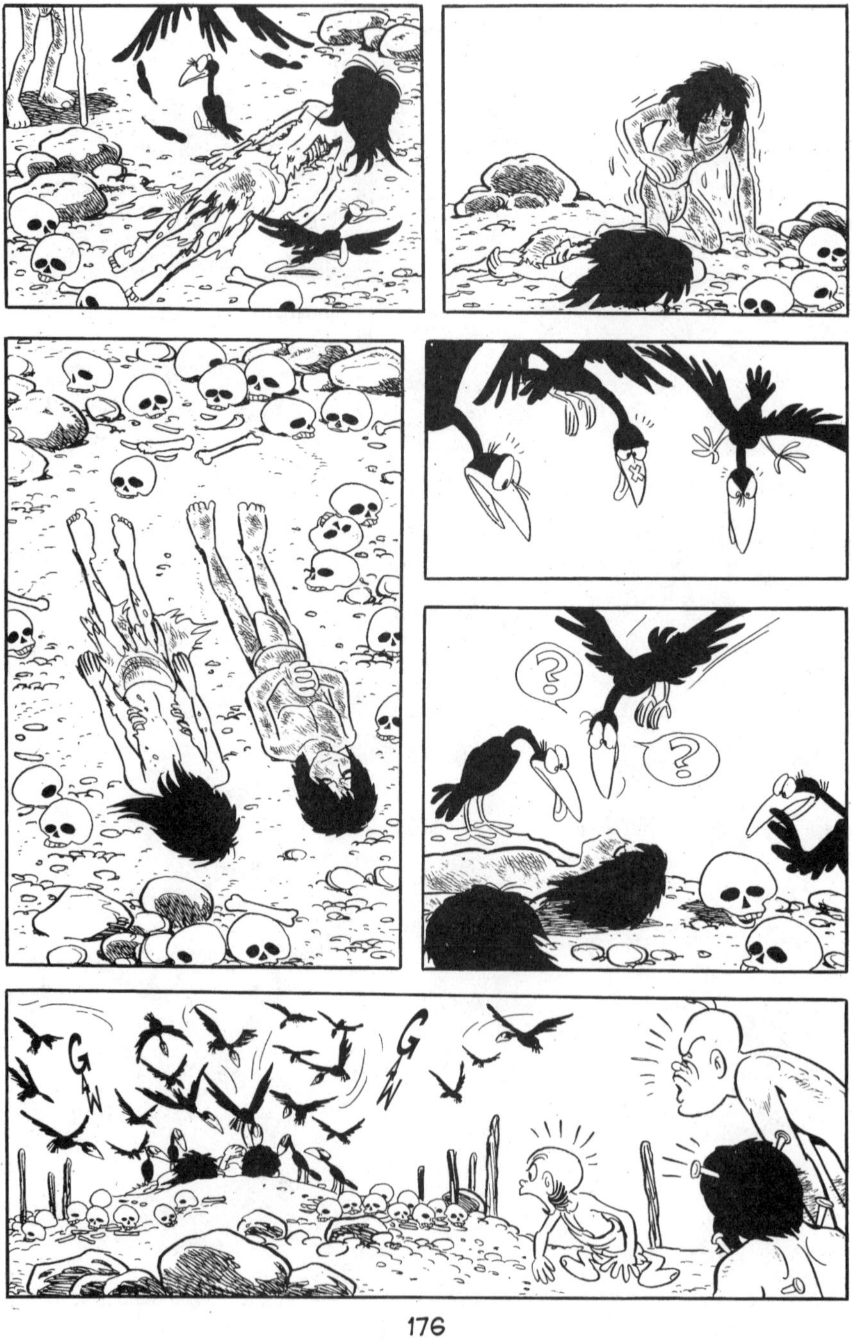
?
?
GAW
G

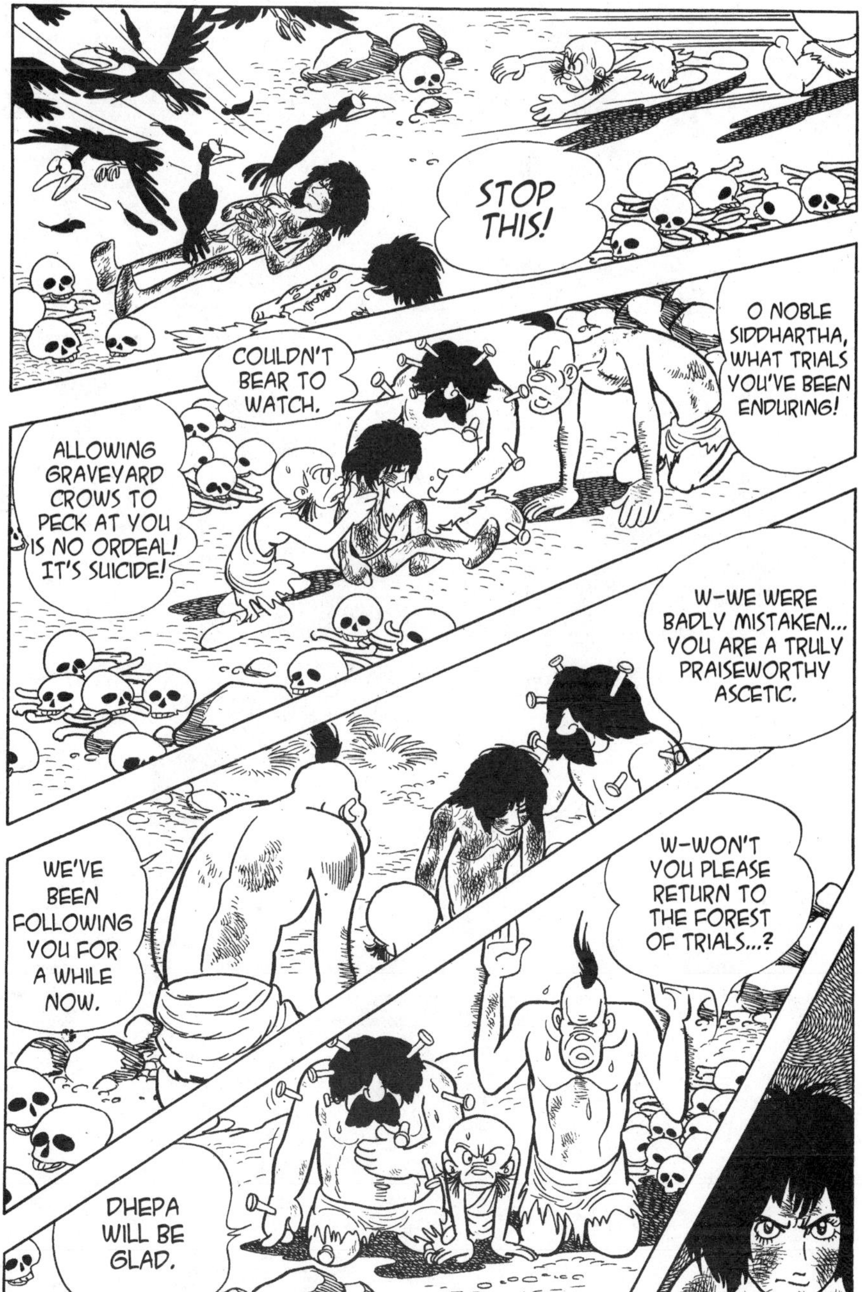
STOP THIS!
COULDN'T BEAR TO WATCH.
O NOBLE SIDDHARTHA, WHAT TRIALS YOU'VE BEEN ENDURING!
ALLOWING GRAVEYARD CROWS TO PECK AT YOU IS NO ORDEAL! IT'S SUICIDE!
W-WE WERE BADLY MISTAKEN... YOU ARE A TRULY PRAISEWORTHY ASCETIC.
WE'VE BEEN FOLLOWING YOU FOR A WHILE NOW.
W-WON'T YOU PLEASE RETURN TO THE FOREST OF TRIALS...?
DHEPA WILL BE GLAD.

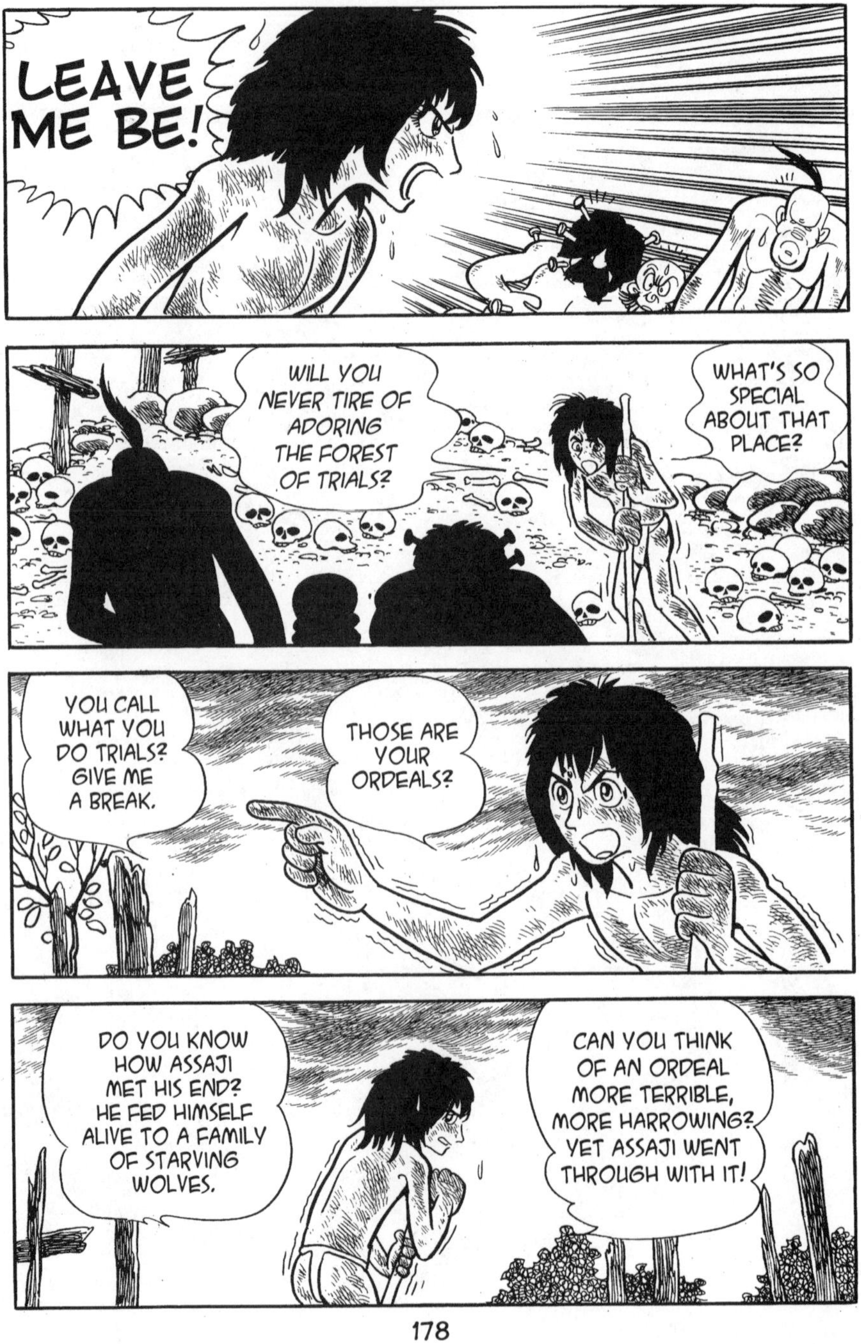
LEAVE ME BE!
WILL YOU NEVER TIRE OF ADORING THE FOREST OF TRIALS?
WHAT'S SO SPECIAL ABOUT THAT PLACE?
YOU CALL WHAT YOU DO TRIALS? GIVE ME A BREAK.
THOSE ARE YOUR ORDEALS?
DO YOU KNOW HOW ASSAJI MET HIS END? HE FED HIMSELF ALIVE TO A FAMILY OF STARVING WOLVES.
CAN YOU THINK OF AN ORDEAL MORE TERRIBLE, MORE HARROWING? YET ASSAJI WENT THROUGH WITH IT!

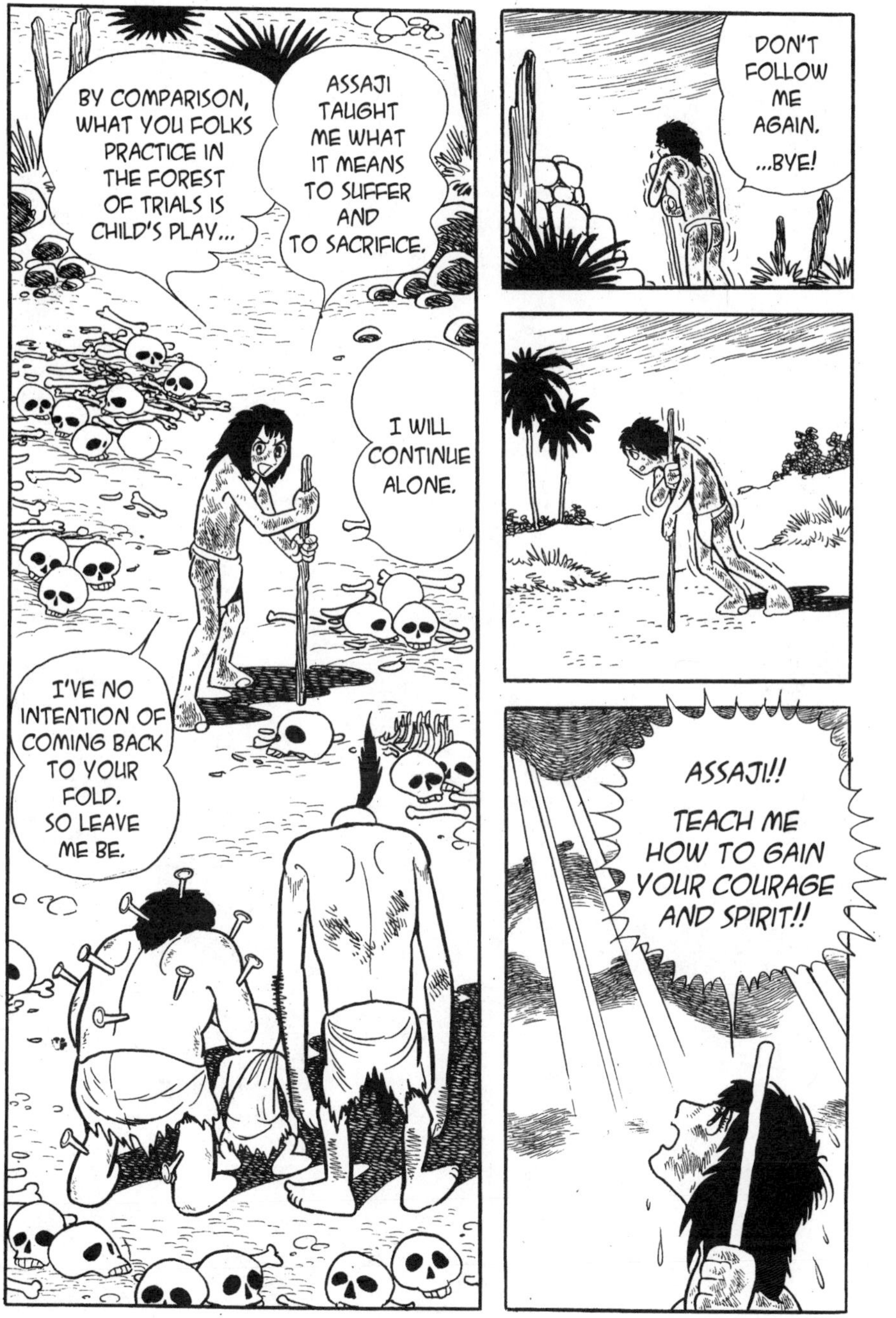
BY COMPARISON, WHAT YOU FOLKS PRACTICE IN THE FOREST OF TRIALS IS CHILD'S PLAY...
ASSAJI TAUGHT ME WHAT IT MEANS TO SUFFER AND TO SACRIFICE.
I WILL CONTINUE ALONE.
I'VE NO INTENTION OF COMING BACK TO YOUR FOLD. SO LEAVE ME BE.
DON'T FOLLOW ME AGAIN.
...BYE!
ASSAJI!!
TEACH ME HOW TO GAIN YOUR COURAGE AND SPIRIT!!

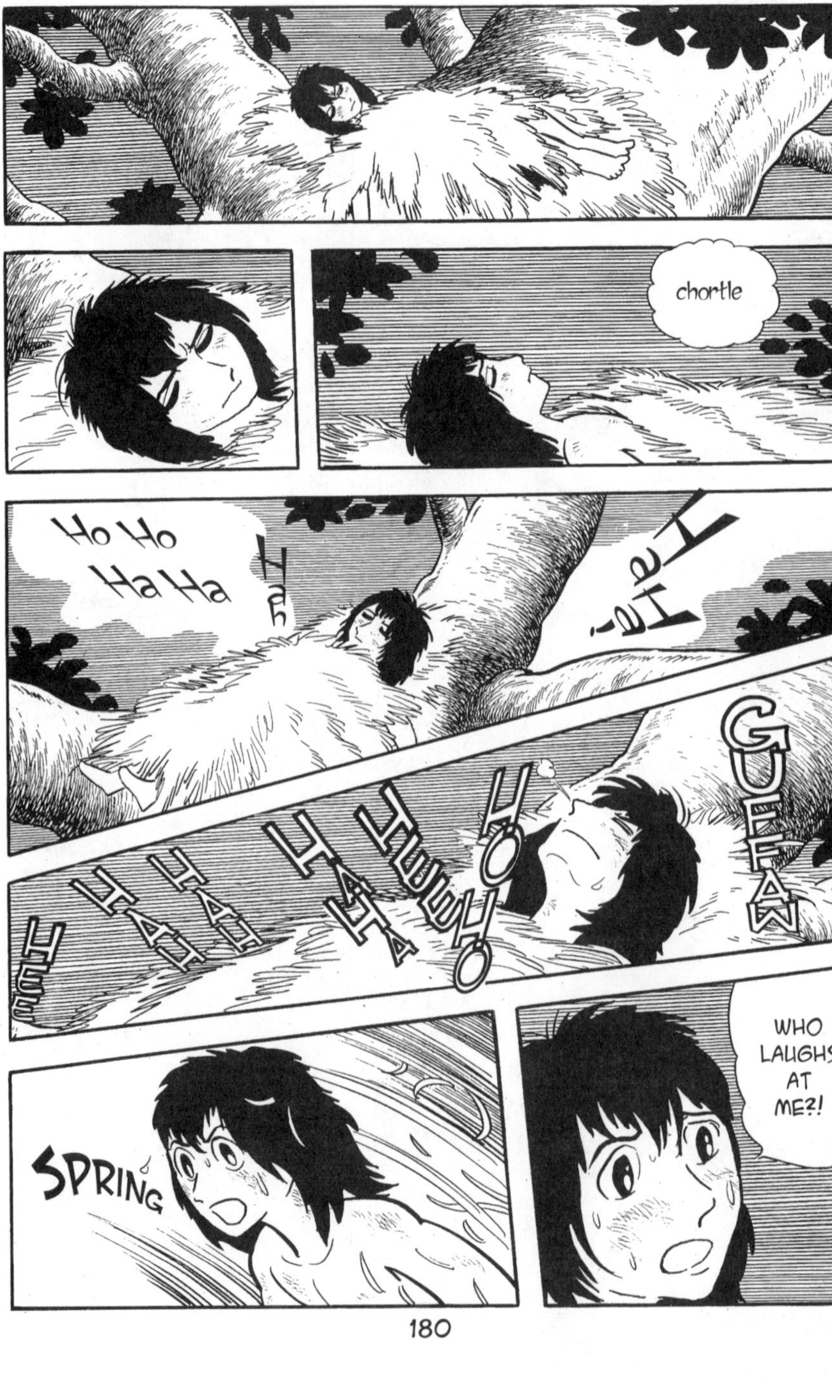
chortle
Ho Ho
Ha Ha
Hah
HaHa!
GUFFAW
SPRING
WHO LAUGHS AT ME?!

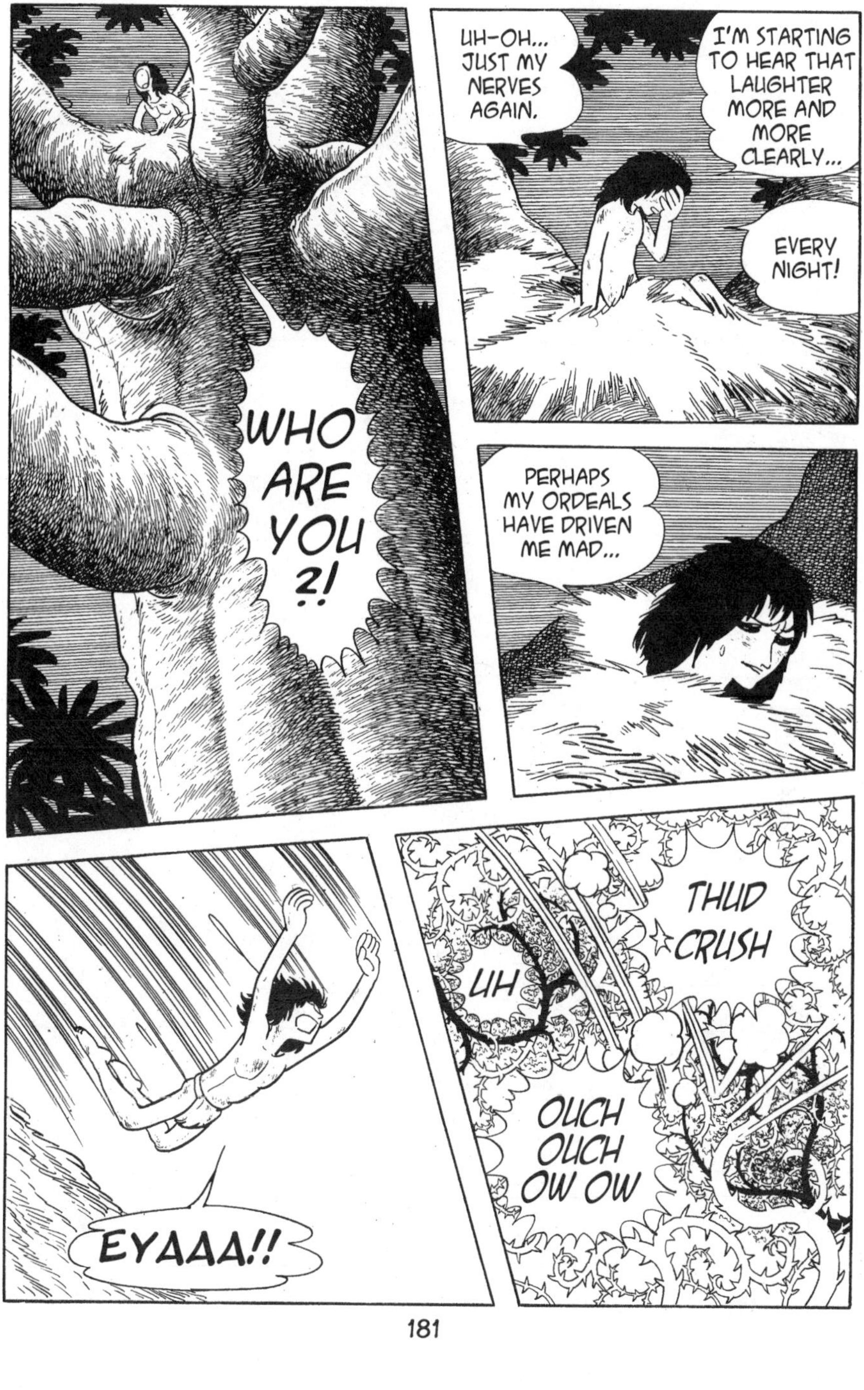
WHO ARE YOU ?!
UH-OH... JUST MY NERVES AGAIN.
I'M STARTING TO HEAR THAT LAUGHTER MORE AND MORE CLEARLY...
EVERY NIGHT!
PERHAPS MY ORDEALS HAVE DRIVEN ME MAD...
EYAAA!!
THUD CRUSH
UH
OUCH OUCH OW OW

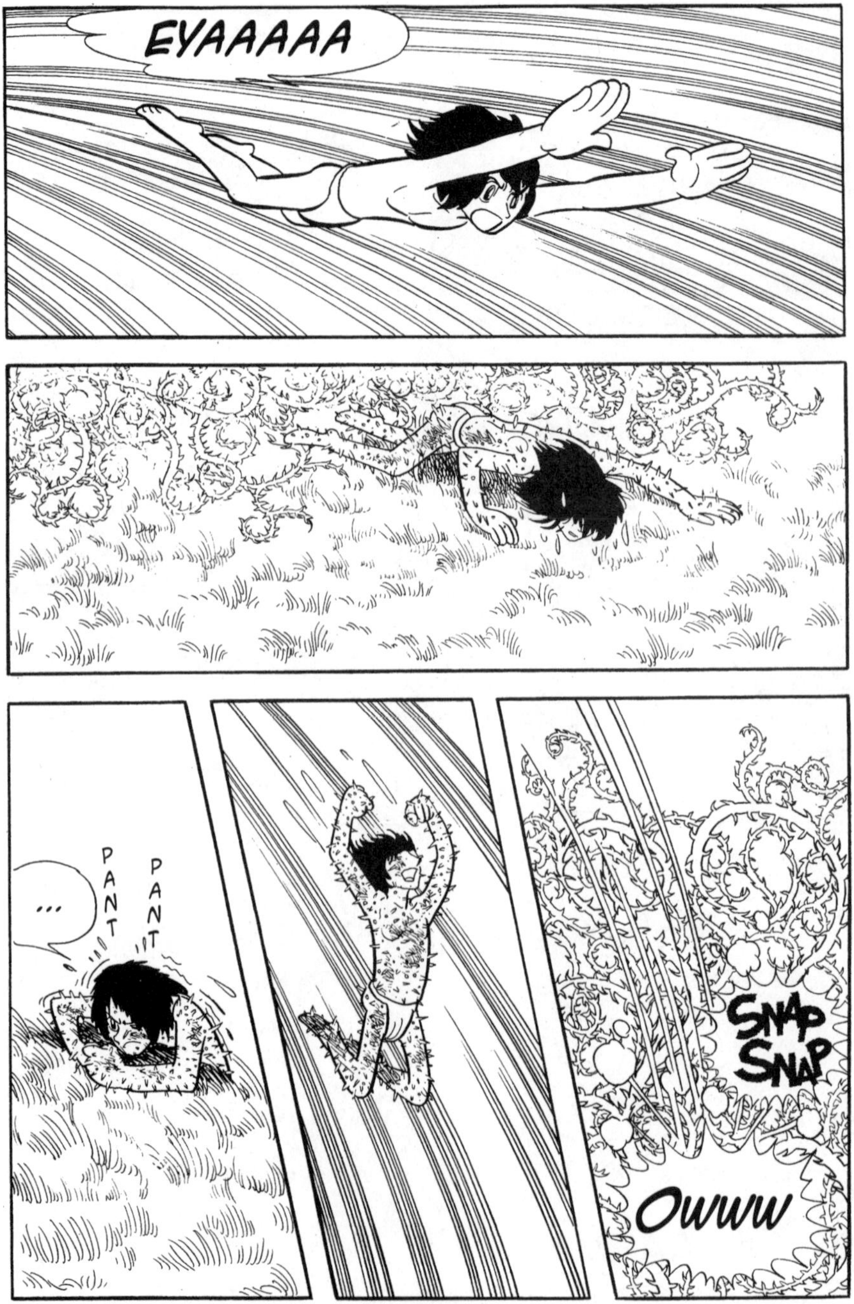

EYAAAAA
...
PANT
PANT
SNAP
SNAP
Owww

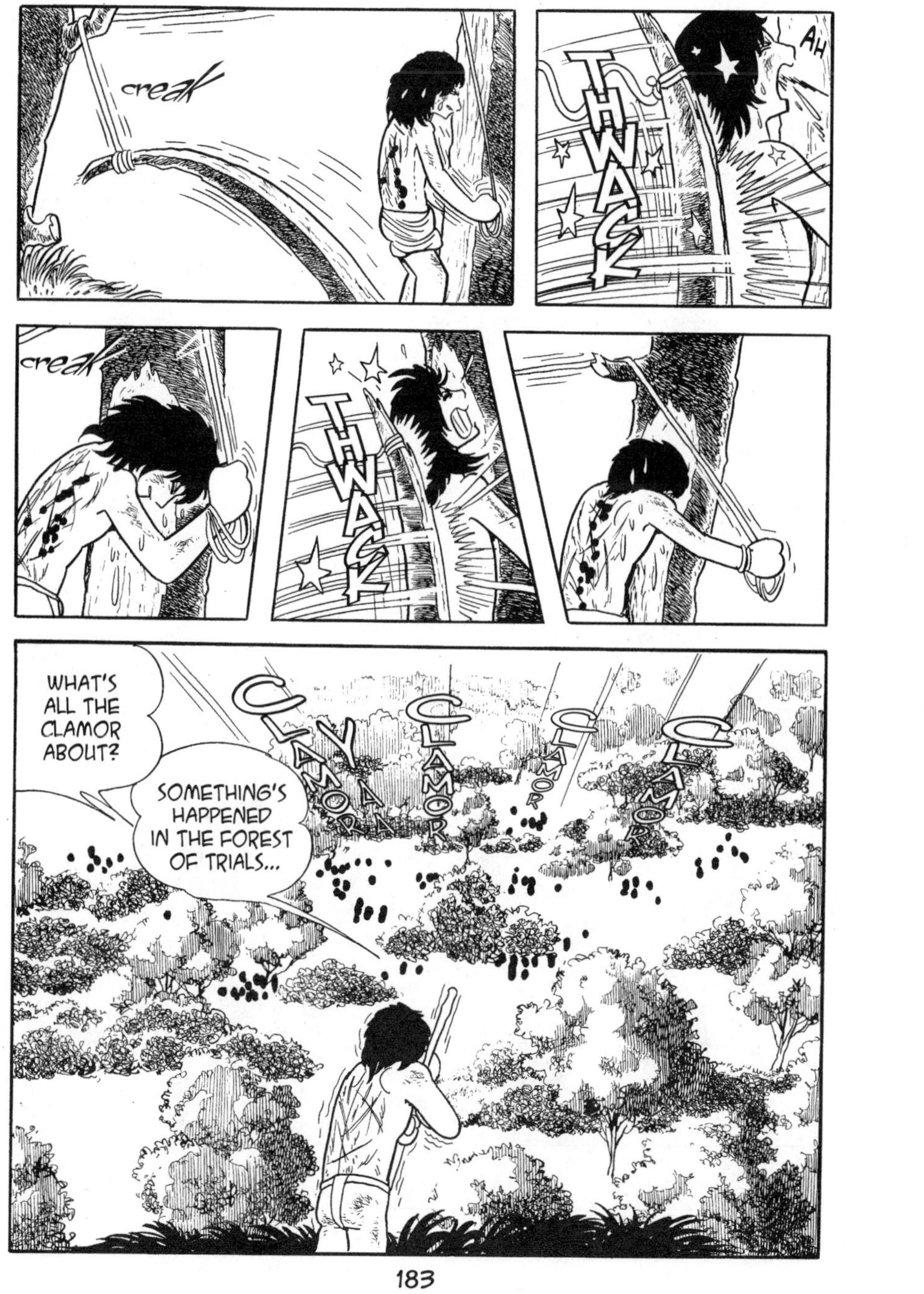
creak
THWACK
AH
creak
THWACK
WHAT'S ALL THE CLAMOR ABOUT?
CLAMOR
YAAA
CLAMOR
CLAMOR
CLAMOR
SOMETHING'S HAPPENED IN THE FOREST OF TRIALS...

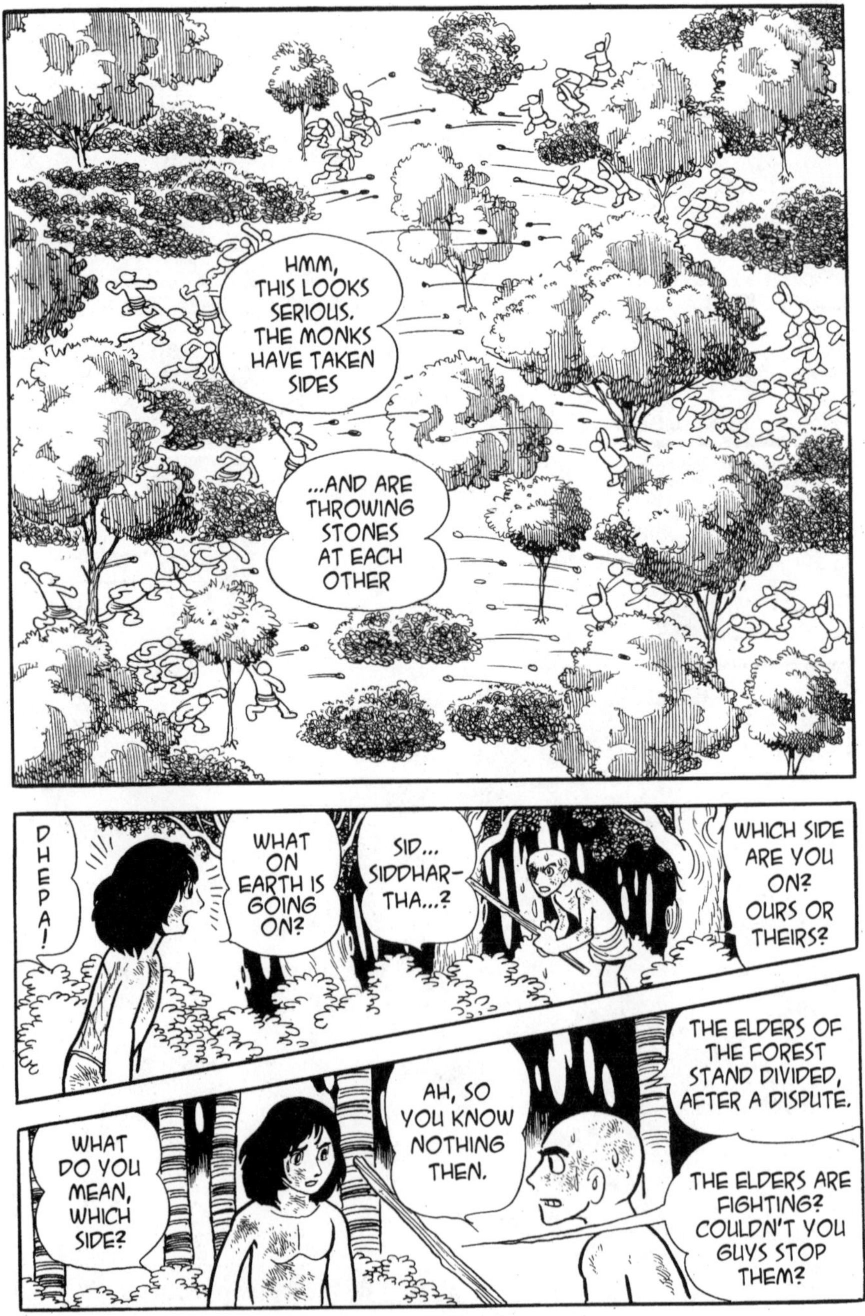
HMM, THIS LOOKS SERIOUS. THE MONKS HAVE TAKEN SIDES
...AND ARE THROWING STONES AT EACH OTHER
DHEPA!
WHAT ON EARTH IS GOING ON?
SID... SIDDHARTHA...?
WHICH SIDE ARE YOU ON? OURS OR THEIRS?
WHAT DO YOU MEAN, WHICH SIDE?
AH, SO YOU KNOW NOTHING THEN.
THE ELDERS OF THE FOREST STAND DIVIDED, AFTER A DISPUTE.
THE ELDERS ARE FIGHTING? COULDN'T YOU GUYS STOP THEM?

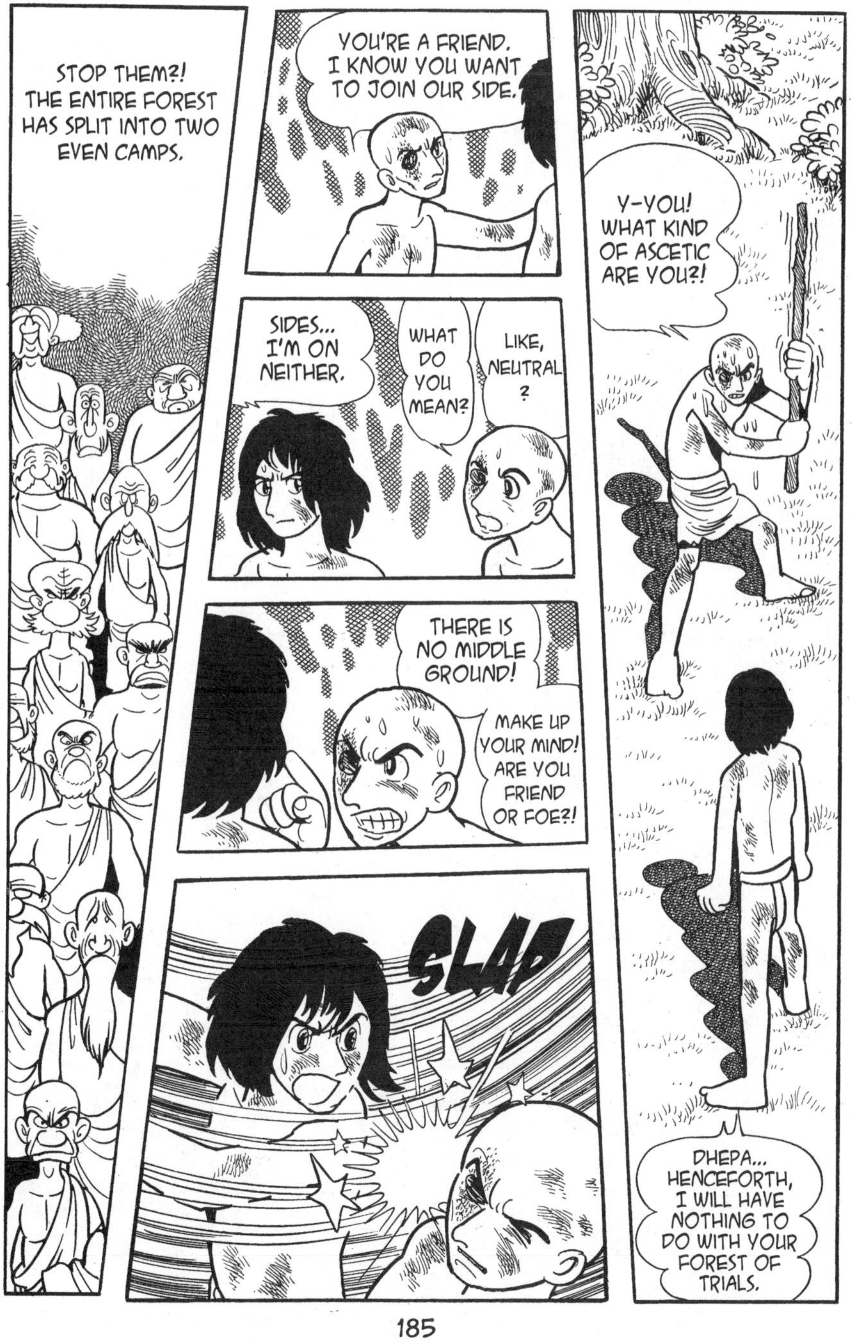
STOP THEM?! THE ENTIRE FOREST HAS SPLIT INTO TWO EVEN CAMPS.
YOU'RE A FRIEND. I KNOW YOU WANT TO JOIN OUR SIDE.
SIDES... I'M ON NEITHER.
WHAT DO YOU MEAN?
LIKE, NEUTRAL?
THERE IS NO MIDDLE GROUND!
MAKE UP YOUR MIND! ARE YOU FRIEND OR FOE?!
SLAP
Y-YOU! WHAT KIND OF ASCETIC ARE YOU?!
DHEPA... HENCEFORTH, I WILL HAVE NOTHING TO DO WITH YOUR FOREST OF TRIALS.

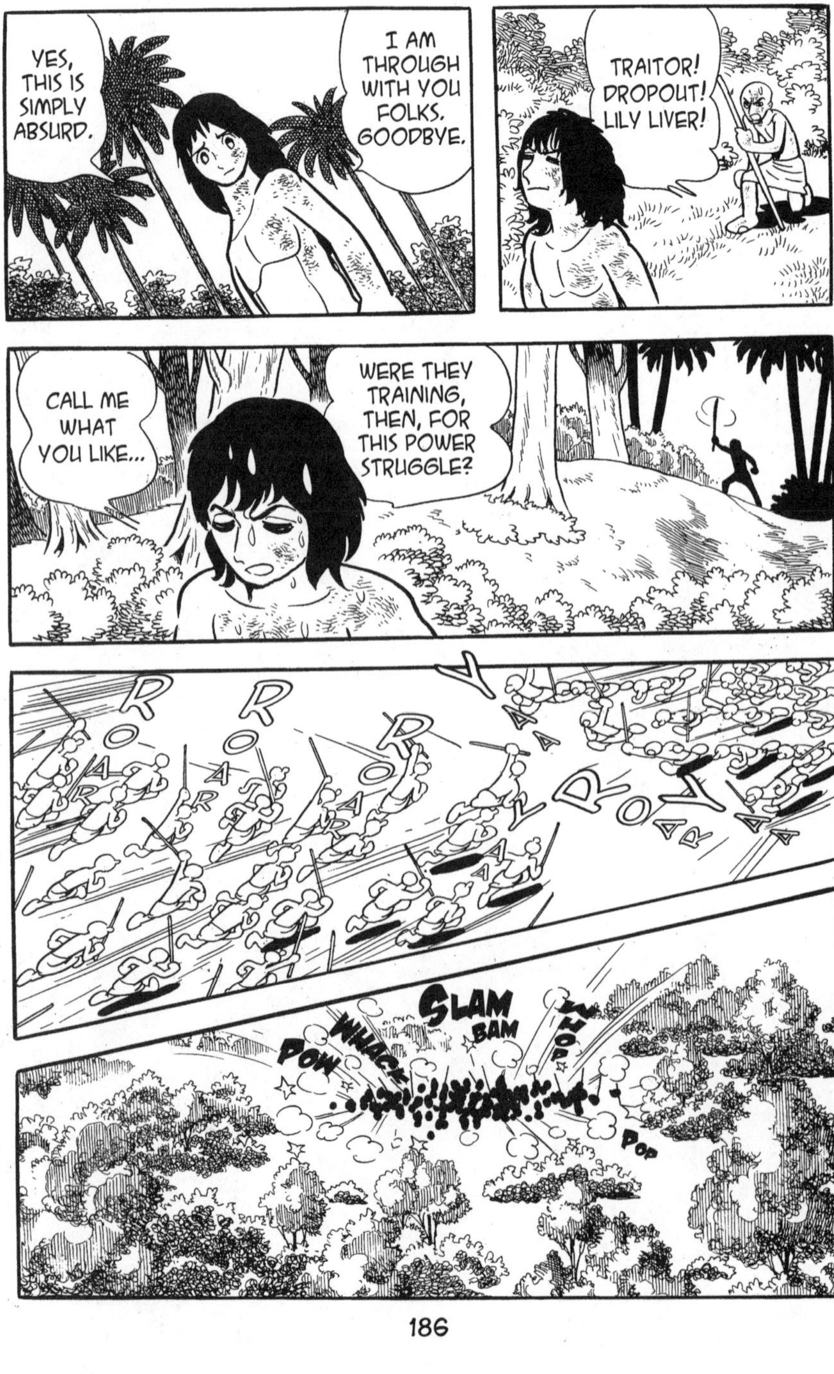
YES, THIS IS SIMPLY ABSURD.
I AM THROUGH WITH YOU FOLKS. GOODBYE.
TRAITOR! DROPOUT! LILY LIVER!
CALL ME WHAT YOU LIKE...
WERE THEY TRAINING, THEN, FOR THIS POWER STRUGGLE?
POW
WHACK
SLAM
BAM
WHOP
POP

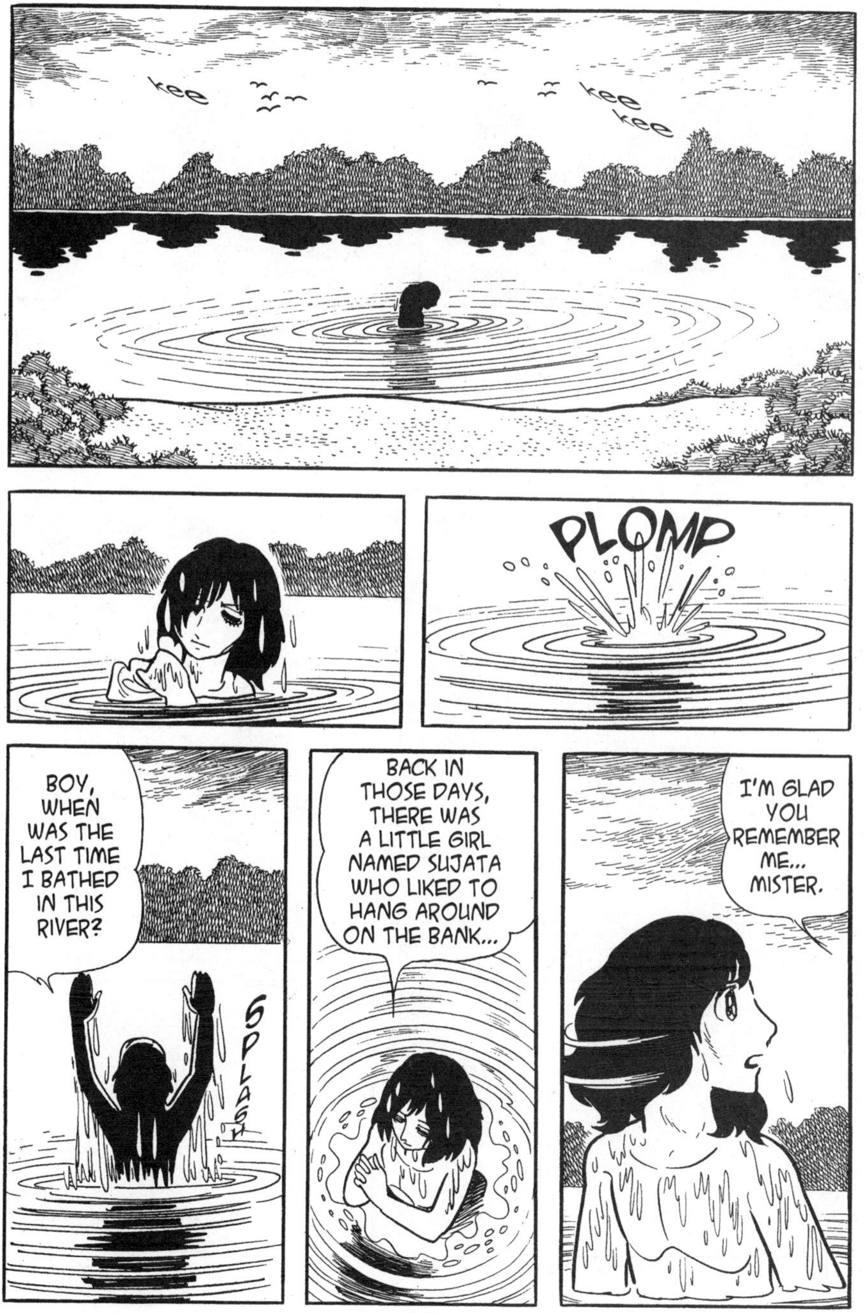
kee
kee
kee
PLOMP
BOY, WHEN WAS THE LAST TIME I BATHED IN THIS RIVER?
SPLASH
BACK IN THOSE DAYS, THERE WAS A LITTLE GIRL NAMED SUJATA WHO LIKED TO HANG AROUND ON THE BANK...
I'M GLAD YOU REMEMBER ME... MISTER.

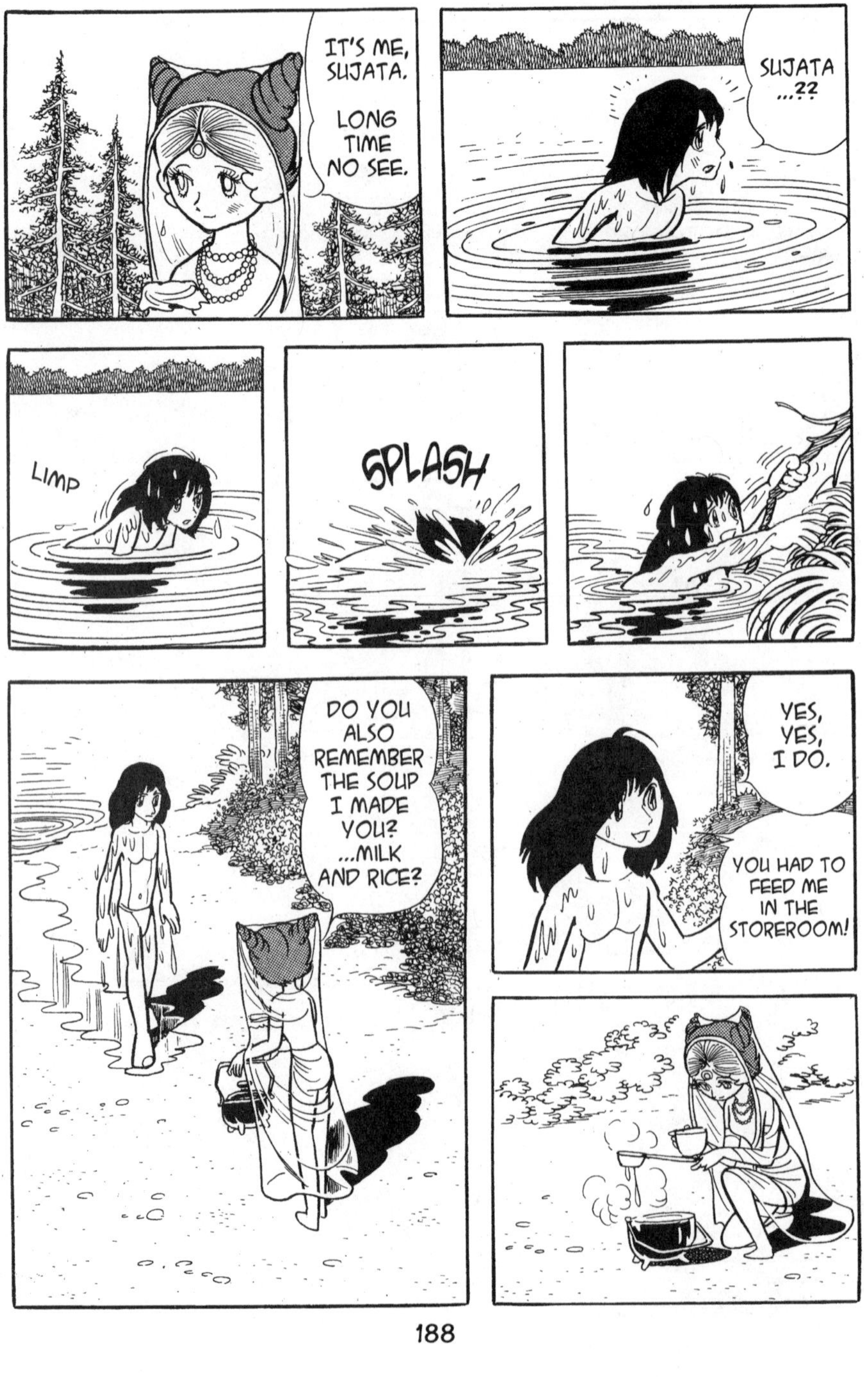
IT'S ME, SUJATA.
LONG TIME NO SEE.
SUJATA ...??
LIMP
SPLASH
DO YOU ALSO REMEMBER THE SOUP I MADE YOU? ...MILK AND RICE?
YES, YES, I DO.
YOU HAD TO FEED ME IN THE STOREROOM!

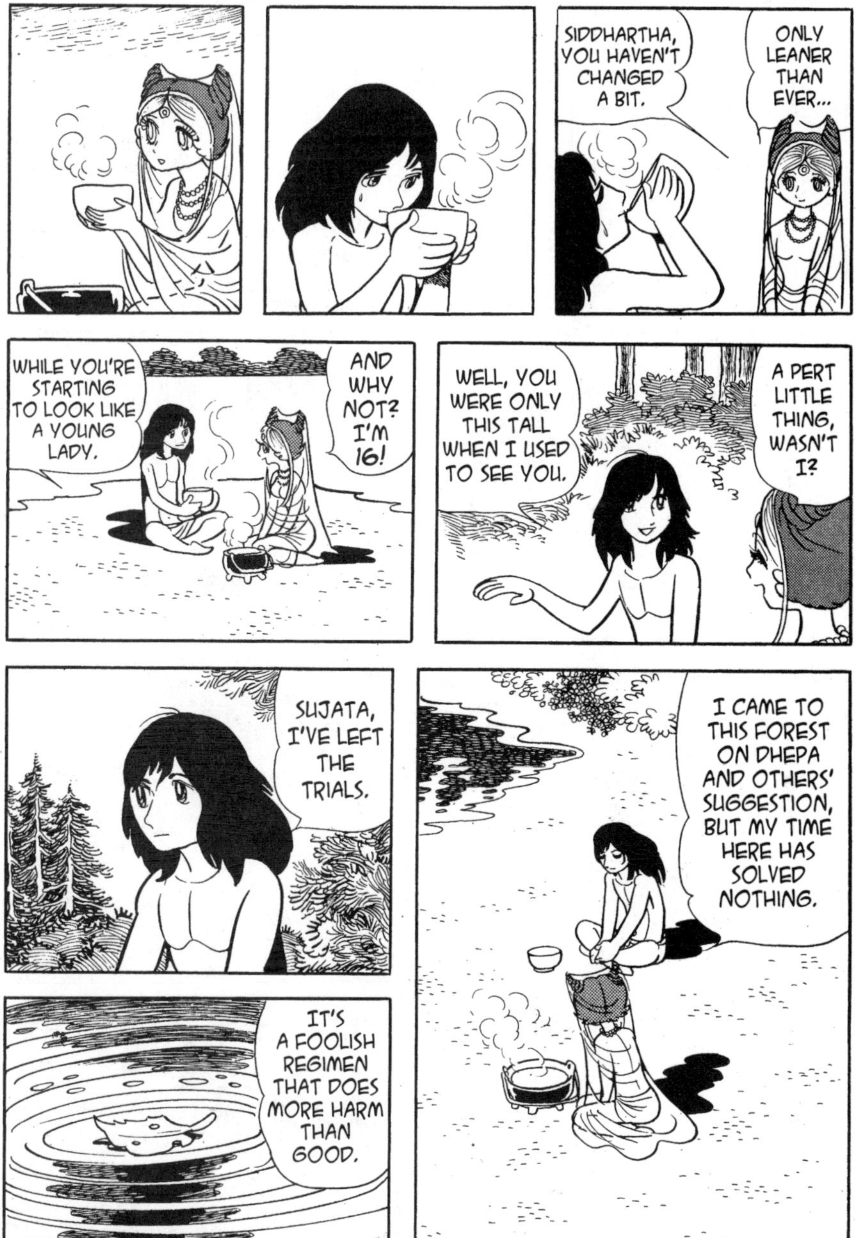
SIDDHARTHA, YOU HAVEN'T CHANGED A BIT.
ONLY LEANER THAN EVER...
WHILE YOU'RE STARTING TO LOOK LIKE A YOUNG LADY.
AND WHY NOT? I'M 16!
WELL, YOU WERE ONLY THIS TALL WHEN I USED TO SEE YOU.
A PERT LITTLE THING, WASN'T I?
SUJATA, I'VE LEFT THE TRIALS.
IT'S A FOOLISH REGIMEN THAT DOES MORE HARM THAN GOOD.
I CAME TO THIS FOREST ON DHEPA AND OTHERS' SUGGESTION, BUT MY TIME HERE HAS SOLVED NOTHING.

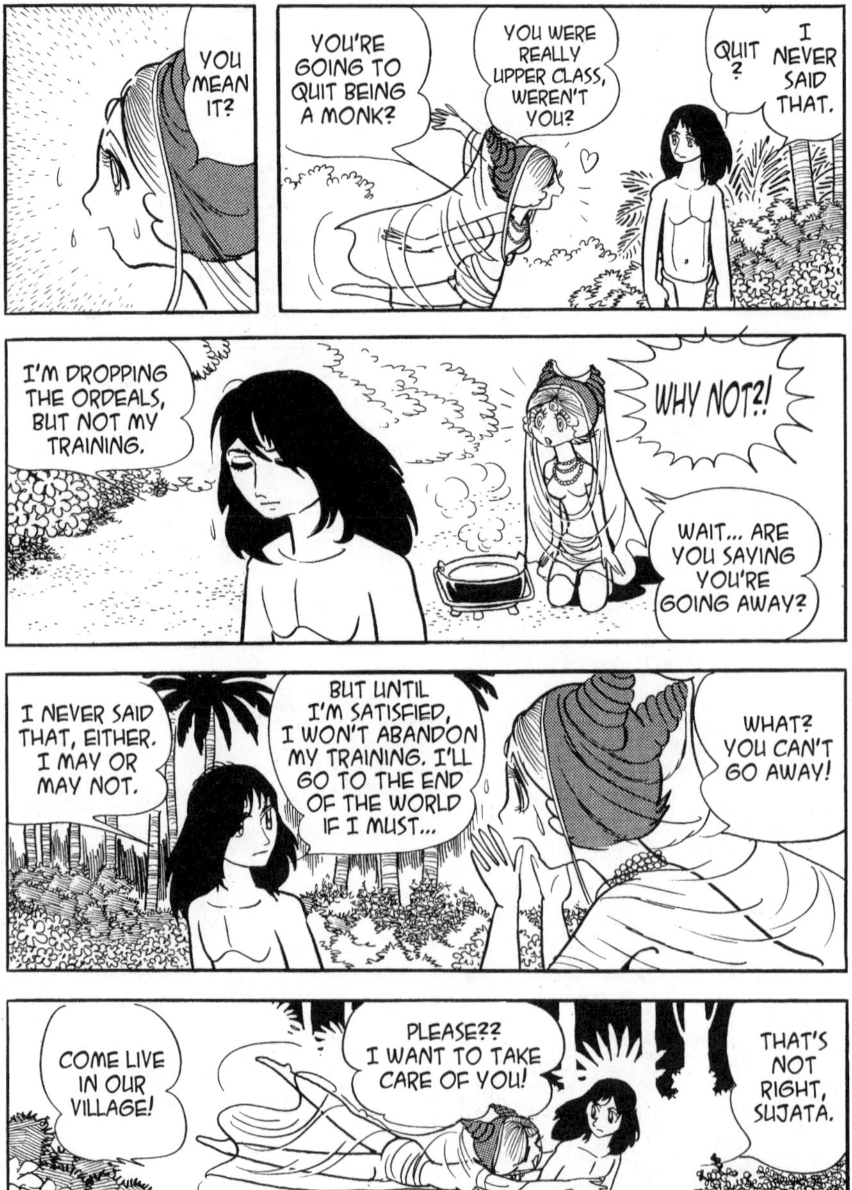
YOU MEAN IT?
YOU'RE GOING TO QUIT BEING A MONK?
YOU WERE REALLY UPPER CLASS, WEREN'T YOU?
QUIT?
I NEVER SAID THAT.
I'M DROPPING THE ORDEALS, BUT NOT MY TRAINING.
WHY NOT?!
WAIT... ARE YOU SAYING YOU'RE GOING AWAY?
I NEVER SAID THAT, EITHER. I MAY OR MAY NOT.
BUT UNTIL I'M SATISFIED, I WON'T ABANDON MY TRAINING. I'LL GO TO THE END OF THE WORLD IF I MUST...
WHAT? YOU CAN'T GO AWAY!
COME LIVE IN OUR VILLAGE!
PLEASE?? I WANT TO TAKE CARE OF YOU!
THAT'S NOT RIGHT, SUJATA.

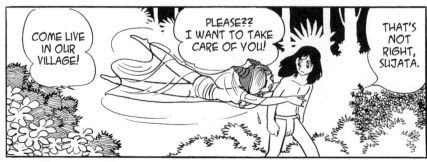

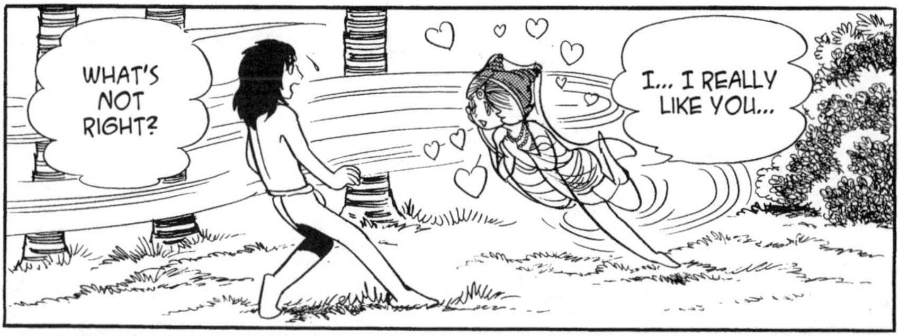
WHAT'S NOT RIGHT?
I... I REALLY LIKE YOU...
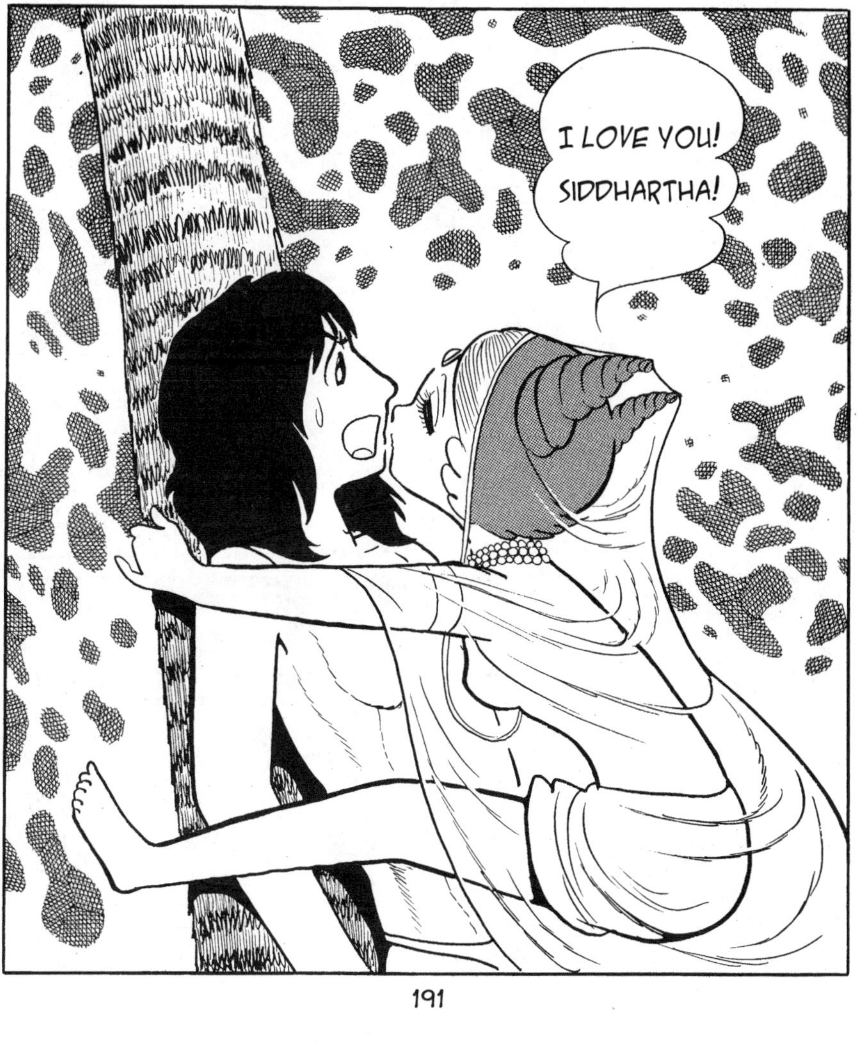
I LOVE YOU! SIDDHARTHA!

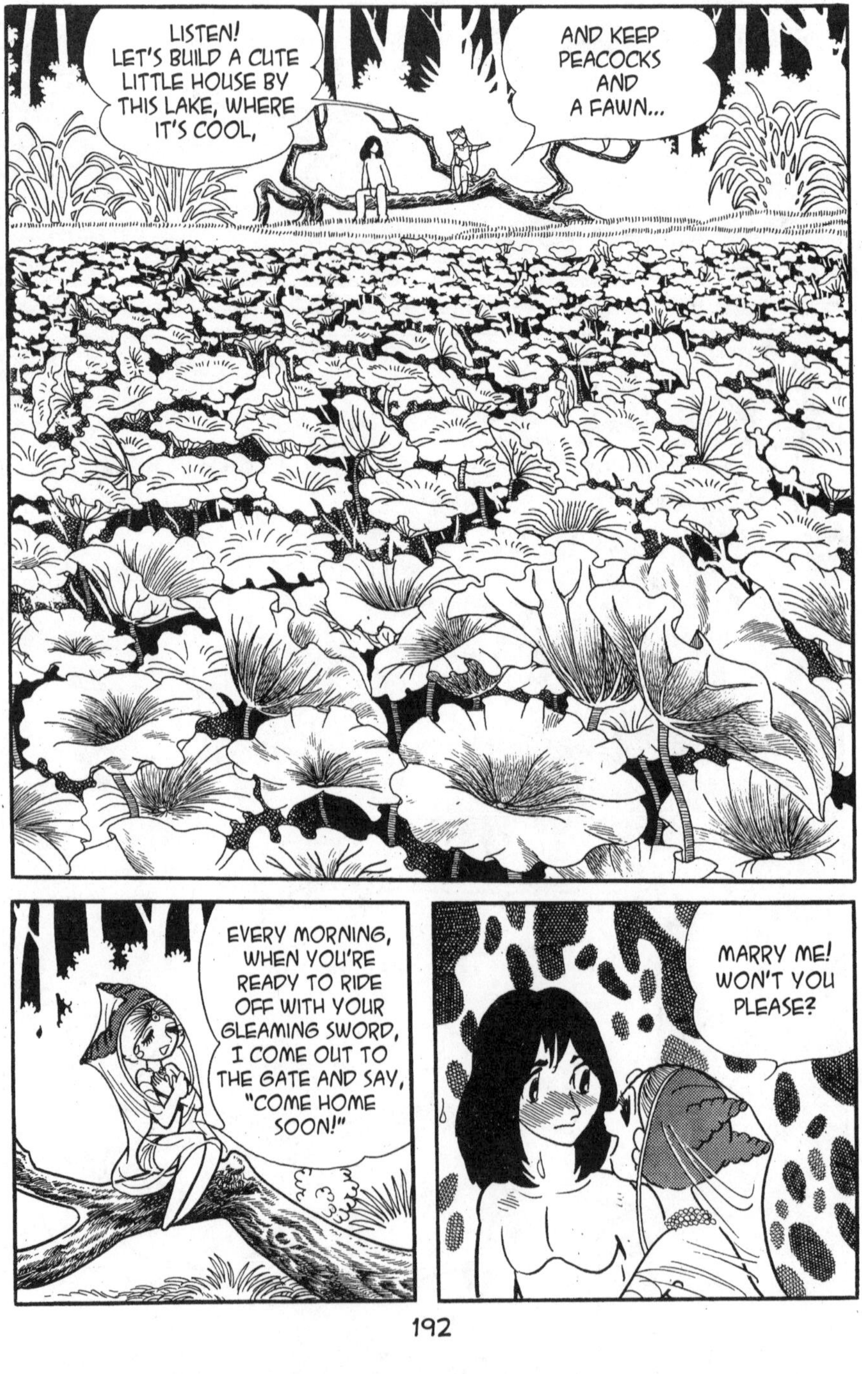
LISTEN! LET'S BUILD A CUTE LITTLE HOUSE BY THIS LAKE, WHERE IT'S COOL,
AND KEEP PEACOCKS AND A FAWN...
EVERY MORNING, WHEN YOU'RE READY TO RIDE OFF WITH YOUR GLEAMING SWORD, I COME OUT TO THE GATE AND SAY, "COME HOME SOON!"
MARRY ME! WON'T YOU PLEASE?

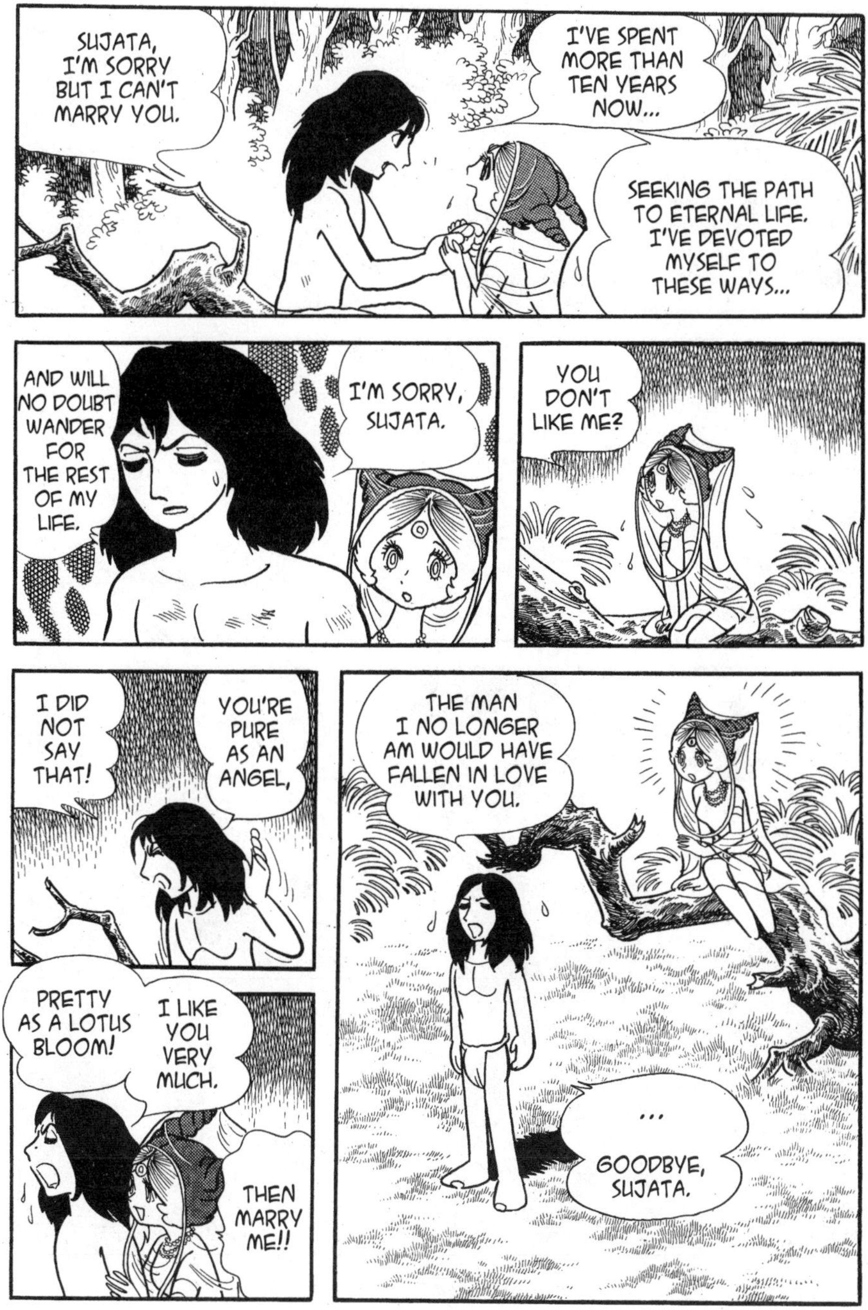
SUJATA, I'M SORRY BUT I CAN'T MARRY YOU.
I'VE SPENT MORE THAN TEN YEARS NOW...
SEEKING THE PATH TO ETERNAL LIFE. I'VE DEVOTED MYSELF TO THESE WAYS...
AND WILL NO DOUBT WANDER FOR THE REST OF MY LIFE.
I'M SORRY, SUJATA.
YOU DON'T LIKE ME?
I DID NOT SAY THAT!
YOU'RE PURE AS AN ANGEL,
PRETTY AS A LOTUS BLOOM!
I LIKE YOU VERY MUCH.
THEN MARRY ME!!
THE MAN I NO LONGER AM WOULD HAVE FALLEN IN LOVE WITH YOU.
... GOODBYE, SUJATA.

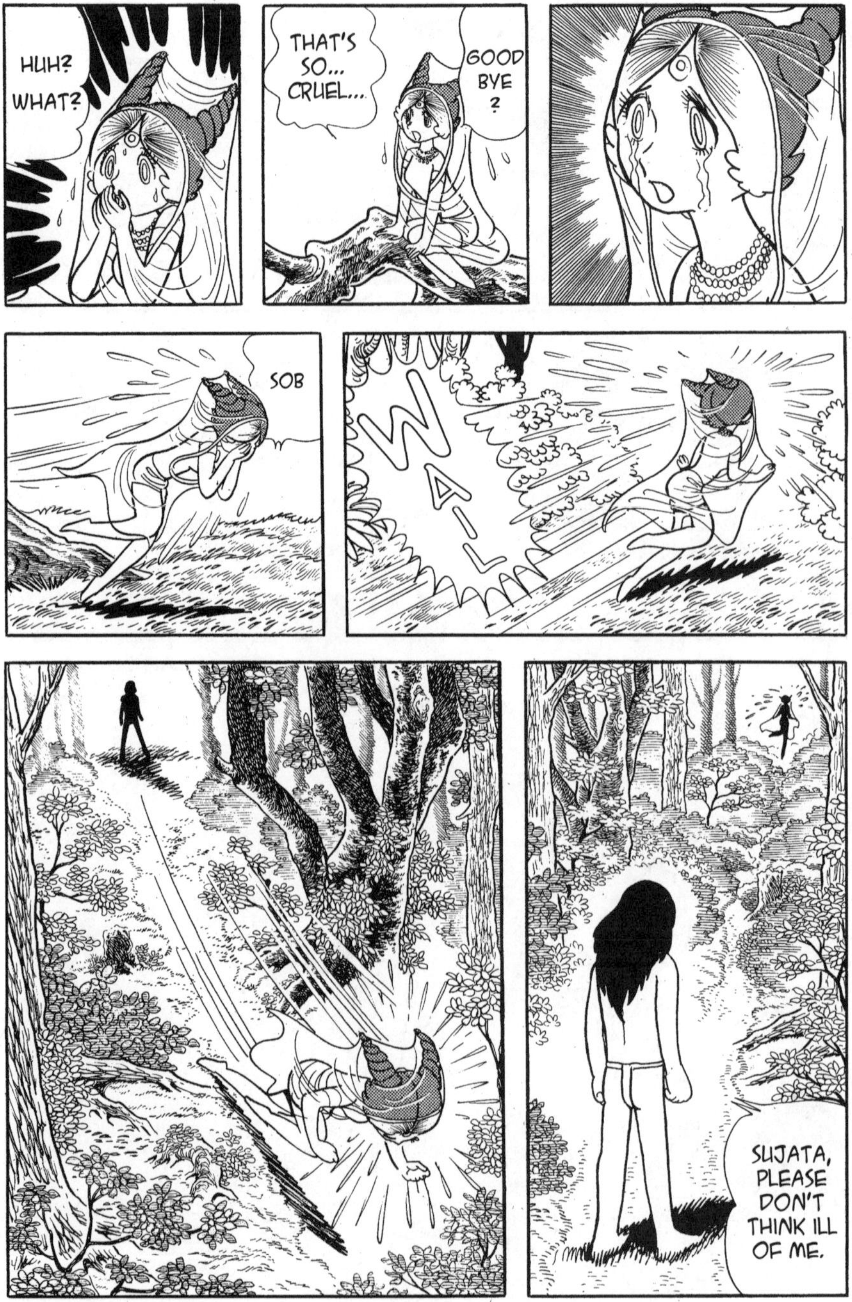
HUH? WHAT?
THAT'S SO... CRUEL...
GOOD BYE?
SOB
WAIL
SUJATA, PLEASE DON'T THINK ILL OF ME.

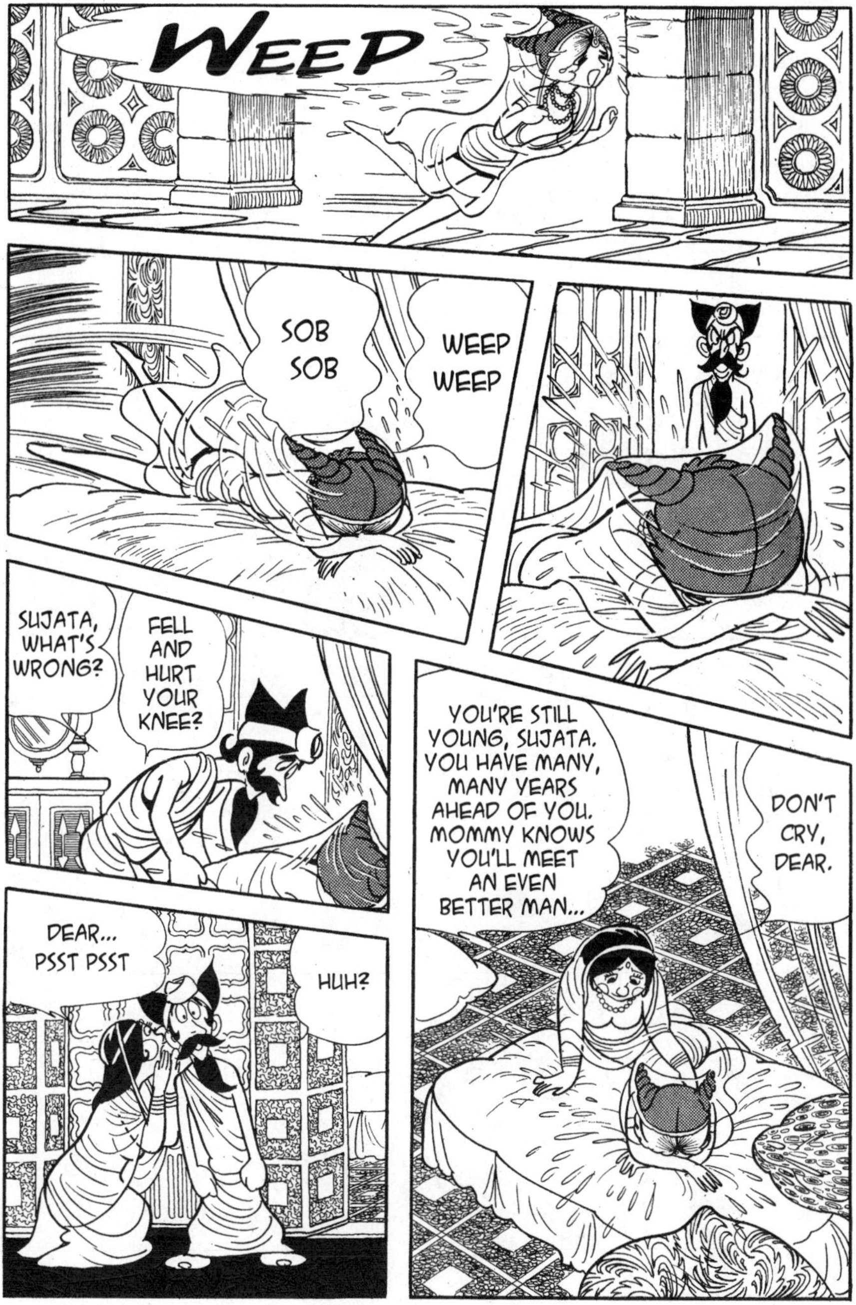
WEEP
SOB SOB
WEEP WEEP
SUJATA, WHAT'S WRONG?
FELL AND HURT YOUR KNEE?
DEAR... PSST PSST
HUH?
DON'T CRY, DEAR.
YOU'RE STILL YOUNG, SUJATA. YOU HAVE MANY, MANY YEARS AHEAD OF YOU. MOMMY KNOWS YOU'LL MEET AN EVEN BETTER MAN...

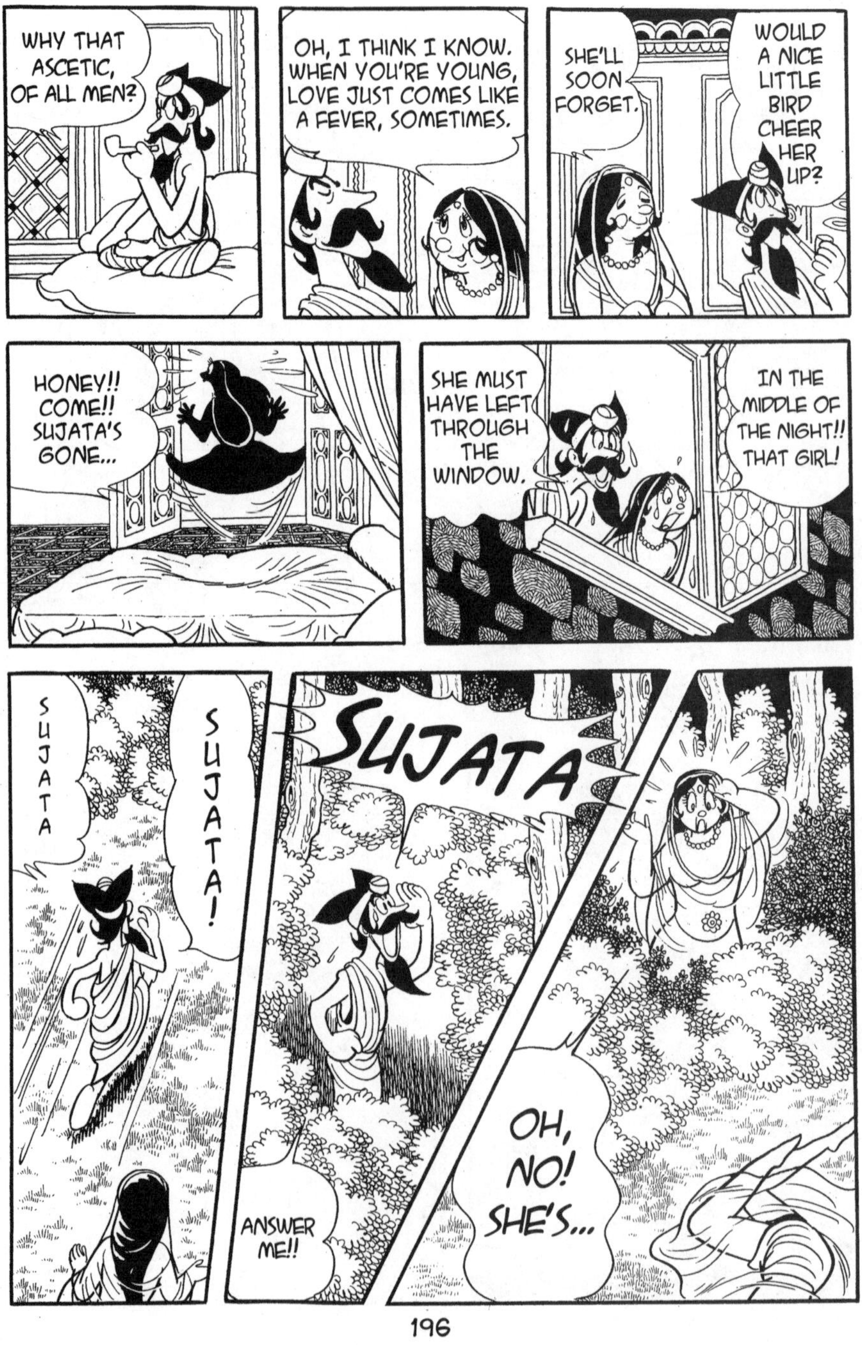
WHY THAT ASCETIC, OF ALL MEN?
OH, I THINK I KNOW. WHEN YOU'RE YOUNG, LOVE JUST COMES LIKE A FEVER, SOMETIMES.
SHE'LL SOON FORGET.
WOULD A NICE LITTLE BIRD CHEER HER UP?
HONEY!! COME!! SUJATA'S GONE...
SHE MUST HAVE LEFT THROUGH THE WINDOW.
IN THE MIDDLE OF THE NIGHT!! THAT GIRL!
SUJATA!
SUJATA
SUJATA
ANSWER ME!!
OH, NO! SHE'S...

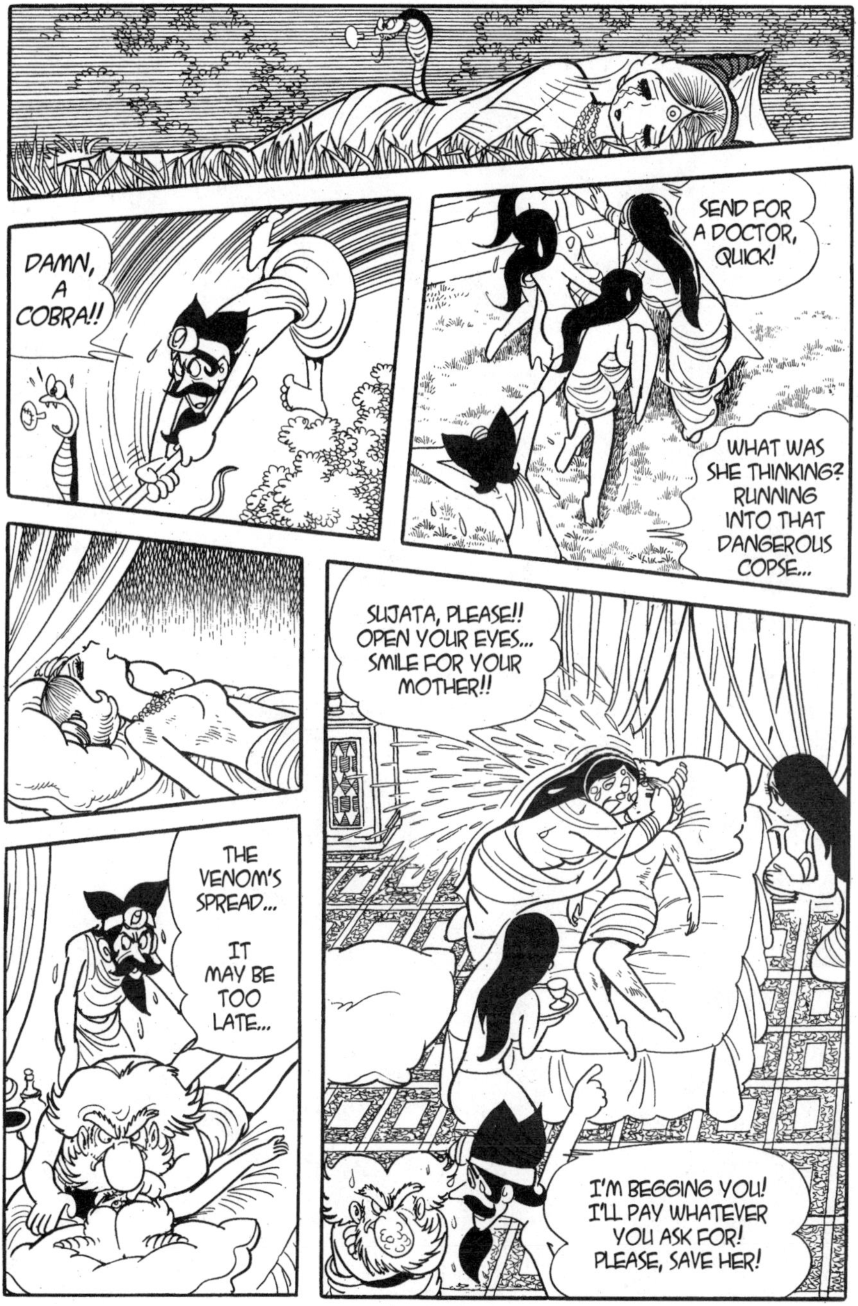
DAMN, A COBRA!!
SEND FOR A DOCTOR, QUICK!
WHAT WAS SHE THINKING? RUNNING INTO THAT DANGEROUS COPSE...
SUJATA, PLEASE!! OPEN YOUR EYES... SMILE FOR YOUR MOTHER!!
THE VENOM'S SPREAD...
IT MAY BE TOO LATE...
I'M BEGGING YOU! I'LL PAY WHATEVER YOU ASK FOR! PLEASE, SAVE HER!

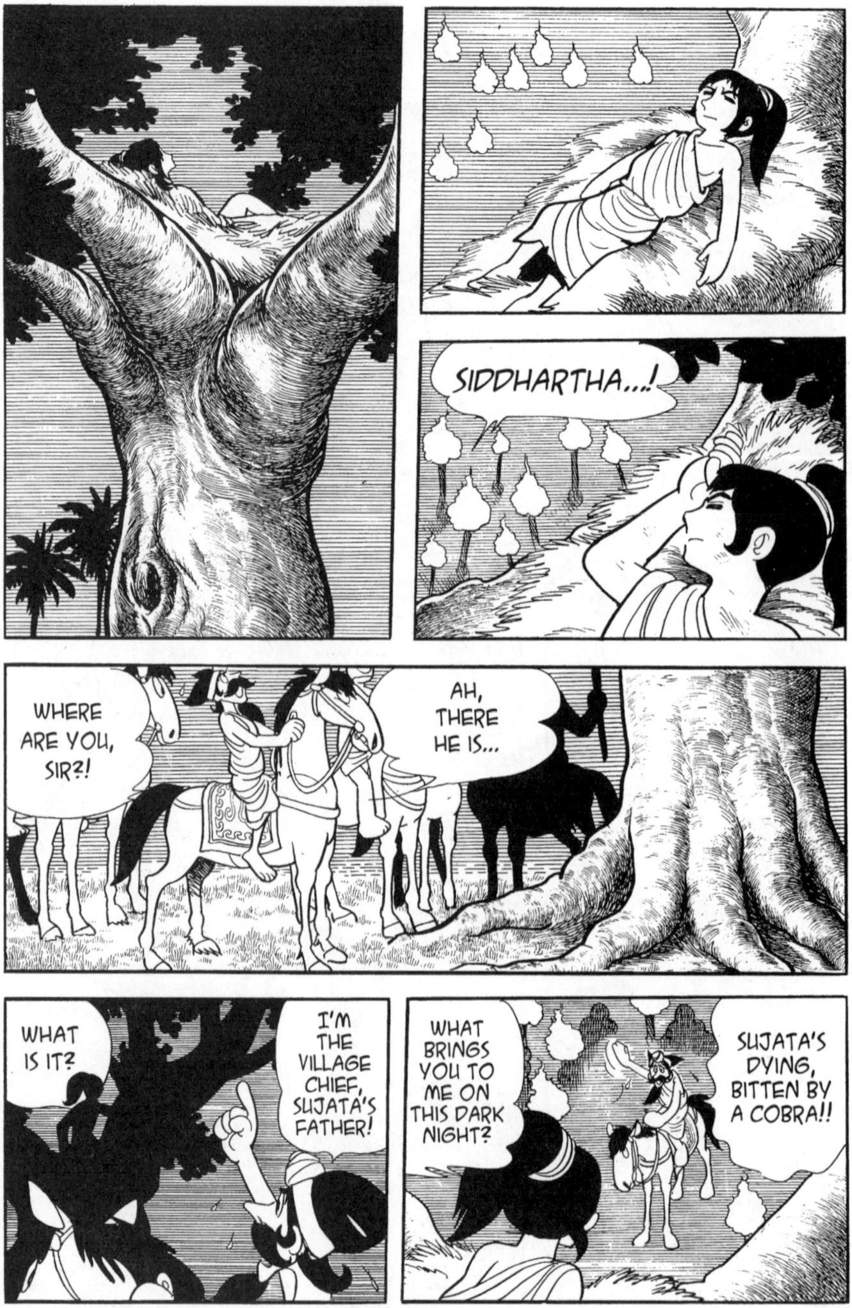
SIDDHARTHA...!
WHERE ARE YOU, SIR?!
AH, THERE HE IS...
WHAT IS IT?
I'M THE VILLAGE CHIEF, SUJATA'S FATHER!
WHAT BRINGS YOU TO ME ON THIS DARK NIGHT?
SUJATA'S DYING, BITTEN BY A COBRA!!

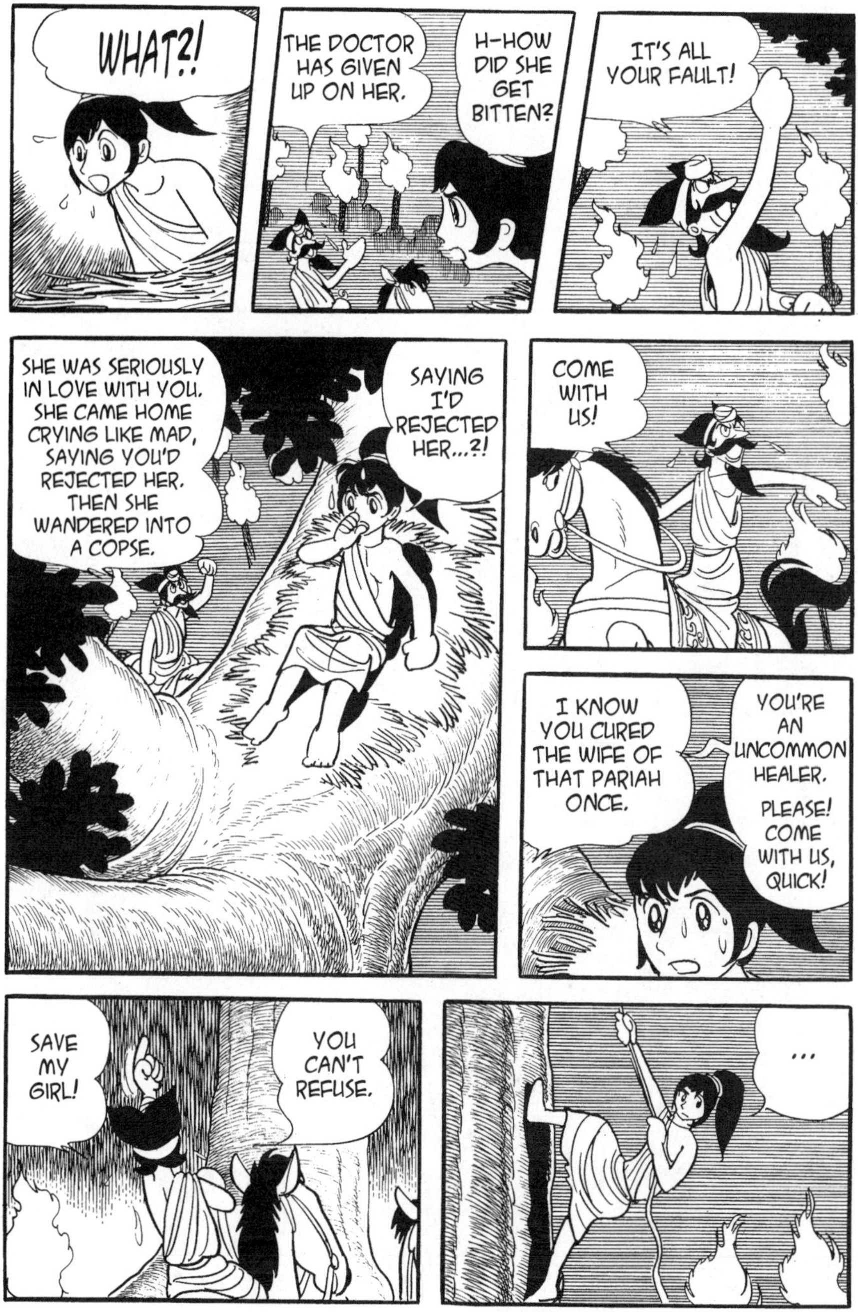
WHAT?!
THE DOCTOR HAS GIVEN UP ON HER.
H-HOW DID SHE GET BITTEN?
IT'S ALL YOUR FAULT!
SHE WAS SERIOUSLY IN LOVE WITH YOU. SHE CAME HOME CRYING LIKE MAD, SAYING YOU'D REJECTED HER. THEN SHE WANDERED INTO A COPSE.
SAYING I'D REJECTED HER...?!
COME WITH US!
I KNOW YOU CURED THE WIFE OF THAT PARIAH ONCE.
YOU'RE AN UNCOMMON HEALER.
PLEASE! COME WITH US, QUICK!
SAVE MY GIRL!
YOU CAN'T REFUSE.
...

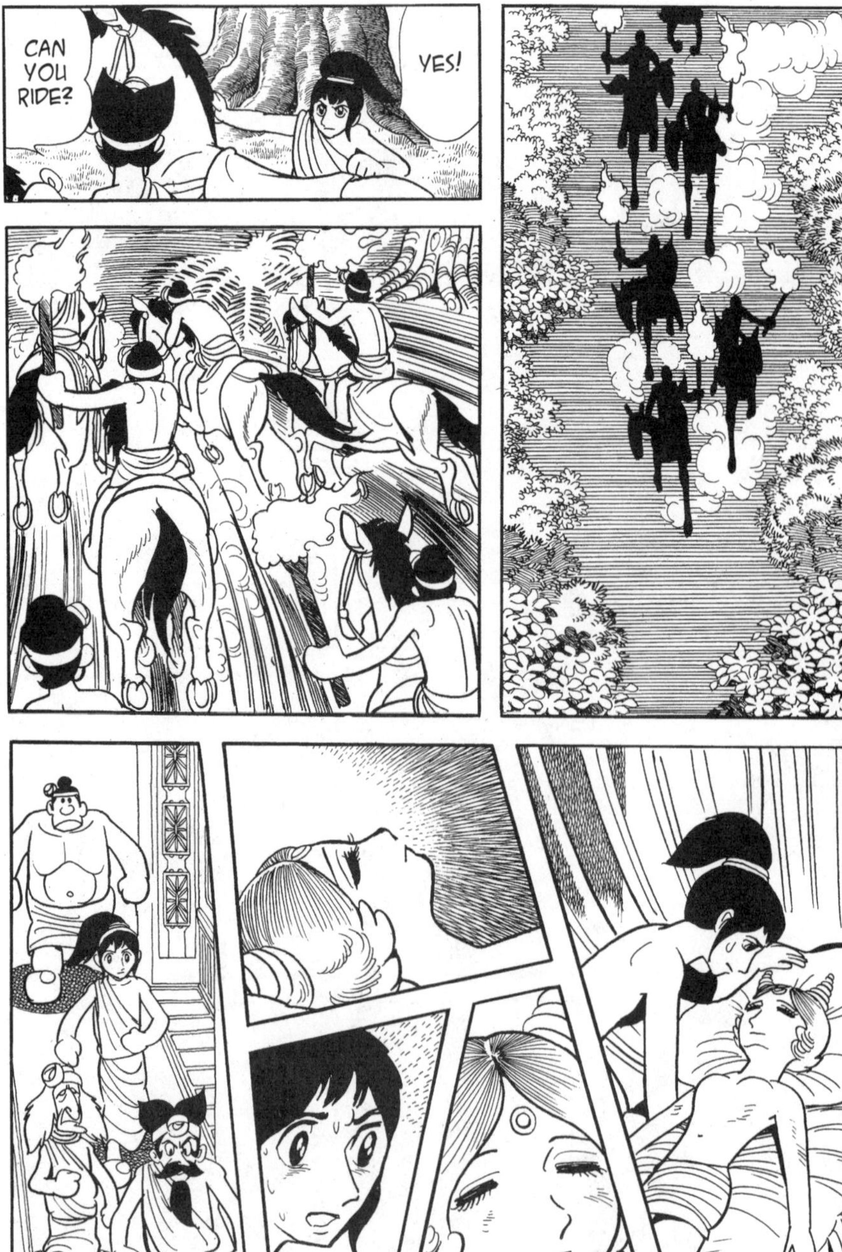
CAN YOU RIDE?
YES!

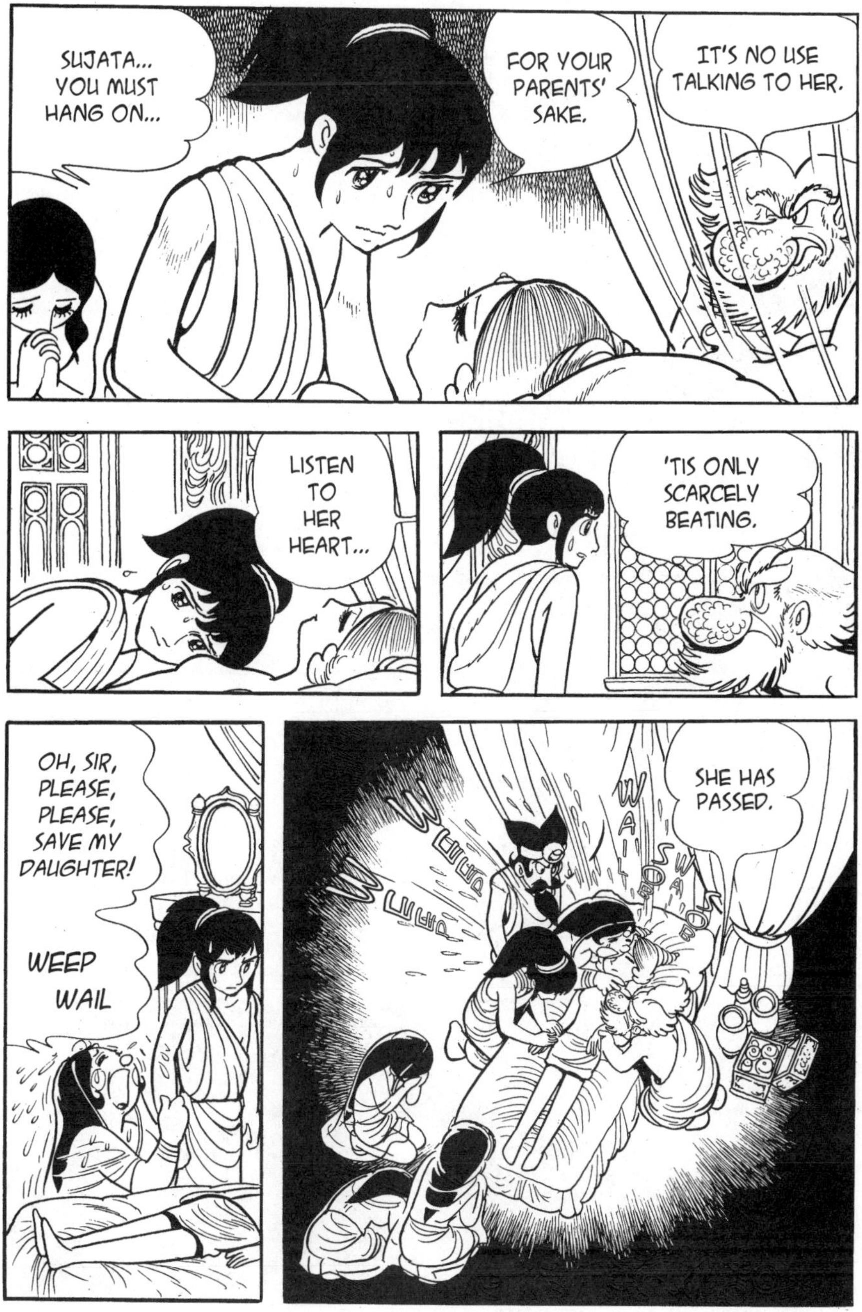
SUJATA... YOU MUST HANG ON...
FOR YOUR PARENTS' SAKE.
IT'S NO USE TALKING TO HER.
LISTEN TO HER HEART...
'TIS ONLY SCARCELY BEATING.
OH, SIR, PLEASE, PLEASE, SAVE MY DAUGHTER!
WEEP
WAIL
SHE HAS PASSED.

IS THERE NO WAY TO BIND THE POOR GIRL'S LIFE TO THIS WORLD?

WILL NO TWINE TIE A LIFE TO A BODY?

WHY MUST IT BE BEYOND US TO HALT DEATH...?

WHEN I SAVED ASSAJI, HE WAS STILL LIVING, AND THE MEDICINE WORKED.

IN HER CASE,

IT'S ALL OVER!

EXCEPT... I'VE BEEN TOLD THAT I HAVE PSYCHIC POWERS.

I RECALL LENDING MY MIND TO BEASTS, FROLICKING AS A BIRD, A RABBIT.

IF ONLY...

MY MIND...

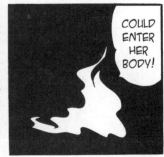

COULD ENTER HER BODY!

202

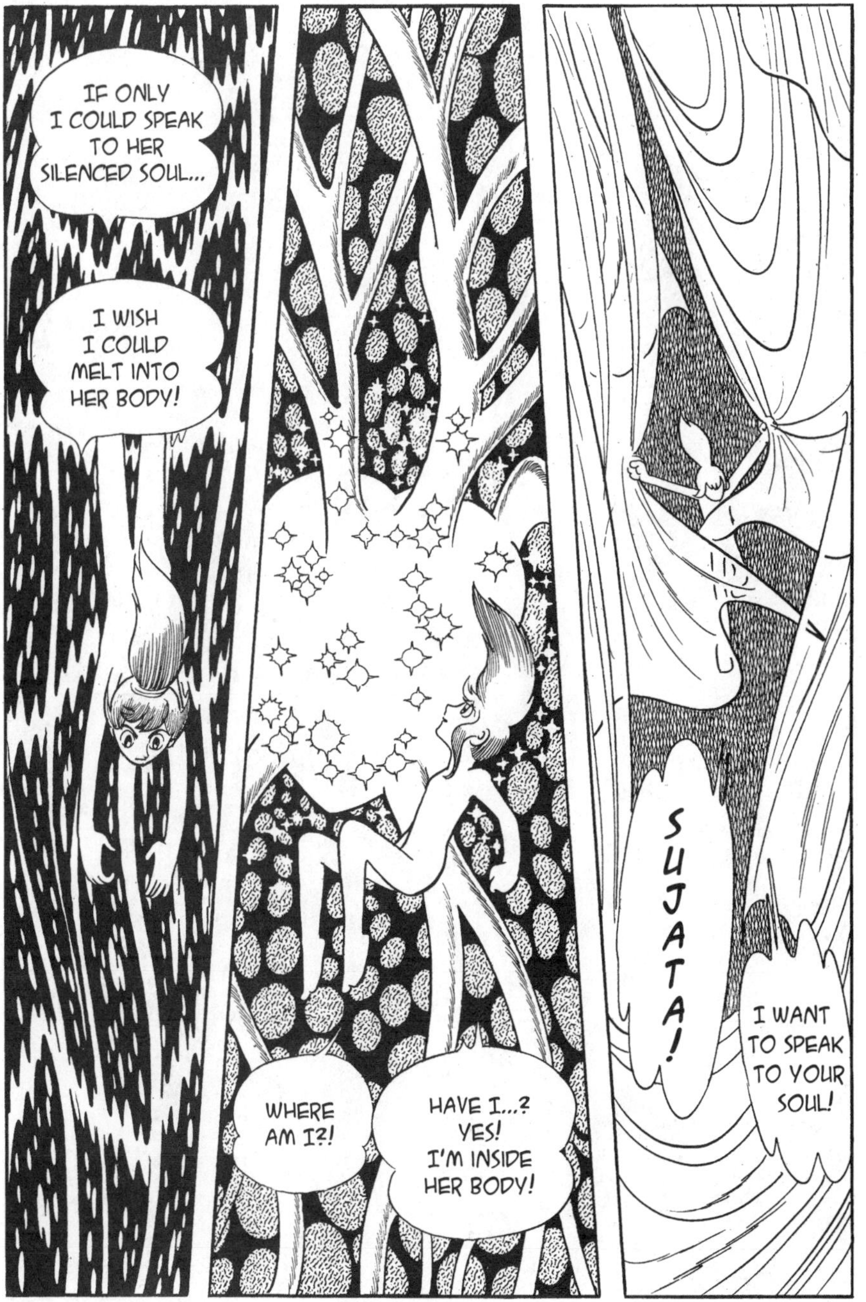
IF ONLY I COULD SPEAK TO HER SILENCED SOUL...
I WISH I COULD MELT INTO HER BODY!
WHERE AM I?!
HAVE I...? YES! I'M INSIDE HER BODY!
SUJATA!
I WANT TO SPEAK TO YOUR SOUL!

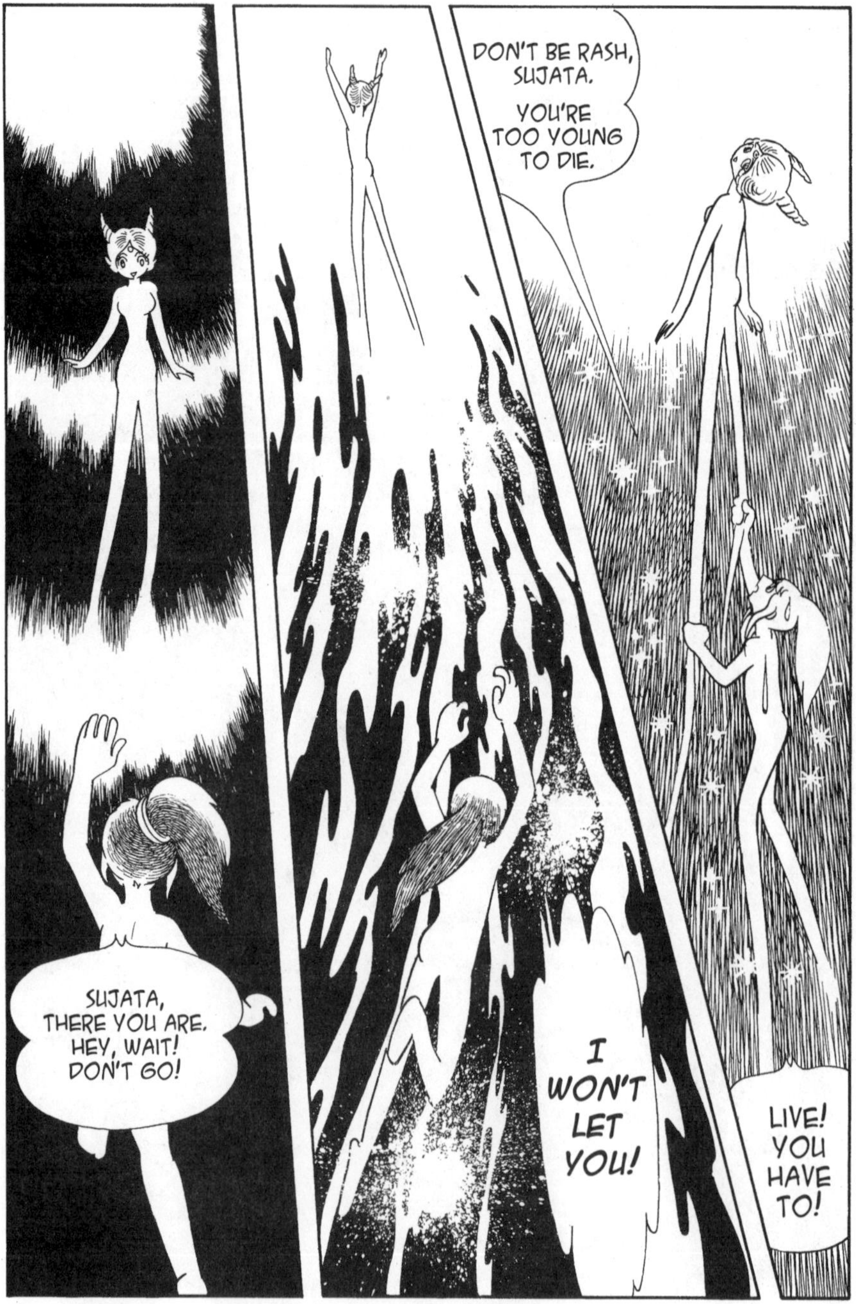
SUJATA, THERE YOU ARE. HEY, WAIT! DON'T GO!
I WON'T LET YOU!
DON'T BE RASH, SUJATA.
YOU'RE TOO YOUNG TO DIE.
LIVE! YOU HAVE TO!

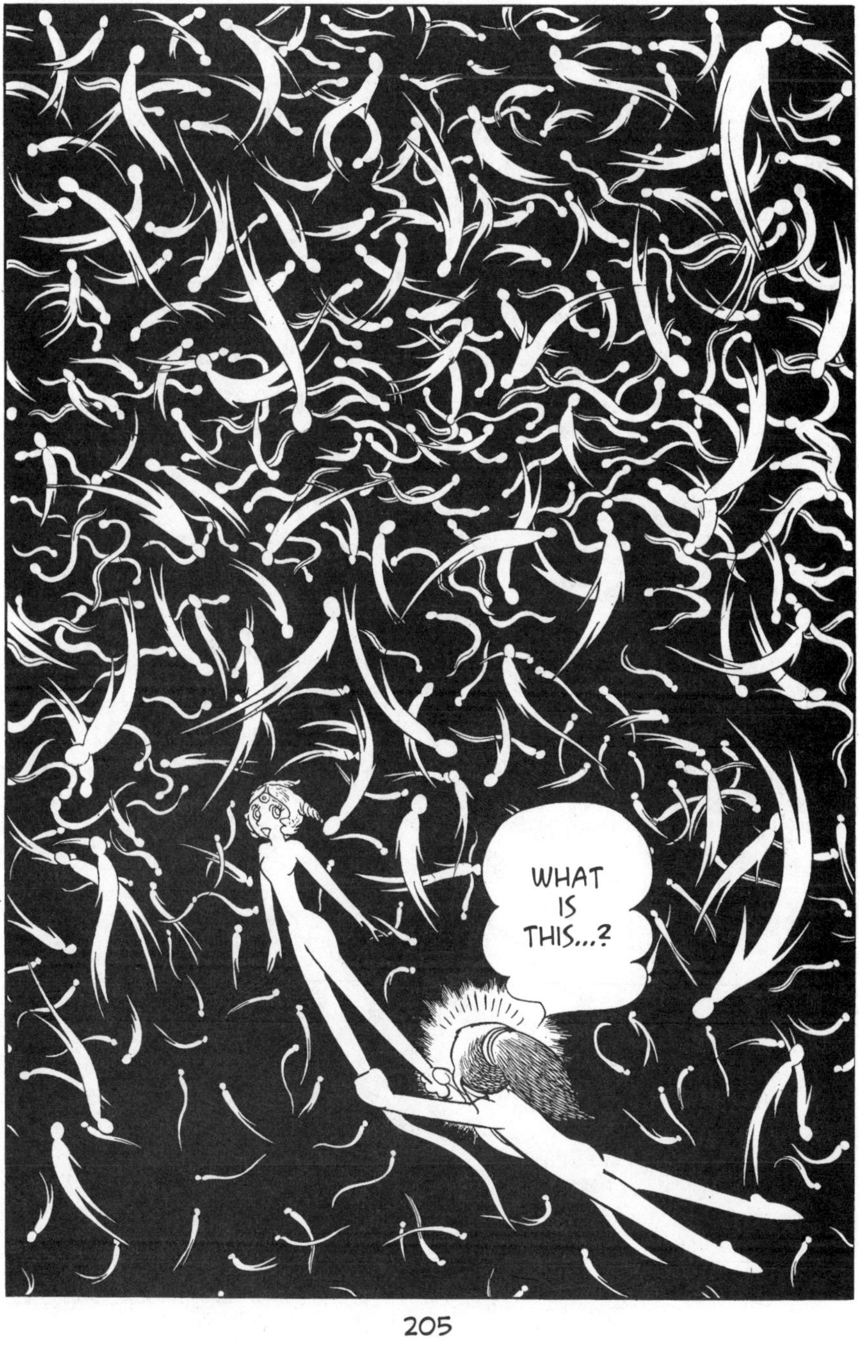
WHAT IS THIS...?

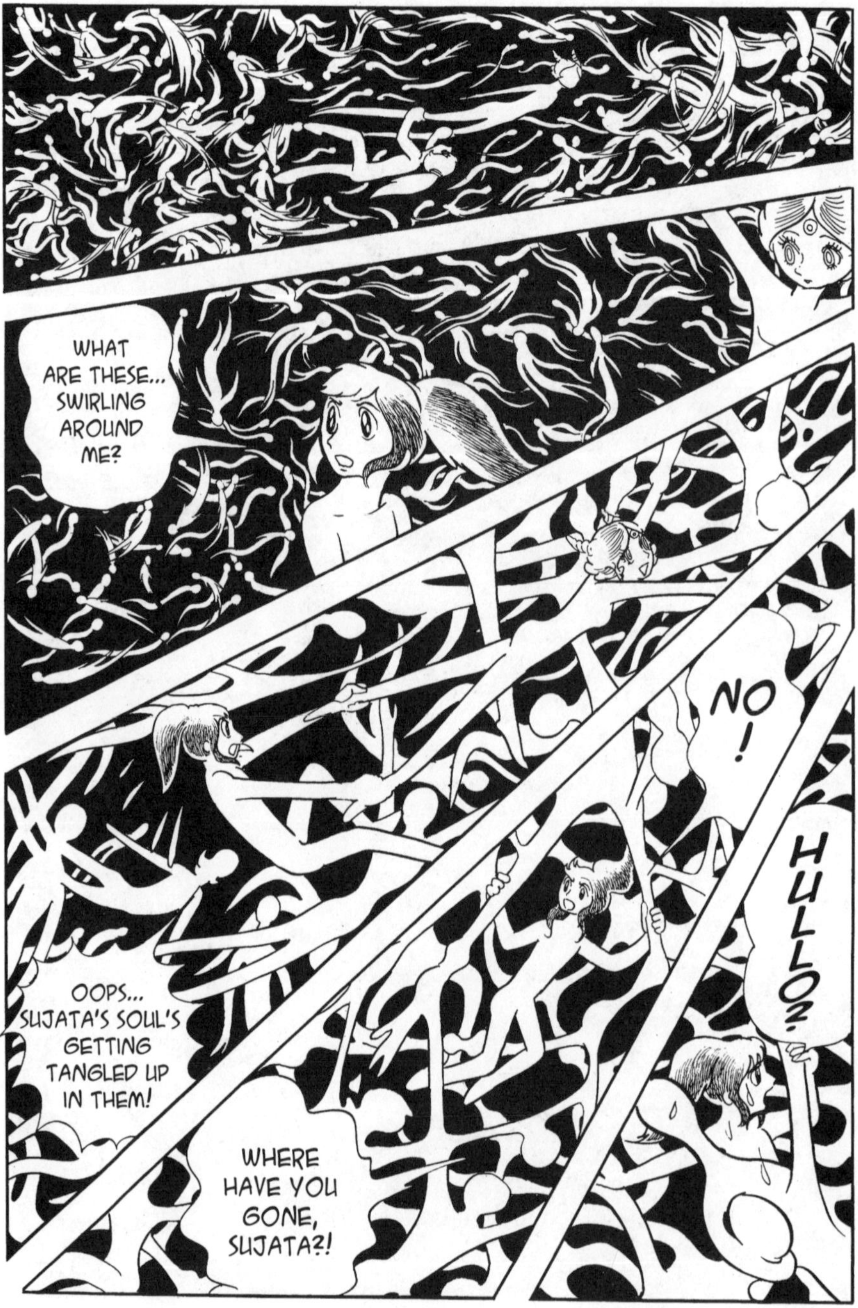
WHAT ARE THESE... SWIRLING AROUND ME?
OOPS... SUJATA'S SOUL'S GETTING TANGLED UP IN THEM!
WHERE HAVE YOU GONE, SUJATA?!
NO!
HULLO?

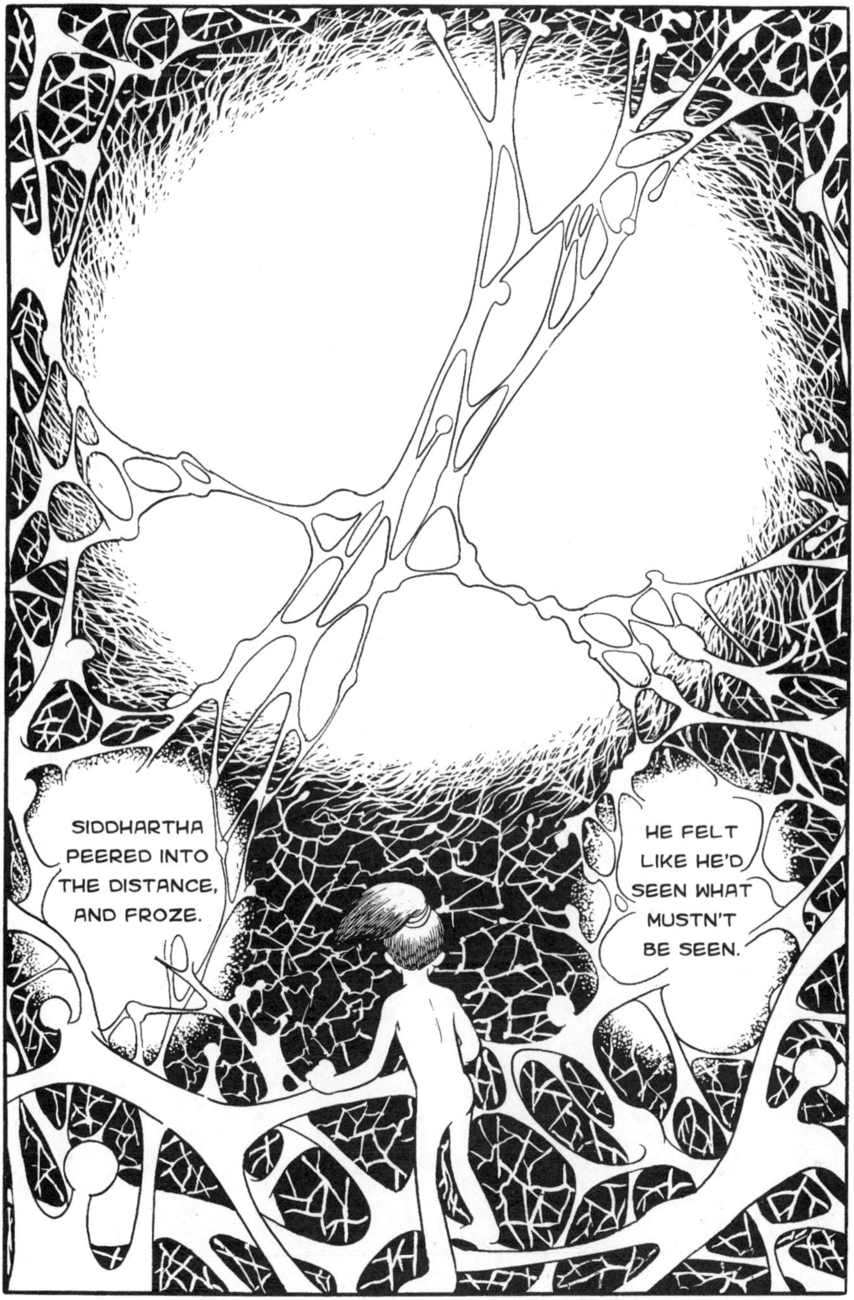
SIDDHARTHA PEERED INTO THE DISTANCE, AND FROZE.
HE FELT LIKE HE'D SEEN WHAT MUSTN'T BE SEEN.

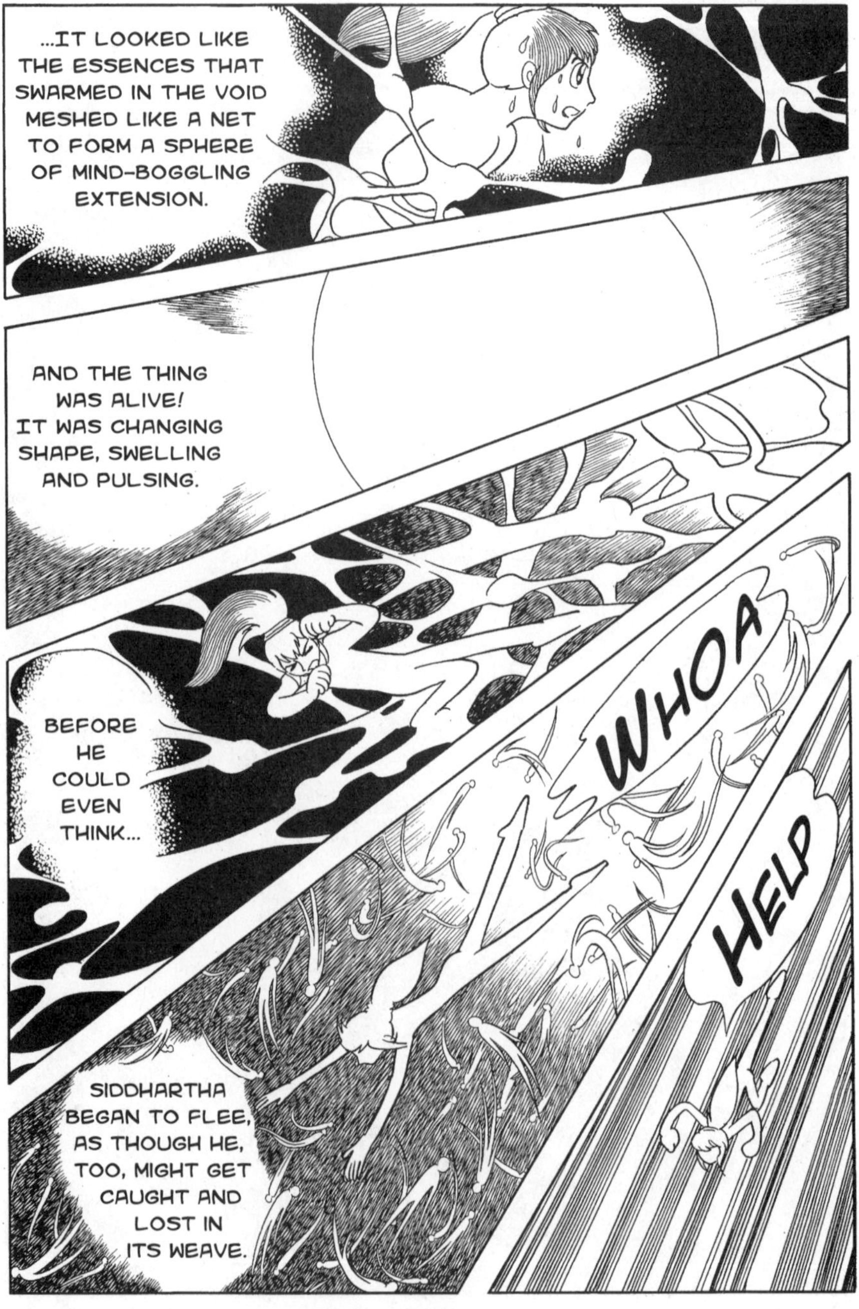
...IT LOOKED LIKE THE ESSENCES THAT SWARMED IN THE VOID MESHED LIKE A NET TO FORM A SPHERE OF MIND-BOGGLING EXTENSION.
AND THE THING WAS ALIVE! IT WAS CHANGING SHAPE, SWELLING AND PULSING.
BEFORE HE COULD EVEN THINK...
WHOA
SIDDHARTHA BEGAN TO FLEE, AS THOUGH HE, TOO, MIGHT GET CAUGHT AND LOST IN ITS WEAVE.
HELP

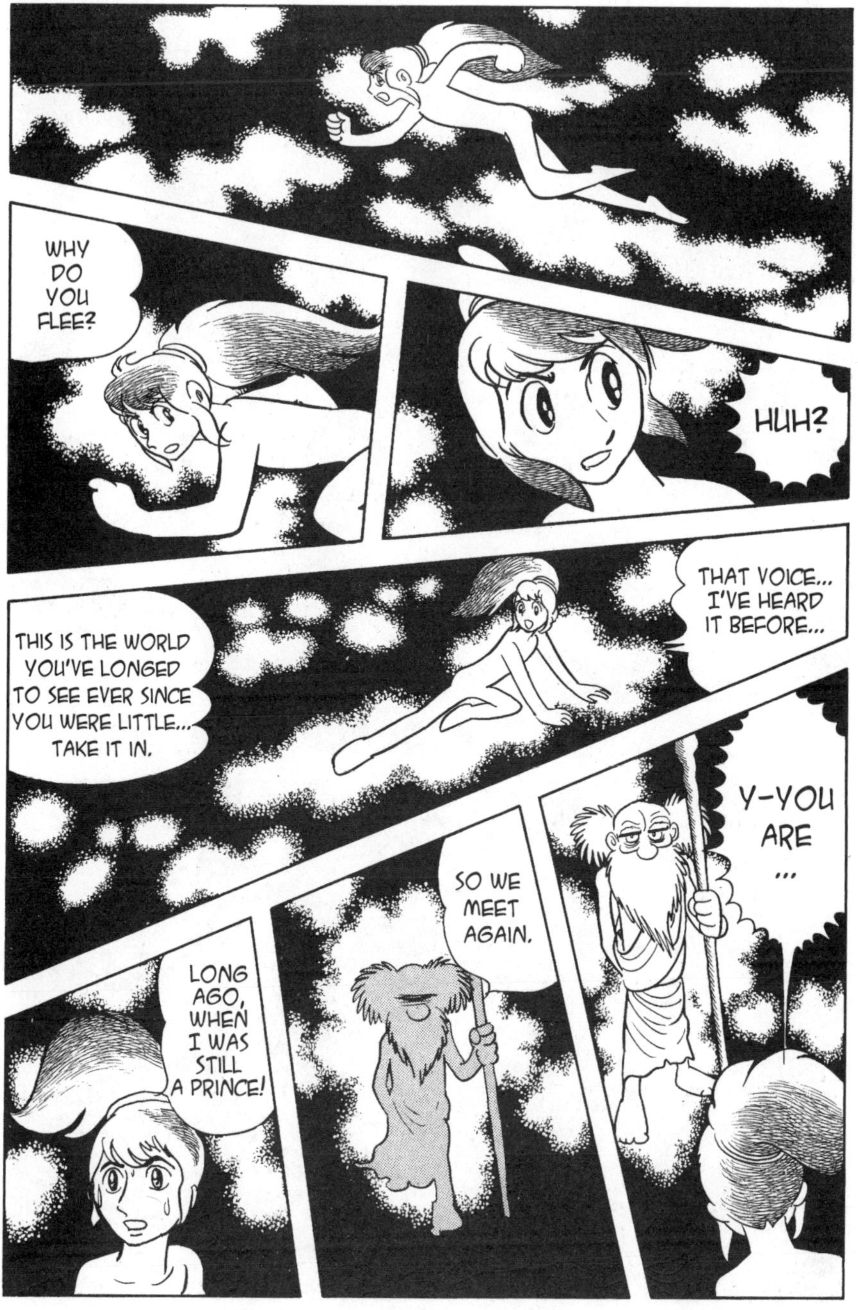
WHY DO YOU FLEE?
HUH?
THIS IS THE WORLD YOU'VE LONGED TO SEE EVER SINCE YOU WERE LITTLE... TAKE IT IN.
THAT VOICE... I'VE HEARD IT BEFORE...
LONG AGO, WHEN I WAS STILL A PRINCE!
SO WE MEET AGAIN.
Y-YOU ARE ...

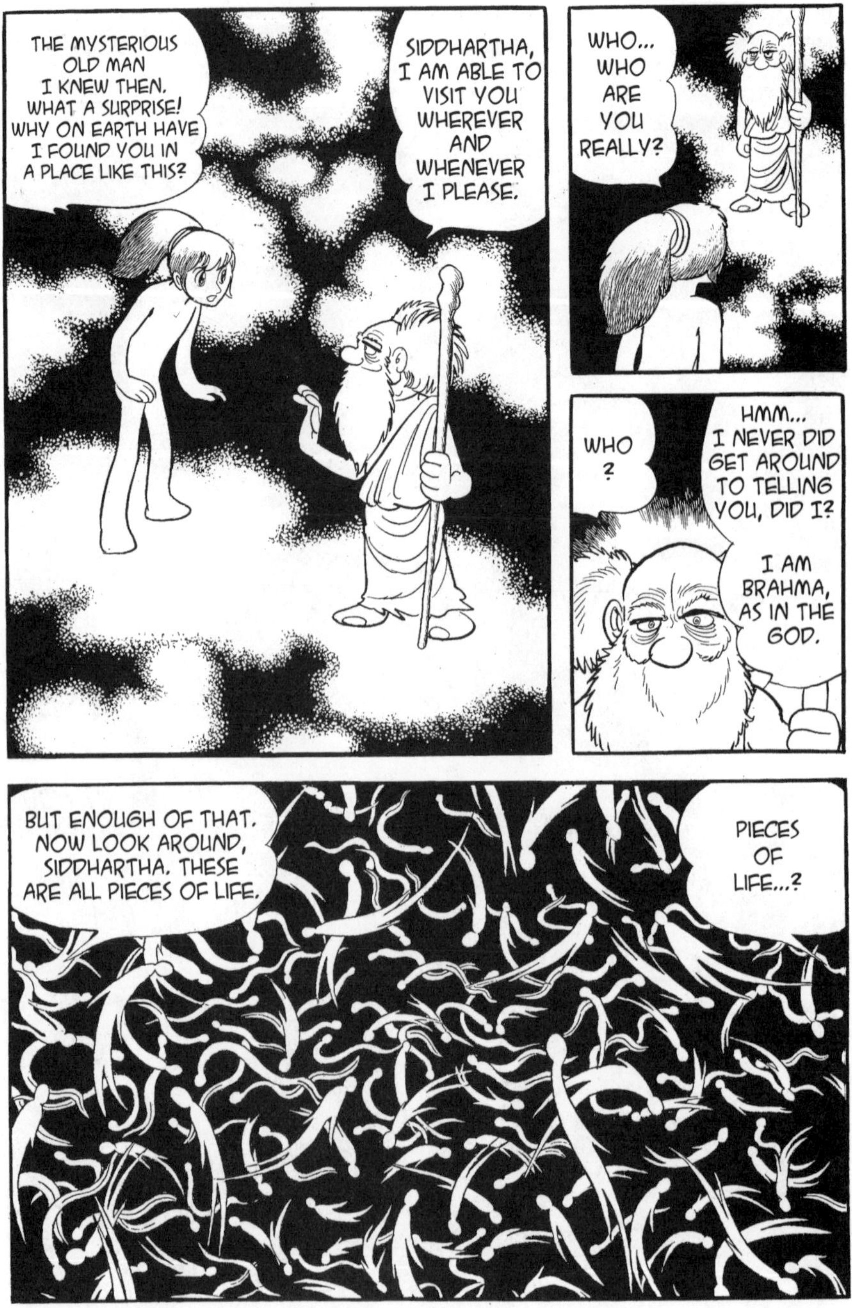
THE MYSTERIOUS OLD MAN I KNEW THEN. WHAT A SURPRISE! WHY ON EARTH HAVE I FOUND YOU IN A PLACE LIKE THIS?
SIDDHARTHA, I AM ABLE TO VISIT YOU WHEREVER AND WHENEVER I PLEASE.
WHO... WHO ARE YOU REALLY?
WHO?
HMM... I NEVER DID GET AROUND TO TELLING YOU, DID I?
I AM BRAHMA, AS IN THE GOD.
BUT ENOUGH OF THAT. NOW LOOK AROUND, SIDDHARTHA. THESE ARE ALL PIECES OF LIFE.
PIECES OF LIFE...?

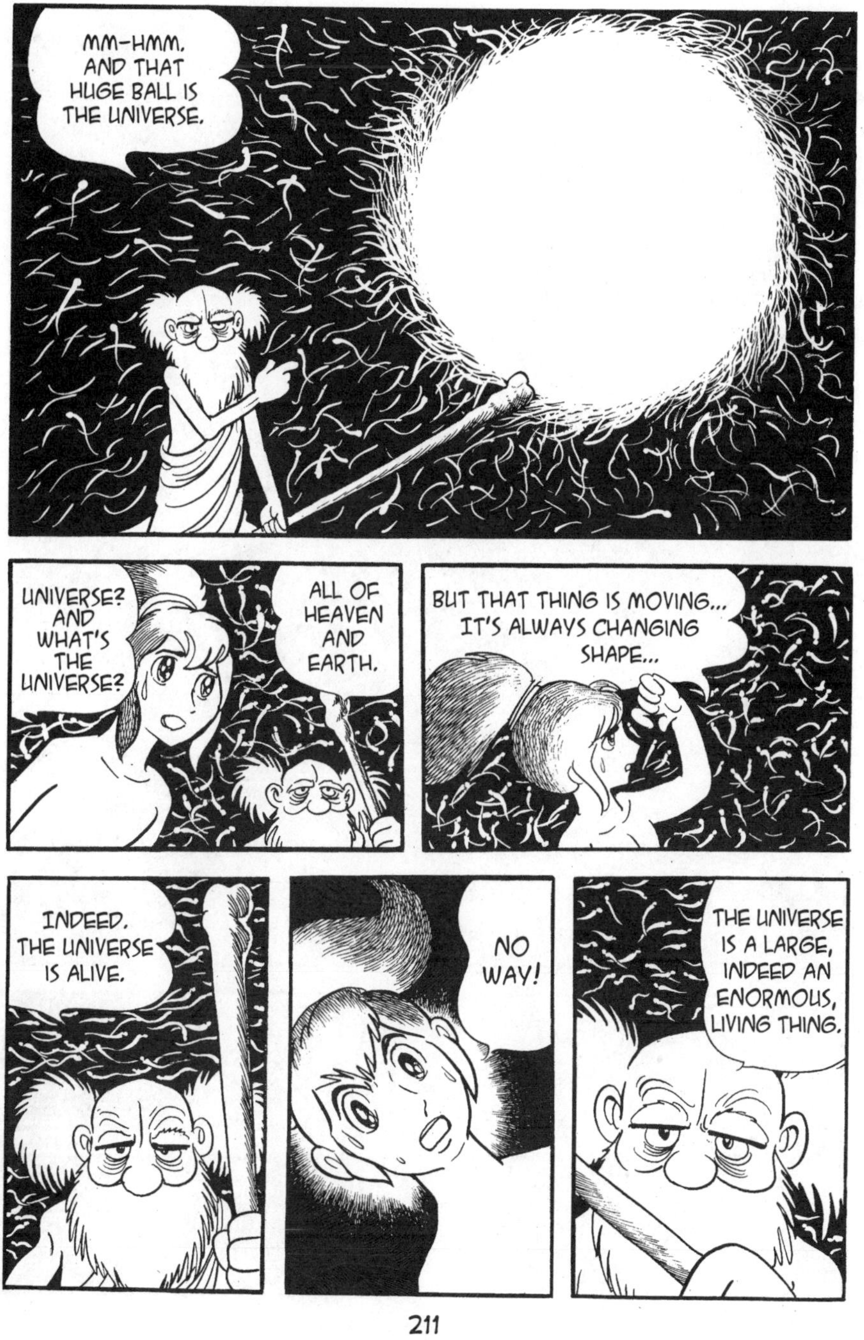
MM-HMM. AND THAT HUGE BALL IS THE UNIVERSE.
UNIVERSE? AND WHAT'S THE UNIVERSE?
ALL OF HEAVEN AND EARTH.
BUT THAT THING IS MOVING... IT'S ALWAYS CHANGING SHAPE...
INDEED. THE UNIVERSE IS ALIVE.
NO WAY!
THE UNIVERSE IS A LARGE, INDEED AN ENORMOUS, LIVING THING.

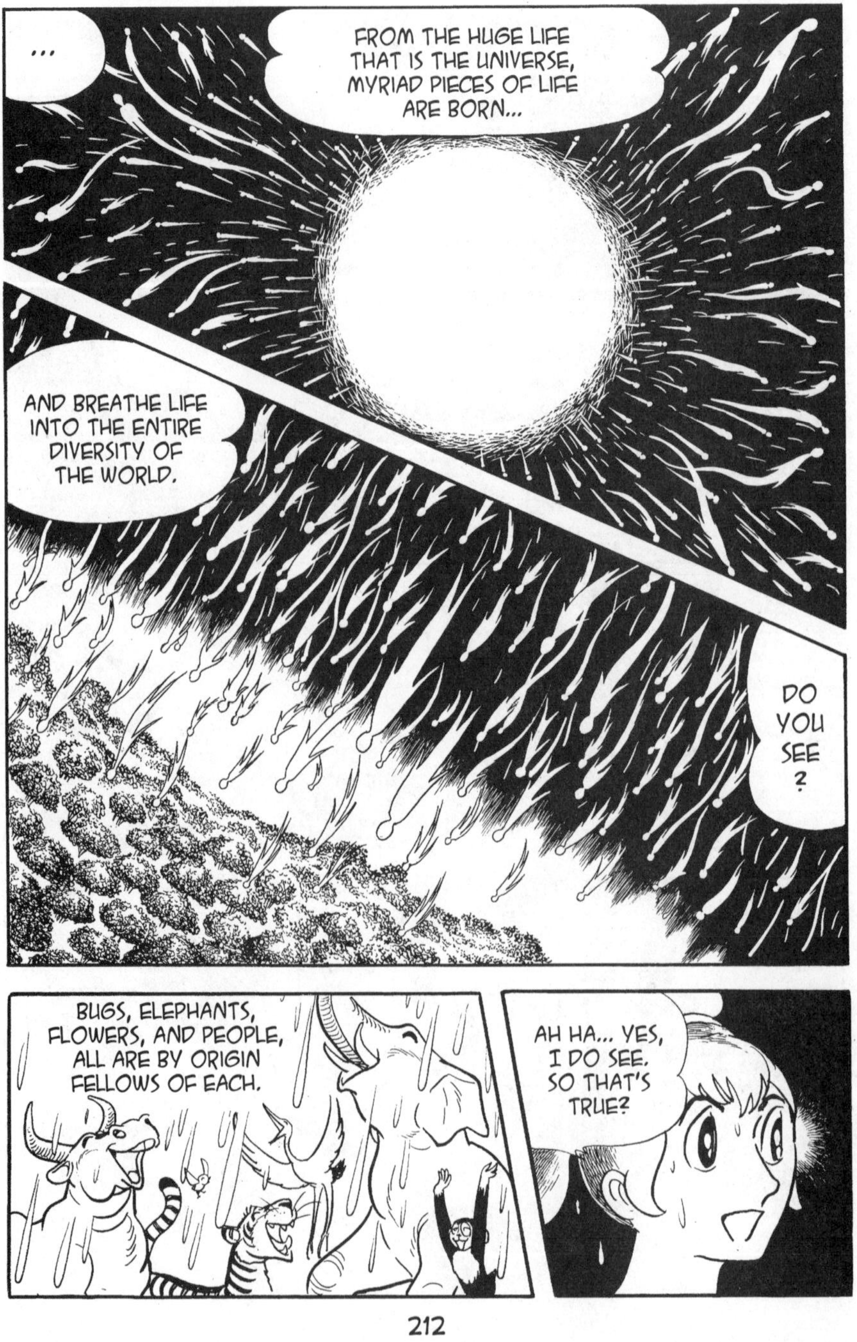
...
FROM THE HUGE LIFE THAT IS THE UNIVERSE, MYRIAD PIECES OF LIFE ARE BORN...
AND BREATHE LIFE INTO THE ENTIRE DIVERSITY OF THE WORLD.
DO YOU SEE?
BUGS, ELEPHANTS, FLOWERS, AND PEOPLE, ALL ARE BY ORIGIN FELLOWS OF EACH.
AH HA... YES, I DO SEE. SO THAT'S TRUE?

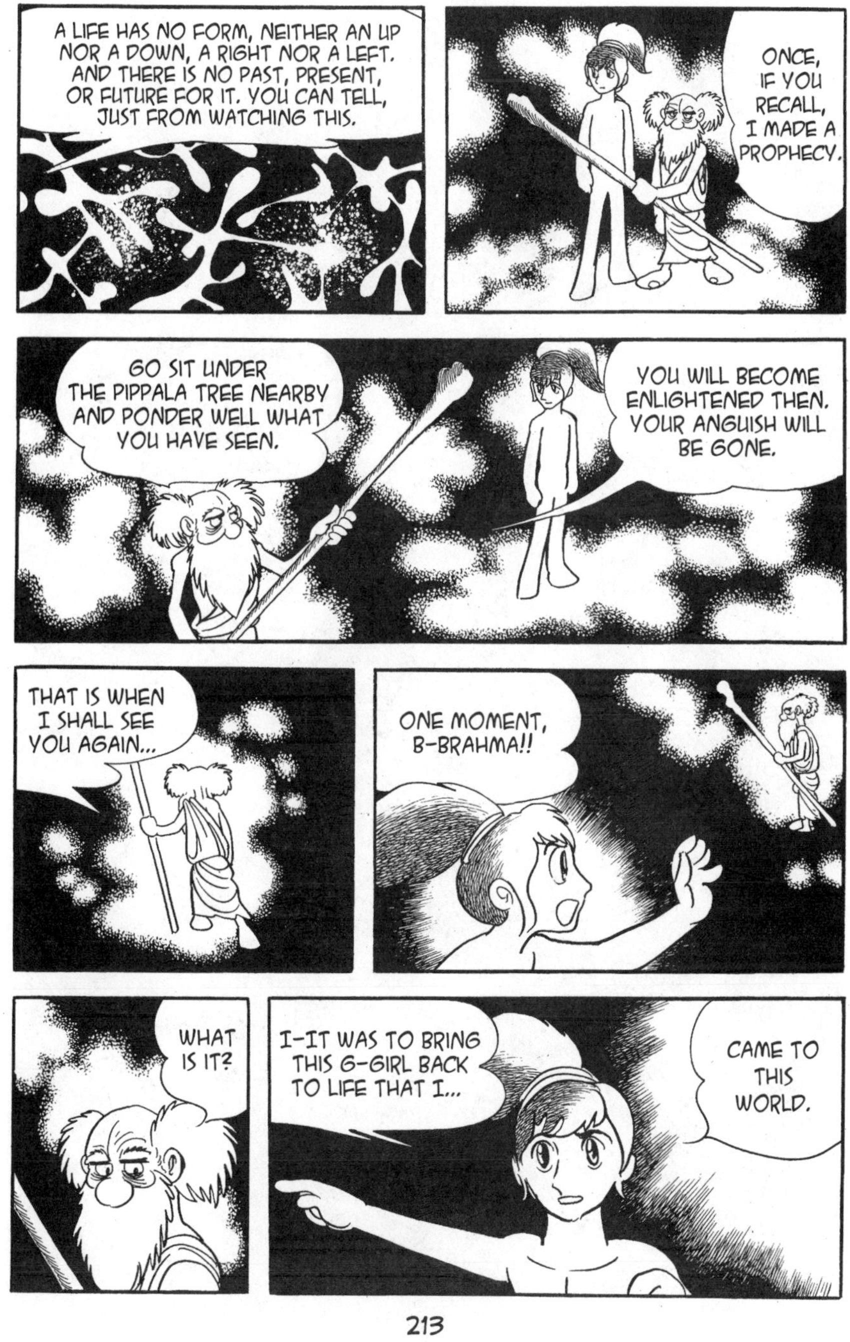
A LIFE HAS NO FORM, NEITHER AN UP NOR A DOWN, A RIGHT NOR A LEFT. AND THERE IS NO PAST, PRESENT, OR FUTURE FOR IT. YOU CAN TELL, JUST FROM WATCHING THIS.
ONCE, IF YOU RECALL, I MADE A PROPHECY.
GO SIT UNDER THE PIPPALA TREE NEARBY AND PONDER WELL WHAT YOU HAVE SEEN.
YOU WILL BECOME ENLIGHTENED THEN. YOUR ANGUISH WILL BE GONE.
THAT IS WHEN I SHALL SEE YOU AGAIN...
ONE MOMENT, B-BRAHMA!!
WHAT IS IT?
I-IT WAS TO BRING THIS G-GIRL BACK TO LIFE THAT I...
CAME TO THIS WORLD.

HMM

HER NAME IS SUJATA.

DO YOU KNOW WHERE SHE IS?

SHE PROBABLY MELTED INTO THAT BALL A WHILE AGO.

EACH PIECE OF LIFE IS THE SAME. TAKE ANY TO BRING HER BACK TO LIFE.

SHE WILL BE BORN ANEW, TO BE EXACT.

CHOOSE ONE THAT PLEASES YOU AND BE ON YOUR WAY.

BUT I CAN'T TELL IF THESE ARE ANIMAL OR HUMAN...

DIDN'T I TELL YOU? ANIMAL, PLANT OR HUMAN, IT'S THE SAME LIFE.

...

THIS ONE!

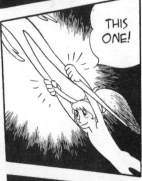

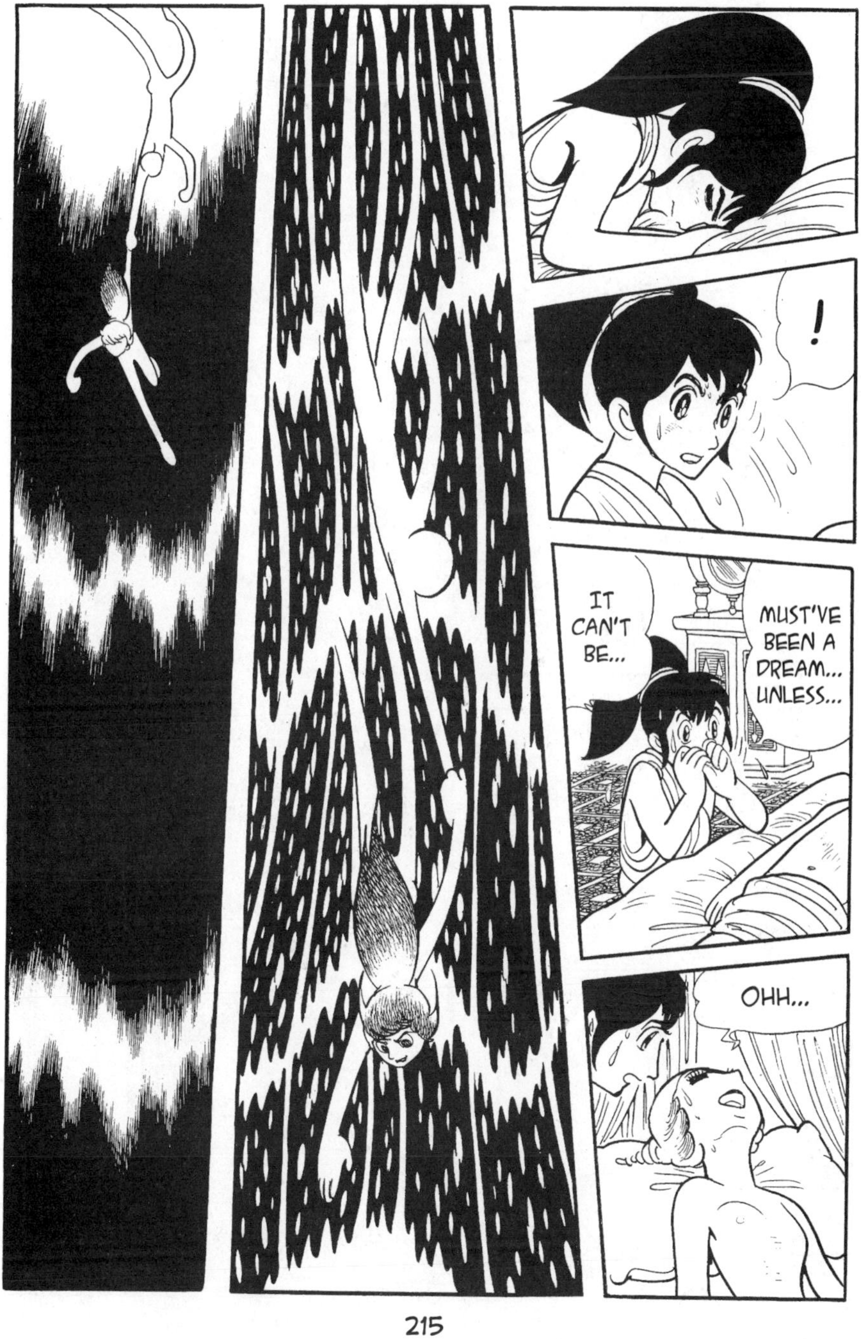
!
IT CAN'T BE...
MUST'VE BEEN A DREAM... UNLESS...
OHH...

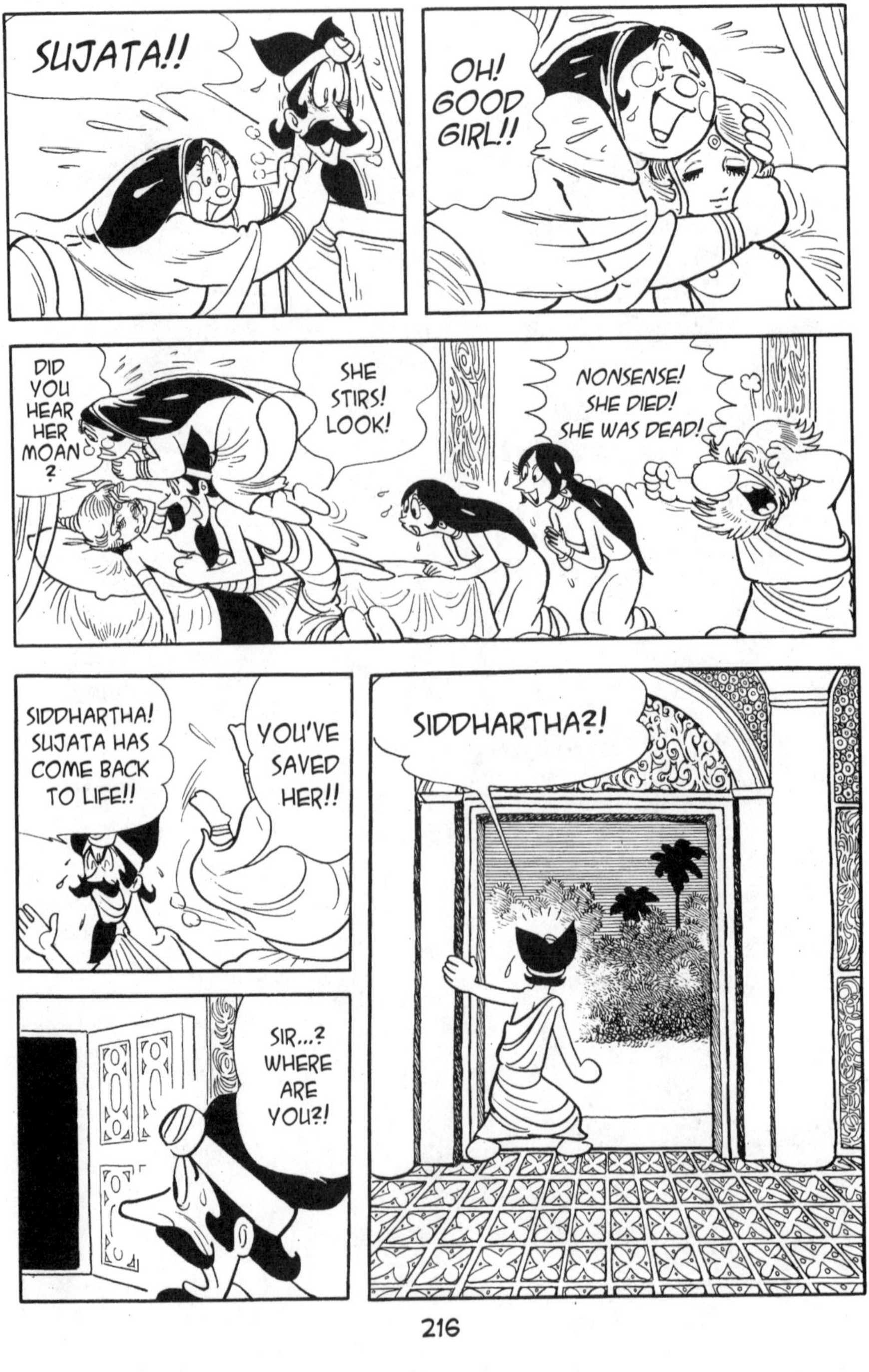
SUJATA!!
OH! GOOD GIRL!!
DID YOU HEAR HER MOAN?
SHE STIRS! LOOK!
NONSENSE! SHE DIED! SHE WAS DEAD!
SIDDHARTHA! SUJATA HAS COME BACK TO LIFE!!
YOU'VE SAVED HER!!
SIR...? WHERE ARE YOU?!
SIDDHARTHA?!

CHAPTER TEN

THE CRYSTAL PRINCE

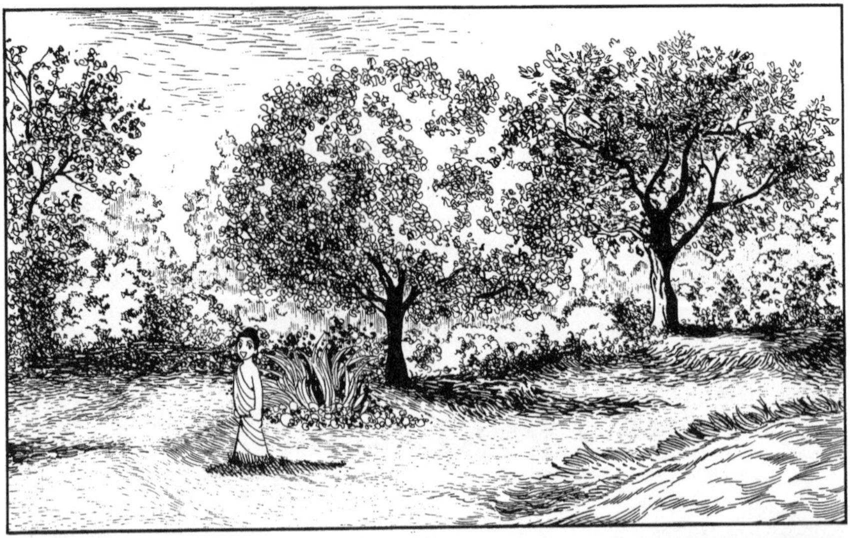

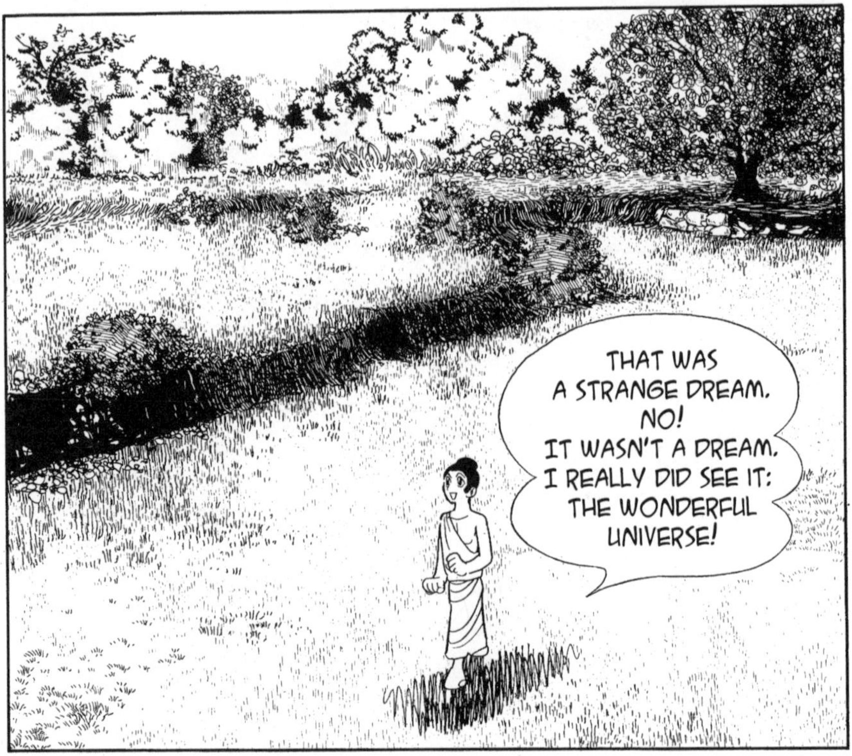
THAT WAS A STRANGE DREAM. NO! IT WASN'T A DREAM. I REALLY DID SEE IT: THE WONDERFUL UNIVERSE!

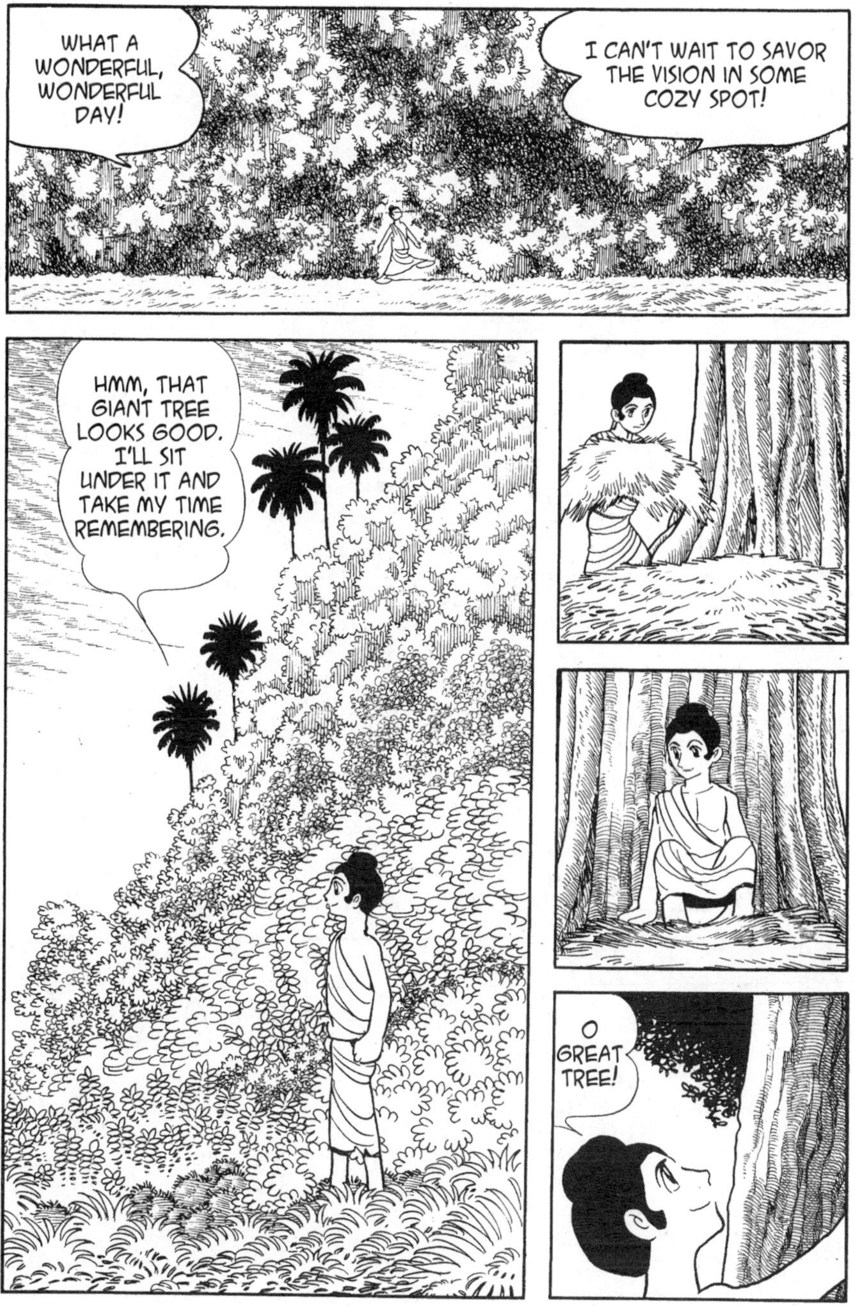
WHAT A WONDERFUL, WONDERFUL DAY!
I CAN'T WAIT TO SAVOR THE VISION IN SOME COZY SPOT!
HMM, THAT GIANT TREE LOOKS GOOD. I'LL SIT UNDER IT AND TAKE MY TIME REMEMBERING.
O GREAT TREE!

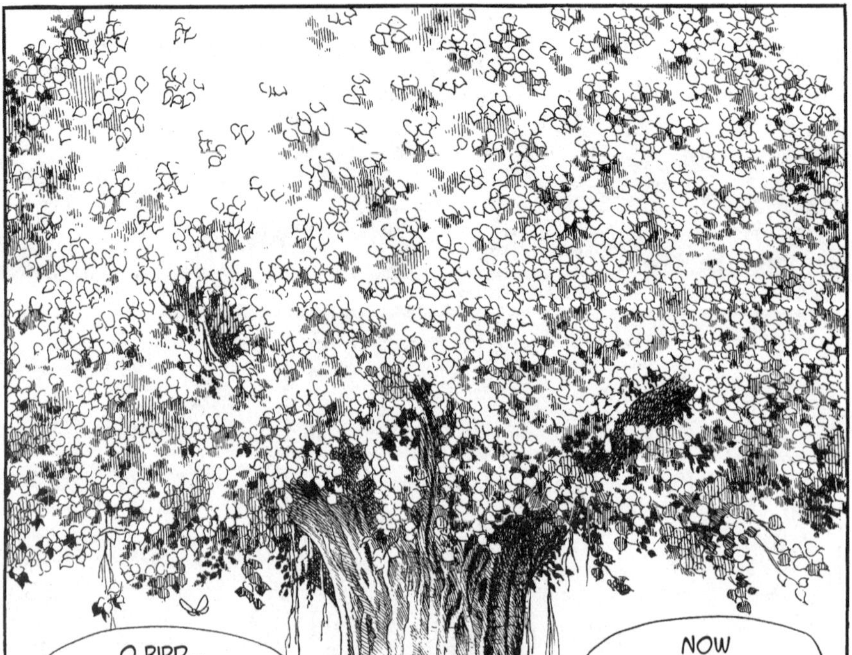
O BIRD... BUTTERFLY! BEE! ANT! AND YE NAMELESS BLADES OF GRASS...
NOW I AM CERTAIN THAT YOU ARE MY BROTHERS AND SISTERS.

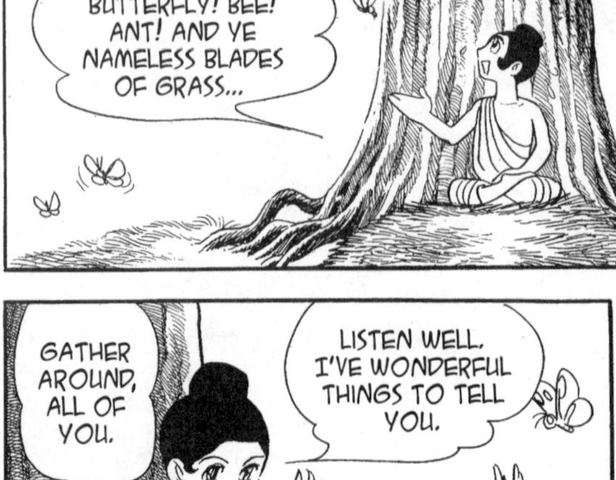
GATHER AROUND, ALL OF YOU.
LISTEN WELL. I'VE WONDERFUL THINGS TO TELL YOU.
Tweet

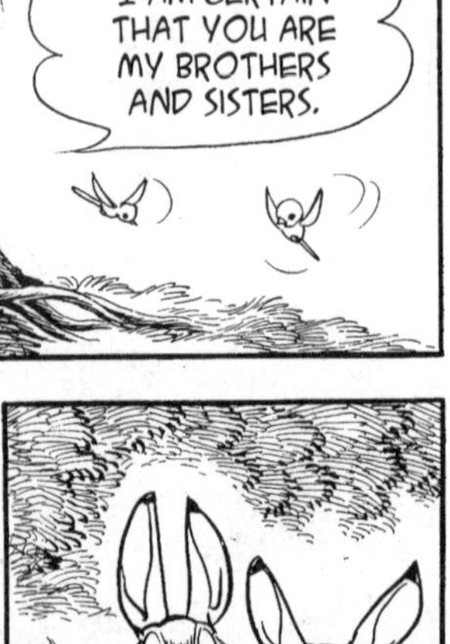

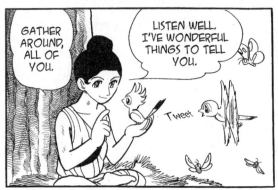

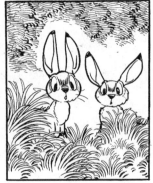

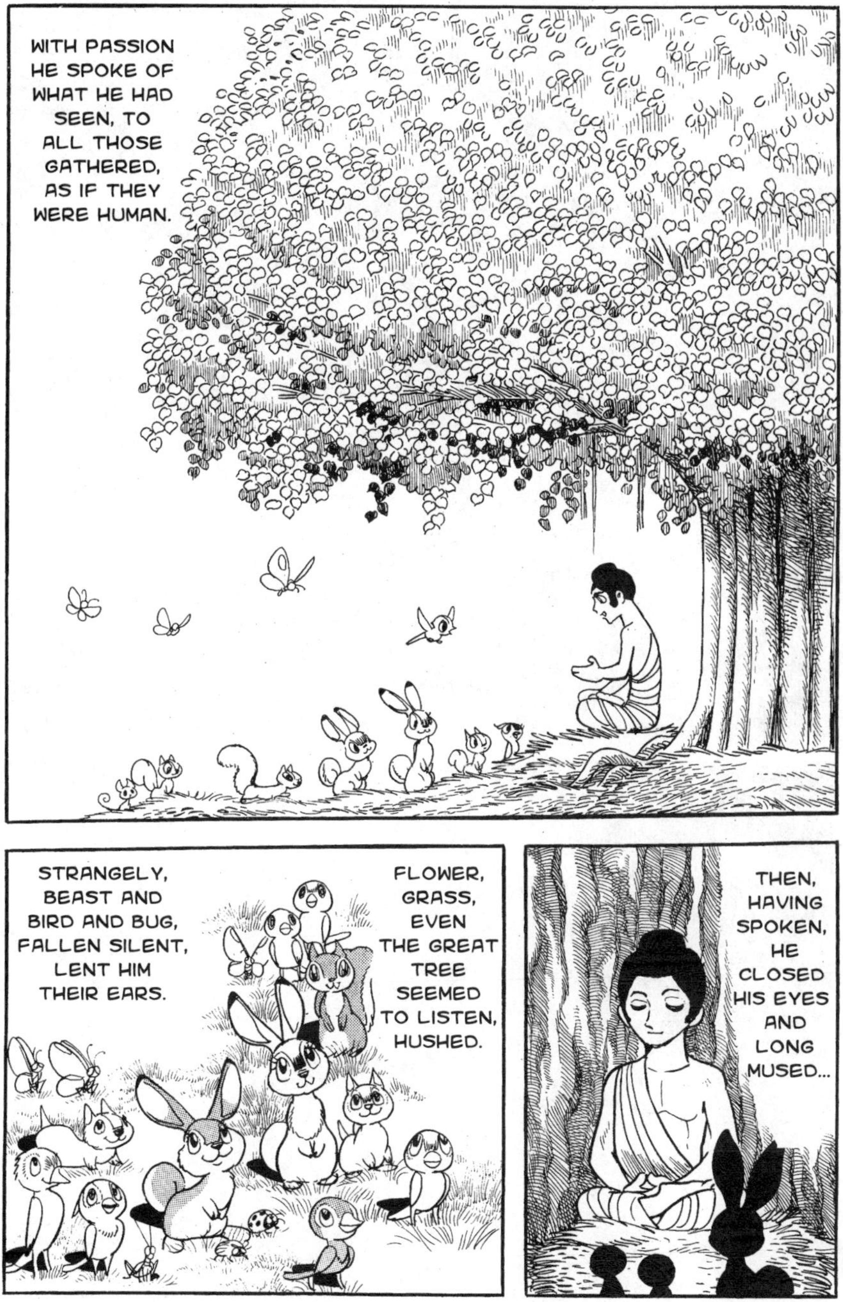
WITH PASSION HE SPOKE OF WHAT HE HAD SEEN, TO ALL THOSE GATHERED, AS IF THEY WERE HUMAN.
STRANGELY, BEAST AND BIRD AND BUG, FALLEN SILENT, LENT HIM THEIR EARS.
FLOWER, GRASS, EVEN THE GREAT TREE SEEMED TO LISTEN, HUSHED.
THEN, HAVING SPOKEN, HE CLOSED HIS EYES AND LONG MUSED...

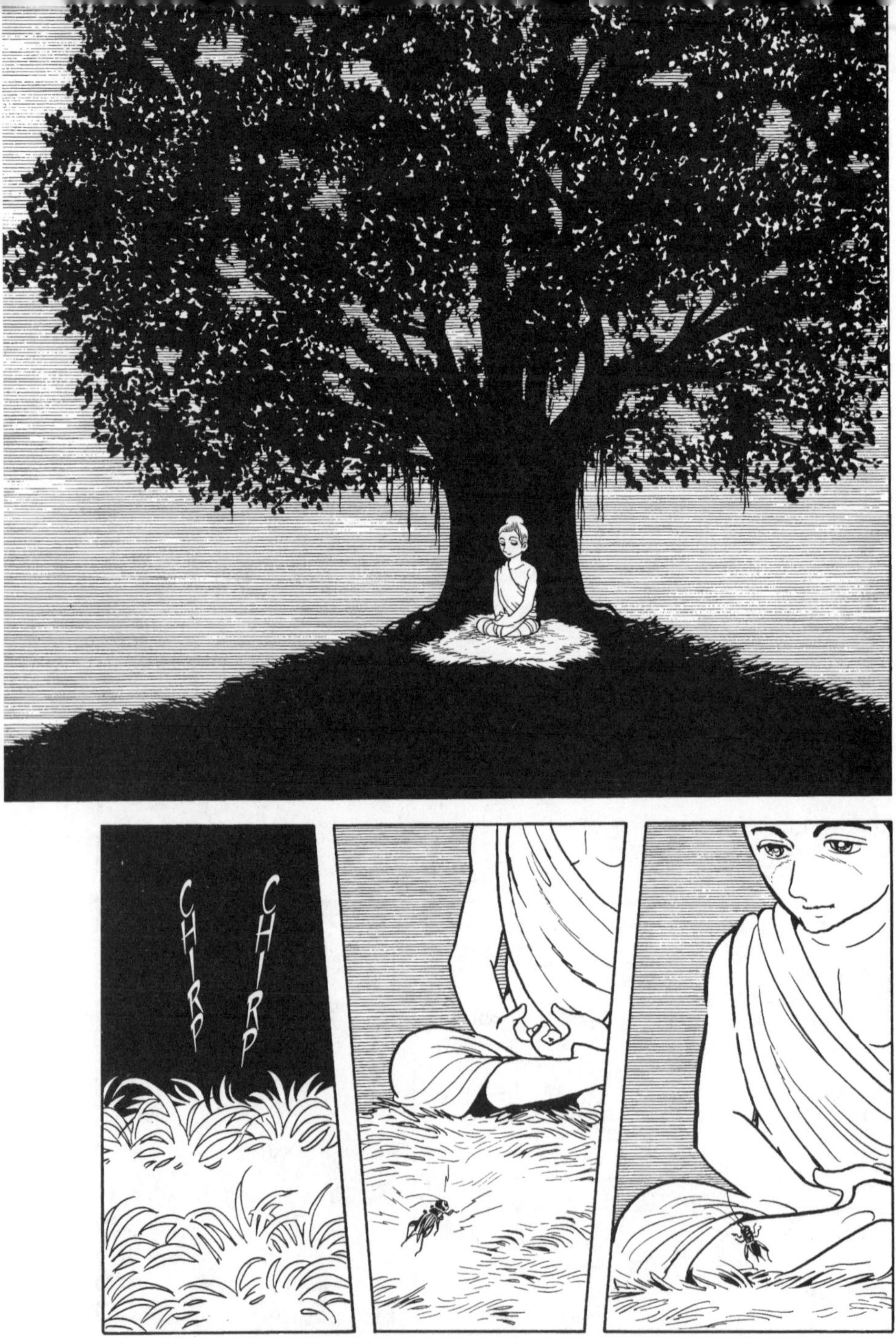
CHIRP
CHIRP

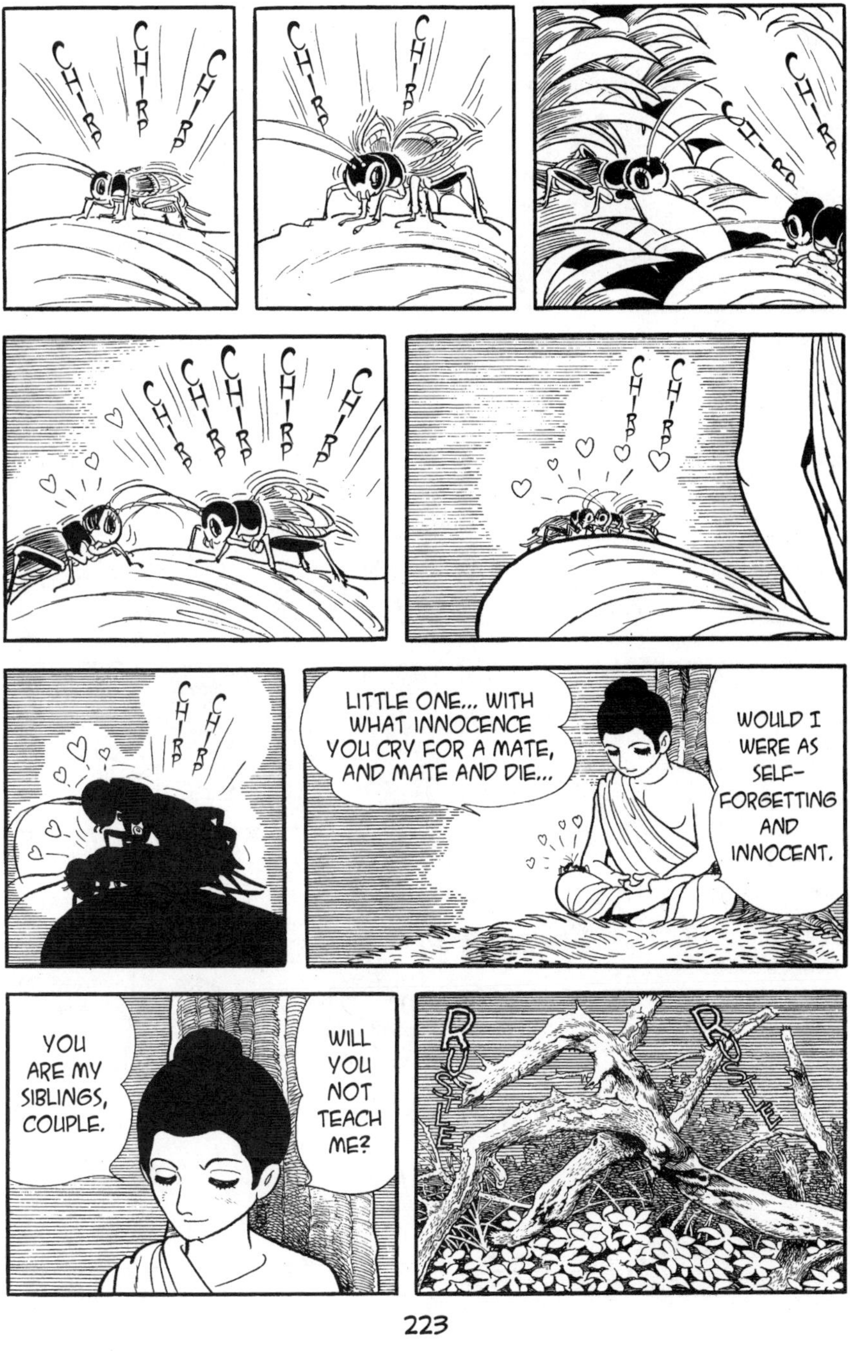
CHIRP
CHIRP
CHIRP
CHIRP
CHIRP
CHIRP
CHIRP
CHIRP
CHIRP
CHIRP
CHIRP
CHIRP
CHIRP
CHIRP
CHIRP
CHIRP
CHIRP
LITTLE ONE... WITH WHAT INNOCENCE YOU CRY FOR A MATE, AND MATE AND DIE...
WOULD I WERE AS SELF-FORGETTING AND INNOCENT.
YOU ARE MY SIBLINGS, COUPLE.
WILL YOU NOT TEACH ME?
RUSTLE
RUSTLE

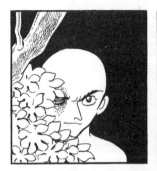

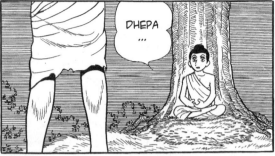

DHEPA ...
WHY ARE YOU HERE?
I THOUGHT I TOLD YOU I NEVER WANTED TO SEE YOU AGAIN.
OR HAVE YOU COME TO JOIN ME UNDER THIS PIPPALA
TO HEAR ME TELL OF THE WONDER-FUL THING I SAW?
NO, THAT'S NOT THE CASE. I HAVE MY PRIDE. I WOULDN'T ASK YOU NOW TO SHARE A TALE WITH ME.
RATHER, I BEAR TIDINGS FOR YOU.
A NEW SAMANNA WHO CAME TO THE FOREST OF TRIALS TODAY BROUGHT US NEWS ...
THAT CONCERNS YOU.

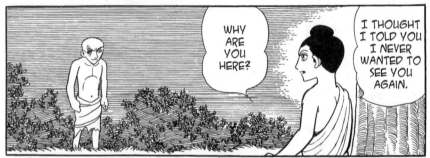

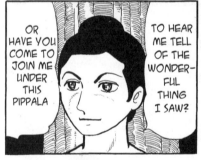

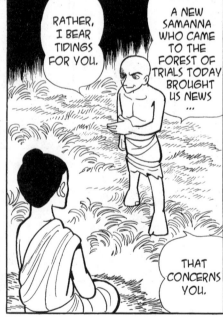

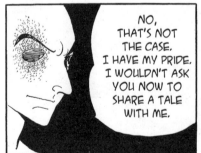

WORD'S THAT YOUR COUNTRY KAPILAVASTU IS NO MORE.

WHAT ?!

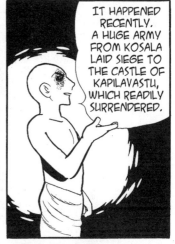

IT HAPPENED RECENTLY. A HUGE ARMY FROM KOSALA LAID SIEGE TO THE CASTLE OF KAPILAVASTU, WHICH READILY SURRENDERED.

RUMOR'S THAT YOU SHAKYA HAVE BEEN MASSACRED AND THAT YOUR PARENTS HAVE BEEN DRAGGED BEFORE KOSALA'S KING PRASENAJIT.

ARE YOU SERIOUS ?!

THAT'S ALL I KNOW. YOU'LL HAVE TO RUSH BACK HOME TO FIND OUT...

WHETHER YOUR PARENTS ARE ALIVE AND WHAT'S BECOME OF YOUR REALM.

WAIT! WHY DID PRASENAJIT SUDDENLY...

225

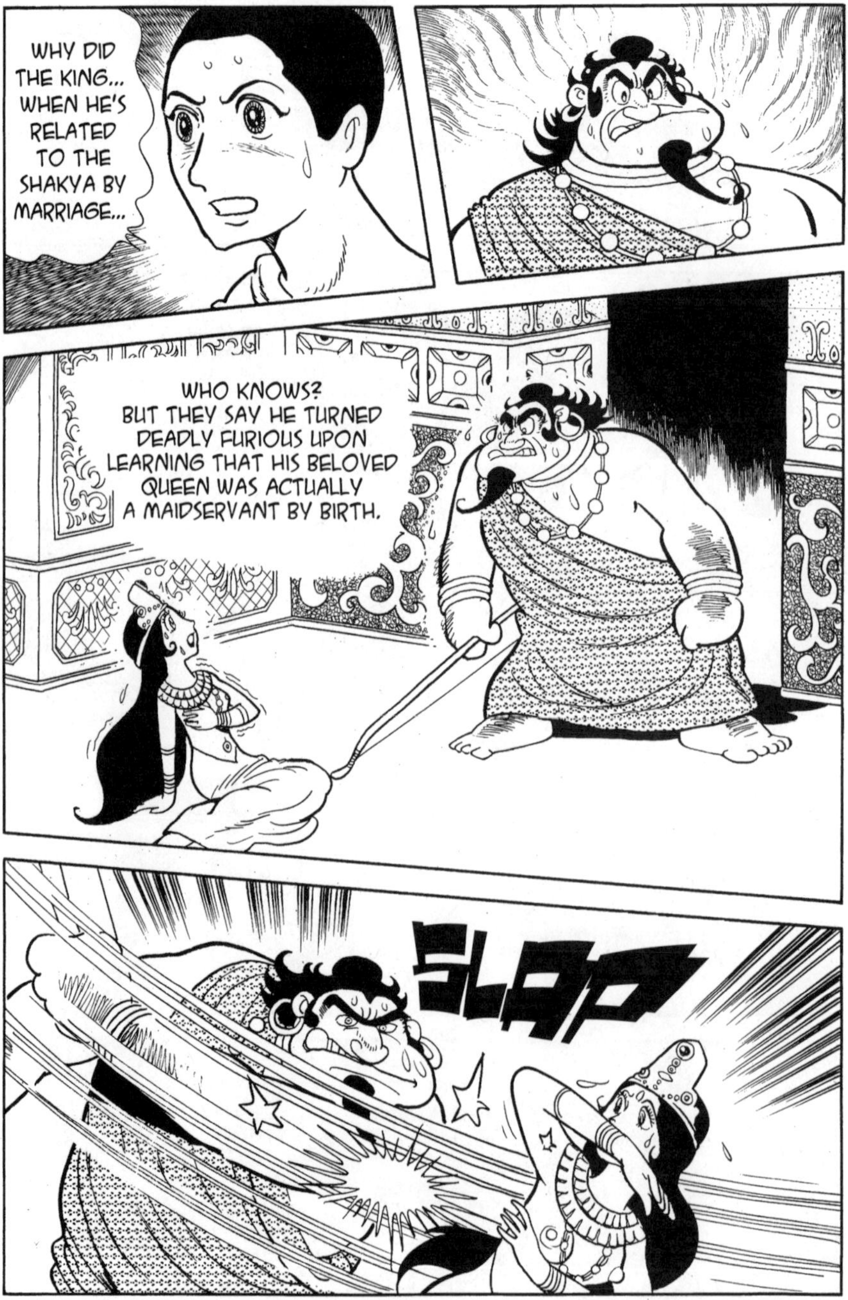
WHY DID THE KING... WHEN HE'S RELATED TO THE SHAKYA BY MARRIAGE...
WHO KNOWS? BUT THEY SAY HE TURNED DEADLY FURIOUS UPON LEARNING THAT HIS BELOVED QUEEN WAS ACTUALLY A MAIDSERVANT BY BIRTH.
SLAP

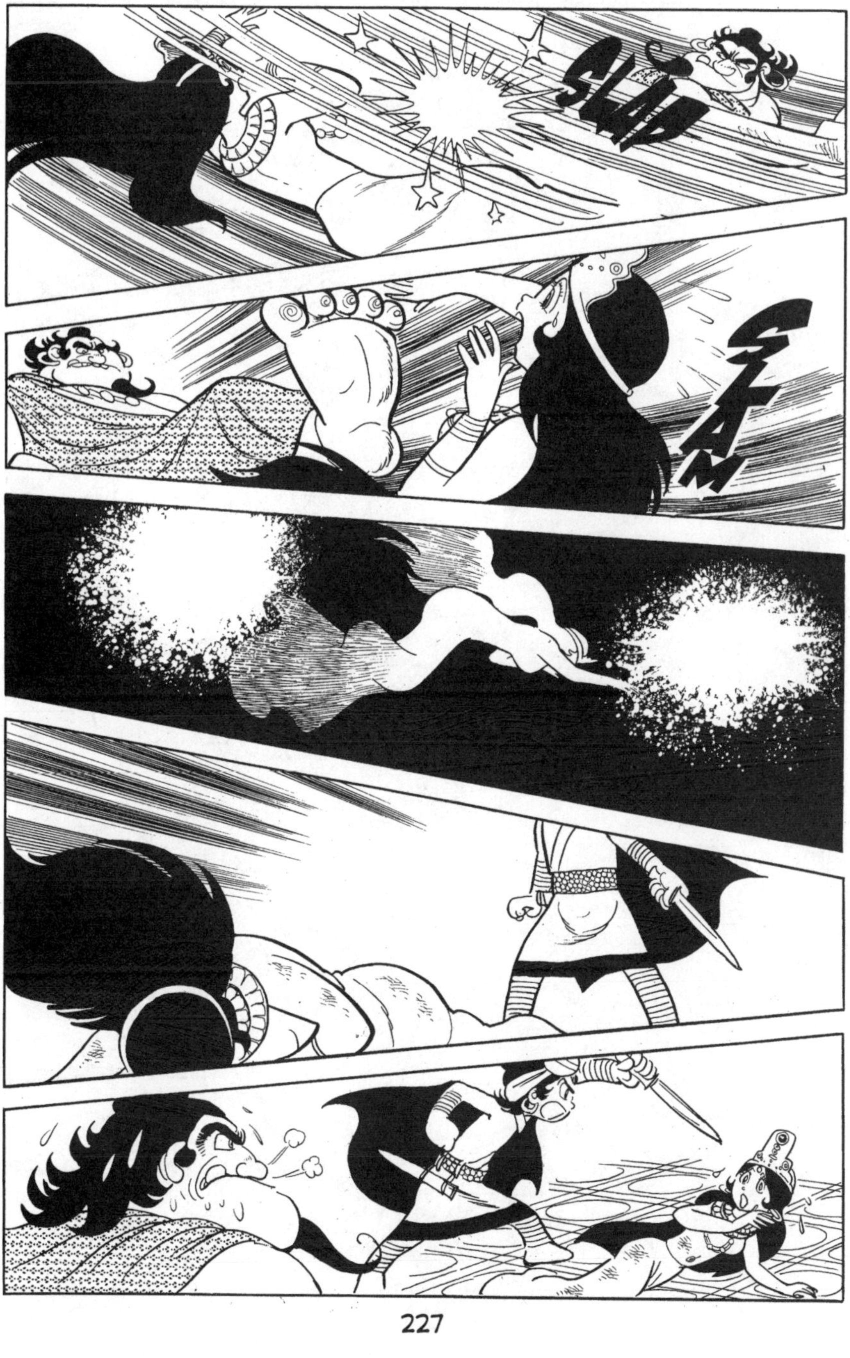
SLAP
SLAM

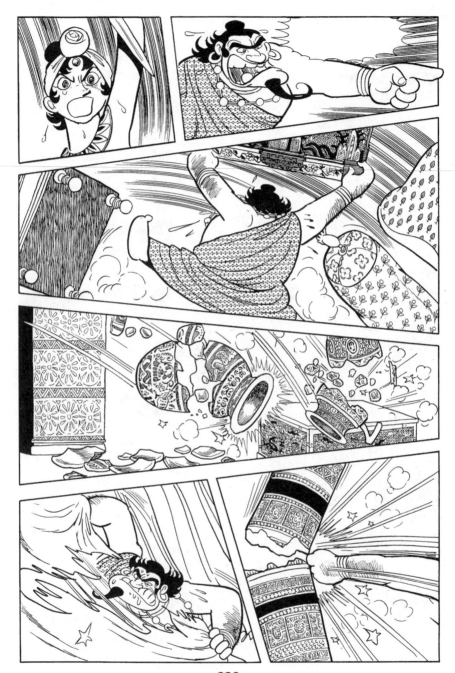

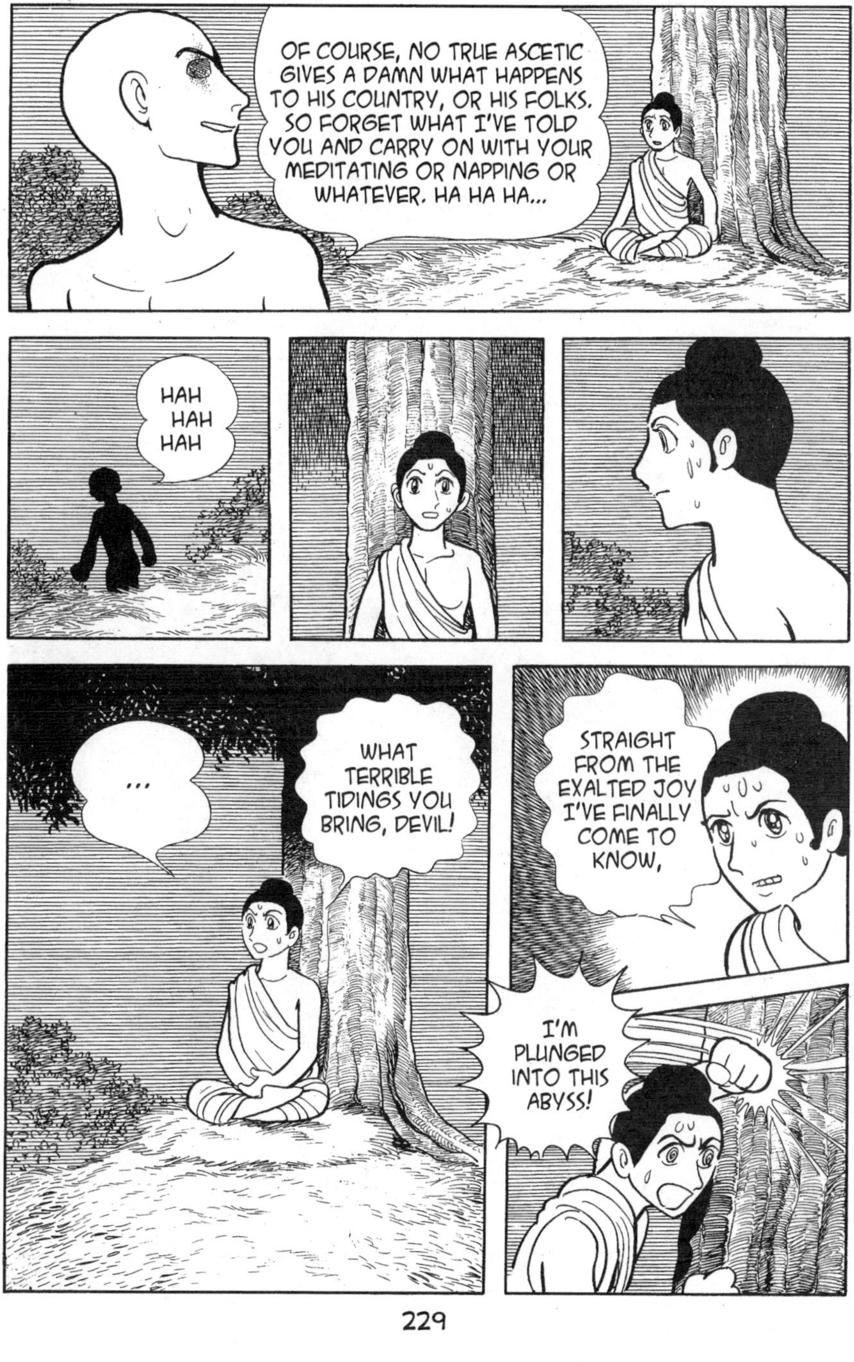
OF COURSE, NO TRUE ASCETIC GIVES A DAMN WHAT HAPPENS TO HIS COUNTRY, OR HIS FOLKS. SO FORGET WHAT I'VE TOLD YOU AND CARRY ON WITH YOUR MEDITATING OR NAPPING OR WHATEVER. HA HA HA...
HAH HAH HAH
...
WHAT TERRIBLE TIDINGS YOU BRING, DEVIL!
STRAIGHT FROM THE EXALTED JOY I'VE FINALLY COME TO KNOW,
I'M PLUNGED INTO THIS ABYSS!

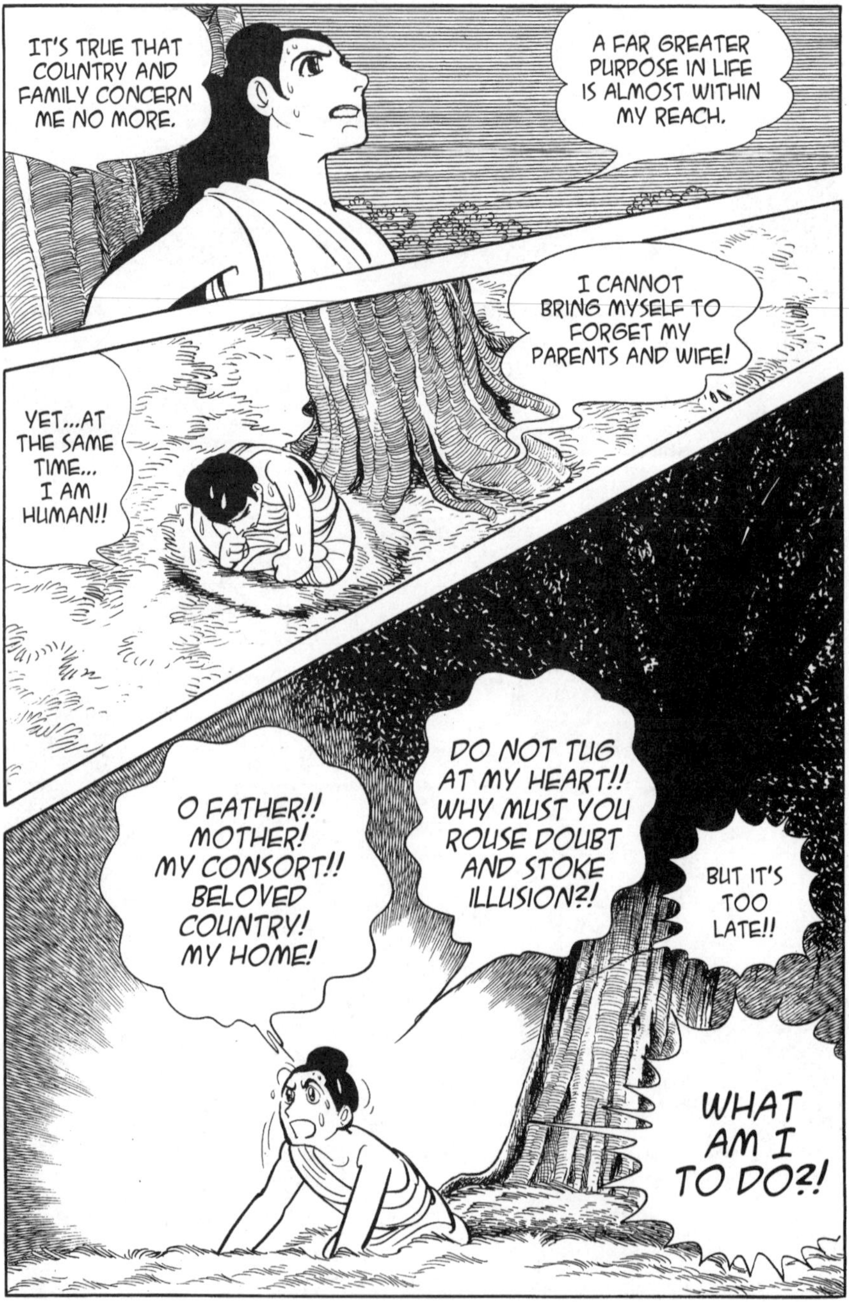
IT'S TRUE THAT COUNTRY AND FAMILY CONCERN ME NO MORE.
A FAR GREATER PURPOSE IN LIFE IS ALMOST WITHIN MY REACH.
I CANNOT BRING MYSELF TO FORGET MY PARENTS AND WIFE!
YET...AT THE SAME TIME... I AM HUMAN!!
O FATHER!! MOTHER! MY CONSORT!! BELOVED COUNTRY! MY HOME!
DO NOT TUG AT MY HEART!! WHY MUST YOU ROUSE DOUBT AND STOKE ILLUSION?!
BUT IT'S TOO LATE!!
WHAT AM I TO DO?!

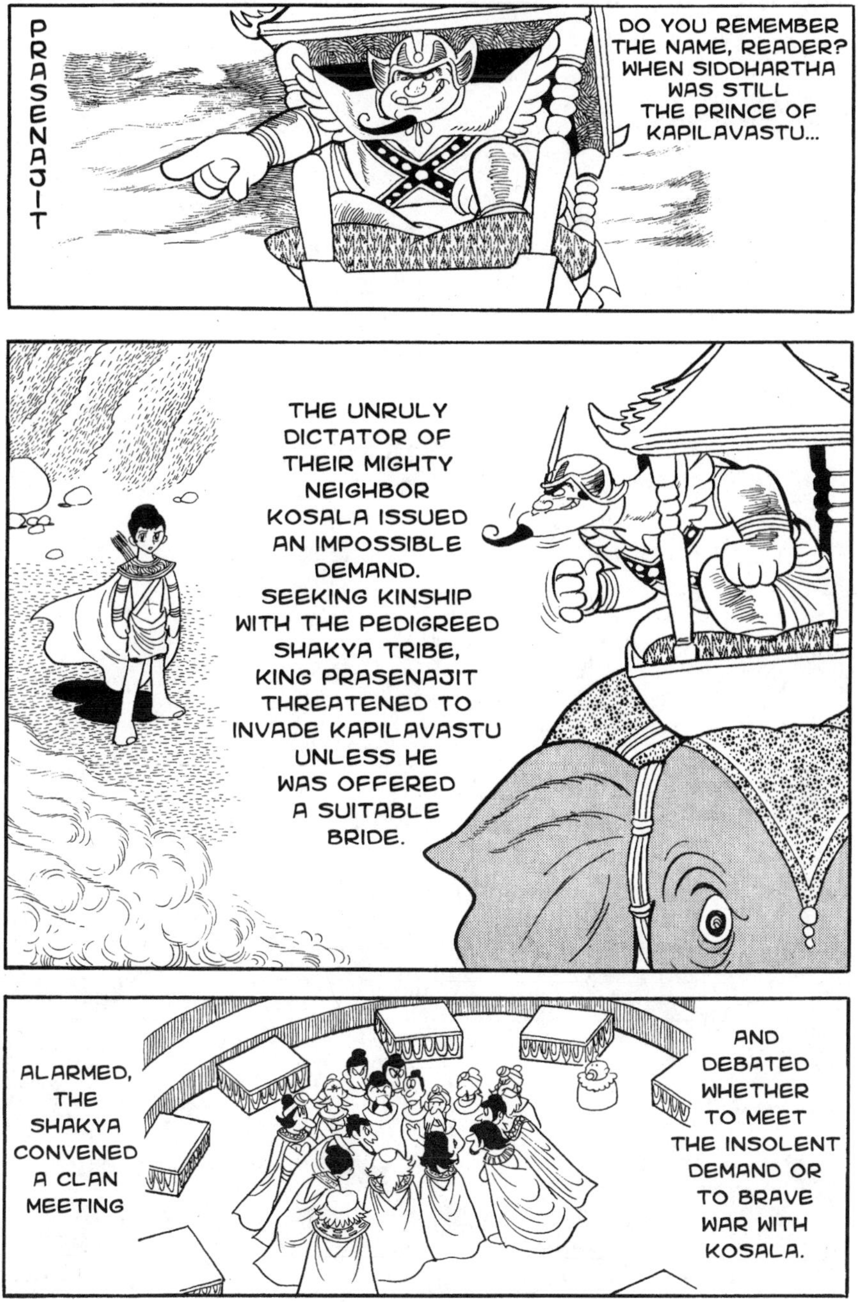
PRASENAJIT
DO YOU REMEMBER THE NAME, READER? WHEN SIDDHARTHA WAS STILL THE PRINCE OF KAPILAVASTU...
THE UNRULY DICTATOR OF THEIR MIGHTY NEIGHBOR KOSALA ISSUED AN IMPOSSIBLE DEMAND. SEEKING KINSHIP WITH THE PEDIGREED SHAKYA TRIBE, KING PRASENAJIT THREATENED TO INVADE KAPILAVASTU UNLESS HE WAS OFFERED A SUITABLE BRIDE.
ALARMED, THE SHAKYA CONVENED A CLAN MEETING
AND DEBATED WHETHER TO MEET THE INSOLENT DEMAND OR TO BRAVE WAR WITH KOSALA.

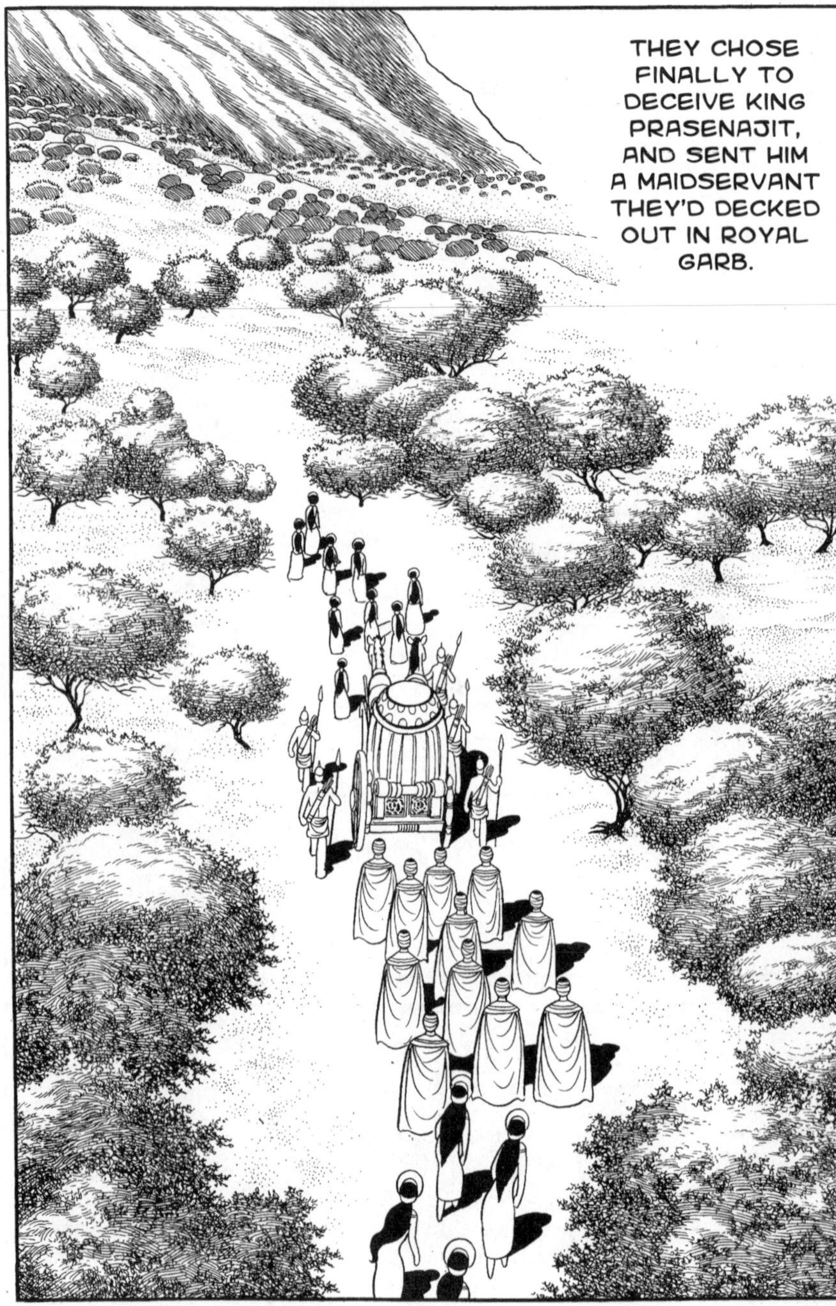
THEY CHOSE FINALLY TO DECEIVE KING PRASENAJIT, AND SENT HIM A MAIDSERVANT THEY'D DECKED OUT IN ROYAL GARB.

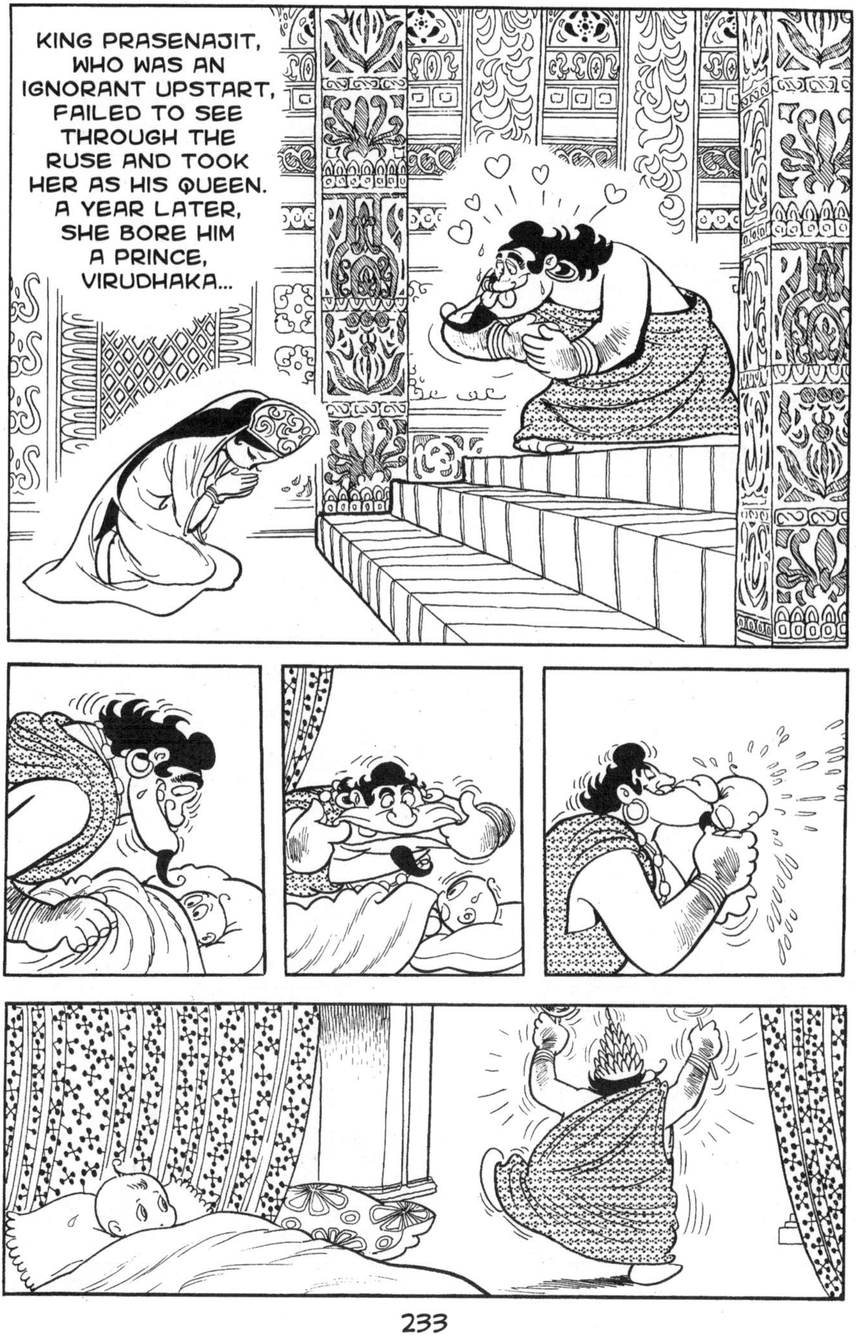
KING PRASENAJIT, WHO WAS AN IGNORANT UPSTART, FAILED TO SEE THROUGH THE RUSE AND TOOK HER AS HIS QUEEN. A YEAR LATER, SHE BORE HIM A PRINCE, VIRUDHAKA...

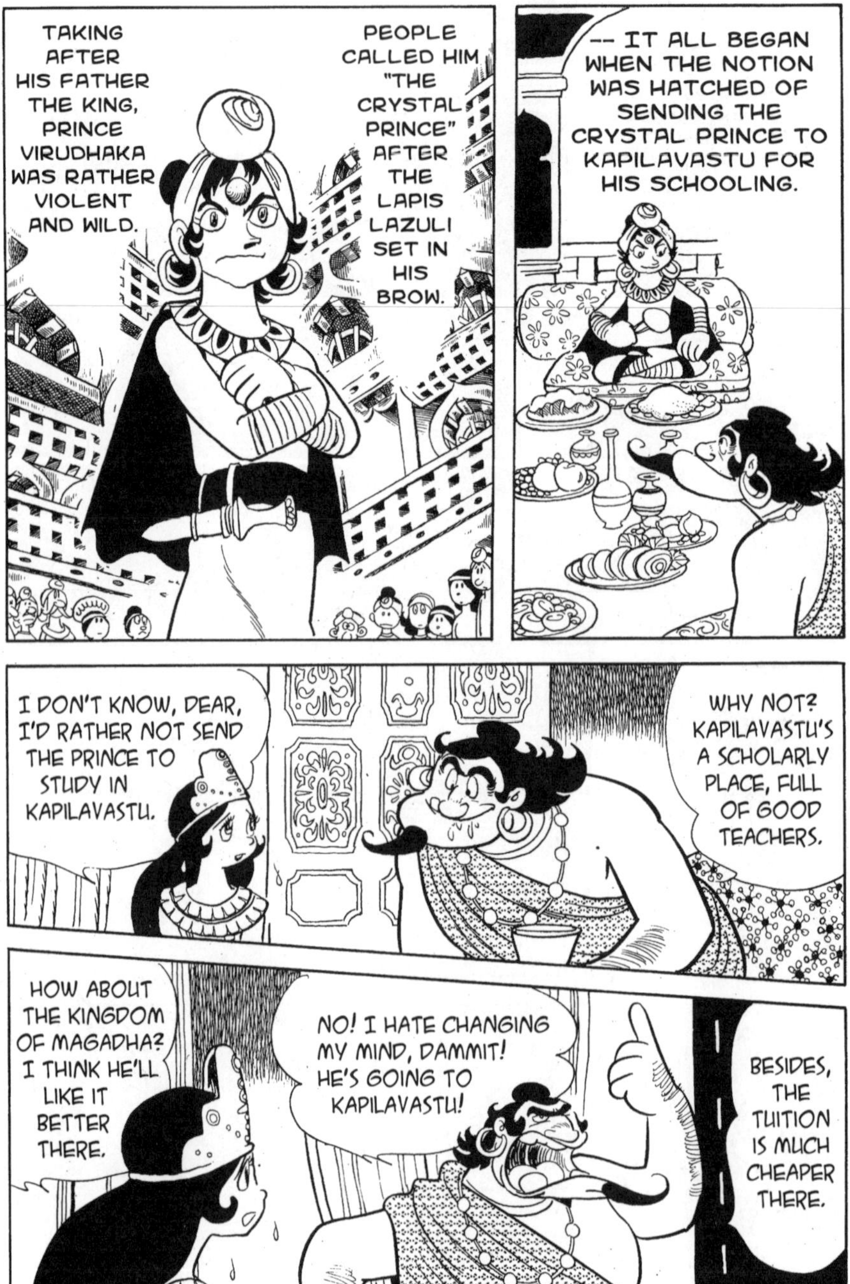
TAKING AFTER HIS FATHER THE KING, PRINCE VIRUDHAKA WAS RATHER VIOLENT AND WILD.
PEOPLE CALLED HIM "THE CRYSTAL PRINCE" AFTER THE LAPIS LAZULI SET IN HIS BROW.
-- IT ALL BEGAN WHEN THE NOTION WAS HATCHED OF SENDING THE CRYSTAL PRINCE TO KAPILAVASTU FOR HIS SCHOOLING.
I DON'T KNOW, DEAR, I'D RATHER NOT SEND THE PRINCE TO STUDY IN KAPILAVASTU.
WHY NOT? KAPILAVASTU'S A SCHOLARLY PLACE, FULL OF GOOD TEACHERS.
HOW ABOUT THE KINGDOM OF MAGADHA? I THINK HE'LL LIKE IT BETTER THERE.
NO! I HATE CHANGING MY MIND, DAMMIT! HE'S GOING TO KAPILAVASTU!
BESIDES, THE TUITION IS MUCH CHEAPER THERE.

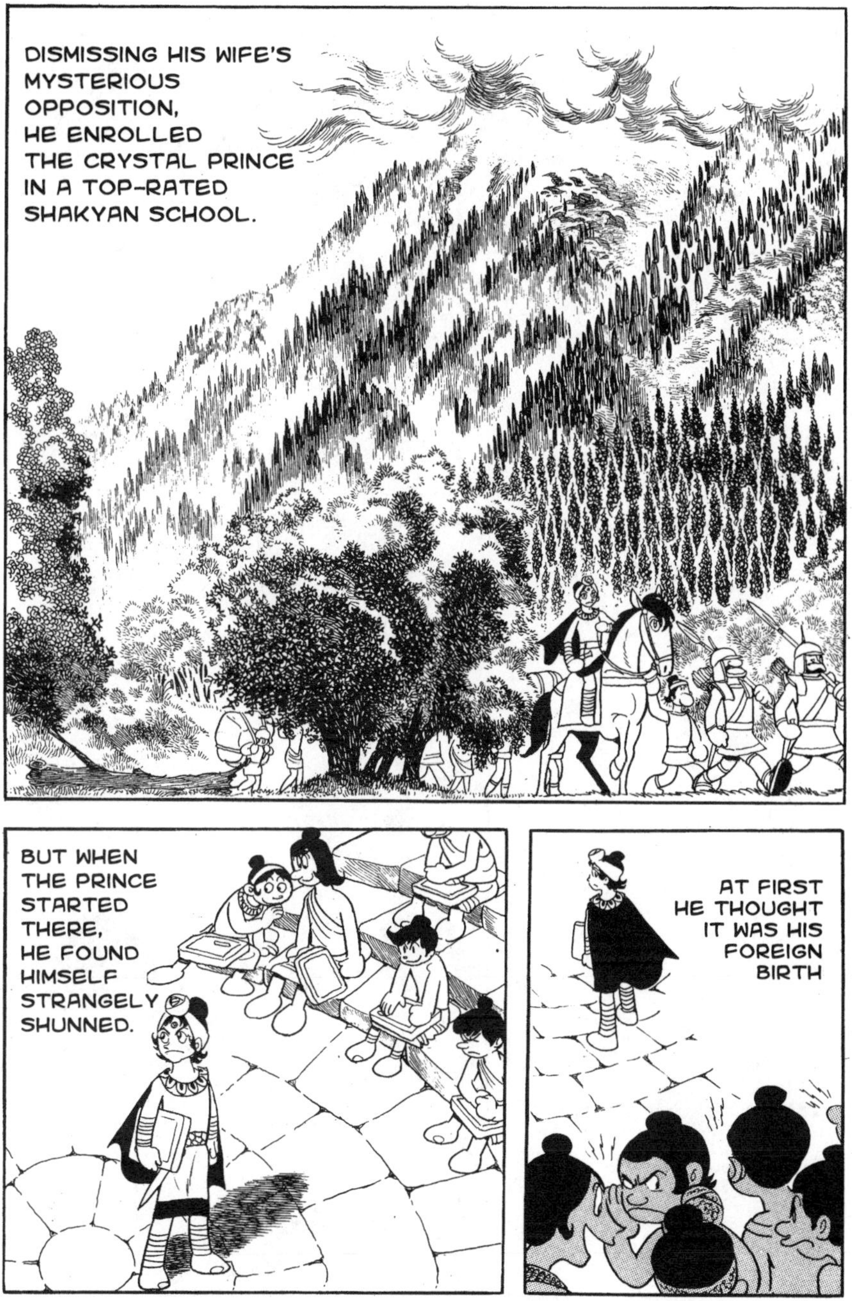
DISMISSING HIS WIFE'S MYSTERIOUS OPPOSITION, HE ENROLLED THE CRYSTAL PRINCE IN A TOP-RATED SHAKYAN SCHOOL.
BUT WHEN THE PRINCE STARTED THERE, HE FOUND HIMSELF STRANGELY SHUNNED.
AT FIRST HE THOUGHT IT WAS HIS FOREIGN BIRTH

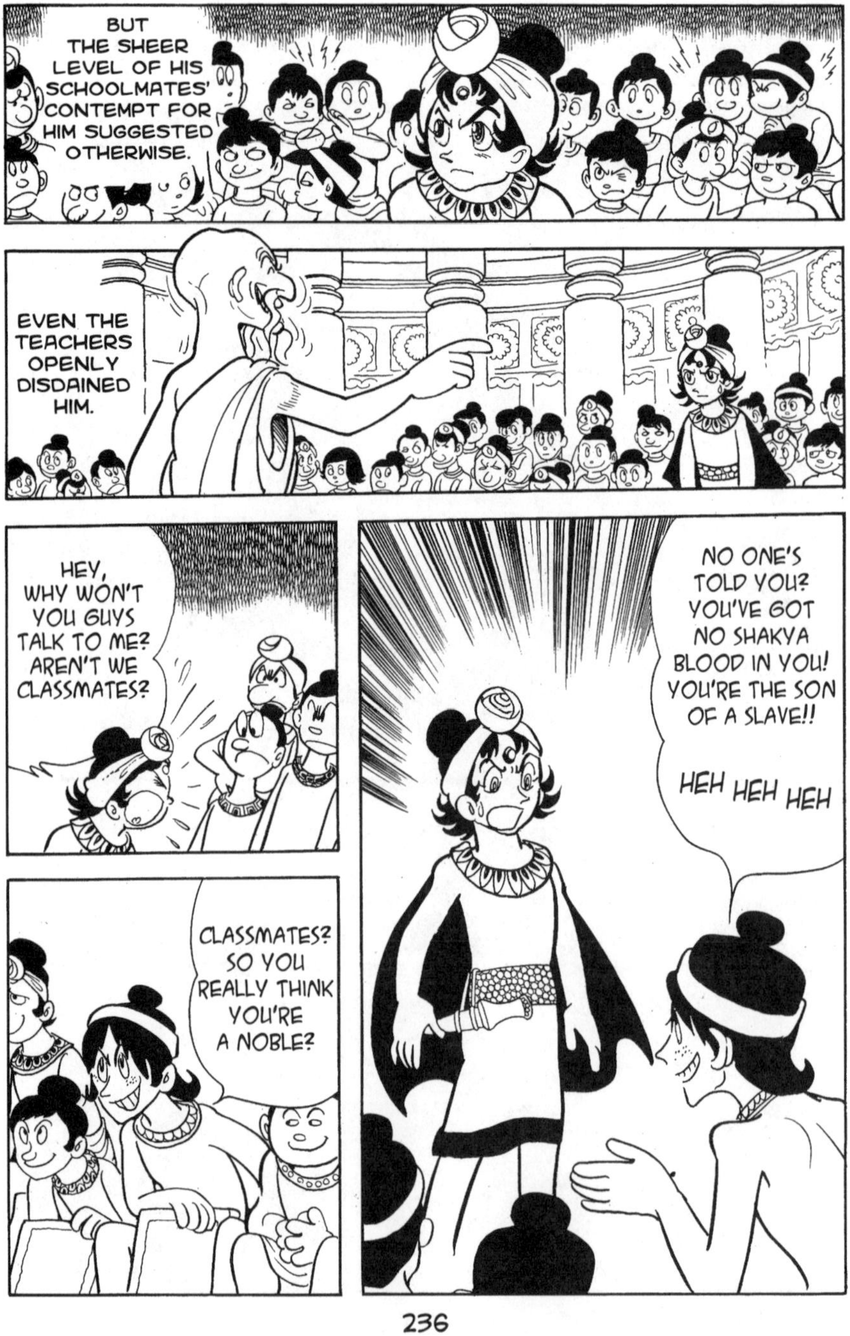
BUT THE SHEER LEVEL OF HIS SCHOOLMATES' CONTEMPT FOR HIM SUGGESTED OTHERWISE.
EVEN THE TEACHERS OPENLY DISDAINED HIM.
HEY, WHY WON'T YOU GUYS TALK TO ME? AREN'T WE CLASSMATES?
CLASSMATES? SO YOU REALLY THINK YOU'RE A NOBLE?
NO ONE'S TOLD YOU? YOU'VE GOT NO SHAKYA BLOOD IN YOU! YOU'RE THE SON OF A SLAVE!!
HEH HEH HEH

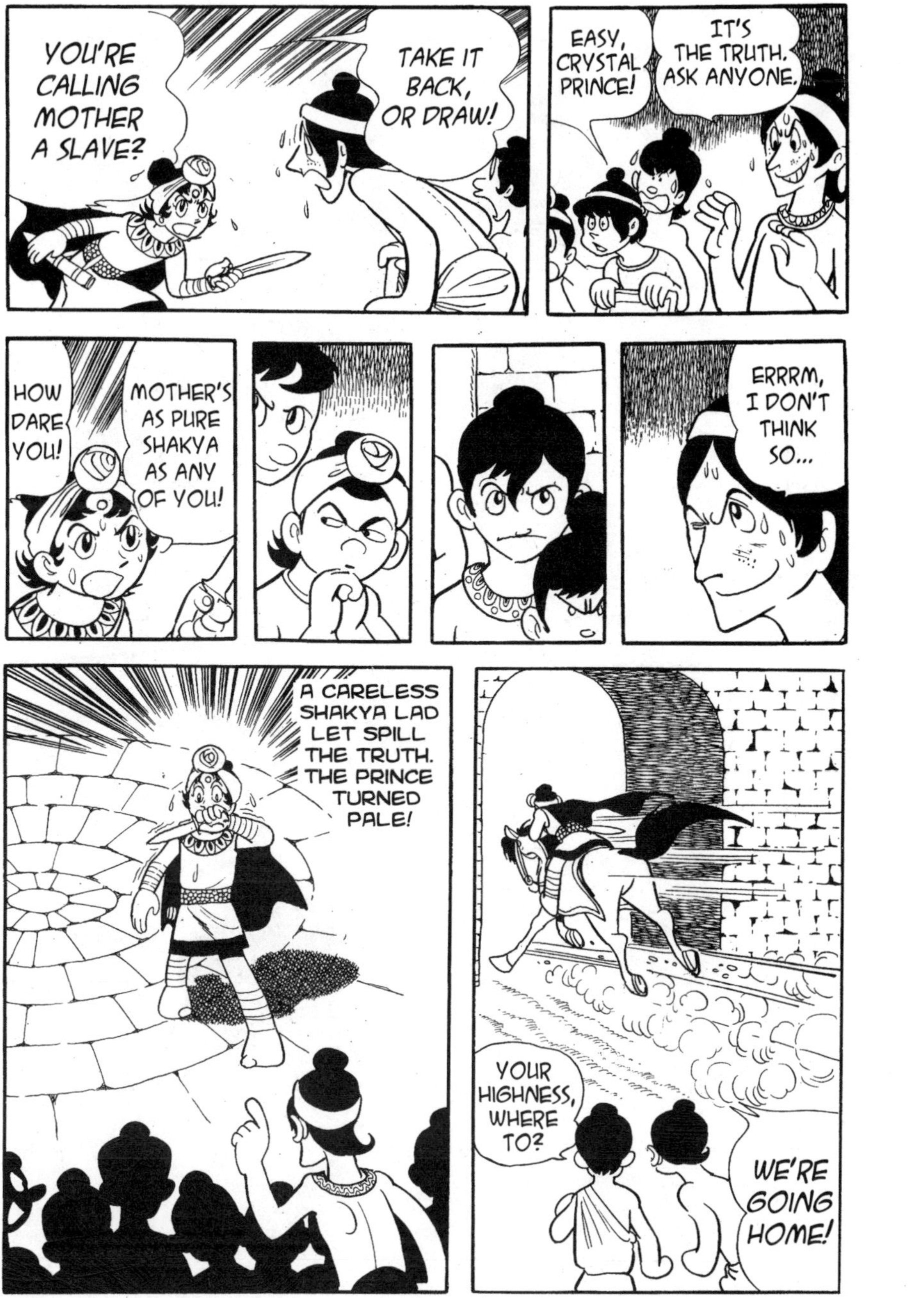
YOU'RE CALLING MOTHER A SLAVE?
TAKE IT BACK, OR DRAW!
EASY, CRYSTAL PRINCE!
IT'S THE TRUTH. ASK ANYONE.
HOW DARE YOU!
MOTHER'S AS PURE SHAKYA AS ANY OF YOU!
ERRRM, I DON'T THINK SO...
A CARELESS SHAKYA LAD LET SPILL THE TRUTH. THE PRINCE TURNED PALE!
YOUR HIGHNESS, WHERE TO?
WE'RE GOING HOME!

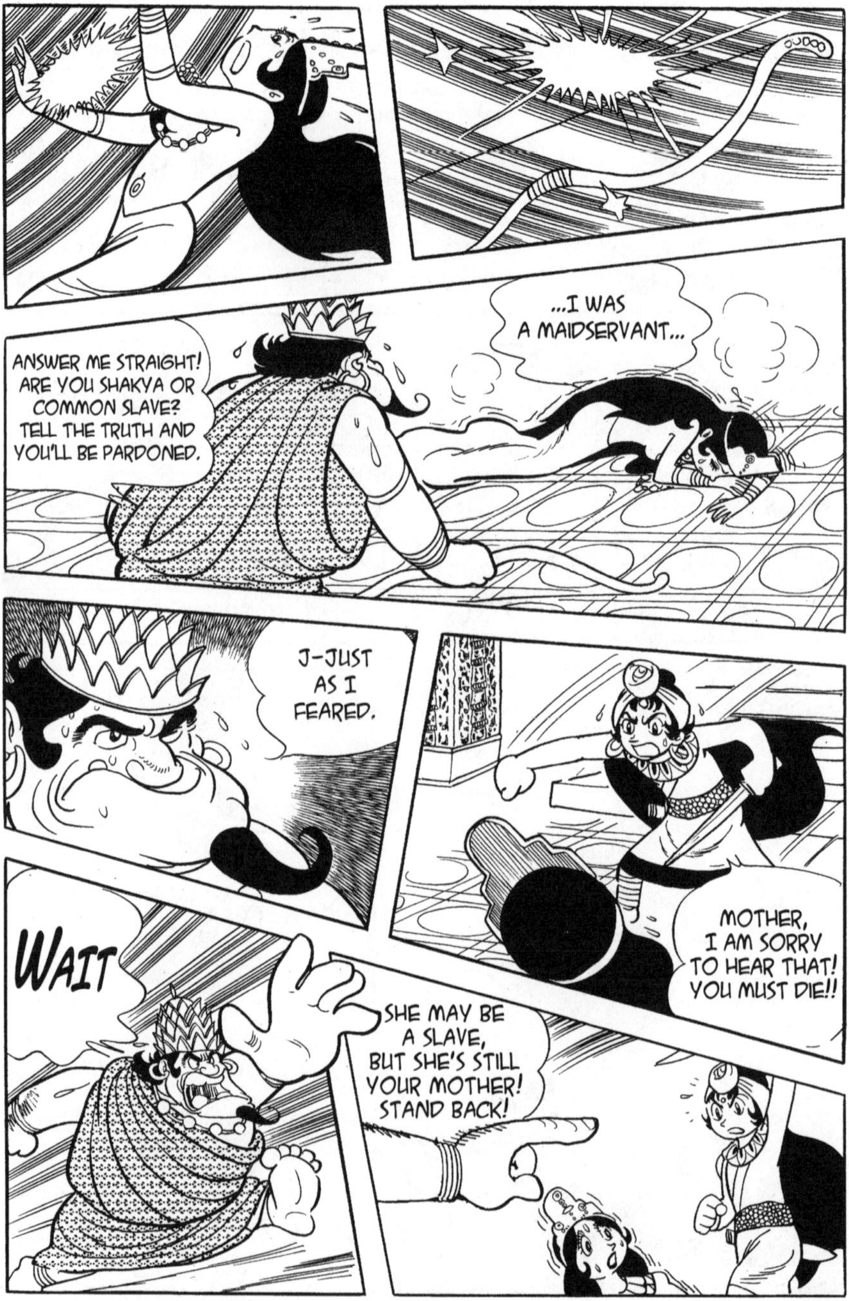

ANSWER ME STRAIGHT! ARE YOU SHAKYA OR COMMON SLAVE? TELL THE TRUTH AND YOU'LL BE PARDONED.
...I WAS A MAIDSERVANT...
J-JUST AS I FEARED.
MOTHER, I AM SORRY TO HEAR THAT! YOU MUST DIE!!
WAIT
SHE MAY BE A SLAVE, BUT SHE'S STILL YOUR MOTHER! STAND BACK!

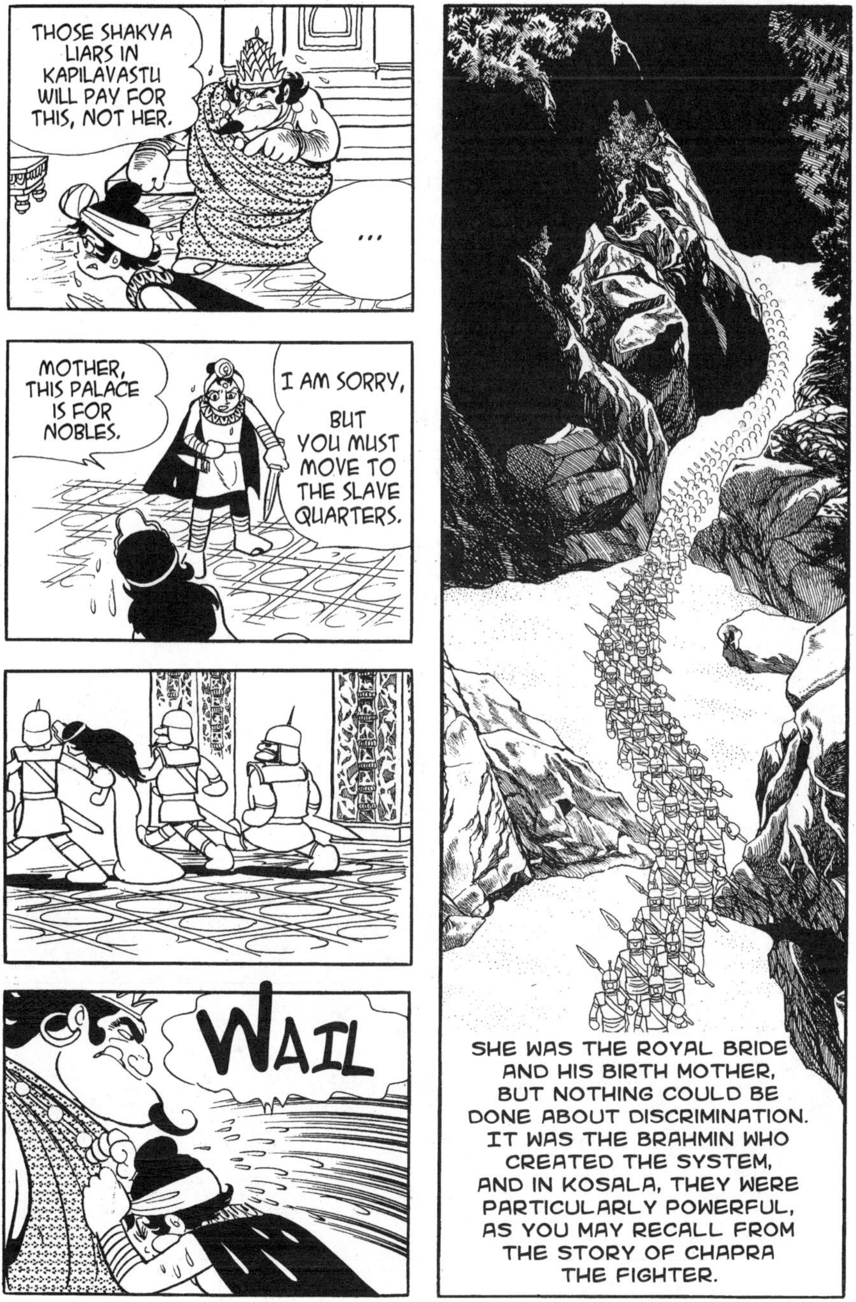
THOSE SHAKYA LIARS IN KAPILAVASTU WILL PAY FOR THIS, NOT HER.
...
MOTHER, THIS PALACE IS FOR NOBLES.
I AM SORRY,
BUT YOU MUST MOVE TO THE SLAVE QUARTERS.
WAIL
SHE WAS THE ROYAL BRIDE AND HIS BIRTH MOTHER, BUT NOTHING COULD BE DONE ABOUT DISCRIMINATION. IT WAS THE BRAHMIN WHO CREATED THE SYSTEM, AND IN KOSALA, THEY WERE PARTICULARLY POWERFUL, AS YOU MAY RECALL FROM THE STORY OF CHAPRA THE FIGHTER.

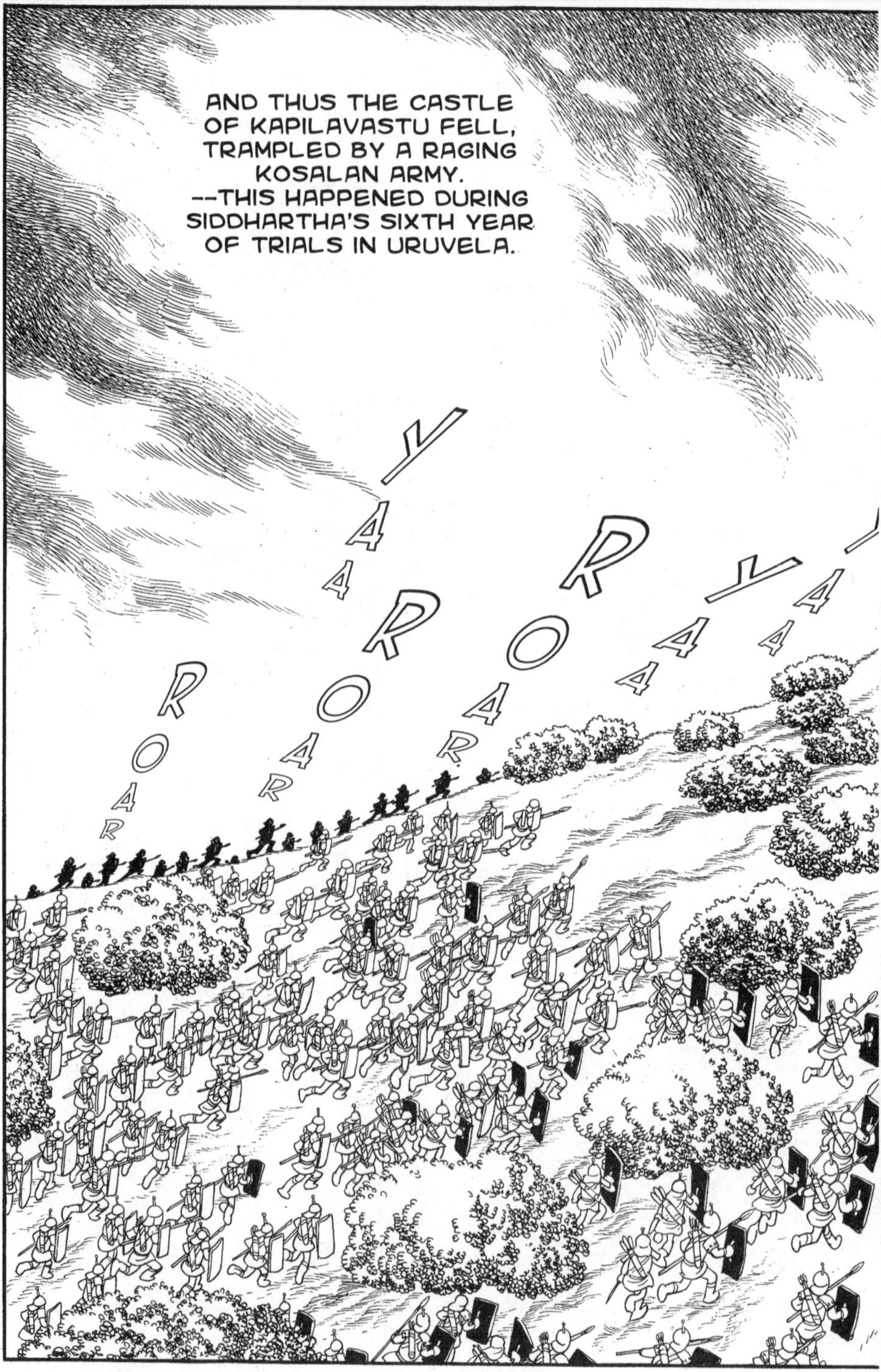
AND THUS THE CASTLE OF KAPILAVASTU FELL, TRAMPLED BY A RAGING KOSALAN ARMY. --THIS HAPPENED DURING SIDDHARTHA'S SIXTH YEAR OF TRIALS IN URUVELA.

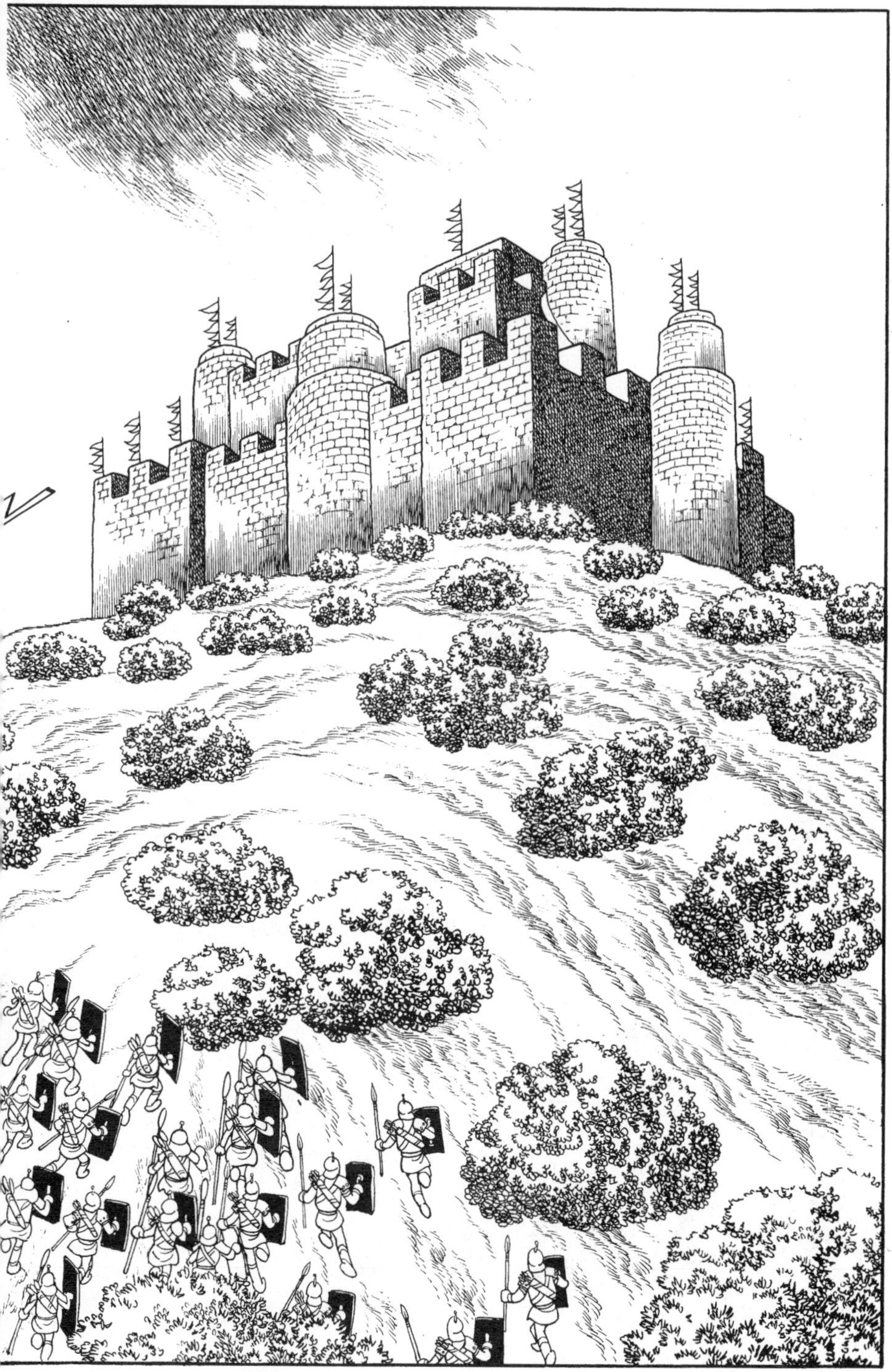

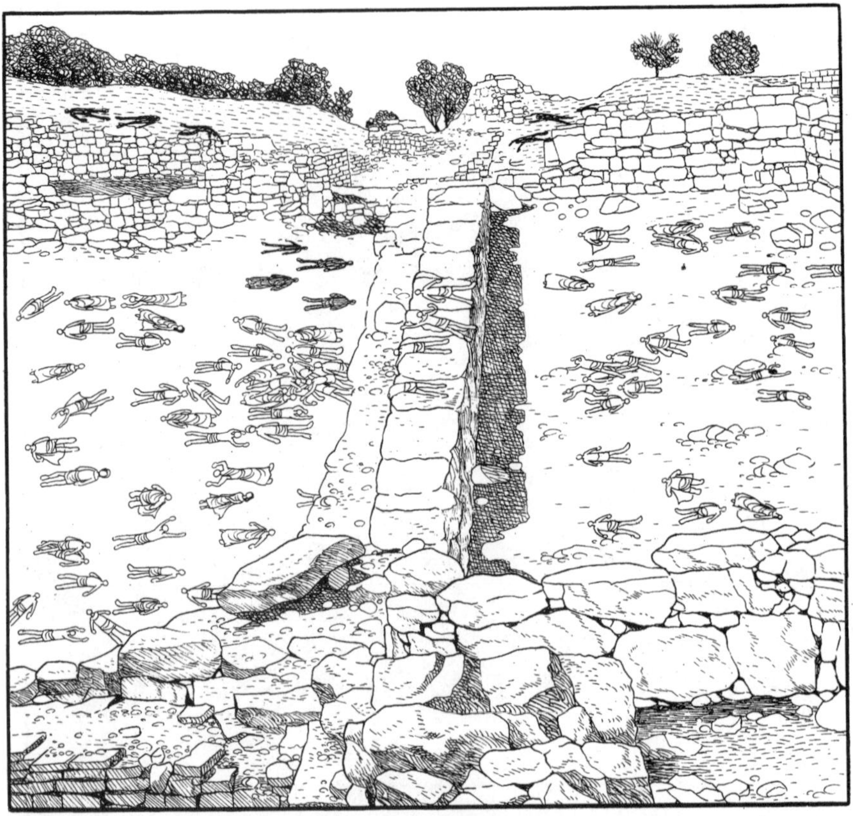

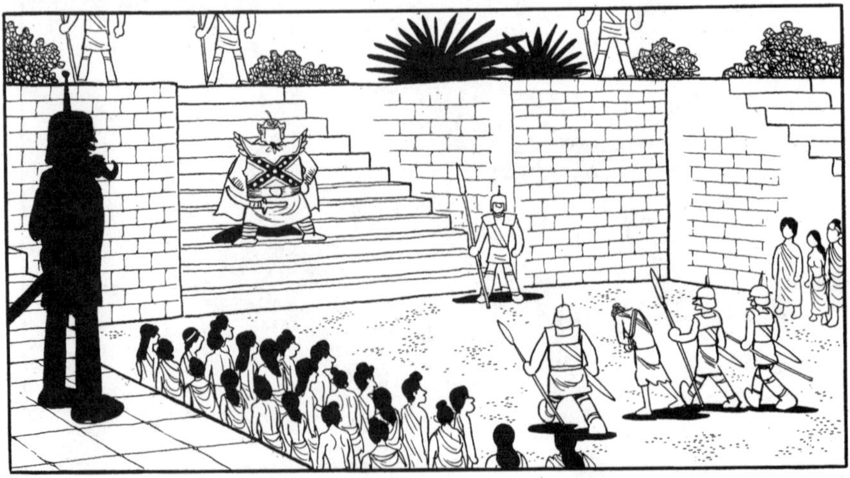

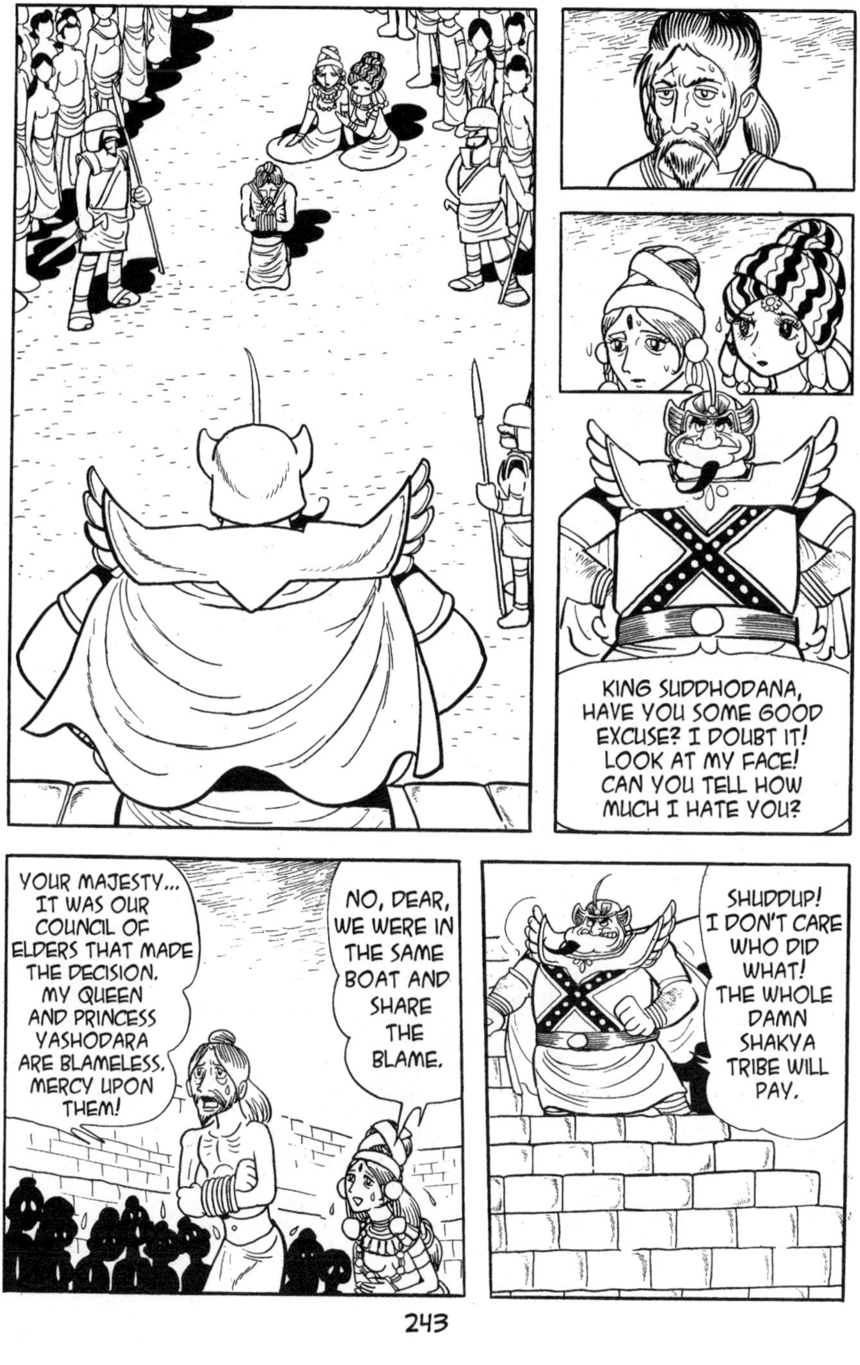

KING SUDDHODANA, HAVE YOU SOME GOOD EXCUSE? I DOUBT IT! LOOK AT MY FACE! CAN YOU TELL HOW MUCH I HATE YOU?
YOUR MAJESTY... IT WAS OUR COUNCIL OF ELDERS THAT MADE THE DECISION. MY QUEEN AND PRINCESS YASHODARA ARE BLAMELESS. MERCY UPON THEM!
NO, DEAR, WE WERE IN THE SAME BOAT AND SHARE THE BLAME.
SHUDDUP! I DON'T CARE WHO DID WHAT! THE WHOLE DAMN SHAKYA TRIBE WILL PAY.

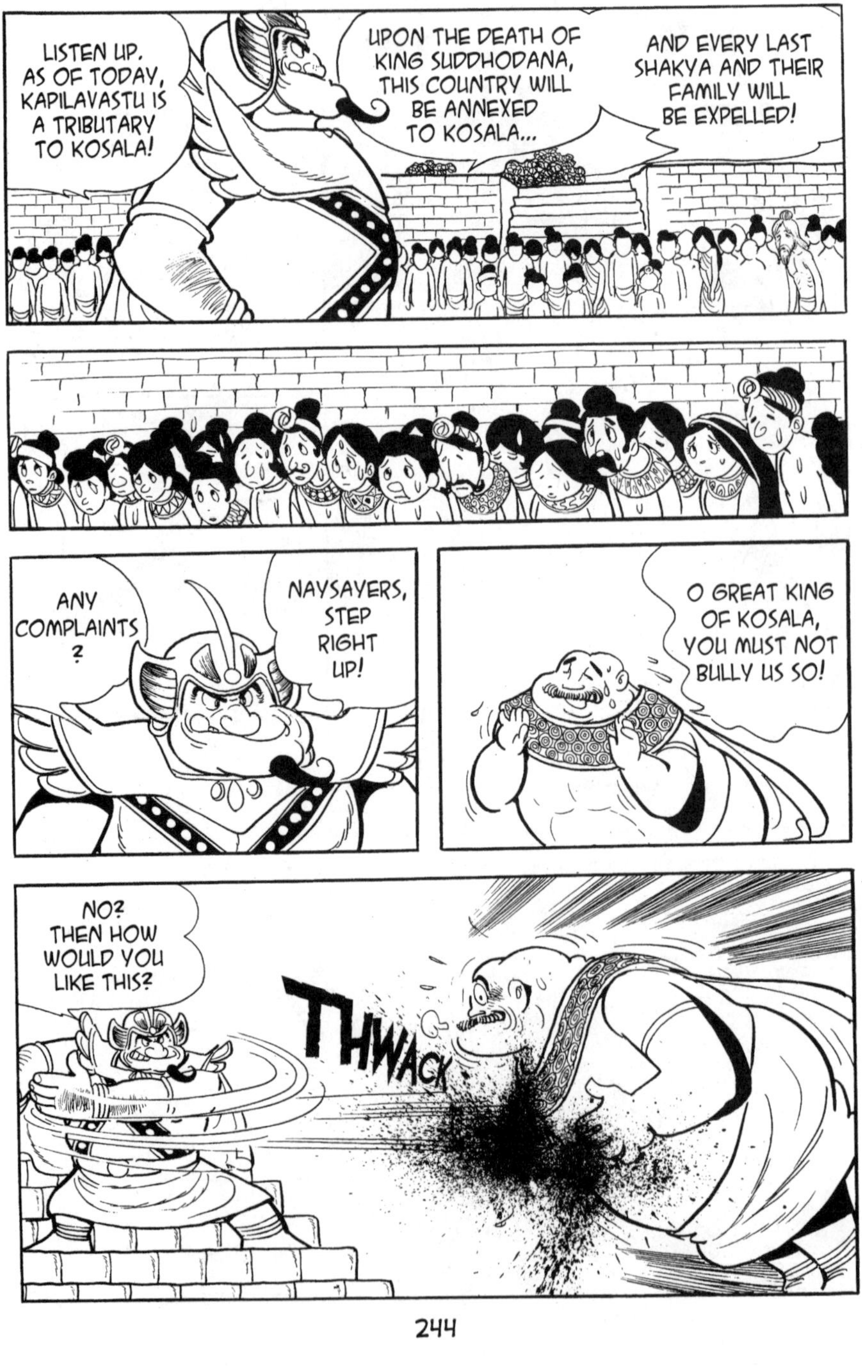
LISTEN UP. AS OF TODAY, KAPILAVASTU IS A TRIBUTARY TO KOSALA!
UPON THE DEATH OF KING SUDDHODANA, THIS COUNTRY WILL BE ANNEXED TO KOSALA...
AND EVERY LAST SHAKYA AND THEIR FAMILY WILL BE EXPELLED!
ANY COMPLAINTS?
NAYSAYERS, STEP RIGHT UP!
O GREAT KING OF KOSALA, YOU MUST NOT BULLY US SO!
NO? THEN HOW WOULD YOU LIKE THIS?
THWACK

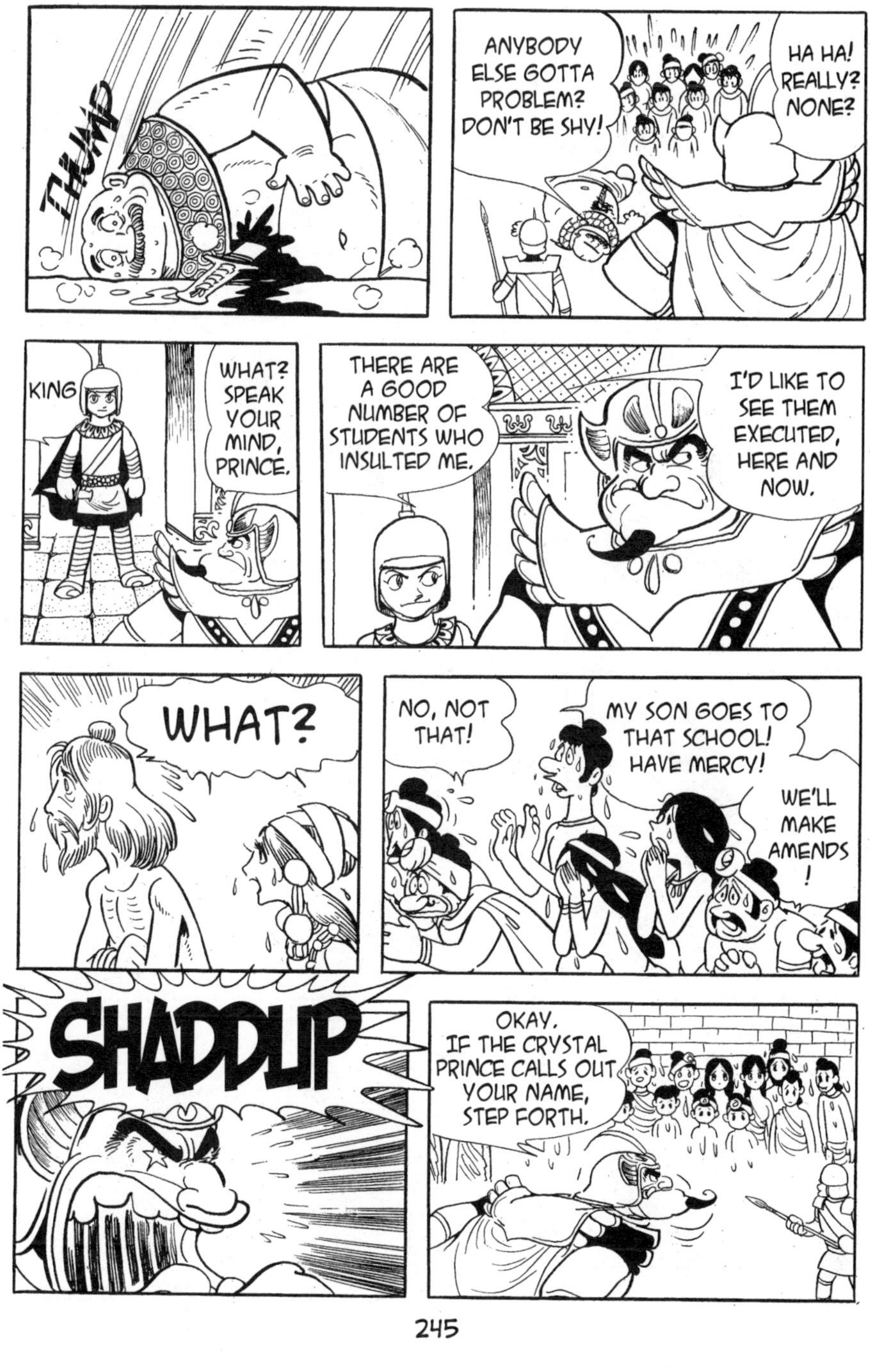
THUMP
ANYBODY ELSE GOTTA PROBLEM? DON'T BE SHY!
HA HA! REALLY? NONE?
KING
WHAT? SPEAK YOUR MIND, PRINCE.
THERE ARE A GOOD NUMBER OF STUDENTS WHO INSULTED ME.
I'D LIKE TO SEE THEM EXECUTED, HERE AND NOW.
WHAT?
NO, NOT THAT!
MY SON GOES TO THAT SCHOOL! HAVE MERCY!
WE'LL MAKE AMENDS!
SHADDUP
OKAY. IF THE CRYSTAL PRINCE CALLS OUT YOUR NAME, STEP FORTH.

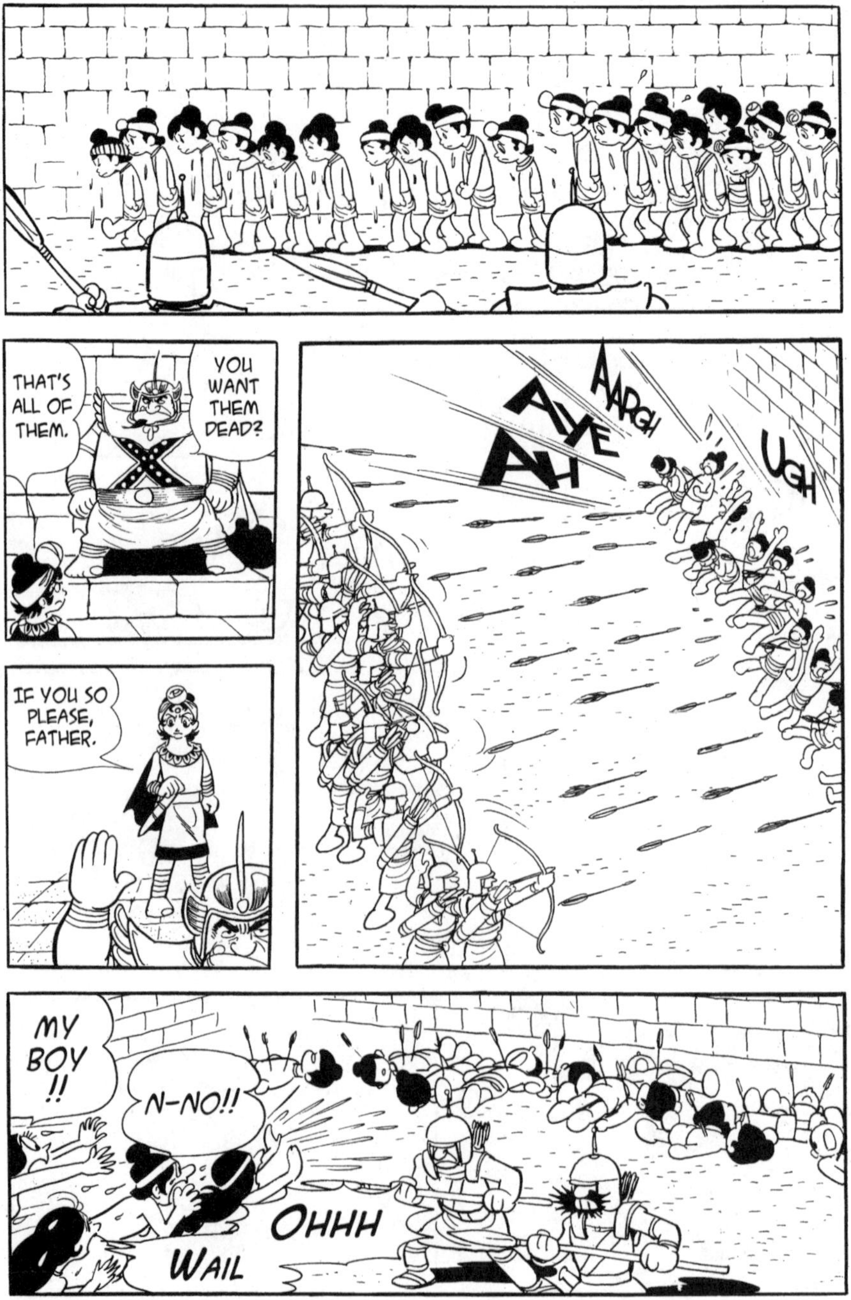
THAT'S ALL OF THEM.
YOU WANT THEM DEAD?
IF YOU SO PLEASE, FATHER.
AARGH
AIYE
AH
UGH
MY BOY !!
N-NO!!
OHHH
WAIL

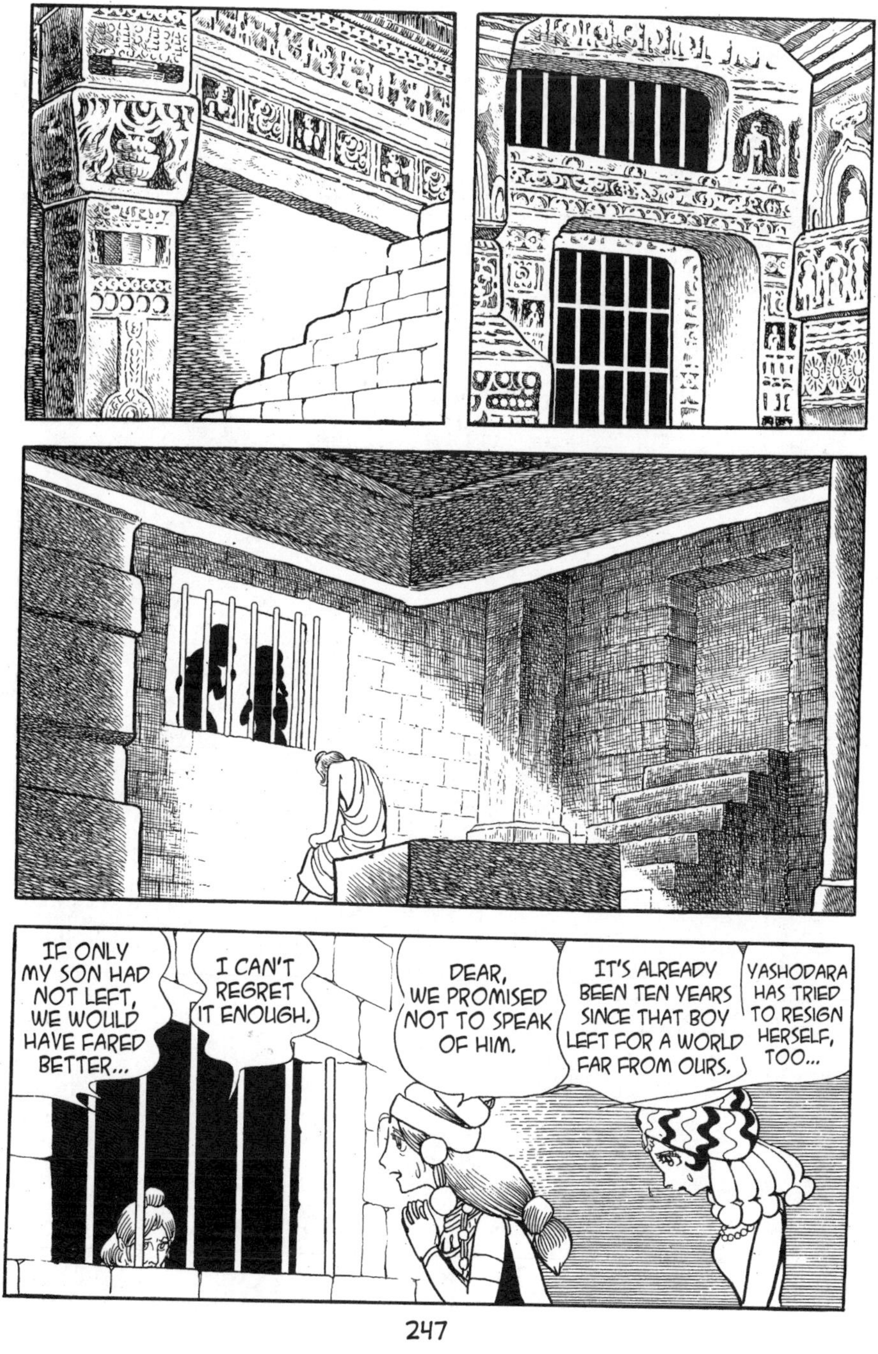
IF ONLY MY SON HAD NOT LEFT, WE WOULD HAVE FARED BETTER...
I CAN'T REGRET IT ENOUGH.
DEAR, WE PROMISED NOT TO SPEAK OF HIM.
IT'S ALREADY BEEN TEN YEARS SINCE THAT BOY LEFT FOR A WORLD FAR FROM OURS.
YASHODARA HAS TRIED TO RESIGN HERSELF, TOO...

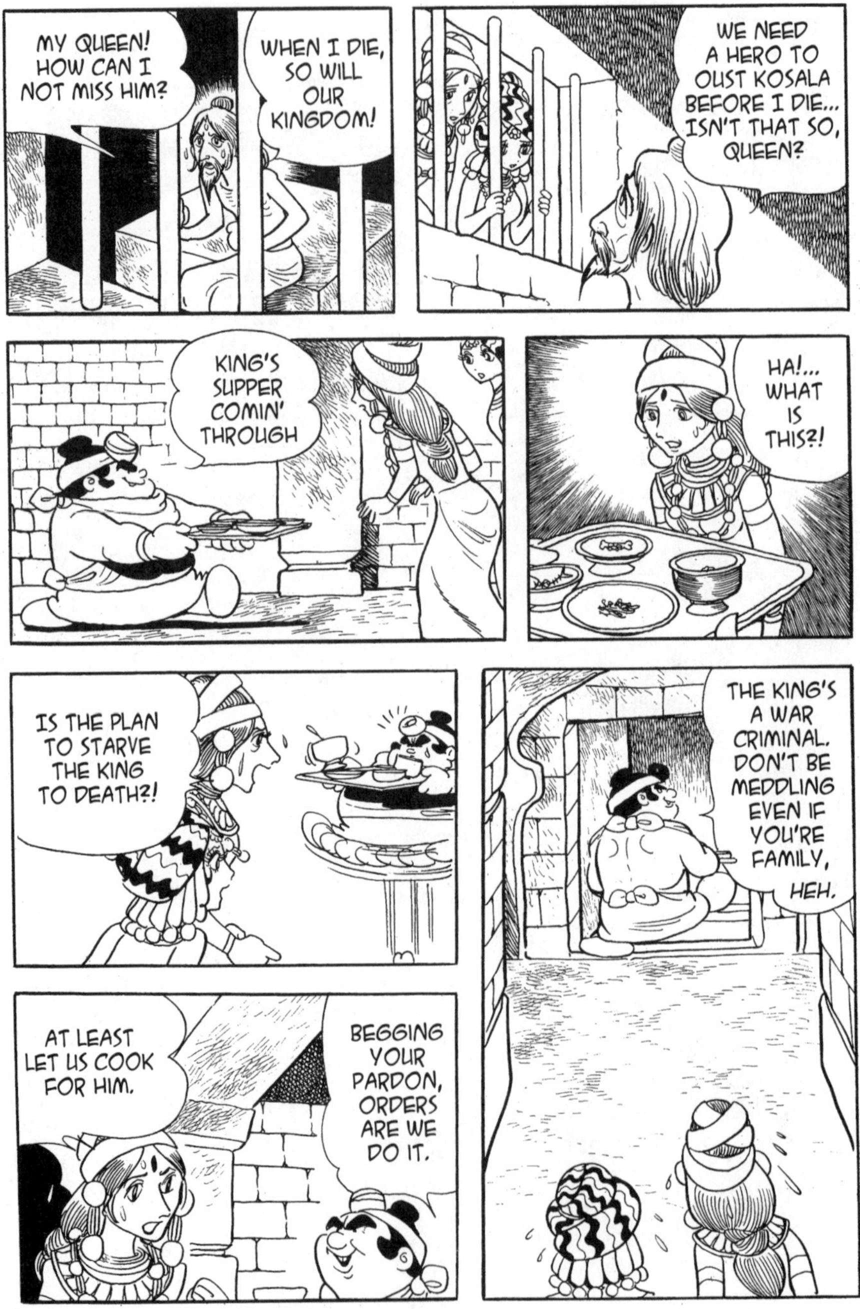
MY QUEEN! HOW CAN I NOT MISS HIM?
WHEN I DIE, SO WILL OUR KINGDOM!
WE NEED A HERO TO OUST KOSALA BEFORE I DIE... ISN'T THAT SO, QUEEN?
KING'S SUPPER COMIN' THROUGH
HA!... WHAT IS THIS?!
IS THE PLAN TO STARVE THE KING TO DEATH?!
AT LEAST LET US COOK FOR HIM.
BEGGING YOUR PARDON, ORDERS ARE WE DO IT.
THE KING'S A WAR CRIMINAL. DON'T BE MEDDLING EVEN IF YOU'RE FAMILY, HEH.

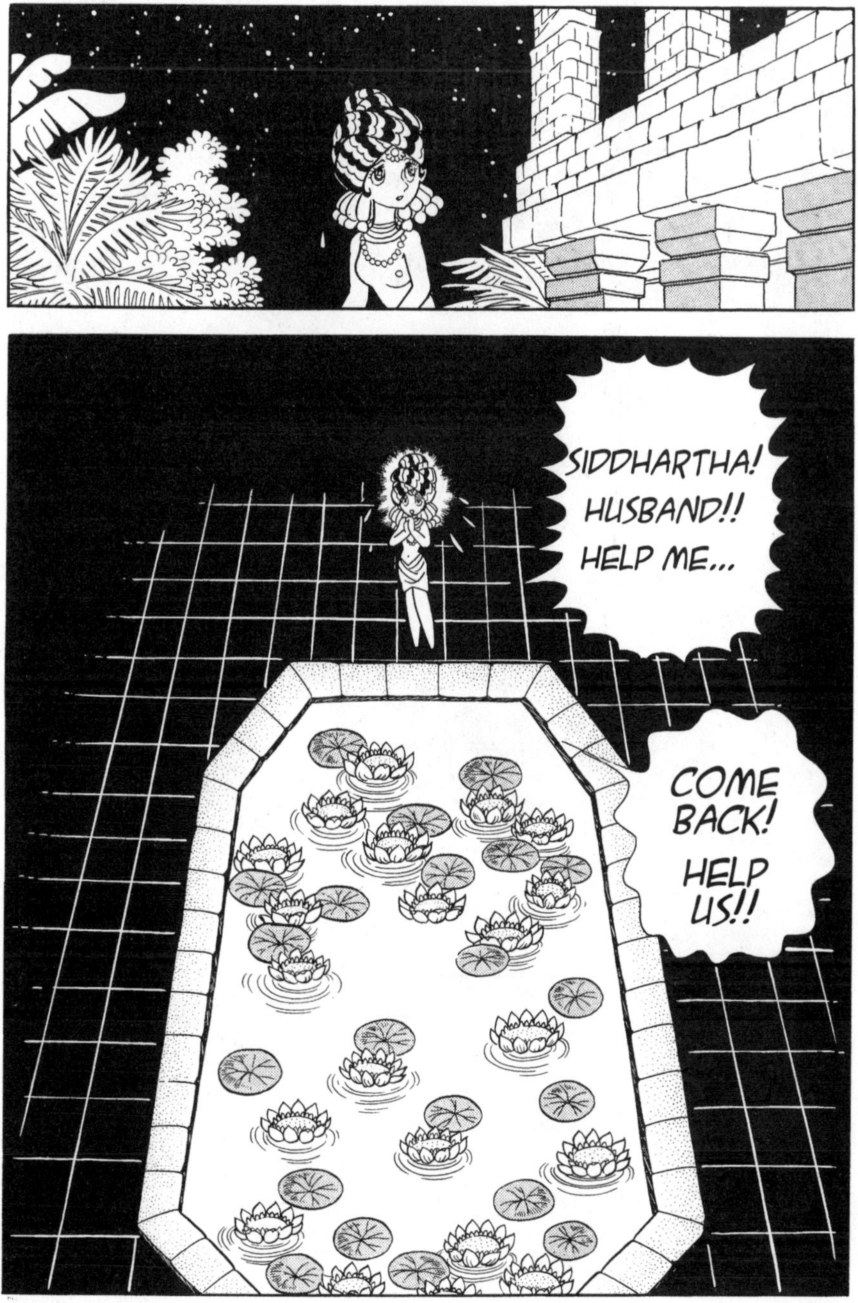
SIDDHARTHA! HUSBAND!! HELP ME...
COME BACK! HELP US!!

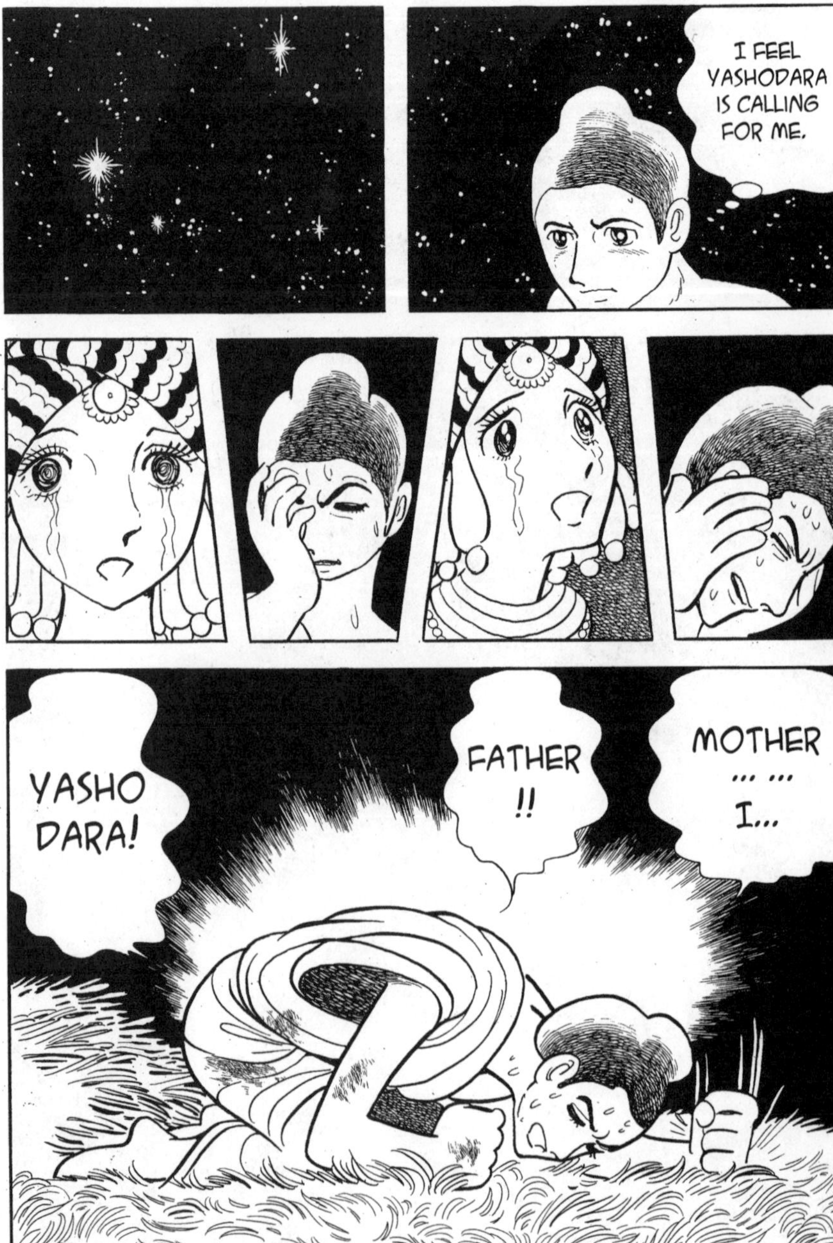
I FEEL YASHODARA IS CALLING FOR ME.
YASHO DARA!
FATHER !!
MOTHER ... ... I...

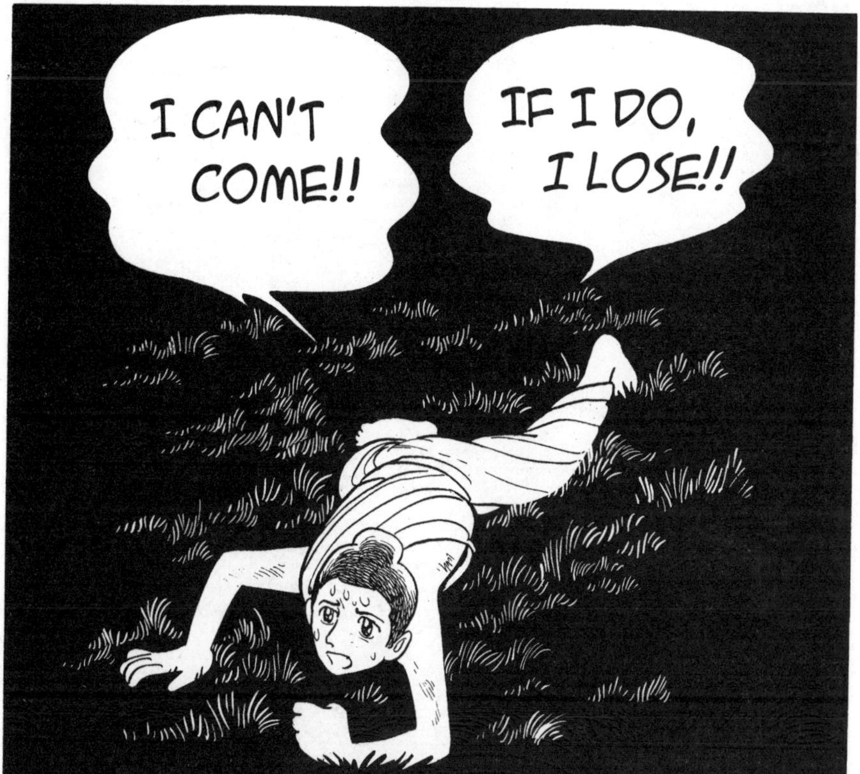
I CAN'T COME!!
IF I DO, I LOSE!!
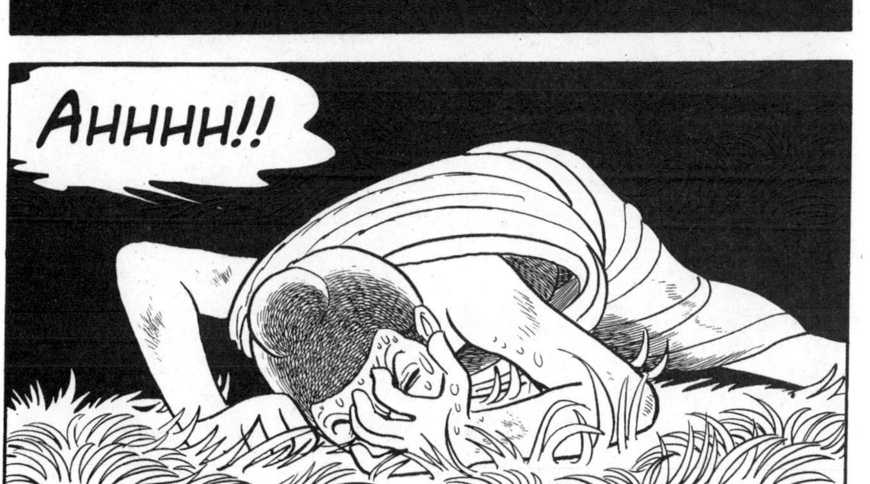
AHHHH!!

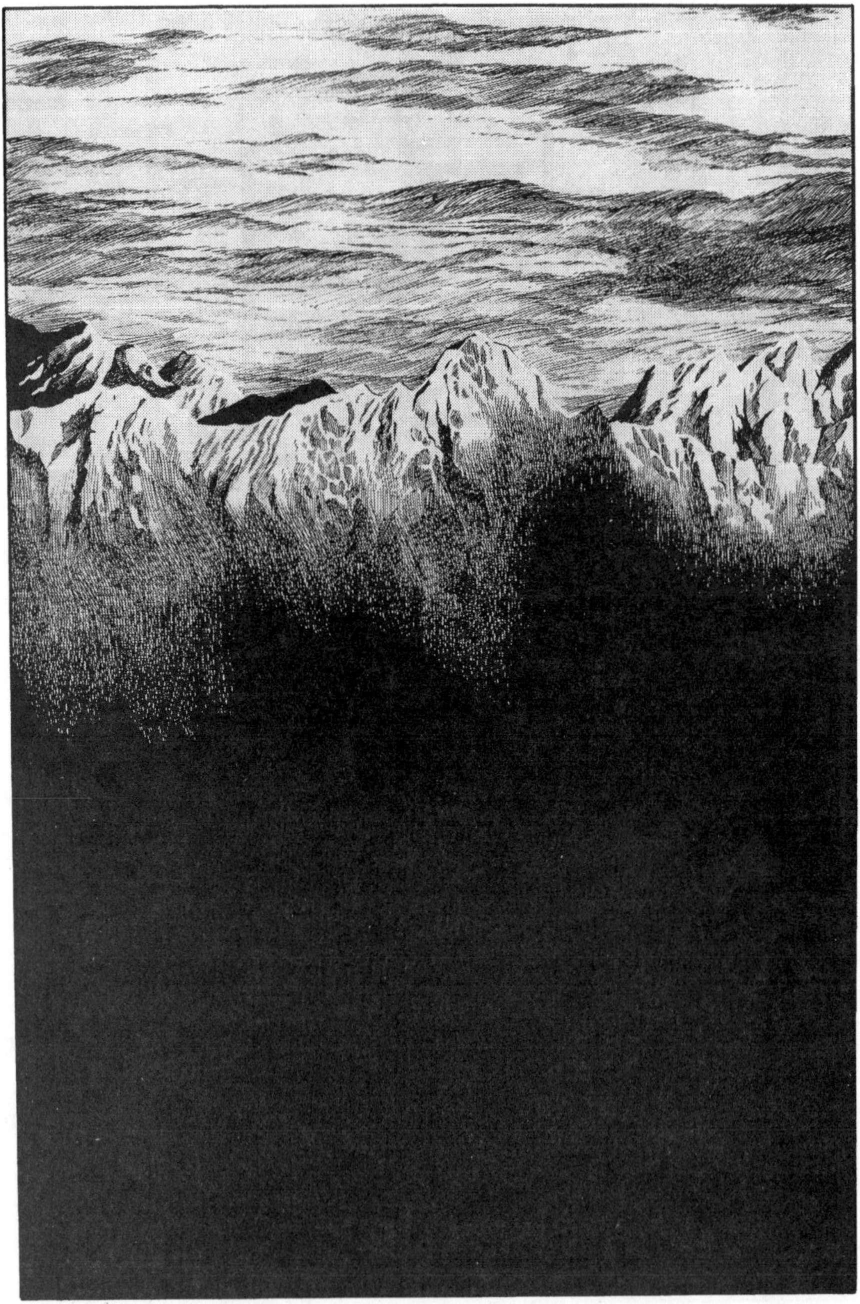

CHAPTER ELEVEN

THE STORY OF YATALA

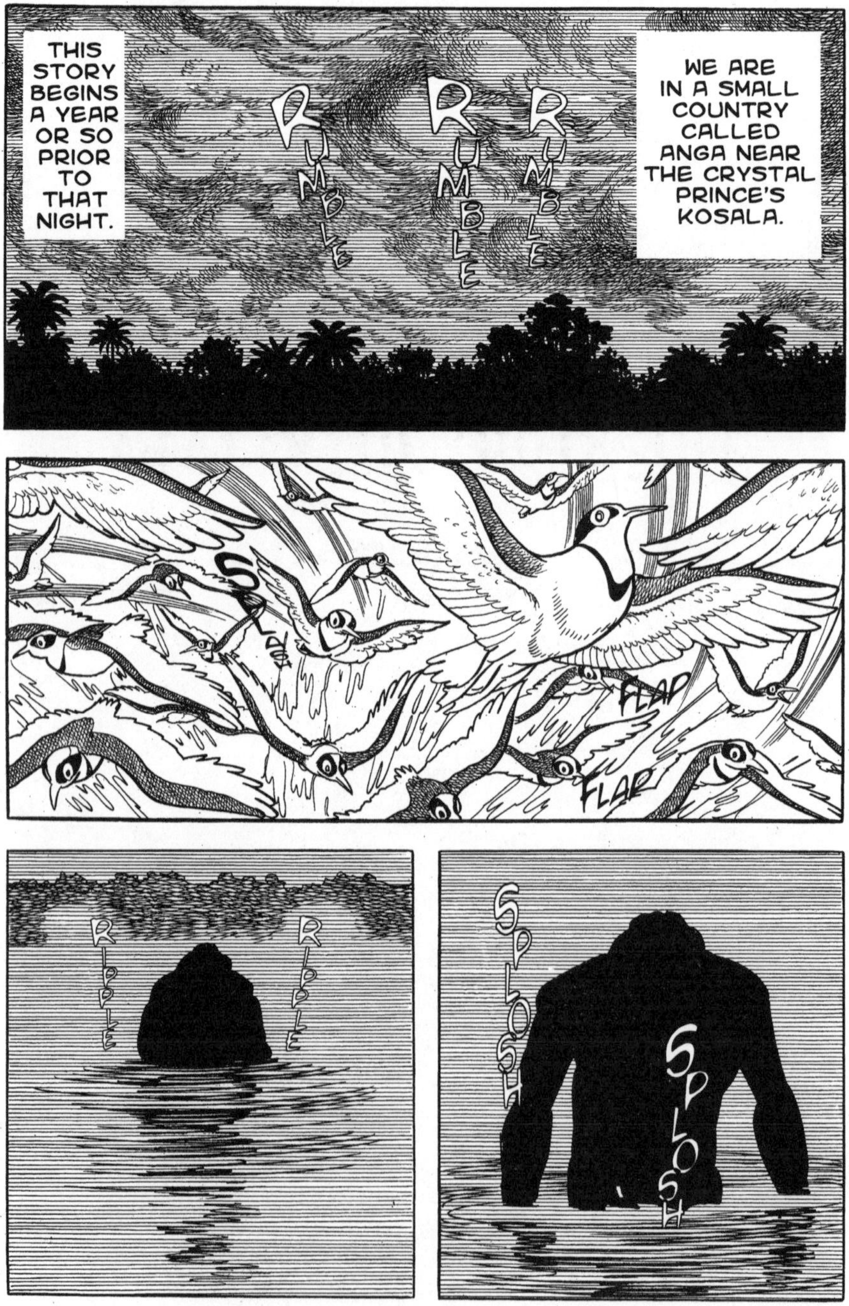
THIS STORY BEGINS A YEAR OR SO PRIOR TO THAT NIGHT.
RUMBLE
RUMBLE
RUMBLE
WE ARE IN A SMALL COUNTRY CALLED ANGA NEAR THE CRYSTAL PRINCE'S KOSALA.
FLAP
FLAP
RIPPLE
RIPPLE
SPLOSH
SPLOSH

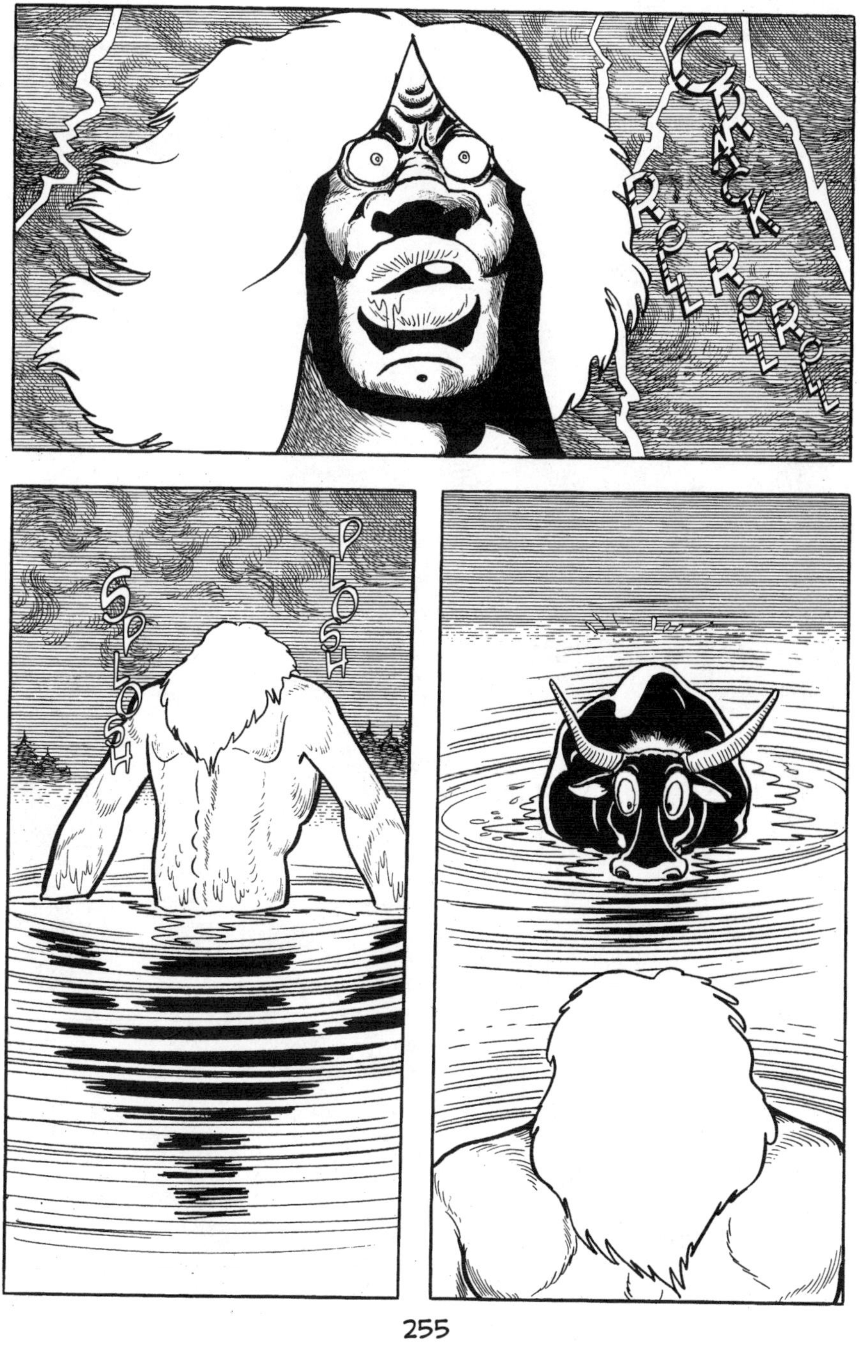
CRACK
ROLL ROLL ROLL
SPLOSH
PLOSH

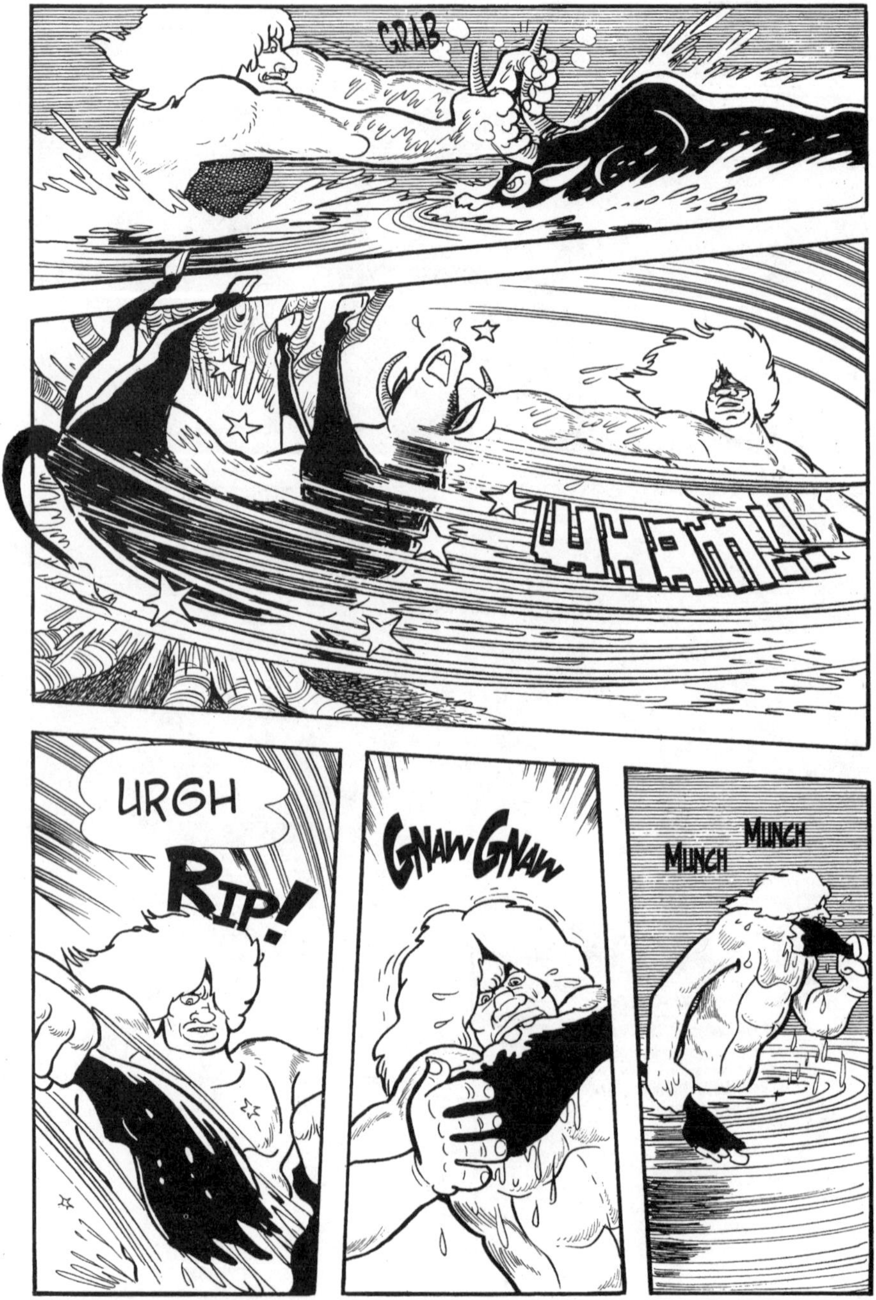
GRAB
WHAM!!
URGH
RIP!
GNAW GNAW
MUNCH
MUNCH

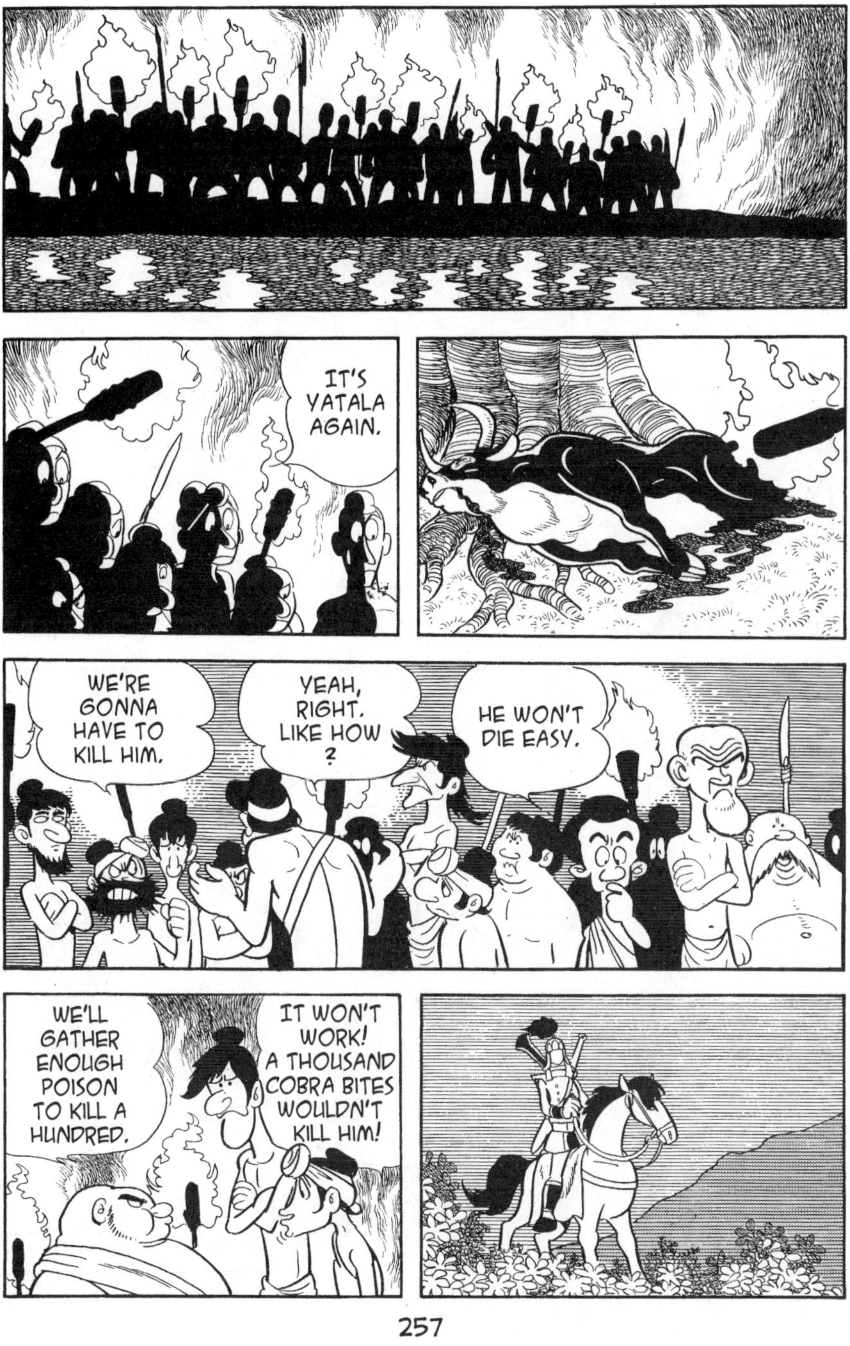

IT'S YATALA AGAIN.
WE'RE GONNA HAVE TO KILL HIM.
YEAH, RIGHT. LIKE HOW ?
HE WON'T DIE EASY.
WE'LL GATHER ENOUGH POISON TO KILL A HUNDRED.
IT WON'T WORK! A THOUSAND COBRA BITES WOULDN'T KILL HIM!

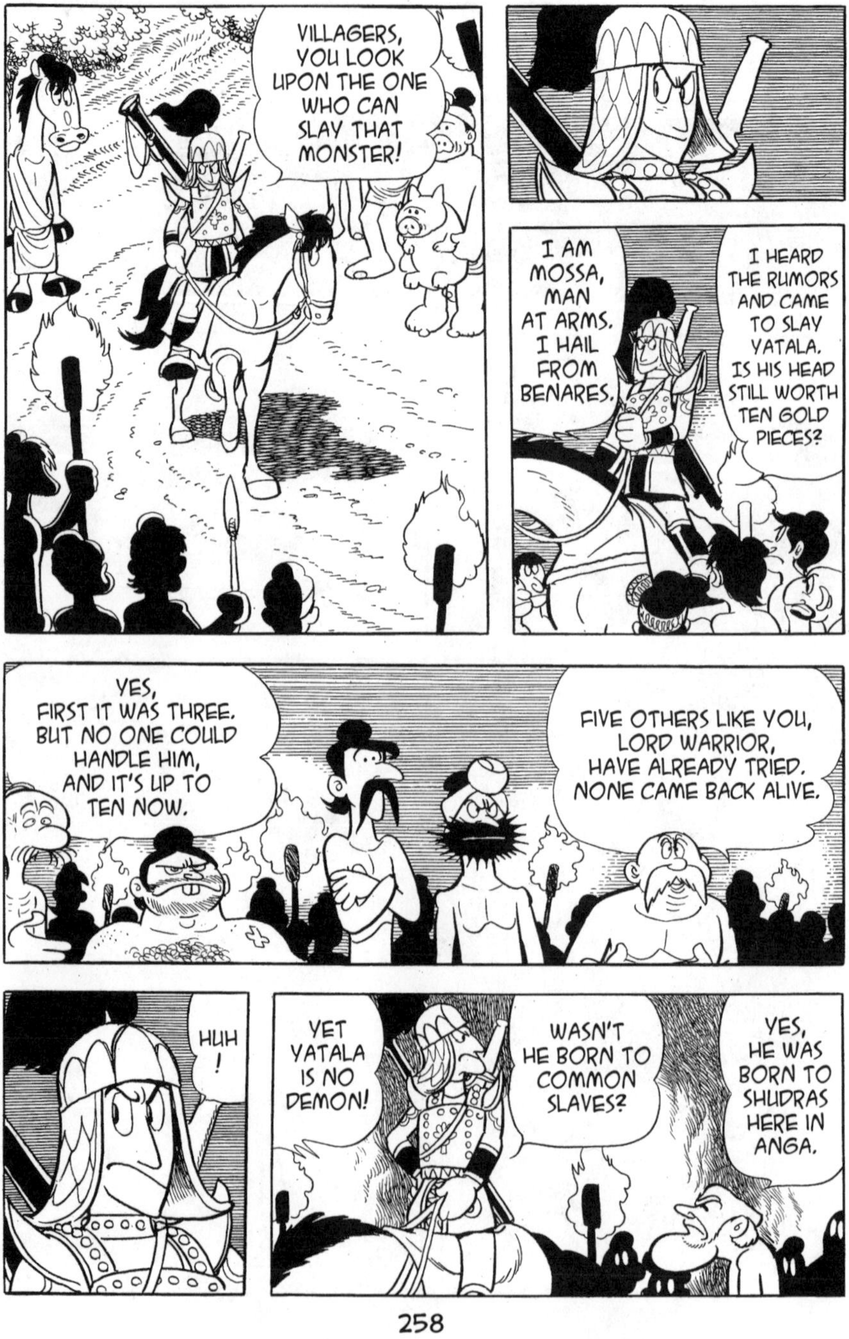
VILLAGERS, YOU LOOK UPON THE ONE WHO CAN SLAY THAT MONSTER!
I AM MOSSA, MAN AT ARMS. I HAIL FROM BENARES.
I HEARD THE RUMORS AND CAME TO SLAY YATALA. IS HIS HEAD STILL WORTH TEN GOLD PIECES?
YES, FIRST IT WAS THREE. BUT NO ONE COULD HANDLE HIM, AND IT'S UP TO TEN NOW.
FIVE OTHERS LIKE YOU, LORD WARRIOR, HAVE ALREADY TRIED. NONE CAME BACK ALIVE.
HUH!
YET YATALA IS NO DEMON!
WASN'T HE BORN TO COMMON SLAVES?
YES, HE WAS BORN TO SHUDRAS HERE IN ANGA.

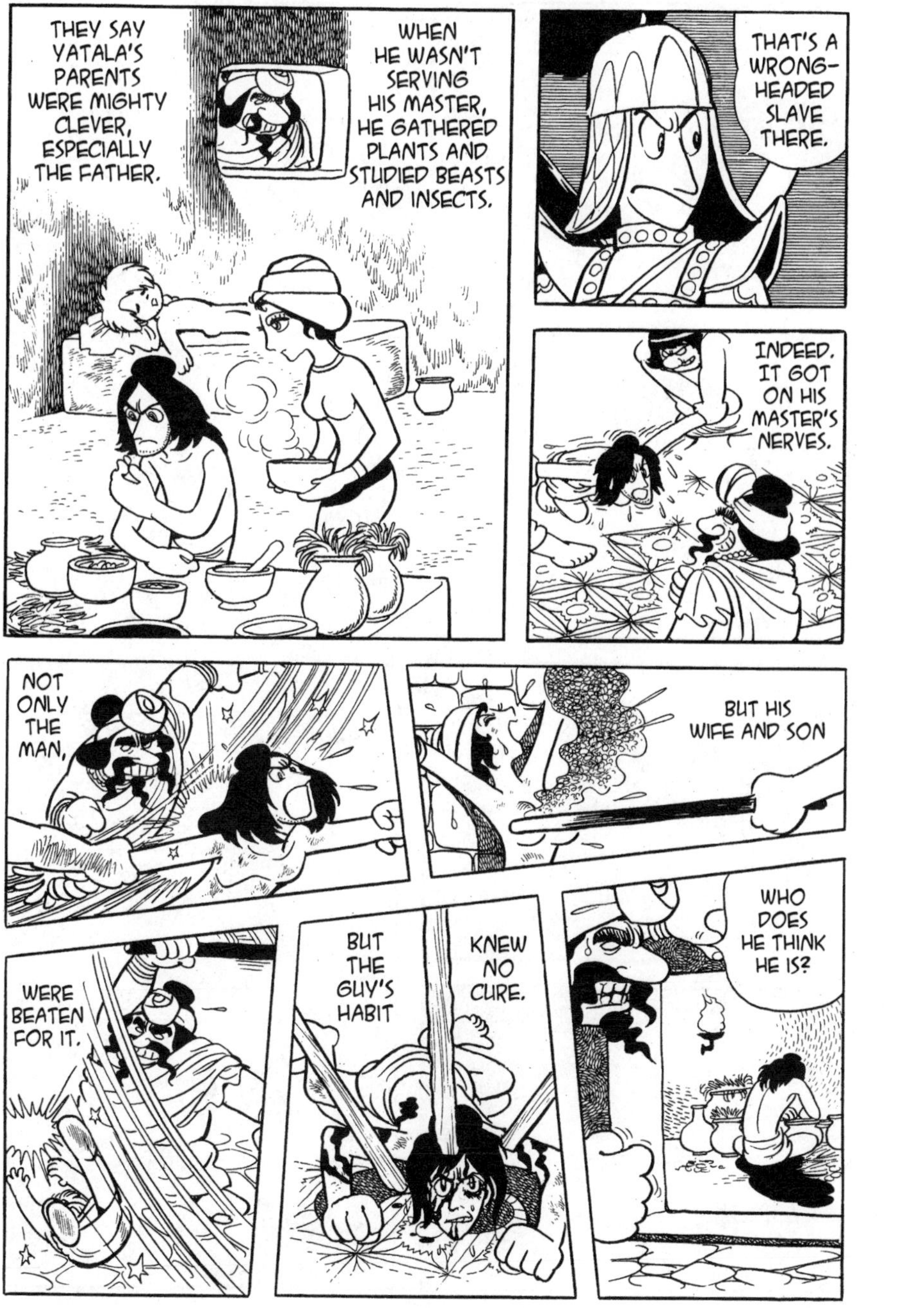
THEY SAY YATALA'S PARENTS WERE MIGHTY CLEVER, ESPECIALLY THE FATHER.
WHEN HE WASN'T SERVING HIS MASTER, HE GATHERED PLANTS AND STUDIED BEASTS AND INSECTS.
THAT'S A WRONG-HEADED SLAVE THERE.
INDEED. IT GOT ON HIS MASTER'S NERVES.
NOT ONLY THE MAN,
BUT HIS WIFE AND SON
WERE BEATEN FOR IT.
BUT THE GUY'S HABIT
KNEW NO CURE.
WHO DOES HE THINK HE IS?

YATALA, LISTEN TO FATHER.

THIS IS A DRUG I MADE FROM HERBS AND THE INNARDS OF BEASTS. DRINK IT EVERY DAY.

WHY?

BECAUSE YOUR MOTHER AND I DON'T WANT YOU TO SUFFER AS WE HAVE.

BY THE TIME YOU'RE A MAN, YOUR BODY WILL BE TOO TOUGH FOR ANY ARROW, WHIP, OR HAIL OF STONE.

I'LL BE STRONGER THAN AN ELEPHANT?

MUCH!

AND YOU'LL KISS THIS SORRY LIFE GOOD-BYE.

WOW!

EVERYONE OUT!

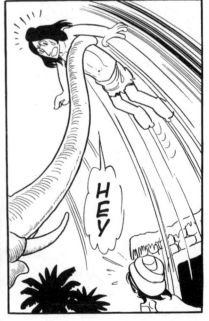

HEY

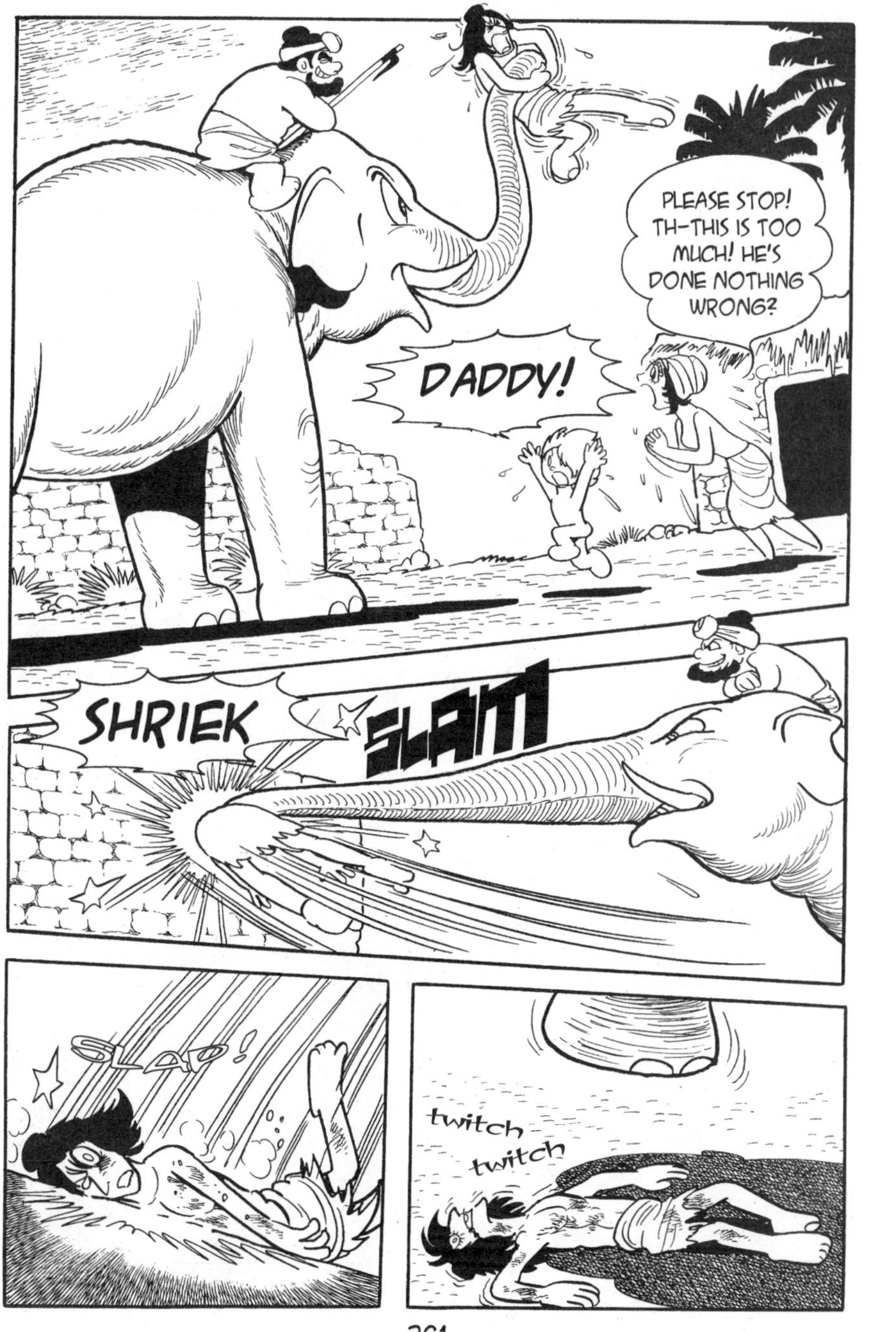
PLEASE STOP! TH-THIS IS TOO MUCH! HE'S DONE NOTHING WRONG?
DADDY!
SHRIEK
SLAM
SLAP!
twitch
twitch

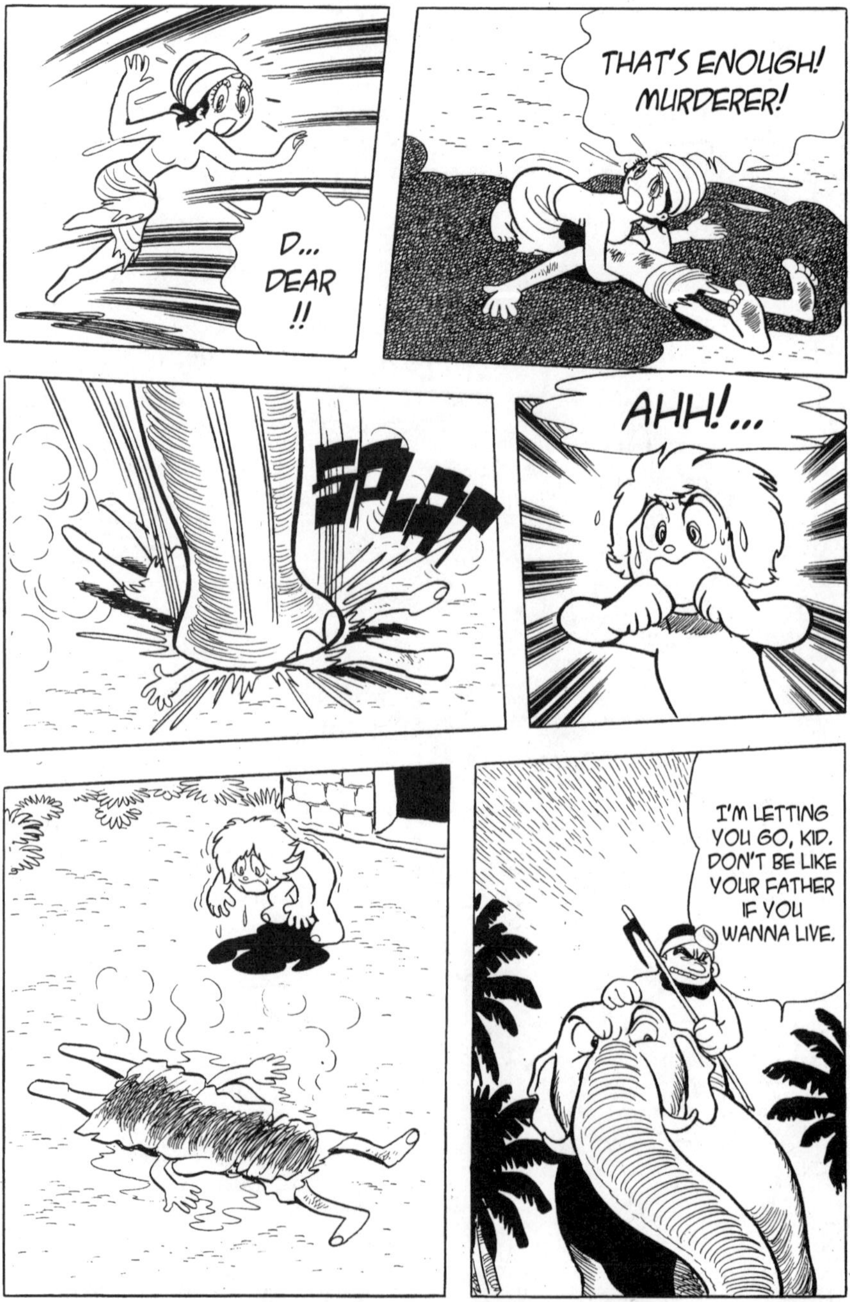
D... DEAR !!
THAT'S ENOUGH! MURDERER!
SPLAT
AHH!...
I'M LETTING YOU GO, KID. DON'T BE LIKE YOUR FATHER IF YOU WANNA LIVE.

AFTER THAT YATALA SPOKE LESS AND LESS,

WHILE HIS EYES BURNED REDDER AND REDDER WITH VENGEANCE.

YEAR BY YEAR

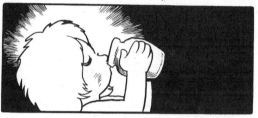

HE GREW TALLER AND TALLER

UNTIL HE WAS A 20-FT MONSTER.

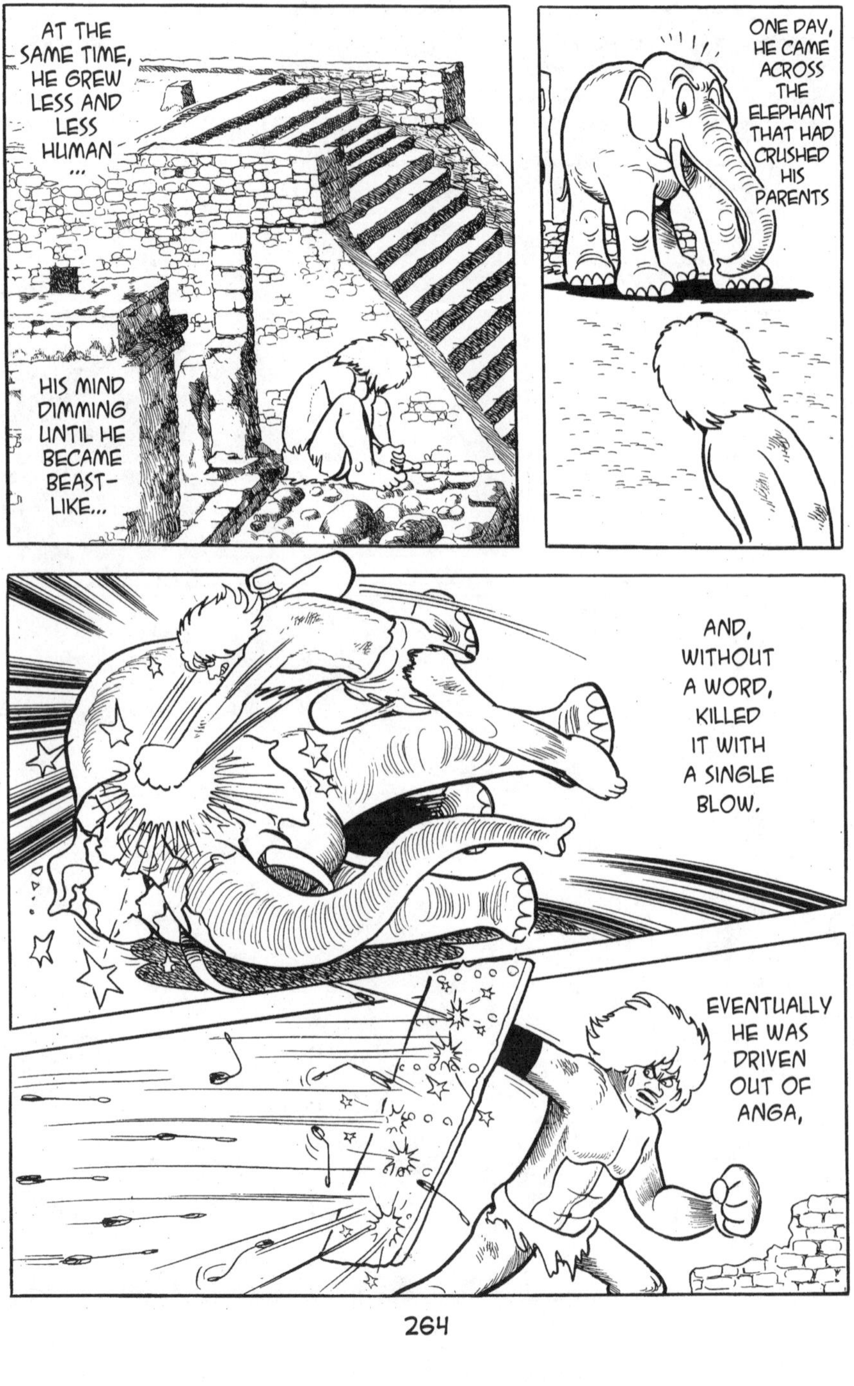
AT THE SAME TIME, HE GREW LESS AND LESS HUMAN ...
HIS MIND DIMMING UNTIL HE BECAME BEAST-LIKE...
ONE DAY, HE CAME ACROSS THE ELEPHANT THAT HAD CRUSHED HIS PARENTS
AND, WITHOUT A WORD, KILLED IT WITH A SINGLE BLOW.
EVENTUALLY HE WAS DRIVEN OUT OF ANGA,

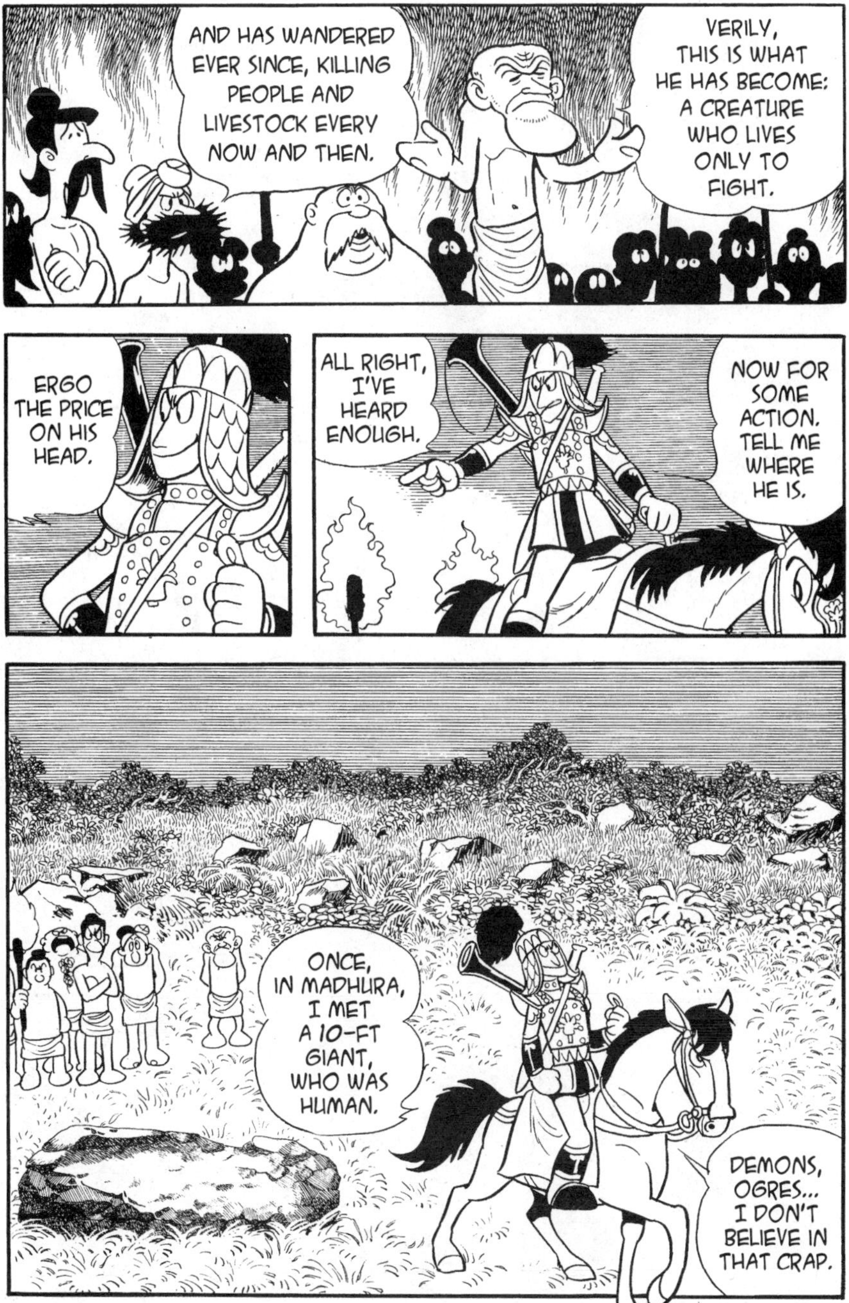
AND HAS WANDERED EVER SINCE, KILLING PEOPLE AND LIVESTOCK EVERY NOW AND THEN.
VERILY, THIS IS WHAT HE HAS BECOME: A CREATURE WHO LIVES ONLY TO FIGHT.
ERGO THE PRICE ON HIS HEAD.
ALL RIGHT, I'VE HEARD ENOUGH.
NOW FOR SOME ACTION. TELL ME WHERE HE IS.
ONCE, IN MADHURA, I MET A 10-FT GIANT, WHO WAS HUMAN.
DEMONS, OGRES... I DON'T BELIEVE IN THAT CRAP.

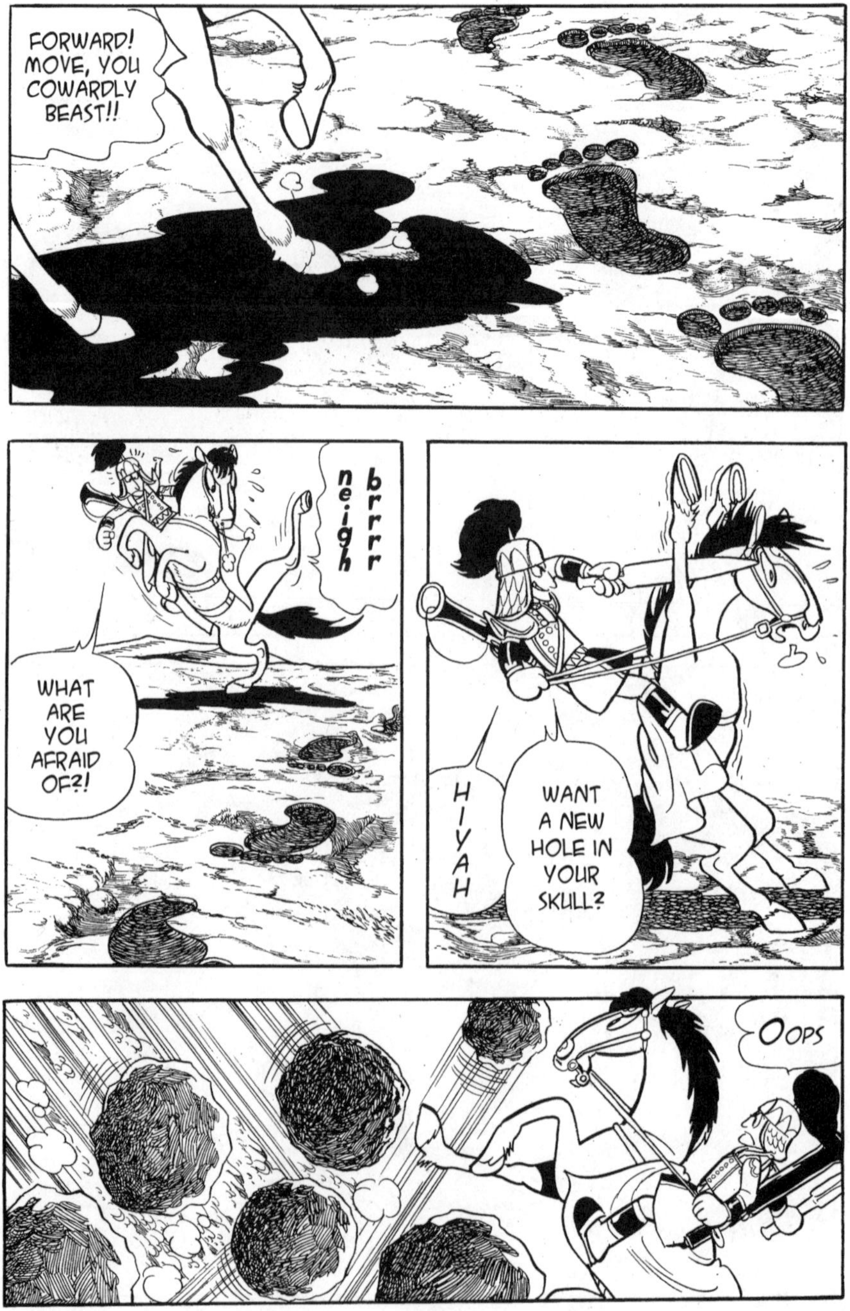
FORWARD! MOVE, YOU COWARDLY BEAST!!
brrrr
neigh
WHAT ARE YOU AFRAID OF?!
HIYAH
WANT A NEW HOLE IN YOUR SKULL?
OOPS

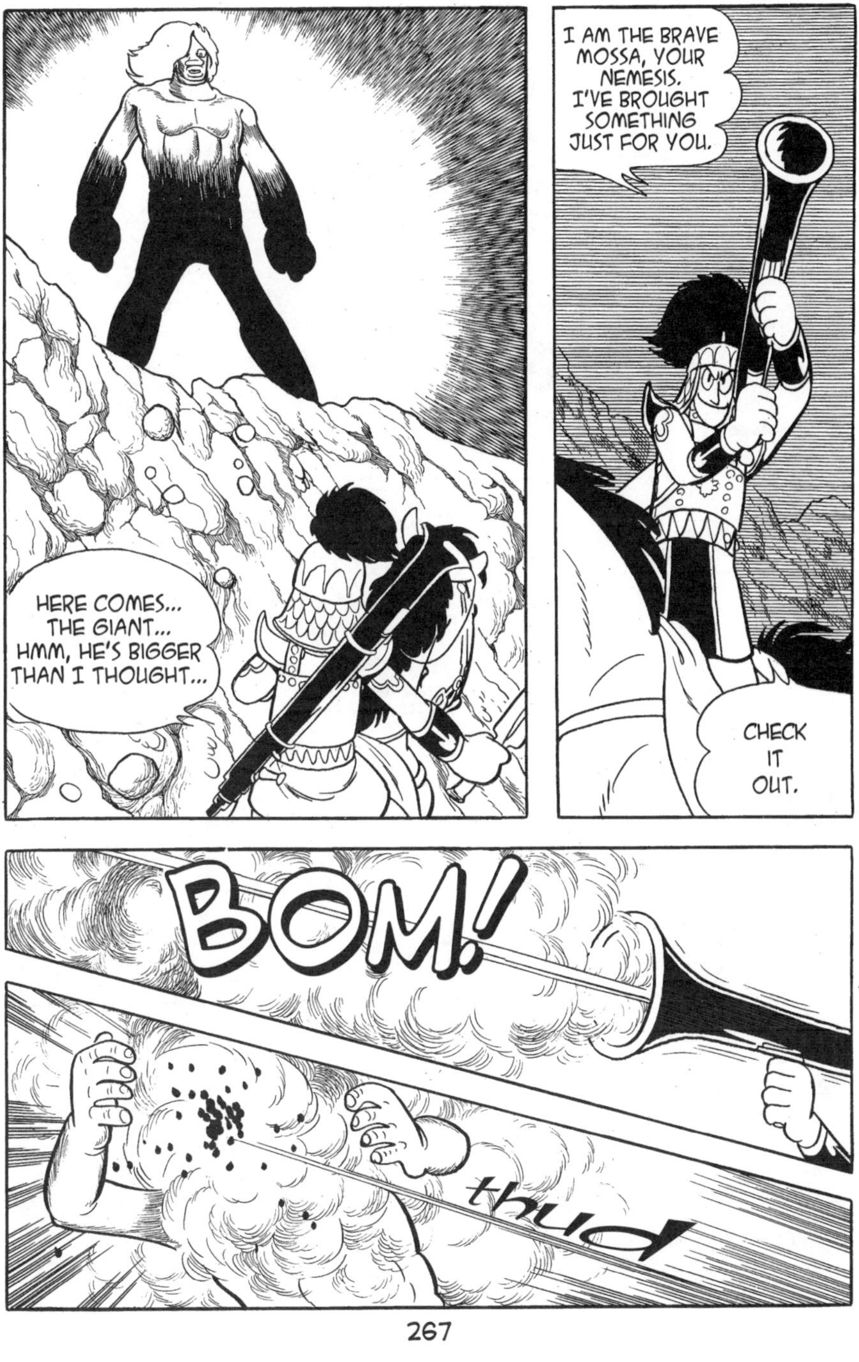
HERE COMES... THE GIANT... HMM, HE'S BIGGER THAN I THOUGHT...
I AM THE BRAVE MOSSA, YOUR NEMESIS. I'VE BROUGHT SOMETHING JUST FOR YOU.
CHECK IT OUT.
BOM!
thud

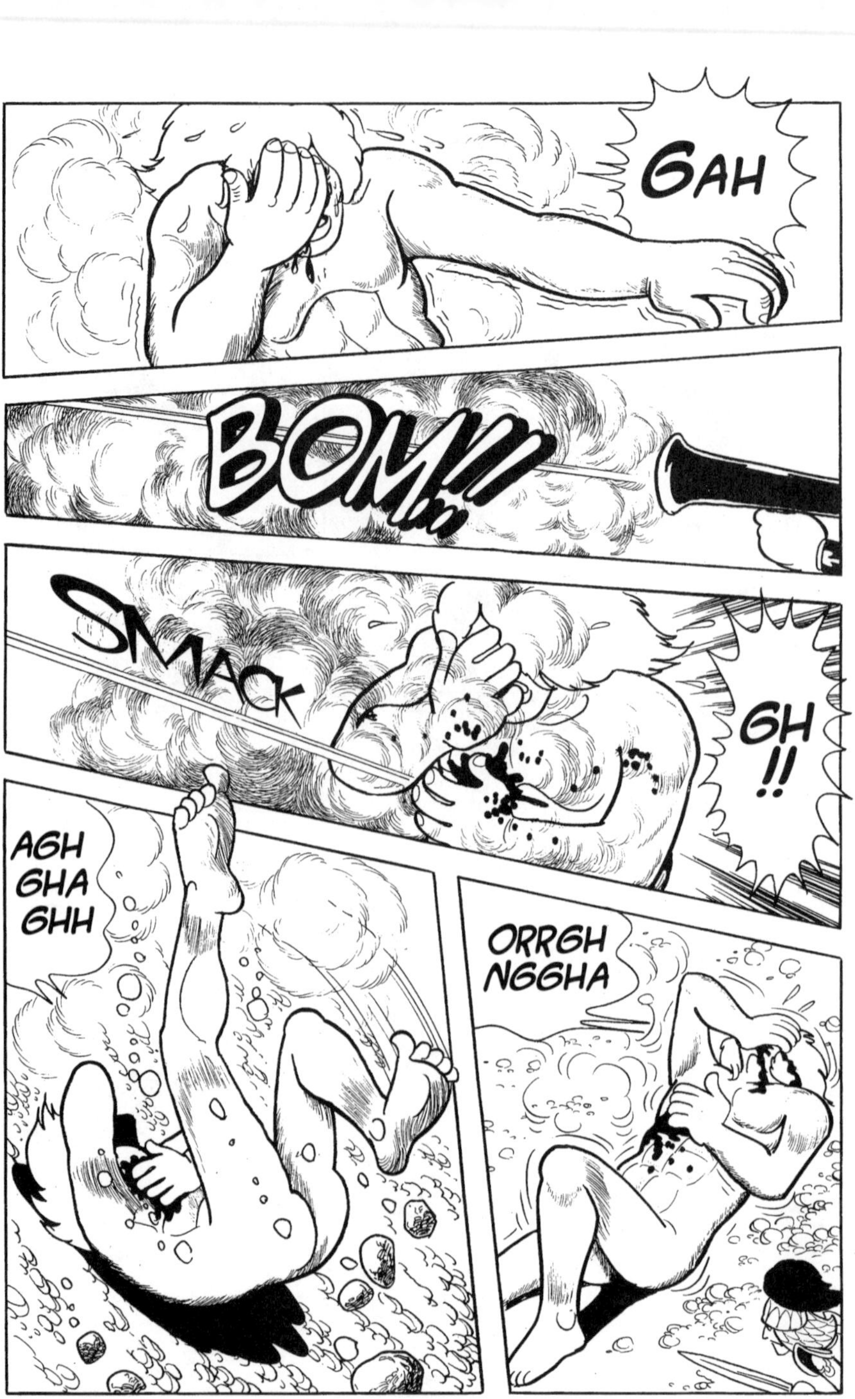
GAH
BOM!!
SMACK
GH !!
AGH GHA GHH
ORRGH NGGHA

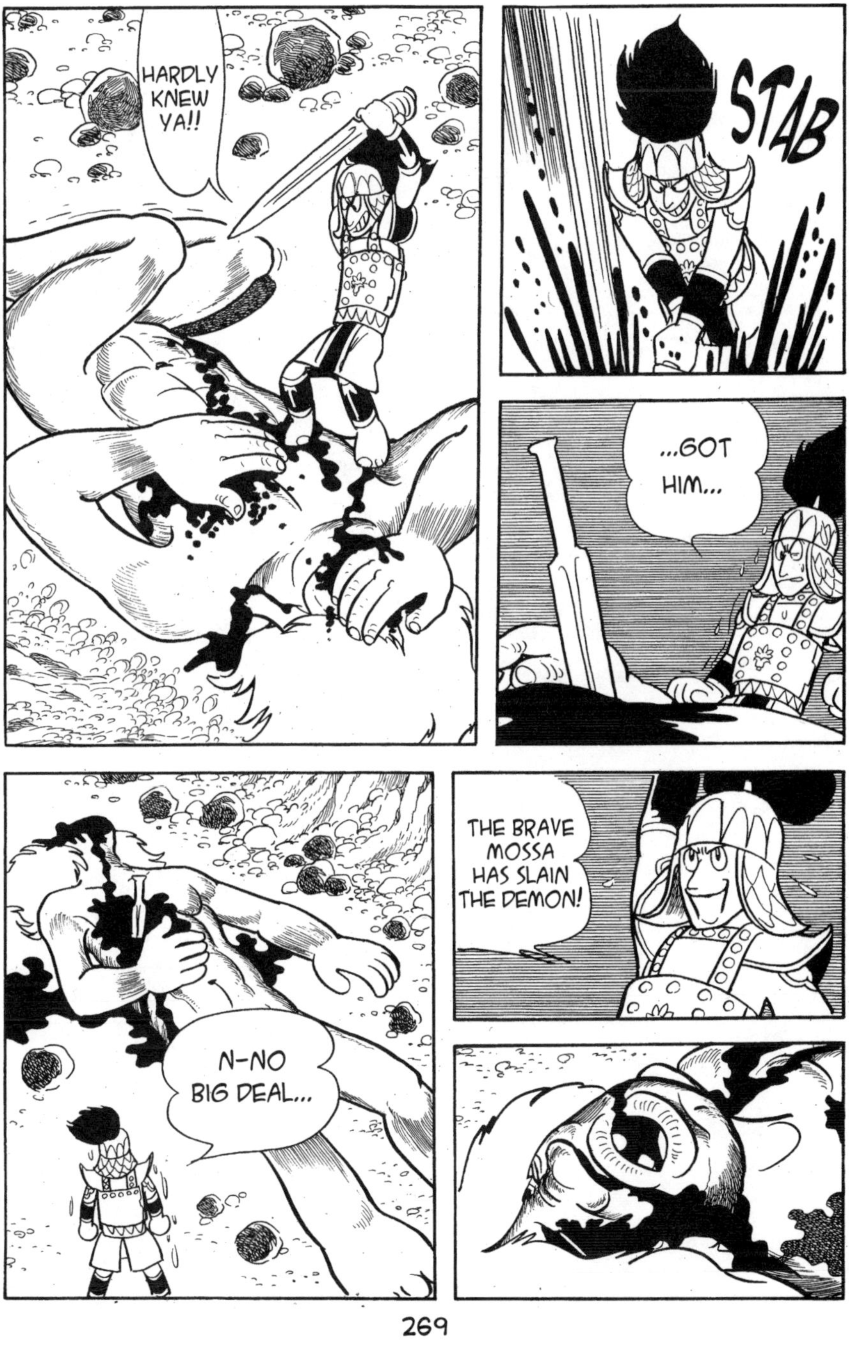
HARDLY KNEW YA!!
STAB
...GOT HIM...
N-NO BIG DEAL...
THE BRAVE MOSSA HAS SLAIN THE DEMON!

SNORE

SNORE

HM?

NO

Y-YOU... HADN'T D-DIED? ...HEY

SQUISHHH

ECK

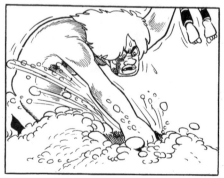

270

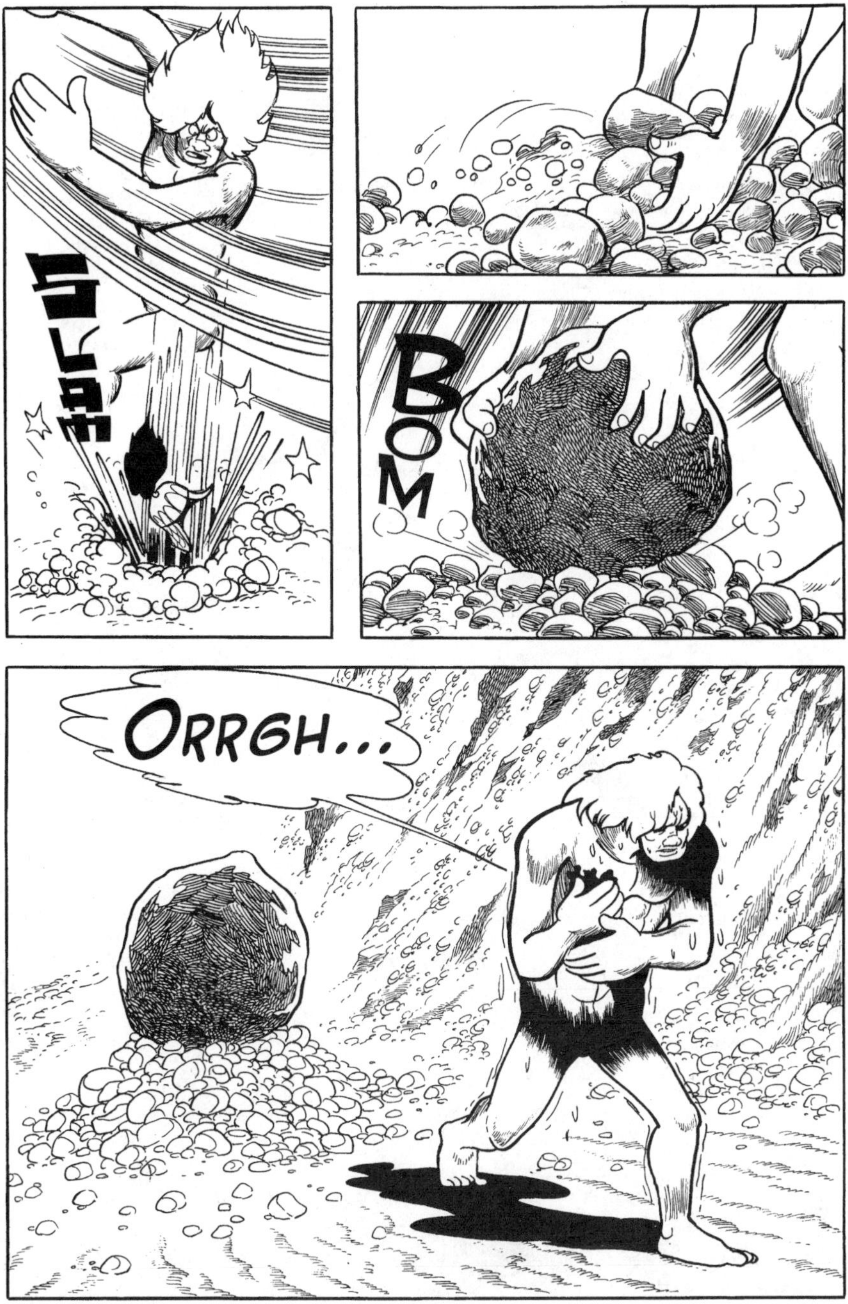
SLAM
BOM
ORRGH...

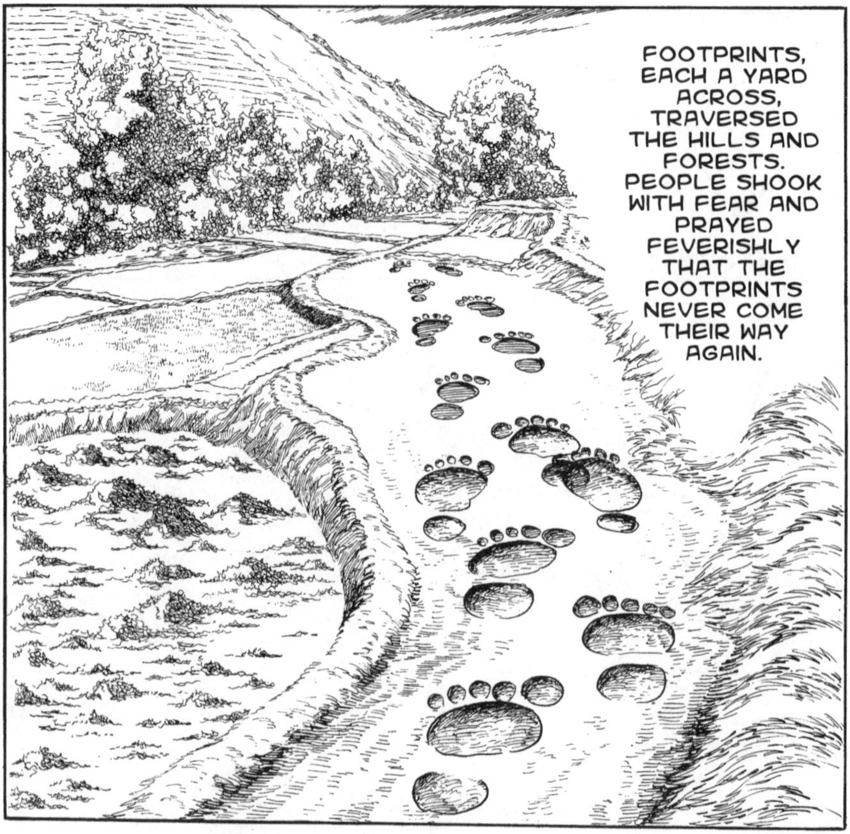
FOOTPRINTS, EACH A YARD ACROSS, TRAVERSED THE HILLS AND FORESTS. PEOPLE SHOOK WITH FEAR AND PRAYED FEVERISHLY THAT THE FOOTPRINTS NEVER COME THEIR WAY AGAIN.

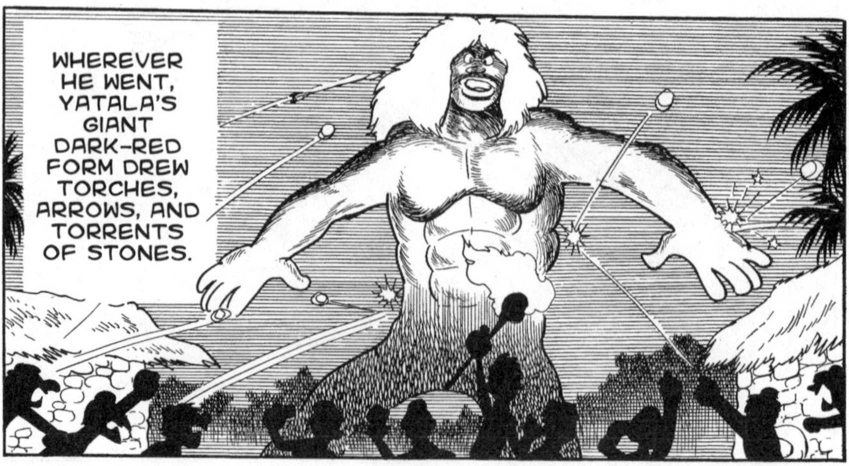
WHEREVER HE WENT, YATALA'S GIANT DARK-RED FORM DREW TORCHES, ARROWS, AND TORRENTS OF STONES.

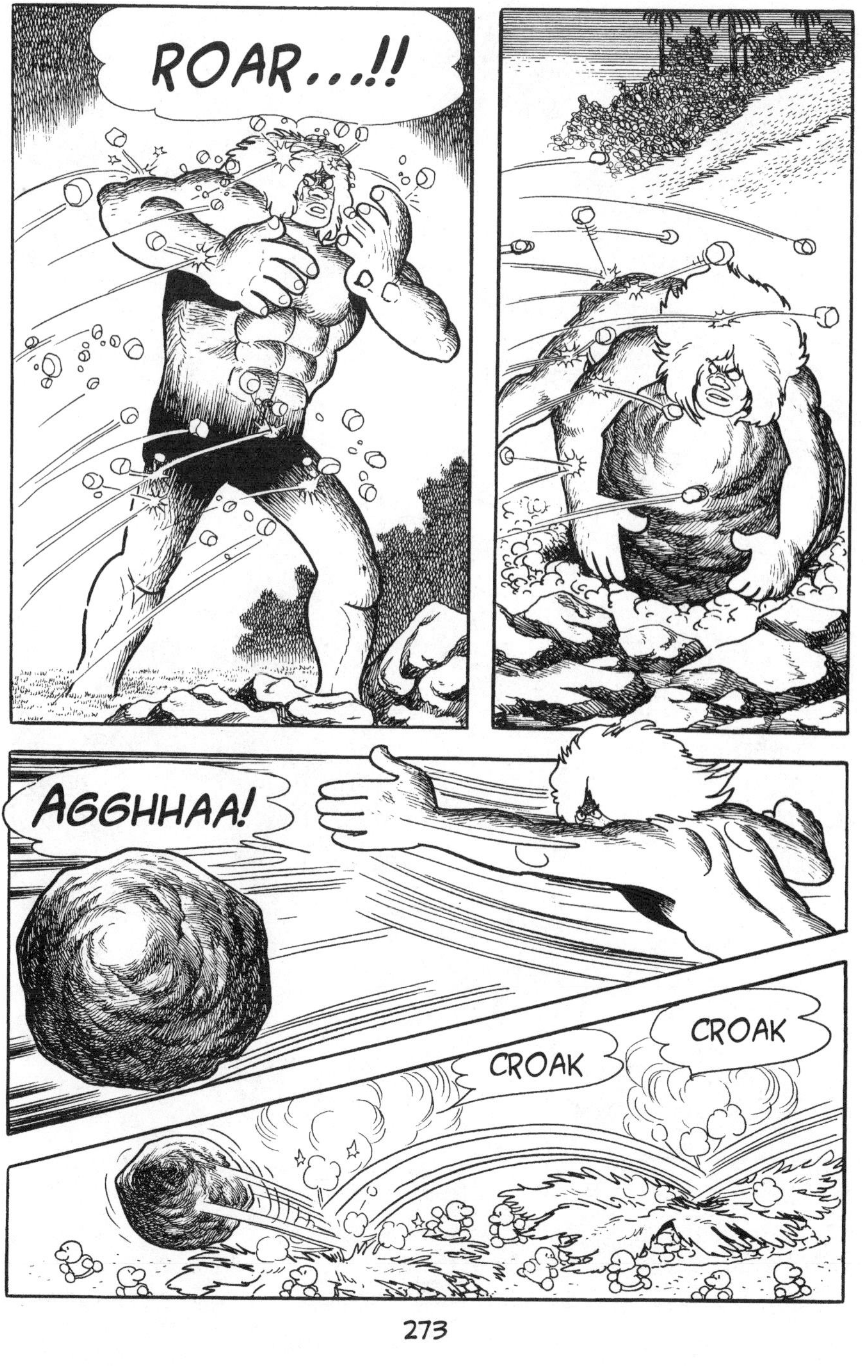
ROAR...!!
AGGHHAA!
CROAK
CROAK

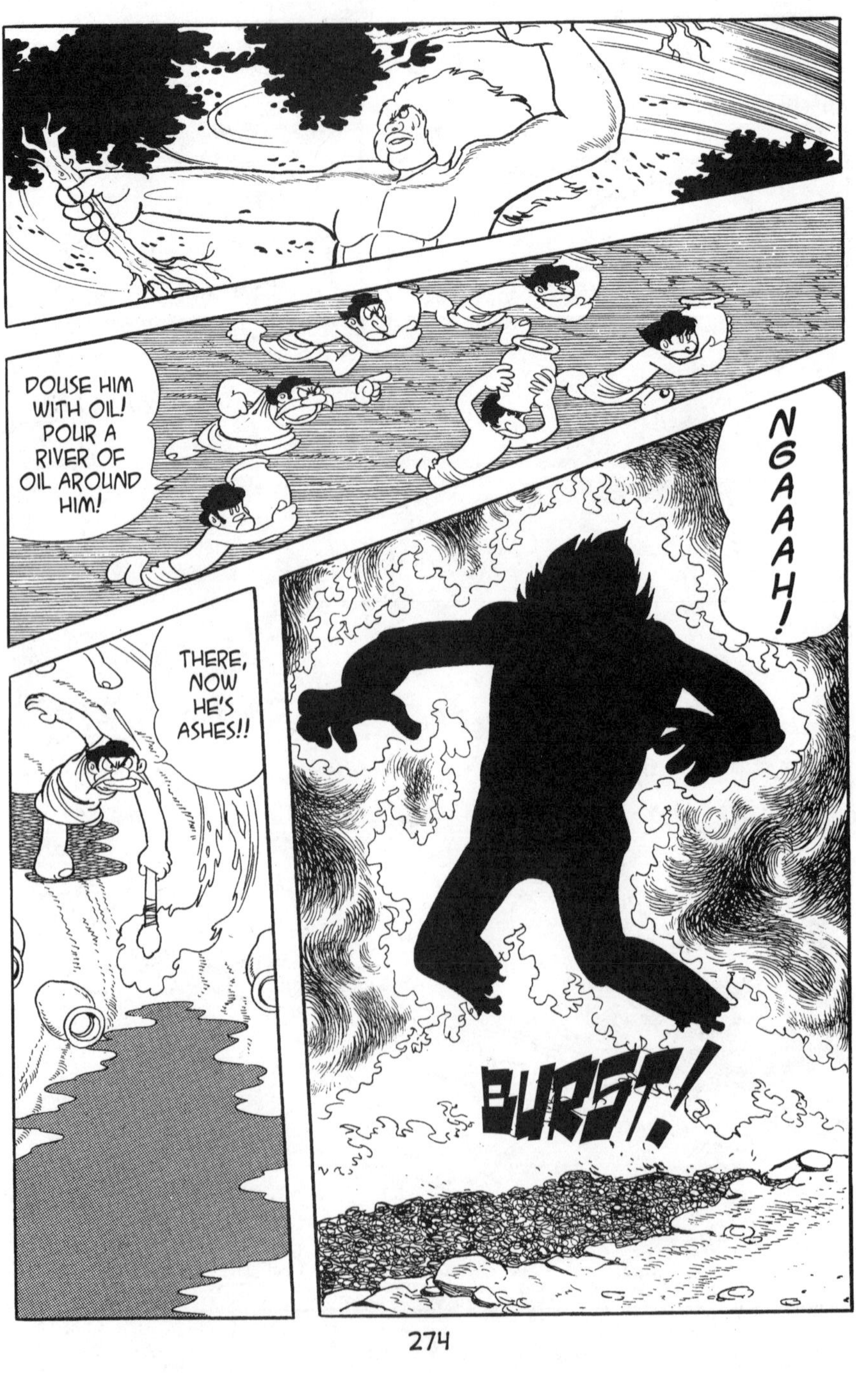
DOUSE HIM WITH OIL! POUR A RIVER OF OIL AROUND HIM!
NGAAAAH!
THERE, NOW HE'S ASHES!!
BURST!

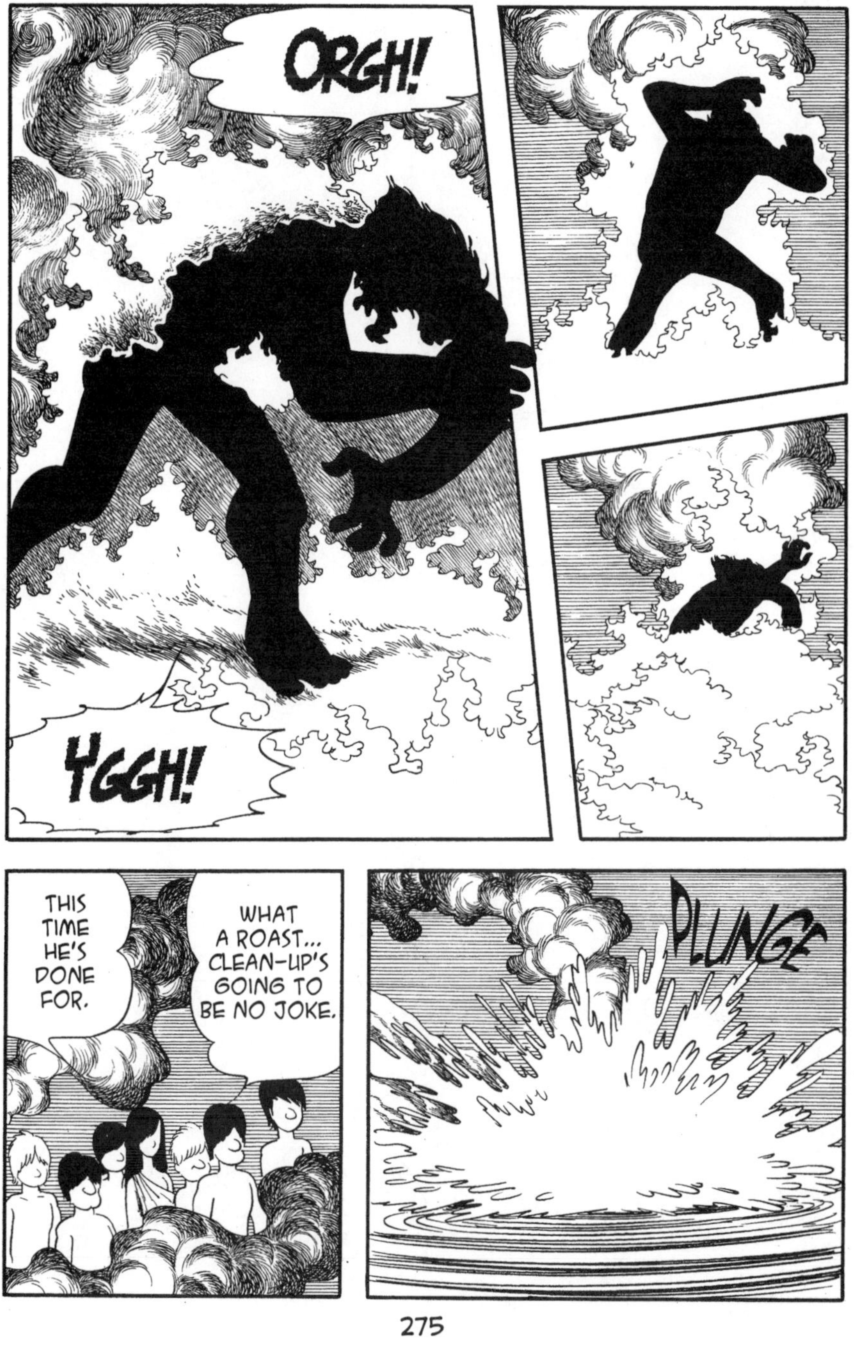
ORGH!
YGGH!
THIS TIME HE'S DONE FOR.
WHAT A ROAST... CLEAN-UP'S GOING TO BE NO JOKE.
PLUNGE

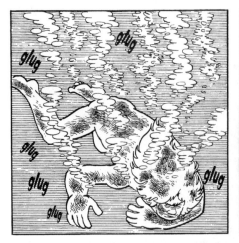

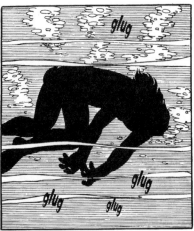

glug
glug
glug
glug
glug
glug
glug
glug
glug
glug
BUT YATALA DID NOT DIE.
HE COULD BE BADLY WOUNDED, HE COULD FALL INTO A COMA, BUT HE ALWAYS LIVED.
LIKE WEEDS THAT GROW BACK WHETHER THEY'RE TRAMPLED OR BURNED, YATALA ENDURED. AND LIVED ON.

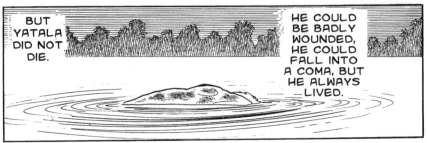

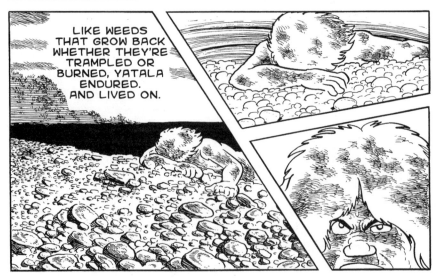

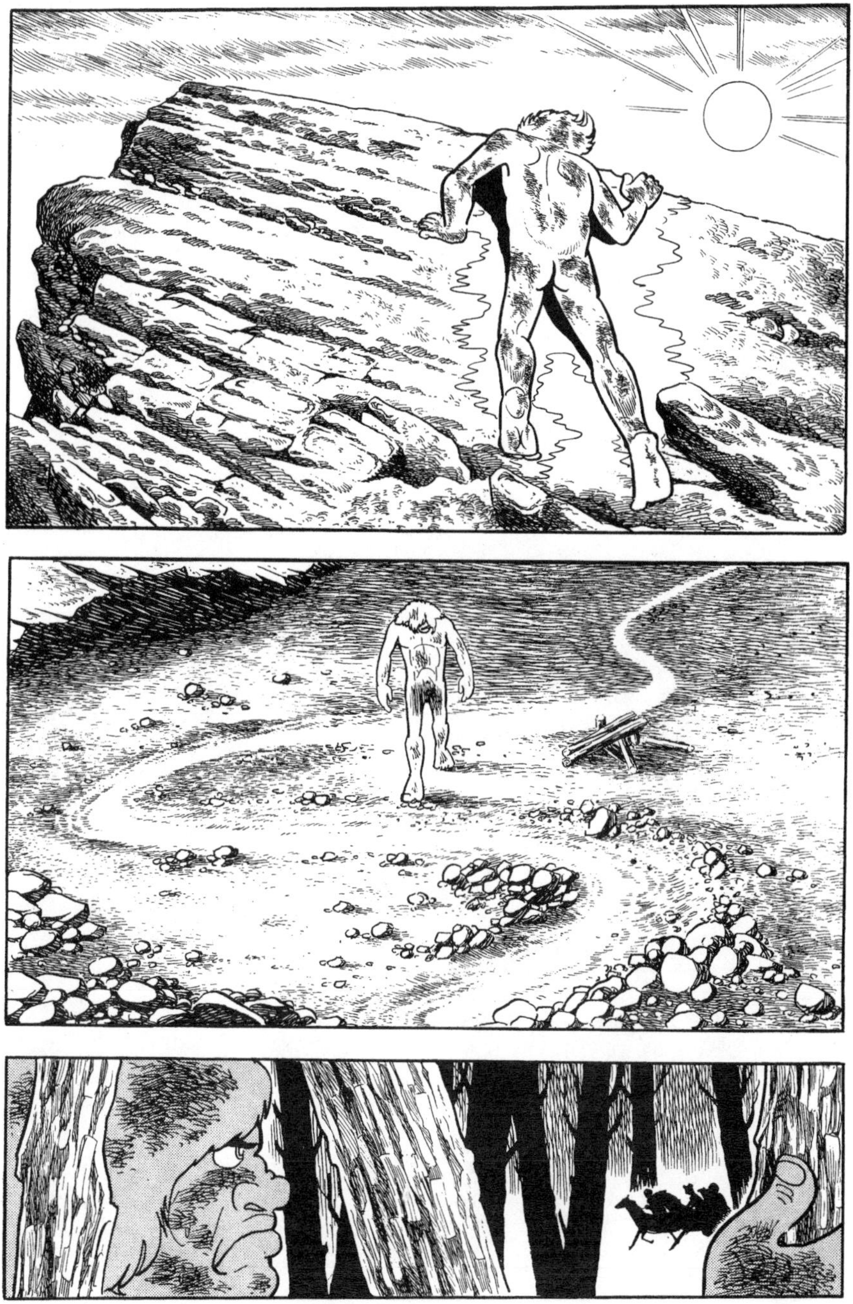

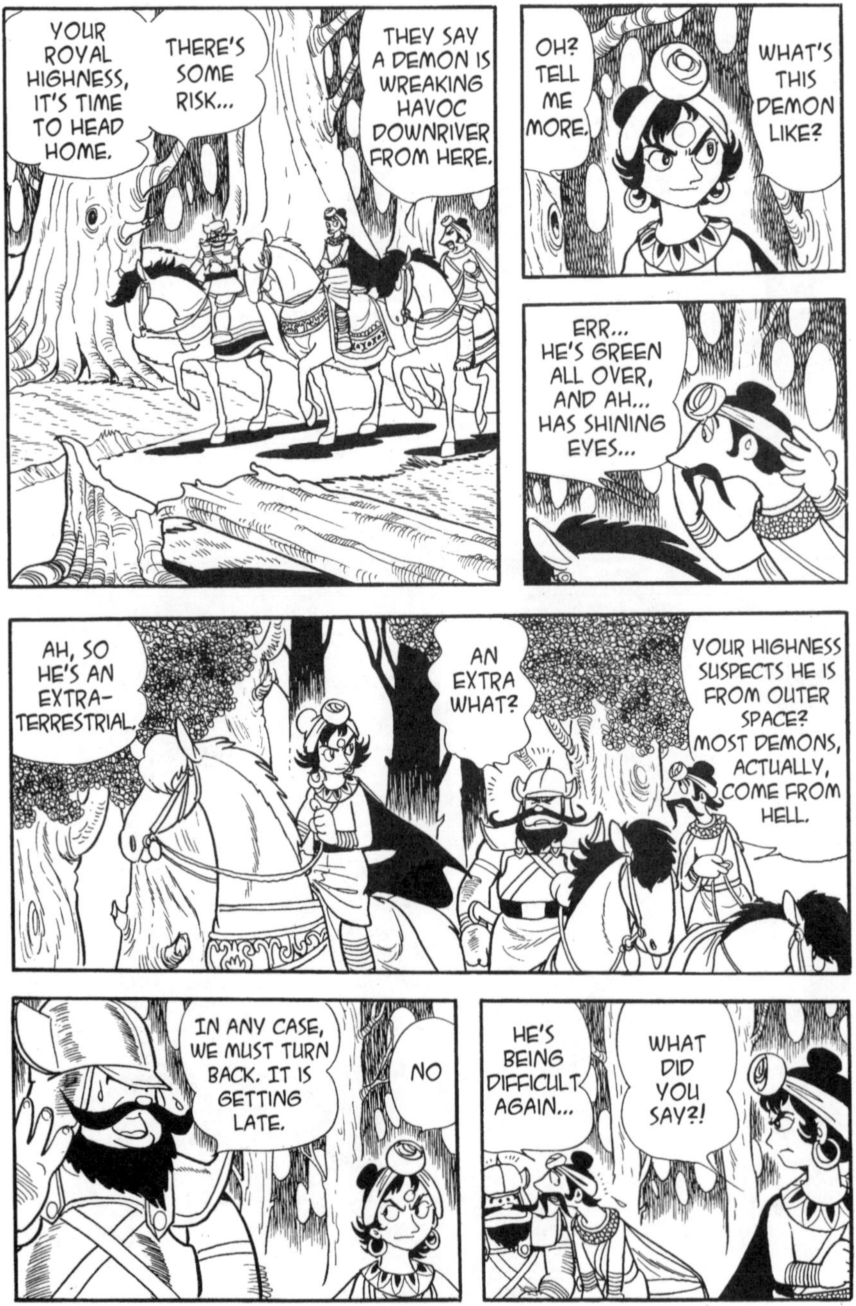

YOUR ROYAL HIGHNESS, IT'S TIME TO HEAD HOME.
THERE'S SOME RISK...
THEY SAY A DEMON IS WREAKING HAVOC DOWNRIVER FROM HERE.
OH? TELL ME MORE.
WHAT'S THIS DEMON LIKE?
ERR... HE'S GREEN ALL OVER, AND AH... HAS SHINING EYES...
AH, SO HE'S AN EXTRA-TERRESTRIAL.
AN EXTRA WHAT?
YOUR HIGHNESS SUSPECTS HE IS FROM OUTER SPACE? MOST DEMONS, ACTUALLY, COME FROM HELL.
IN ANY CASE, WE MUST TURN BACK. IT IS GETTING LATE.
NO
HE'S BEING DIFFICULT AGAIN...
WHAT DID YOU SAY?!

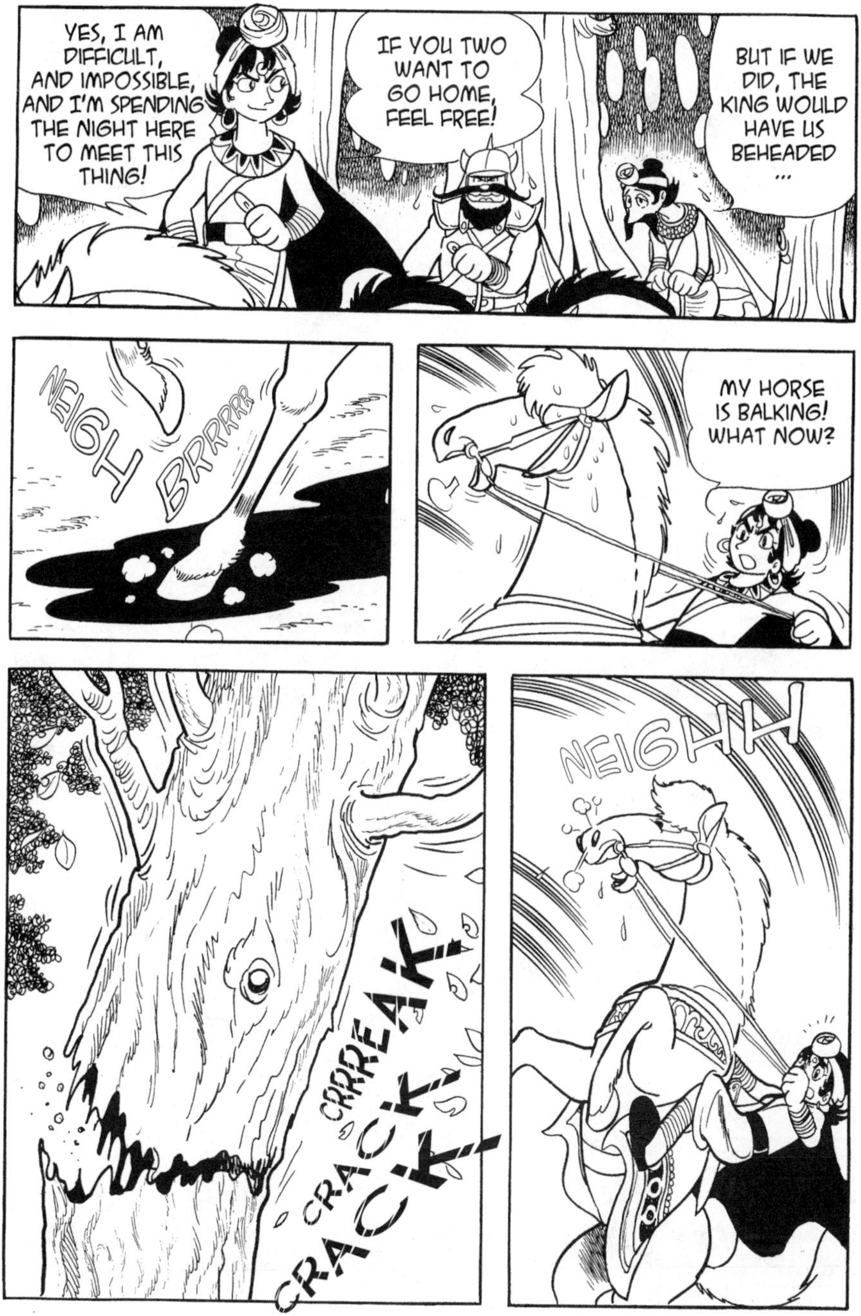
YES, I AM DIFFICULT, AND IMPOSSIBLE, AND I'M SPENDING THE NIGHT HERE TO MEET THIS THING!
IF YOU TWO WANT TO GO HOME, FEEL FREE!
BUT IF WE DID, THE KING WOULD HAVE US BEHEADED ...
NEIGH
BRRRRR
MY HORSE IS BALKING! WHAT NOW?
CRRREAK
CRACK
CRACK
NEIGHH

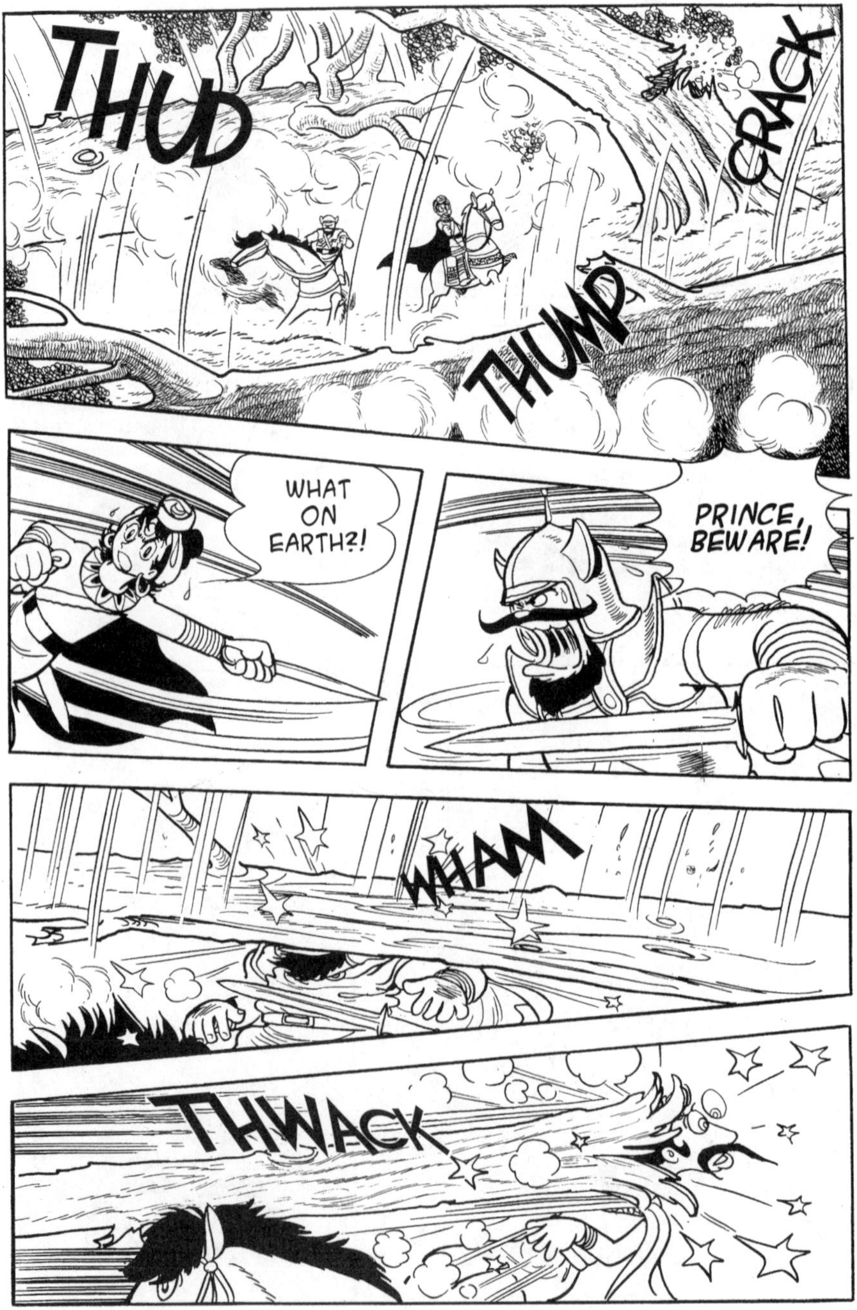
THUD
CRACK
THUMP
WHAT ON EARTH?!
PRINCE, BEWARE!
WHAM
THWACK

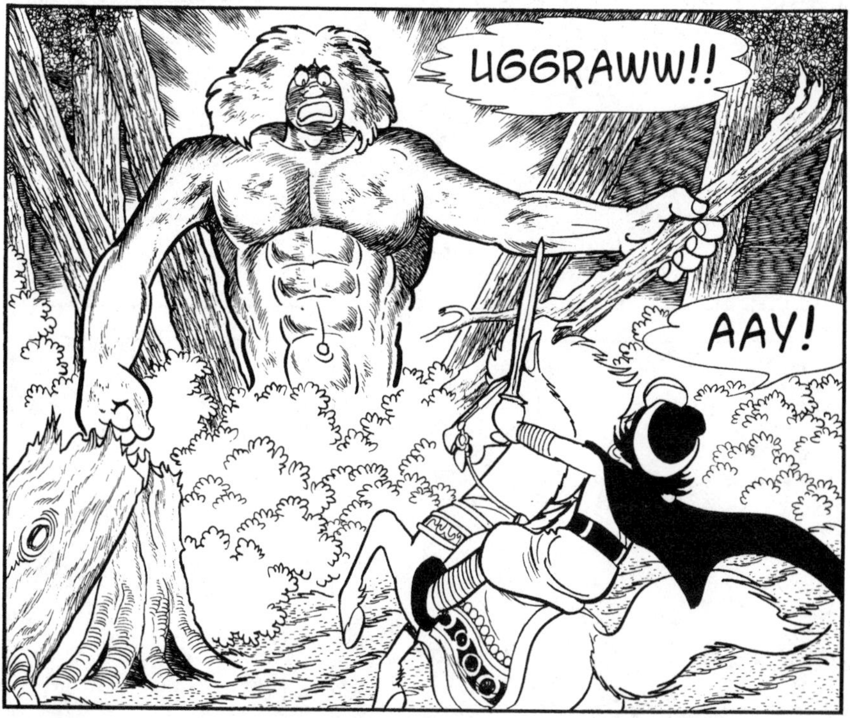
UGGRAWW!!
AAY!

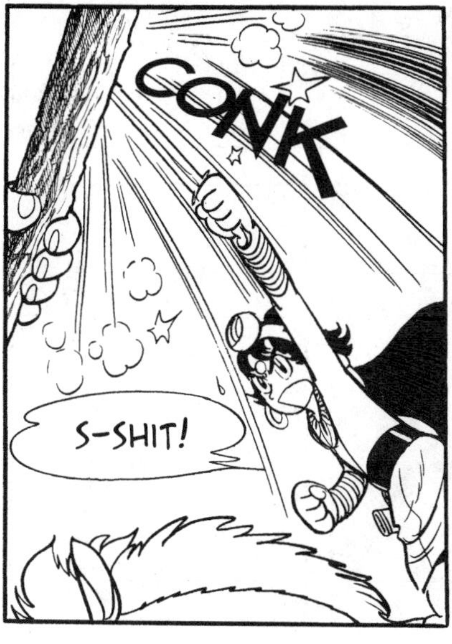
CONK
S-SHIT!

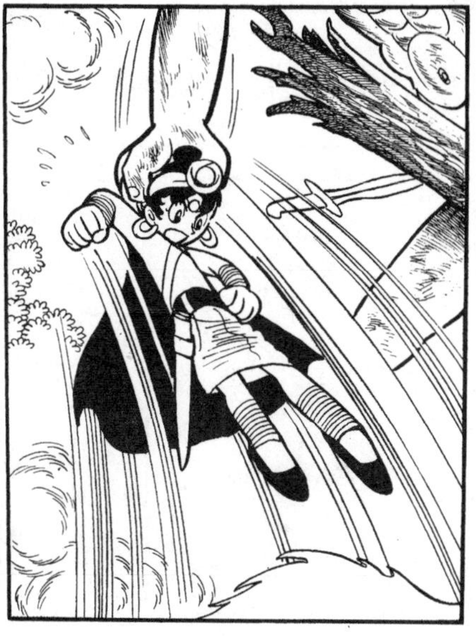

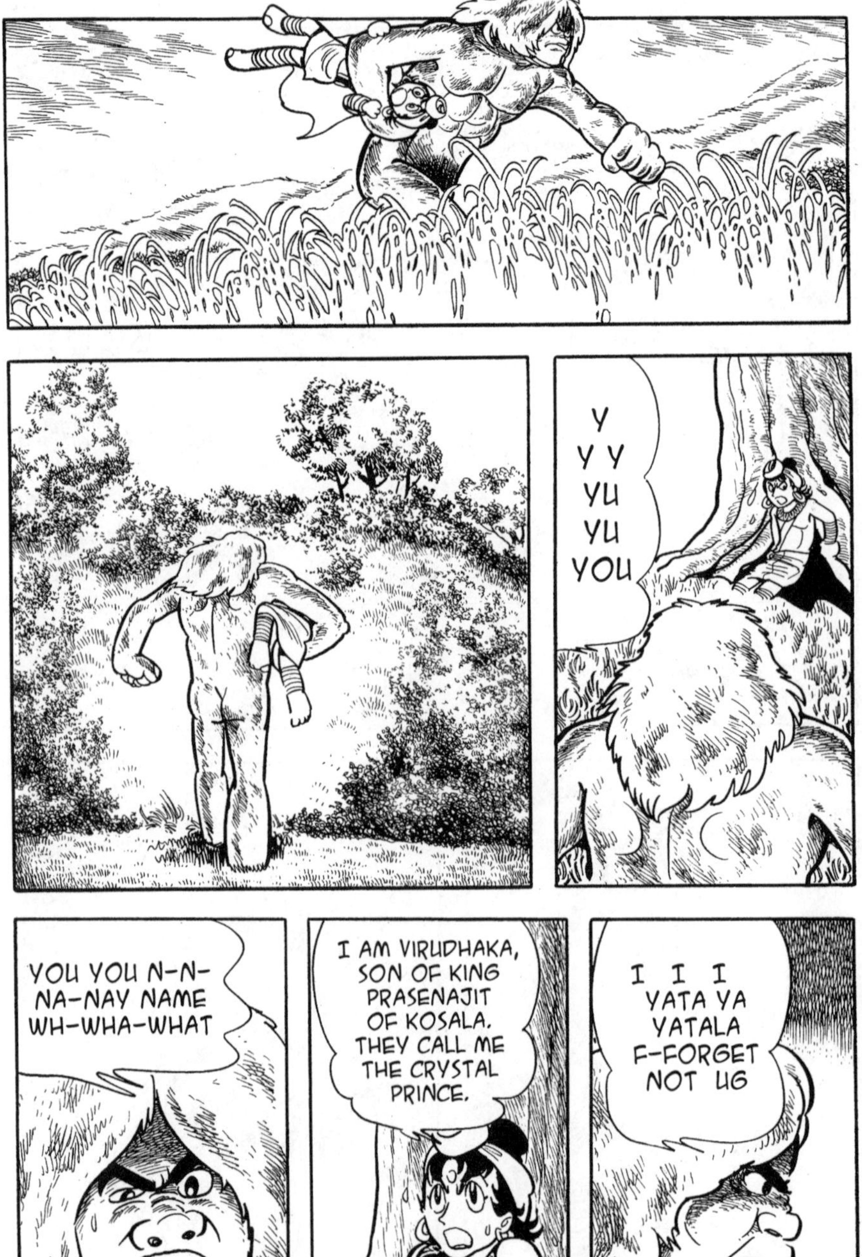
Y Y Y YU YU YOU
YOU YOU N-N-NA-NAY NAME WH-WHA-WHAT
I AM VIRUDHAKA, SON OF KING PRASENAJIT OF KOSALA. THEY CALL ME THE CRYSTAL PRINCE.
I I I YATA YA YATALA F-FORGET NOT UG

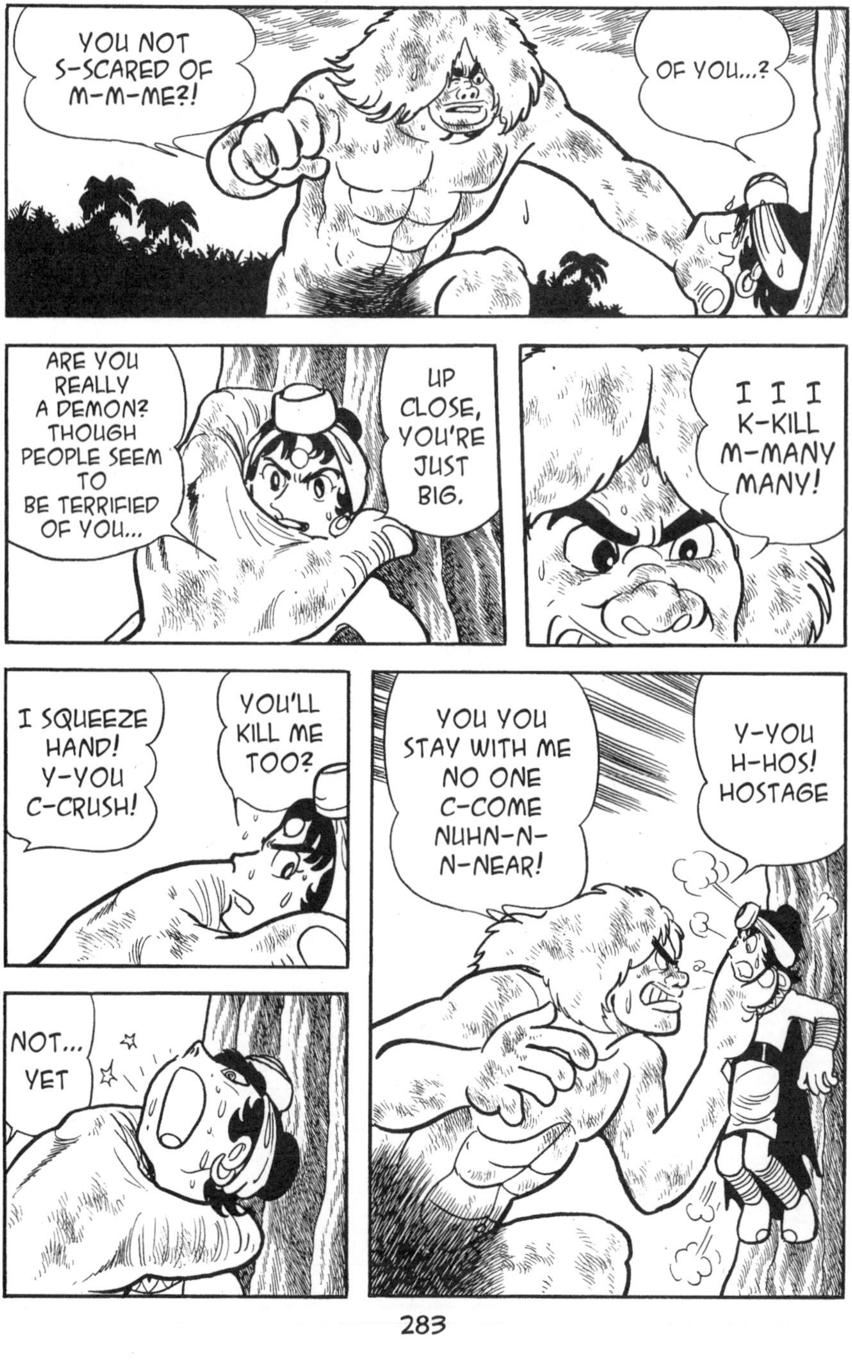
YOU NOT S-SCARED OF M-M-ME?!
OF YOU...?
ARE YOU REALLY A DEMON? THOUGH PEOPLE SEEM TO BE TERRIFIED OF YOU...
UP CLOSE, YOU'RE JUST BIG.
I I I K-KILL M-MANY MANY!
I SQUEEZE HAND! Y-YOU C-CRUSH!
YOU'LL KILL ME TOO?
NOT... YET
YOU YOU STAY WITH ME NO ONE C-COME NUHN-N-N-NEAR!
Y-YOU H-HOS! HOSTAGE

ME, YOUR HOSTAGE? THINK YOU'LL EVER GET AWAY WITH THAT?

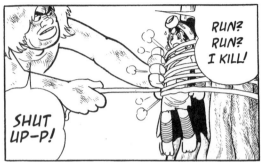

RUN? RUN? I KILL!

SHUT UP-P!

WHAT ARE YOU AFTER? WHAT IS IT YOU WANT? MONEY? OR IS THIS SOME SORT OF REVENGE?

... ...

HEY, ANSWER ME!

MOST WISHES, I CAN GRANT!

THE CRYSTAL PRINCE OF KOSALA KNOWS HOW TO HONOR A PROMISE. WHATEVER YOU ASK FOR, YOU WILL GET, I SAY. I GIVE YOU MY WORD!

SAY SOMETHING.

284

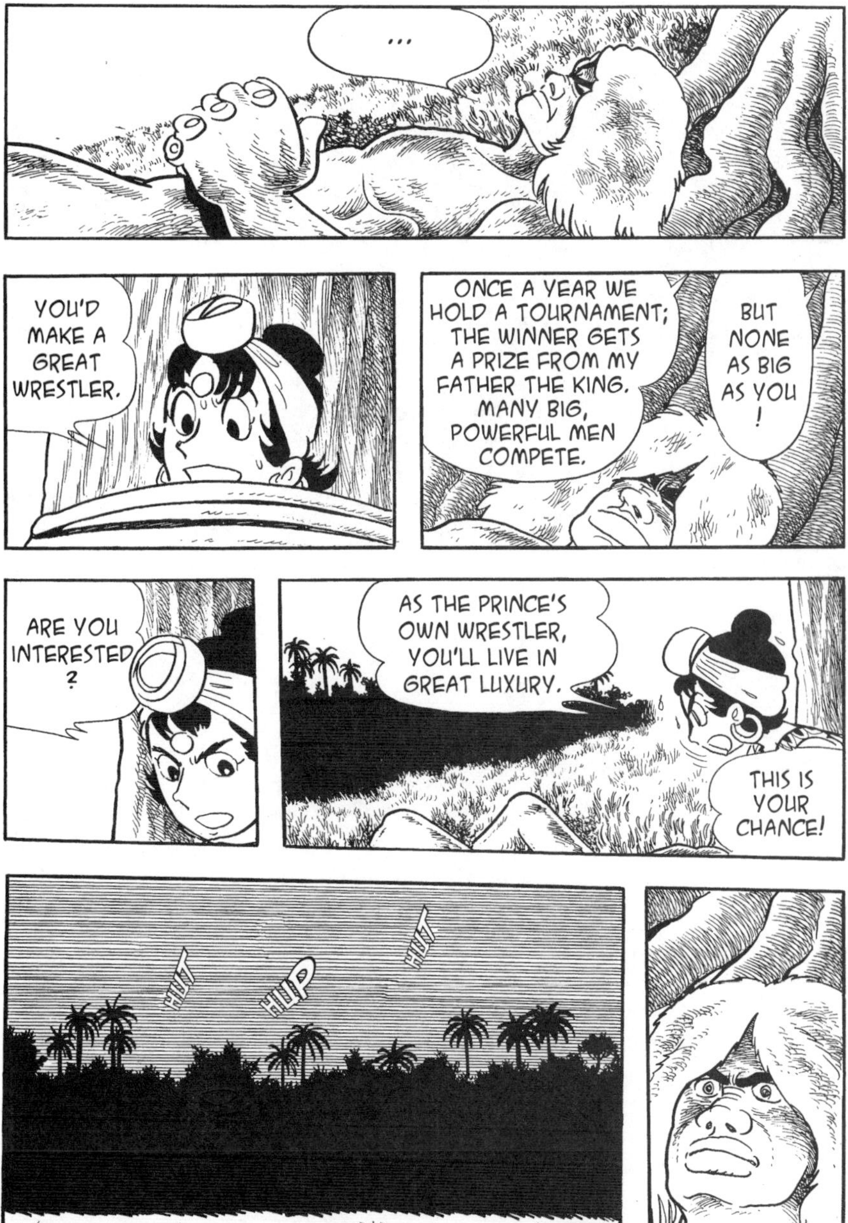
...
YOU'D MAKE A GREAT WRESTLER.
ONCE A YEAR WE HOLD A TOURNAMENT; THE WINNER GETS A PRIZE FROM MY FATHER THE KING. MANY BIG, POWERFUL MEN COMPETE.
BUT NONE AS BIG AS YOU !
ARE YOU INTERESTED ?
AS THE PRINCE'S OWN WRESTLER, YOU'LL LIVE IN GREAT LUXURY.
THIS IS YOUR CHANCE!
HUT
HUP
HUT

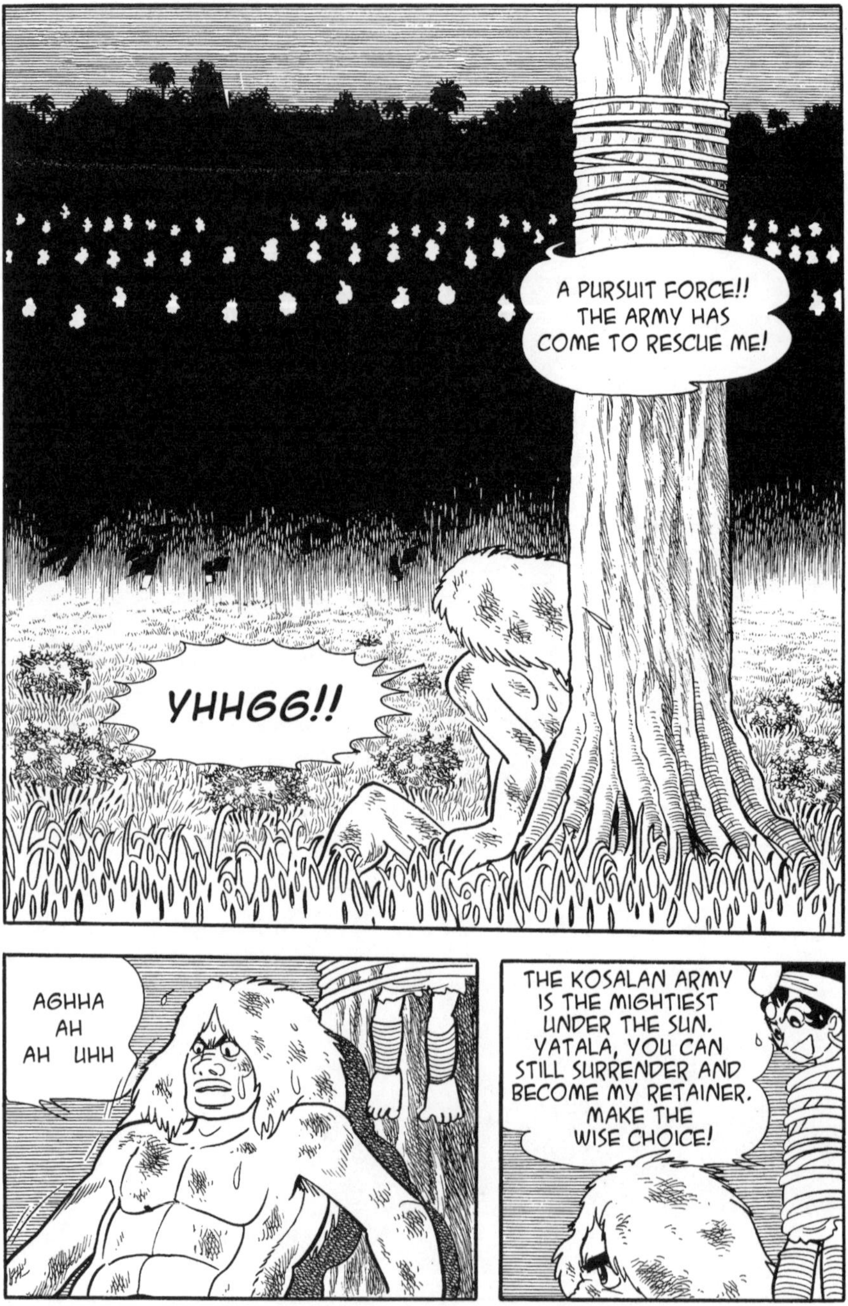
A PURSUIT FORCE!! THE ARMY HAS COME TO RESCUE ME!
YHHGG!!
AGHHA AH AH UHH
THE KOSALAN ARMY IS THE MIGHTIEST UNDER THE SUN. YATALA, YOU CAN STILL SURRENDER AND BECOME MY RETAINER. MAKE THE WISE CHOICE!

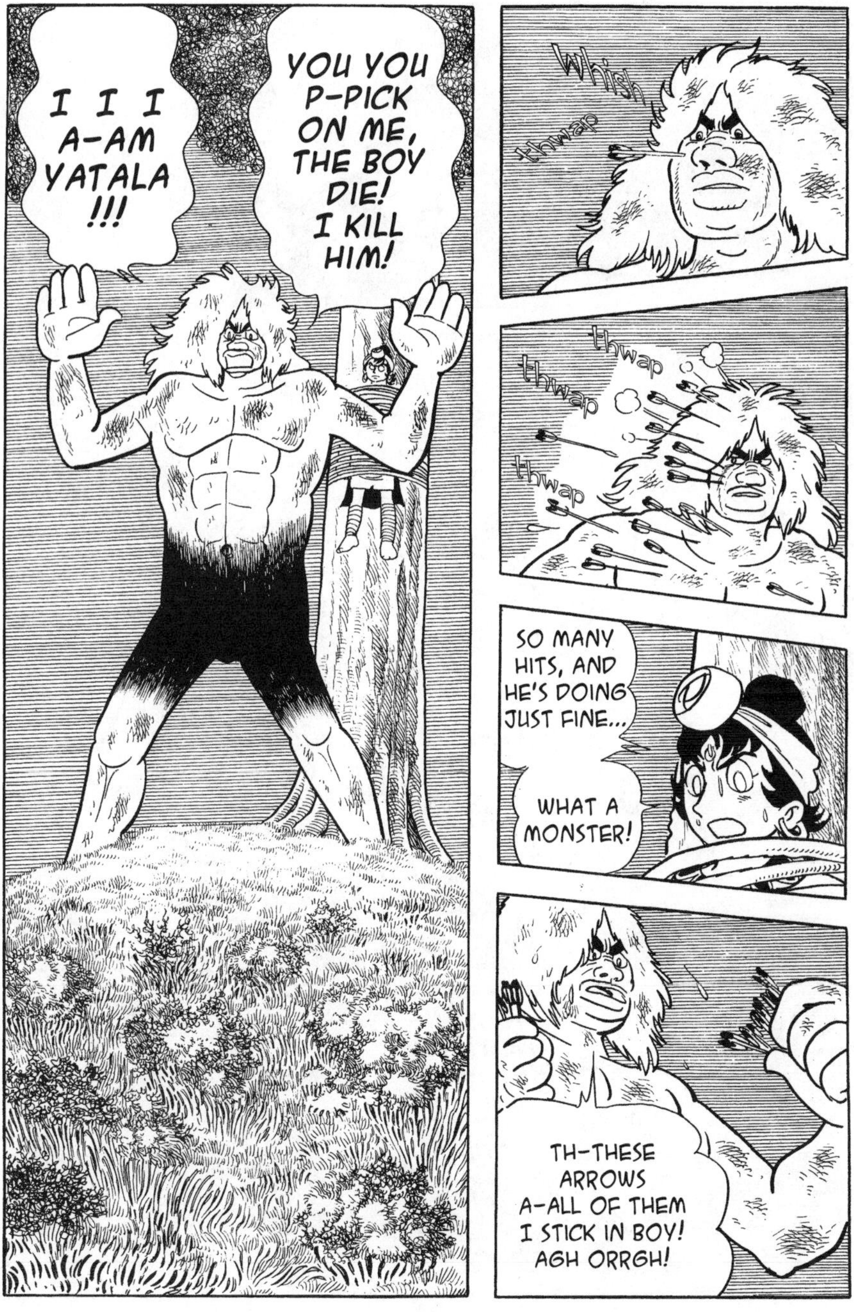
I I I A-AM YATALA !!!
YOU YOU P-PICK ON ME, THE BOY DIE! I KILL HIM!
Whish
thwap
thwap
thwap
thwap
SO MANY HITS, AND HE'S DOING JUST FINE...
WHAT A MONSTER!
TH-THESE ARROWS A-ALL OF THEM I STICK IN BOY! AGH ORRGH!

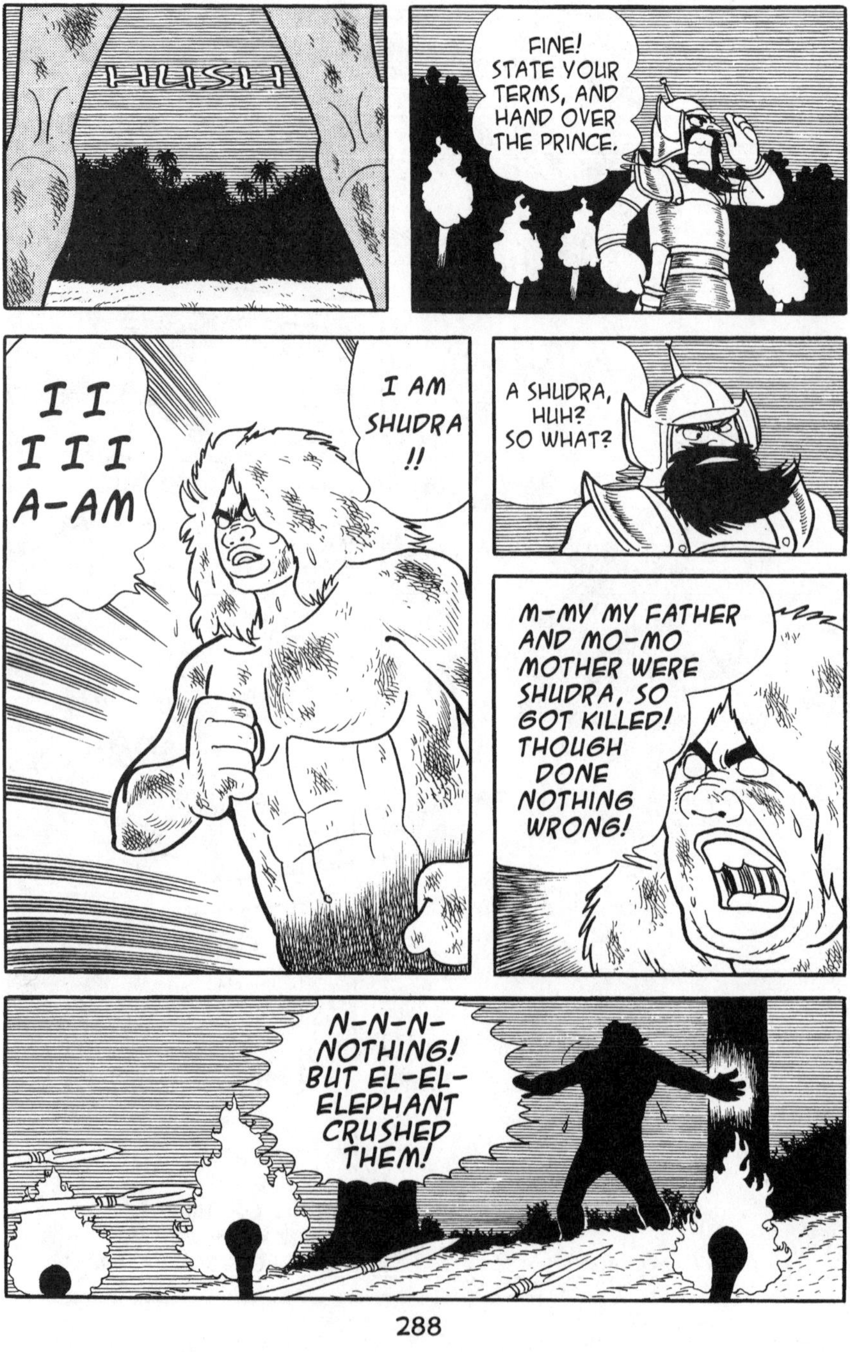
HUSH
FINE! STATE YOUR TERMS, AND HAND OVER THE PRINCE.
I I I I I A-AM
I AM SHUDRA !!
A SHUDRA, HUH? SO WHAT?
M-MY MY FATHER AND MO-MO MOTHER WERE SHUDRA, SO GOT KILLED! THOUGH DONE NOTHING WRONG!
N-N-N-NOTHING! BUT EL-EL-ELEPHANT CRUSHED THEM!

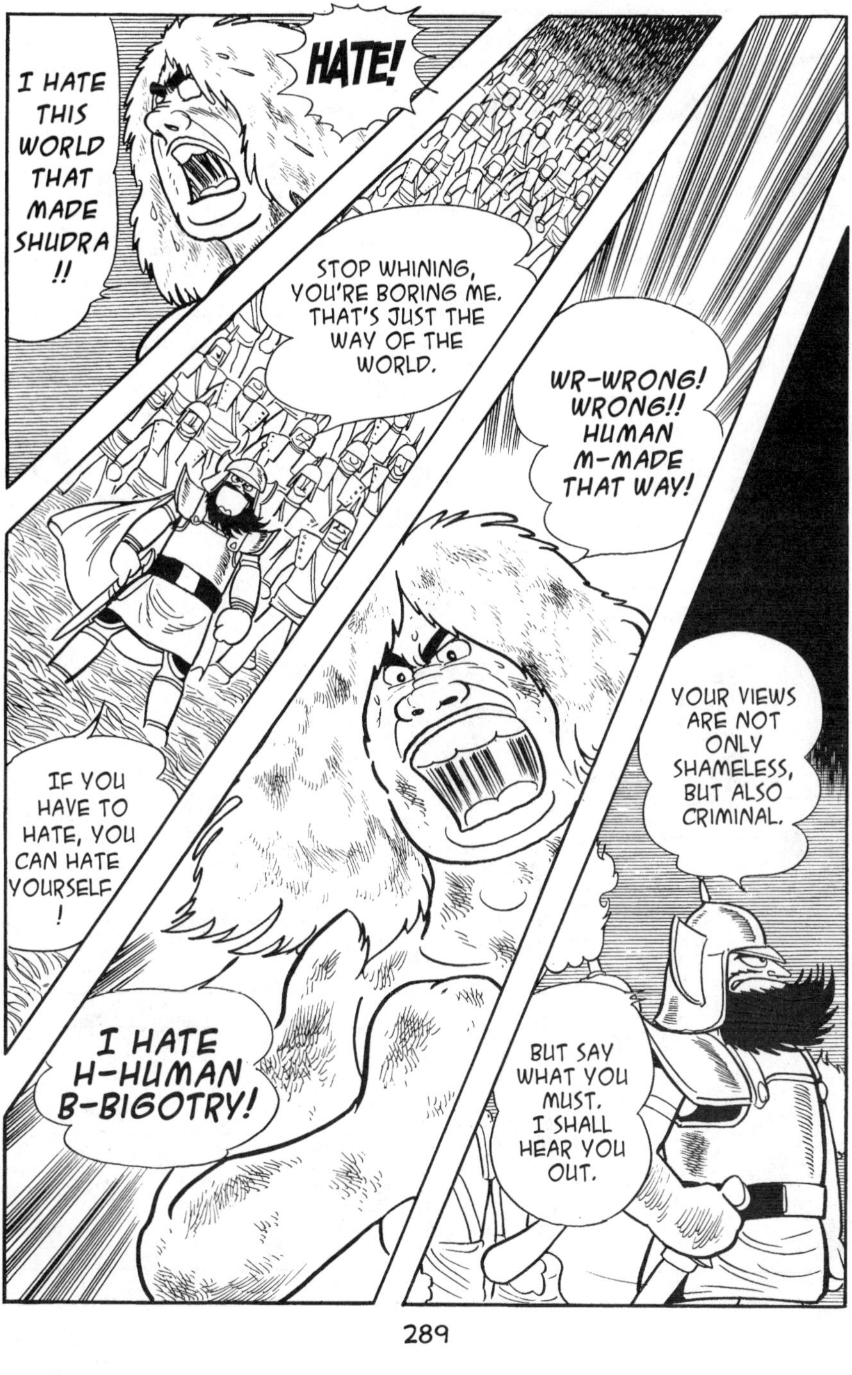
I HATE THIS WORLD THAT MADE SHUDRA!!
HATE!
STOP WHINING, YOU'RE BORING ME. THAT'S JUST THE WAY OF THE WORLD.
IF YOU HAVE TO HATE, YOU CAN HATE YOURSELF!
WR-WRONG! WRONG!! HUMAN M-MADE THAT WAY!
I HATE H-HUMAN B-BIGOTRY!
YOUR VIEWS ARE NOT ONLY SHAMELESS, BUT ALSO CRIMINAL.
BUT SAY WHAT YOU MUST. I SHALL HEAR YOU OUT.

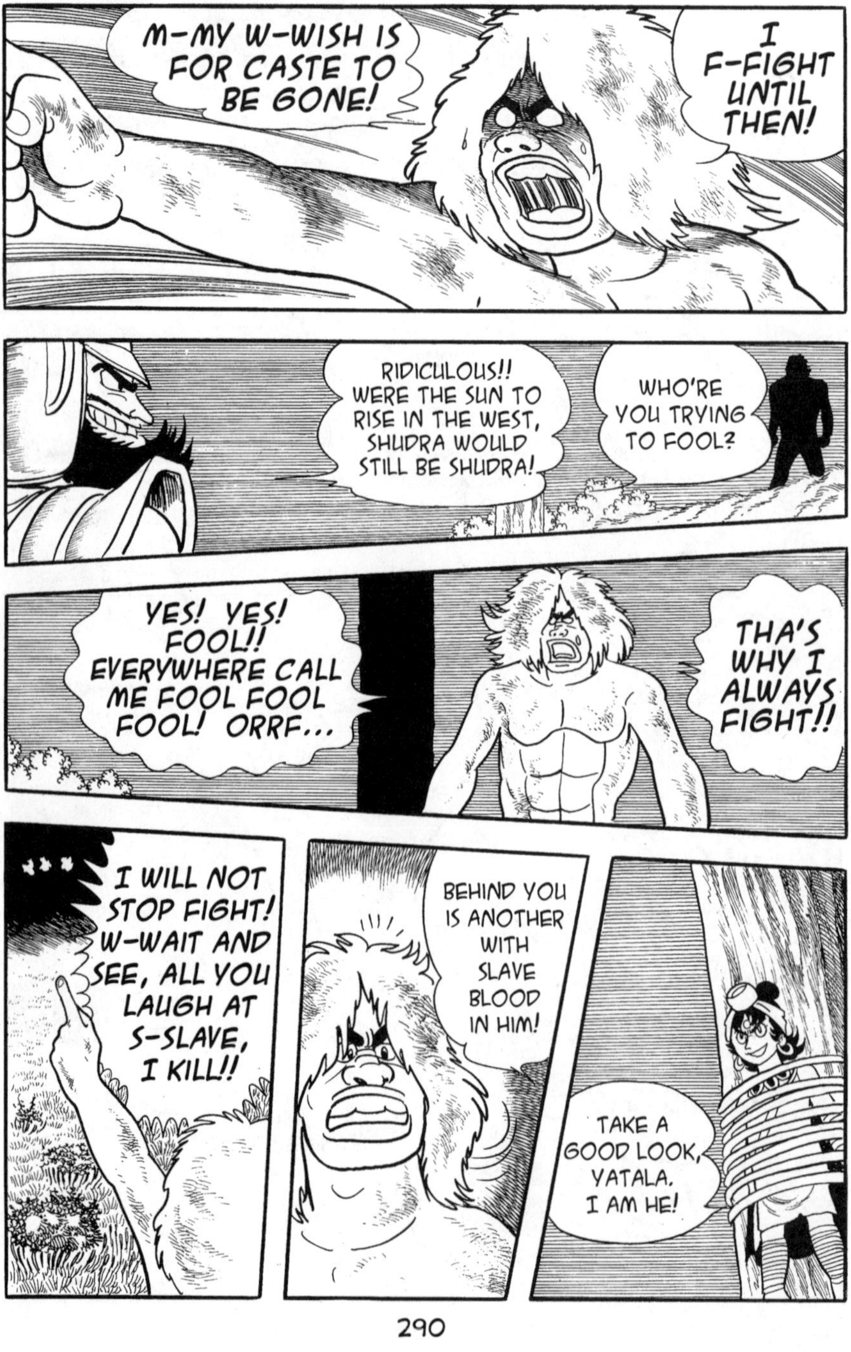

M-MY W-WISH IS FOR CASTE TO BE GONE!
I F-FIGHT UNTIL THEN!
RIDICULOUS!! WERE THE SUN TO RISE IN THE WEST, SHUDRA WOULD STILL BE SHUDRA!
WHO'RE YOU TRYING TO FOOL?
YES! YES! FOOL!! EVERYWHERE CALL ME FOOL FOOL FOOL! ORRF...
THA'S WHY I ALWAYS FIGHT!!
I WILL NOT STOP FIGHT! W-WAIT AND SEE, ALL YOU LAUGH AT S-SLAVE, I KILL!!
BEHIND YOU IS ANOTHER WITH SLAVE BLOOD IN HIM!
TAKE A GOOD LOOK, YATALA. I AM HE!

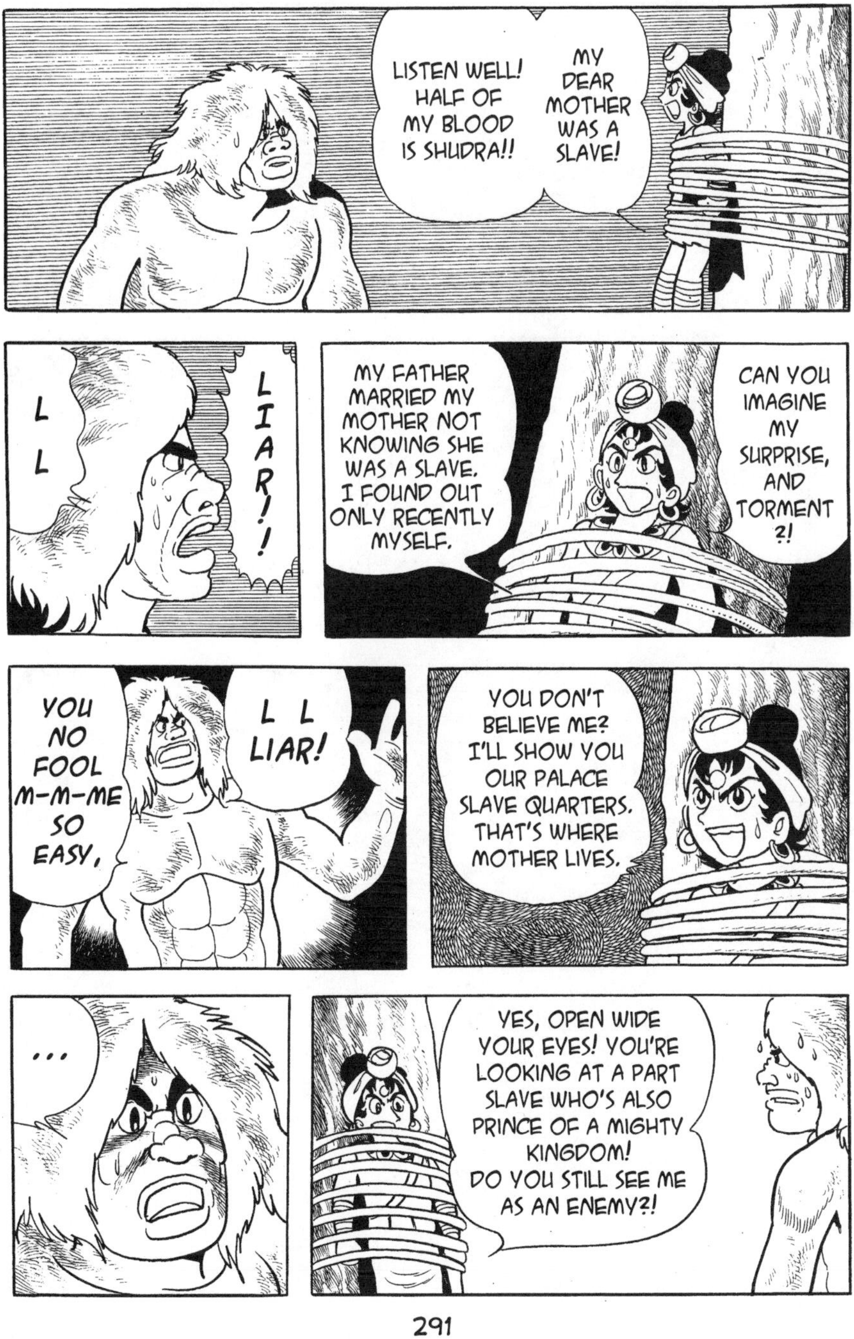
LISTEN WELL! HALF OF MY BLOOD IS SHUDRA!!
MY DEAR MOTHER WAS A SLAVE!
L
L
LIAR!!
MY FATHER MARRIED MY MOTHER NOT KNOWING SHE WAS A SLAVE. I FOUND OUT ONLY RECENTLY MYSELF.
CAN YOU IMAGINE MY SURPRISE, AND TORMENT?!
YOU NO FOOL M-M-ME SO EASY,
L L LIAR!
YOU DON'T BELIEVE ME? I'LL SHOW YOU OUR PALACE SLAVE QUARTERS. THAT'S WHERE MOTHER LIVES.
...
YES, OPEN WIDE YOUR EYES! YOU'RE LOOKING AT A PART SLAVE WHO'S ALSO PRINCE OF A MIGHTY KINGDOM! DO YOU STILL SEE ME AS AN ENEMY?!

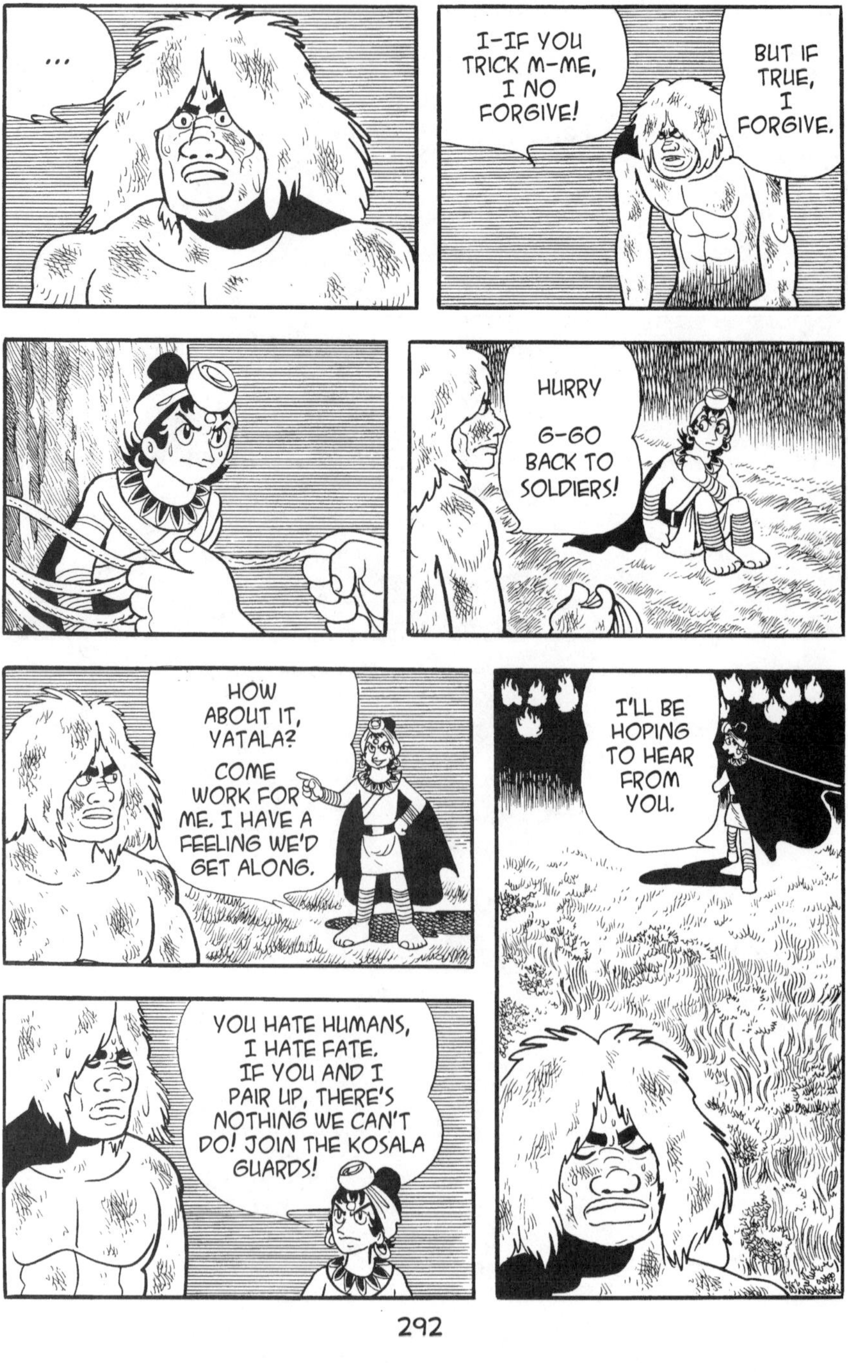
...
I-IF YOU TRICK M-ME, I NO FORGIVE!
BUT IF TRUE, I FORGIVE.
HURRY
6-GO BACK TO SOLDIERS!
HOW ABOUT IT, YATALA?
COME WORK FOR ME. I HAVE A FEELING WE'D GET ALONG.
I'LL BE HOPING TO HEAR FROM YOU.
YOU HATE HUMANS, I HATE FATE. IF YOU AND I PAIR UP, THERE'S NOTHING WE CAN'T DO! JOIN THE KOSALA GUARDS!

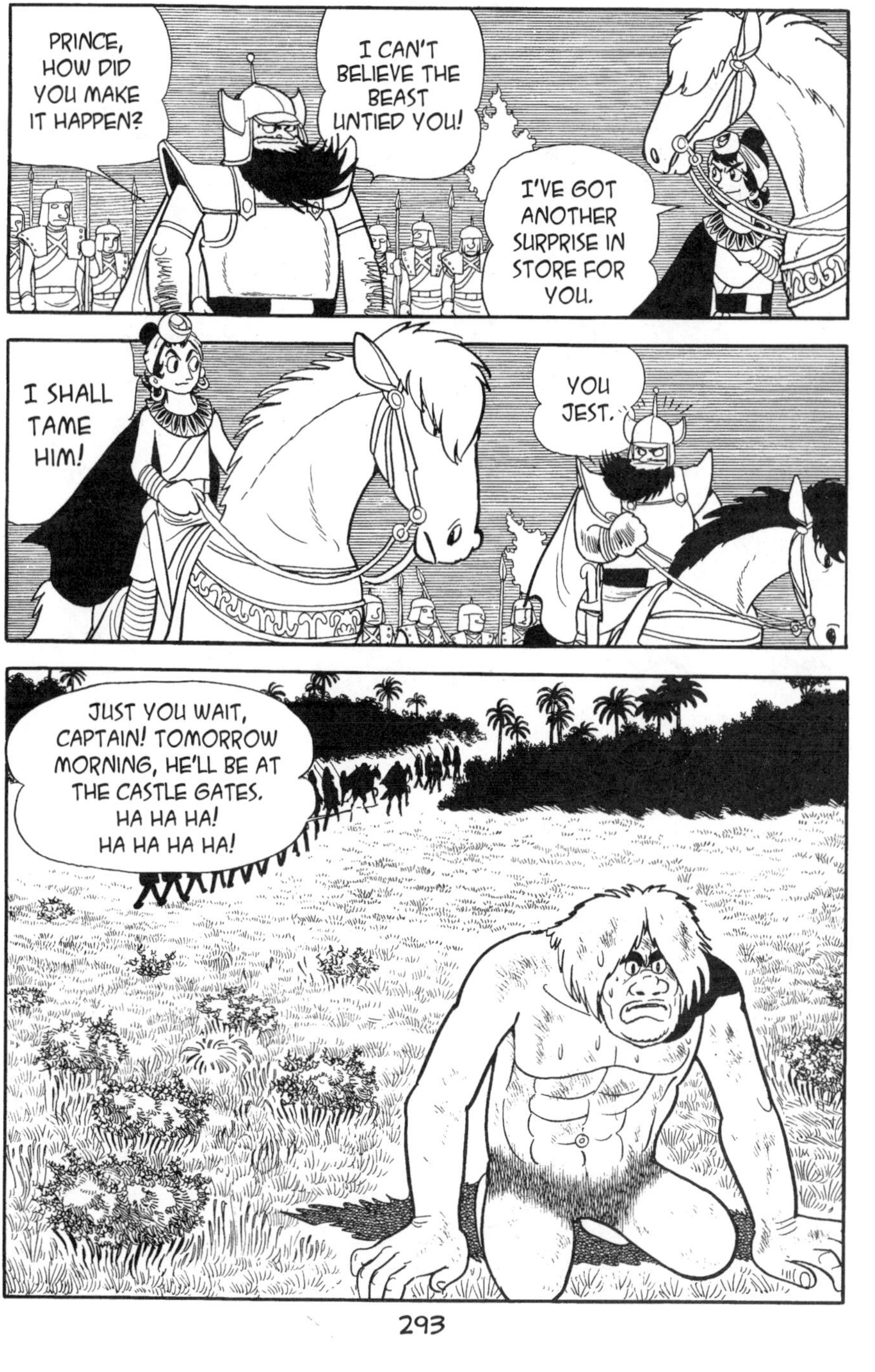
PRINCE, HOW DID YOU MAKE IT HAPPEN?
I CAN'T BELIEVE THE BEAST UNTIED YOU!
I'VE GOT ANOTHER SURPRISE IN STORE FOR YOU.
I SHALL TAME HIM!
YOU JEST.
JUST YOU WAIT, CAPTAIN! TOMORROW MORNING, HE'LL BE AT THE CASTLE GATES. HA HA HA! HA HA HA HA!

EGADS!
HELP!!
ROAR!!
C-C-CRYSTAL P-P-PRINCE !!!
WHOA!

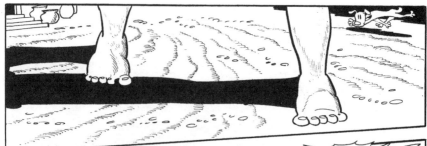

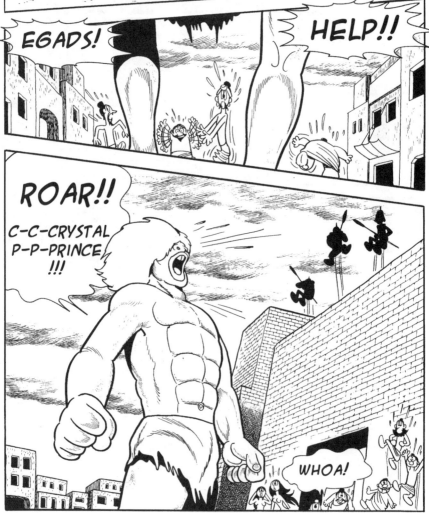

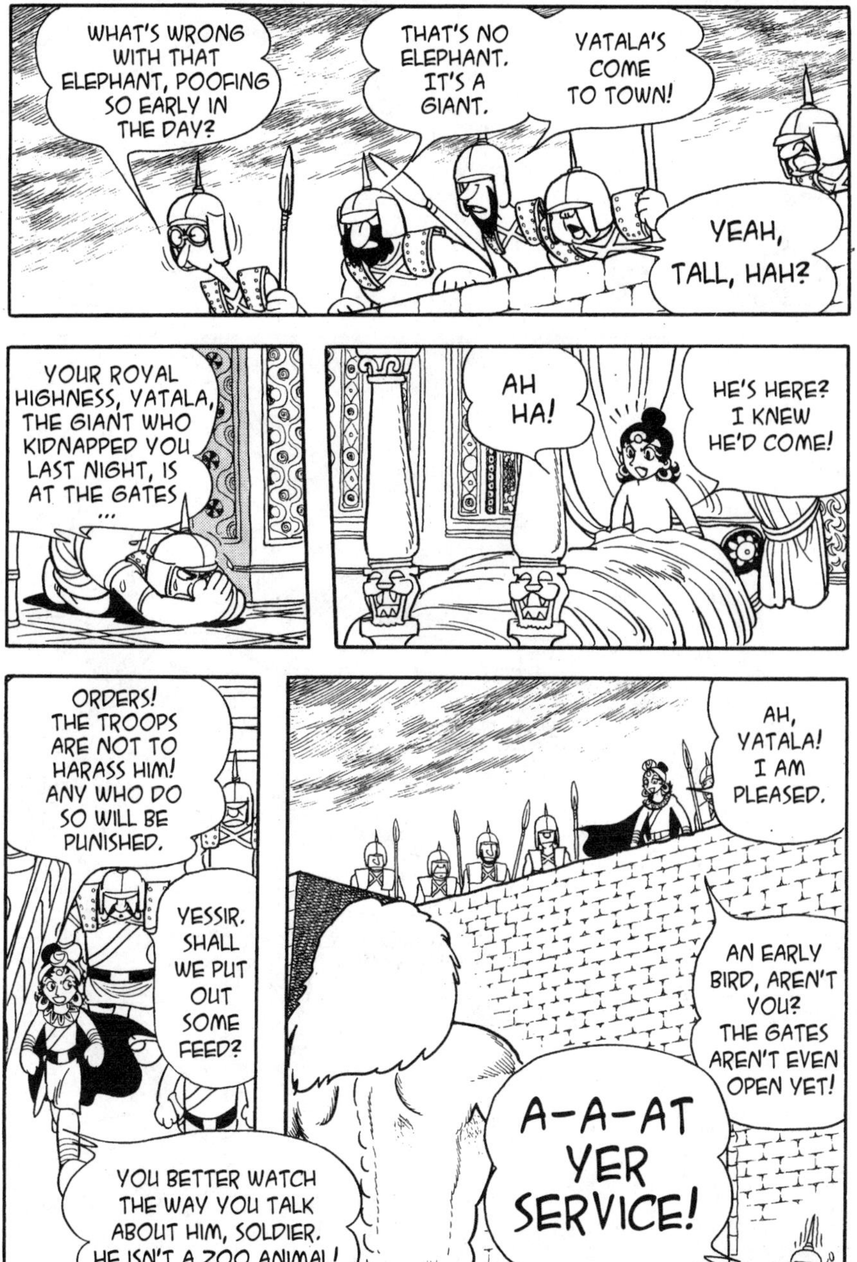
WHAT'S WRONG WITH THAT ELEPHANT, POOFING SO EARLY IN THE DAY?
THAT'S NO ELEPHANT. IT'S A GIANT.
YATALA'S COME TO TOWN!
YEAH, TALL, HAH?
YOUR ROYAL HIGHNESS, YATALA, THE GIANT WHO KIDNAPPED YOU LAST NIGHT, IS AT THE GATES ...
AH HA!
HE'S HERE? I KNEW HE'D COME!
ORDERS! THE TROOPS ARE NOT TO HARASS HIM! ANY WHO DO SO WILL BE PUNISHED.
YESSIR. SHALL WE PUT OUT SOME FEED?
YOU BETTER WATCH THE WAY YOU TALK ABOUT HIM, SOLDIER. HE ISN'T A ZOO ANIMAL!
AH, YATALA! I AM PLEASED.
AN EARLY BIRD, AREN'T YOU? THE GATES AREN'T EVEN OPEN YET!
A-A-AT YER SERVICE!

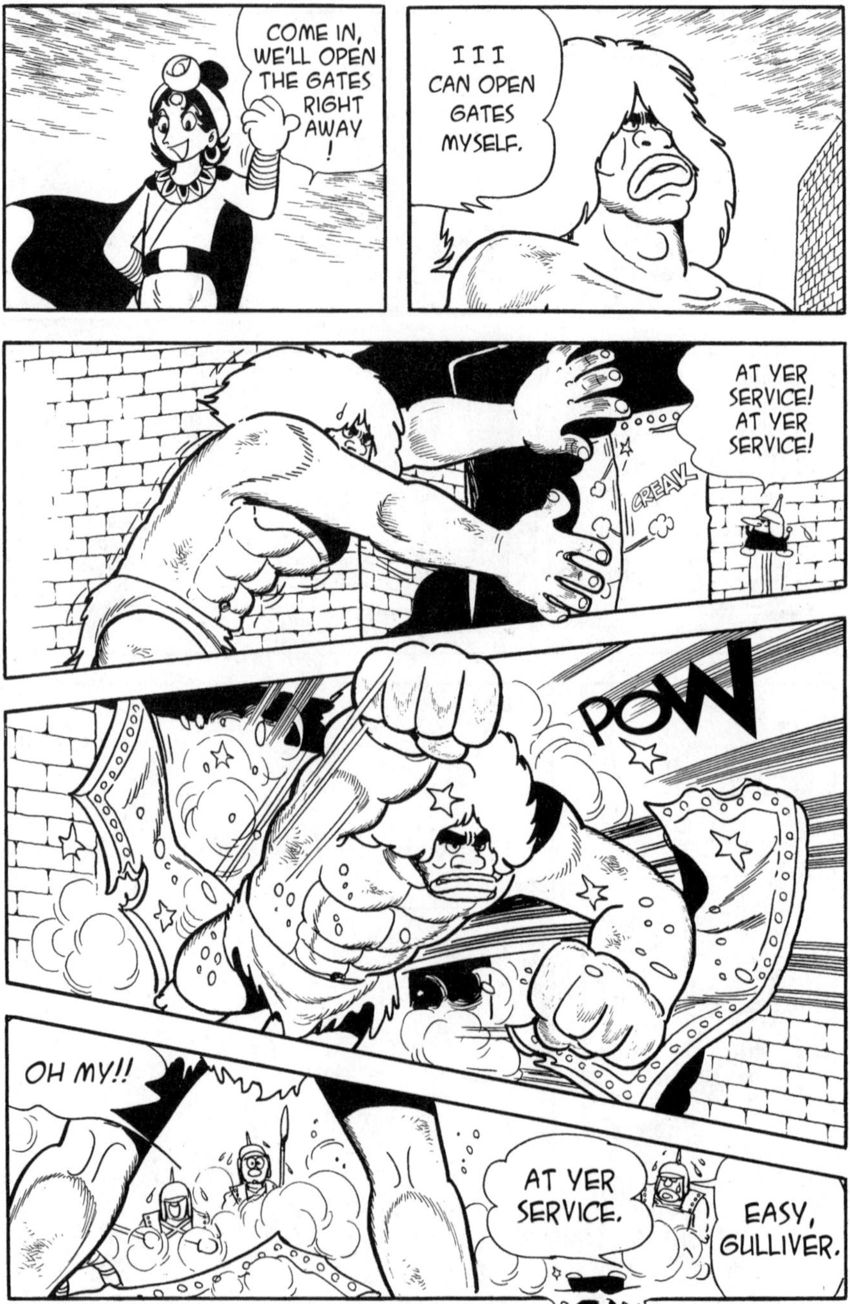
COME IN, WE'LL OPEN THE GATES RIGHT AWAY !
I I I CAN OPEN GATES MYSELF.
AT YER SERVICE! AT YER SERVICE!
CREAK
POW
OH MY!!
AT YER SERVICE.
EASY, GULLIVER.

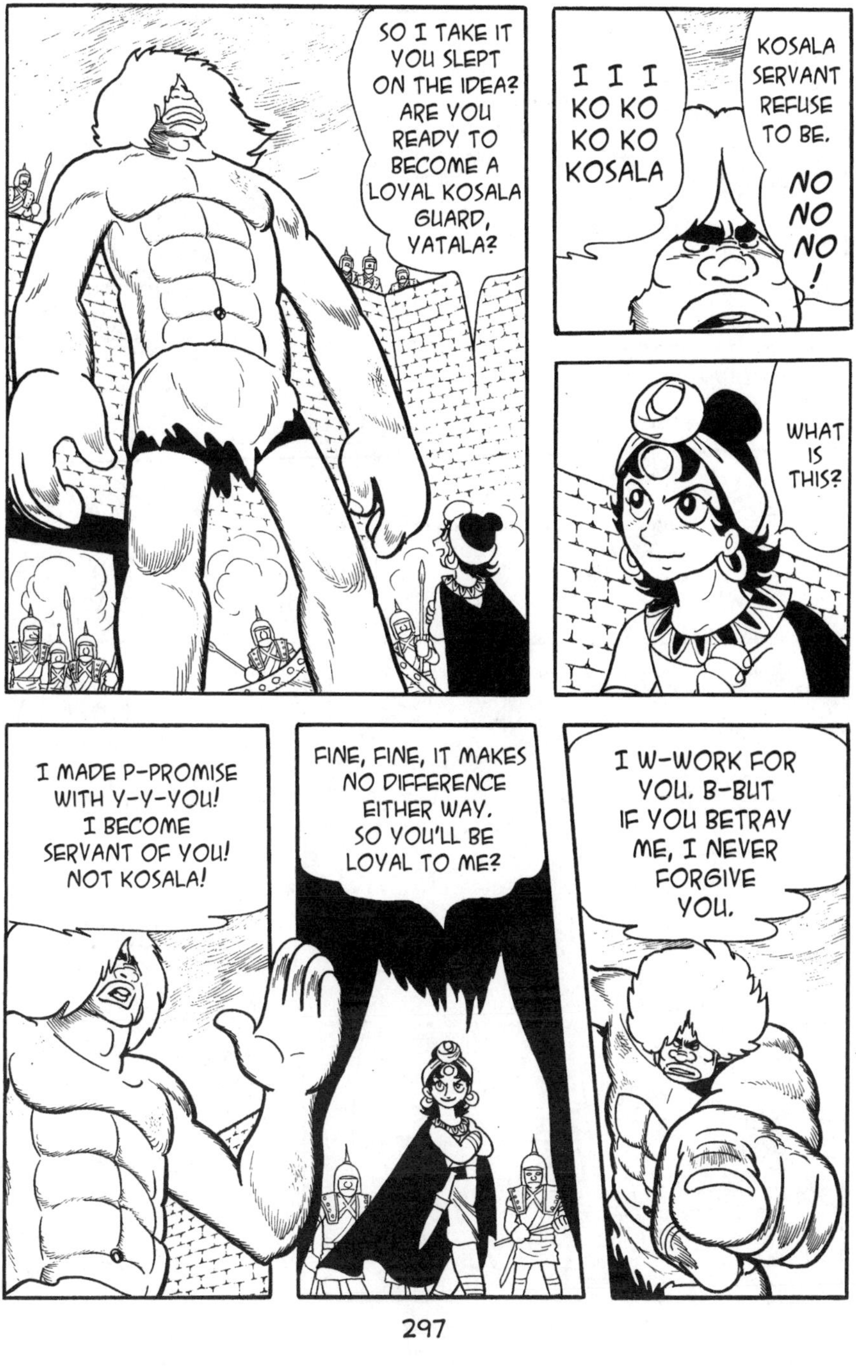
SO I TAKE IT YOU SLEPT ON THE IDEA? ARE YOU READY TO BECOME A LOYAL KOSALA GUARD, YATALA?
I I I KO KO KO KO KOSALA
KOSALA SERVANT REFUSE TO BE.
NO NO NO!
WHAT IS THIS?
I MADE P-PROMISE WITH Y-Y-YOU! I BECOME SERVANT OF YOU! NOT KOSALA!
FINE, FINE, IT MAKES NO DIFFERENCE EITHER WAY. SO YOU'LL BE LOYAL TO ME?
I W-WORK FOR YOU. B-BUT IF YOU BETRAY ME, I NEVER FORGIVE YOU.

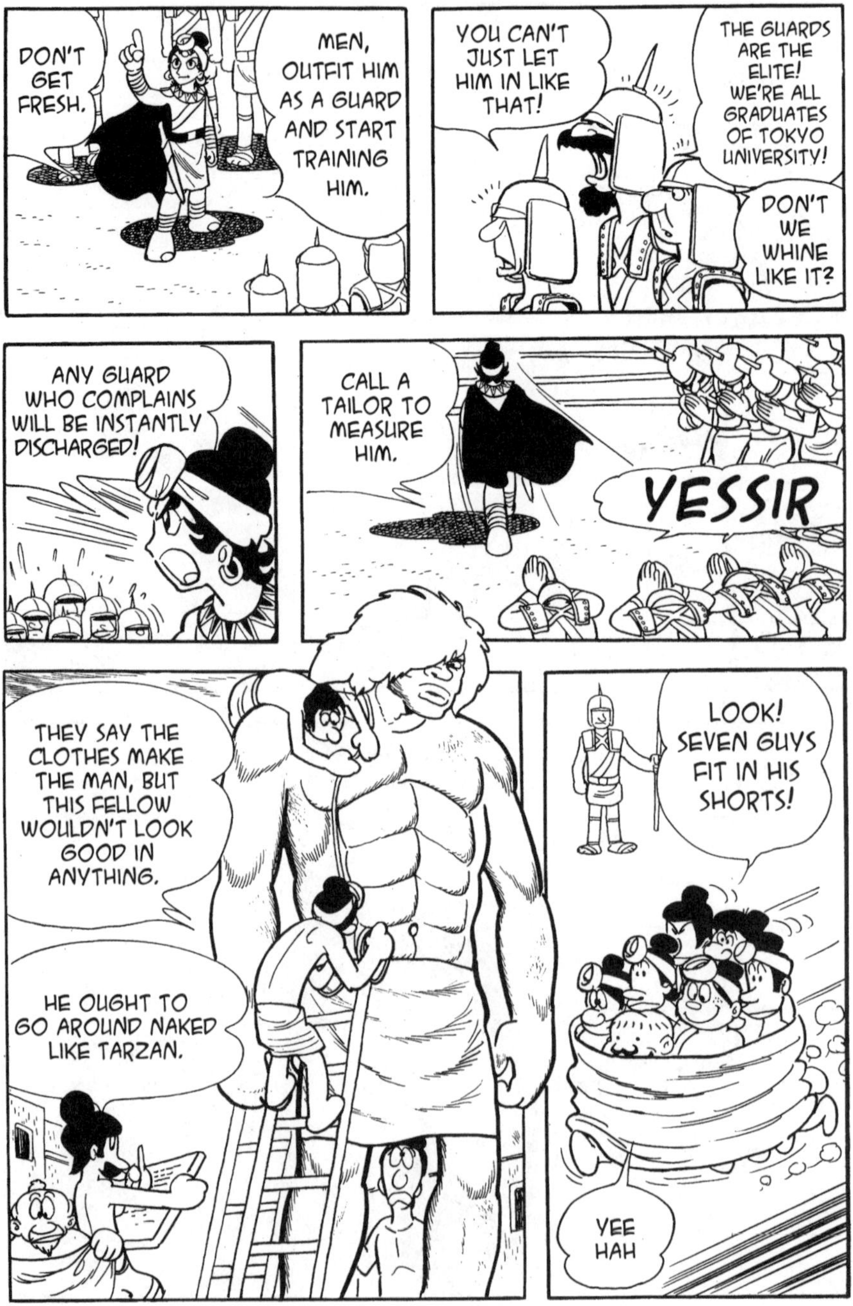
DON'T GET FRESH.
MEN, OUTFIT HIM AS A GUARD AND START TRAINING HIM.
YOU CAN'T JUST LET HIM IN LIKE THAT!
THE GUARDS ARE THE ELITE! WE'RE ALL GRADUATES OF TOKYO UNIVERSITY!
DON'T WE WHINE LIKE IT?
ANY GUARD WHO COMPLAINS WILL BE INSTANTLY DISCHARGED!
CALL A TAILOR TO MEASURE HIM.
YESSIR
THEY SAY THE CLOTHES MAKE THE MAN, BUT THIS FELLOW WOULDN'T LOOK GOOD IN ANYTHING.
HE OUGHT TO GO AROUND NAKED LIKE TARZAN.
LOOK! SEVEN GUYS FIT IN HIS SHORTS!
YEE HAH

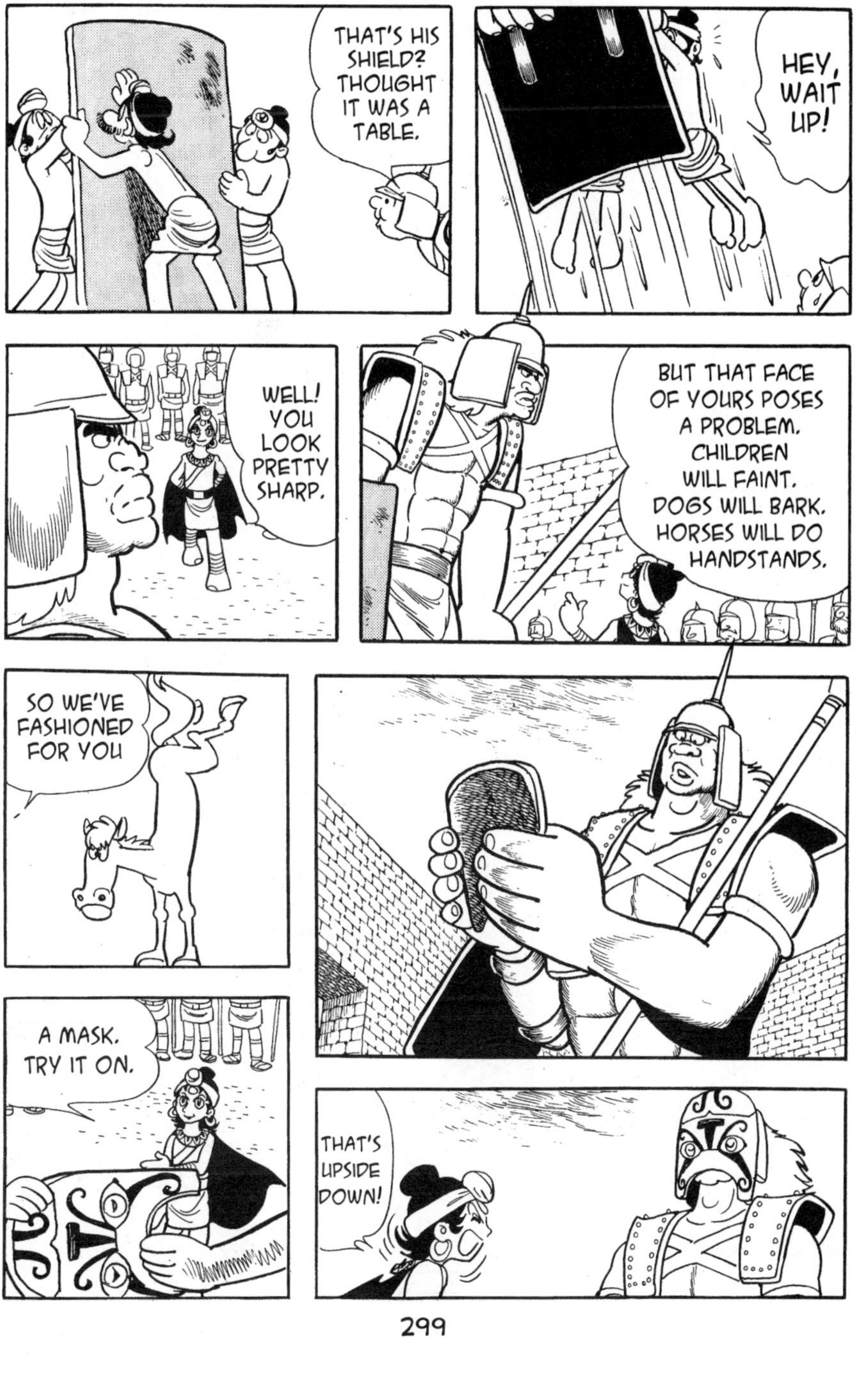
THAT'S HIS SHIELD? THOUGHT IT WAS A TABLE.
HEY, WAIT UP!
WELL! YOU LOOK PRETTY SHARP.
BUT THAT FACE OF YOURS POSES A PROBLEM. CHILDREN WILL FAINT. DOGS WILL BARK. HORSES WILL DO HANDSTANDS.
SO WE'VE FASHIONED FOR YOU
A MASK. TRY IT ON.
THAT'S UPSIDE DOWN!

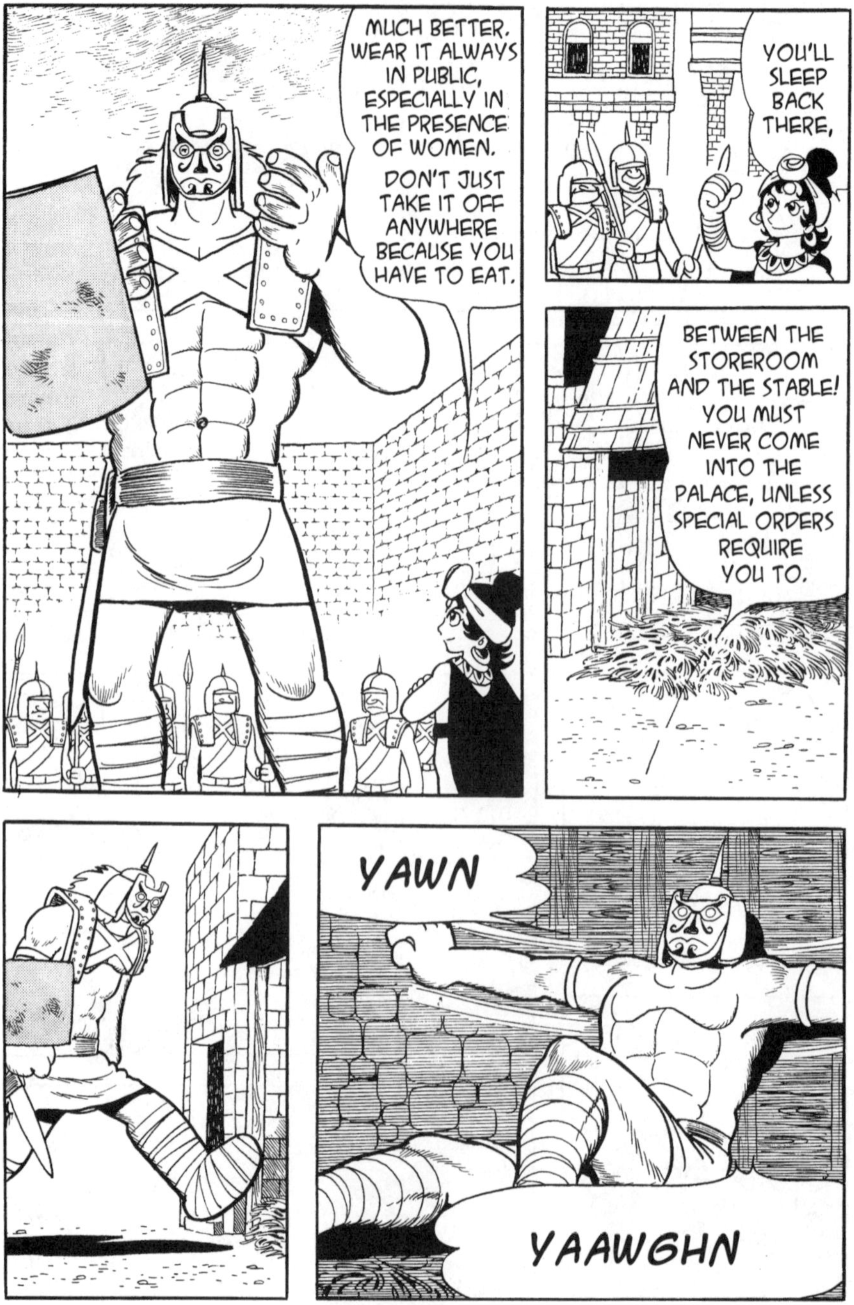
MUCH BETTER. WEAR IT ALWAYS IN PUBLIC, ESPECIALLY IN THE PRESENCE OF WOMEN.
DON'T JUST TAKE IT OFF ANYWHERE BECAUSE YOU HAVE TO EAT.
YOU'LL SLEEP BACK THERE,
BETWEEN THE STOREROOM AND THE STABLE! YOU MUST NEVER COME INTO THE PALACE, UNLESS SPECIAL ORDERS REQUIRE YOU TO.
YAWN
YAAWGHN

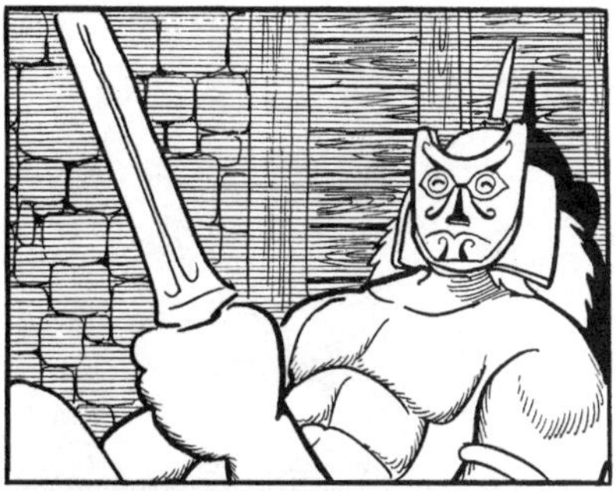

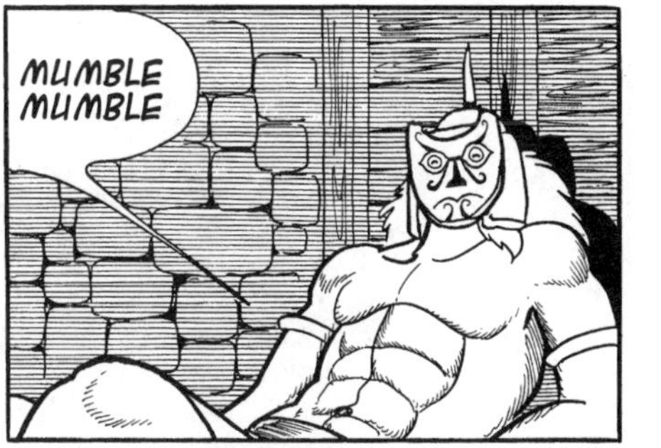
MUMBLE
MUMBLE

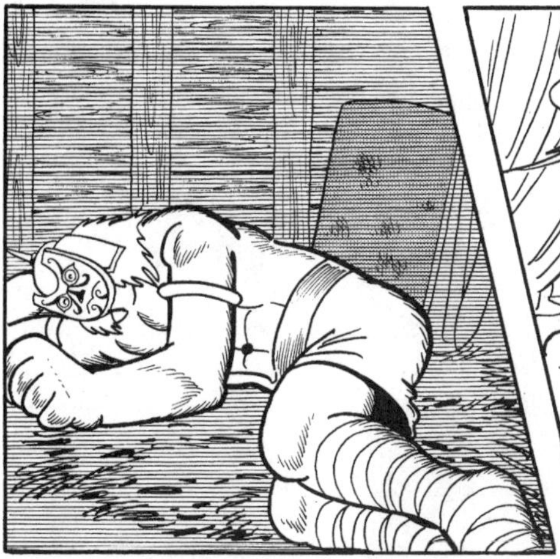

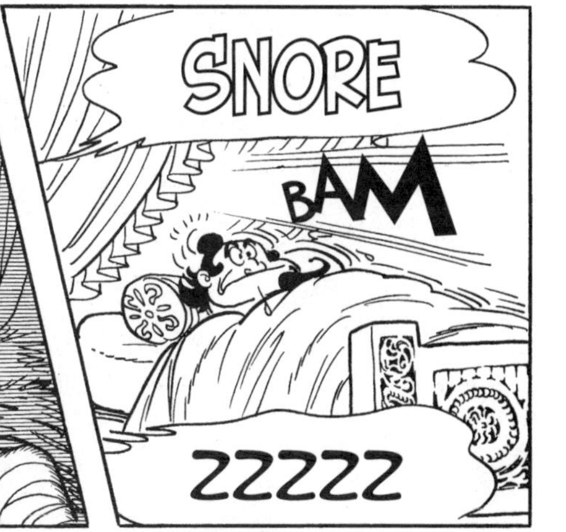
SNORE
BAM
ZZZZZ

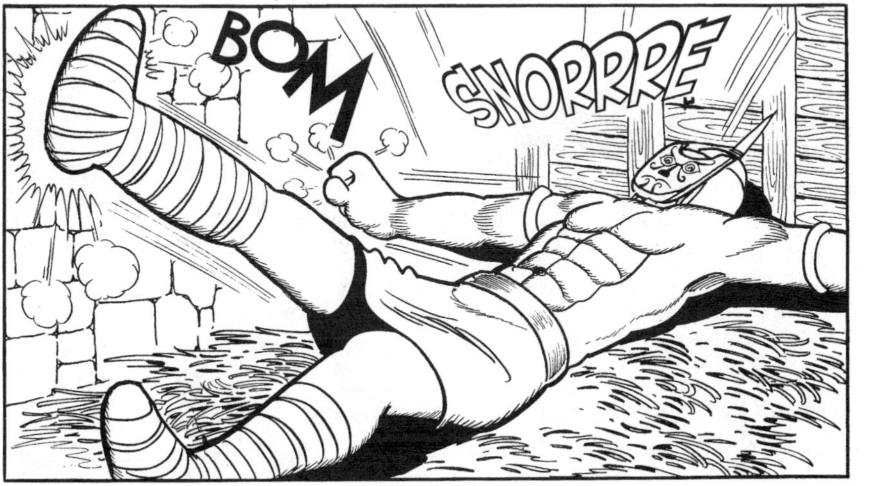
BOM
SNORRRE

PRINCE!

PRINCE CRYSTAL!

WHY'D YOU BRING THAT DANGEROUS THING HOME!

HE'S MY VASSAL, FATHER.

HIS FOOT KNOCKED AGAINST MY LIVING ROOM WALL...

AND LOOK WHAT HAPPENED. IT'S FULL OF CRACKS.

FATHER, THAT GIANT, TAMED, WILL DO US GOOD.

OH, BUT HE'LL DO MORE HARM.

HE WON'T EVEN MAKE A GOOD PRO WRESTLER. HE HASN'T THE LOOKS!

WHICH I DID...

FATHER, EVER SINCE WE CONQUERED KAPILAVASTU, THE KINGDOM OF MAGADHA HAS BEEN ON ALERT.

MAGADHA IS RULED BY NO PIPSQUEAK, BUT BY THE FAMED KING BIMBISARA! SOONER OR LATER, OUR TWO KINGDOMS WILL LOCK HORNS. THAT WILL SURELY BE A FIGHT TO THE DEATH.

WE'LL FIGHT THEM IF WE MUST.

MAGADHA HAS MORE ELEPHANTS THAN US. THEY ALSO HAVE MORE, IF NOT BETTER, TROOPS THAN KOSALA.

IF WE TRAIN THAT GIANT...

HE'LL BE OUR PRIZE WEAPON.

HE'LL BE OUR SUPERHERO? HE'LL FIGHT FOR THE GOOD GUYS?

FATHER, LEAVE THE GIANT TO ME.

SIGH FINE.

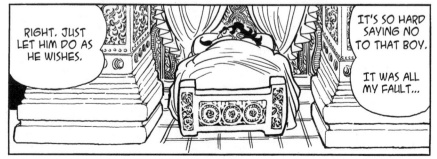

RIGHT. JUST LET HIM DO AS HE WISHES.

IT'S SO HARD SAYING NO TO THAT BOY.

IT WAS ALL MY FAULT...

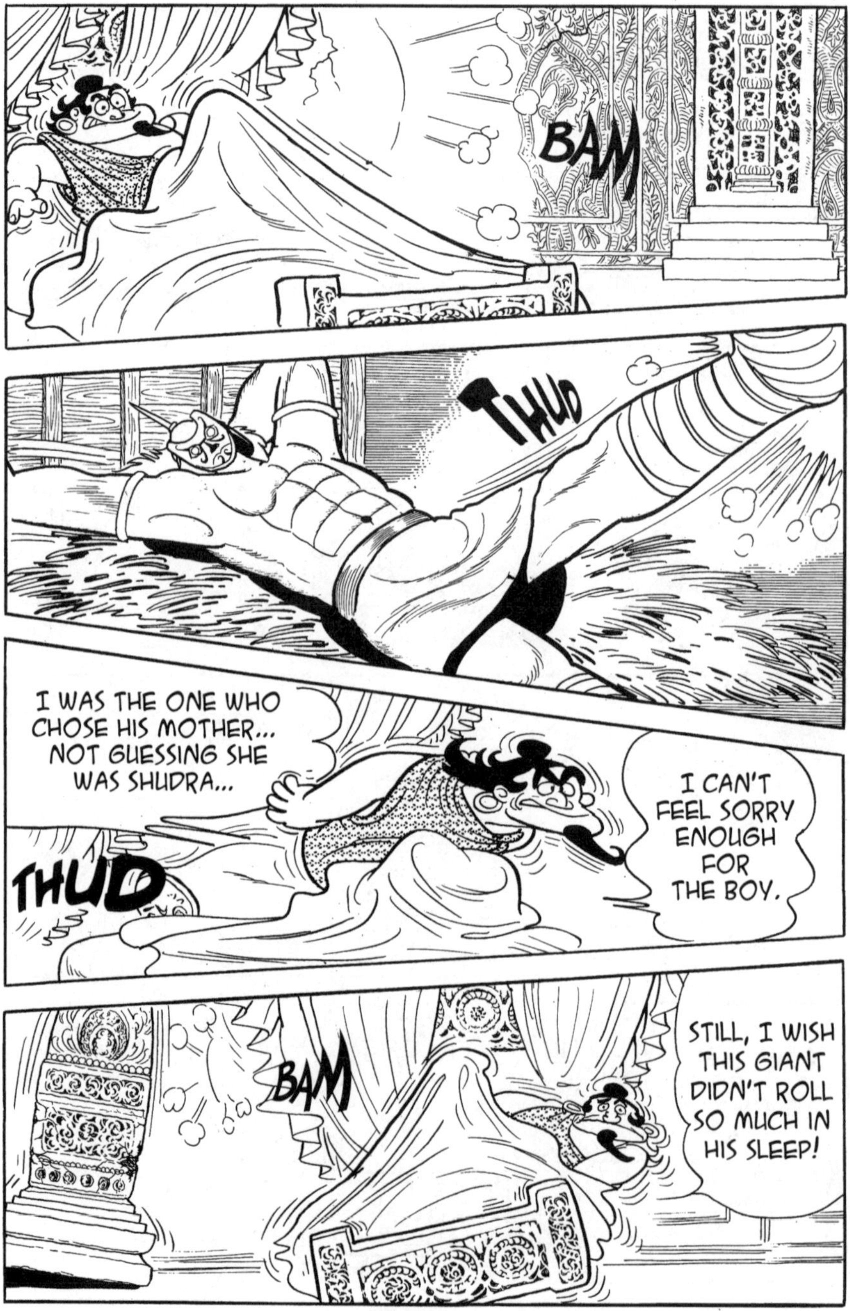
BAM
THUD
I WAS THE ONE WHO CHOSE HIS MOTHER... NOT GUESSING SHE WAS SHUDRA...
THUD
I CAN'T FEEL SORRY ENOUGH FOR THE BOY.
BAM
STILL, I WISH THIS GIANT DIDN'T ROLL SO MUCH IN HIS SLEEP!

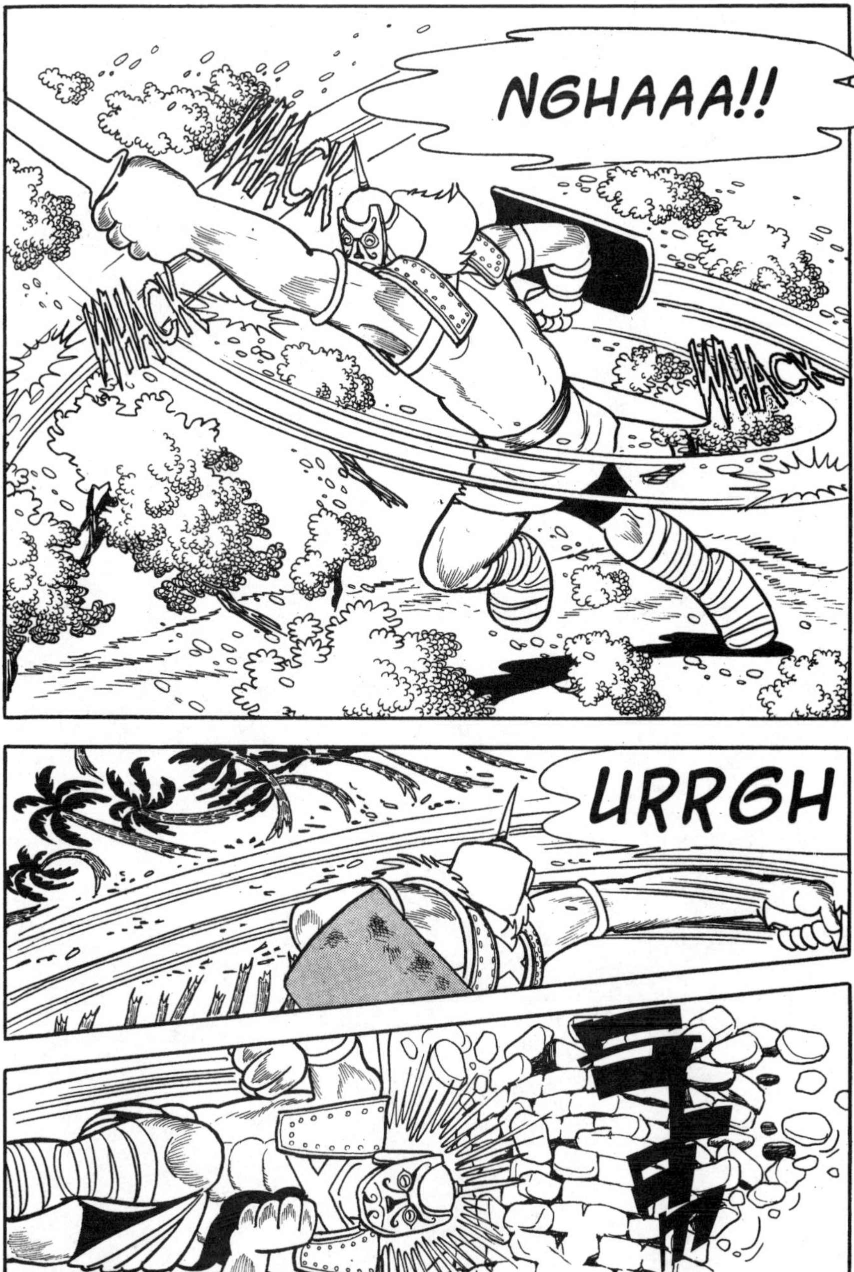
WHACK
NGHAAA!!
WHACK
WHACK
URRGH

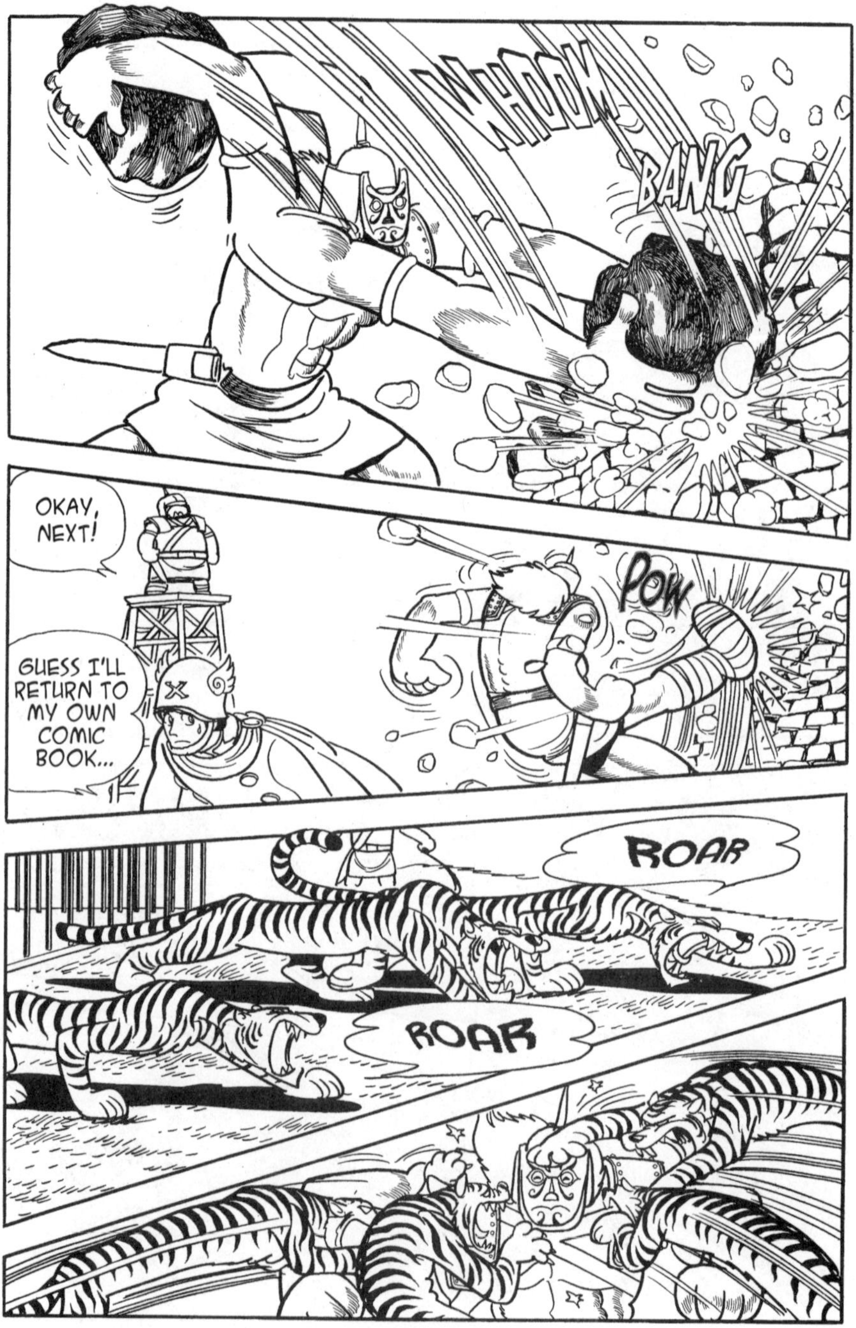
WHOOOM
BANG
OKAY, NEXT!
POW
GUESS I'LL RETURN TO MY OWN COMIC BOOK...
ROAR
ROAR

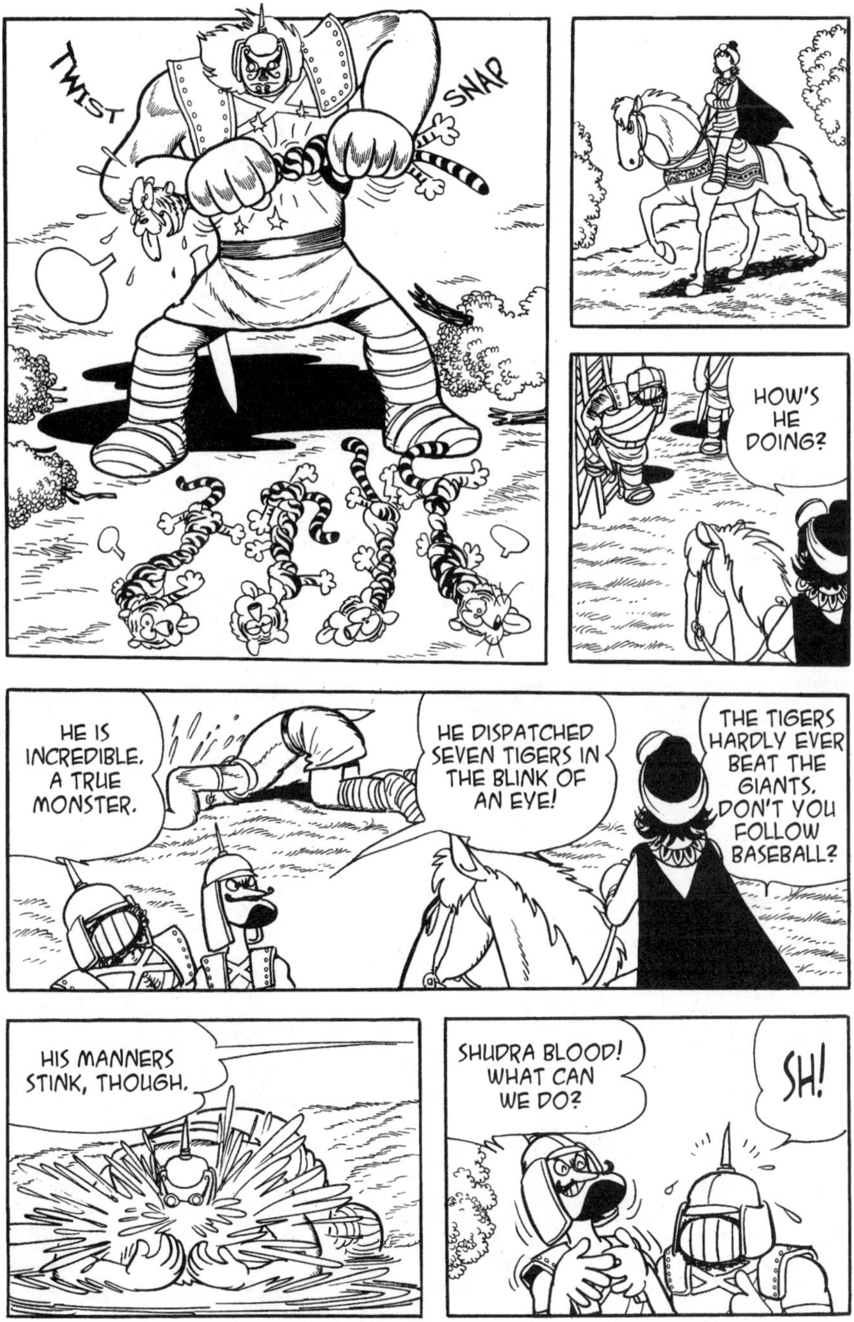
TWIST
SNAP
HOW'S HE DOING?
HE IS INCREDIBLE. A TRUE MONSTER.
HE DISPATCHED SEVEN TIGERS IN THE BLINK OF AN EYE!
THE TIGERS HARDLY EVER BEAT THE GIANTS. DON'T YOU FOLLOW BASEBALL?
HIS MANNERS STINK, THOUGH.
SHUDRA BLOOD! WHAT CAN WE DO?
SH!

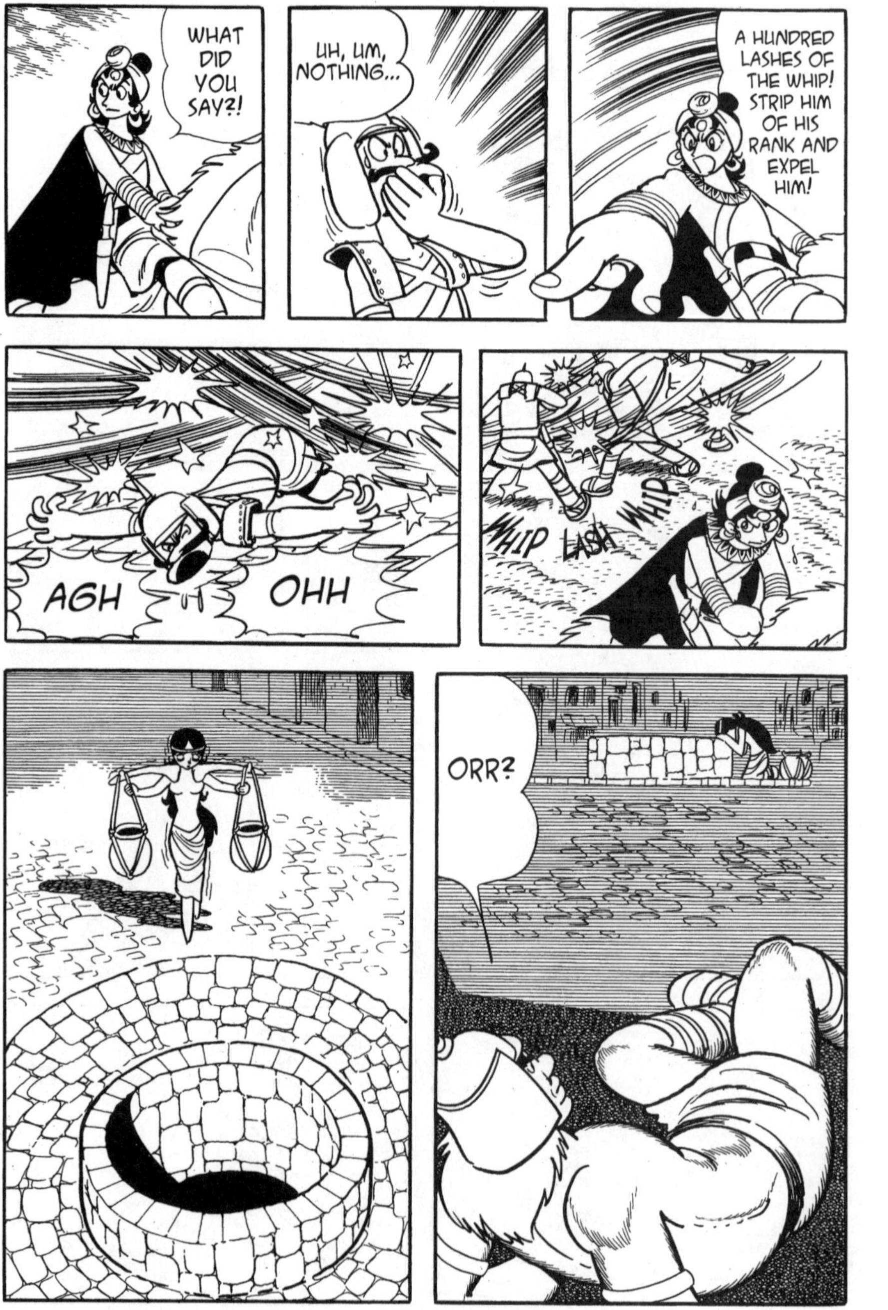
WHAT DID YOU SAY?!
UH, UM, NOTHING...
A HUNDRED LASHES OF THE WHIP! STRIP HIM OF HIS RANK AND EXPEL HIM!
AGH
OHH
WHIP
LASH
WHIP
ORR?

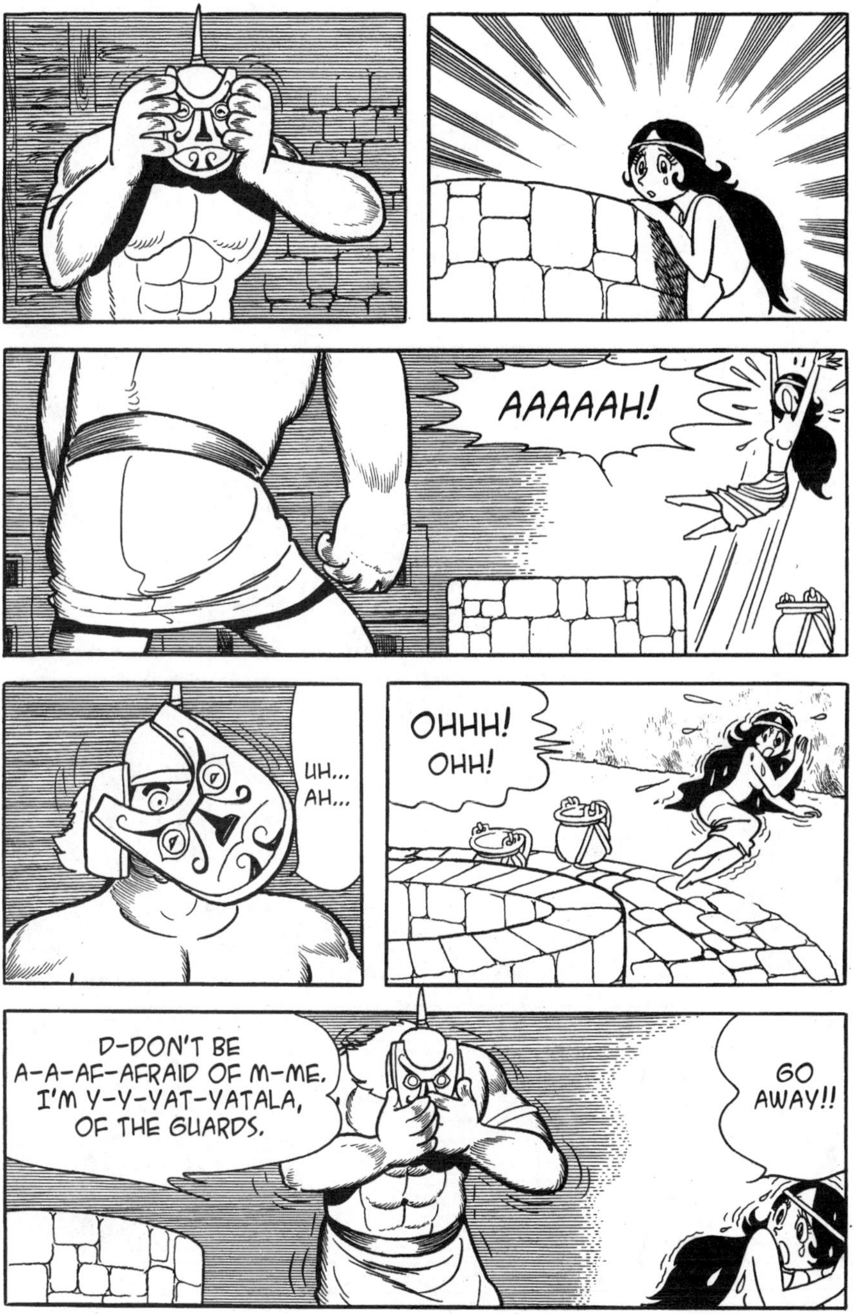
AAAAAH!
UH... AH...
OHHH! OHH!
D-DON'T BE A-A-AF-AFRAID OF M-ME. I'M Y-Y-YAT-YATALA, OF THE GUARDS.
GO AWAY!!

Y-YOU WERE CRYING, C-CRYING AT THE WELL.

YOU CRY, S-SO SAD. YOU CRY S-SO SA-SA-SADLY. WHY C-C-CRY?

AY!

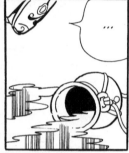

...

I D-DRAW W-WATER FOR YOU. I D-DRANK YOUR WATER... S-S-SORRY.

...?

UHR?

Y-YOUR FACE, J-JUST LIKE CRYSTAL PRINCE. S-SAME FACE!!

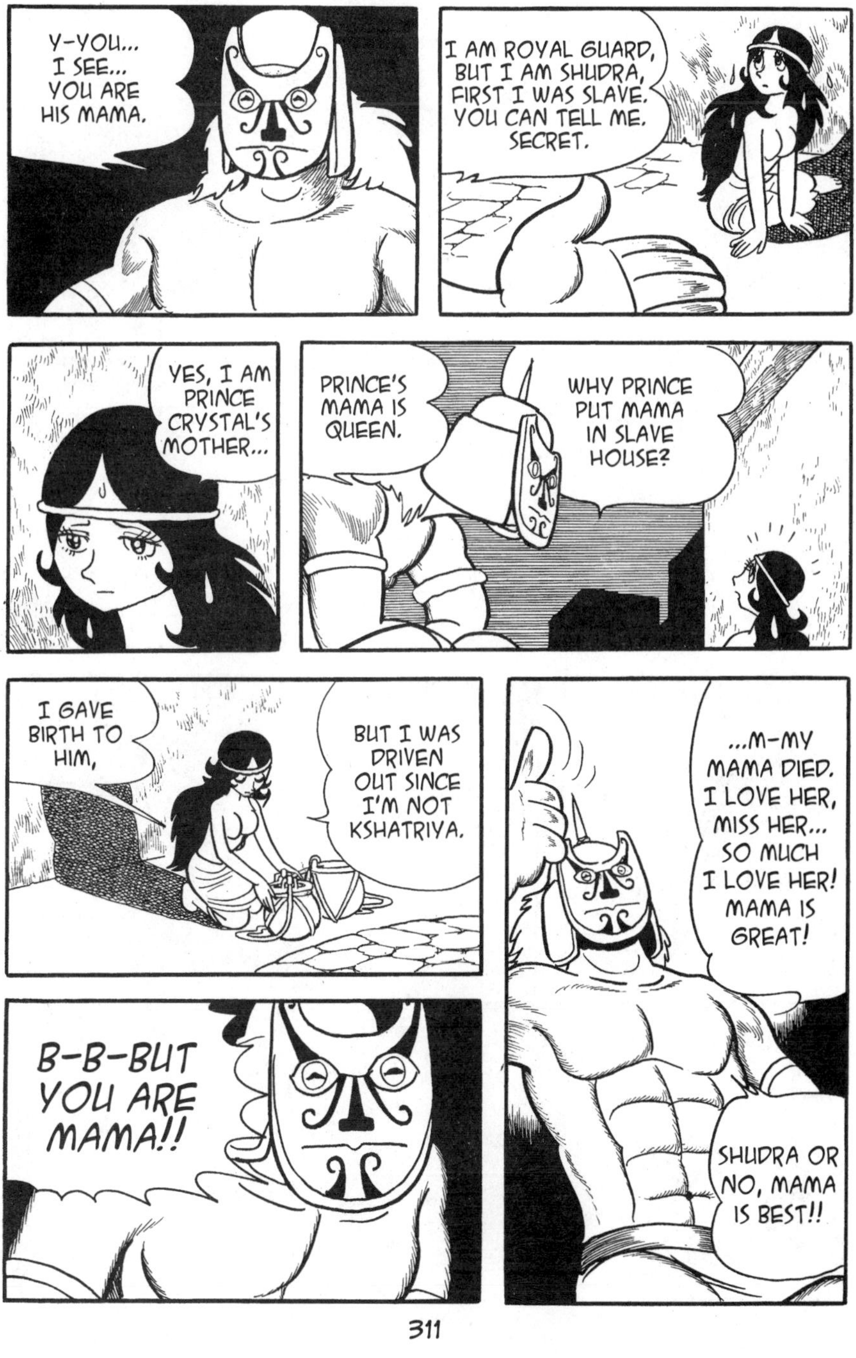
Y-YOU... I SEE... YOU ARE HIS MAMA.
I AM ROYAL GUARD, BUT I AM SHUDRA, FIRST I WAS SLAVE. YOU CAN TELL ME. SECRET.
YES, I AM PRINCE CRYSTAL'S MOTHER...
PRINCE'S MAMA IS QUEEN.
WHY PRINCE PUT MAMA IN SLAVE HOUSE?
I GAVE BIRTH TO HIM,
BUT I WAS DRIVEN OUT SINCE I'M NOT KSHATRIYA.
B-B-BUT YOU ARE MAMA!!
...M-MY MAMA DIED. I LOVE HER, MISS HER... SO MUCH I LOVE HER! MAMA IS GREAT!
SHUDRA OR NO, MAMA IS BEST!!

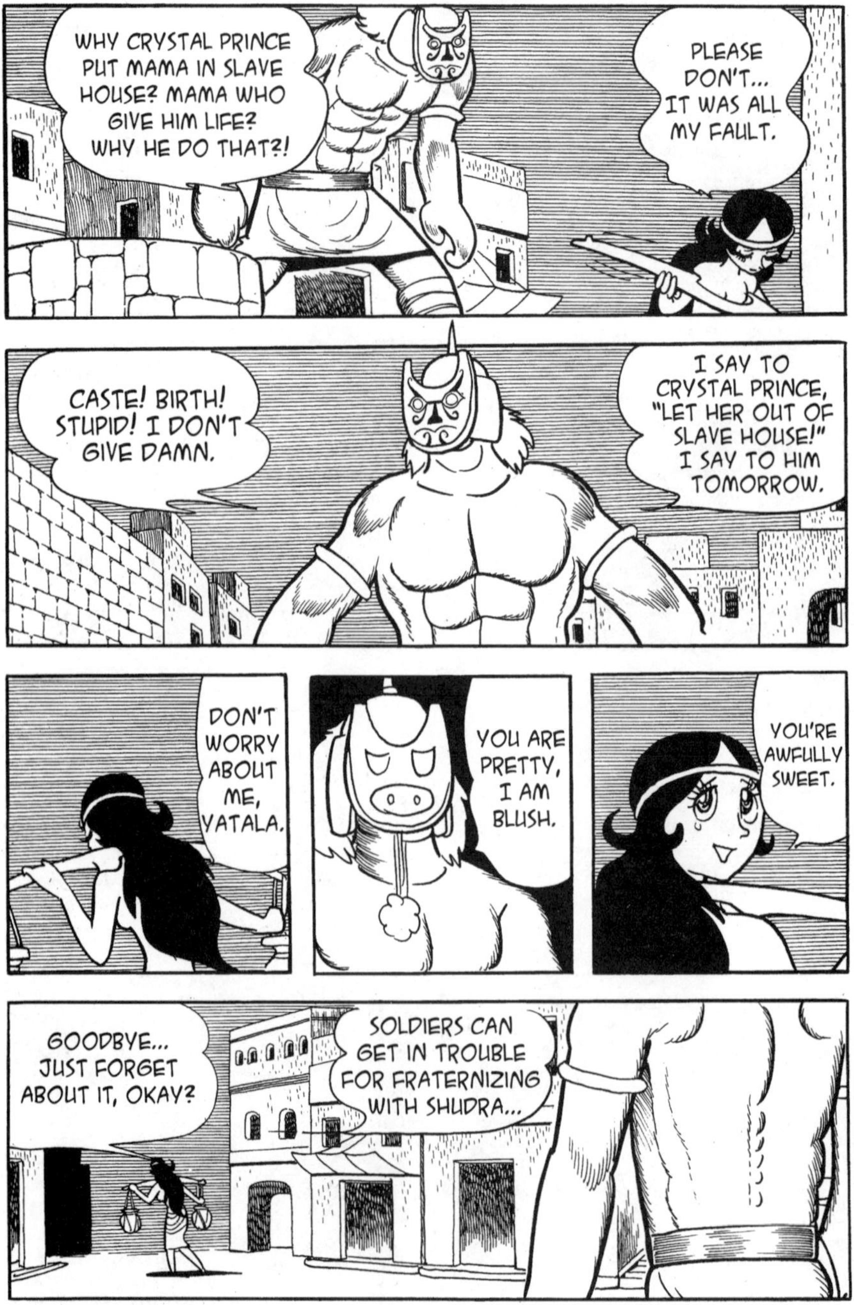
WHY CRYSTAL PRINCE PUT MAMA IN SLAVE HOUSE? MAMA WHO GIVE HIM LIFE? WHY HE DO THAT?!
PLEASE DON'T... IT WAS ALL MY FAULT.
CASTE! BIRTH! STUPID! I DON'T GIVE DAMN.
I SAY TO CRYSTAL PRINCE, "LET HER OUT OF SLAVE HOUSE!" I SAY TO HIM TOMORROW.
DON'T WORRY ABOUT ME, YATALA.
YOU ARE PRETTY, I AM BLUSH.
YOU'RE AWFULLY SWEET.
GOODBYE... JUST FORGET ABOUT IT, OKAY?
SOLDIERS CAN GET IN TROUBLE FOR FRATERNIZING WITH SHUDRA...

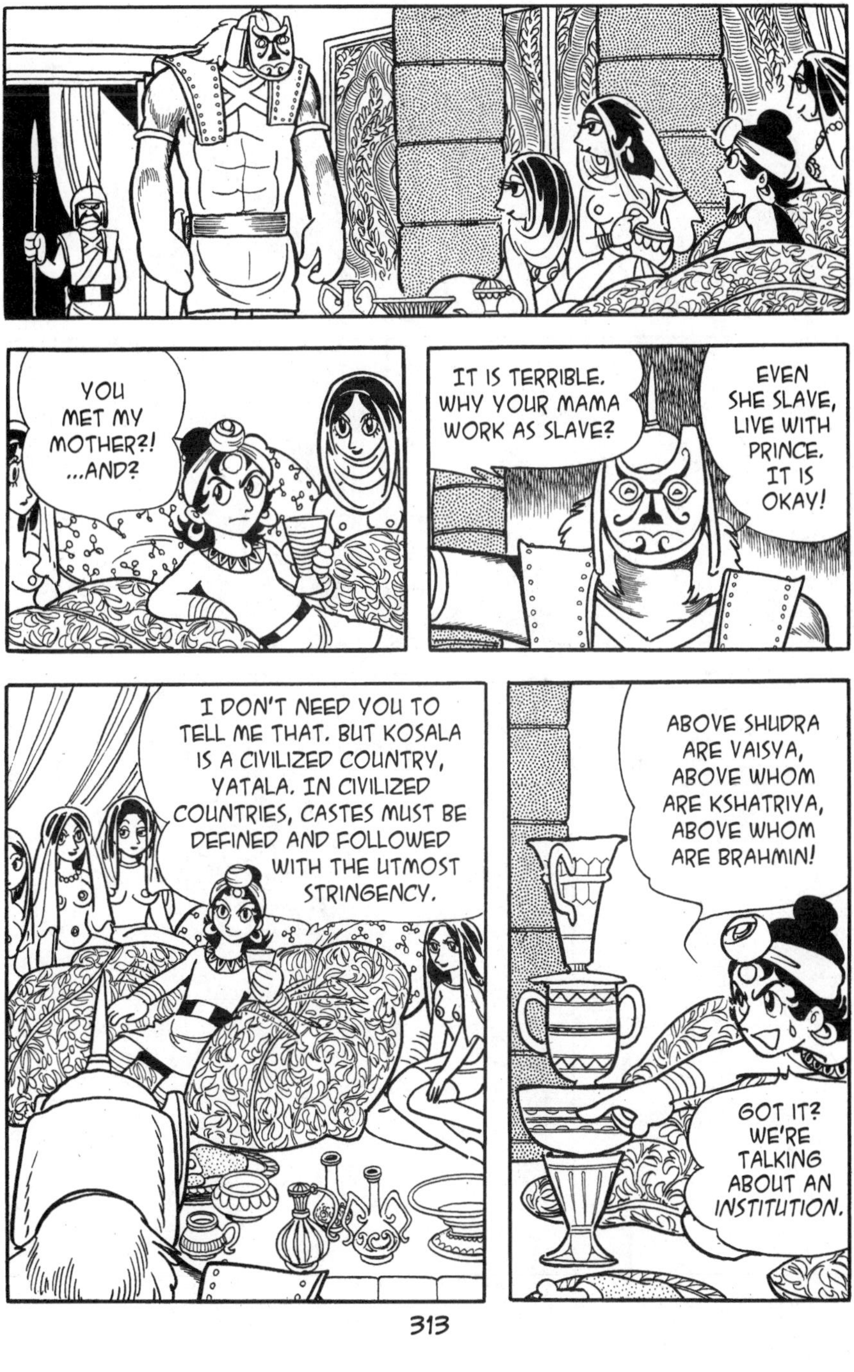
YOU MET MY MOTHER?! ...AND?
IT IS TERRIBLE. WHY YOUR MAMA WORK AS SLAVE?
EVEN SHE SLAVE, LIVE WITH PRINCE. IT IS OKAY!
I DON'T NEED YOU TO TELL ME THAT. BUT KOSALA IS A CIVILIZED COUNTRY, YATALA. IN CIVILIZED COUNTRIES, CASTES MUST BE DEFINED AND FOLLOWED WITH THE UTMOST STRINGENCY.
ABOVE SHUDRA ARE VAISYA, ABOVE WHOM ARE KSHATRIYA, ABOVE WHOM ARE BRAHMIN!
GOT IT? WE'RE TALKING ABOUT AN INSTITUTION.

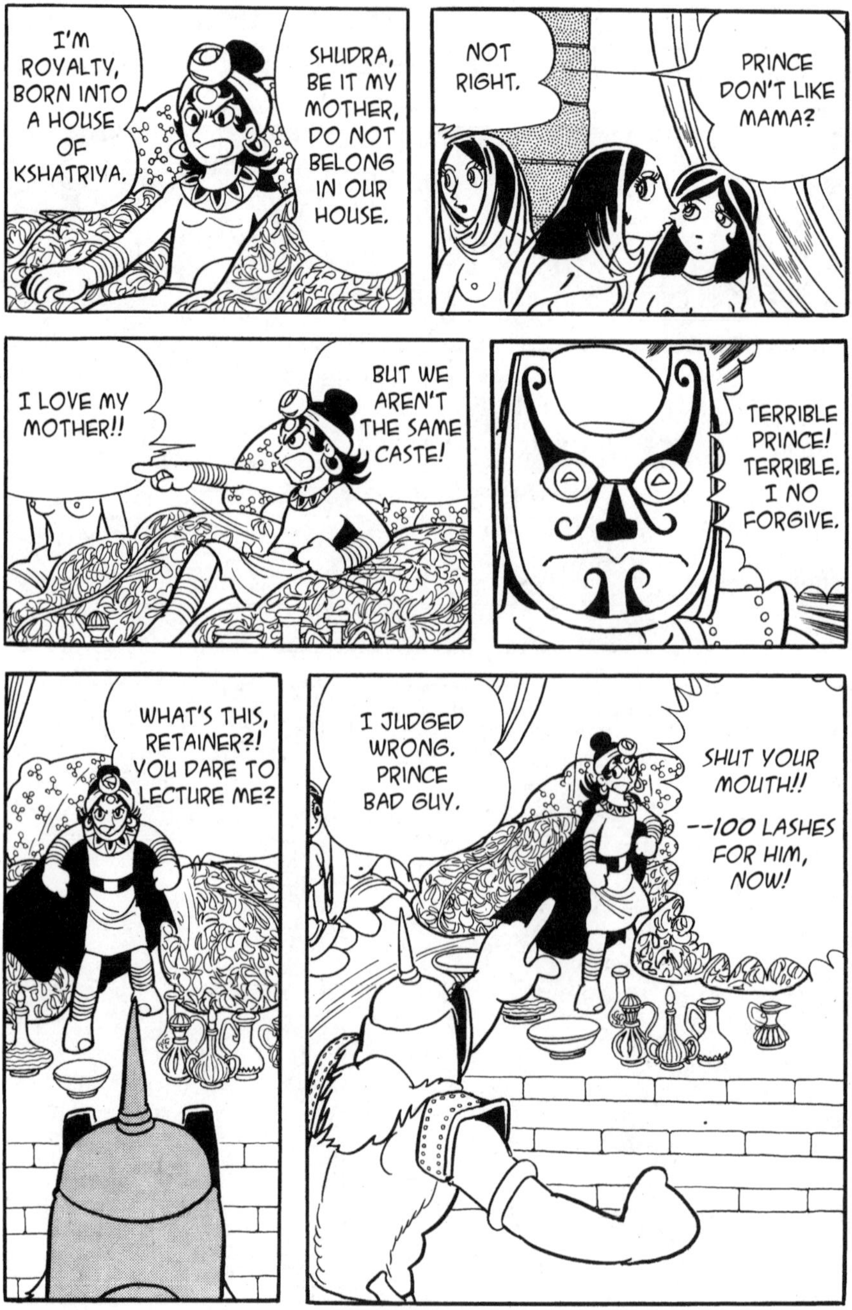
I'M ROYALTY, BORN INTO A HOUSE OF KSHATRIYA.
SHUDRA, BE IT MY MOTHER, DO NOT BELONG IN OUR HOUSE.
NOT RIGHT.
PRINCE DON'T LIKE MAMA?
I LOVE MY MOTHER!!
BUT WE AREN'T THE SAME CASTE!
TERRIBLE PRINCE! TERRIBLE. I NO FORGIVE.
WHAT'S THIS, RETAINER?! YOU DARE TO LECTURE ME?
I JUDGED WRONG. PRINCE BAD GUY.
SHUT YOUR MOUTH!!
--100 LASHES FOR HIM, NOW!

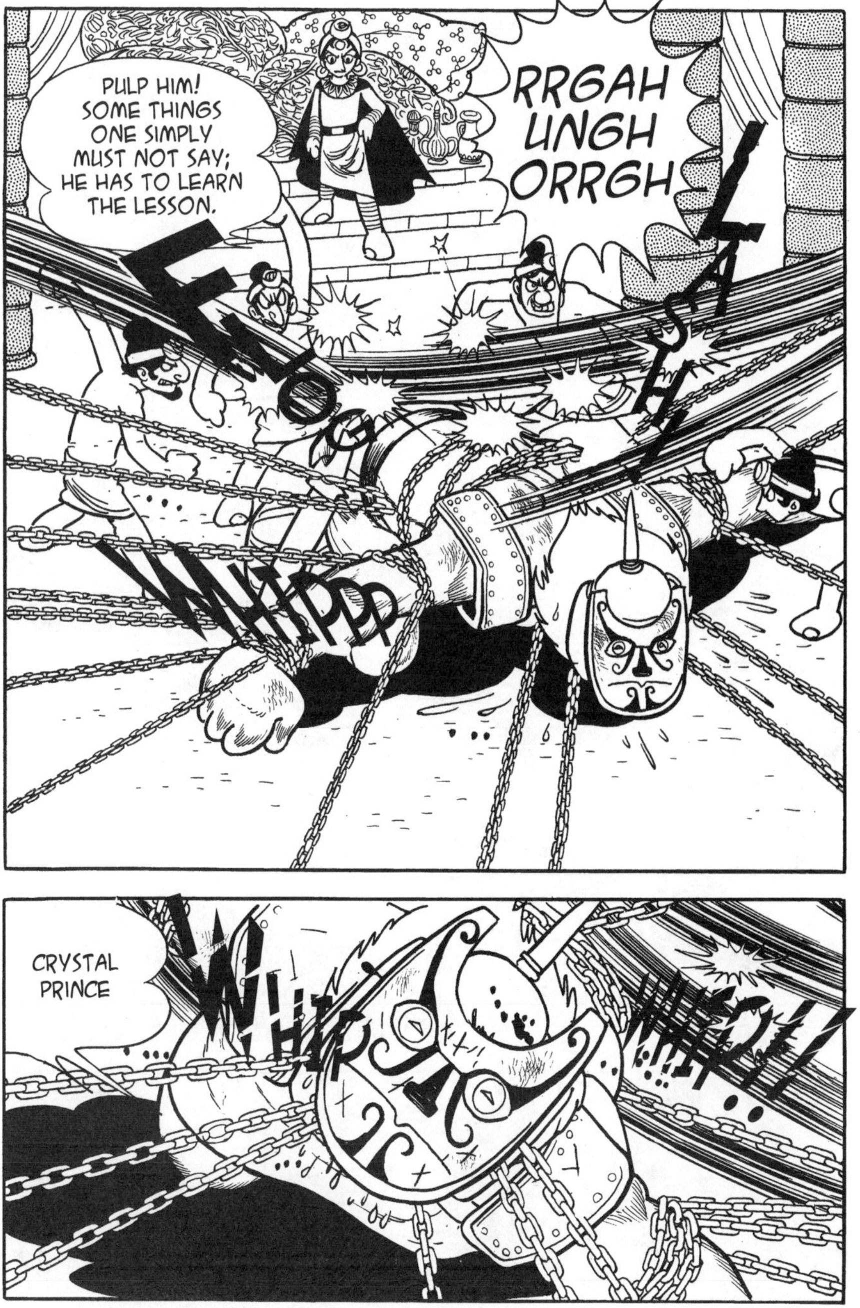
PULP HIM! SOME THINGS ONE SIMPLY MUST NOT SAY; HE HAS TO LEARN THE LESSON.
RRGAH UNGH ORRGH
LASH!
WHIPPP
CRYSTAL PRINCE
WHIP

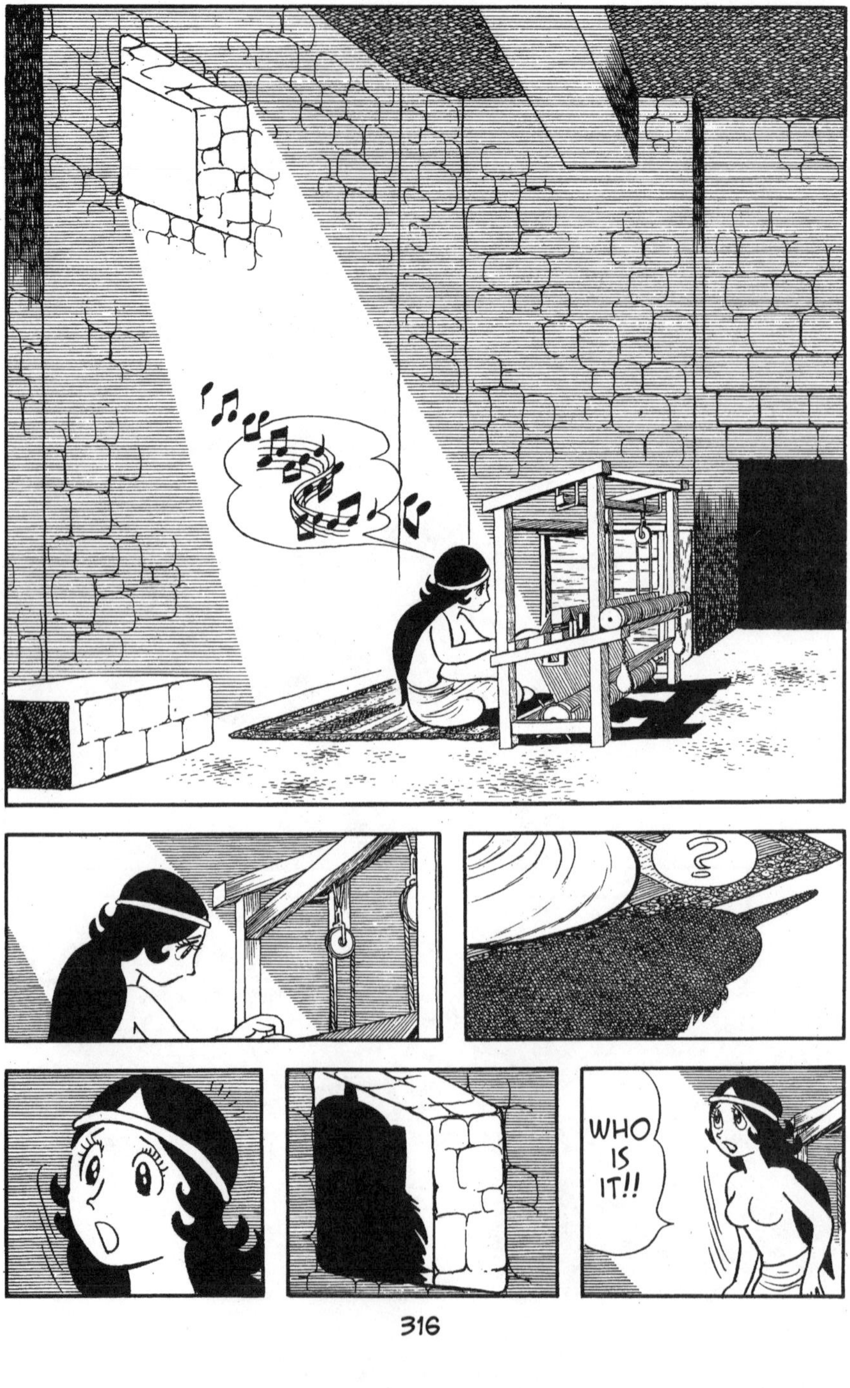
?
WHO IS IT!!

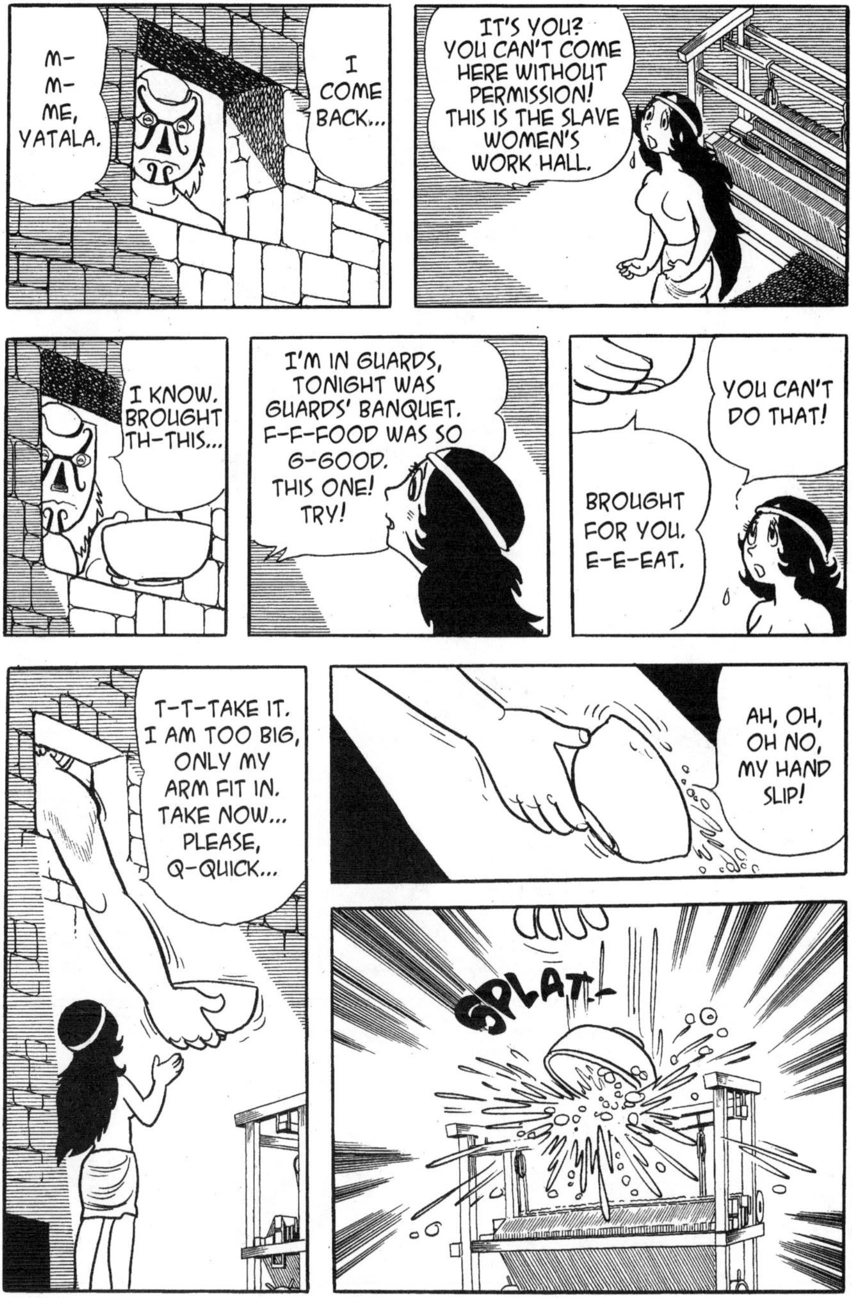
M-
M-
ME, YATALA.
I COME BACK...
IT'S YOU? YOU CAN'T COME HERE WITHOUT PERMISSION! THIS IS THE SLAVE WOMEN'S WORK HALL.
I KNOW. BROUGHT TH-THIS...
I'M IN GUARDS, TONIGHT WAS GUARDS' BANQUET. F-F-FOOD WAS SO G-GOOD. THIS ONE! TRY!
BROUGHT FOR YOU. E-E-EAT.
YOU CAN'T DO THAT!
T-T-TAKE IT. I AM TOO BIG, ONLY MY ARM FIT IN. TAKE NOW... PLEASE, Q-QUICK...
AH, OH, OH NO, MY HAND SLIP!
SPLAT!

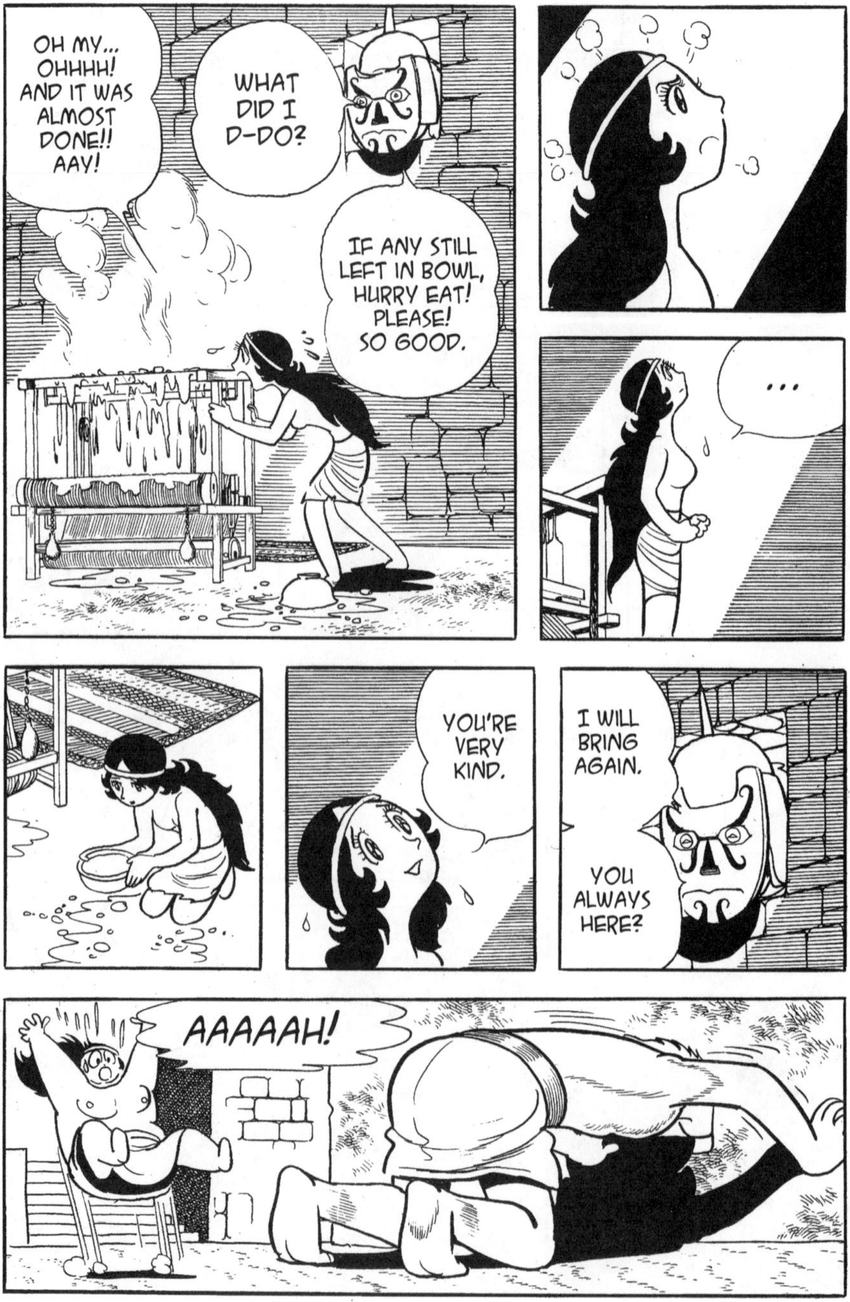
OH MY... OHHHH! AND IT WAS ALMOST DONE!! AAY!
WHAT DID I D-DO?
IF ANY STILL LEFT IN BOWL, HURRY EAT! PLEASE! SO GOOD.
...
YOU'RE VERY KIND.
I WILL BRING AGAIN.
YOU ALWAYS HERE?
AAAAAH!

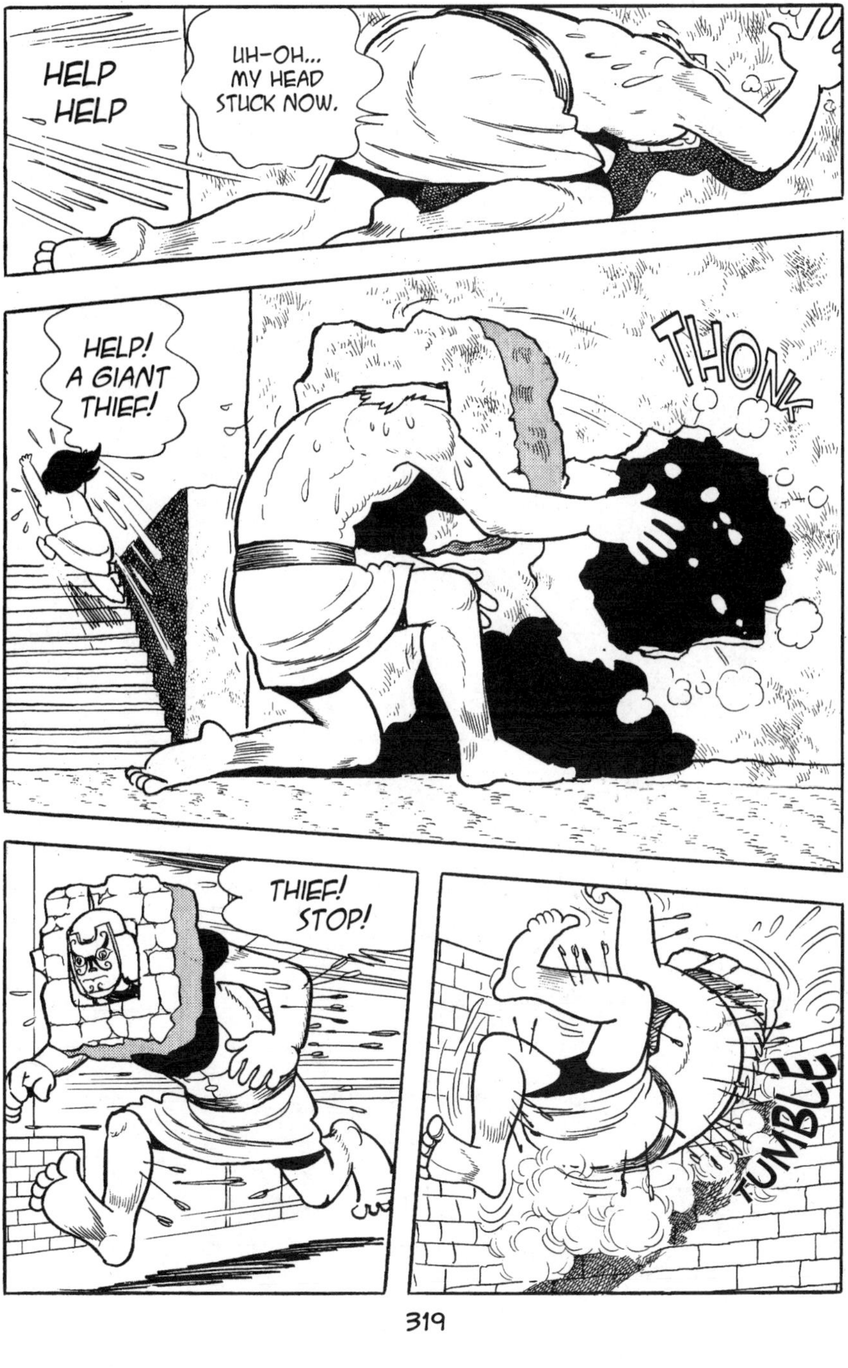
HELP
HELP
UH-OH... MY HEAD STUCK NOW.
HELP! A GIANT THIEF!
THONK
THIEF! STOP!
TUMBLE

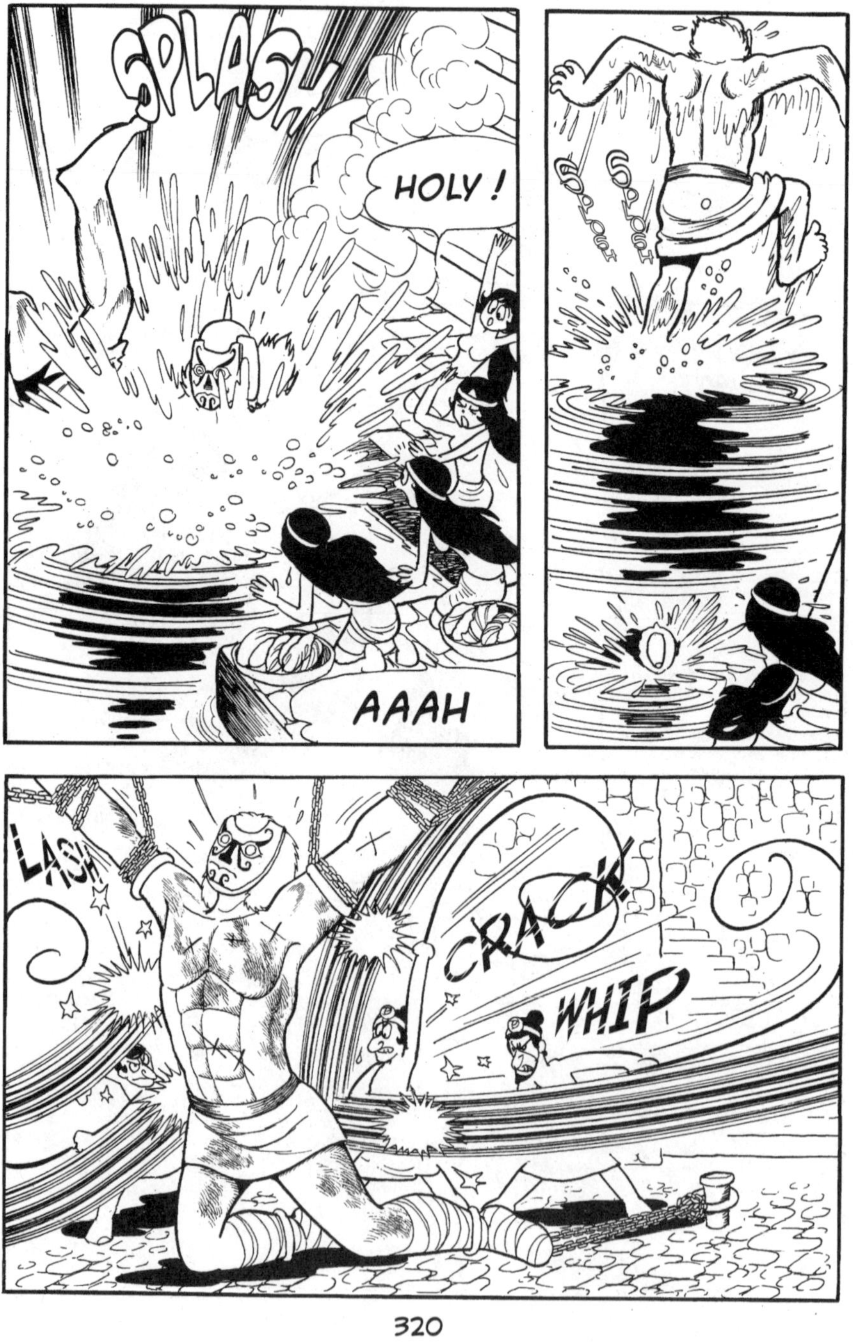
SPLASH
HOLY !
AAAH
SPLOSH
SPLOSH
LASH
CRACK
WHIP

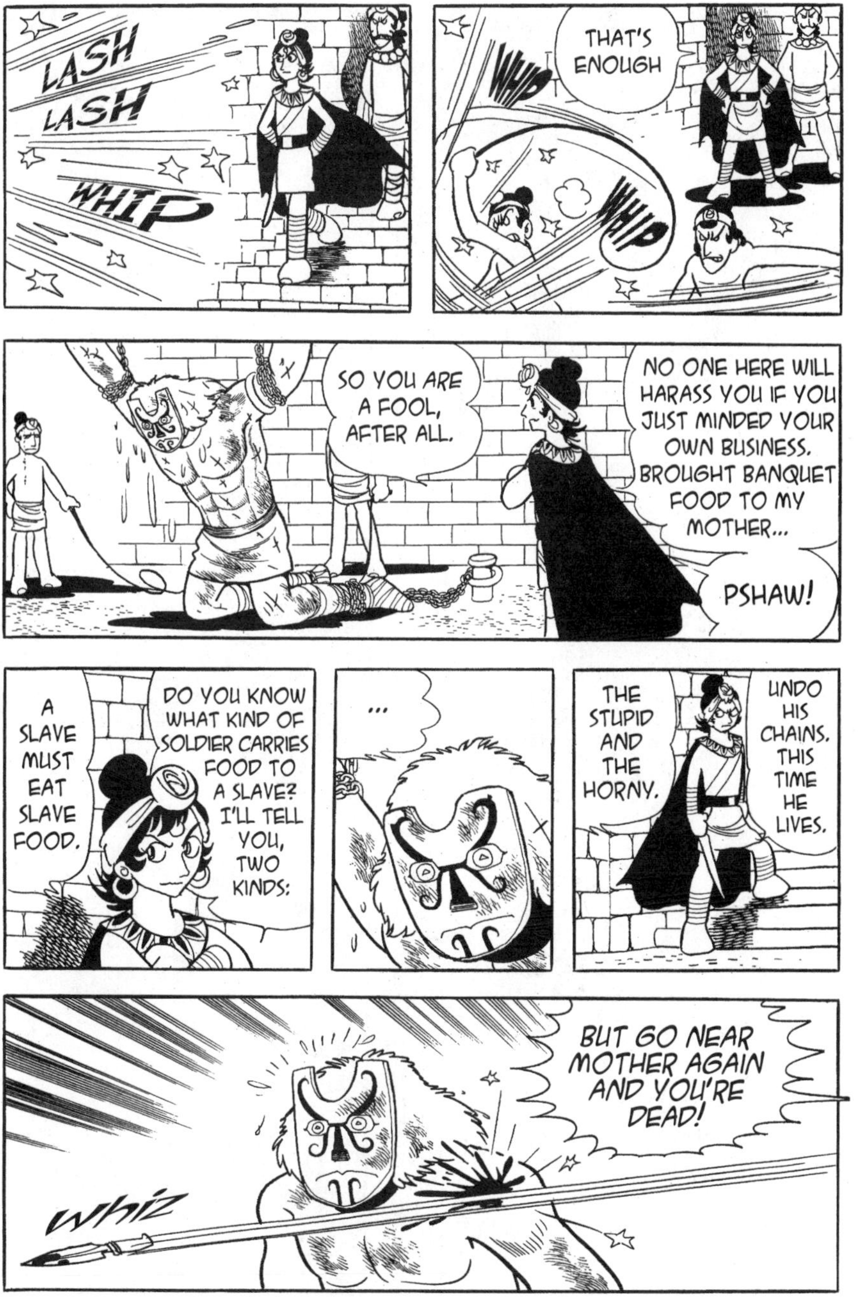
LASH
LASH
WHIP
THAT'S ENOUGH
WHIP
WHIP
SO YOU ARE A FOOL, AFTER ALL.
NO ONE HERE WILL HARASS YOU IF YOU JUST MINDED YOUR OWN BUSINESS. BROUGHT BANQUET FOOD TO MY MOTHER...
PSHAW!
A SLAVE MUST EAT SLAVE FOOD.
DO YOU KNOW WHAT KIND OF SOLDIER CARRIES FOOD TO A SLAVE? I'LL TELL YOU, TWO KINDS:
...
THE STUPID AND THE HORNY.
UNDO HIS CHAINS. THIS TIME HE LIVES.
BUT GO NEAR MOTHER AGAIN AND YOU'RE DEAD!
whiz

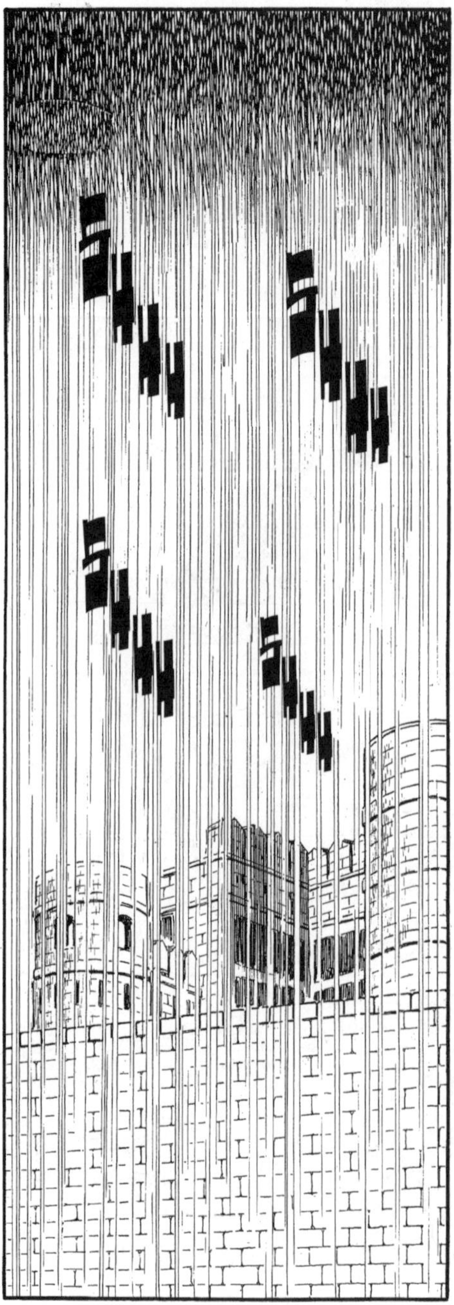
SHHH
SHHH
SHHH
SHHH

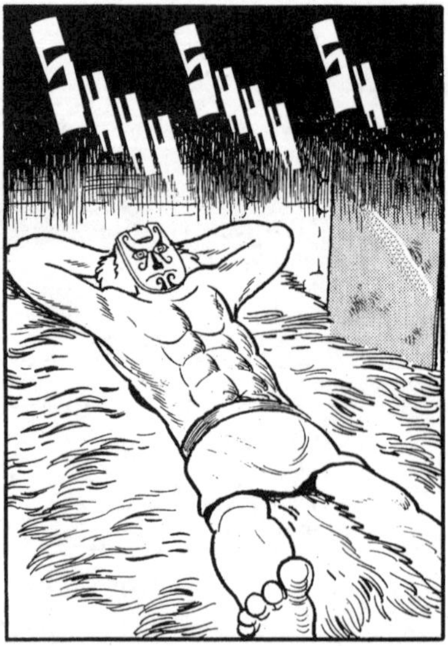
SHHH
SHHH
SH

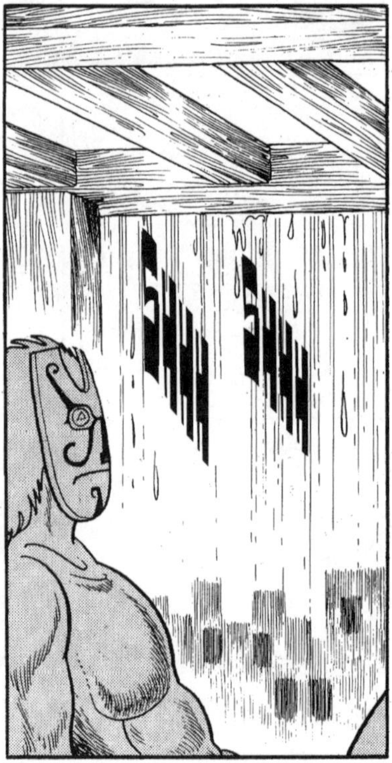
SHHH
SHHH

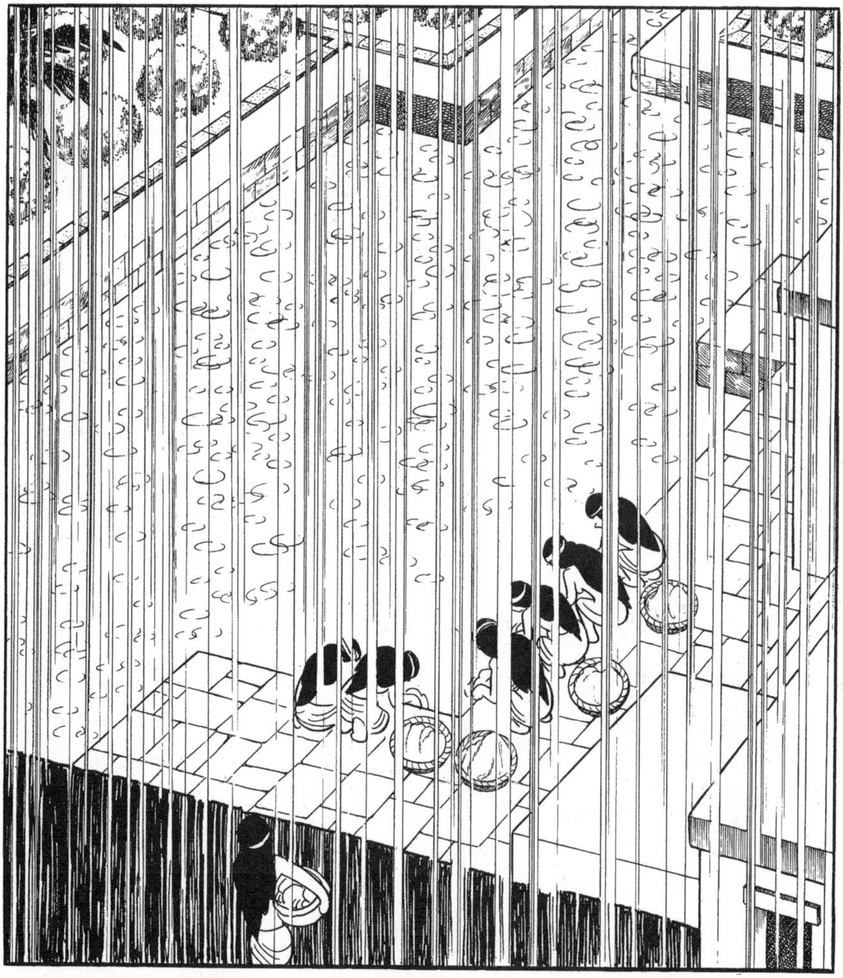
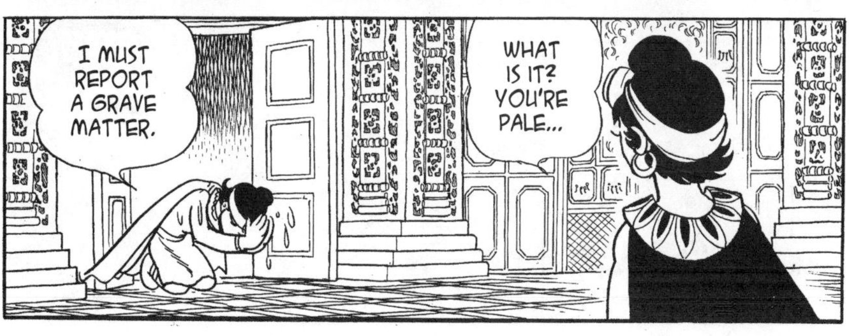
I MUST REPORT A GRAVE MATTER.
WHAT IS IT? YOU'RE PALE...

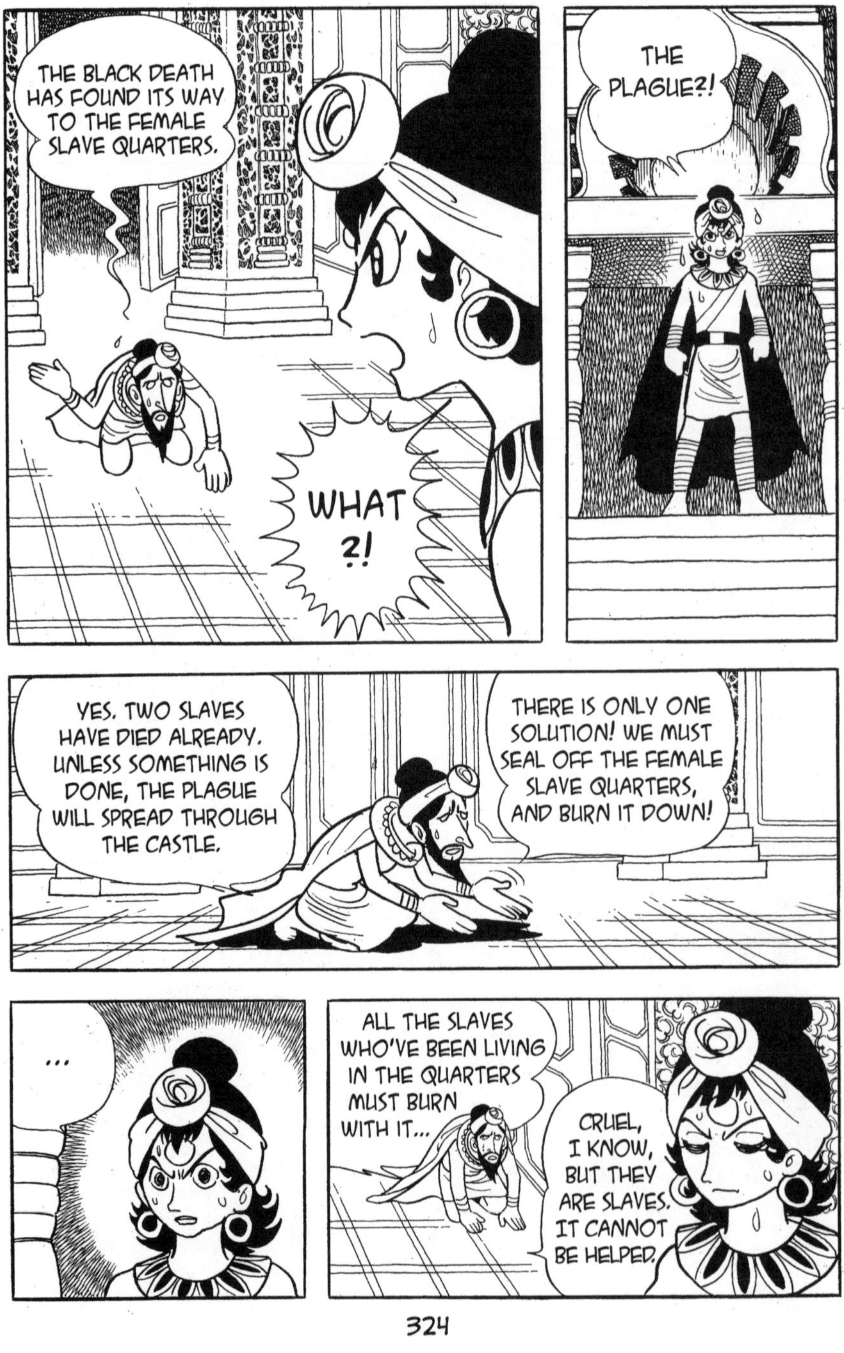
THE BLACK DEATH HAS FOUND ITS WAY TO THE FEMALE SLAVE QUARTERS.
WHAT ?!
THE PLAGUE?!
YES. TWO SLAVES HAVE DIED ALREADY. UNLESS SOMETHING IS DONE, THE PLAGUE WILL SPREAD THROUGH THE CASTLE.
THERE IS ONLY ONE SOLUTION! WE MUST SEAL OFF THE FEMALE SLAVE QUARTERS, AND BURN IT DOWN!
...
ALL THE SLAVES WHO'VE BEEN LIVING IN THE QUARTERS MUST BURN WITH IT...
CRUEL, I KNOW, BUT THEY ARE SLAVES. IT CANNOT BE HELPED.

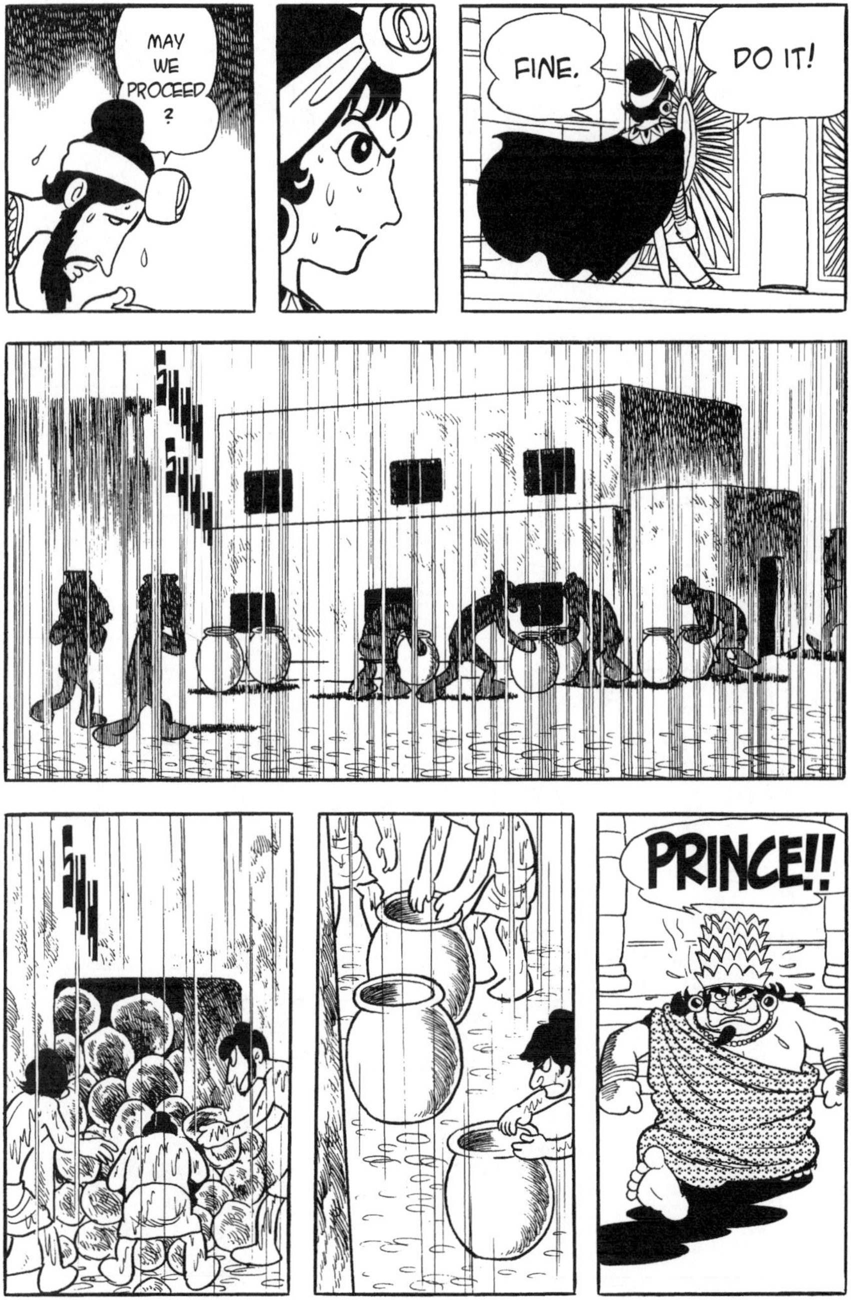
MAY WE PROCEED?
FINE.
DO IT!
SHHH SHHH
SHH
PRINCE!!

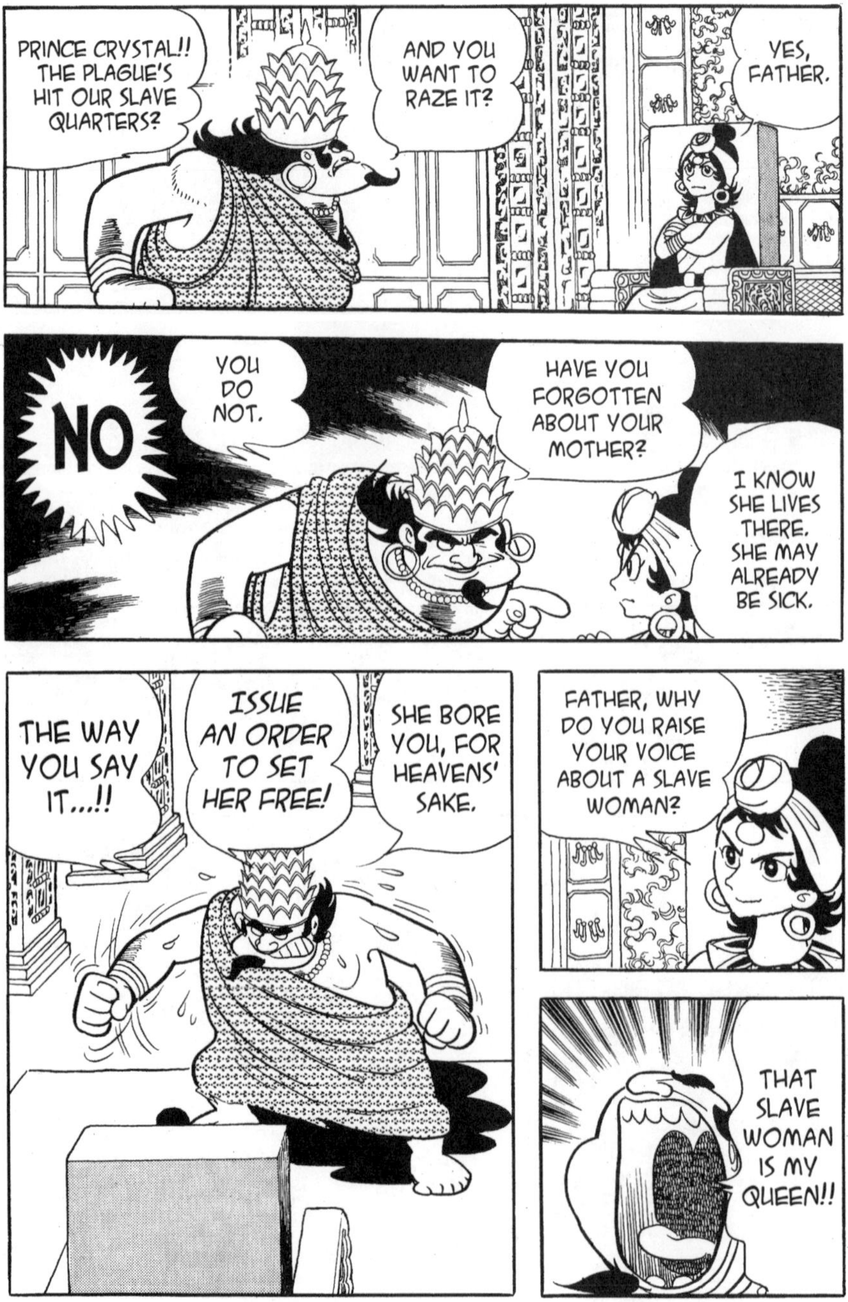
PRINCE CRYSTAL!! THE PLAGUE'S HIT OUR SLAVE QUARTERS?
AND YOU WANT TO RAZE IT?
YES, FATHER.
NO
YOU DO NOT.
HAVE YOU FORGOTTEN ABOUT YOUR MOTHER?
I KNOW SHE LIVES THERE. SHE MAY ALREADY BE SICK.
THE WAY YOU SAY IT...!!
ISSUE AN ORDER TO SET HER FREE!
SHE BORE YOU, FOR HEAVENS' SAKE.
FATHER, WHY DO YOU RAISE YOUR VOICE ABOUT A SLAVE WOMAN?
THAT SLAVE WOMAN IS MY QUEEN!!

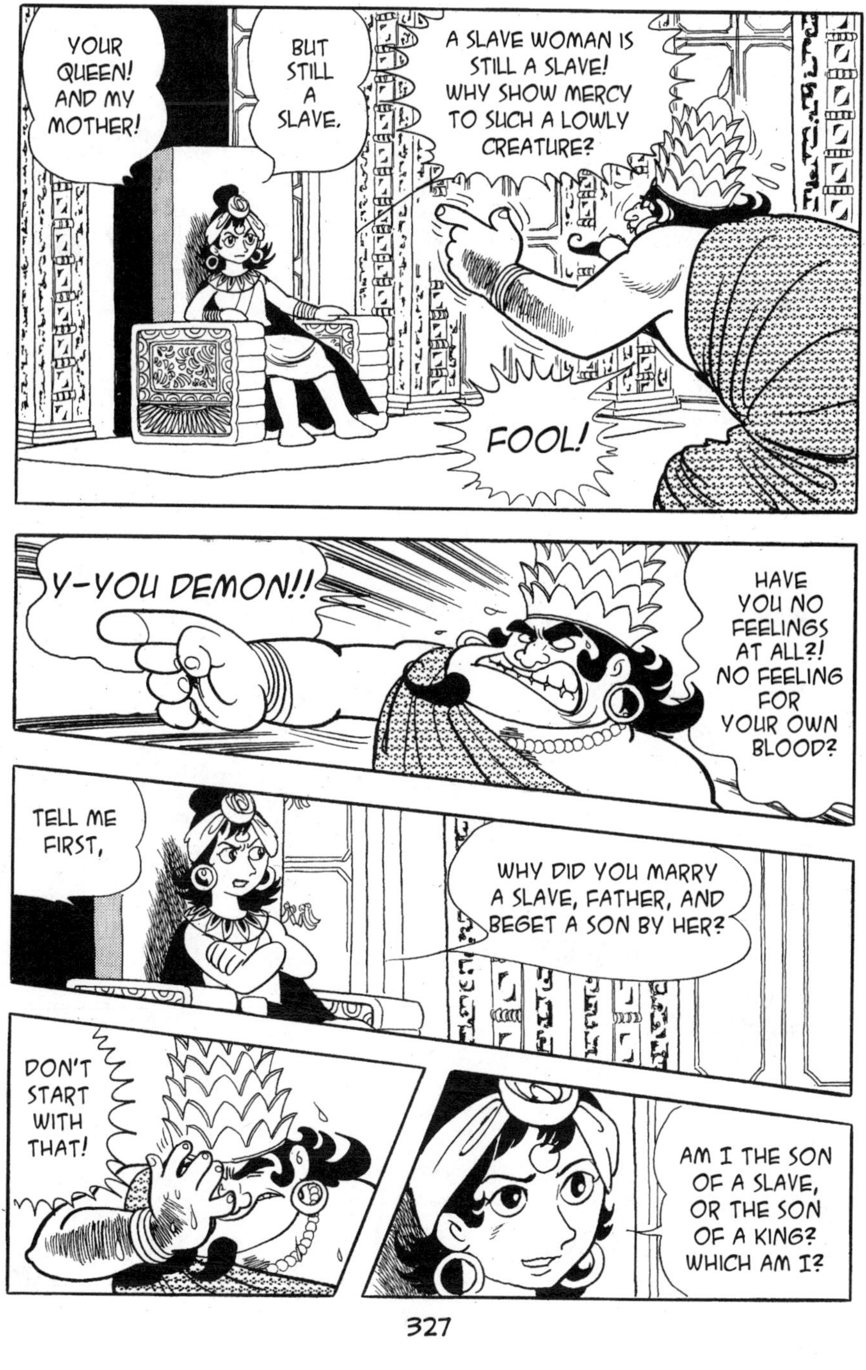
YOUR QUEEN! AND MY MOTHER!
BUT STILL A SLAVE.
A SLAVE WOMAN IS STILL A SLAVE! WHY SHOW MERCY TO SUCH A LOWLY CREATURE?
FOOL!
Y-YOU DEMON!!
HAVE YOU NO FEELINGS AT ALL?! NO FEELING FOR YOUR OWN BLOOD?
TELL ME FIRST,
WHY DID YOU MARRY A SLAVE, FATHER, AND BEGET A SON BY HER?
DON'T START WITH THAT!
AM I THE SON OF A SLAVE, OR THE SON OF A KING? WHICH AM I?

THE SON OF A KING, OF COURSE!

THEN, KING, DO NOT WEEP FOR A SLAVE!! LET US RULE AS WE MUST.

THE TEN SLAVES HAVE BEEN TRAPPED IN.

OK

POUR THE OIL AND SET IT ALIGHT. BURN THE PLACE DOWN.

FATHER, IF YOU HAVE NO OTHER BUSINESS, PLEASE WITHDRAW.

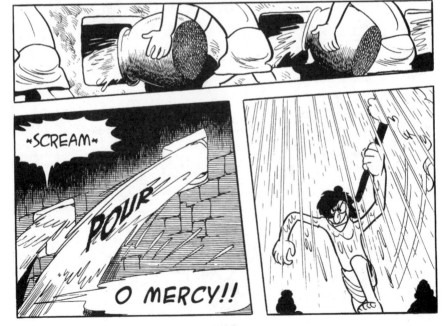

SCREAM

POUR

O MERCY!!

328

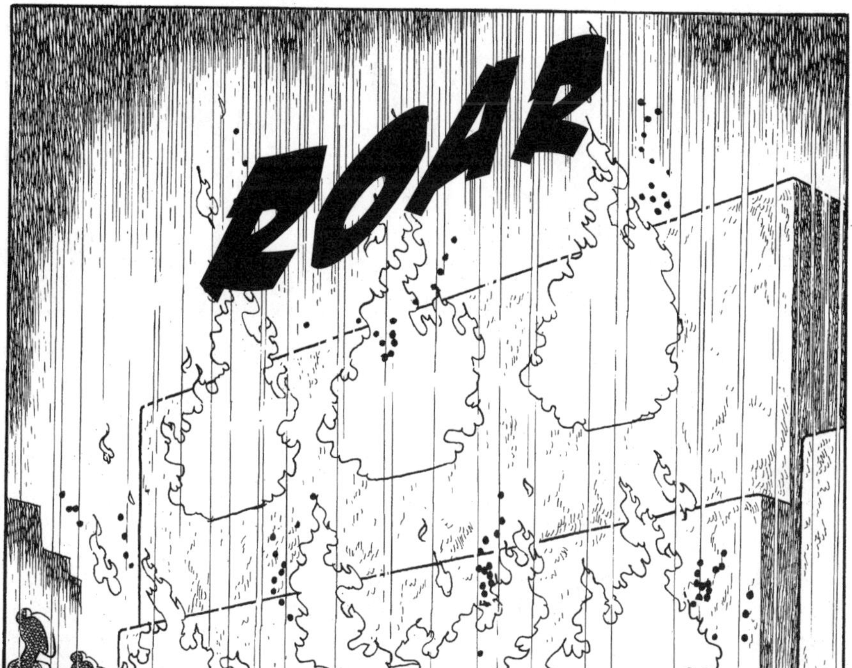
ROAR
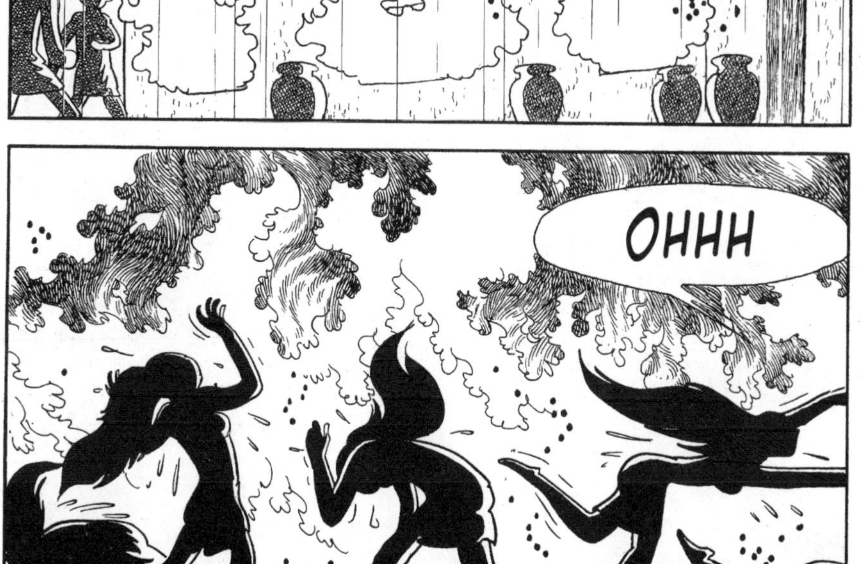
OHHH

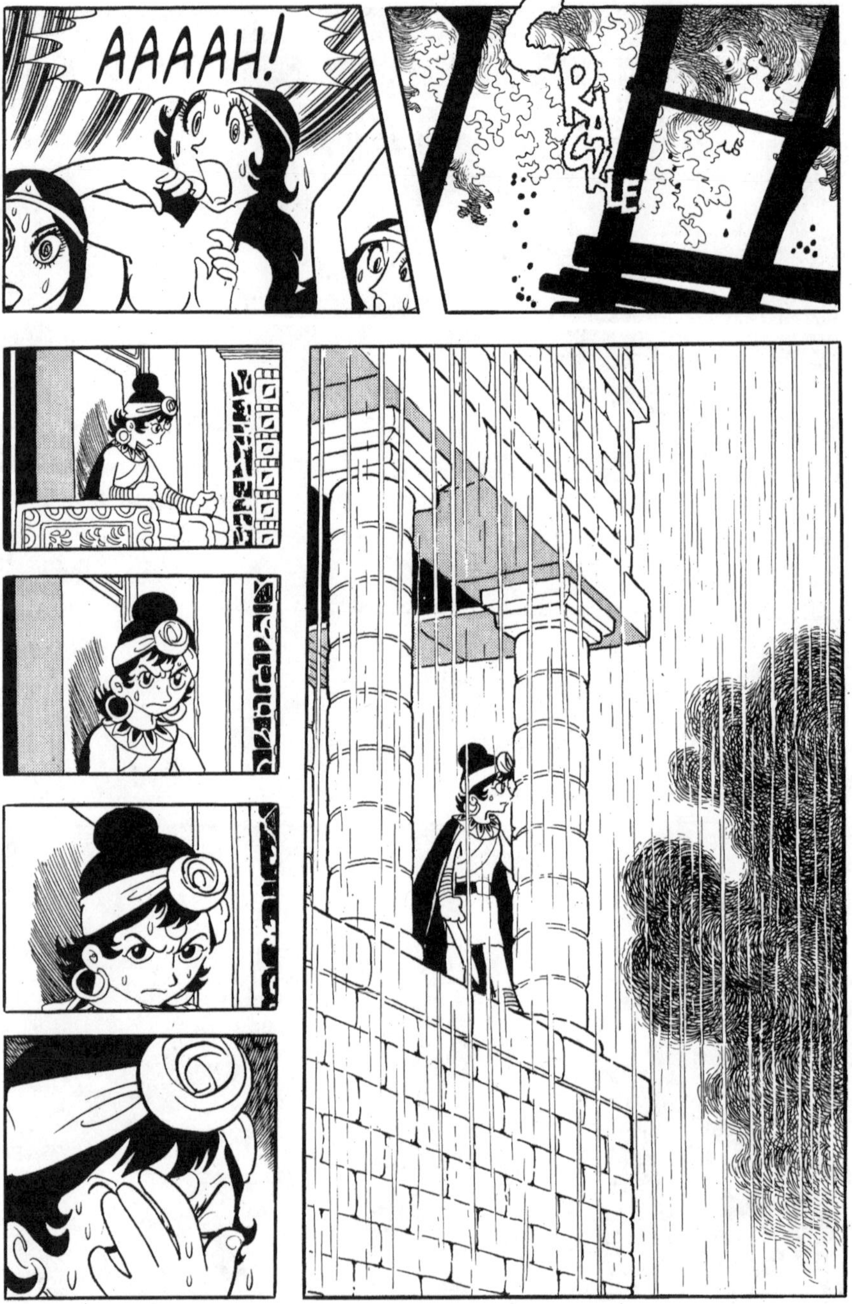
AAAAH!
CRACKLE

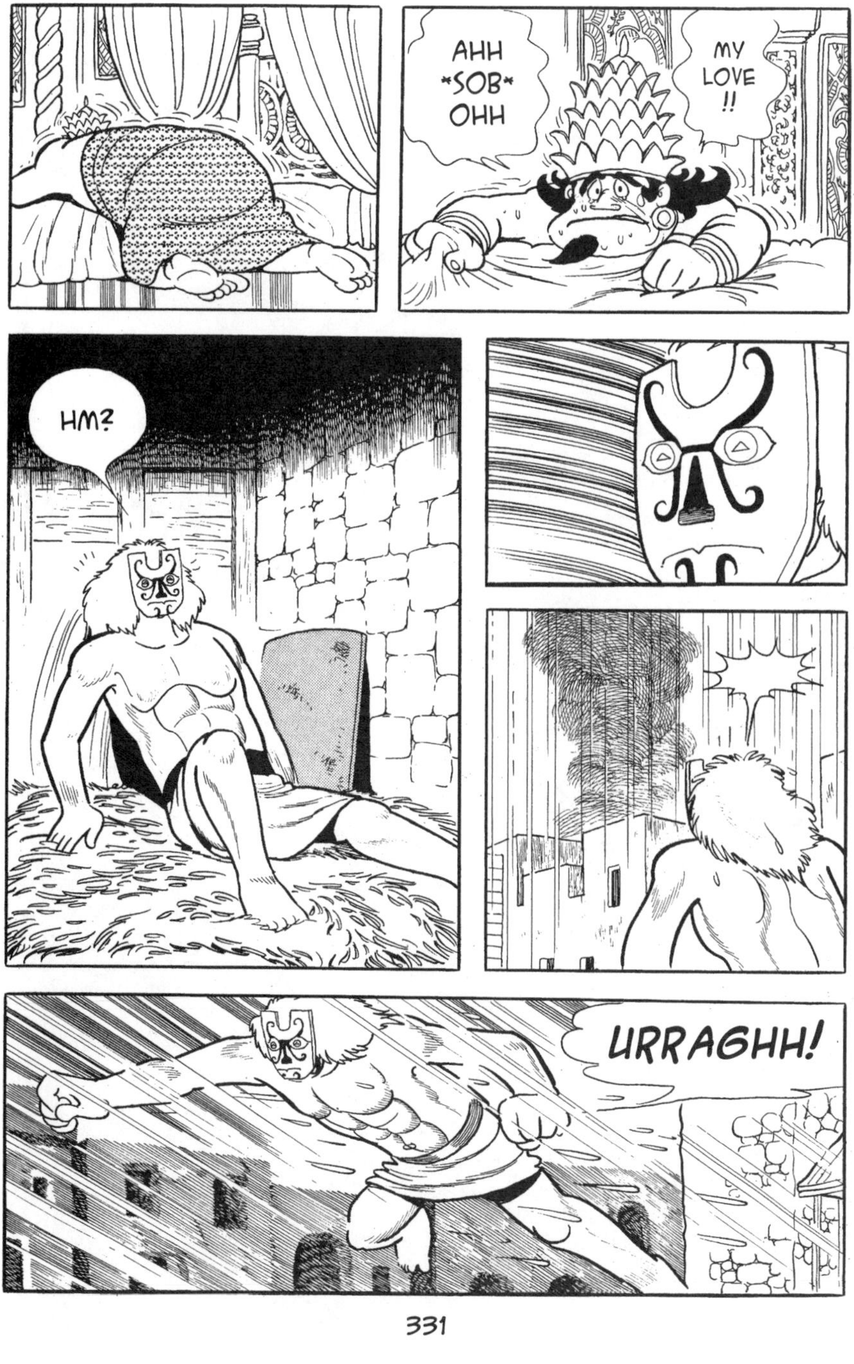
AHH *SOB* OHH
MY LOVE !!
HM?
URRAGHH!

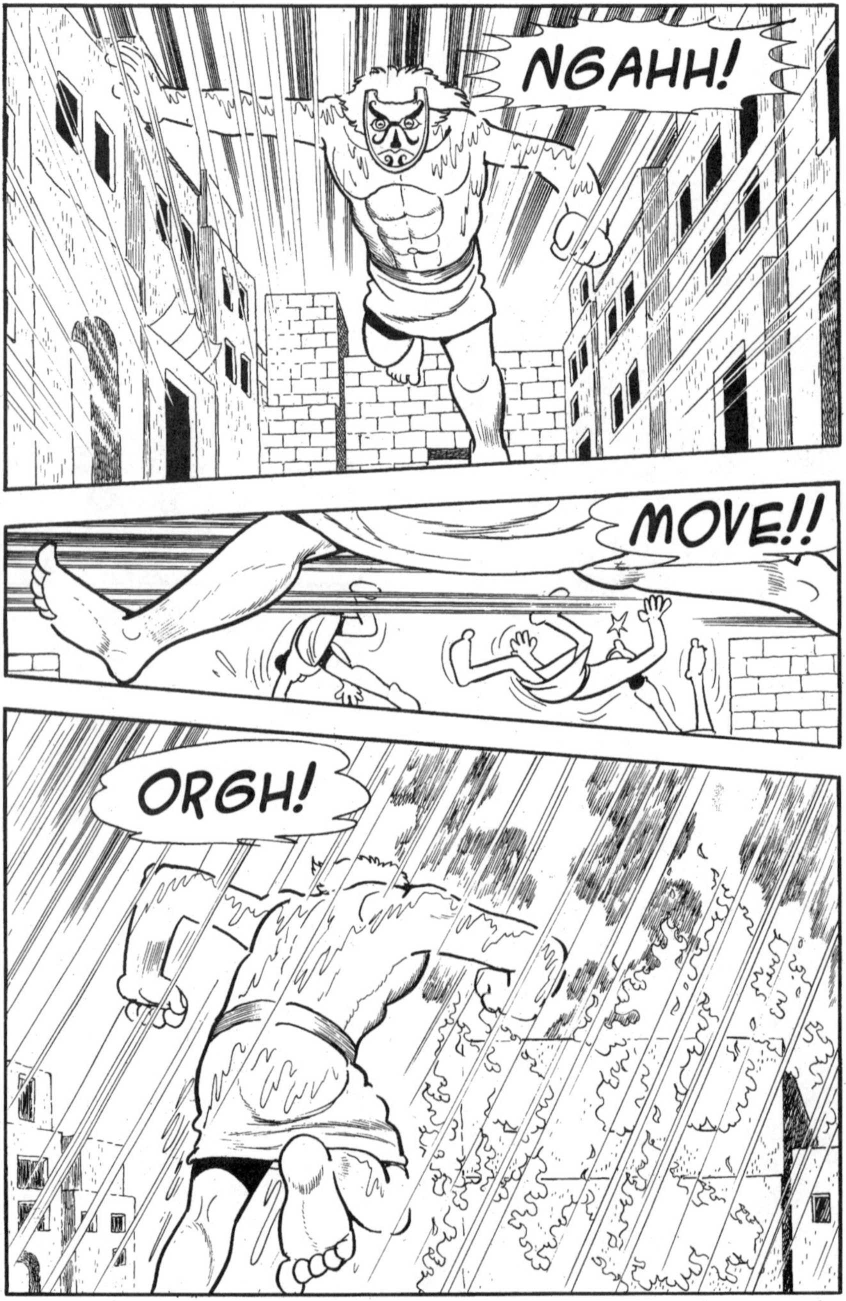
NGAHH!
MOVE!!
ORGH!

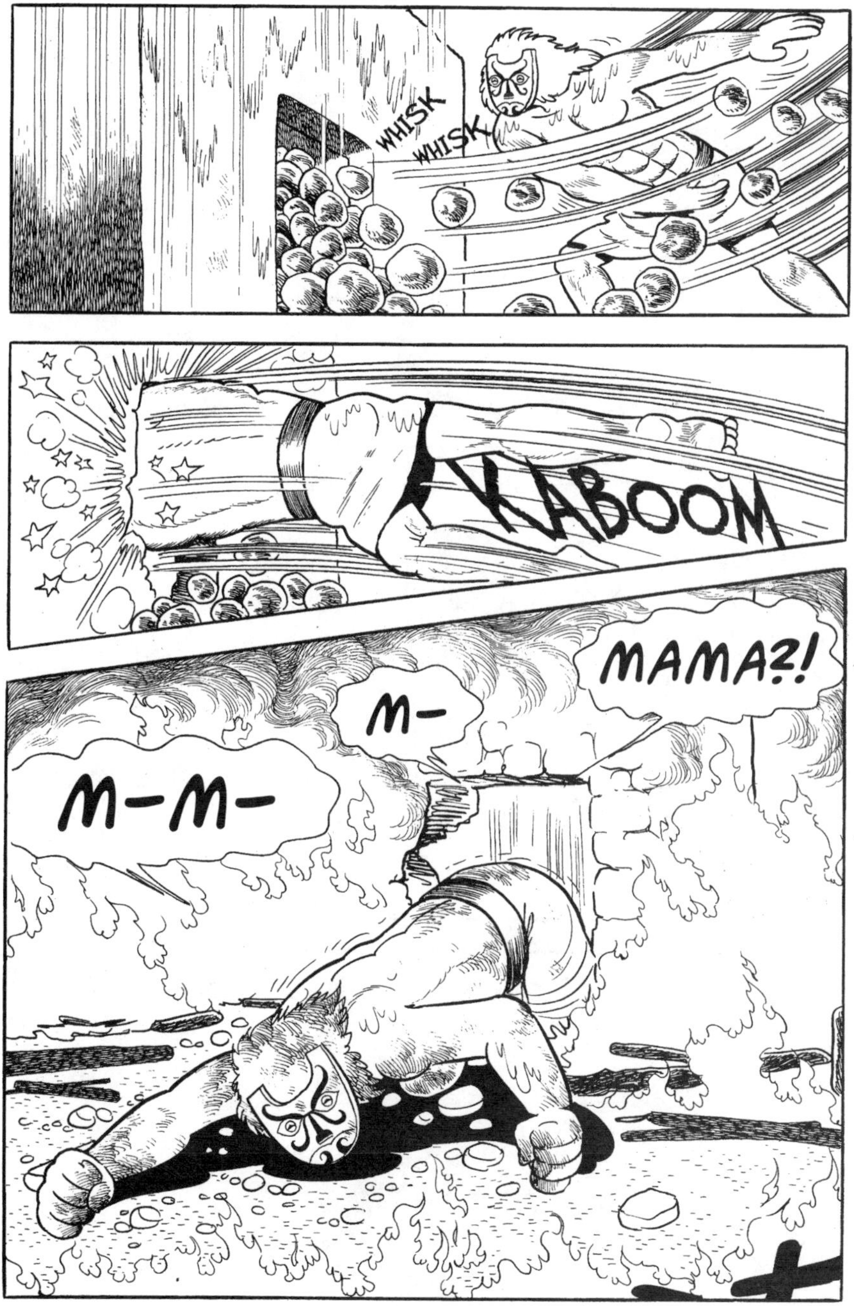
WHISK
WHISK
KABOOM
M-M-
M-
MAMA?!

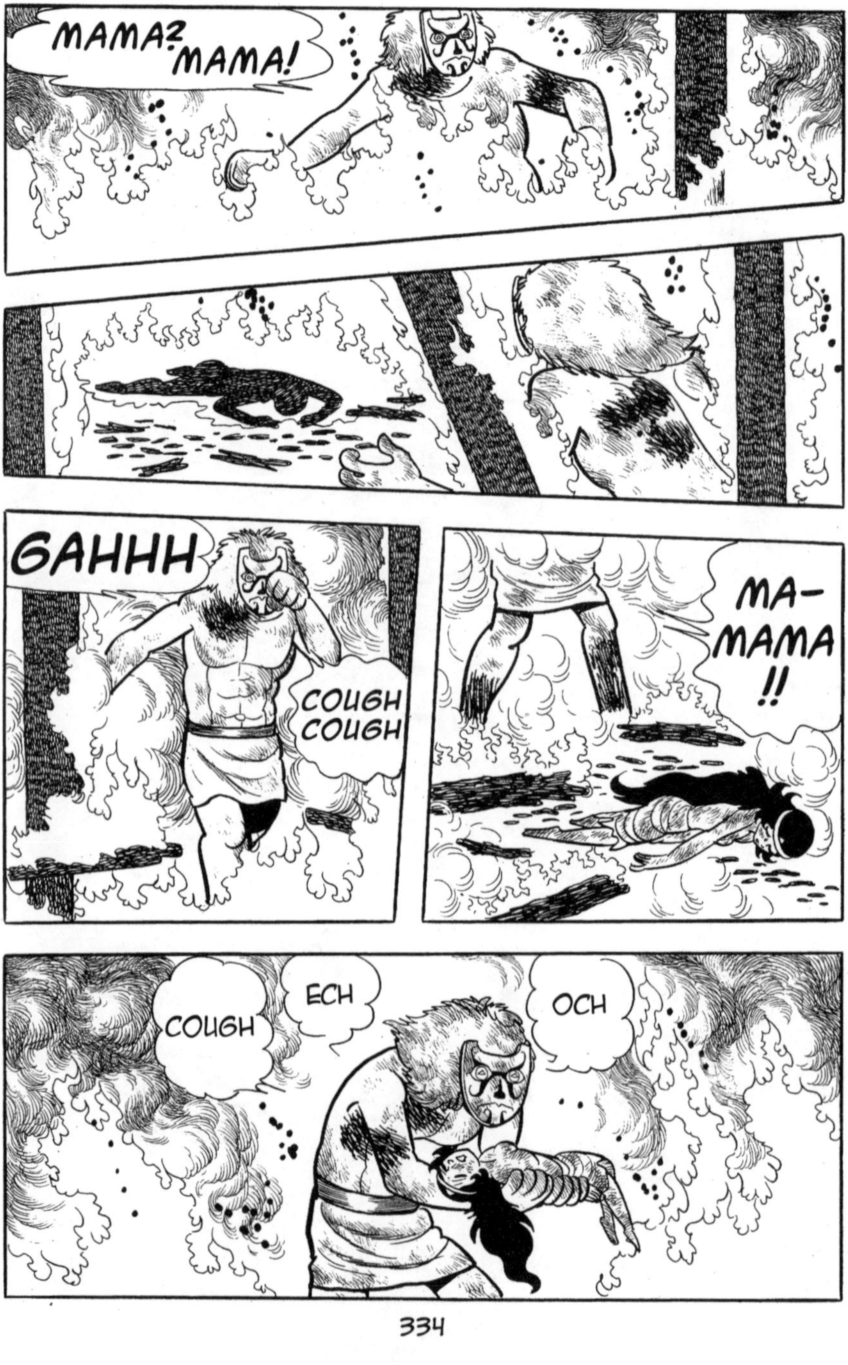
MAMA? MAMA!
GAHHH
COUGH COUGH
MA-MAMA !!
COUGH
ECH
OCH

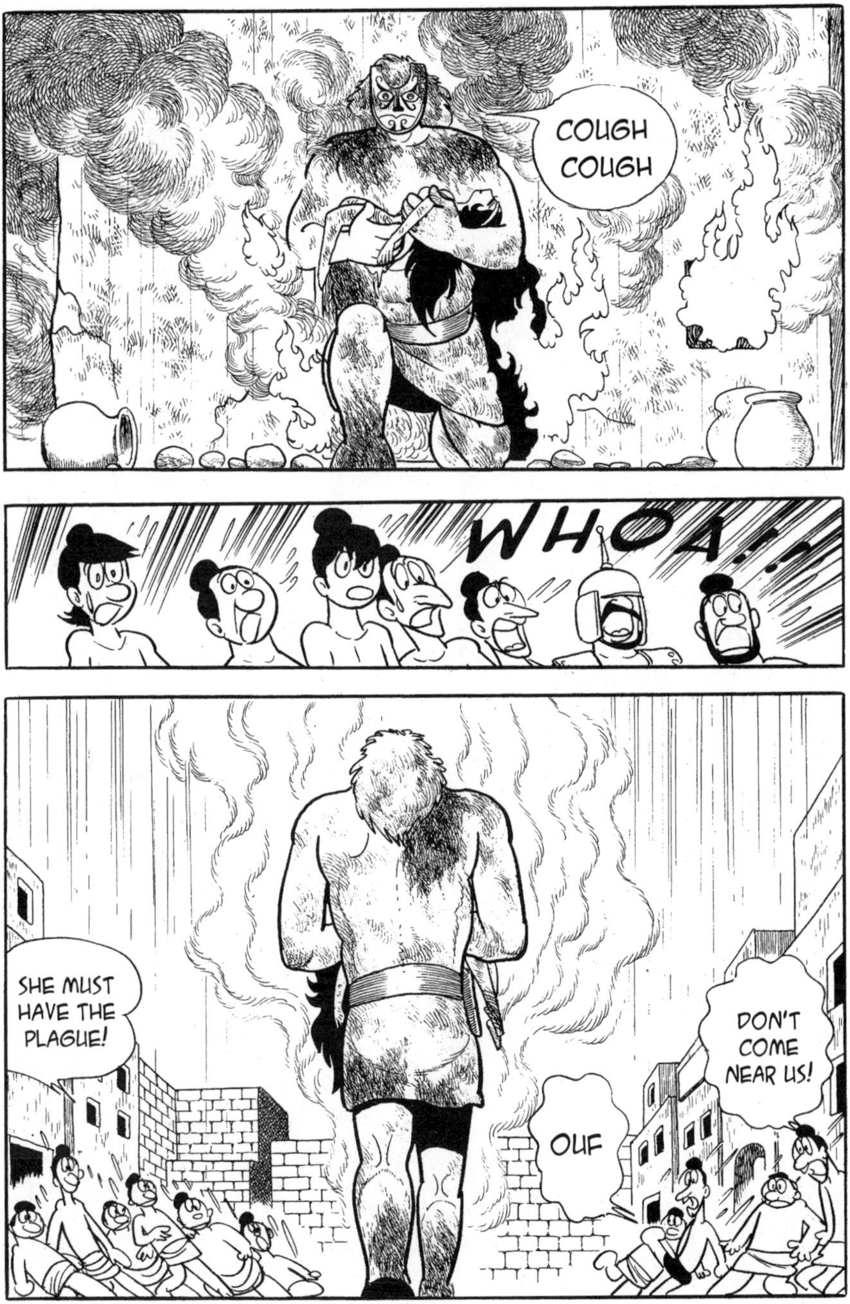
COUGH COUGH
WHOA!!
SHE MUST HAVE THE PLAGUE!
OUF
DON'T COME NEAR US!

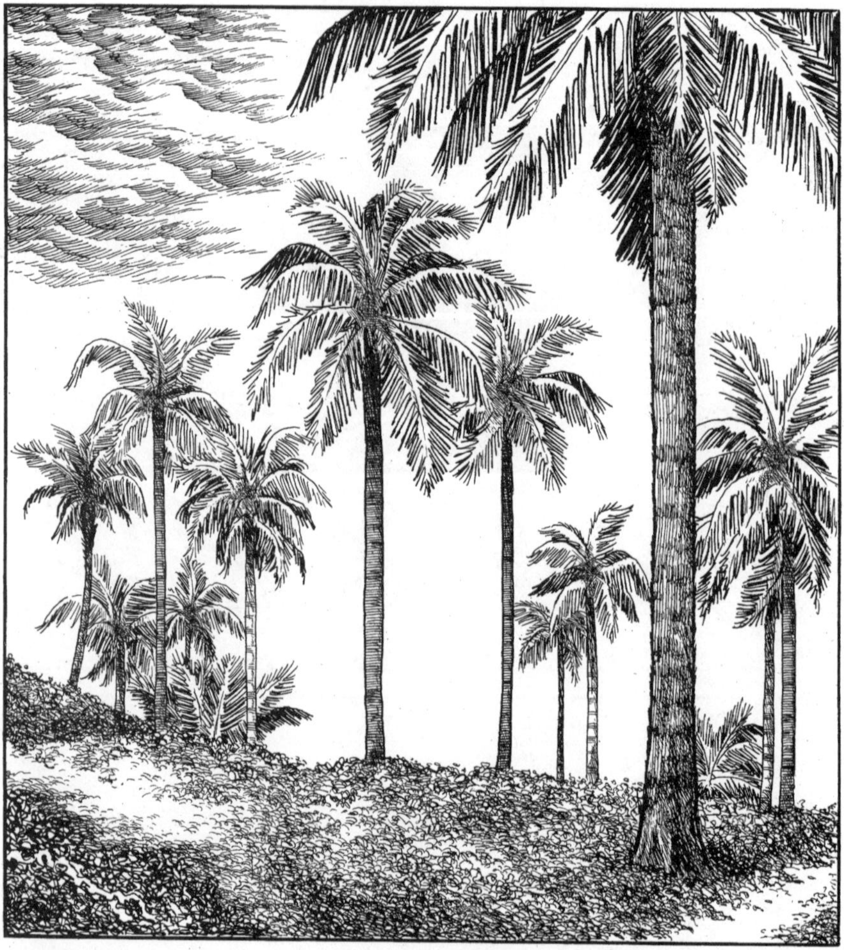
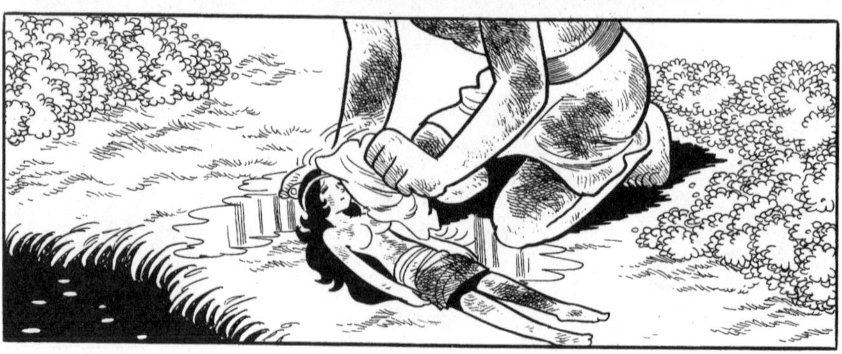

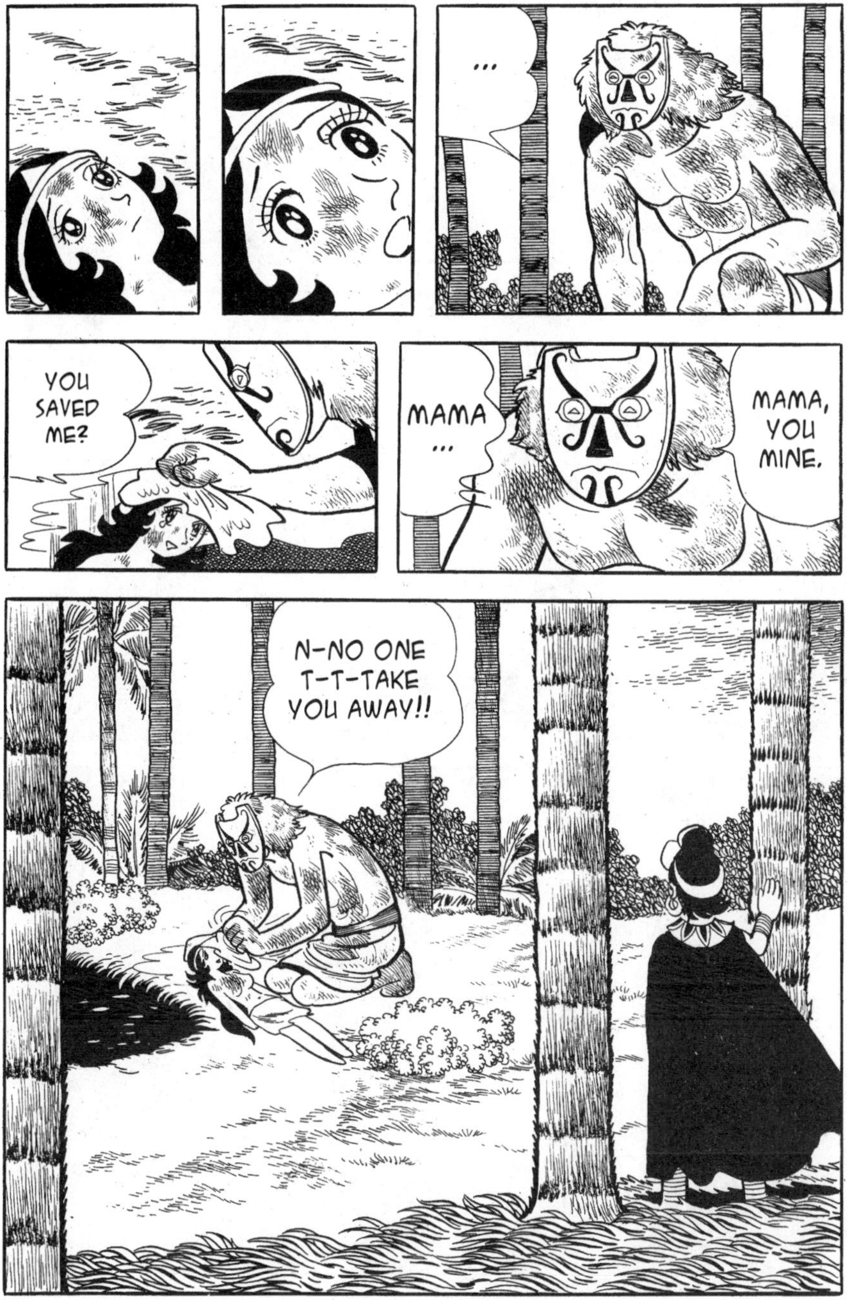
...
YOU SAVED ME?
MAMA ...
MAMA, YOU MINE.
N-NO ONE T-T-TAKE YOU AWAY!!

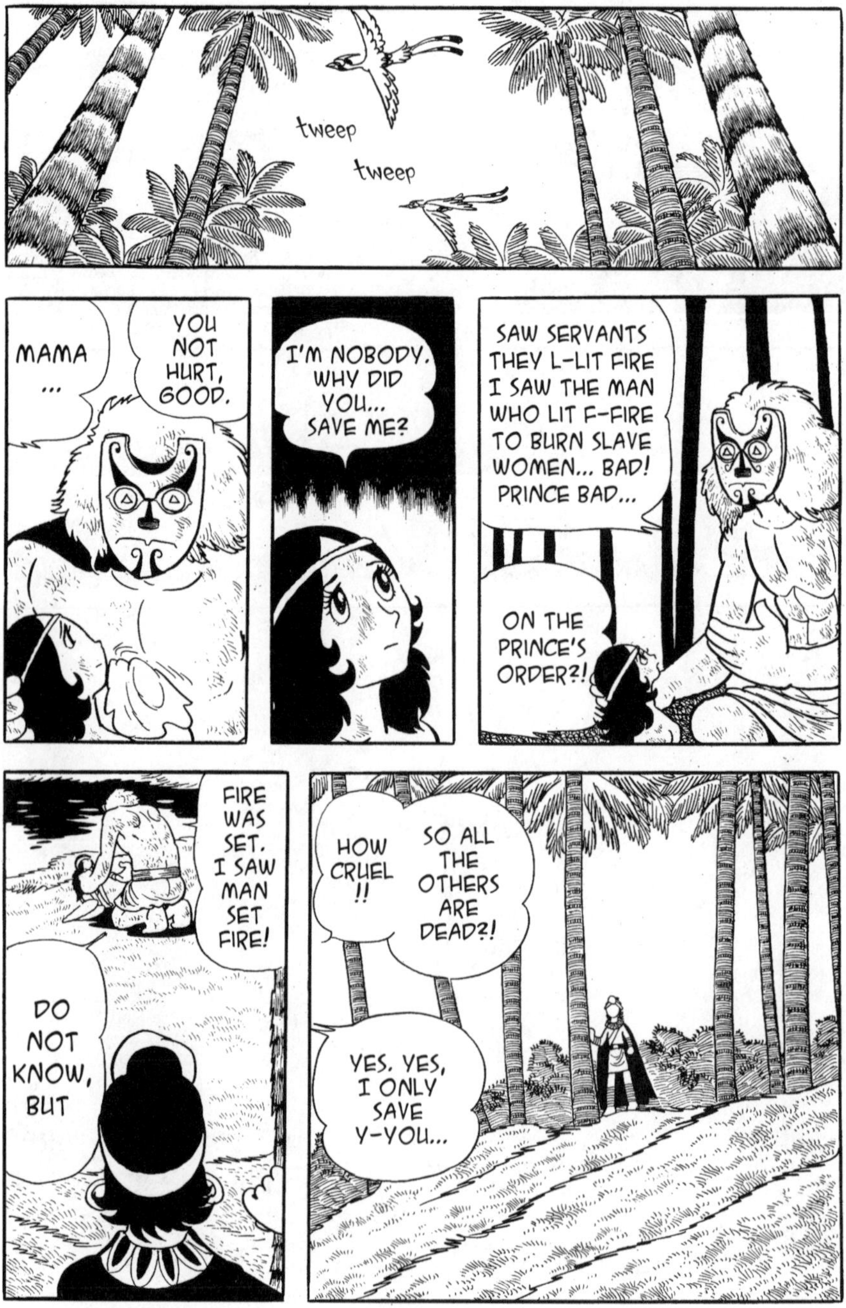
tweep
tweep
MAMA ...
YOU NOT HURT, GOOD.
I'M NOBODY. WHY DID YOU... SAVE ME?
SAW SERVANTS THEY L-LIT FIRE I SAW THE MAN WHO LIT F-FIRE TO BURN SLAVE WOMEN... BAD! PRINCE BAD...
ON THE PRINCE'S ORDER?!
FIRE WAS SET. I SAW MAN SET FIRE!
DO NOT KNOW, BUT
HOW CRUEL !!
SO ALL THE OTHERS ARE DEAD?!
YES. YES, I ONLY SAVE Y-YOU...

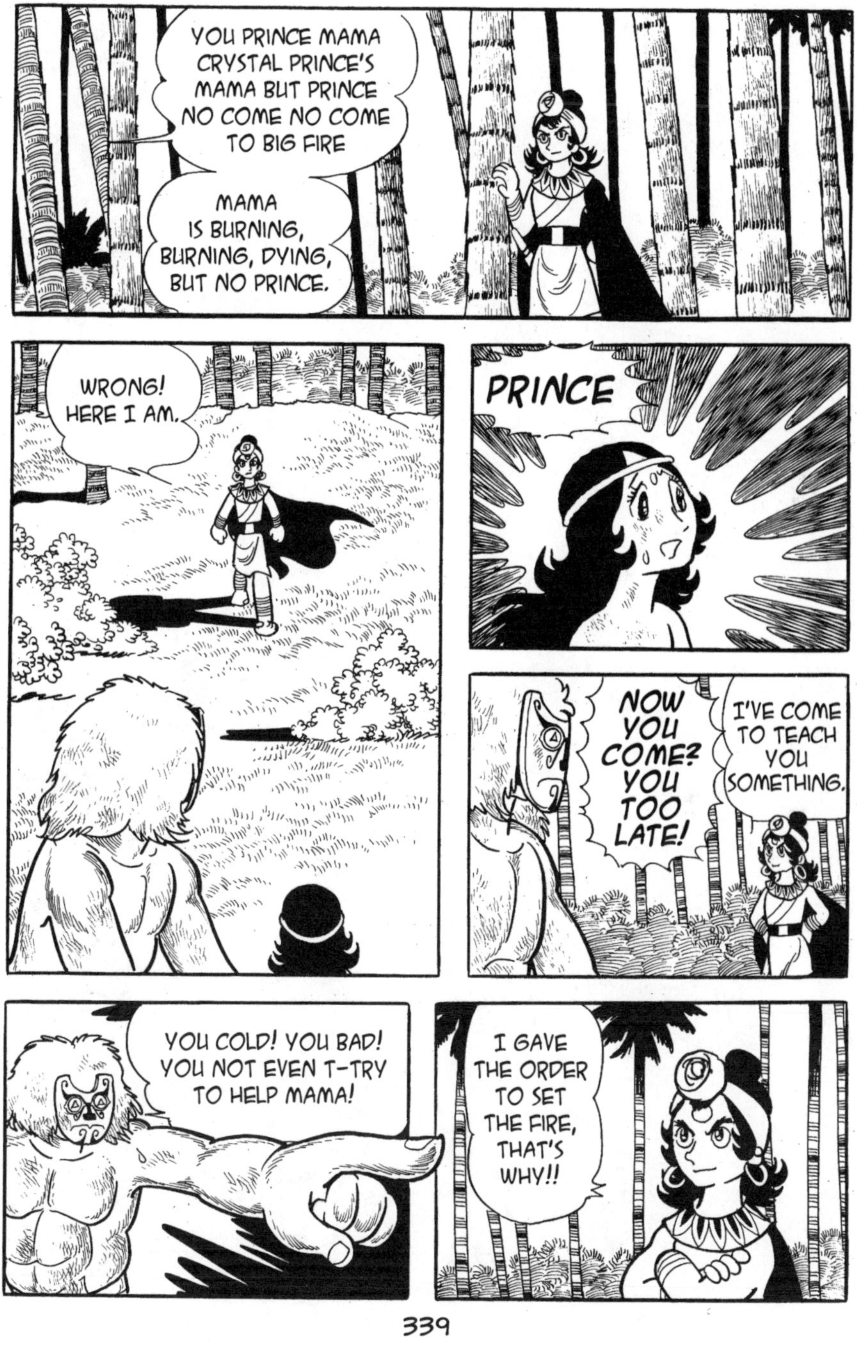
YOU PRINCE MAMA CRYSTAL PRINCE'S MAMA BUT PRINCE NO COME NO COME TO BIG FIRE
MAMA IS BURNING, BURNING, DYING, BUT NO PRINCE.
WRONG! HERE I AM.
PRINCE
NOW YOU COME? YOU TOO LATE!
I'VE COME TO TEACH YOU SOMETHING.
YOU COLD! YOU BAD! YOU NOT EVEN T-TRY TO HELP MAMA!
I GAVE THE ORDER TO SET THE FIRE, THAT'S WHY!!

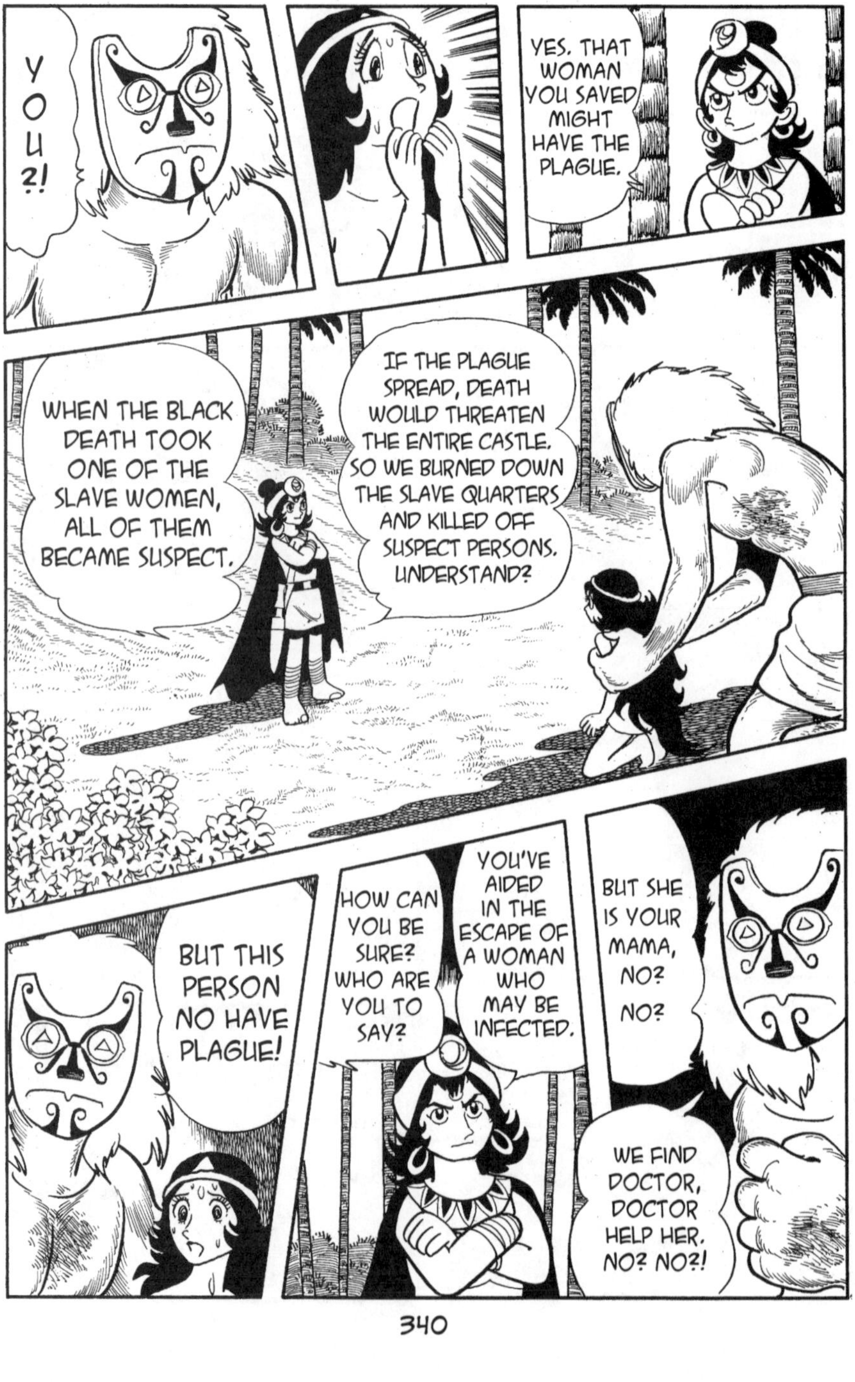
YOU?!
YES. THAT WOMAN YOU SAVED MIGHT HAVE THE PLAGUE.
WHEN THE BLACK DEATH TOOK ONE OF THE SLAVE WOMEN, ALL OF THEM BECAME SUSPECT.
IF THE PLAGUE SPREAD, DEATH WOULD THREATEN THE ENTIRE CASTLE. SO WE BURNED DOWN THE SLAVE QUARTERS AND KILLED OFF SUSPECT PERSONS. UNDERSTAND?
BUT THIS PERSON NO HAVE PLAGUE!
HOW CAN YOU BE SURE? WHO ARE YOU TO SAY?
YOU'VE AIDED IN THE ESCAPE OF A WOMAN WHO MAY BE INFECTED.
BUT SHE IS YOUR MAMA, NO?
NO?
WE FIND DOCTOR, DOCTOR HELP HER. NO? NO?!

A DOCTOR FOR A SLAVE? YOU MAKE ME LAUGH.

BUT NOW, THERE'S NO NEED EITHER TO KILL HER.

ORDERS, YATALA. TAKE THIS WOMAN SOMEPLACE FAR AWAY, AND LEAVE HER THERE SO SHE CAN DIE ALONE WITHOUT INFECTING ANYONE.

WHA... WHAT?!! AB–AB– ABANDON MAMA? TERRIBLE! HOW CAN YOU DO!

I AM PRINCE. IS IT RIGHT FOR A PRINCE TO JEOPARDIZE HIS WHOLE CASTLE, NAY, A CITY OF PEOPLE,

TO TRY TO SAVE HIS OWN KIN?

LET US GO, YATALA...

THE PRINCE IS RIGHT...

IF MAMA NOT SICK! I COME AFTER YOU.

JUST SHUT UP AND GO.

YATALA, COME BACK TO THE CASTLE AFTERWARDS. THAT'S AN ORDER.

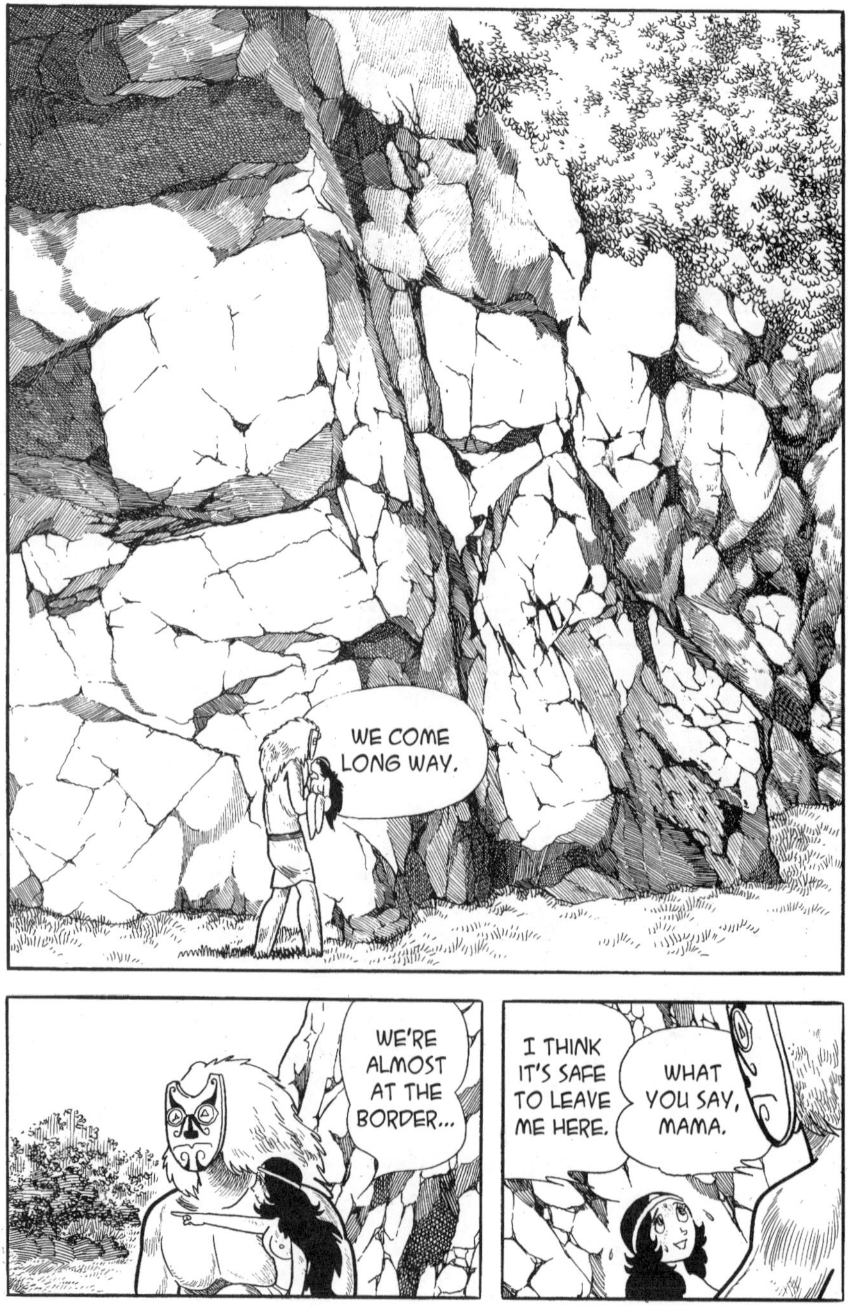
WE COME LONG WAY.
WE'RE ALMOST AT THE BORDER...
I THINK IT'S SAFE TO LEAVE ME HERE.
WHAT YOU SAY, MAMA.

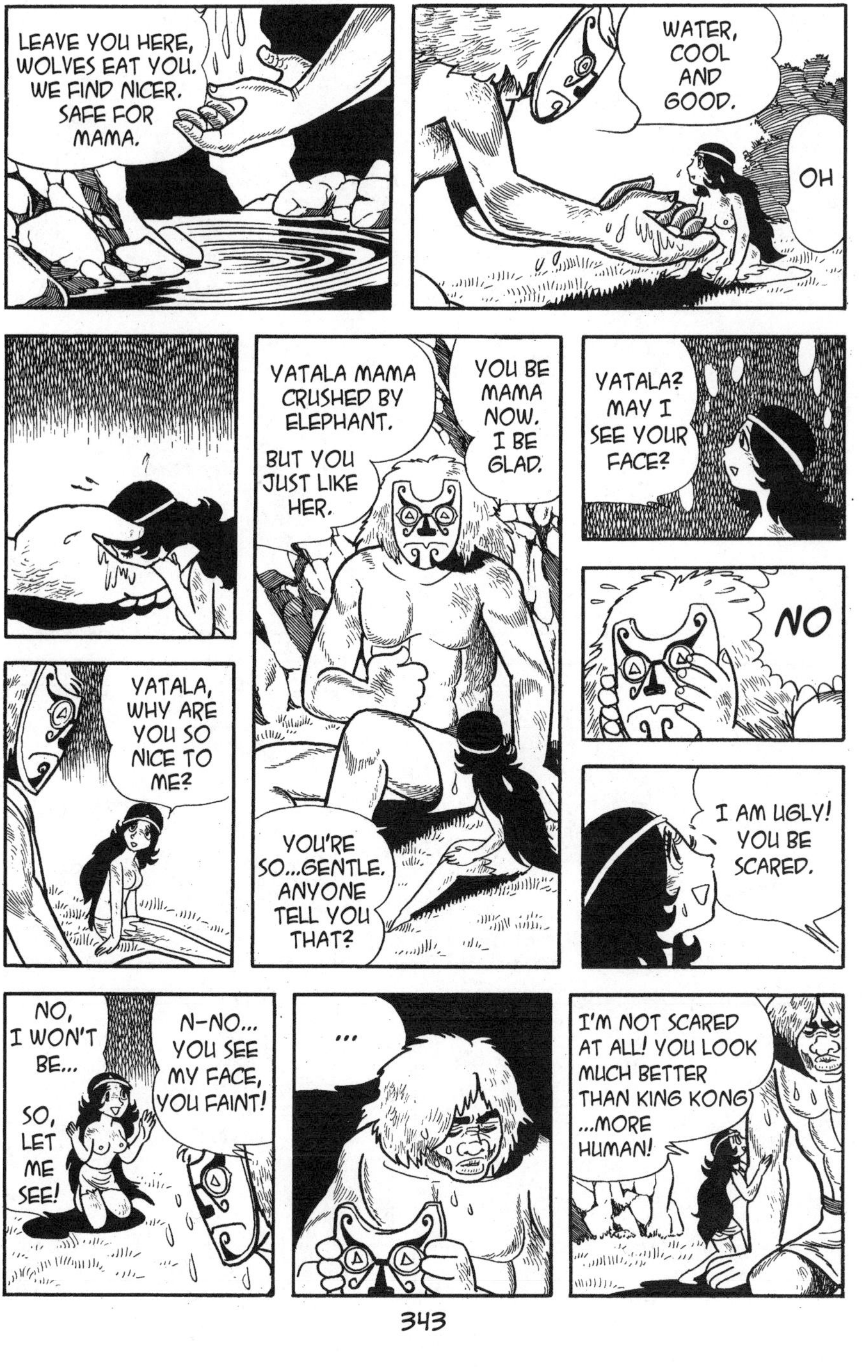

LEAVE YOU HERE, WOLVES EAT YOU. WE FIND NICER. SAFE FOR MAMA.
WATER, COOL AND GOOD.
OH
YATALA MAMA CRUSHED BY ELEPHANT.
BUT YOU JUST LIKE HER.
YOU BE MAMA NOW. I BE GLAD.
YATALA? MAY I SEE YOUR FACE?
YATALA, WHY ARE YOU SO NICE TO ME?
YOU'RE SO...GENTLE. ANYONE TELL YOU THAT?
NO
I AM UGLY! YOU BE SCARED.
NO, I WON'T BE...
SO, LET ME SEE!
N-NO... YOU SEE MY FACE, YOU FAINT!
...
I'M NOT SCARED AT ALL! YOU LOOK MUCH BETTER THAN KING KONG ...MORE HUMAN!

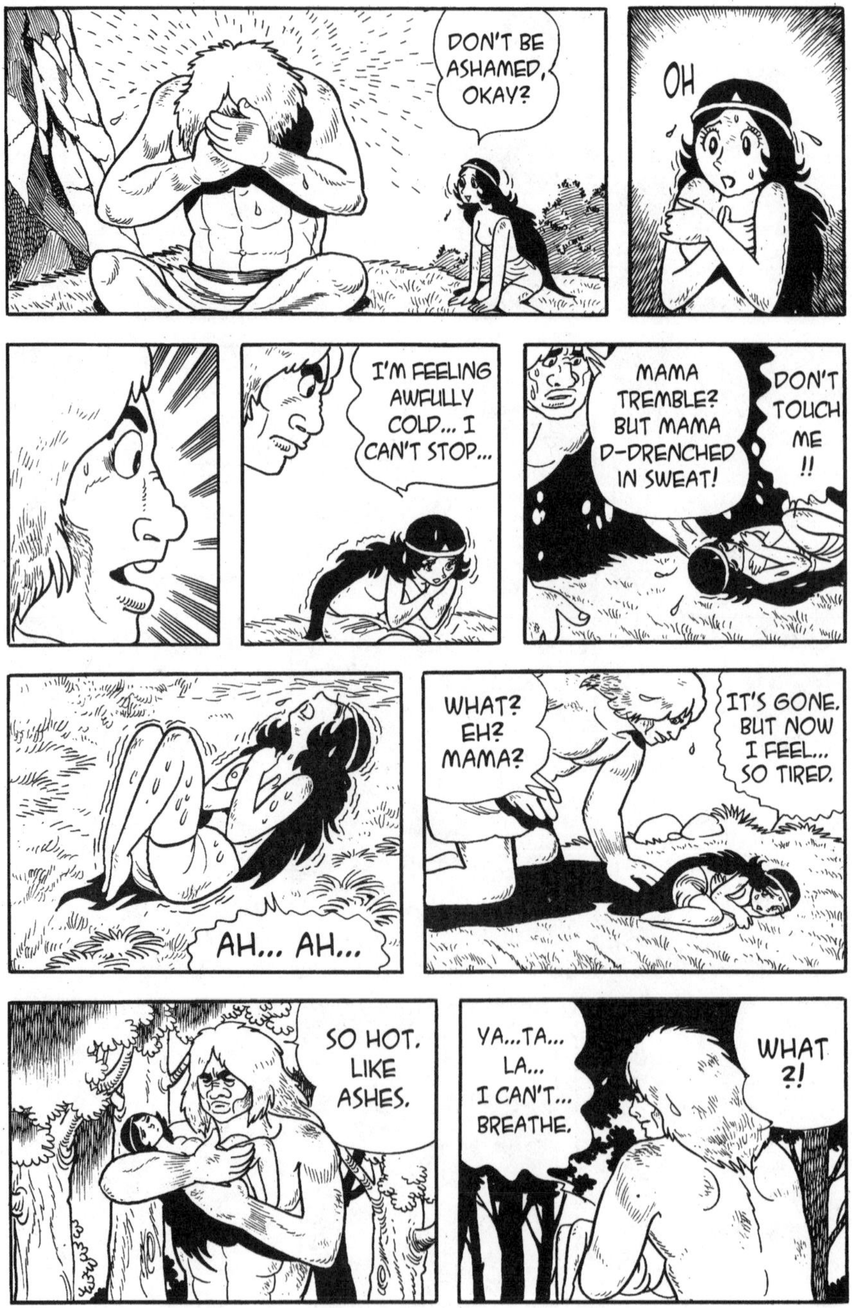
DON'T BE ASHAMED, OKAY?
OH
I'M FEELING AWFULLY COLD... I CAN'T STOP...
MAMA TREMBLE? BUT MAMA D-DRENCHED IN SWEAT!
DON'T TOUCH ME !!
AH... AH...
WHAT? EH? MAMA?
IT'S GONE. BUT NOW I FEEL... SO TIRED.
SO HOT. LIKE ASHES.
YA...TA... LA... I CAN'T... BREATHE.
WHAT ?!

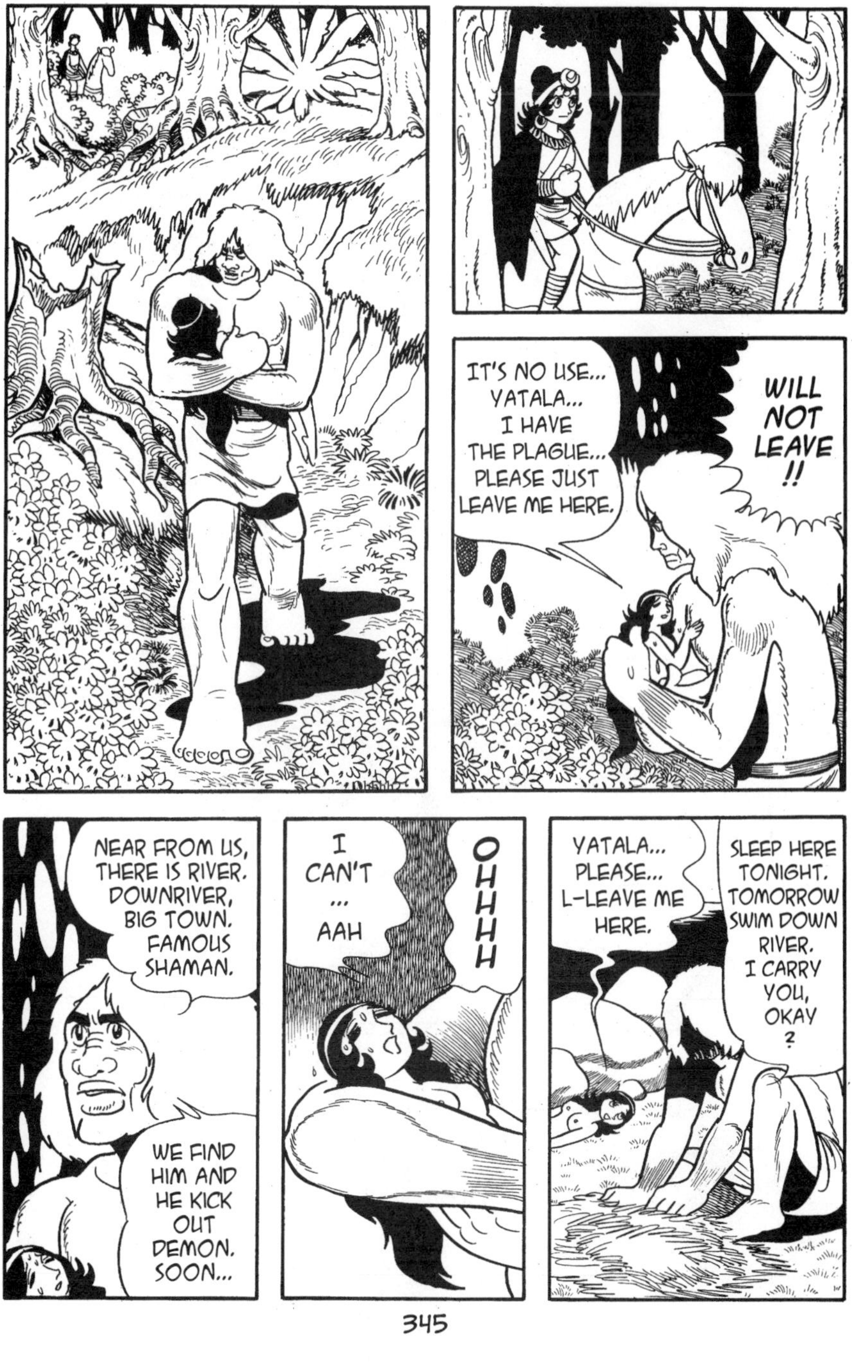
IT'S NO USE... YATALA... I HAVE THE PLAGUE... PLEASE JUST LEAVE ME HERE.
WILL NOT LEAVE !!
NEAR FROM US, THERE IS RIVER. DOWNRIVER, BIG TOWN. FAMOUS SHAMAN.
WE FIND HIM AND HE KICK OUT DEMON. SOON...
I CAN'T ... AAH
OHHHH
YATALA... PLEASE... L-LEAVE ME HERE.
SLEEP HERE TONIGHT. TOMORROW SWIM DOWN RIVER. I CARRY YOU, OKAY ?

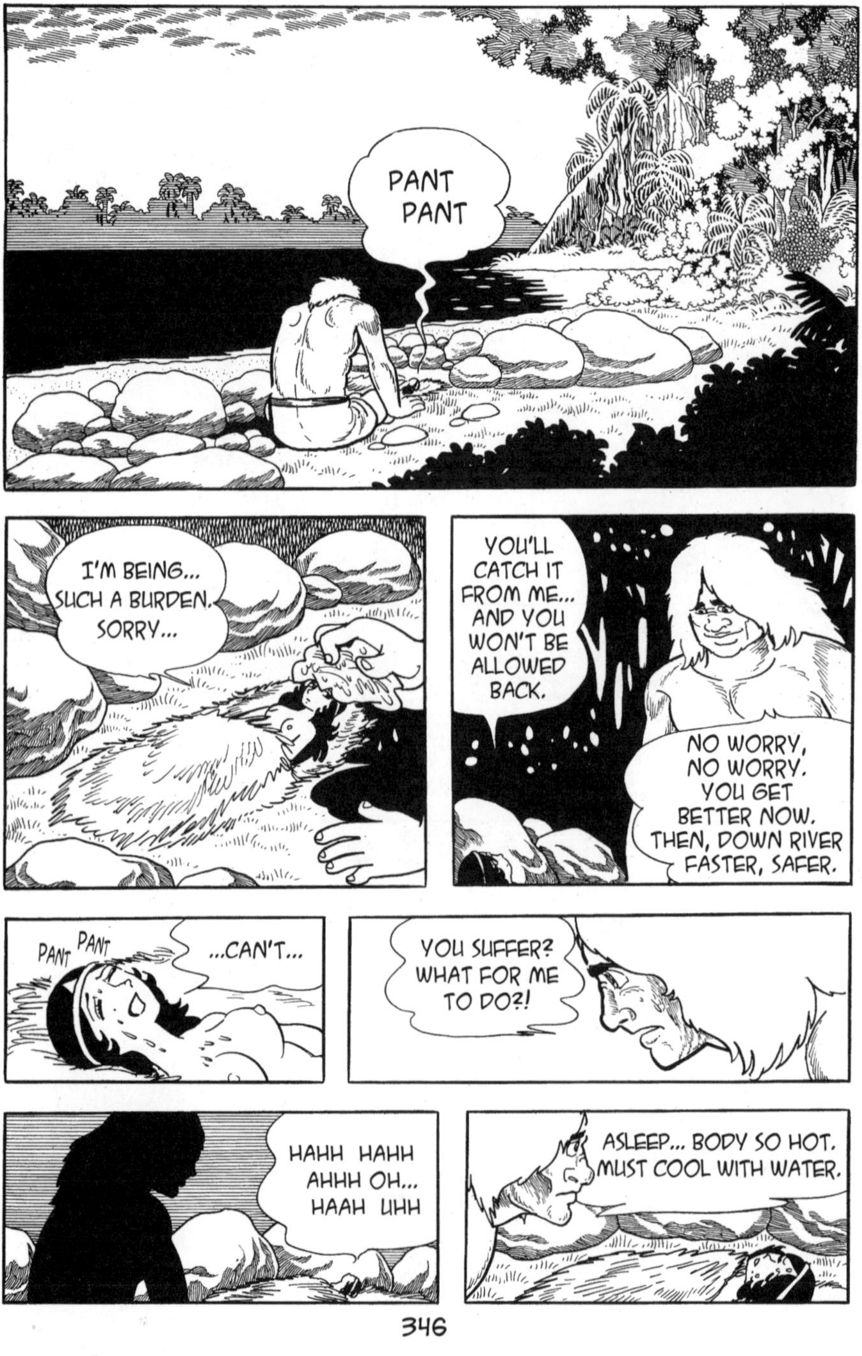
PANT
PANT
I'M BEING... SUCH A BURDEN. SORRY...
YOU'LL CATCH IT FROM ME... AND YOU WON'T BE ALLOWED BACK.
NO WORRY, NO WORRY. YOU GET BETTER NOW. THEN, DOWN RIVER FASTER, SAFER.
PANT PANT
...CAN'T...
YOU SUFFER? WHAT FOR ME TO DO?!
HAHH HAHH AHHH OH... HAAH UHH
ASLEEP... BODY SO HOT. MUST COOL WITH WATER.

PLUCK

SO MANY FISH I CAUGHT, MAMA. YUMMY. I COOK IT SOFT, VERY SOFT. FOUND SOME HERBS, TOO.

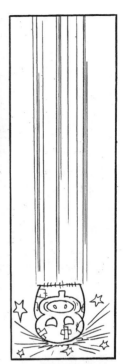

OH HO! FOOD!!

MAMA ?!

EYES OPEN, MAMA! EYES OPEN!

AAAAAH!

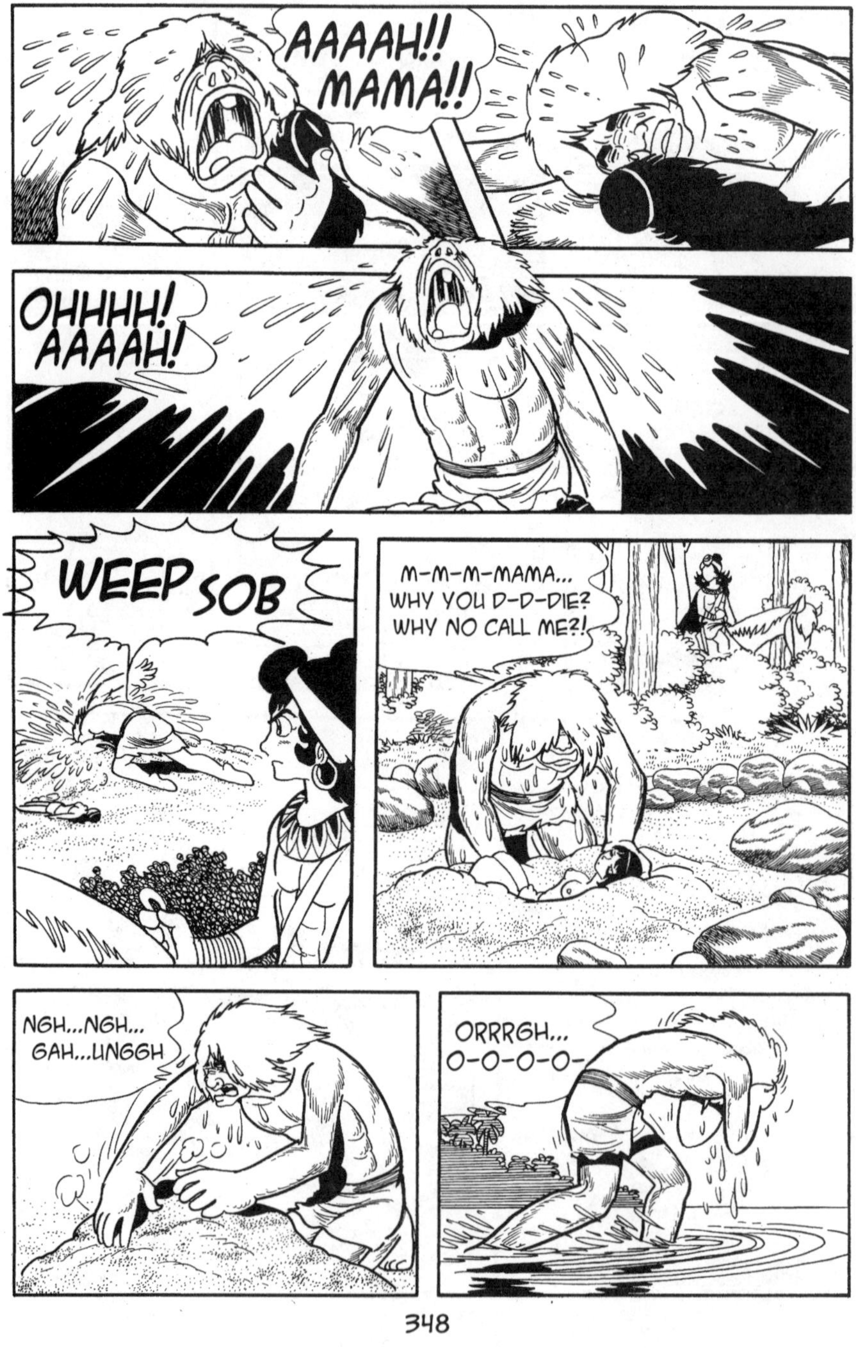
AAAAH!! MAMA!!
OHHHH! AAAAH!
WEEP SOB
M-M-M-MAMA... WHY YOU D-D-DIE? WHY NO CALL ME?!
NGH...NGH... GAH...UNGGH
ORRRGH... O-O-O-O-

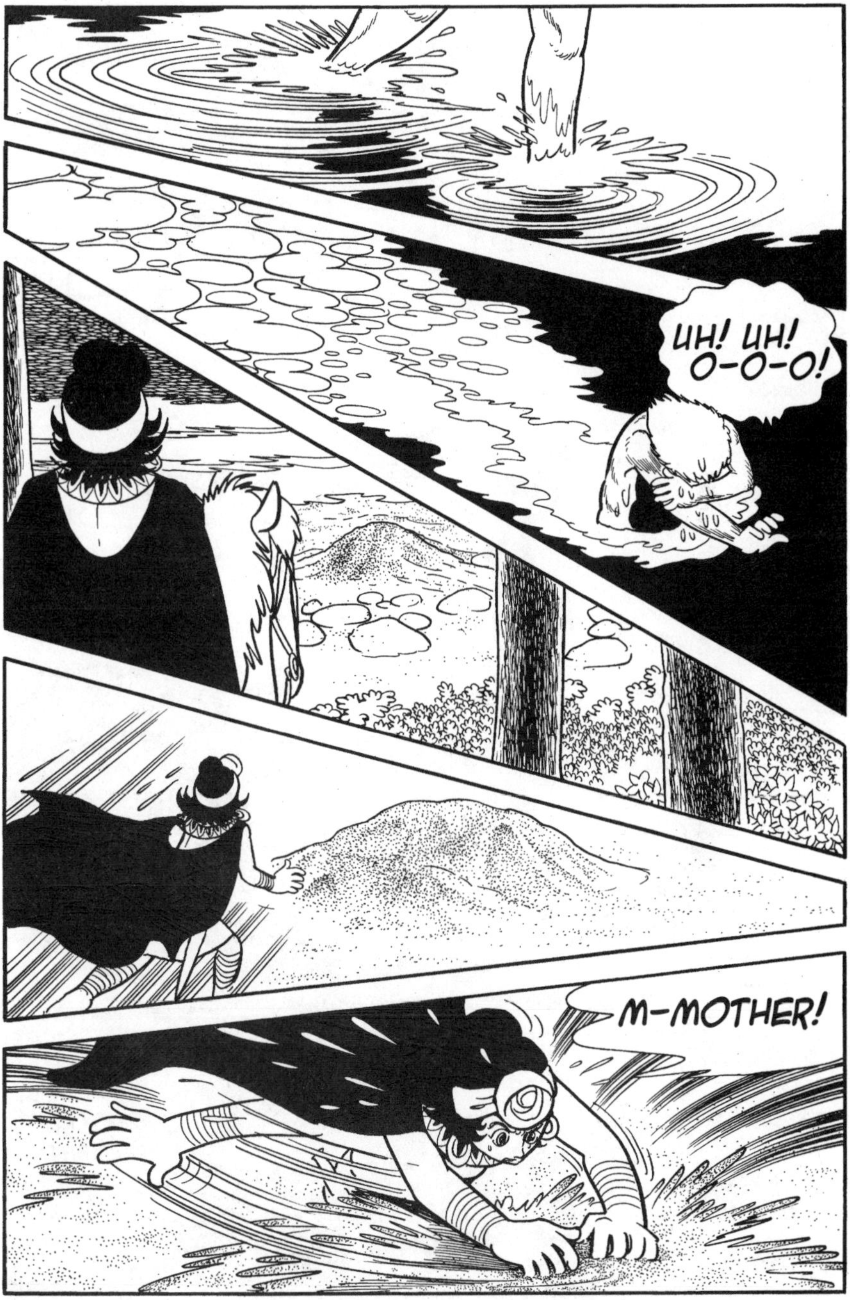
UH! UH! O-O-O!
M-MOTHER!

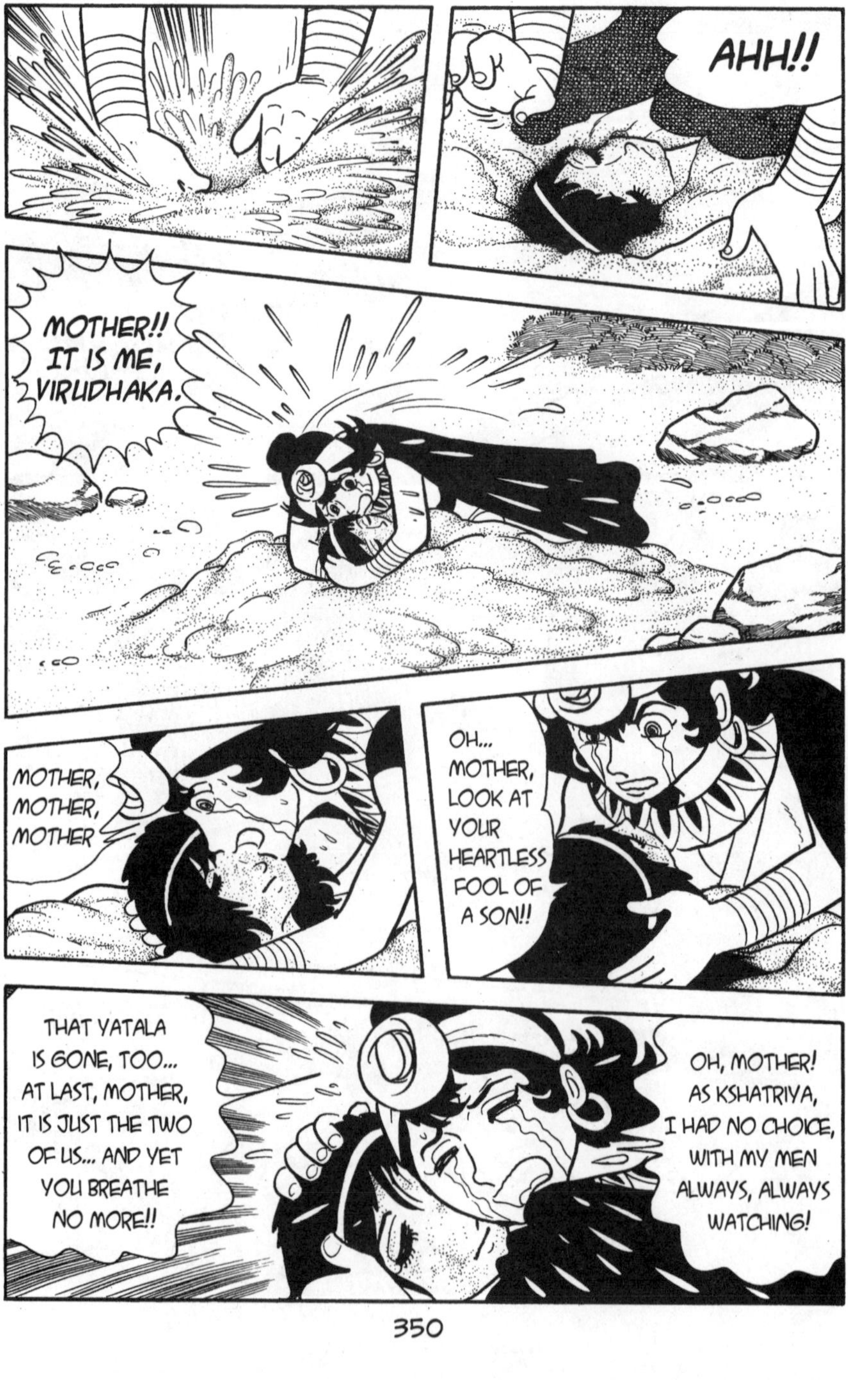
AHH!!
MOTHER!! IT IS ME, VIRUDHAKA.
MOTHER, MOTHER, MOTHER
OH... MOTHER, LOOK AT YOUR HEARTLESS FOOL OF A SON!!
THAT YATALA IS GONE, TOO... AT LAST, MOTHER, IT IS JUST THE TWO OF US... AND YET YOU BREATHE NO MORE!!
OH, MOTHER! AS KSHATRIYA, I HAD NO CHOICE, WITH MY MEN ALWAYS, ALWAYS WATCHING!

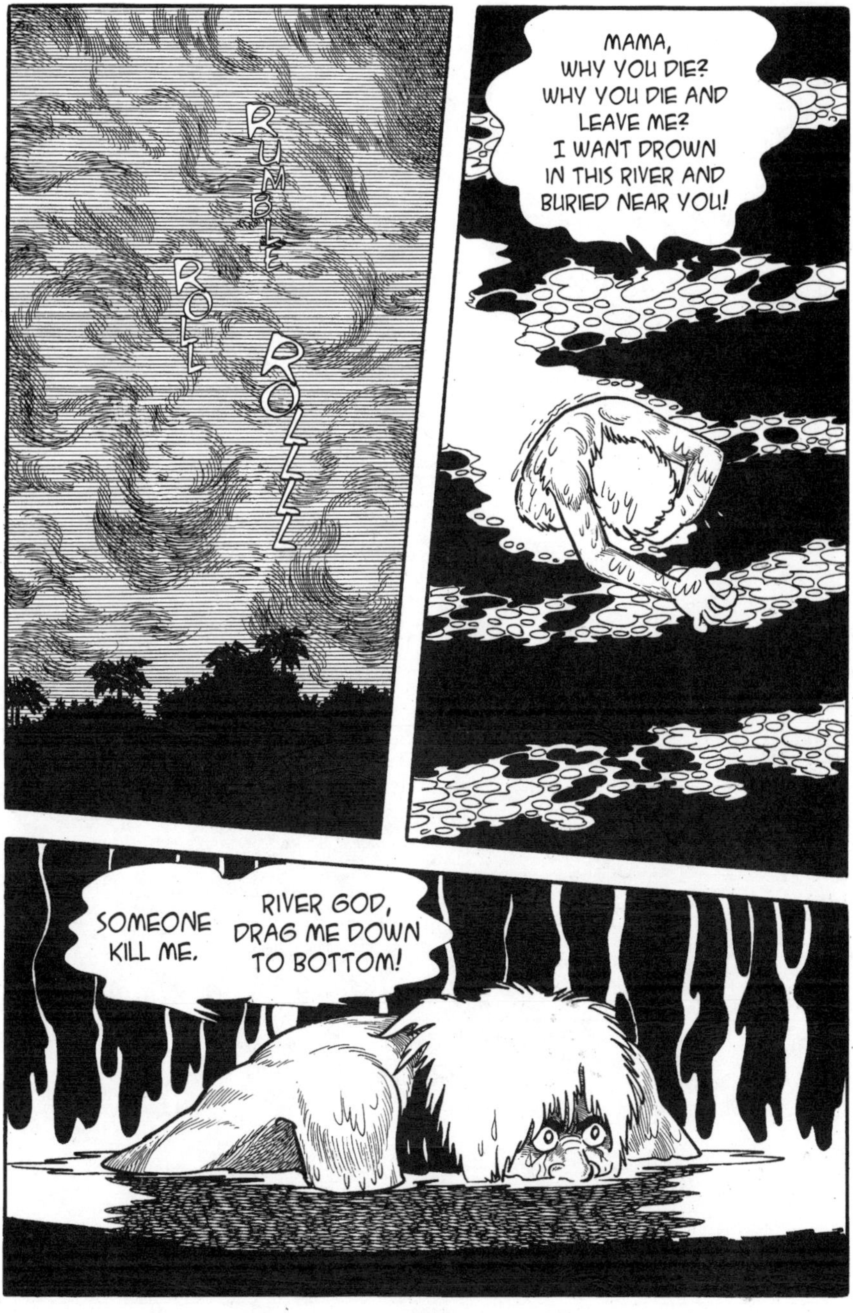
RUMBLE
ROLL
ROLLL
MAMA, WHY YOU DIE? WHY YOU DIE AND LEAVE ME? I WANT DROWN IN THIS RIVER AND BURIED NEAR YOU!
SOMEONE KILL ME.
RIVER GOD, DRAG ME DOWN TO BOTTOM!

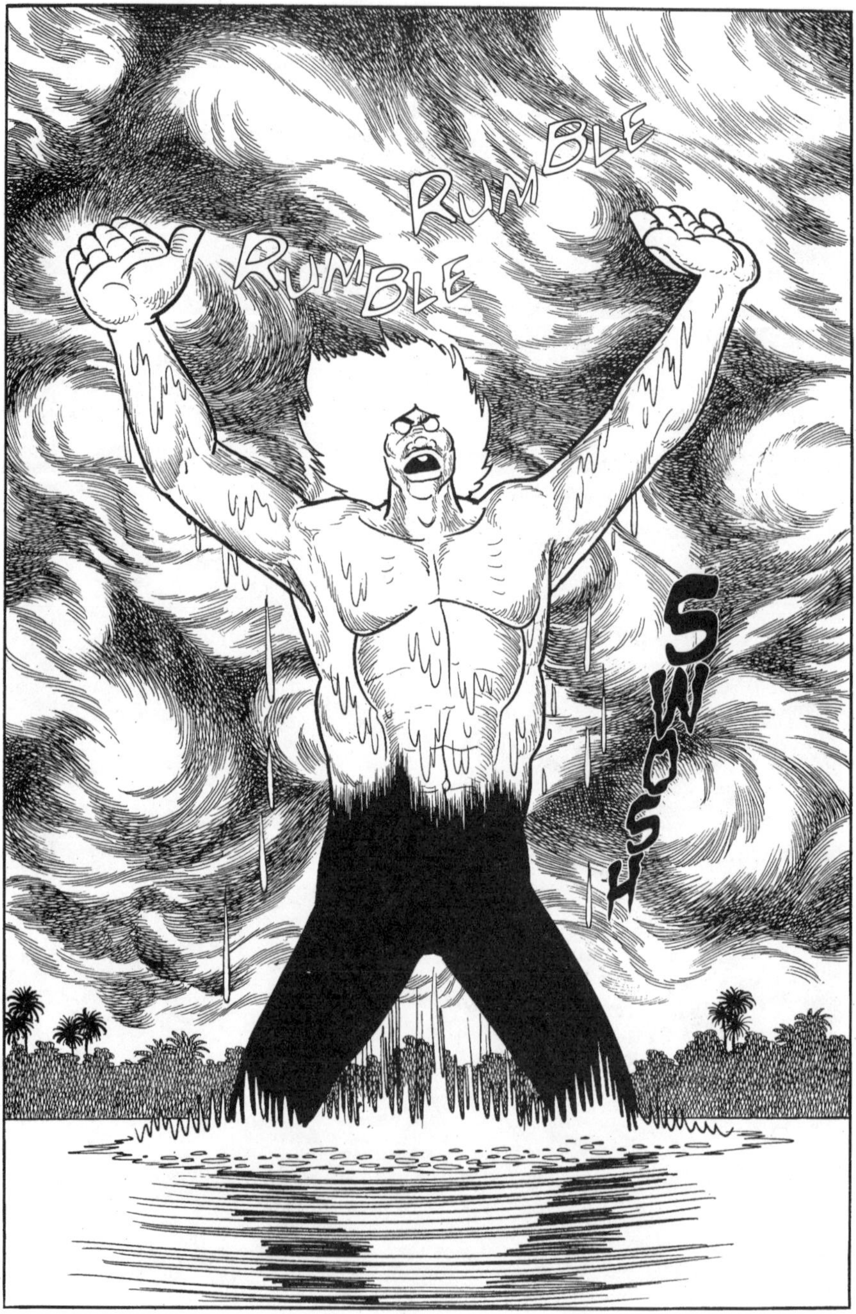
RUMBLE
RUMBLE
SWOSH

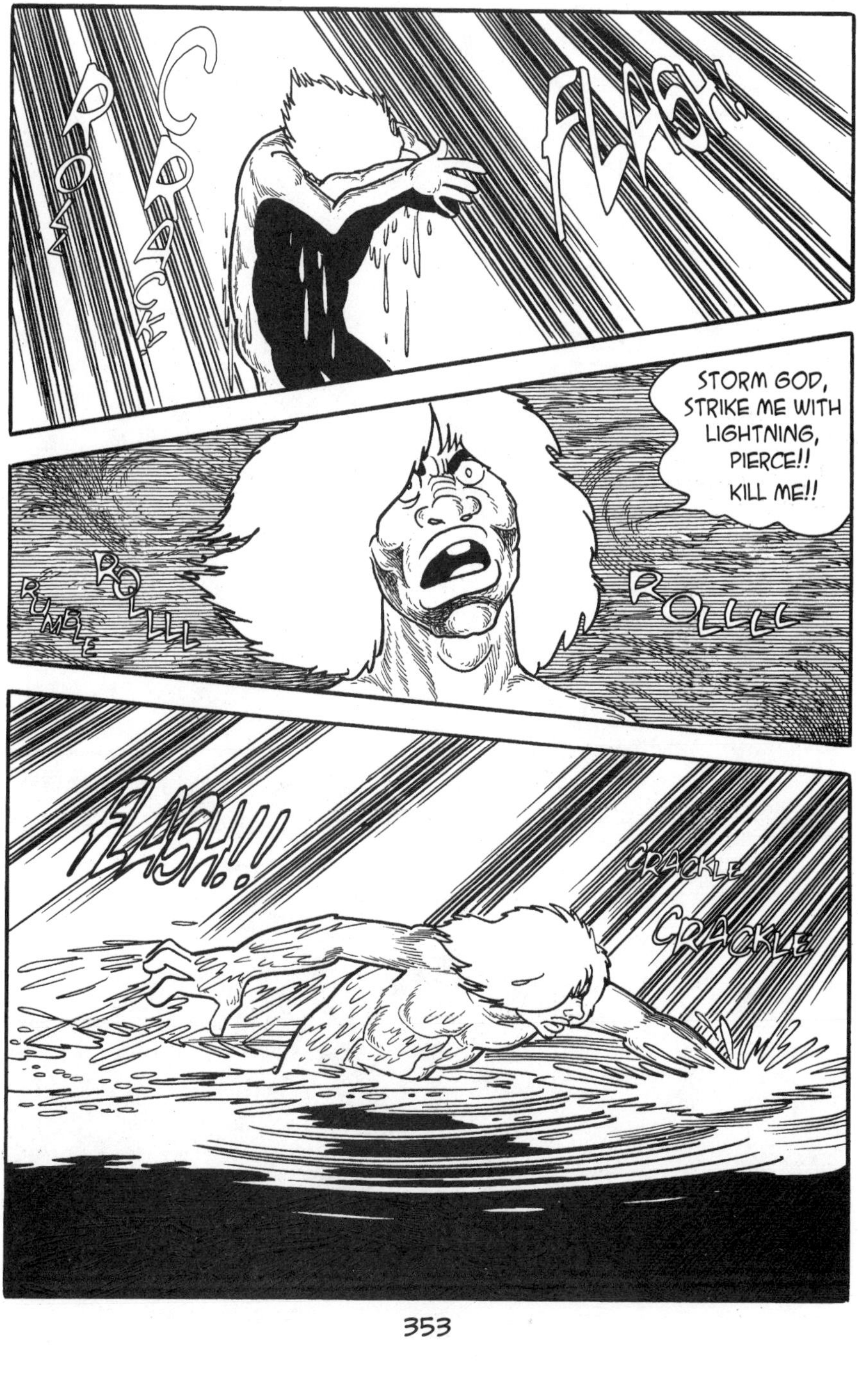
ROLL
CRACK!
FLASH!
STORM GOD, STRIKE ME WITH LIGHTNING, PIERCE!! KILL ME!!
RUMBLE
ROLLLL
ROLLLLL
FLASH!!
CRACKLE
CRACKLE

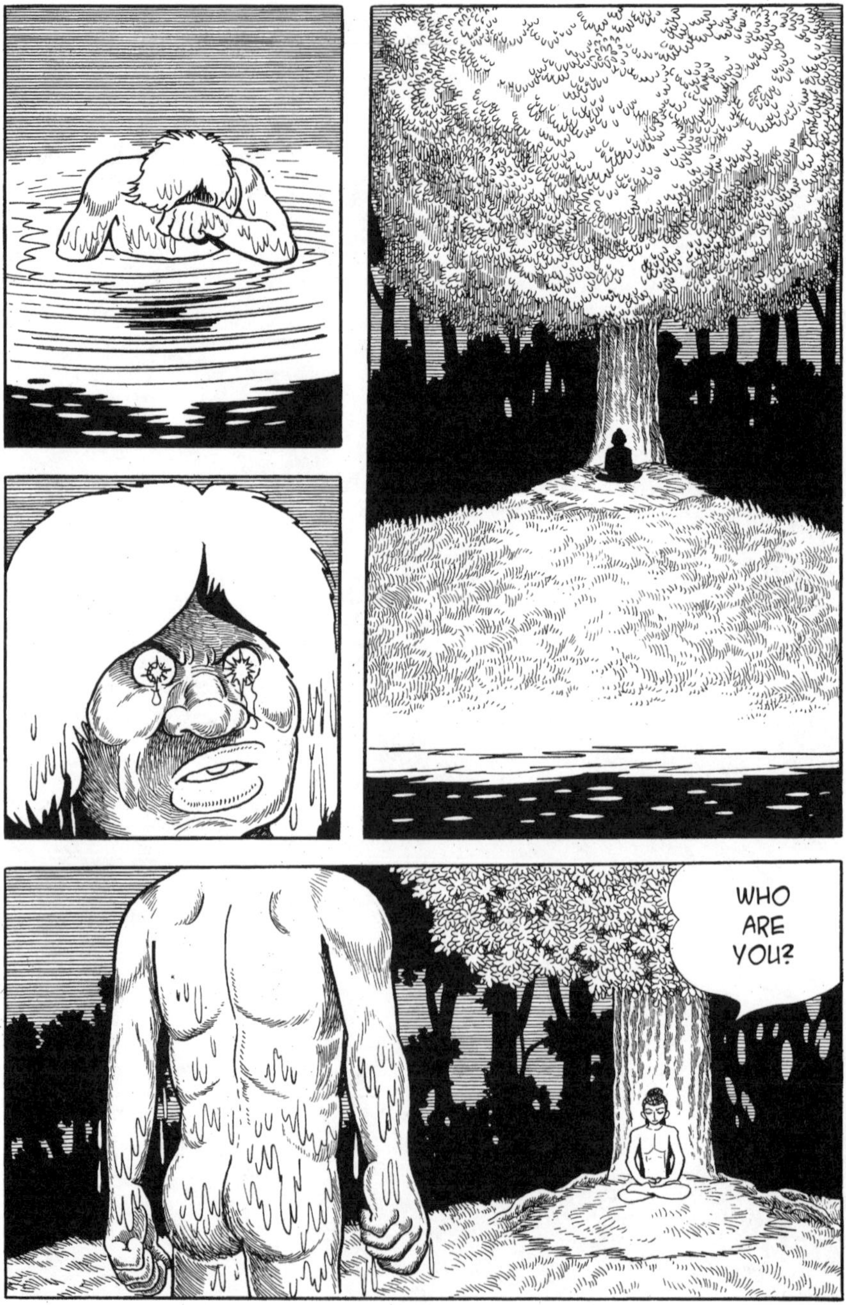
WHO ARE YOU?

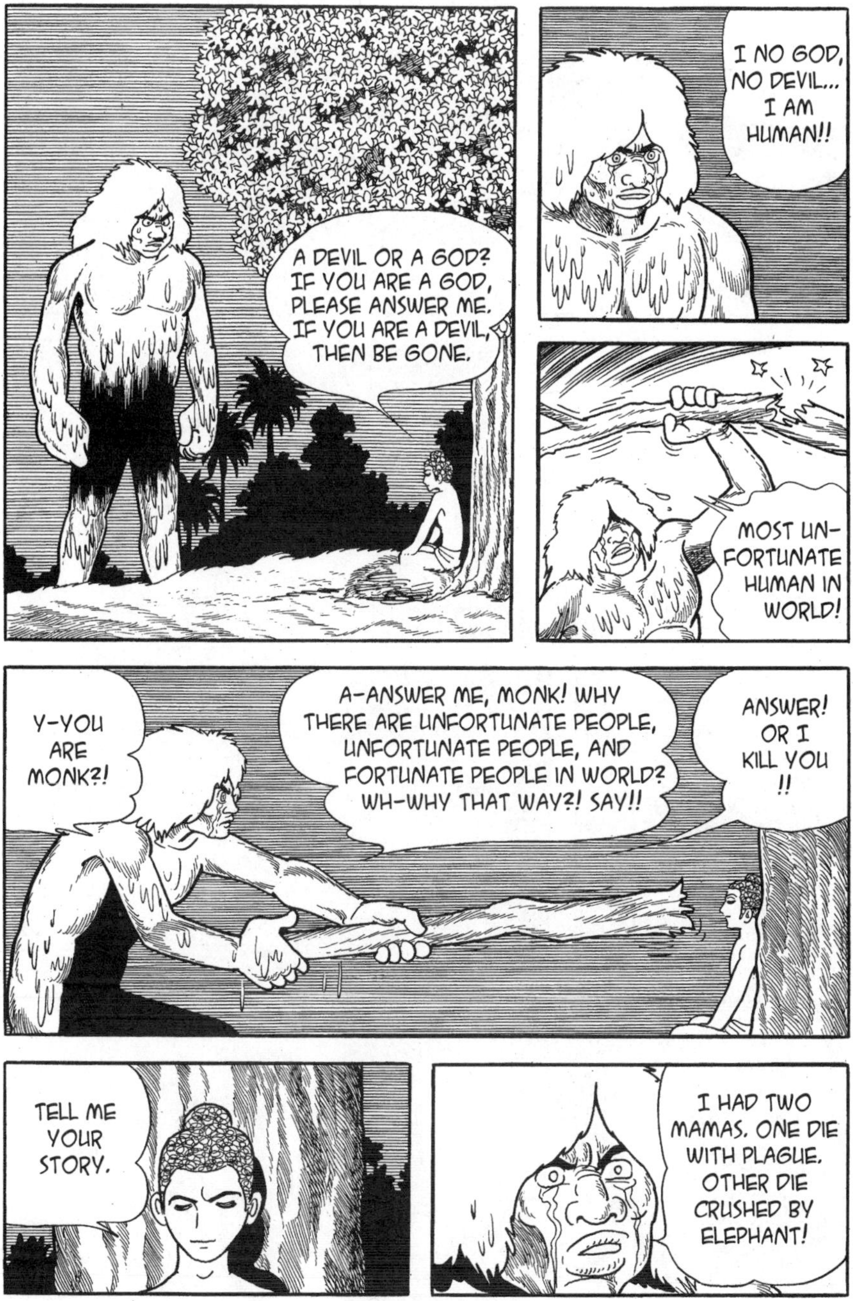
A DEVIL OR A GOD? IF YOU ARE A GOD, PLEASE ANSWER ME. IF YOU ARE A DEVIL, THEN BE GONE.
I NO GOD, NO DEVIL... I AM HUMAN!!
MOST UN-FORTUNATE HUMAN IN WORLD!
Y-YOU ARE MONK?!
A-ANSWER ME, MONK! WHY THERE ARE UNFORTUNATE PEOPLE, UNFORTUNATE PEOPLE, AND FORTUNATE PEOPLE IN WORLD? WH-WHY THAT WAY?! SAY!!
ANSWER! OR I KILL YOU !!
TELL ME YOUR STORY.
I HAD TWO MAMAS. ONE DIE WITH PLAGUE. OTHER DIE CRUSHED BY ELEPHANT!

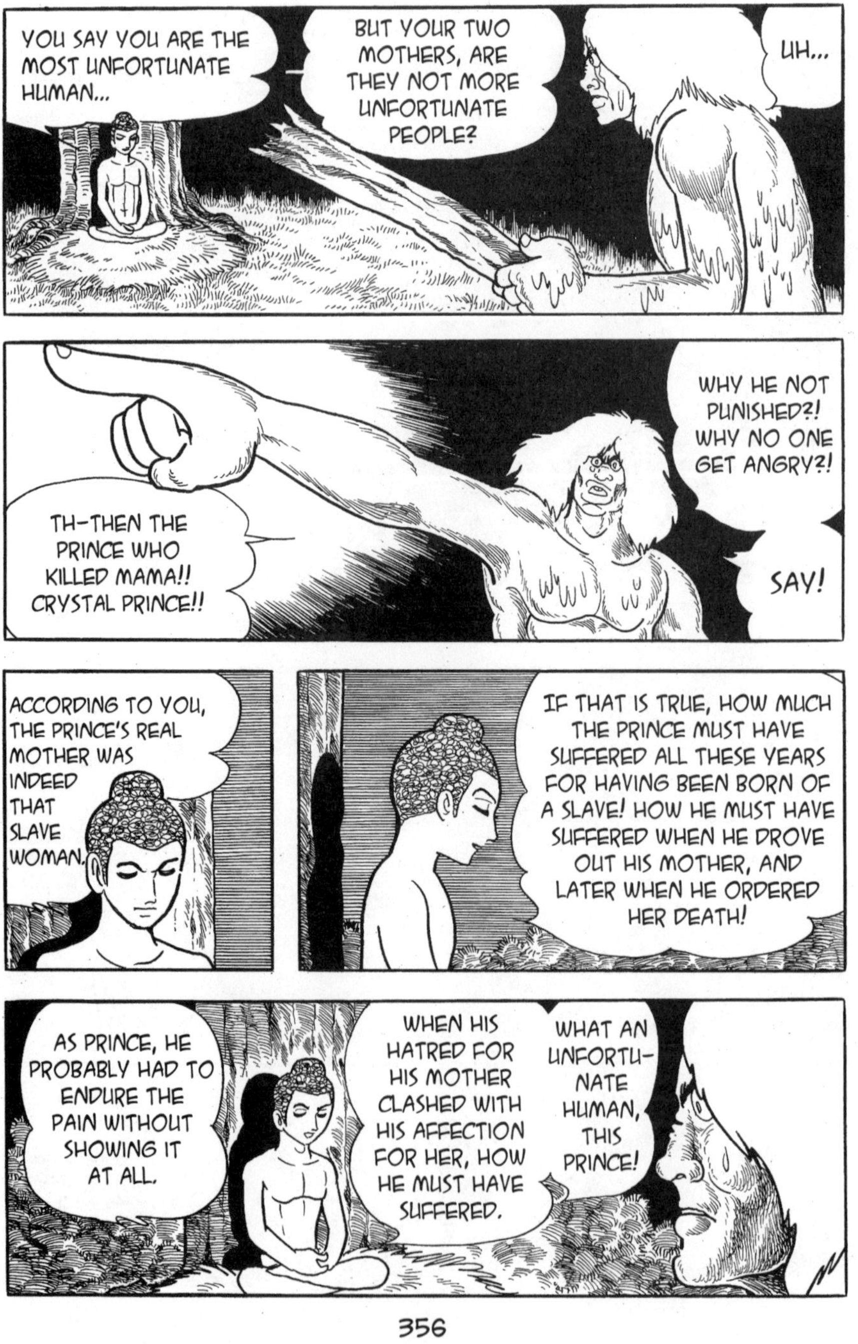
YOU SAY YOU ARE THE MOST UNFORTUNATE HUMAN...
BUT YOUR TWO MOTHERS, ARE THEY NOT MORE UNFORTUNATE PEOPLE?
UH...
TH-THEN THE PRINCE WHO KILLED MAMA!! CRYSTAL PRINCE!!
WHY HE NOT PUNISHED?! WHY NO ONE GET ANGRY?!
SAY!
ACCORDING TO YOU, THE PRINCE'S REAL MOTHER WAS INDEED THAT SLAVE WOMAN.
IF THAT IS TRUE, HOW MUCH THE PRINCE MUST HAVE SUFFERED ALL THESE YEARS FOR HAVING BEEN BORN OF A SLAVE! HOW HE MUST HAVE SUFFERED WHEN HE DROVE OUT HIS MOTHER, AND LATER WHEN HE ORDERED HER DEATH!
AS PRINCE, HE PROBABLY HAD TO ENDURE THE PAIN WITHOUT SHOWING IT AT ALL.
WHEN HIS HATRED FOR HIS MOTHER CLASHED WITH HIS AFFECTION FOR HER, HOW HE MUST HAVE SUFFERED.
WHAT AN UNFORTU-NATE HUMAN, THIS PRINCE!

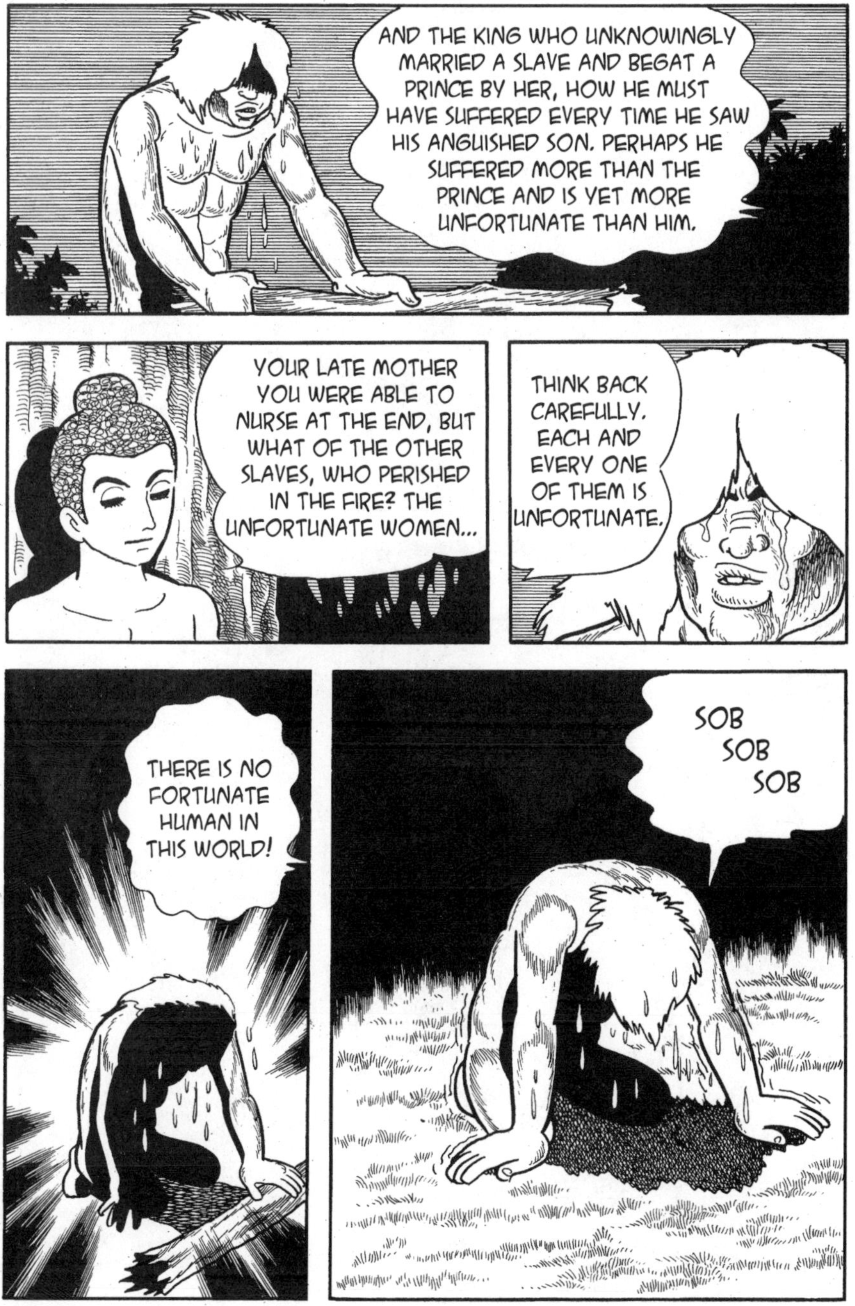
AND THE KING WHO UNKNOWINGLY MARRIED A SLAVE AND BEGAT A PRINCE BY HER, HOW HE MUST HAVE SUFFERED EVERY TIME HE SAW HIS ANGUISHED SON. PERHAPS HE SUFFERED MORE THAN THE PRINCE AND IS YET MORE UNFORTUNATE THAN HIM.
YOUR LATE MOTHER YOU WERE ABLE TO NURSE AT THE END, BUT WHAT OF THE OTHER SLAVES, WHO PERISHED IN THE FIRE? THE UNFORTUNATE WOMEN...
THINK BACK CAREFULLY. EACH AND EVERY ONE OF THEM IS UNFORTUNATE.
THERE IS NO FORTUNATE HUMAN IN THIS WORLD!
SOB SOB SOB

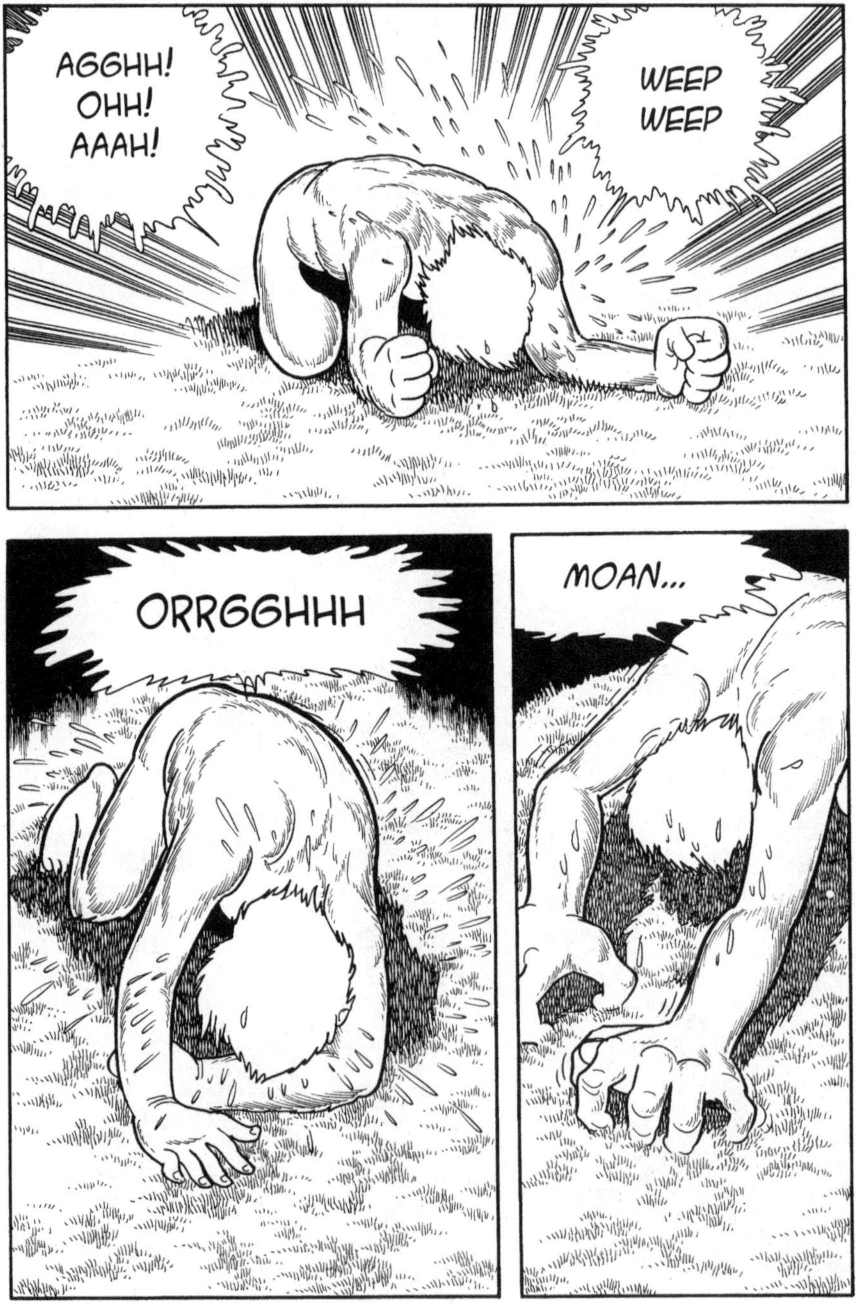
AGGHH! OHH! AAAH!
WEEP WEEP
ORRGGHHH
MOAN...

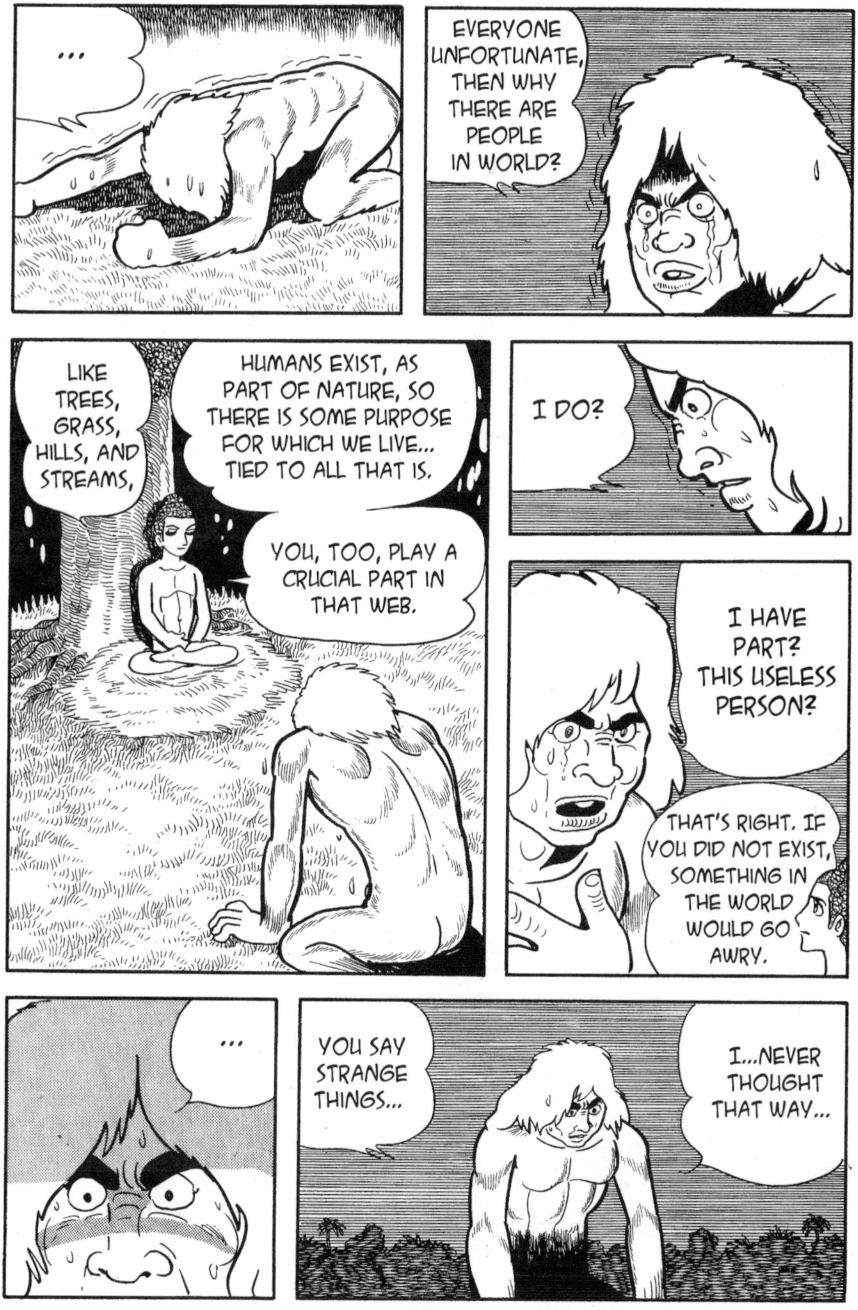
...
EVERYONE UNFORTUNATE, THEN WHY THERE ARE PEOPLE IN WORLD?
LIKE TREES, GRASS, HILLS, AND STREAMS,
HUMANS EXIST, AS PART OF NATURE, SO THERE IS SOME PURPOSE FOR WHICH WE LIVE... TIED TO ALL THAT IS.
YOU, TOO, PLAY A CRUCIAL PART IN THAT WEB.
I DO?
I HAVE PART? THIS USELESS PERSON?
THAT'S RIGHT. IF YOU DID NOT EXIST, SOMETHING IN THE WORLD WOULD GO AWRY.
...
YOU SAY STRANGE THINGS...
I...NEVER THOUGHT THAT WAY...

THEN... HOW I LIVE FROM NOW?

BEHOLD THE RIVER.

A TRULY GREAT THING. FOR COUNTLESS CENTURIES, IT HAS FLOWED THE WAY NATURE ORDAINED IT TO.

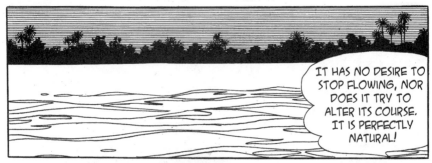

IT HAS NO DESIRE TO STOP FLOWING, NOR DOES IT TRY TO ALTER ITS COURSE. IT IS PERFECTLY NATURAL!

WHAT'S MORE, IT IS VAST AND BEAUTIFUL... IT IS APPRECIATED. AND IT GIVES.

LIKE THE RIVER, YOU ARE HUGE. BUT YOU WILL ALSO BE GREAT LIKE IT IF YOU LIVE RIGHTLY.

YOU... TELL ME YOUR NAME ...

MY NAME IS SIDDHARTHA.

SIDDHARTHA! YOU GREAT HUMAN.

I WANT BE YOUR DISCIPLE. MAKE ME DISCIPLE, PLEASE.

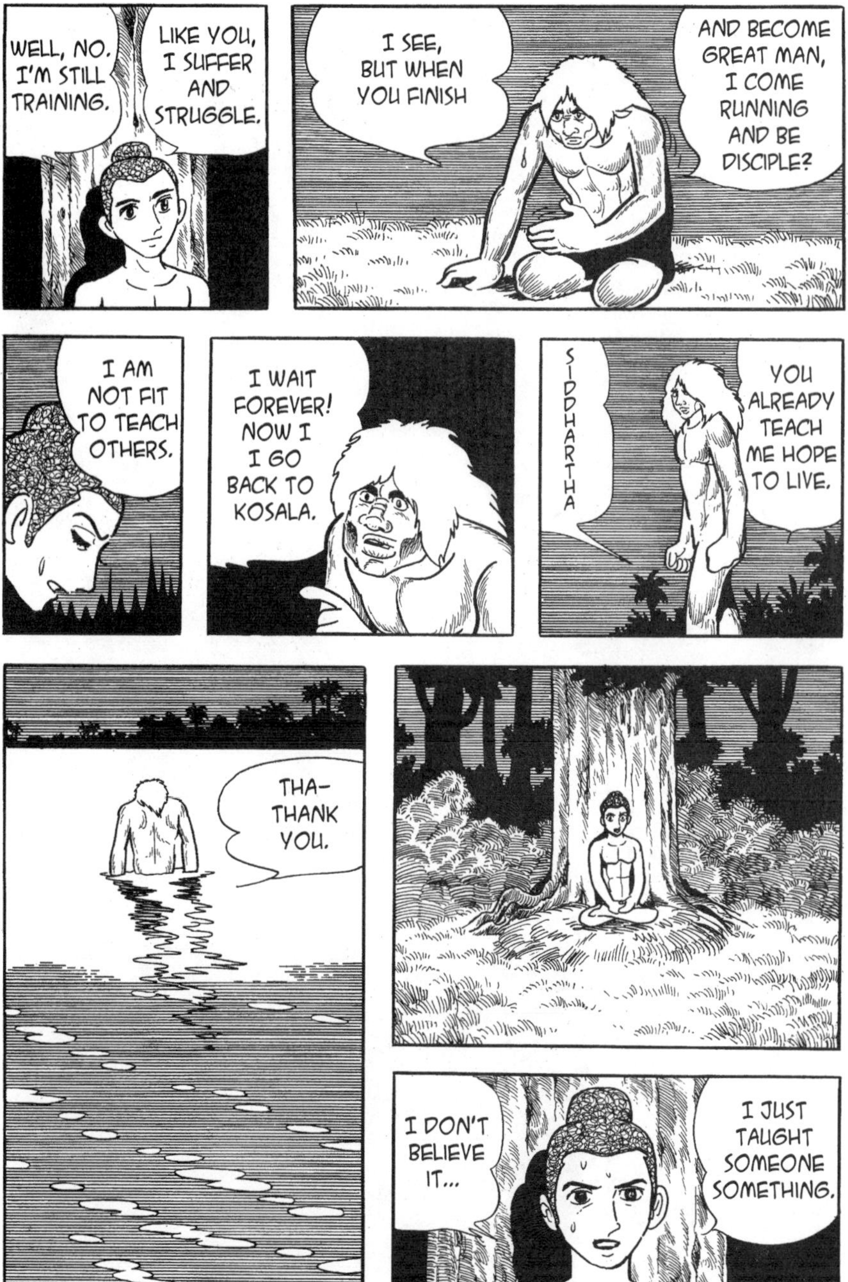
WELL, NO. I'M STILL TRAINING.
LIKE YOU, I SUFFER AND STRUGGLE.
I SEE, BUT WHEN YOU FINISH
AND BECOME GREAT MAN, I COME RUNNING AND BE DISCIPLE?
I AM NOT FIT TO TEACH OTHERS.
I WAIT FOREVER! NOW I I GO BACK TO KOSALA.
SIDDHARTHA
YOU ALREADY TEACH ME HOPE TO LIVE.
THA- THANK YOU.
I DON'T BELIEVE IT...
I JUST TAUGHT SOMEONE SOMETHING.

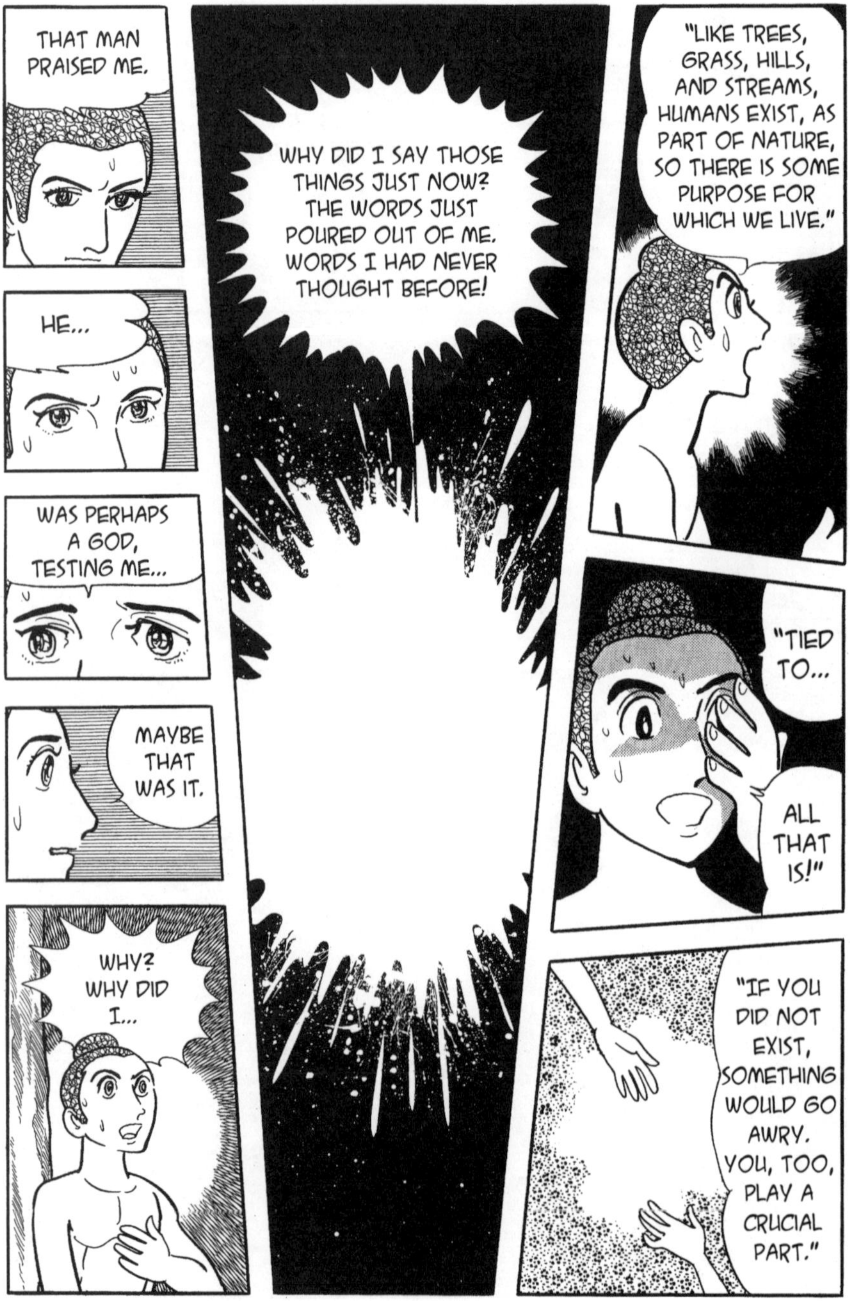

THAT MAN PRAISED ME.
HE...
WAS PERHAPS A GOD, TESTING ME...
MAYBE THAT WAS IT.
WHY? WHY DID I...
WHY DID I SAY THOSE THINGS JUST NOW? THE WORDS JUST POURED OUT OF ME. WORDS I HAD NEVER THOUGHT BEFORE!
"LIKE TREES, GRASS, HILLS, AND STREAMS, HUMANS EXIST, AS PART OF NATURE, SO THERE IS SOME PURPOSE FOR WHICH WE LIVE."
"TIED TO...
ALL THAT IS!"
"IF YOU DID NOT EXIST, SOMETHING WOULD GO AWRY. YOU, TOO, PLAY A CRUCIAL PART."

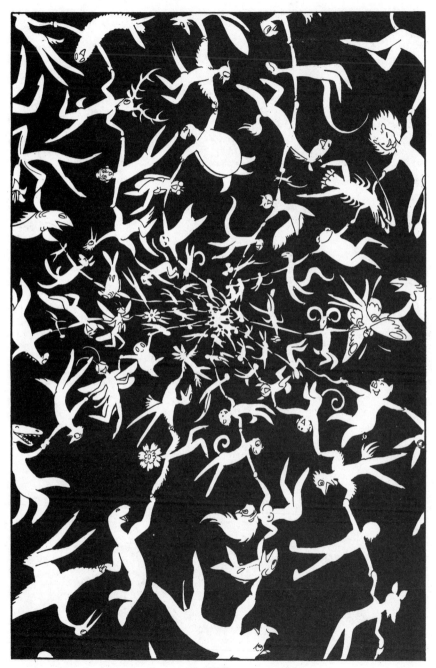

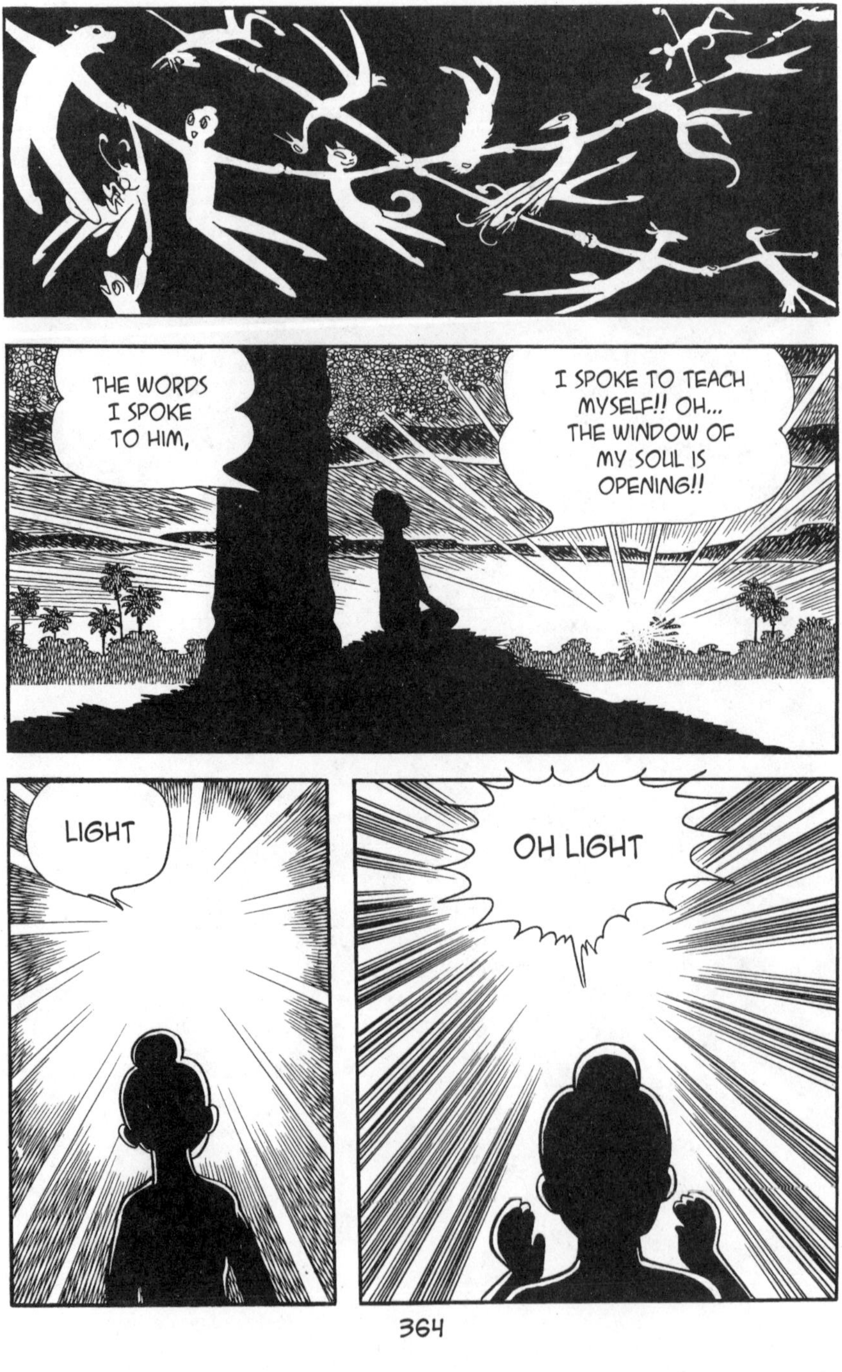
THE WORDS I SPOKE TO HIM,
I SPOKE TO TEACH MYSELF!! OH... THE WINDOW OF MY SOUL IS OPENING!!
LIGHT
OH LIGHT

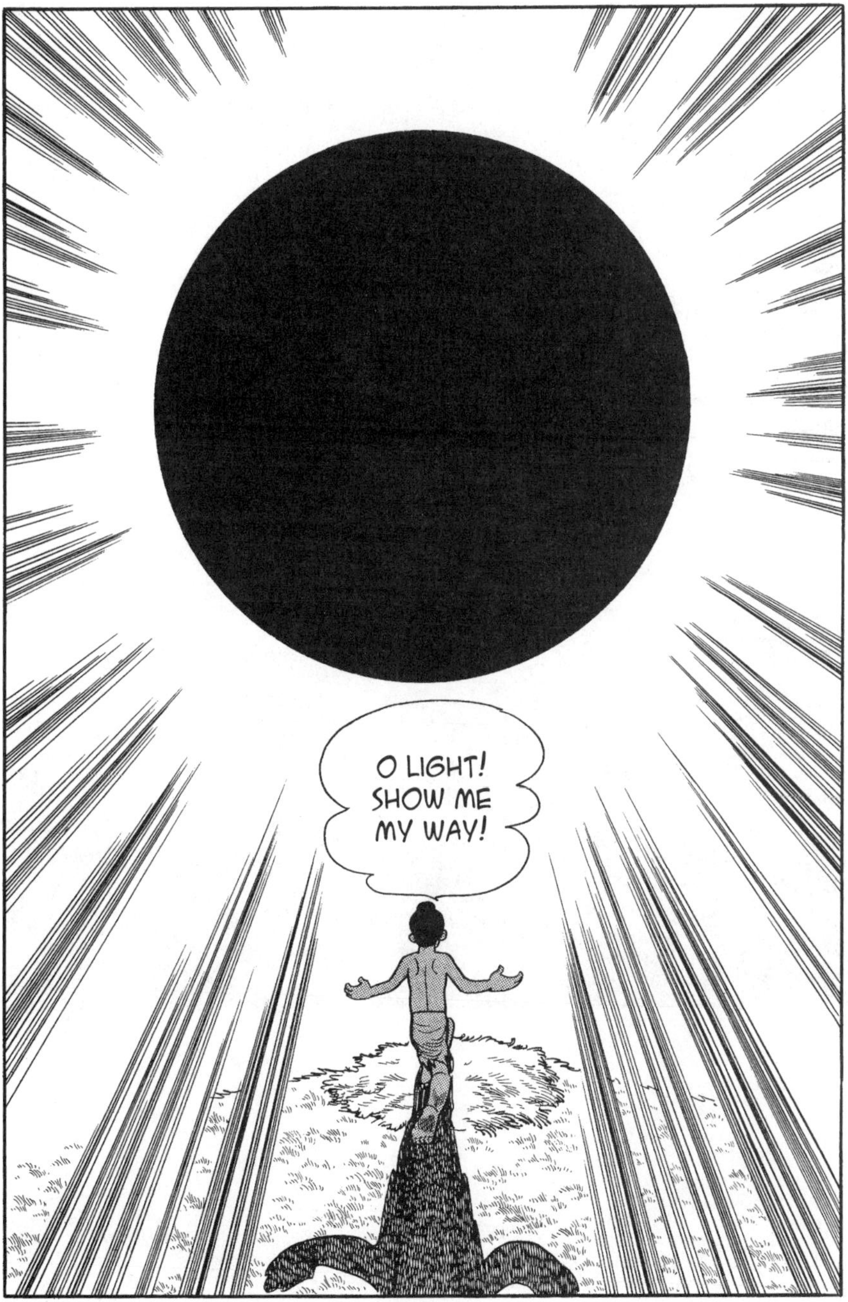
O LIGHT! SHOW ME MY WAY!

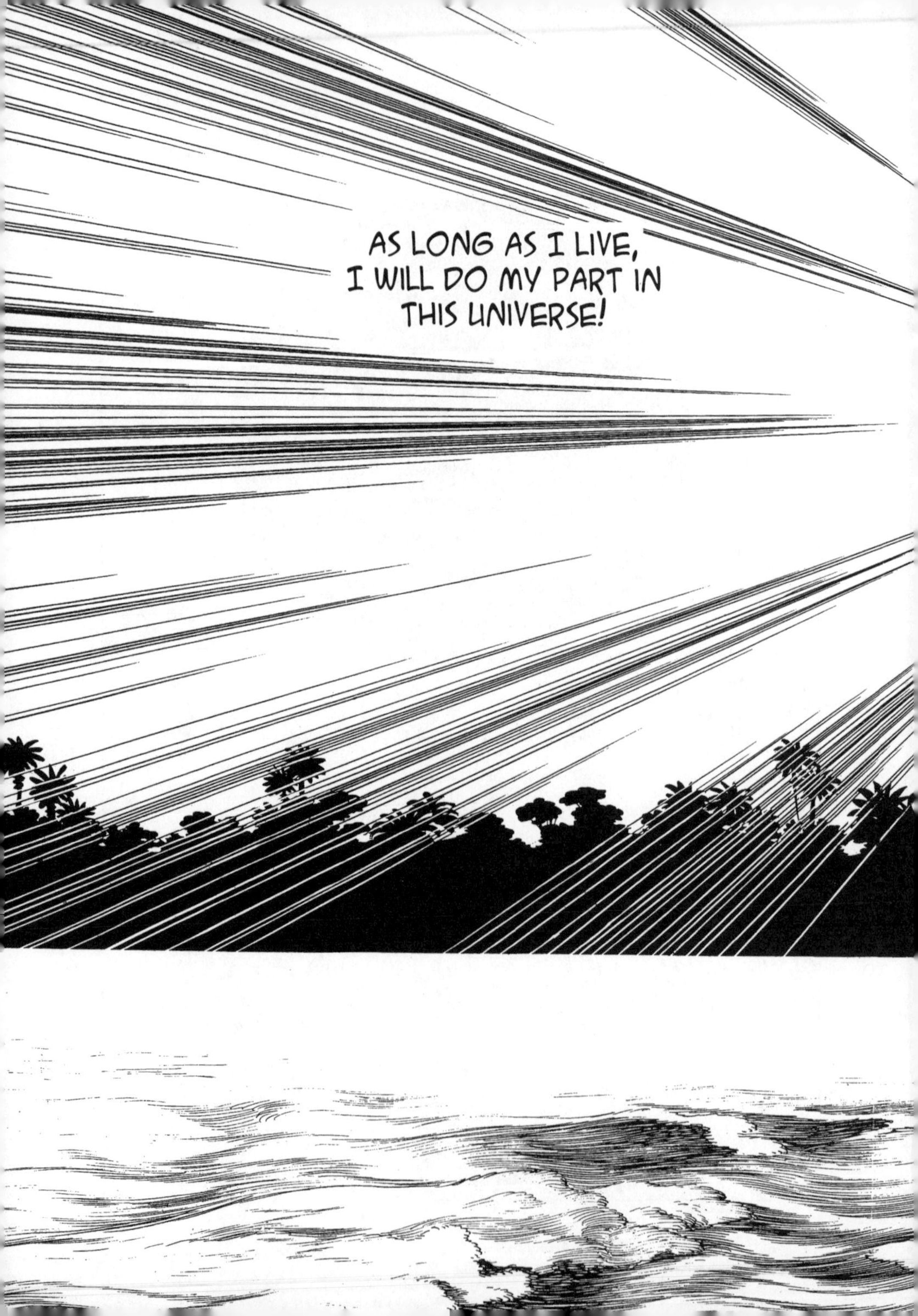
AS LONG AS I LIVE, I WILL DO MY PART IN THIS UNIVERSE!

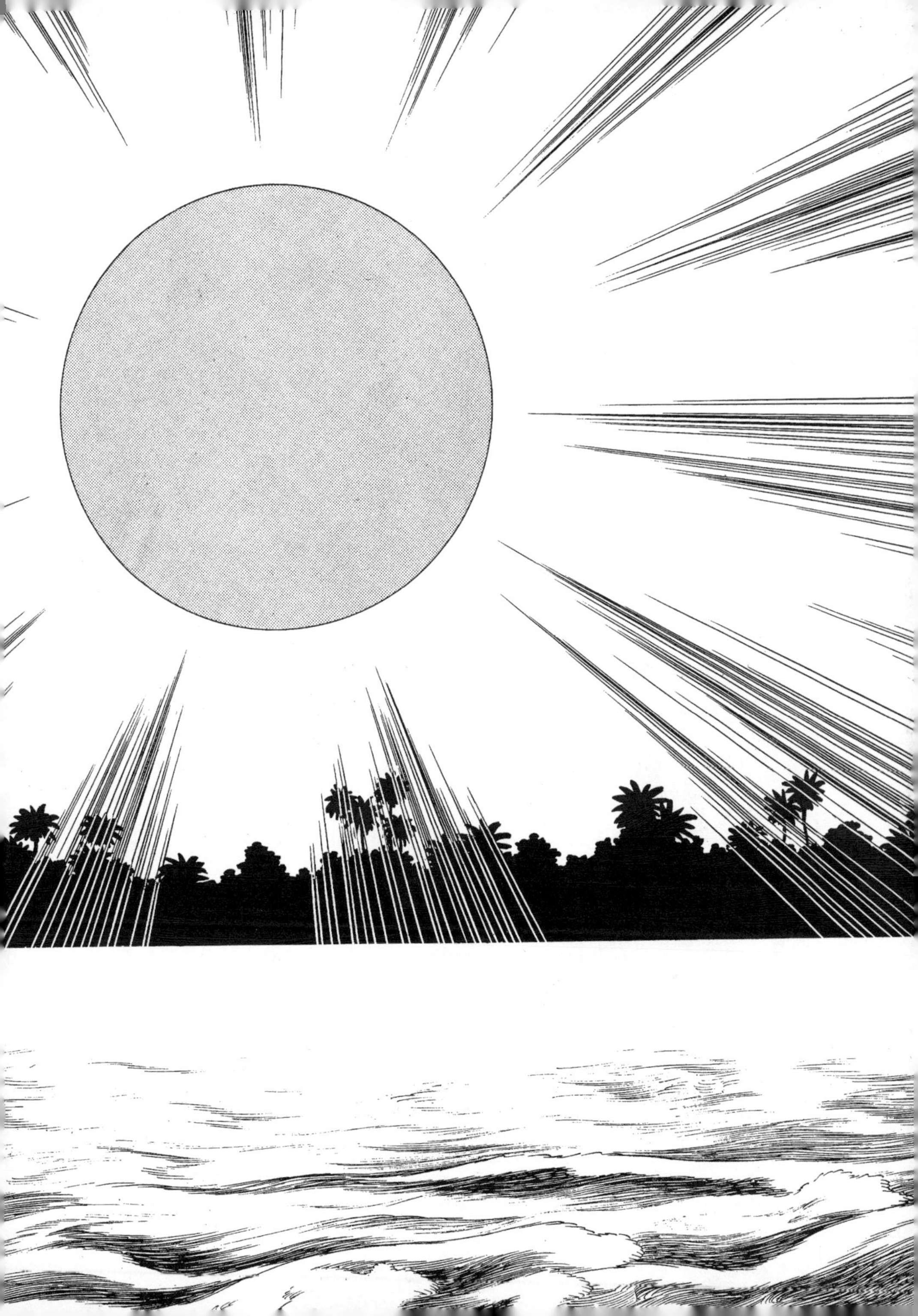

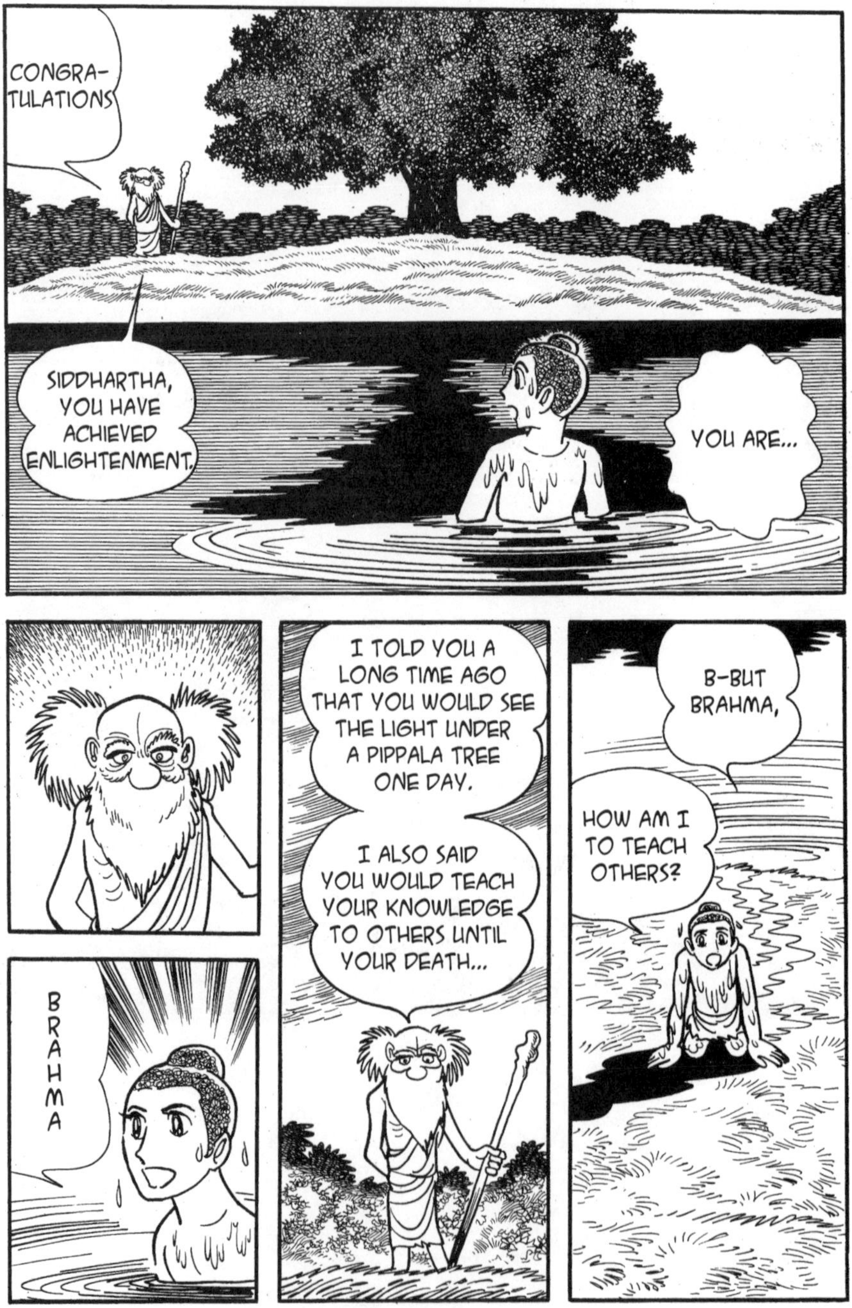
CONGRA-TULATIONS
SIDDHARTHA, YOU HAVE ACHIEVED ENLIGHTENMENT.
YOU ARE...
B R A H M A
I TOLD YOU A LONG TIME AGO THAT YOU WOULD SEE THE LIGHT UNDER A PIPPALA TREE ONE DAY.
I ALSO SAID YOU WOULD TEACH YOUR KNOWLEDGE TO OTHERS UNTIL YOUR DEATH...
B-BUT BRAHMA,
HOW AM I TO TEACH OTHERS?

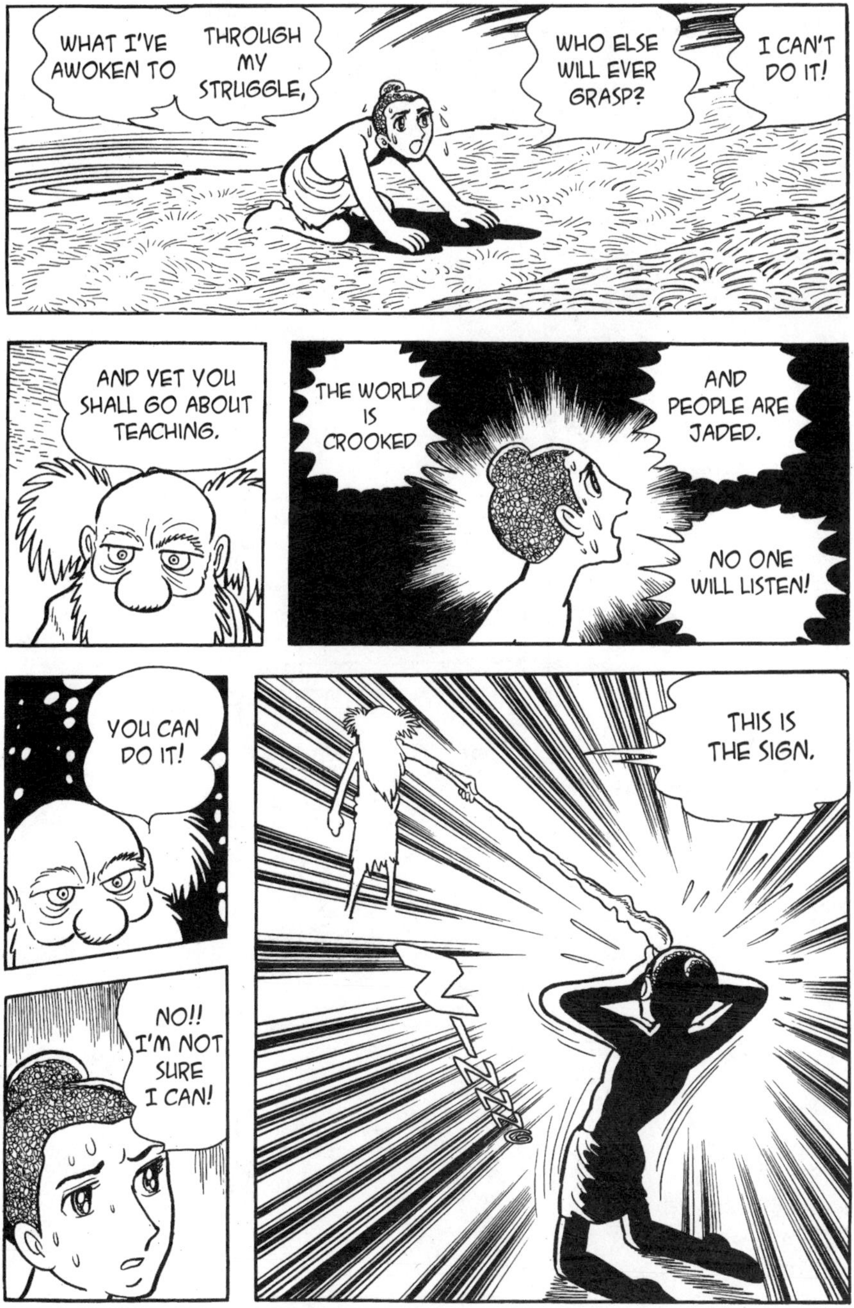
WHAT I'VE AWOKEN TO
THROUGH MY STRUGGLE,
WHO ELSE WILL EVER GRASP?
I CAN'T DO IT!
AND YET YOU SHALL GO ABOUT TEACHING.
THE WORLD IS CROOKED
AND PEOPLE ARE JADED.
NO ONE WILL LISTEN!
YOU CAN DO IT!
NO!! I'M NOT SURE I CAN!
THIS IS THE SIGN.

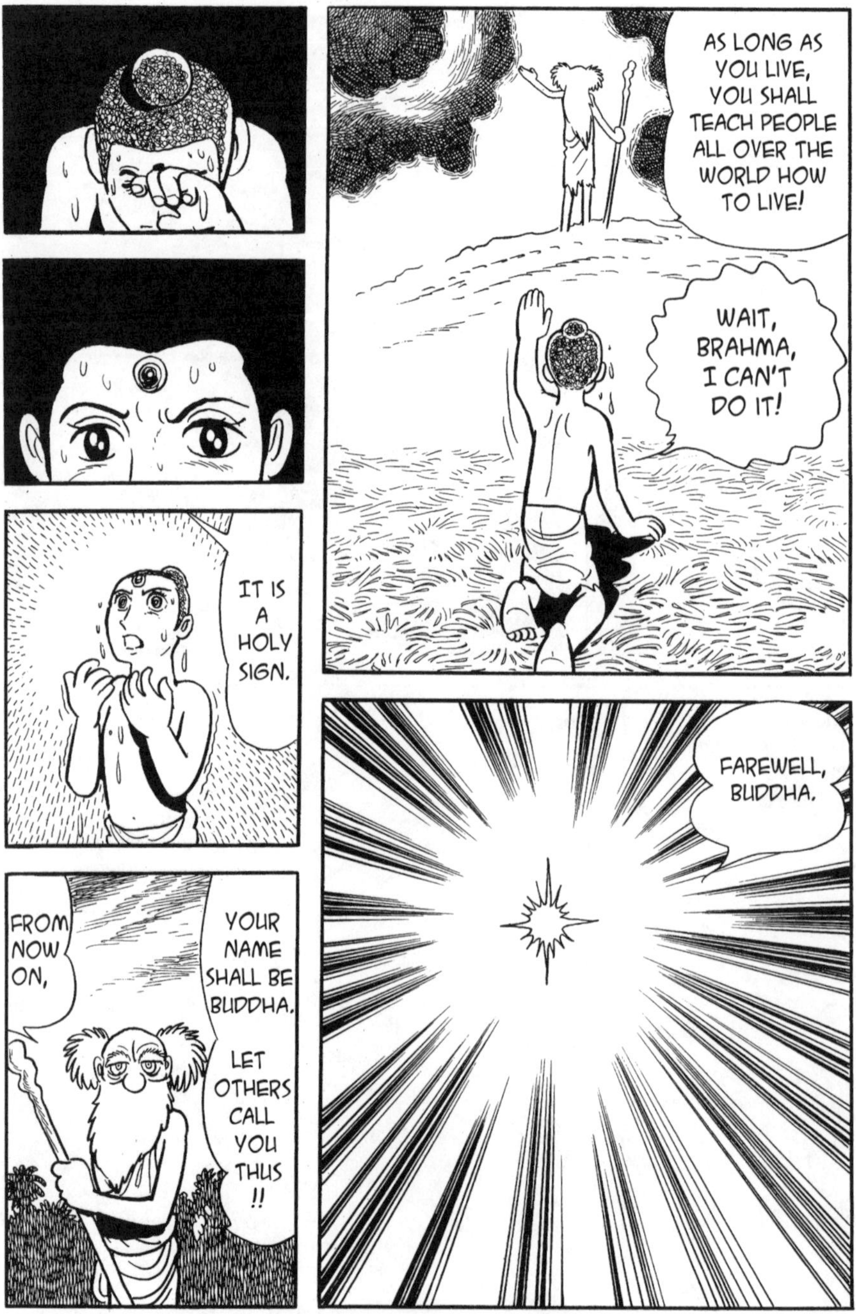
IT IS A HOLY SIGN.
FROM NOW ON,
YOUR NAME SHALL BE BUDDHA.
LET OTHERS CALL YOU THUS !!
AS LONG AS YOU LIVE, YOU SHALL TEACH PEOPLE ALL OVER THE WORLD HOW TO LIVE!
WAIT, BRAHMA, I CAN'T DO IT!
FAREWELL, BUDDHA.

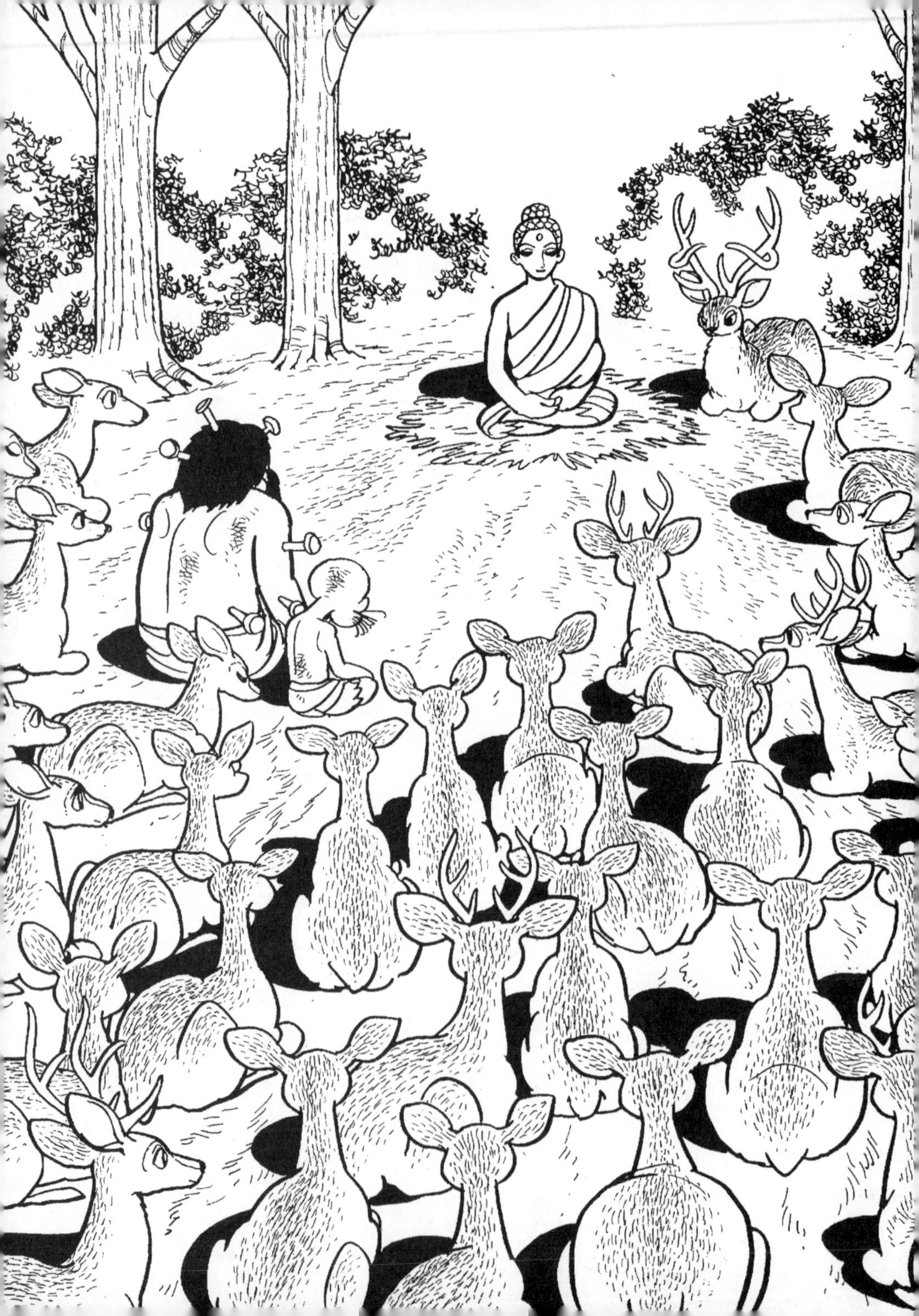

BUDDHA
OSAMU TEZUKA

Vol.**5**: *DEER PARK*
Vol.**6**: *ANANDA*

IN VOLUME 5, THE BUDDHA ACCEPTS A DEER AS HIS FIRST DISCIPLE. DEVADATTA, NOW A CUNNING YOUTH, PAIRS UP WITH THE EQUALLY STREET-SMART TATTA.

IN VOLUME 6, THREE BRAHMIN BROTHERS TEST BUDDHA'S WISDOM, AND DEVADATTA'S HALF-BROTHER ANANDA, A CRIMINAL PROTECTED BY A SHE-DEVIL, JOINS THE FRAY.

V

READ

"A rousing tale of intrepid heroes, horrid villains and wicked supernatural creatures. A fast read."
—*Publishers Weekly*

"Enormously entertaining" —*Orlando Sentinel*

"A swashbuckling fantasy...action is always center stage...intense...dreamlike."
—*Seattle Times*

"Japan's answer to *The Lord of the Rings*"
—*The Globe and Mail*

THE GUIN SAGA

KAORU KURIMOTO

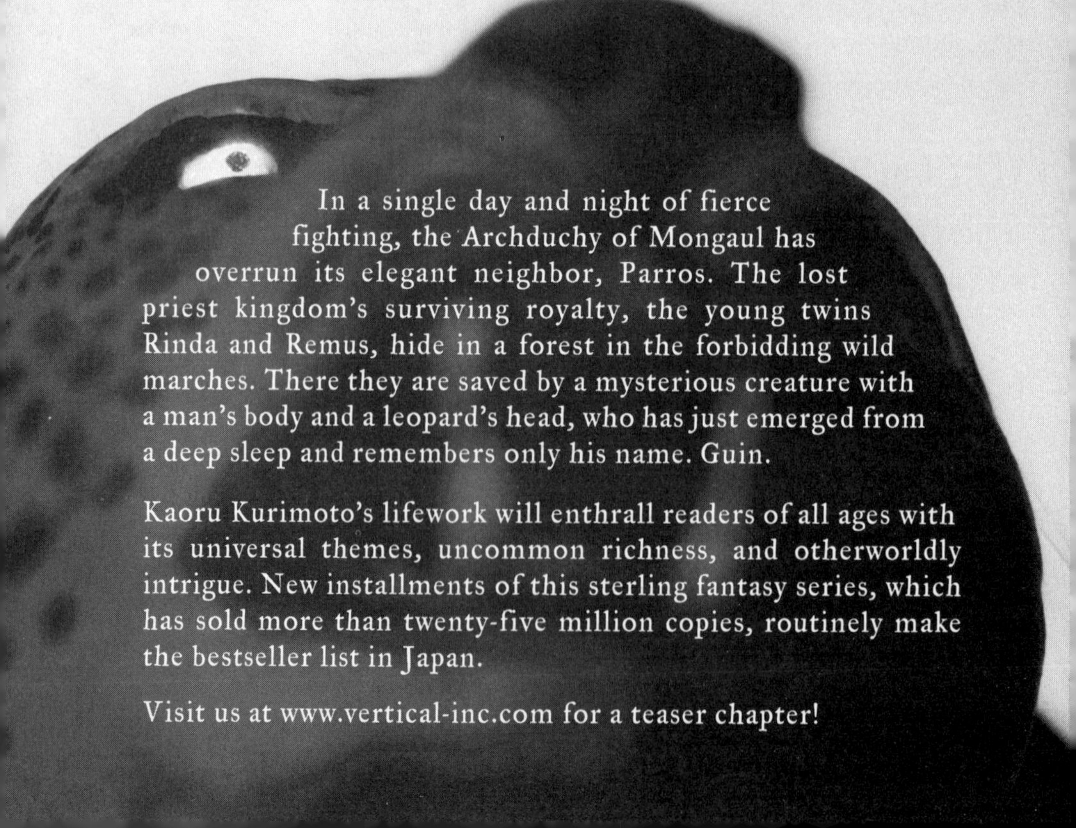

In a single day and night of fierce fighting, the Archduchy of Mongaul has overrun its elegant neighbor, Parros. The lost priest kingdom's surviving royalty, the young twins Rinda and Remus, hide in a forest in the forbidding wild marches. There they are saved by a mysterious creature with a man's body and a leopard's head, who has just emerged from a deep sleep and remembers only his name. Guin.

Kaoru Kurimoto's lifework will enthrall readers of all ages with its universal themes, uncommon richness, and otherworldly intrigue. New installments of this sterling fantasy series, which has sold more than twenty-five million copies, routinely make the bestseller list in Japan.

Visit us at www.vertical-inc.com for a teaser chapter!